KU-515-356

A New Book of
Middle Eastern Food

Claudia Roden was born and brought up in Cairo. She finished her education in Paris and later studied art in London. Starting as a painter she was drawn to the subject of food partly through a desire to evoke a lost heritage – one of the pleasures of a happy life in Egypt. The local delight in food, like the light, colour and smells and the special brand of hospitality, warmth and humour, has left a permanent impression.

With her bestselling classic, *A Book of Middle Eastern Food* (Penguin 1970, revised edition *A New Book of Middle Eastern Food,* 1985), first published in 1968, Claudia Roden revolutionized Western attitudes to the cuisines of the Middle East. Her intensely personal approach and her passionate appreciation of the dishes delighted readers, while she introduced them to a new world of foods, both exotic and wholesome. The book received great critical acclaim, and the publication of the new enlarged edition was enthusiastically welcomed. Josceline Dimbleby in the *Sunday Telegraph* said, 'A Book of Middle Eastern Food ... is still one of my favourite books; beautifully written, interesting and evocative with excellent recipes ... I was delighted to see that there is now a new enlarged edition of the book with many more delights'.

Mrs Roden continued to write about food with a special interest in the social and historical background of cooking. In 1981 Penguin reissued her delightful book *Coffee*. This was followed in 1982 by *Picnic*, a cornucopia of a book with hundreds of recipes and ideas for everything from picnics to wedding parties and barbecues and background stories the world over. The book is forever featured in newspapers and magazines year after year when the season for alfresco eating is on.

Then came the BBC television series, *Mediterranean Cookery with Claudia Roden*, and the accompanying book entitled *Claudia Roden's Mediterranean Cookery*. Her latest book is *The Book of Jewish Food*, which is published by Viking and forthcoming in Penguin.

In 1992, she won the Glenfiddich Trophy, the top prize in the Glenfiddich Awards.

Claudia Roden

A NEW BOOK OF
MIDDLE EASTERN FOOD

New and enlarged edition

PENGUIN BOOKS

PENGUIN BOOKS

Published by the Penguin Group
Penguin Books Ltd, 27 Wrights Lane, London W8 5TZ, England
Penguin Putnam Inc., 375 Hudson Street, New York, New York 10014, USA
Penguin Books Australia Ltd, Ringwood, Victoria, Australia
Penguin Books Canada Ltd, 10 Alcorn Avenue, Toronto, Ontario, Canada M4V 3B2
Penguin Books (NZ) Ltd, Private Bag 102902, NSMC, Auckland, New Zealand

Penguin Books Ltd, Registered Offices: Harmondsworth, Middlesex, England

First published as *A Book of Middle Eastern Food*
by Thomas Nelson 1968
Published in Penguin Books 1970
Revised edition published as *A New Book of Middle Eastern Food*
by Viking 1985
Published in Penguin Books 1986
15

Drawings by Murray Zanoni

Printed in England by Clays Ltd, St Ives plc

December 2001

To
Paul, Simon, Nadia and Anna

━━━◆◆◆━━━

Contents

Contents

Acknowledgements

I gratefully extend my thanks to the many people of the Middle East who so generously contributed recipes, advice and their culinary experience, and whose enthusiasm and strong conviction of the value of their culinary tradition were the origin of this book.

I wish to thank my parents, my father, whose enjoyment of life and appreciation of Middle Eastern food inspired me to perpetuate the tradition, and my mother, who advised and guided me throughout.

I wish to thank my husband, my brothers, Ellis and Zaki Douek, and their wives for their constant sympathetic support, encouragement and valuable advice, many friends for their interest and gracious sampling of my food, and my children, who allowed me to write the book.

Of those who contributed recipes, I am particularly indebted to Mrs Iris Galante, Mrs Lily Galante, my aunt Régine Douek, Mrs R. Afif, Mrs Irene Harari, Mrs I. Laski and Mrs S. Gaon.

I would like to express my warmest appreciation of the overwhelming generosity I encountered at the various Arab and North African Embassies, and the Islamic Centre, and for the recipes, help and advice given to me by members of the embassy staffs and their wives, some of whom extended the hospitality of their homes.

I am equally indebted to the Israeli Embassy for their generous advice, and to the Israeli Government Tourist Office for supplying me with recipes.

I wish to extend my deepest gratitude to Miss Belinda Bather, whose rich experience was the major source of the Turkish recipes, and to Mrs V. Afsharian who contributed many Persian dishes.

I wish to record my gratitude to Professor A. J. Arberry, with whose kind permission I have been able to include many recipes from al-Baghdadi's medieval manual and various culinary poems which he translated, and to Monsieur Maxime Rodinson, from whose valuable studies in Arab culinary history and analysis and extracts from the *Wusla il al Habib* I have drawn much information.

9

I also wish to acknowledge my debt to certain Arab, Turkish and Persian cookery books which I have studied. *

Finally, I wish to thank my editor, Helena Radecka, for her constant invaluable guidance from the early stages of my project, and for her enthusiasm and understanding throughout. Without her the book would not have been as it is.

I have many more people to thank for this new edition. I cannot name all those who gave recipes and helped in different ways but I remember them all gratefully, especially Amin Hadad who invited me into the kitchen of the Fakhreldine, the late Josephine Salam who taught me a great deal and Sami Zubeida. My greatest debt is to Jill Norman who gave much valued advice. The brilliant studies of Maxime Rodinson continue to be an inspiration; his works are the source of much of my information about the history of Arab food. I have special thanks for Eleo Gordon who has seen this edition to press.

* A list of cookery books on the Middle East is given on page 526.

Using the Book

Recipes are designed to serve 6 people generously unless otherwise stated. Teaspoons, tablespoons and teacups are of the sizes most commonly found in English households. With some exceptions, quantities and measures need not be interpreted with too much precision.* They should be used as a guide, and after the initial trying out of a new recipe, readers are encouraged to trust their taste and to taste often, and allow themselves a certain freedom in preparation. This is in the spirit of a cuisine which is rich in regional differences.

Some variations are given but many more exist, according to region and even to individual families. Another cook might use slightly different ingredients (or the same in varying proportions) for a dish similar to one I have given, equally successfully. On a different day, when in a different mood, or with a different appetite, I myself might prepare the same dish in a different manner from that which I have recorded.

It is quite possible to substitute oil for butter in almost every dish, even in *fila* pastry, without in any way spoiling the dish. The latest findings on healthy eating indicate that we should reduce our consumption of butter.

Three tomatoes can sometimes be used instead of one, and onions and garlic may be used abundantly or omitted entirely without spoiling a dish. Parsley may be used when fresh coriander or chervil is not available, turmeric may occasionally be substituted for saffron, and cinnamon and allspice may often be interchanged. Soups may be made thick or thin, and salads more or less lemony, according to taste.

---

* For instance, where a recipe calls for 120 g (4 oz) almonds, a 100-g packet will usually do perfectly well.

□ On the Merits of Trusting Your Taste*

A Governor came to Akshehir who was rather eccentric.

'If anyone knows a good dish,' said he, 'I wish he would write out the recipe and we will make a Cookery Book.'

He made the suggestion to one of the principal men of the town, who passed it on to the Khoja.

Next day the Khoja met this man and said, 'Do you know I was thinking all night about what you told me. I have invented a rare dish – one that no one has ever heard of – quite delicious!'

When the man asked what it was, he said, 'You must make a batter of garlic and honey.'

The man, who was a bit of a fool, went off at once, and happening to meet the Governor, said to him, 'We have a Khoja in the town, a man of much experience and quite an original character.' He then proceeded to give him the Khoja's recipe.

Now, the Governor was by no means as intelligent as he was supposed to be. He answered, 'How extraordinary! You don't say so!' and at once hurried home and gave orders to the cook that he was to try it for supper.

Of course it was disgusting.

The Governor was very angry and told the man who had mentioned the Khoja to him, to bring him to Government House.

'So you are the man who invented a dish of garlic and honey?' he asked.

'Your very humble servant,' replied the Khoja, 'unworthy though I be to have done such a thing.'

'Very well,' said the Governor, and gave orders that he should be made to eat some on an empty stomach next morning.

As he turned it over in his mouth he made horrible grimaces at the nasty taste, and the Governor said, 'What are you making those faces for? Enjoy yourself. Take your fill of this dish you invented. Perhaps it tastes differently to the man who made it.'

'Your Excellency!' said the Khoja, 'this invention of mine was only a theory. I had never tasted the thing before. Now I have, and I see that theory and practice are quite different things. I don't like it, either.'

---

* Henry D. Barnham (trans.), *Tales of Nasr-ed-Din Khoja.*

Introduction (1968)

My compilation of recipes is the joint creation of numerous Middle Easterners who, like me, are in exile, either forced and permanent, or voluntary and temporary. It is the fruit of nostalgic longing for, and delighted savouring of a food that was the constant joy of life in a world so different from the Western one. The Arab sayings, 'He who has a certain habit will have no peace from it', and 'The dancer dies and does not forget the shaking of his shoulders', apply to us.

The collection began fifteen years ago with a recipe for *ful medames*. I was a schoolgirl in Paris then. Every Sunday I was invited together with my brothers and a cousin to eat *ful medames* with some relatives. This meal became a ritual. Considered in Egypt to be a poor man's dish, in Paris the little brown beans became invested with all the glories and warmth of Cairo, our home town, and the embodiment of all that for which we were homesick.

Our hosts lived in a one-room flat, and were both working, so it was only possible for them to prepare the dish with tinned *ful*. Ceremoniously, we sprinkled the beans with olive oil, squeezed a little lemon over them, seasoned them with salt and pepper, and placed a hot hard-boiled egg in their midst. Delicious ecstasy! Silently, we ate the beans, whole and firm at first; then we squashed them with our forks and combined their floury texture and slightly dull, earthy taste with the acid tang of lemon, mellowed by the olive oil; finally, we crumbled the egg, matching its earthiness with that of the beans, its pale warm yellow with their dull brown.

Since that time, I and many relatives (Sephardic Jews), acquaintances and friends, exiled from our Middle Eastern homelands, have settled in various countries. We have kept in close touch by letter and occasional visits. Some of us have tried to re-create certain aspects of the way of life to which we were accustomed after centuries of integrated life in the Ottoman and Arab worlds, in particular the food, which meant so much in the Middle East and has come to mean even more in exile.

It has been, for me, a matter of great delight to acquire an extra

13

recipe from some relative passing through London, a well-known ex-restaurateur from Alexandria, or somebody's aunt in Buenos Aires – another treasure to pass on to the Middle Eastern community in Paris, Geneva or Milan.

Friday night dinners at my parents, and gatherings of friends at my own home have been opportunities to rejoice in our food and to summon the ghosts of the past.

Each dish has filled our house in turn with the smells of the *Muski*, the Cairo market, of the *corniche* in Alexandria, of Groppi's and the famous Hati Restaurant. Each dish has brought back memories of great and small occasions, of festivals, of the emotions of those times, and of the sayings invariably said. They have conjured up memories of street vendors, bakeries and pastry shops, and of the brilliant colours and sounds of the markets. Pickles and cheeses have re-created for us the atmosphere of the grocery shop round the corner, down to which a constant flow of baskets would be lowered from the windows above, descending with coins, and going up again with food. It is these smells, emotions, habits and traditions, attached and inseparable from our dishes, a small part of our distinctive culture, that I have tried to convey with the food.

At first, on leaving Egypt, I imagined our food to be uniquely Egyptian. In Europe, I discovered that the Turks claimed most of our dishes, and that the Syrians, Lebanese and Persians claimed the rest, leaving us with only a few specialities, our 'national dishes'. Nearly all our food was common to other Middle Eastern countries, so to write about 'our food' was to write about Middle Eastern food generally. I have not been able to disentangle what is an Egyptian culinary tradition from a Turkish, Persian or Syrian one, and I have had to include various countries which I did not intend to at first, but which were necessary to make a complete and comprehensible picture of what was originally my 'family's food'. The countries which imposed themselves were, in a broad sense, the countries of the Middle East.

The Middle East is a broad and fluid term which today means different things to different people. Its more recent history and events, tragic, intricate and tumultuous, have made it, for all those who have any mild involvement with it, loaded with explosive emotion. I cannot attempt in this book of food to make any sort of political or geographical definition, since even the latter is tragically complex and unsettled.

Introduction (1968)

The region embraces many different countries, races and religions. The people call themselves 'orientals', a term more often used in the West when referring to the Far East. The area is one of geographical, climatic, human and social contrasts. It has been the birthplace of our present civilization, and the battle-ground of most of the creeds, philosophies and religions which form the basis of those now occupying the minds of much of the world today.

Some parts of the Middle East are racially pure, such as those inhabited by Bedouin Arabs. Others, such as the Mediterranean coast, inhabited by people loosely termed 'Levantines', are extremely mixed in racial origin, nationality and religion, embodying the numerous human changes brought about by various empires, invasions, foreign settlers and traders. A name invented by my community for these people is 'Bazramites'.

With a few exceptions, the Arabic language is spoken throughout the region in its numerous and varied dialects. The religion is that of Islam, but each country until recently sheltered a large number of small communities of Christians and Jews, and various small sects and factions of these.

Here is my choice of countries included in this book: Syria, the Lebanon, Egypt, Iran, Turkey, Greece, Iraq, Saudi Arabia, the Yemen, the Sudan, Algeria, Tunisia, Morocco and Israel. Their cooking is inextricably linked.

Although the Balkan countries have adopted culinary traditions from their former Ottoman rulers, I have not included them, since they are now far removed from the Middle East, and they have not notably fed many dishes back to the common pool. I have dealt with Greece in as much as its tradition is almost identical with the Turkish one.

I have treated the food of the individual countries arbitrarily, giving preference and most careful scrutiny to all aspects of food belonging to my own personal background, but, I hope, doing justice to the food of other countries too. Iran, the Lebanon, Syria, Turkey and Morocco I found ready to pour out an abundant variety of splendid recipes, while other countries, possessing a poorer and more limited range, had only a few dishes to offer.

The early sources of my collection of recipes have been my family and my own community from Egypt; people who were either born in Egypt or who had lived, themselves and their forefathers, for centuries in various countries of the Middle East, and had come to settle in

Egypt. Their culture and traditions ran parallel to, and were part of, wider national traditions.

To explore the food of the different countries was made easy for me by the fact that we were particularly spoilt in the very cosmo-politan atmosphere of Egypt, which contained communities of other Middle Eastern nationals. My own family has a Syrian and a Turkish branch, and many of my relatives have married into fam-ilies coming from the Lebanon, North Africa and Iran. This enabled us to savour the best of many worlds.

I was extremely lucky in having the help of Turks, Syrians, Iranians, Lebanese, Saudi Arabians, Armenians, Israelis and North Africans, whom I met in London and with whom I spent long, rich and interesting hours, taking in their experience, watching them cook, sampling the dishes they prepared for me before trying them myself. All those who contributed recipes have a feeling for, and deep understanding of food.

Most of these people explained in the minutest detail the washing and the handling of ingredients, the feel, the smell and the colour of the food – but usually omitted quantities, weights and cooking times. I learnt that to some 'leave it a minute' meant an hour, that 'five spoonfuls' was in order to make a round figure or because five was for them a lucky number, and that a pinch could be anything from an eighth of a teaspoon to a heaped tablespoon.

Remarking how delicious the dishes they described were, they related the circumstances in which they used to prepare them. It gave them, I think, as much pleasure to describe the recipes as it gave me to record them. Through them I have gathered humble peasant food, flamboyant Mediterranean dishes, the elaborate dishes developed during the times of the Great Empires as well as the everyday dishes of the middle classes throughout the Middle East.

I have tried to be faithful to the old traditions of cooking, but I have also introduced dishes in which the European influence of the present century can be felt. These I have classed as modern dishes or modern variations.

I have tried to trace the origins of dishes and to understand their variations, to detect the influences brought about by conquering nations, mass emigrations and religious prohibitions, and I have discovered that, to a certain extent, I can only guess at these.

I was thrilled to find at the British Museum library and at the

Introduction (1968)

School of Oriental Languages two medieval cookery manuals (see page 522), one translated by Professor A. J. Arberry, and the other with an analysis and extracts translated into French by M. Maxime Rodinson. I could not resist including recipes from both those books. I have quoted them with the kind permission of the authors, as they are so clearly and beautifully described. Out of well over two hundred recipes, I have chosen a few, some because they were so familiar that it was interesting to compare them with the modern variations they inspired, others simply because they appealed to me, and I would like to be permitted to return them to the culinary repertoire of the Middle East. Since exact measures are not given, I have indicated the quantities that I would personally choose through my own experience of cooking.

With this collection of dishes I wish to offer what to me is a treasure, the detailed and simple explanation of the way in which the women of the Middle East (and, of course, the professional male cooks) have prepared their food for centuries, some even since Pharaonic times. I would like to pass on the experience which has been transferred from mother and mother-in-law to daughter and daughter-in-law, with the keen encouragement of their husbands, fathers and brothers.

Middle Eastern cooking, though sometimes elaborate, is easy. Some of the dishes, such as stuffed vine leaves, may take some time to prepare; but if you consider cooking to be a pleasurable and creative activity, you are adding to the enjoyment of serving and eating the dish the peace and pleasure derived from rolling up the leaves. Women in the West like to knit while watching television, or while sitting with their children. Could rolling vine leaves and stuffing tomatoes not be yet another such soothing activity?

The preparation of most of these dishes is short and simple. Some require lengthy cooking, but these often need very little work and hardly any attention. They can usually be cooked a day in advance and become richer in this way. Sometimes the cooking time can be greatly reduced by the use of modern labour-saving devices such as electric blenders or pressure cookers.

Middle Eastern food is economical, lamb and minced meat being the favourite meats. The recipes can give inspiration for subtle and exciting ways of cooking familiar and cheaper cuts of meat. Alcohol, which usually brings up the cost of cosmopolitan *haute cuisine*, is

17

absent (except for in a few modern dishes), owing to its prohibition by Muslim dietary law.

The vegetables, used because of their abundance in the Middle East, are available almost everywhere in Britain today, either imported or home grown.

Spices can be found in most supermarkets as well as in Greek and Indian shops. Some ingredients, such as vine leaves, pine nuts and *fila* pastry, not generally available in ordinary shops, can usually be found in all Greek shops or where there are Greek or Cypriot communities, and in some continental delicatessens.

I have included with my recipes a few tales, poems and descriptions of ceremonies, rituals and myths, customs and manners, all relating to food. I believe that they will make the dishes more interesting and familiar by placing them in their natural and traditional setting, and add to the pleasure of eating them.

I have allowed myself to include riddles, proverbs and sayings, in the hope that through them a little of the wit and spirit of the peoples of the Middle East may be discovered. Although I have used instances of my own experience, and songs and proverbs of particular regions, these are not foreign to other parts of the Middle East, but common and general.

In particular, I have included stories of Goha, the folk hero of the Middle East, sometimes called Goha Ibn Insh'Allah al Masri in Egypt, and known in various countries as Joha, Abbu Nawwas and Nasr-ed-Din Khoja. He is, in turn, an itinerant *imam* (priest), a peasant, a *qadi* (judge), husband, donkey-man and court buffoon.

Since the Arabic names of the dishes vary a little from one country to another, I have chosen to use those by which they are most familiarly known in Egypt, except in cases of particularly national specialities.

Introduction to the New Edition

Since it first came out in 1968, *A Book of Middle Eastern Food* has become an important part of my life. It has meant a continuing involvement with the area which holds my roots and for which I have a special tenderness. People always talk to me about food, to enthuse or to complain, and those who come from the Middle East reveal their passions and offer culinary secrets. I am invited to eat and to watch people cook and I have correspondents in different countries. My pockets are full of cooking instructions obtained at a chance meeting and my drawers full of recipes written in different hands. Over the years I have amassed a great deal of new material. Most of it has been incorporated in this revised and expanded edition.

Many new recipes appear in every chapter. On two or three occasions a recipe has been replaced by a better one of the same dish, and there are many additional regional variations. I have also made changes throughout the book, mainly in the form of suggestions for an alternative ingredient, a new flavouring or an easier method of cooking and quantities of butter or oil have occasionally been reduced in accordance with today's ideas about health. These improvements are the result of fifteen years' further experience.

Otherwise, I have left the recipes as they were, with the voice and the idiosyncracies of those who told them. The amateur way in which they are described as I first heard them best reflects the rich and varied character of a very personal and much-loved cuisine passed down by generations in the family. I have not tried to correct spelling, pronunciations or names, for this is an area of great complexity with differences from one country to another. For instance, the name of Egyptian bean rissoles varies from one part of the country to another; it is *falafel* in Alexandria and *ta'amia* in Cairo, while the same dish is *megadarra* in Egypt and *mudardara* in Lebanon. This is not a scholarly book and I have not followed a system, merely written a name as I remember it and as it sounded to me.

To make room for as many new recipes as possible, I have taken out some of the least interesting ones which had been entered more for the record than for their gastronomic value. Many of the Israeli recipes have gone because they are no longer in fashion in Israel. Trends there will be dealt with in a new book I am preparing on Jewish food.

In the choice of new recipes, I have taken into account the greater familiarity with and enthusiasm for Oriental food and the new readiness to try unusual combinations of ingredients. There have been many changes since I started working on the first edition. At that time people wondered with barely veiled horror whether my book was to be about sheeps' eyes and testicles. Their perception of this type of food was not very different from what the explorer Charles Montagu Doughty, who travelled in Arabia around 1876, described as lambs sitting on mountains of rice in a sea of fat. In his view the Arabs were better at making love than food. The image lingered, tinged perhaps with a little prejudice for a weaker and colonized civilization.

These days, most people are familiar with the 'Arabian Delights' which are regularly featured in magazines. The smoke of roasting lamb wafts into the streets of London and many a suburban kitchen is filled with the smells of Cairo, Fez and Baghdad. Health food shops and delicatessens sell burghul, halva, tahina and couscous, while packets of pitta bread quickly disappear from supermarket shelves.

It is worth noting that Middle Eastern food was already in fashion a long time ago. Interest in the cuisine has mirrored the relationship between Europe and the followers of Islam and the relative prestige of their two cultures. It has depended on war and peace, on politics and commerce and also on the spirit of Europe, whether it cultivated the senses or denied them, whether it was hedonist or puritan. In the full-blooded Middle Ages when Islam was in its Golden Age with the most advanced civilization in the world, Middle Eastern food had the greatest impact on cooking in Europe.

At that time Christian Europe looked on the Infidels with fear and horror as pillaging and ravaging barbarians and cruel despots, but at the same time it was impressed by their wealth and power. Chroniclers wrote of the magnificent courts and of the loves and excesses of the Caliphs. Travellers and merchants told of the extraordinary and exquisite foods they were served while they sat on a rug near a fountain in a fruit garden. While worrying about the odious enemy, Europe fantasized about its fabulous riches, of harems and serails, bazaars and minarets, about fierce warriors who chopped off heads, and passionate lovers. The Crusades created an even more avid interest, a mixture of hate for the enemy and fascination for its exotic culture. Popular curiosity was captivated by the philosophical and scientific knowledge of the Islamic civilization. The courts and the upper classes imitated its ways and its fashions. The cooking, too, was a stimulus and an inspiration which brought new ways of looking at food. *

When commerce flourished between East and West, rice, almonds, pine kernels and other nuts and dried fruits, such as prunes, raisins, apricots and dates, arrived from the Levant with the aromatics which play an important part in Oriental cooking. Rose water and orange blossom essence, tamarind and all types of seeds, plants and bark appeared in Europe. The Crusaders, Orientalized by years spent in the Levant, often with a local cook in their employ, brought home the ways of handling them. There are still traces of this early influence in the most English of foods: in Christmas pudding and mince pies, marzipan, and in rice pudding, and it is a curious thought that our famous brown sauces and the mint and

* Maxime Rodinson has developed this theme in a general way in his book *La Fascination de l'Islam* (Maspero, 1980).

vinegar sauce for lamb perpetuate the lustre of ancient Persia on our everyday tables.

In the last few years I have become increasingly aware of the debt owed by early European cookery to the Arab tradition. I have come across recipes here and there in old English and French cookery books which are almost identical to those featured in early Islamic manuscripts. They make use of rice and ground almonds or milk of almonds, of the same mixtures of spices and aromatics and the whole range of dried fruits and nuts which were part of the early trade with the Levant. At the enchanting medieval banquet given by Lorna Sass (author of *To the King's Taste*, Richard II's book of feasts and recipes, and *To the Queen's Taste*), which Audrey Ellison helped to prepare in London in 1978, I felt that I was the guest who was the most familiar with the chicken cooked in milk and honey with pine nuts, the delicately spiced fruit and salmon pie and the dried fruit tart.

In a paper for the 'Accademia Italiana della Cucina' in 1967, the eminent French Orientalist Maxime Rodinson summarized his demonstrations of the Oriental legacy to European cooking and traced the etymology of the names of many dishes in early Latin and European cookery books to Persian and Arab origins. The legacy came partly through Arabic books on dietetics and medicine which had a considerable influence in Europe well into the eighteenth century.

In the twelfth or thirteenth century a book of Arab dietetics was translated into Latin in Venice by a certain Jambobinus of Cremona, who called it *Liber de Ferailis et Condimentis*. This translation was one of the earliest 'cookery books' of medieval Europe. The original author was Ibn Jazla, a doctor of Baghdad who died in the year 1100. Jambobinus used eighty-three of his recipes, kept their Arab names and indicated whether they were good for the stomach and noted their effect on various organs and functions as well as on the temperament. Many of these recipes were to reappear in other Latin cookery books with or without dietic information and later in Italian, French and English translations, where their origin remains detectable by their names, the Oriental ingredients and the way the method is described.

Ibn Jazla was not the only source of Arab recipes in European cookery books. Many recipes were known. Much later, in the early sixteenth century, Andrea Alpago, a Venetian doctor and scholar who had spent thirty years in the Orient, translated the works of the Arab doctor and philosopher Avicenna, who was born in 980. He used Arab books on dietetics to give information about the dishes quoted by Avicenna and put this material under Glossaries to each volume of the huge treatise on medicine written by Avicenna.

Not many of the old Oriental dishes have survived from the Middle Ages, but each generation has revived a few or picked up new ones. Eliza Acton, Mrs Beeton, Mrs Leyel and other cookery writers each offered a few exotic recipes to make people dream of the *Arabian Nights*. Elizabeth David finally lifted the veil from the food which she learned about when she lived in Cairo, Alexandria and Greece. It is her *Book of Mediterranean Food* which slightly eased my nostalgic sickness, and her brilliance and integrity which inspired me to write. In the early edition she intimated that there were many more dishes in the Near East which needed to be discovered: that was the spark that fired me.

These days, with the proliferation of Middle Eastern restaurants, we have Oriental dishes on our streets. Just as the French Revolution brought the chefs from aristocratic homes across the Channel to England, so the tumultuous and tragic events which have ripped the Middle East apart have caused the exodus of cooks and restaurateurs from several countries. Many Lebanese, Cypriot, Greek and Turkish restaurants have opened their doors in the past few years and, more recently, a few Iranian, Egyptian and North African restaurants have begun to offer their own particular specialities. In France the political convulsions which brought the Pieds Noirs from North Africa have caused 'la conquête de la France par le couscous'.

Turkish restaurants have long been established here but it is the Lebanese restaurants which have made the greater impact recently. Theirs has been called the 'pearl of the Arab kitchen'. In its position as gateway to the Mediterranean and its role of intermediary between East and West, and because of an early tourist trade, Lebanon has had to groom its food to appeal to Western tastes. It inherited from the Phoenicians the art of trading and the art of pleasing and from the Arabs their hospitality, while its long association with France has brought ways of refining the Arab kitchen.

Unfortunately, apart from Turkey and Lebanon, there is no real restaurant tradition in the Middle East. Such establishments have developed historically from street food with a few chairs placed beside a movable stall. Their menus of meats grilled over embers, salads and rice still belong more to the street, while the vast and rich repertoire of home cooking with its regional and community variations has stayed in the family.

The main purpose of this book has remained to winkle out these recipes from village or backwater obscurity and from the jealous protection of a privileged household.

General Features of Middle Eastern Food

I have noted a few general features of Middle Eastern cooking which may help to form a better understanding of the character of this cuisine.

Cooking fats used in most countries in the past were rather heavy. In particular, *alya*, the rendered fat from a sheep's or lamb's tail, was extremely popular. Many of the medieval recipes I have included start with 'melt tail' or 'fry in tail'. They refer to *alya*. As a special refinement it was sometimes coloured red or yellow. Today, although this fat is still used for cooking in a few districts, it has generally been replaced by a clarified butter called *samna*, ordinary butter, margarine and oil.

Samna, the most favoured, is butter (usually made from buffaloes' milk) which has been melted over boiling water and clarified by straining it through thin dampened muslin. The impurities which cause butter to burn and darken are eliminated, as well as much of the water content. It is rich and strong with a distinctive taste, and a little of it will give the same result as a much larger quantity of butter. It also keeps well. A type of *samna* sold in jars in Indian shops in England is called *ghee*. (See also page 64.)

The usual oils are olive, cotton seed, nut, corn and sesame. Olive oil is preferred for dishes which are to be eaten cold and for frying fish.

As a general rule, people like to fry or sauté their meat and vegetables before adding water to make stews and soups. These acquire a darker colour and a richer flavour, while the meat, sealed by the preliminary frying, retains its juices. The Moroccans of Fez are an exception; their pale, delicate lamb stews are distinguished from those of the inhabitants of other Moroccan towns. They do not fry the ingredients, but cook them from the start in water with a little oil, relying on the stocks which result, and the variety and quality of the other ingredients, to give colour, texture and body to their dishes. To them it is a crime against refinement to fry meats or vegetables destined for a stew.

The utensils and the type of heat available have to a large extent determined the style of cooking. Ovens have only recently been introduced in most homes. In the past, cooking was generally done over a type of primus called a *fatayel*. It was a long, slow procedure, and pans were sometimes left to simmer overnight. This habit has remained to the present day, although the necessity may have passed, and it is more usual for food to be prepared over heat than for it to be baked or roasted in an oven.

It was customary in the past, and to a lesser degree it still is even today, to send certain dishes to be cooked in the ovens of the local bakery. This was a feature of the way of life. People hurried about in the streets with huge trays or casseroles, sometimes balancing them on their heads. Life at the ovens bustled with activity and humour. I am told of great-aunts who sealed their pans with a paste made of flour and water, ostensibly in order to cook the dish under pressure, but also to ensure that no one introduced an unwholesome, impure or prohibited ingredient out of spite. Many people specified precisely in what position they wanted their pans placed in the enormous ovens. Others, perfectionists, sat by the ovens on wicker stools throughout the cooking time, watching their food and giving directions for the pans to be moved this way and that, in order to vary the degree of the heat. Today, dishes which would in the past have gone to the district oven (such as a roast leg of lamb surrounded by all its vegetables) are cooked in domestic ovens, but slowly, as before.

Another factor which helped to perpetuate the tradition of slow, lengthy cooking, as well as that of the more elaborate dishes which require time and craftsmanship, is the social custom which has kept women in the home until very recently.

Precision and timing are not important and no harm is done if a dish is left to simmer for an hour longer and the meat is so tender that it has fallen off the bone or the lentils have disintegrated. Nor is there any liking for red meat or underdone vegetables – unless they are eaten completely raw which is also popular.

Grilling little morsels over charcoal is associated everywhere with Muslim cooking. Skewer cookery, whether it is meat, chicken or fish kebabs (generally believed to have been developed by Turks on the field of battle), is the most popular street food in every Middle Eastern country and it is not only street vendors who are masters of the art of using the heat from dying embers.

Throughout the area, lamb is the favourite meat and the most available, but it is only in the desert lands that it is eaten in great quantities. Because of the dietary laws of the predominant religion of Islam, generally no pork is used and no wine. Even where meat is not out of reach because of the cost, it is stretched to go far in a stew or sauce or as part of the filling in vegetables, with 250 g (½ lb) serving on average four people. A wide variety of vegetables are eaten raw or cooked in olive oil to be served cold. They are also stuffed and appear in stews or as pickles. Fruits are used in many different ways. Wheat is the staple cereal of the countryside, rice is the urban one to serve as a side dish and base to most foods. Beans of all types, split peas, chick peas and lentils, have been part of the diet since time immemorial. Much is made of them; the choice depends on what grows locally. There are noodles and very thin spaghetti. A meal without bread to dip in is unthinkable and some people cannot enjoy anything without it.

Nuts have been used since ancient times in a variety of dishes and in unexpected ways. One of the regional characteristics which denotes the nationality of the cook is the selective use of nuts. Where an Egyptian or Syrian would use ground almonds or pine nuts to thicken a sauce such as *tarator* (page 218) or almond sauce (page 424), a Turk would use ground walnuts. Iranians also use ground walnuts, for example in their *faisinjan* sauce (page 242) for chicken or duck, in the same way as they are used for the Circassian chicken (page 95). In Iran, pomegranate or sour cherry sauce is added to the walnut sauce, while in Turkey it is sprinkled with the favourite garnish of red paprika melted in oil.

In most countries, it is customary to place a bowl of fresh yoghourt on the table, to be eaten with such varied foods as *eggah*, pilavs, stuffed vegetables, salads and kebabs. It is sometimes flavoured with salt, mint and crushed garlic. In Turkey, yoghourt is used extensively as a bed for meat or vegetables, or to be poured over salads, eggs, vegetables, rice, almost anything in fact. It is also used as a cooking liquid, particularly in the Lebanon, Turkey and Iran.

Each country has developed its own special way of making a

paper-thin pastry. The most usual is to pull out a soft dough as much as it can possibly be stretched; another is to make very thin pancakes with a batter. With melted butter brushed in between leaves, the result is a type of puff pastry.

People do not usually eat puddings or sweets at meal time. They are usually reserved for visitors and festive occasions. Each country has many types of milk pudding and each has an assortment of pastries stuffed with nuts and bathed in syrup.

Flavours range from delicate and subtle to fierce and powerful. Persians favour dishes delicately balanced in between sweet and sour, cooked with vinegar, lemon and sugar, and the juice of sour pomegranates. They share with Moroccans a predilection and a skill for combining the textures and flavours of meats and fruits. All these tastes have been adopted to some degree in the neighbouring countries.

Garlic is generally liked, both raw and fried. Many will put a whole head in the ashes of a fire to mellow and soften to a cream.

The sharp taste of lemons or limes can be tasted in many salads and cooked dishes. A rather musty taste is obtained by Iranians and Iraqis with a dried variety, and a subdued one by Moroccans with lemons pickled in brine. The scents of rose and orange blossom water are evident in sweet dishes which are sometimes made with honey instead of sugar. The Orient is so partial to the sensual pleasures of perfumes and aromatics that the widest possible variety of herbs, spices, woods, and essences are used in the kitchen. They are an expression of the voluptuous Semitic taste for pleasure and the happy life which even the ascetic puritans do not attempt to resist.

Taste and pleasure are not the only considerations, for good healthy eating is part of the Arab philosophical doctrine of the perfect concordance of the elements of the universe with those of human nature. In the past medical men wrote books on dietetics; today those who can, strive for a balanced diet.

Understanding a Cuisine – National and Regional Differences

Having collected a rich and extraordinary assortment of recipes from a great number of people, many of whom did not know the origins of their favourite dishes, and had picked them up at some point in their wanderings – from a place they had visited, from a relative or a chance acquaintance, I tried to give them a national identity. It was impossible to class them by countries because of the overlap and similarities; there would be too much repetition. Instead, a picture emerged of one culinary tradition; very poor in parts, extremely varied and rich in others and with more regional than national variations. There were often more differences between town and country than across a border, and neighbouring towns in the same country sometimes had different specialities while the main towns of different countries had the same foods.

The reasons for this are to be found in the geography and history of the area. The geographical differences are extremely wide; there are large, empty deserts and lush countryside, great rivers and arid hills, green mountains, marshlands and long coastlines. Not every country has inherited a bit of each, nor do they have the same produce. Their cooking reflects those differences but it also mirrors the ramified complexities of the past. The result of a shared history and the unifying influences of the Arab and Islamic and later Ottoman empires with their inherent divisions, bitter struggles and conflicts, has been the development of one culinary tradition that can be divided into four main branches. Of these, the most exquisite and refined and one of the least known abroad is the Iranian cuisine, which is the ancient source of much of the *haute cuisine* of the Middle East. It is based on long-grain rice, which grows around the Caspian Sea. This is served at every meal, cooked to the highest standard of perfection and accompanied by a variety of sauces or mixed with meats, vegetables, fruits and nuts.

In Syria, Lebanon and Jordan the cooking is much the same, for boundaries here are only recent. It is in this patchwork of creeds and communities where Arab revival and consciousness first took root that what is known as 'Arab' food is at its best. Urban cooking is based on rice, country food on cracked wheat. It is no accident that the area has been called the 'Fertile Crescent' for the soil bears the richest variety and quality of vegetables and fruits. Although some of their neighbours with a sheep-farming economy laugh at the 'vegetable-eaters', theirs is nevertheless the most popular cuisine of the Arab world.

Turkish cooking is the one which has influenced most countries abroad and which we have known longest and best, for the Ottoman

Empire expanded over an enormous territory for hundreds of years, leaving its traces on the tables of such countries as Bulgaria, Romania, Yugoslavia, Hungary, Greece, Cyprus, Crete, Egypt, parts of Russia and North Africa. In all these countries you will find the same kebabs and rice and wheat dishes, savoury pies and yoghourt salads and the nutty, syrupy pastries with paper-thin or shredded dough.

The fourth distinctive cooking style is that of North Africa, where Moroccan cuisine is especially magnificent. It is based on the couscous of the original Berber inhabitants with centuries-old echoes from Spain, Portugal and Sicily and the more recent influence of France. Remarkably, it bears the strongest signs of inheritance from ancient Persia in the art of combining ingredients and mixing spices.

I was tempted to learn more about the origins of the dishes. The search became fascinating, although it was soon clear that, to a certain extent, it would be impossible to determine their true sources. The same recipes seemed to turn up in several countries. One could not be certain as to when exactly they had come or from where, and who had introduced them to whom. But it was a thrill to discover a dish mentioned in some historical or literary work, in a poem or in a proverb, and to conjure up the circumstances of its arrival in a particular place, to guess which battle and which conquering general had brought it, and to wonder why one country had adopted it while another had rejected it.

The history of this food is that of the Middle East. Dishes carry the triumphs and glories, the defeats, the loves and sorrows of the past. We owe some to an event, or to one man; the Caliph who commissioned it, the poet who sang it, or the *Imam* who 'fainted on receiving it'.

Nothing was more valuable to me in my pursuit, nor more exciting, than the discovery of writings by the French Orientalist, Professor Maxime Rodinson, on the history of Arab food. I am much indebted to him and in particular to his study of early culinary manuscripts. I have dealt with these in greater detail in this new edition for they have not ceased to fascinate me.

A Cuisine Shaped by a Tumultuous History

A look into the past of the Middle East, a region strategically located athwart the crossroads of great cultures, shows it constantly beset by endless currents and cross-currents, great and small wars and all-embracing empires with factional and dynastic rivalries. All this, with the shifting allegiances, cultures and subcultures and people spilling from one part to another, has affected the kitchen very much to its advantage. Here is its story.

The early origins of Middle Eastern food can be found in Bedouin dishes and the peasant dishes of each of the countries involved. In the case of Egypt, one can go back as far as Pharaonic times to find the foods still eaten by the Egyptians today: roast goose, *melokhia* soup, *bamia* and *batarekh*. In his *Dictionary of the Bible*, J. Hastings writes that the 'Hebrews in the wilderness looked back wistfully on the cucumbers, melons, leeks, onions and garlic of Egypt; all of these were subsequently cultivated by them in Palestine'. He also lists other foods mentioned in the Bible, such as varieties of beans and lentils, chick peas, bitter herbs (still eaten today in the Passover ritual), olives, figs, grapes and raisins, dates, almonds and nuts. These were prepared in a manner similar to that of the Egyptians, probably remembered by the Jews from their time in Egypt. One speciality the Hebrews adopted was a fish, split open, salted and dried in the sun. It was very useful to take on long journeys, and it is still considered a great delicacy all over the Middle East.

Little is known about what the other ancient inhabitants of the Middle East ate – the Syrians, Lydians, Phrygians, Cappadocians, Armenians, Assyrians, Babylonians, Cilicians and Mesopotamians. But one can assume that these prosperous, civilized states have had highly developed and luxurious culinary traditions, undoubtedly influenced by Greek and Roman customs, which fused together at different times during their history of invasions and conquests. The inhabitants of the arid desert areas of Arabia and the Sahara produced the spartan food still popular with the Bedouins today.

The Persian Influence

The Persian Empire of *c.* 500 B.C. was the earliest empire to envelop the region. Macedonian Greeks followed to radiate their culture,

culinary and other. As the Romans and Parthians fought for domi-
nance, the states they governed assimilated their traditions – and
their cooking. And while these empires were won and lost, the
character and style of Middle Eastern food was born.

It is in the Persia of the Sassanid period (third to seventh century)
that it blossomed. The reign of King Khusrow I inaugurated the most
brilliant period of the Sassanid era, and with it the decline of
Byzantine power. Alexander the Great and his successors had made
part of Persia, as well as parts of India, Hellenic strongholds. The
debris of Hellenic civilization remained for many centuries, min-
gling and fusing with the Persian and Indian civilizations. There was
crossfertilization in the kitchen as there was with philosophies,
myths and cultures. Similarities in food in these countries today,
particularly between India and Persia, bear witness to these early
influences.

In the reign of Khusrow II (early seventh century), Byzantium was
finally defeated, and the Persian generals conquered Antioch,
Damascus, Jerusalem and Alexandria. The triumphs of this great
king were matched by his growing cruelty, vanity and greed. Enormous sums were spent on his pleasures and those of his court.
Persian tales and legends describe his fantastic banquets, lavishly
laid, dazzling with luxury and extravagance. In his book *L'Iran sous
les Sassanides*, Arthur Christensen describes some of the dishes
popular at the time, and the court's favourite recipes. It is then that
some of the dishes so familiar today made their first appearance. A
'dish for the King' consisted of hot and cold meats, rice jelly, stuffed
vine leaves, marinated chicken and a sweet date purée. A 'Khorassa-
nian dish' was composed of meat grilled on the spit and meat fried in
butter with a sauce. A 'Greek dish' was made with eggs, honey,
milk, butter, rice and sugar – a sort of rice pudding. A 'Dehkan dish'
consisted of slices of salted mutton with pomegranate juice, served
with eggs.

Young kid was popular, so was beef cooked with spinach and
vinegar. All kinds of game and poultry were eaten; in particular,
hens fed on chenevis were hunted and 'frightened' before they were
killed, and then grilled on the spit. The lower part of the chicken's
back was considered the tastiest. Today it is still a delicacy, sometimes called 'the mother-in-law's morsel'. Meat was marinated in
yoghourt and flavoured with spices. Many different kinds of almond
pastry were prepared, jams were made with quinces, dates stuffed

with almonds and walnuts. All this is still done today. Our dishes were savoured by Khusrow and his favourite wife, Shirin.

The decline of the Sassanids had started by the end of Khusrow's reign, but even after this grandiose empire had crumbled, its music and its food survived. Many Arab and Turkish dishes today betray their origins by their Persian names.

Dishes Spread to the Far Corners of the Islamic Empire

The spread of Islam was the most important factor in the development of a gastronomy comparable to that of France and China. The death of the Prophet Muhammad in Arabia in the year A.D. 632 was followed by victorious wars waged by the followers of his faith. Bedouin Arabs burst out of the Arabian Peninsula, conquered one territory after another, converted it to Islam and established an enormous Islamic Empire stretching across Asia, North Africa, Spain and Sicily. Wherever they went with their sword the Arabs brought their tastes and those of the countries they conquered, amalgamating and spreading the foods from one part of the empire to another.

In the early days, during the Umayyad period when Damascus was the capital of the empire, the Arab tribes, led by the family of Muhammad, established themselves as a ruling class, separate and above their conquered subjects. The Bedouin warriors, quartered in their great army encampments, ate only once a day and kept aloof and superior with high standards of restraint and strict, austere living. Their primitive tastes collided with the local Byzantine and Persian hedonism. They ate very simple foods which combined ingredients of agricultural and pastoral origin. Preparation was elementary – the Bedouin diet consisted of bread and dates; of mutton, with some goat and camel meat, and the milk of these animals; with the occasional game and wild berries found in the desert. The settled agricultural populations ate chicory, beets, gourds, courgettes, marrow, cucumber, leeks, onions and garlic, olives, palm hearts, broad beans, lemons, pomegranates and grapes. A gruel called *harira* was made of dried barley meal to which water, butter or fat were added, and flour was cooked in milk. Spices were hardly used, even though the Arabs were engaged in transporting them to Europe. They obtained too high a price on the Roman market to be used locally.

The tastes of the Prophet prevailed. His favourite dishes, *tharid*, bread crumbled in a broth of meat and vegetables, and *hays*, a mixture of dates, butter and milk, were still popular. Muhammad had a special liking for sweetmeats and honey and he was fond of cucumbers. He also liked fat meat. When a lamb or a kid was being cooked, he would go to the pot, take out the shoulder and eat it. It is said that he never ate reclining, for the angel Gabriel had told him that such was the manner of kings. He used to eat with his thumb and his two forefingers; and when he had done, he would lick them, beginning with the middle one.

Over the years, Arab ranks were infiltrated and diluted by Byzantine, Persian and the other conquered peoples. The subject classes, slowly working their way up through the evolving Islamic society to a footing of equality with the Arabs, came at last to constitute the new society themselves. The Abbasid régime was one of Persian ascendancy in which Persians flooded into Islam, transporting with them the core of their civilization. The Arabs, dazzled by the aristocratic brilliance of the Persians they had conquered, adopted their dishes with their traditions of chivalry and good living. The other subject nations, Asian, Aramean, Egyptian and Greek, later also came to the fore, bringing their own sometimes prestigious culinary heritage to the now cosmopolitan society.

Thus the Arabs, even though their own cooking was rudimentary, brought about the marriage of cooking styles of the ancient Mediterranean and the Near East and the opulent cooking of Persia.

The Golden Age

In the Abbassid period from the ninth to the twelfth century, the Golden Age of Islam, cooking was transformed into an art which reached magnificent heights. The Islamic Empire occupied far-flung areas of the world – Egypt, and all of North Africa, nearly all Spain, the islands of Sicily and Crete, with a few southern Italian towns, besides the north of Arabia, Syria, Armenia, the south-east part of the Caucasus, Mesopotamia and Iraq, Persia and Afghanistan. It was the most powerful influence in the world. Mecca was its religious centre and Baghdad was the capital, the cultural and political hub. The creative culinary genius flourished especially under the reign of Harun-al-Rashid (786–801). Culinary literature proliferated and reached the level of an art. There were two parallel trends. One, the result of the interest in food of the Abbassid upper classes, written by them or for them, was a princely activity devoted to the refinement of pleasure and to setting high standards of taste and *savoir-vivre* for the élite – poets, astrologers, astronomers, scholars, princes and even Caliphs took pleasure in writing about food. The other was the development of a branch of medicine: dietetics, and this was the work of doctors concerned with health.

Gastronomy was especially esteemed in this rich period of Arab history when the search for the most delicious combinations of food, according to increasingly subtle criteria, formed the preoccupation of a distinguished society of gourmets. The banquets at the royal courts of the Caliphs of Baghdad were proverbial for their variety and lavishness. The Caliphs commissioned people to invent dishes, to write poems about foods and to sing their praise at gatherings which became legendary. Mas'údí, a writer of the time, describes one such event at the court of Mustakfi, the Caliph who was blinded and deposed in 946, in his *Meadows of Gold*. I quote from Professor Arberry's translation:

One day Mustakfi said: 'It is my desire that we should assemble on such and such a day, and converse together about the different varieties of food, and the poetry that has been composed on this subject.' Those present agreed; and on the day prescribed Mustakfi joined the party, and bade every man produce what he had prepared. Thereupon one member of the circle spoke up: 'O Commander of the Faithful, I have some verses by Ibn al-Mu'tazz in which the poet describes a tray containing bowls of *kämakh*.'

Ibn al-Mu'tazz too had been a tragic prince who ruled for one day only and was put to death in 908. The poem, about a tray of hors d'oeuvre, described the different elements in an ardent and sensuous manner. Others followed with long poems to the glory of many delicacies in terms of ecstatic love.

Another recited a work by the poet, astrologer and culinary expert Husain al-Kushâjim, describing a table of delicacies, of roast kid, partridges, chickens, *tardina, sanbusaj, nad, buran* and sweet lozenges. Another then stood up and recited a poem of Ibn al-Rumi, describing *wast*. Another quoted Ibrāhīm of Mosul on the marvel of *sanbusaj*. Yet others glorified *harisa, madira, judhaba* and *qata'if*. Each time, Mustakfi ordered that everything that had been mentioned in the poem should be served. They ate to the sound of music and sweet maidens' voices. Never had the narrator seen the Caliph so happy since the day of his accession. To all present, revellers, singers and musicians, he gave money and gifts. Sadly, the narrator adds, this Caliph was one day to be seized by Ahmad ibn Abi Shajâ' Mu'izz al-dawla the Buwayhid, who had his eyes 'put out'.

A ruling class had emerged whose members led a life of luxury and who devised a code of *savoir-vivre*. Manuals on how to be a connoisseur appeared. In *Meadows of Gold* Mas'ūdi advised people to read his other work *Ahbar Az-Zaman*, unfortunately lost, in which, he says,

One can be instructed in detail on the variety of wines, on desserts, on the manner of arranging them in baskets or on plates, either piled up in pyramids, or otherwise, a culinary summary the knowledge of which is essential and which cannot be ignored by a well-bred man. One can also read about the new fashions in the way of dishes, the art of combining aromas and spices for the seasoning; subjects of conversation, as well as the way to wash one's hands in the presence of one's host.

Development and Character of the Court Cuisine*

In 1949 Professor Maxime Rodinson published 'Recherches sur les documents Arabes relatifs à la cuisine' in the *Revue des études islamiques*. In this sociological and philological study of the history of food in the Arab world, he discusses early culinary literature, analyses cookery manuals (see page 22) and describes the court cuisine of the twelfth and thirteenth centuries. In what follows I have also made use of the information he gives in the entry 'Ghidha' in the *Encyclopaedia of Islam*.

He describes the many changes in the new empire, which affected food habits. The spread of food products was one. Products which had formerly been grown only in one part of the area now spread throughout it. Rice is a good example. It originated in India and was grown in Syria, Iraq and Iran before Islam. Now it spread as a crop all

* A version of this section of my Introduction has been published in *Petits Propos Culinaires*, 6 (1980).

over the Arab world and became a popular food as far away as Spain (although it did not quite take the place of wheat, which was a commodity traded on a large scale everywhere). Sugar, introduced to Iran from India shortly before the Muslim conquest, spread after this through the whole of the Mediterranean.

Large-scale transport brought food from one part of the empire to another; truffles from the desert, olive oil from Syria, dates from Iraq, coffee from Arabia. Later, a wide range of ingredients was introduced from places outside the empire. Spices such as pepper, ginger, cinnamon, cloves, cardamom, cumin, coriander, betel, musc, mastic and nutmeg were brought from China, India and Africa. In the twelfth century, dried and salted fish, honey and hazelnuts came from Russia and the Slav countries, cheese from Sicily and Crete, wine, chestnuts and saffron from the South of France.

Increased travel meant that cooks from parts renowned for their food were employed in distant regions. In the Middle Ages, Egyptian cuisine and cooks had a high reputation. So did the cooks of Bolu in Turkey. And there were massive migrations, with immigrants introducing their traditional dishes into their new habitat. The rulers had huge, well-equipped and well-stocked kitchens, staffed by numerous cooks and their assistants, in which all types of dishes could be attempted.

By the tenth century there was a new prosperous élite in Baghdad which aspired to refinement and had strict rules in this matter. Their quest for the grand, the exotic and the unusual led them to the adoption of the cuisines of foreigners whose civilizations enjoyed in their eyes a certain prestige for the power and glory which they had formerly enjoyed. Hence the vogue for Iranian dishes, and later the fashion for things Turkish. The European influence began to be evident in the period of the Crusades ('Franc' dishes appear in the *Wusla*).

Characteristics of the New Court Cuisine

The cookery manuals naturally dealt with the new cuisine which was constantly developing in the kitchens of the courts, and which was much being discussed. It had not been handed down from the past and therefore needed to be recorded.

Introduction to the New Edition

What was the style of this princely cuisine? The following features characterized it.

1. *It used expensive ingredients which only a few could afford.* Some of these were rare and came from far, such as spices; others were newly grown on Arab soil, such as rice and sugar. Chicken and lamb were used; and so were locally grown vegetables, but the more common ones such as okra, beans and figs were not.

Everyone knew which were the foods of the poor and which of the rich. (Proverbs, songs and popular literature express this awareness.) Meat and rice were for the rich; lentils, beans and honey for the poor. Although these latter foods retained their popularity, they were stigmatized in a book by al-Jahiz as the food of misers and were almost ignored in the manuscripts we have mentioned. When simple local dishes were included, they were glamorized; for example, the melted down lamb's-tail fat was perfumed with a variety of aromatics as well as with quince and apple and dried coriander, aniseed, onion, cinnamon and mastic, and was coloured red and yellow. Bedouin dishes with dates were made grand by replacing the stones with blanched almonds. Traditional peasant dishes with wheat and lentils were enriched with meat and delicately spiced.

2. *Techniques were elaborate and sophisticated.* Methods of preserving with salt and vinegar, lemon juice and mustard were inherited from the Ancient East and from classical civilizations. Fruit was crystallized in honey. Smoke-drying was said in Egypt to be a Greek process. (In the past they had dried meat by hanging thin strips in the open or preserved it by burying it in fat.) Ancient ways were moulded to the new demands of the court – a general characteristic style developed with flavours even from as far as Spain and Turkistan, with regional variations.

3. *The grander dishes were Iranian.* Their origins are revealed in the Arab repertoire today by their names ending in *-ak* and *-aj*. Techniques of cooking and elegant ways were adopted from conquered Iran, which had been the most prestigious civilization in the area.

4. *Koranic prohibitions were observed.* Koranic regulations and prohibitions advised by the pious specialists on religious questions were followed. No pork was used and no wine.

5. *Newly acquired tastes became fashionable.* The taste for highly spiced foods and sweet things appeared at a more advanced stage of Muslim civilization; it was simply a continuation of the

tastes of classical antiquity. So was the taste for sweet and sour which came via Iran.

6. *Visual appeal was important.* Saffron and turmeric were used for colour, and much care was taken to give delight in presentation. Counterfeit dishes such as mock brains and an omelette in a bottle were devised as pleasant surprises.

7. *Complexity was valued.* Complexity in flavour was valued for its own sake, quite apart from the actual flavour itself. Aromatics were used in tiny quantities but in a great number and a variety of combinations. All the spices already mentioned were combined with herbs such as parsley, mint, rue, thyme, lavender, mallow, purslane, bay and tarragon. Poppy and sesame seeds, fenugreek, rose petals and rose buds were used. The result was delicate and subtle, and, if we go by the tastes handed down, not too strong or too hot.

Complexity in form was also esteemed. Confections which required skill, application and time were well considered, especially if they were small and beautifully shaped. Vegetables were hollowed out and stuffed, tiny pies were filled, elegant little parcels were made with wrappings of pastries or leaves.

The Place of Dietetics and Medical Books

Dietetics were at the same time a branch of medicine and a form of culinary literature.

Anecdotes of the period depict doctors sitting at the tables of Caliphs to advise them on what was good for them. (Maimonides sat for al-Malik al Afdal.)

The educated classes paid a great deal of attention to dietetic precepts so that this science was of great importance. It stemmed for the most part from the scientific medicine systematized by the Greeks and was based on the theory of humours, from which all kinds of conclusions had been reached on the nature of each food and its suitability to one or another human temperament. It incorporated local popular ideas – that dates cause ophthalmia but are good for childbirth, for instance – and penetrated deeply among the masses.

Arab books on dietetics preceded medical books, and all the early books of medicine contained a long chapter enumerating, usually in alphabetical order, the attributes and faults of each food from the point of view of bodily and spiritual well-being. They also gave recipes, which were much like those which went round the courts, and accompanied them by critical advice on what was good for the liver and the heart.

Culinary Literature Disappears; Cooking Styles Continue

Arab culinary literature faded with the decline of this brilliant civilization and of the Abbassid dynasty which was marked by the fall of Baghdad in 1258 at the hands of the Mongols. Gastronomy continued to have its enthusiasts, but with the growth of religious puritanism they became more discreet. Its authors were no longer the aristocratic arbiters of taste but obscure people who painstakingly recorded recipes for their own use and the instruction of their servants.

Some of al-Baghdadi's recipes for stews could be word for word instructions for an Iranian *khoresh* or a Moroccan *tagine* of today; and we still make in my family many of the dishes described in the *Wusla*. As for the methods, grinding fine, rolling into balls or oblongs, pounding in the mortar, simmering long in broth, cutting up in lozenges, bathing in syrup – every touch and movement required are those employed today. As in the past, milk puddings are thickened with ground rice and cornflour or semolina; and the same honeyed pastries filled with chopped nuts are the usual fare of vendors in the street, to be kept preciously in boxes for festive occasions or the much-appreciated visit of an unexpected guest.

The Ottoman Empire

The next empire to pick up the immense culinary fund from the derelict Caliphate was the great Turkish Ottoman Empire in the fourteenth century. The Turks made their first appearance in the ninth century as slave soldiers (Mameluks), drawn from the steppe-lands of Central Asia for the regular armies of the empire. These Turkish slaves came to wield great power, and after ruling with a number of small local dynasties they were in control of the whole Islamic realm. A nomadic branch, the Osmanlis, or Ottomans, were to establish the most powerful Muslim and indeed world empire in history, pushing the boundaries into the heart of Europe.

Fierce and warlike by nature, they had little sophistication by way of food (their shish kebabs are said to have originated on the battlefields when their invading armies had to camp outdoors in tents awaiting a new assault). The Sultan's table, nevertheless, soon took on the lustre and glamour of the Abbassid banquets. At first the Turks took the Persian cuisine as their model but gradually they developed one of their own based on the foods they adopted from the welter of different peoples, creeds and ethnic groups of their empire, and especially those of their slaves who were palace cooks. The extraordinary amalgam of dishes was the result of the unique character of the empire and its ruling class whose members entered as the Sultan's slave and remained a slave all their lives as part of the Ottoman Slave Household. This institution was so superior in discipline and in organizational efficiency that it allowed the empire to survive for centuries. The more able recruits were subjected to a strict course of training and turned into courtiers, husbands of princesses, even Grand Viziers. The profession of public slave on a high level was dangerous, all-important and glorious, indeed the most splendid profession in the empire and it was open exclusively to children born of infidels.

The royal family, the Sultan's wives, palace and government officers, the standing army – all were slaves and descendants of slaves. The Sultan himself was the son of a slave. Most were Christians or their children and had been captured in battle or bought in markets from Barbary pirates and Krim Tartars. Some had been given as gifts by Venetian traders. They had been plucked from Caucasian highlands, from Russian forests and Eurasian steppe-lands, and some came from Western Europe (a few as volunteers). Wrenched from all family ties and roots, they were more ready to serve loyally. As blue eyes, rosy cheeks and fair hair increased in the mixed population of the greatest Muslim state, so a wide variety of foods remembered from far-off lands entered the culinary pool.

The first Turkish-born cooks employed in the Palace of Topkapi were from Bolu, the mountain region where the Sultans went hunting. According to legend they were so pleased with the young men who cooked their meats for them in the open that they brought them back to the Palace.

Introduction to the New Edition

In this extraordinary society food was all-important. The insignia of the Janissary force was the pot and spoon which symbolized a standard of living higher than that of other troops. The titles of its officers were drawn from the camp kitchen, from 'First Maker of Soup' to 'First Cook' and 'First Carrier of Water', and the sacred object of the regiment was the stew pot around which the Janissaries gathered, not merely to eat but to take counsel among themselves.

The courts of the glamorous and romantic Sultans such as Mehmed the Conqueror and Suleiman the Magnificent were notorious for their luxury and devotion to the pleasures of the table. In their kitchens dishes from all over the world were developed and perfected. Cooks were recruited from the provinces or learned their trade early on as slave page-boys in the palace school, where they were taught to sharpen knives and swords, to mix drinks and cook the Sultan's favourite dishes for his sumptuous banquets. The most powerful Grand Vizier of all time, Mehmed Koprulu, started off as a young cook. Cooking was one of the most important of the arts and everyone, poet, astrologer, physician or prince, wrote recipes, songs and poems about food.

The sixteenth-century Turkish poet Revani, in his *Işret Nāme*, deals with festive themes, and writes of the glorious banquets of the time: cultured revellers seated in a circle around crystal cups and flagons, each excelling in some art or other, debating a point of literature or philosophy, while a few musicians play the plaintive melodies of the East, a singer tells of tragic loves and a fair young cupbearer goes her rounds. He also describes the various delicacies which figure at these banquets: sausages lying as if they were serpents keeping guard over a treasure, roast fowl dancing with delight to see the wine, grains of rice like pearls, saffron dishes like yellow-haired beauties, *börek* which might flout the sun, *chorek* shaped like the moon, jelly on which the almond fixeth her eyes, *qada'if* like a silver-bodied loveling.

By the nineteenth century the decline of the Ottoman Empire was marked by corruption, inefficiency and brutality, and the society was by then based on sectarian allegiances. While the different countries struggled to break free with the impulse of modern European nationalism, they looked in their own particular traditions for their pleasures.

Pre-Ottoman and pre-Islamic foods such as the Berber couscous and the Egyptian *ful medames* were celebrated with greater fervour

41

and the small sects and communities clung to their differences, making their specialities a proof of identity.

But the Turks have nevertheless left their traces on the tables of the countries they conquered – not only in the Middle East but also in the Balkans, in Bulgaria, Romania, Serbia, Yugoslavia and Hungary, Greece, Cyprus, Crete and parts of Russia, as an agreeable compensation for past tyrannies and spilt blood. In their own country, the old court cuisine is represented mainly in Istanbul and by the restaurant trade, while the cooking of Anatolia remains largely unknown in its great regional diversity.

The traditions of the aristocratic cuisine are kept going by what remains of an old and prestigious trade: the profession of cook or chef, which has never been equalled anywhere else in the Middle East. In the heart of Anatolia, near the Lake Abant, lies the *vilayet* of Bolu from where cooks were recruited to serve in the Royal Palace or the houses of the nobles. Leaving the fields to be tilled by women, the young men of Bolu came to Istanbul where, as apprentices to one of their relatives, they learnt the secrets of the trade. At the age of twelve or thirteen, boys were sent to Istanbul to work in the kitchens near their fathers, uncles or cousins, who taught them what no stranger was allowed to learn.

At the age of eighteen or nineteen, a young man, by then a fully fledged cook, would blushingly ask the masters for permission to visit the village. There he would marry, leave his wife and come back to his kitchen in Istanbul. This is how a closed society of chefs was formed. Although nowadays the trade is not so jealously guarded, the really good cooks still come from the region of Bolu and especially from the villages of Gerede and Mengen.

The writer Emine Foat Tugay writes about these famous chefs in her family chronicle *Three Centuries* (1963), where she says:

Turkish cooking of the past ranked among the great cuisines of the world. Much of it has disappeared together with the excellent chefs, who had learnt their trade as apprentices in konaks and palaces, where they had to satisfy the exigent palates of their masters. They gradually worked their way up under the master chef from scullery-boy or apprentice to become third, second, and finally first assistant cook. After ten or twelve years the chef would declare his first assistant capable of working on his own account. The young cook then invited all the other chefs to a dinner which he prepared single-handed. He would choose all the most difficult dishes, and anxiously awaited their verdict, since it was they and they only who were empowered to declare him a master cook. If the dinner won the approval of the chefs, they would present him with a large silver watch on a thick silver chain, and would wrap around him, from the waist downwards, a wide striped cotton cloth which took the place of an apron, an insignia of his new status. Henceforth he was their equal.

Every cook in Turkey is a native of the province of Bolu. They never marry anyone outside their own village, and leave their wives at home to look after their fields and to bring up the children. They take leave once a year, for two or three months, and call in a colleague of equal capacity to replace them in the interval. This custom still holds good nowadays, though otherwise the system which I have mentioned has disappeared so completely that even the now middle-aged do not remember it. The old chefs almost always brought their complete staffs with them when they were appointed and took them away with them when they left.

New Trends

After the collapse of the Ottoman Empire in the early part of this century, the identity of the Arabic-speaking world crystallized as an Arab world and at the same time the influence of Europe became very important. People came to settle from all over the world. It was the Middle East of Lawrence Durrell, the Alexandria where Greek and Italian were spoken on the *corniche*, the Lebanon where most people spoke French. Italy was in Libya, the British were everywhere, the Maghreb was French. In this cosmopolitan and Europeanized climate, Western food, especially French cuisine, was considered more desirable. Restaurants and caterers offered European menus. Food in general tended to become lighter and cooking fats more digestible. Dishes appeared in which the tastes of East and West had fused. A handful of cookery books in Arabic featured dishes such as *roly-poly bel costarda* (a type of swiss roll) and *macaroni al Italiani*. The Grand Hotel of Khartoum offered a menu devised in the time of Gordon which was very reminiscent of British Rail fare, although clients could be served local food on request.

Each country began to follow its own gastronomic way and cultivate its peasant or regal past, its Arab identity or its closeness to Europe. Traditional local dishes were more openly appreciated but many countries were too poor to make the most of their gastronomic heritage. Women went out to work when they could and impoverished bourgeoisies could no longer keep up old standards with a cuisine which required the skill of patient hands, nor could they always find the good ingredients.

Socialism and Islamic egalitarianism have created a new mood in the kitchen. Ideology has elevated peasant food and 'cheap, quick and easy' things have become respectable. Presumably it is not so easy to persuade hostile servants to spend hours pounding and stuffing. The humble food which had been stigmatized in the past as low class and miserly has now become fashionable. It had probably always been the preferred 'family food' with the special touch usually bestowed on what is for the nearest and dearest, but now it has also become the food for entertaining. It is rich in grains, beans and vegetables and very healthy.

The oil-rich countries, generally those with a starker diet and rudimentary methods of cooking, can afford to import culinary talent from their poorer but more sophisticated neighbours. People in Egypt complain that the Saudis are taking away their family cooks. And with the new mobility of businessmen, professionals, technicians and all types of workers within the Arab world, there is a greater familiarity with the styles of cooking from one part to another. A few recipes have been widely adopted and popularized (some appear on menus of international hotels). The trouble is that when they become standardized, something is lost and false trimmings appear.

Social Aspects

The activities of cooking and eating reflect many subtly intricate facets of the Middle Eastern character and way of life. They are intensely social activities, while the dishes hold within them centuries of local culture, art and tradition.

Hospitality is a stringent duty all over the Middle East. 'If people are standing at the door of your house, don't shut it before them', and 'Give the guest food to eat even though you yourself are starving', are only two of a large number of sayings which serve to remind people of this duty, a legacy of nomadic tribal custom when hospitality was the first requirement for survival.

Sayings of Muhammad in the Quran, folk proverbs, religious,

mystical and superstitious beliefs set up rules of social *savoir-vivre* to the minutest detail – sweetly tyrannical, immutable and indisputable rules of civility and manners – to dictate the social behaviour of people towards each other, and sometimes submerge and entangle them in social obligations.

The ultimate aim of civility and good manners is to please: to please one's guest or to please one's host. To this end one uses the rules strictly laid down by tradition: of welcome, generosity, affability, cheerfulness and consideration for others.

People entertain warmly and joyously. To persuade a friend to stay for lunch is a triumph and a precious honour. To entertain many together is to honour them all mutually. The amount of food offered is a compliment to the guest and an indication of his importance. Failure to offer food and drink shows a dislike of visitors and brings disrepute to the host.

It is equally an honour to be a guest. Besides the customary obligations of cordiality and welcome, there is the need for the warmth of personal contact and cheerful company, the desire to congregate in groups, and the wish to please. It is common when preparing food to allow for an extra helping in case an unexpected guest should arrive. Many of the old recipes for soups and stews carry a note at the end saying that one can add water if a guest should arrive. When a meal is over there should always be a good portion of food left, otherwise one might think that someone has not been fully satisfied and could have eaten more.

The host should set before his guest all the food he has in the house, and apologize for its meagreness, uttering excuses such as: 'This is all the grocer had', or 'I was just on my way down to the confectioner's', or 'For the past two weeks I have been preparing for my niece's wedding and have not had time to make anything else'.

If a guest comes unexpectedly, the host must never ask why he has come, but receive him with a smiling face and a look of intense pleasure. After a ceremony of greetings, he should remark on the pleasure of seeing him and the honour of such a visit. The guest should never say right away why he has come, if there is a reason, but first inquire about the family, friends and affairs of his host. The latter must treat his guests as though he were their servant; to quarrel with them would be a disgrace. He must never argue with them about politics or religion, but should always acquiesce. He must never ask his guests if they would like food or drink, but provide these automatically, insisting that they have them and ignoring repeated refusals.

'The first duty of a host is cheerfulness' is a maxim strictly abided by. A host must amuse and entertain, provide light gossip, jokes, and, occasionally, riddles and a little satire. He may also offer a tour of the house and an inspection of new acquisitions.

A guest, in turn, must also play his role correctly. He should 'guard his voice, shorten his sight and beautify (praise) the food'. That is, although he must commend everything, exclaim in admiration and congratulate, he should not look about too much, nor inspect too closely. The Quran advises him to talk nicely and politely: 'Sow wheat, do not sow thorns; all the people will like you and love you.' 'Don't enter other people's houses, except with permission and good manners.' 'Beautify your tongue and you will obtain what you desire.'

A guest must at first refuse the food offered to him, but eventually give in on being urgently pressed. In particular, he must never refuse dishes which have already been sampled by others of the company, as this would put them in an uncomfortable position. If he comes invited, he must bring a present, and if this happens to be a box of confectionery, the host must open it immediately and offer him some.

The Quran advises that 'It is not right for a man to stay so long as to incommodate his host'. When a guest leaves, he must bless his host and he is under an obligation to speak well of him to others.

However, this beautifully laid-out pattern has its pitfalls. The wrong sort of admiration might be mistaken for envy, and give rise to a fear of the 'evil eye', of which it is said that 'half of humanity dies'. Folklore provides phrases to avoid this. The words 'five on your eye' are equivalent to the Western 'touch wood'. Blessings uttered towards various saints and the invocation of the name of God also act as a protection from evil. The person who is the object of admiration may protect himself by denouncing the reality of his good fortune and protesting that he has also been the victim of various misfortunes. However, a remark of admiration directed towards a personal possession may oblige the owner to offer it instantly and pressingly.

Cooks always cook to suit the taste of those who will eat the food. They need and expect approval. Often, dishes for the evening are lengthily discussed in the morning. Husbands express their wishes as to what they would like for dinner, and while they are eating, often remark on the success of the dish. However, a few husbands of my acquaintance believe that they must criticize something in a meal or complain that the dish requires a little more of one thing or another, thereby preventing their wives from becoming complacent.

Cooks are constantly coaxed and encouraged to surpass themselves and to perfect family favourites. Cooking ability is rated highly among female accomplishments. One Arab saying goes: 'A woman first holds her husband with a pretty face, then by his tummy and lastly with the help of a *sheb-sheb* (a wooden slipper).'

Cooking is often done in company. Mothers and daughters, sisters, cousins and friends love to talk about what they will serve their family for lunch or dinner, and they sit with or help each other to prepare delicacies which require time and skill. At all special occasions, such as family gatherings and national or religious holidays, the hostess can count on the help of many eager and generous relatives and friends, who come to help prepare the food, sometimes two or three days ahead. If they are unable to be present at the preparations, they will often send a plateful of their own particular speciality instead.

People always turn to food to mark important events. Weddings, circumcisions, religious festivals, new arrivals, in fact most occasions call for a particular dish or delicacy, or even a whole range of specialities. If these are lacking when it is customary to include them, it is a cause for offence and gossip. Criticism and disapproval are feared most by those who wish to impress and do the right or customary thing. This accounts for the fact that parties, though often extraordinarily lavish and varied, are also repetitive within each community. No table could be without stuffed vine leaves, *kahk*, *ma'amoul* or *baklava* and the usual range of delicacies. How fearful one is of the critical gaze of a guest searching for some speciality which is missing from the table!

It is said that there is a language of flowers. In the Middle East there exists a language of food. A code of etiquette for serving and presenting particular dishes expresses subtle social distinctions. Which piece, of what, and in what order, gives away the status of the person who is being served. There are rules of procedure according to social and family status and age. A dignitary or the head of the family is served the best helping first. A guest who comes seldom or who comes from afar is served before one who is a regular and familiar visitor to the house. A bride-to-be is served ceremoniously at the house of her husband-to-be. But when she is married, her status drops considerably at the table (as it does everywhere else), to rise again when she is expecting a baby. Then, she is often pampered and allowed to indulge in extravagant yearnings. If she then gives birth to a son, her status remains high.

A person of 'low extraction' who insists on sitting next to one of high birth or importance might be asked: 'What brought the sardine to the red mullet?' A proverb advises men to pay respect to status, and to give to each according to his station: 'Divide the meat and look at the faces.' And a saying describes this regard: 'When a wealthy man comes to a feast, the host tells some poor man to get up and give his place to the newcomer.'

In some parts of the Middle East where folklore is rich in beliefs about the evil eye, *djinns* and omens, some foods are believed to have magical powers.

Garlic is believed by some to ward off the evil eye and is sometimes hung at the front door of a house to protect its inhabitants. For its disinfectant qualities it is hung on a string around children's necks during epidemics. In some parts, people do not eat brains for fear of becoming as stupid as the animal; in others, they eat them to fortify their own brains and become more intelligent. Some do not eat the hearts of birds in case they might acquire their timidity.

Certain beliefs are uncommon and localized, and few people will have even heard of them. Others are widespread in all the countries and communities. One of these is that eating yellow things will result in laughter and happiness; another, that eating honey and sweet things will sweeten life and protect one from sadness and evil. Predictably, things coloured black, such as very black aubergines, are considered by some to be unlucky, while green foods encourage the repetition of happy and prosperous events.

In the past, some foods were believed to have aphrodisiac qualities. Sheikh Umar Ibn Muhammed al Nefzawi, in his now famous sixteenth-century book, *The Perfumed Garden*, recommends various foods as a cure for impotence or as powerful sexual stimulants. For the former, he recommends eating 'a stimulant pastry containing honey, ginger, pyrether, syrup of vinegar, hellebore, garlic, cinnamon, nutmeg, cardamoms, sparrows' tongues, Chinese cinnamon, long pepper, and other spices'; also 'nutmeg and incense mixed with honey'. Of foods which 'all learned men' acknowledge to have a positive effect in stimulating amorous desires are: an asparagus omelette, a fried-onion omelette, camel's milk mixed with honey, eggs boiled with myrrh, coarse cinnamon and pepper, eggs fried in butter, then immersed in honey and eaten with a little bread, and simply plain chick peas. He assures his readers that 'the efficacy of all these remedies is well known, and I have tested them'. Even today, a certain belief in the aphrodisiac powers of some foods still exists.

Cooking in the Middle East is deeply traditional and non-intellectual – an inherited art. It is not precise and sophisticated like Chinese cooking, nor is it experimental and progressive like American cooking today. Its virtues are loyalty and respect for custom and tradition, reflected in the unwavering attachment to the dishes of the past. Many have been cooked for centuries, from the time they were evolved, basically unchanged.

Yet each cook feels that within the boundaries of tradition she can improvise. She can pit her artfulness and wits, her sensuous feeling for the food, its texture and aroma, to create a unique and exquisite dish with the imprint of her own individual taste.

Of the people who have given me recipes, most added remarks such as: 'Personally, I like to add a little mint', implying that this was their own innovation; or 'I always put double the usual amount of ground almonds', meaning that they are extravagant; or 'I use dry breadcrumbs instead of soaked bread', to show their ingenuity; or, with a touch of guilt, 'I use stock cubes instead of making a chicken stock because it is easier, but I find it very acceptable'. Somebody even devised a way of stuffing courgettes without actually doing so, by curling slices around a compact ball of meat and rice filling and securing them tightly with a toothpick.

Nevertheless, if I suggested to those same people a totally new taste or a totally new form or method for a dish, they were mildly outraged or laughed incredulously at the folly of such a suggestion.

A certain malleability and a capacity to absorb new cultures while still remaining true to themselves have enabled the people of the Middle East to adopt dishes brought back by the Moors from Spain, those introduced by the Crusaders, Greek dishes, North African dishes such as couscous and, more recently, French, Italian and even English dishes, and then to adapt them to suit local tastes.

Of the dishes created by the local way of life and general character are the large variety of *mezze*, served before a meal, or to accompany drinks at any time of the day. These reflect the passion that the Middle Eastern peoples have for leisure and the importance they attach to their peace of mind, the luxury of tranquil enjoyment which they call *keif*. It is for them a delight to sit at home on their balconies, in their courtyards, or at the café, slowly sipping drinks and savouring *mezze*.

The numerous stuffed *mahshi*, *börek*, *sanbusak* and pastries, all requiring artful handiwork, denote a local pride in craftsmanship and skill. The smaller they are the more esteemed, for it is more difficult and it takes longer. The traditional decoration of dishes down to the humblest sauce or soup with a dusting of red paprika or brown cumin and a sprinkling of chopped parsley is the result of a love of beauty and ornamentation, the same that has produced the luscious Islamic decorative arts. The sensuous blue and green patterns of the ceramics are echoed in the green chopped pistachios and pale chopped blanched almonds adorning cream puddings. The criss-cross wooden patterns of the balconies behind which the women used to hide haunt the lozenge shapes of *basbousa* and *baklava*. The colours of confectioneries, syrups and pickles are those of the brilliant dresses which appear at *mûlids* (festivals).

The Traditional Table

Before proceeding to the table, guests are entertained in a different room, where they often sit on sofas at floor level. A maid comes round with a large copper basin and flask, pouring out water (sometimes lightly perfumed with rose or orange blossom) for the guests to wash their hands. A towel is passed round at the same time.

Dining tables are low and round – large metal trays resting on a type of stool, or on short, carved, folding wooden legs, sometimes inlaid with mother of pearl and tortoise-shell. The trays themselves are of copper, brass or silver, beaten and engraved, sometimes inlaid with silver or other metals. Thin threads of the metal are beaten into crevices with a little hammer, making traditional oriental decora-

tive patterns and writings: words of blessing, charms against the evil
eye and words in praise of Allah. Usually several tables are placed in
the room, and the diners sit around them on cushions.

Several bowls containing a variety of dishes are placed on each
table for guests to enjoy the pleasure of deciding which dish to start
with, and with which delicacy to follow.

Before the meal is started, the word *Bismillah* (In the name of
God!) is uttered by all.

In eating, a strict code of etiquette is observed. It is related that the
Imam Hassan (son of Ali) listed twelve rules of etiquette to be
observed.

The first four are *necessary*, namely: to know that God is the Provider;
to be satisfied with what he has provided; to say 'In the name of God!'
when beginning to eat and to say 'To God be thanks!' when you finish.
The next four are *customary*, and it is well to observe them, though they
are not required: to wash the hands before eating; to sit at the left of the
table; to eat with three fingers; and to lick the fingers after eating. The
last four are rules of particular politeness: to eat out of the dish that is
immediately in front of you and out of your own side of the dish; to take
small pieces; to chew the food well; and not to gaze at the others at the
table with you. These twelve rules form the traditional basis for the
table manners of the majority of the people.

Besides these rules, there are other, subtler points of *savoir-vivre*.
It is tolerated to eat with five fingers when eating food of a not too
solid consistency, such as couscous.

It is considered sociable and polite to detach choice morsels such
as chicken hearts or livers, or fish roes, and to offer these to a
neighbour.

If one feels satiated, one should nevertheless continue to nibble at
a dish from which others are still eating, since if one person stops
eating, everyone else may feel compelled to stop too, and the dish
will be removed from the table.

One must lick one's fingers at the end of a meal only. To do so
before would be a sign that one had finished.

One must always talk about pleasant and joyful things and never
introduce a sad or bitter note into the conversation. One must be
cheerful and entertaining, and remark on the perfection of dishes,
saying, 'Your fingers are green!' if the hostess has prepared them or
helped in their preparation; and 'May your table always be generous
to all!' – a phrase entertaining the hope that one will be asked to eat
there again soon.

Sometimes, in parts where women have not yet become emancipated, men only are invited. Islam looks upon women with suspicion. According to Muslim tradition, the Prophet Muhammad said: 'I have not left any calamity more hurtful to man than woman.' In some parts, women are believed to have more power to cast the evil eye, so they are served first, before their look of longing can have a harmful effect on the food.

If two people have eaten together, they are compelled to treat each other well, as the food contains a conditional curse. This is alluded to in the sayings: 'God and the food will repay him for it', and 'Cursed, son of a cursed one, is he who eats food and deceives him who shared it with him'. Host and guest in particular are tied in a relationship governed by this conditional curse.

When the meal is finished, guests leave the table to go through the hand-washing ceremony again and to partake of coffee or tea.

Similar rules to these are added to Western manners in homes where Western habits of eating have been adopted. Actions and words reveal an attachment to ancient tradition. At buffet dinner parties in our house, for example, the guests stood far away from the table and had to be urged and pressed to eat. Although the mechanics of the European table, the knife and fork, and the table napkin, had been adopted, the old, Middle Eastern manners and rules of *bienséance* remained.

To those of the Middle East who might misunderstand my motives and feel offended, as I believe some will, by my description of 'table manners', I would like to say that the manner of eating with the fingers is most delicate and at least as refined as any belonging to the culture of the West, and I have only respect for the elegance of these rules of *savoir-vivre*.

In her beautiful *Three Centuries* Emine Foat Tugay describes the customary hospitality of the aristocratic Ottoman families in the early part of this century, especially during the month of Ramadan, when gates and house doors would be opened to the public:

An Imam and a muezzin were engaged for the whole month at our house, and the latter would chant the call to evening prayer from the top of the stairs leading into the garden. Prayer-rugs facing south-east towards Mecca had been spread in the main hall for the men, and the drawing-rooms were similarly prepared for the women. As soon as a cannon boomed, announcing that the sun had set, the fast was broken with olives and bread, prior to the short evening prayer. The household, with its resident guests and any strangers who had come in, then sat down at different tables to *iftar*, as the first meal after the fast is called. The men were all served in the selamlik, whether they were known to my father or not. He dined separately with his guests, but the food was the same for all. Strange women did not often come to iftar, nevertheless a table was always ready for the *Allah misafiri*, the guests of God. Special dishes were served at iftar. Black and green olives, several kinds of sliced cheese, a variety of jams, very thin slices of a sausage made of mutton, and the dried meat of mutton or turkey, the two last-named being the only foods flavoured with garlic which were ever eaten in the konaks, had been placed, each one separately, in tiny dishes before each plate. Goblets containing sherbet always stood beside the glasses for water. The meal invariably began with soup, followed by eggs cooked either with cheese or meat, sausage, or dried meat, and usually ended after a large number of courses with the serving of *güllaj*, a sweet made from thin wafers of starch. Two hours after sunset, the muezzin again chanted his call to the last prayer of the day, the *Yatsi Namaz*. During Ramazan only, another prayer, the *Teravi Namaz*, immediately follows the yatsi, both together lasting over an hour. My father, with his sons and household and those of his guests who wished to participate, never missed any of these prayers. I used to pray with the other women in the drawing-room, where screens placed in front of the wide-open double doors enabled them to hear the recitations without being seen. Those who fast are permitted two meals only, the *sahur*, an hour before sunrise, and the iftar at sunset. During the interval nothing may pass down the throat, even smoking being prohibited, since smoke can be swallowed. The iftars which I have known, generous and ample as they were, would have seemed paltry in comparison with some of the gargantuan meals of former times. The following anecdote, related by Colonel Aziz Bey in my hearing, will give some idea of an iftar in those days.

During Sultan Mahmud II's reign, at the beginning of the nineteenth century, the Sheyh-ul-Islam, Meki Efendi, was famed for the excellence of his table. The Sultan, hearing of this, decided to put to the test the Sheyh's reputation of being both a generous host and himself a gourmet of superb excellence. Unannounced, he arrived one evening in Ramazan, with a retinue of forty, to partake of the iftar at Meki Efendi's yali. The Sheyh-ul-Islam was quietly sitting in his room beside a window which looked out on the Bosphorus, reading the Qur'an. When his servants informed him of the Sultan's arrival, he closed the holy book, kissed and lifted it to his forehead, then placed it on a high shelf. Turning to his servants he said: 'Have the iftar served in the selamlik, and the sahur in the harem to the family.' He then went down to meet his unexpected guests. The food was so abundant that, after justice had been done to each superlative dish, all were more than satisfied. After the sweetmeats had been served, cut-glass bowls containing stewed sour cherries (*vishne*) were set down to refresh jaded palates. The Sultan, astonished that the bowls all began to drip and dissolve, wanted to know why this was happening. Meki Efendi humbly explained that the bowls were made of ice, which had been specially preserved in pits and was every day carved and adorned with intricate patterns by specialized craftsmen. The Sultan laughed and had to admit that even his own table could not boast of such luxury as this.

On a much smaller scale our own table, in readiness for any uninvited guests, was laid for sixteen every day. Without counting my father, who only lunched at home on Fridays, we were already six, my mother, three children, and two governesses. Poor Halil (then in an invalid chair for his tubercular back) ate separately. The ladies who dropped in to lunch usually brought their own children. Hala Hanim, for instance, never came without her daughter and two granddaughters. There were rarely empty seats at table. Simultaneously with ours, a second table presided over by the bacis was laid in another room for such guests as might be considered to be 'below the salt'. They were served by younger girls. At our table the three specially trained *sofracis*** were reinforced by at least as many other maids. The enormous platters of food were handed round once (there were no second helpings) and then passed to an under-maid who waited outside the dining-room, to be taken to the bacis' table. Food was so abundant that when we had finished the dishes were still more than half-full. The staff had their meals, cooked specially for them, in the servants' hall in the basement. For each meal the cooks prepared food for twenty-five at the master's table and for forty indoor and outdoor servants; these had only five courses. They began with either soup, eggs, or a pastry stuffed with cheese, had a meat course, a vegetable dish served separately, the inevitable pilav made of rice, and lastly either a sweet or fruit.

Our 'frugal' meals of six courses, which had so shocked my mother's family, always began with either fish, eggs, or *börek*, a dish comprising various kinds of pastry stuffed with cheese and herbs, or spiced minced meat. Then came meat or fowl with potatoes and salad, two vegetable courses, the first eaten cold and cooked in oil, the second in butter and served hot, pilav, each day a different kind, and either a milk pudding or pastry soaked in syrup. Fruit always finished off the meal. Coffee was served in the drawing-room or in summer in the entrance hall, which was delightfully cool.

Everyone publicly washed their hands before and after each meal, either in a passage beside the dining-room, which was lined with marble basins and taps, or inside, where the maids offered silver ewers and basins to the senior guests. In my mother's youth one maid had held the basin, a second poured water, and a third offered the towel. She had

* Servants.

simplified the process; the same maid held the basin in her left hand and poured out with her right. If the guest was important enough, we children deferentially handed the towels instead of this office being performed by a servant.

☐ *Shams-Eddin Mohamet Hafiz was one of the greatest poets of Persia. He was widely respected by all Persians, and lived in his native Shiraz during the fourteenth century A.D.*

On a visit to nearby Isfahan he was the house guest of Ali Agha Isfahani, the most prominent merchant of Isfahan. Elated by this great honour bestowed on him Ali Agha instructed his wife that nothing but the best of food be prepared by her chefs during the Hafiz visit and only the most prominent guests should be invited to the banquets performed almost every night during this visit.

Needless to say that various dishes were prepared and they were all one better than the other. So during the first banquet while Hafiz really enjoyed the meal he ended up by shaking his head and saying how much he missed the banquets and parties of Shiraz. This led Ali Agha to believe that his wife was not making enough effort to please the palate of the great Poet and requested her to double the amount of food and the variety for the next evening. But again after enjoying the meal Hafiz shook his head and passed the same remarks about the parties of Shiraz. And this went on for several nights afterwards. While Ali Agha's household were doubling and tripling the amount of food their eminent guest was passing the same remarks. At last Ali Agha was on the point of bursting and he took his courage into his hands and asked Hafiz as to where they were lacking to please him. Hafiz replied, 'You are not displeasing me. On the contrary you are almost embarrassing me by offering and wasting so much food every evening. And how can I stay at your home as long as I desire while this goes on!' That taught Ali Agha the art of preparing the adequate food for each occasion.*

Muslim Dietary Laws

A note on Muslim dietary laws is relevant in a book of food which has been influenced by them.

* A story told by Joseph Shamoon.

The religion of Islam is the most important part of Middle Eastern culture and the main foundation of the customs and traditions of the region. The code of religion is derived mainly from the Quran, which serves the faithful as a model and rule of life in every particular.

The Quran consists of a collection of the revelations or commands which the Prophet Muhammad received through the Angel Gabriel as messages from God, and which he delivered to those about him, on Divine direction. As Muhammad received the messages in moments of Divine inspiration he recited them to those of his Companions, or followers, who were with him, and who wrote them down on any object available, such as a stone or a piece of cloth.

These fragments were copied and preserved after the Prophet's death, to be compiled and collected later by a certain Zayd b. Thabit. The *Suras*, or chapters, were not arranged in chronological order and are out of their original context. Without the certainty of the occasion and period at which they were revealed, it is possible to interpret them in different ways. To appreciate them, one should be aware of the social environment of the time, and of the influence of the customs and superstitions of previous centuries.

Muhammad mentioned food many times throughout the Quran, and insisted particularly on its beneficial character as a gift from God. He repeated injunctions about kinds of food permitted and not permitted.

So eat of what God has given you, lawful or good, and give thanks for God's favour if Him it is you serve.

Say I find not in that which is revealed to me aught forbidden for an eater to eat thereof, except that it be what dies of itself, or blood poured forth, or flesh of swine – for that surely is unclean – or what is a transgression other than (the name of) God having been invoked in it. But whoever is driven to necessity, not desiring nor exceeding the limit, then surely thy Lord is Forgiving, Merciful.

In actual fact, the following are forbidden:

1. animals dead before they are slaughtered, or those killed for reasons other than that of food;
2. blood;
3. pig's flesh;
4. animals slaughtered as an offering to a pagan deity or in the name of the deity;
5. alcoholic or fermented liquids, and all inebriating liquors,

although they were favoured at first. They are forbidden in cooking, too.

An animal that is killed for the food of man must be slaughtered in a particular manner: the person who is about to do it must say: 'In the name of God, God is most great!' and then cut its throat.

These dietary laws are observed in varying degrees of laxity throughout the Muslim world. It is very uncommon for people to eat pork. Some Muslims drink wine, liqueurs and other types of alcohol, and some use them in their food. This is quite common practice today in Turkey, but generally, cooking with wine and alcohol is more an individual and personal preference, rather than a national or traditional characteristic.

Flavourings, Condiments and Perfumes

No one who has walked through a Middle Eastern spice street can ever forget the intoxicating effect of mingled scents nor the extraordinary displays of knotted roots, bits of bark and wood, shrivelled pods, seeds, berries, translucent resins, curious-looking plants, bulbs, buds, petals, stigmas, even beetles.

Practically every main town in the Middle East has its *attarine* or spice street in the *soukh* or bazaar, where rows of very small shops (some as small as cupboards) sell spices and aromatics. Vendors lay them out with art to tempt those passing by with their delicate shades of gold and brown and their enigmatic shapes. They sometimes roast, grate or crush them to a powder in a mortar, on demand, and sift them through a fine sieve as they did centuries ago. They fill little cones made out of tightly rolled pieces of newspaper and offer them as though they were magic potions.

The Orient is renowned for its delight in incense, perfumes and aromatic flavourings. Since early times it was part of the spice route between the Far East, Central Africa and Europe. The local taste for spices and for sweet dishes was inherited from Ancient Egypt and the Graeco-Roman world when spices are thought to have been used also to mask the smell of slightly 'off' meat. Long before Islam, Arabia was already known as the land of spices, and Herodotus wrote that the whole country was scented with spices and exhaled a marvellously sweet odour. The country, however, was only the transit area – as were Persia and Ethiopia – for the transport trade between East and West when spices were the most highly prized merchandise because of their small volume and high prices. Their commerce which was kept going in a small way even throughout the Muslim conquests flourished especially during the Crusades. The middlemen, Arabs, Persians and Saracen merchants (the last mainly Syrians and Jews), fiercely guarded their monopoly and their sources of supply. Saracen ships brought spices from China, Tibet, Malacca, Java and Sumatra as well as India and Ceylon and the east coast of Africa through the Persian Gulf and the Red Sea. Trading posts were established everywhere and when the Arab conquests interrupted business relations with Europe, the Jews became the middlemen. Goods were transferred to camels following the caravan routes through the Arabian desert to Palestine and Syria, or came via Cairo in boats on the Nile. Trading ships waited in the Mediterranean to carry them into Europe through the ports of Venice and Genoa. It is not surprising that the intermediaries should have succumbed to the attractions of their precious merchandise. A certain magic still surrounds the use of spices and aromatics, which are not only used for their taste but also for their medicinal, therapeutic and even sometimes aphrodisiac value. For they are variously believed to increase the appetite, help digestion or calm the nerves, to be good for the heart and circulation, to be antitoxic or sexually stimulating and even to kill microbes. Attributes are well-founded or romantic; ginger is said to make people loving, rose water to give a rosy outlook, dill and aniseed to have digestive qualities, and garlic to be both health-giving and an antiseptic.

Almost everything that can add a touch of flavour or aroma is used in cooking. The aromatic plants most commonly used are flat-leafed parsley, coriander (sometimes called 'Arab parsley') and mint. Oregano, wild marjoram, thyme and dill, fenugreek, bay, celery, fennel, chives and tarragon, purslane and rue also play their part. Herbs are so popular that they are sometimes placed in a bunch on the table for people to pick at. Fresh coriander is used liberally in salads as well as stews, mint marries happily with yoghourt, dill is especially popular in Turkey and Iran.

All the usual spices come into use: saffron, turmeric, cumin, coriander, cinnamon, nutmeg, allspice, cloves, ginger, cardamom, caraway, aniseed, sesame, poppy seed, fennel, dill, fenugreek and mustard seeds, peppercorns, cayenne and paprika – all these have an important place. Each country has its favourites and its own special mixtures and combinations.

Some Less Common Flavourings

BOIS DE PANAMA (also called saponaria) is a pale dry wood which, when boiled in water, produces a thick white foam. It is used to make the cream called *naatiffe* for *karabij* (page 476).

MAHLAB is black cherry kernels and gives a special taste to breads and pastries. It is sometimes sold already ground.

MASTIC (sometimes wrongly called gum arabic, which is glue). The hard resin of the acacia tree is sometimes used as chewing gum with a little piece of ordinary wax to soften it. It must be pulverized before it is used to flavour puddings. Years ago it also sometimes went into stews.

MUSK, which comes from the abdominal scent glands of the male musk deer of the Himalayas, gives a heavy scent to puddings. Abel – musk seeds (*ambrette*) are a substitute flavouring.

ORANGE BLOSSOM WATER lends a delicate perfume to syrups, pastries and puddings. You may add a drop or two to water and Turkish coffee, a tablespoonful to a salad dressing or a stew. A teaspoon in a coffee cup of boiling water, with or without sugar, makes the soothing and digestive 'white coffee' of Lebanon. Only a diluted form of the strong distilled essence is obtainable in this country. It was used here a good deal as a flavouring centuries ago but in recent years has been sold as a toiletry article by chemists.

PEPPERS. Many types of peppers are used. Besides the black pepper berry and the weaker white pepper seed freed from its powerful wrinkled black skin, there are grey peppers called cubebs and long peppers which look like a black catkin, both of which are not as strong as the black berries. All these are best bought whole and used freshly ground. There is also the dried red pepper or pimento of which there are many varieties – all of the capsicum family. Dried and ground it ranges from the mild, sweet red pepper and paprika to the very fiery cayenne or chilli powders.

POMEGRANATE SEEDS. The juicy, shiny pink seeds of the fresh fruit are sprinkled on salads and on tahina sauce for fish. Cut the fruit in half, scoop out the seeds and discard the bitter-tasting pith. Dried wild seeds give a sharp flavour to hummus and tahina.

POMEGRANATE SYRUP is made from the juice of sour rather than sweet fruits boiled down to a thick syrup. Much used in Iranian cooking.

ROSE BUDS. A powerfully aromatic variety of rose from Damascus is used to perfume strong spice mixtures. In Egypt we used to leave rose buds about in little plates to embalm the air.

ROSE WATER. Diluted rose petal essence is used to scent syrups, pastries and puddings and all types of hot and cold drinks. Often used together with orange blossom water, when it is the weaker of the partnership and can therefore be used less sparingly.

SAHLAB – the bulb of a type of orchid – is used in powder form to thicken milk and lend it a special flavour.

SHAMAR in Arabic, *mavro* in Greek, is found here in Indian shops as onion seed. It is mixed in among sesame seeds on bread and *kahk* (page 436).

SUMAC (or *summak*) is a sourish, dark, browny-red seed which is ground to a powder. Iranians use it frequently and provide it in restaurants particularly to flavour kebabs. Iraqis use it too and Lebanese and Syrians sprinkle it on salads or on fish. Juice can be extracted by soaking cracked seeds (about 120 g/4 oz) in 350 ml (12 fl oz) of water for 20 minutes, then straining and squeezing the juice out. It is often used instead of lemon juice.

TAMARIND. You can find this in Indian shops, sold partly dried as a sticky mass of broken pods with fibres and seeds. Macerated in hot water these produce a sour, dark brown juice. Used with sugar it gives a pleasant sweet and sour taste.

A commercial paste and tamarind balls are easier to use and a reasonably good substitute.

TAHINA PASTE is the oily meal which results from crushing sesame seeds. It is used both raw and cooked for sauces.

LEMONS PRESERVED IN SALT. The French name for this North African speciality is *citrons confits*. It is much used as a condiment to flavour chicken dishes and all sorts of stews and sometimes to enliven a salad. Use ripe lemons or limes. Wash them well. Cut them in four – in two if they are limes – but not right through. Let them hold together at the stem end. Sprinkle salt inside the slits. (Use about 120 g (4 oz) salt for 1 kg (2 lb) lemons.) Put them in a wide-necked jar. Press the lemons down hard with a weight like a stone (well washed). The salted juices which are gradually released, augmented by the juice of other lemons, preserve the peels which soften and mellow and are ready in a month. You may use them whole or chopped up or the peel alone without the pulp. The juice can be used as a seasoning.

NOUMI BASRA (IN IRAQ) OR OMAN LEMONS (IN IRAN). These small, brown, dried limes which give a sharp musty flavour to Iranian and Iraqi soups and stews can now be bought whole or ground in some Indian and Oriental stores, but you can make them yourself by letting fresh limes dry out. It takes several months for them to be completely dry and hard and very dark brown inside. The time depends on the weather. It is best to put them out in the sun to begin with and leaving them on radiators also helps. They are ready when they sound hollow when you tap them on the table. You may use them whole – pierced with a fork when the skin softens with cooking, or cracked open with a hammer or a pestle and mortar, in which case people who are specially fond of them may like to have them in their serving. Otherwise you may add them in ground form. One lime is usually enough for a stew for 6.

DIBBIS, or date syrup, is an Iraqi sweetening agent made by boiling dates until they form a pulpy mass. In the past it was poured into a basket strainer. Another basket was inverted over this and they were placed between two boards by means of which the juice was expressed. (People stood and jumped on top.) It was then poured on to trays, allowed to evaporate in the sun and the thick syrup which resulted was stored in tins and jars.

The syrup, which looks like thick brown treacle, keeps well and is used in savoury as well as sweet dishes. It is not easy to find here at the moment. People like to mix it with tahina and eat this with bread.

SAMNA (clarified butter) is also used for its distinctive flavour. To clarify butter, heat it slowly in a pan until it is thoroughly melted and bubbling, then chill it until it is firm. Transfer carefully to another pan leaving behind the residue at the bottom. Melt the butter again and when it froths strain it through a fine cloth into a jar. (See also page 24.)

Make a large quantity, it keeps for months (actually, years). It gives a special acid taste to food and does not burn.

Some people flavour the butter as it bubbles with aromatics such as fenugreek, caraway or cardamom seeds. Use 1–2 tablespoons of seeds to 250 g/8 oz butter.

Spice Mixtures

Every household has favourite spice mixtures which they blend to taste and keep in jars as a ready condiment or flavouring. A few are made to be eaten with bread. This is broken into pieces, dipped in olive oil and then in the condiment to pick it up.

There are classic mixtures which vendors make up and which are often simply called 'the three spices' or 'the four spices'. In Egypt what we called *les quatre épices* was a ground mixture of cloves, cinnamon, nutmeg and pepper. 'Four spices' in Tunisia may mean cinnamon, pepper, rose buds and paprika, and in Morocco it may be cloves, nutmeg, ginger and pepper. 'Curry mixtures' of varying compositions popular in the regions neighbouring India are similar to those of that country.

RAS EL HANOUT. Grocers in North Africa stake their reputation on a 'house blend' which according to folklore may contain up to a hundred aromatics but in reality contains around twelve. The 'grocer's head', as it is called, generally includes cinnamon bark, whole nutmeg, dried rose buds, pieces of dried ginger, cloves, cubebs and different peppers – sometimes the golden green Spanish fly, renowned for its 'aphrodisiac' qualities. They are pounded together in a mortar as required.

ZAHTAR. A mixture of thyme and salt or *sumac*, which occasionally contains toasted sesame, is sold in little paper cornets to dip bread into.

Relishes

Some spice mixtures are made into a paste with oil or tomato concentrate or something moist. A covering layer of oil stops them spoiling.

HARISSA. This famous pimento paste gives a fiery taste and a red colour to many foods in North Africa. It can be bought here ready made but this will not have the special perfume of the home-made variety. To make it you will need: 250 g (8 oz) fresh or dried fiery red chilli peppers, 1 medium-sized whole head garlic, 1 tablespoon dried coriander (pulverized), 1 tablespoon caraway seeds, 1 tablespoon dried mint, 3 tablespoons or more fresh coriander leaves and 1 tablespoon salt, plus a little olive oil.

Remove stems and seeds and soak dried chillis in water for an hour. Drain and pound with the rest of the ingredients or put through a food processor, moistening with a little olive oil, to obtain a thick paste. This will keep well in a jar in the refrigerator if it is covered with a new layer of oil every time it is used. Use very little at a time. As you can imagine, it is very powerful.

TABIL. A Tunisian mixture of fresh coriander, caraway seeds, garlic and red peppers, both sweet and fiery, ground or pounded to a paste.

ZHUG. I tasted this relish in Israel, where it was brought by Yemenite immigrants. It is so strong that a tiny drop picked up on the tip of my little finger set my throat on fire.

Grind and blend the following to a paste: 1 teaspoon black pepper, 1 teaspoon caraway seed, 3–4 cardamom pods, 4 strong dried peppers soaked in water for an hour, 1 whole head garlic, a good bunch of coriander leaves and salt. Use it to flavour soups and stews or simply to dip your bread in.

A teaspoon of this mixed with 2 tablespoons fenugreek seeds and the mashed pulp of a large tomato makes another relish called *hilbeh*.

☐ *The Loan of a Cauldron**

One day the Khoja asked a neighbour for the loan of a cauldron. After he had done with it, he put a small saucepan inside and took it back to the owner. When the man saw the small saucepan, he said, 'What is this?' and the Khoja answered, 'Your cauldron has had a baby.'

'That's good news!' said the man, and accepted it with pleasure.

One day the Khoja wanted to borrow the cauldron again and took it home with him.

The owner waited a long time, but he noticed that the cauldron did not come back. Then he went round to the Khoja and knocked at his door. When the Khoja came and asked him what he wanted, he answered, 'I want that cauldron.'

'Accept my sincere condolences,' said the Khoja, 'the cauldron is dead!'

'What!' said his neighbour in the greatest amazement – 'dead! Whoever heard of a cauldron dying?'

'Strange! – strange!' replied the Khoja. 'You could believe that the cauldron had a baby, and yet you do not believe that it could die!'

* Barnham (trans.), *Tales of Nasr-ed-Din Khoja.*

Hors d'Œuvre

Mezze

Mezze are one of the most delightful features of Middle Eastern food – not least because they are meant to be enjoyed in an unhurried way – indeed they are almost a way of life. From the cafés by the Nile to mountain resorts in the Lebanon and palatial villas in Morocco and Persia, savouring *mezze* with an ouzo, a beer, a syrup or a coffee can be a delight approaching ecstasy, part sensual, part mystical. The pleasure of savouring the little pieces of food is accompanied by feelings of peace and serenity, and sometimes by deep meditation.

Mezze are ideally suited to the Western way of life. A small assortment can be served with drinks at parties, and a wider choice provides an exciting buffet dinner. One alone provides a first course.

There are many different kinds of *mezze*, simple and elaborate.

Nuts of all types; salted and soaked chick peas; olives; cucumbers cut into long thin slices and sprinkled with salt half an hour before serving; quartered tomatoes; pieces of cheese cut into small cubes or long sticks, sometimes grilled or fried – these provide *mezze* which require little or no work.

Salads are popular as *mezze*. So is every type of pickle. Sauces or dips made with tahina (sesame meal), chick peas and aubergines are greatly favoured. They are eaten with little pieces of Arab bread.

Myriad 'miniature foods', sometimes exact but diminished replicas of main dishes of meat, chicken and fish, can be served. Favourites are grilled or fried chicken livers, fried cubes of lamb's or calf's liver served hot or cold, small minced meat, chicken or fish balls, and little savoury pastries such as *börek* (page 135) and pies.

Stuffed vine leaves are popular in all their forms. So are *ta'amia* or *falafel* in Egypt (page 86), and an assortment of fresh herbs in Persia (page 69).

In this chapter, I shall give the dishes which are more commonly thought of as hors d'œuvre dishes, although some of them are also served as salads or as accompaniments to main dishes. Other *mezze* will be found in the chapters on salads, savouries and pickles. Recipes for meat, chicken and fish balls, and other dishes in the meat, poultry and fish chapters can also be reduced in size and served as an appetizer or first course. *Hamine* eggs, for instance (page 187), or boiled or deep-fried eggs sprinkled with cumin, make good *mezze*. They will be found in the chapter on egg dishes.

When preparing an assortment of appetizers, arrange them so that you make the most of the colour and texture of each, by its contrast or affinity to its neighbour. Place the small, sharply defined shapes of fish sticks or *ta'amia*, for instance, next to smooth, pale sauces and dips. Set shiny black olives next to faintly beige tahina cream, and light green cucumber fingers beside a gently tinted aubergine purée. If necessary, decorate the *mezze* with chopped parsley, tomato and onion slices, radishes, gherkins, lemon wedges, paprika, olives, almonds or chick peas.

Limit your selection of *mezze* with strict self-discipline if you are serving them before a large meal, or appetites may easily be spoilt.

In the recipes which follow, quantities given are quite large, designed for 6 people who will be offered only one, or perhaps two, dishes. Reduce the quantity by half if you wish, as is customary, to serve a larger variety.

A Bowl of Fresh Herbs

In Persia fresh herbs are served as *mezze*, and a bowl containing a varied assortment of these is placed on the table at most meals.

An ancient custom is for women to eat the herbs with bread and cheese at the end of a meal. According to an old belief, this will help them to keep their husbands away from a rival. Job's tears and mandrake in particular should turn him against a 'co-wife'.[*]

Wash a few sprigs of fresh parsley, mint, chives, cress, dill, coriander, tarragon, spring onions – in fact any fresh herbs you like which are available – and arrange them in a bowl.

□ *Persian saying: 'Even the worm inside a stone eats herbs.'*

Raw and Vinegared Vegetables

A selection of beautifully cut raw vegetables to nibble at is a very good thing to offer before a meal.

An alternative is to turn them into instant pickles. Have carrots, turnips, cauliflower, celery stalks and cucumber, all cut into thin sticks, slices or florets. Sprinkle generously with salt and let the juices run out for an hour. Then moisten with wine vinegar and leave for a further hour before serving.

The most popular street food of Iraq is called *abiadh al bedh*. It is pushed around the streets of Baghdad in carts piled high with neatly arranged arrays of hard-boiled eggs, pickles, beetroot, tomatoes, spring onions and all types of seasonal vegetables, with lavish

[*] Donaldson, *The Wild Rue*.

decorations of parsley, chives and other herbs. The vendor picks pieces on demand, slices and seasons them and rolls them up in a piece of bread.

Wara Einab
Dolma or Stuffed Vine Leaves

Popular in every country throughout the Middle East, stuffed vine leaves are a most intriguing and delightful delicacy. There are numerous variations. As a general rule, minced meat is used in the making of hot *dolma*, and cold *dolma* are made without meat. Nevertheless, left-over vine leaves stuffed with meat are sometimes eaten cold and, invariably, they turn out to be delicious.

The leaves can be bought preserved in brine in all Greek and Oriental stores, and they are also sold in tins in many delicatessens. But if you can, it is best to use fresh ones.

Hot Stuffed Vine Leaves

250 g (8 oz) preserved, drained vine leaves
120 g (4 oz) long-grain rice
250 g (8 oz) beef or lamb, minced
1 tomato, skinned and chopped
1 small onion, finely chopped
3 tablespoons finely chopped parsley
3 tablespoons finely chopped celery leaves (optional)
Salt and black pepper
2 tablespoons tomato concentrate (optional)
2 tomatoes, sliced (optional)
2 cloves garlic, halved or slivered
Juice of 1 lemon, or more

If using vine leaves preserved in brine, put them in a large bowl and pour boiling water over them. Make sure that the water penetrates well between the layers, and let the leaves soak for 20 minutes. Drain. Soak in fresh cold water, then drain again, and repeat the process once more. This will remove excess salt.

If using fresh vine leaves, soften them by plunging them, a few at a time, in boiling water for a few minutes until they become limp, then drain.

Soak and wash the rice in boiling water, and then rinse it under the cold tap. Drain it well. In a large bowl, mix the rice with the meat, chopped tomato, onion, parsley, celery, salt and pepper. Add 2 tablespoons or more tomato concentrate for a particularly Greek flavour.

Place one leaf on a plate vein side up. Place 1 heaped teaspoon of the filling in the centre of the leaf near the stem edge. Fold the stem end up over the filling, then fold both sides towards the middle and roll up like a small cigar. Squeeze lightly in the palm of your hand. This process will become very easy after you have rolled a few.

Fill the rest of the leaves in the same way. Continue until all the filling is used up.

Line the bottom of a large saucepan with a layer of tomato slices or left-over vine leaves to prevent the stuffed leaves from sticking to the pan and burning. Pack the stuffed leaves in tight layers on top, pushing small pieces of garlic here and there between them. Sprinkle with lemon juice and add about 150 ml (¼ pint) water. Some cooks mix a little saffron with the water to give a pale yellow colour to the cooked filling, but in my opinion this is unnecessary since it does not seem to improve the taste and the leaves themselves give a beautiful pale lemon colour to the rice anyway.

Put a small plate over the rolled leaves to prevent them from coming undone, and cover with a lid. Cook the leaves over very gentle heat for at least 2 hours, or until tender, adding water gradually as it becomes absorbed. The cooking time can be reduced to 20 minutes if a pressure cooker is used, but the taste is improved by the long simmering.

Turn out on to a serving dish and serve hot.

≈ A Lebanese variation adds 4 or more cloves of garlic (crushed) in addition to the slivered ones and a tablespoon of crushed dried mint with a little water about 20 minutes before the end of cooking time.
≈ Others, including Persians, Lebanese and Greeks, like to add about ½ teaspoon ground cinnamon to the filling.

Cold Stuffed Vine Leaves

This is an exquisite dish in which the delicate aromas of the spices blend with the taste of the vine leaves against a background of acid lemon and sweet garlic. In Egypt this version is called 'false' or 'lying' because there is no meat, but nevertheless most people prefer it.

250 g (8 oz) preserved, drained vine leaves
250 g (8 oz) long-grain rice
2–3 tomatoes, skinned and chopped
1 large onion, finely chopped, or 4 tablespoons finely chopped spring onions
2 tablespoons finely chopped parsley
2 tablespoons dried crushed mint

¼ level teaspoon ground cinnamon
¼ level teaspoon ground allspice
Salt and black pepper
2 tomatoes, sliced (optional)
3–4 cloves garlic (optional)
150 ml (¼ pint) olive oil
¼ teaspoon powdered saffron or turmeric (optional)
1 teaspoon sugar
Juice of 1 lemon, or more

Prepare the leaves as described in the previous recipe. Soak and stir the rice in boiling water, and then rinse it under the cold tap. Drain it thoroughly. In a bowl, mix the rice with the tomatoes, onion or spring onions, parsley, mint, cinnamon, allspice and salt and pepper to taste.

Stuff the leaves with this mixture and roll them up as described in the previous recipe. Pack them tightly in a large pan lined with tomato slices or left-over, torn or imperfect vine leaves, occasionally slipping a whole clove of garlic in between them if you like.

Mix the olive oil with 150 ml (¼ pint) water and the saffron, if used. Add the sugar and lemon juice, and pour the mixture over the stuffed leaves. Put a small plate on top of the leaves to prevent them unwinding, cover the pan, and simmer very gently for at least 2 hours, until the rolls are thoroughly cooked; add water occasionally, a coffee cup at a time, as the liquid in the pan becomes absorbed. Cool in the pan before turning out. Serve cold.

≈ Iranians like to add about 2 tablespoons chopped dill and 90 g (3 oz) seedless raisins or currants to the filling.

≈ Another variation which adds a new element to the texture uses hummus or chick peas. Soak about 60 g (2 oz) in water overnight. Then crush them in a mortar and add them to the filling. In this case use 60 g (2 oz) less rice.

≈ Pine nuts (about 60 g/2 oz) can also be added, and make a delicious variation.

≈ In Iraq, Swiss chard or spinach leaves are used instead of vine leaves when these are not available.

Aubergine Purée

This way of preparing aubergines, sometimes called 'poor man's caviar', is a favourite all over the Middle East.

3 aubergines	1–2 cloves garlic, crushed
3 tablespoons olive oil	Juice of 1 lemon, or more
2–3 tablespoons chopped parsley	Salt and black pepper

The best way of preparing this purée is to grill the aubergines over charcoal, which gives them a distinctive flavour. However, it will probably be more convenient to grill them under a grill or place them over a gas flame; either way is very successful. Sear them until the skins are black and start to blister, and the flesh feels soft and juicy. Rub the skins off under the cold tap, taking care to remove any charred particles. Gently squeeze out as much of the juice as possible, since it is rather bitter.

Put the aubergines in a bowl and mash them with a fork, or pound them to a smooth paste in a mortar. An electric blender will give excellent results. Add the oil gradually, beating all the time. Then add the remaining ingredients, mixing vigorously to blend them into the purée. Taste and add more lemon juice, garlic or seasonings as you wish.

Serve as an appetizer or salad.

≈ Many people these days find it easier to roast the aubergines in a very high oven until they soften – instead of grilling. It is a good idea to put 2 small onions in to soften with the aubergines. Chop them up and mix them into the aubergine purée.

≈ A lovely salad can also be made by stirring into the purée 3 large peeled and chopped tomatoes and a small grated onion.

Aubergine Purée with Yoghourt

A similar recipe to this one, called *buran*, is to be found in al-Baghdadi's thirteenth-century cookery manual. Fried meat balls are added to the purée, and the dish is seasoned with ground cumin and cinnamon.

3 aubergines	1–2 cloves garlic, crushed
3 tablespoons olive oil	Salt
300 ml (½ pint) yoghourt	2 tablespoons finely chopped
Juice of 1 lemon	parsley (optional)

Cook and peel the aubergines as described in the previous recipe, and squeeze them to remove the bitter juices.

Mash them with a fork in a bowl or put through a blender. Add the olive oil gradually, beating constantly. Then add the yoghourt and mix vigorously until it is thoroughly blended with the aubergine purée. Mix in the remaining ingredients (except parsley), spoon into a serving bowl and garnish with chopped parsley if desired. Serve cold.

≈ A very pleasant alternative to yoghourt is fresh single cream. Stir in about 150 ml (¼ pint). Add lemon and garnish. There is no need for oil.

≈ For a Tunisian touch, stir in a bit of *harissa* (page 65).

Fried Aubergines with Yoghourt

3 aubergines	2 cloves garlic, crushed
Salt	300 ml (½ pint) yoghourt
Oil	Dried crushed mint, to garnish

Cut the aubergines into 1-cm- (½-inch-) thick slices. Sprinkle them with salt and leave them in a colander for about ½ hour to allow the bitter juices to drain away. Rinse them with cold water and wipe dry.

Fry the aubergine slices in hot oil for a few minutes on each side until lightly browned. Add the crushed garlic and fry for a minute or two longer until golden and aromatic. Remove the aubergine slices and garlic, and drain on absorbent paper. Allow to cool.

Season the yoghourt with salt. (Some people prefer to add the crushed garlic raw to the yoghourt instead of frying it with the aubergines.) Arrange and spread alternate layers of yoghourt and fried aubergine slices in a dish. Start with a layer of yoghourt, and top the dish with yoghourt too. Garnish with dried crushed mint and serve as an appetizer or salad.

Gebna Beida
White Cheese

1½ litres (4 pints) milk	4 tablespoons liquid essence of
1 tablespoon salt, or more	rennet*

* Rennet contains rennin from the stomach of the calf. It coagulates the milk proteins, and activates the curd.

74

Use at least 4 pints of milk as the amount of cheese produced even from this quantity is really quite small.

Pour the milk into a saucepan and heat gently. Add the salt and liquid rennet, and continue to heat the milk slowly until you can just bear to keep your finger in it without feeling any sting. Do not cover the pan as condensed steam would spoil the process, and do not allow the milk to become too hot as this will cause failure. Boiling would ruin it.

Turn off the heat and cover the pan with a cloth. The milk will separate into curds and whey. Leave undisturbed for at least 6 hours or overnight.

Pour the mixture into a colander or large sieve lined with thin damp muslin, and let it drain overnight. The following day, turn out the piece of cheese formed into a small round wicker or plastic basket with little holes in it. This will allow it to dry out further and will give it the shape and texture of the basket. Leave the cheese for another whole day. Then turn the beautiful, porcelain-white cheese out on to a plate and serve as an appetizer with olives. It is also delicious sliced and fried with eggs when it is a few days old and rather dry.

≈ The same cheese, made with little or no salt, is excellent eaten with jam.

□ *As soon as Goha discovered that someone had stolen the piece of salted cheese from his lunch box, he ran to the fountain. 'What are you doing here?' asked a friend. 'I am waiting for the one who stole my cheese. I always come here as soon as I have eaten some.'*

Fried or Grilled Cheese

A hard dry goat cheese is the best for this. Greek cheeses such as Halumi, Kephalotyri and Kasseri, which are hard and salty, or the popular Kashkaval, are delicious cut into cubes or slices, grilled or fried, and served with a squeeze of lemon juice.

Grill the cheese over charcoal or under the grill, turning it over once, until the skin begins to blister, becomes spotted with brown and starts to melt. Alternatively, fry the cheese in very hot oil or butter, rolling the pieces in flour first if you like. Serve very hot, sprinkled with lemon juice.

This idea can be adapted to other cheeses, such as Gruyère or hard Cheddar.

Fried cheese used to be served in cafés in Cairo in two-handled frying pans straight from the fire, to be eaten with bread and a squeeze of lemon.

Sidqi Effendi, in his Turkish cookery manual written in the nineteenth century, gives this recipe for grilling cheese. 'Put a portion of cheese in silver paper. Wrap it up and put it over a fire. When the paper starts to glow the cheese is ready to eat and deliciously creamy . . . This is good food which enhances sex for married men.'

Aubergine Slices with Onions and Tomatoes

This is an elegant buffet version of *Imam Bayildi* (page 367).

3 medium-sized aubergines	Salt and pepper
2 onions, coarsely chopped	A small bunch of parsley, finely
Olive or a light vegetable oil	chopped
2 cloves garlic, crushed	2 tablespoons pine nuts
1 large tin peeled tomatoes	

Cut the aubergines into 1½-cm (½-inch) slices. Sprinkle generously with salt and let them sweat in a colander for about an hour.

For the filling, fry the onions in 2 tablespoons oil until golden. Add the garlic and stir. When the aroma rises, add the peeled tomatoes with only half their juice. Season to taste with salt and pepper and cook until the liquid is reduced, then stir in the parsley.

Rinse the salt off the aubergines and gently squeeze a few slices at a time together between the palms of your hands to get rid of some of their juices. Deep fry quickly in very hot oil (this so they absorb much less of it), turning over once, until just coloured. Press on absorbent paper, then arrange on a large serving dish.

Spread a little of the filling over each slice. Toast the pine nuts over low heat in a frying pan with no oil, shaking it until they are lightly browned. Sprinkle them over the filling.

Serve cold.

≈ Lately, on the advice of a Turkish lady, I have been stewing the aubergine slices in tomato juice with a drop of oil instead of frying them – which is lighter and also very good.

Hors D'Œuvre

Fried Liver Pieces, hot or cold

4–6 slices calf's or lamb's liver
2 tablespoons olive oil
2 tablespoons wine vinegar
Salt and black pepper
Oil
Juice of ½ lemon

2 tablespoons finely chopped
 parsley (optional)
1 small mild onion, thinly sliced
 (optional)
A good pinch of ground cumin
 (optional)

Calf's liver is tastier than lamb's, but of course very much more expensive. Wash the liver, cut it into small, neat pieces, and remove any sinews or membranes. Mix the olive oil, vinegar and seasonings, to make a marinade. Marinate the liver for an hour, or longer if possible.

Drain the liver pieces well. Fry them in hot oil, turning the pieces once, for only a minute or two so that they are well done on the outside but still very juicy inside. (Liver dries very quickly and is not good overcooked.) Cook a little longer if serving cold. The liver pieces can equally well be grilled gently. In this case, they should be eaten hot.

Serve sprinkled with lemon juice; if you like, garnish the liver pieces with chopped parsley and very thin slices of Spanish onion. They are also good lightly dusted with cumin.

≈ A Moroccan way is to add a good sprinkling of paprika, cumin and coriander to the frying oil.

□ *A Recipe for Cooking Liver**

One day the Khoja bought some liver, and as he was carrying it away a friend met him and asked how he meant to cook it.

'Oh! as usual,' answered he.

'No!' said his friend, 'there is a very nice way of doing it. Let me describe it to you.'

He did so, but the Khoja said, 'I cannot remember all these details. Write down the recipe on a piece of paper and I will cook the liver accordingly.'

His friend wrote it down and handed it to him.

He was proceeding home deep in thought when a hawk pounced down, took the liver out of his hand, and flew off with it.

* Barnham (trans.), *Tales of Nasr-ed-Din Khoja.*

The Khoja, however, did not seem to mind, for he held out the recipe and called to the hawk, 'What is the use of your doing that? You can't enjoy it, because I have got the recipe here.'

Onions with Vinegar

It is said that the Prophet Muhammad did not like the smell of onions although he liked to eat them, and he therefore asked people not to attend the mosque smelling of onion or garlic. Even today, people are sometimes turned away from holy places for this reason. Although according to numerous sayings and proverbs, onions have a low rating in Arab folklore, they are very much appreciated and often eaten raw, quartered or sliced.

A Persian way of serving onions is called *sarkeh piaz*.

2 large mild onions	2–3 tablespoons wine vinegar
Salt	1 tablespoon dried crushed mint

Slice the onions into half-moon shapes. Sprinkle with a little salt, add the vinegar and mint. Toss the onions in this seasoning, and leave them to stand for at least 1 hour before serving. They will become soft, lose much of their pungency and absorb the other flavours.

They can then be served as an appetizer, or be placed in little bowls on the table to accompany a main dish.

□ *Arab saying: 'He fasted for a year, then he broke his fast on an onion.' (Implying that it was not worth fasting.)*

Brain Salad

Brains are considered a great delicacy by many people in the Middle East. A Syrian student I met in London admitted to cooking and eating three sets a day in his bed-sitting room, such was his passion for them.

In some parts of the Middle East, it is believed that they feed one's own brain and render one more intelligent. In other places, it is thought that eating brains reduces one's intelligence to that of the animal, and people who hold such beliefs cannot be persuaded to touch them.

2 sets calf's brains or 4 sets lamb's
   brains
Salt
Vinegar
½ large mild onion or 4–6 spring
   onions, finely chopped
Juice of ½–1 lemon, or more

4–6 tablespoons olive oil
Black pepper
2–3 tablespoons finely chopped
   parsley
½ teaspoon ground cumin
   (optional)

Brains should be cooked when they are very fresh, preferably on the day they are bought. Soak them for 1 hour in cold water with salt and 1 tablespoon vinegar. Carefully remove the thin outer membranes, and wash under cold running water. Simmer gently for 10 minutes in salted water to which you have added a teaspoon of vinegar.

In the meantime, marinate the chopped onion in lemon juice. Drain the brains and let them dry. Slice them. They should be firm enough to keep their shape. Arrange the slices in a single layer in a shallow serving dish.

Stir the olive oil into the onion and lemon mixture, season to taste with salt and pepper, and sprinkle it over the brains. Garnish the dish with chopped parsley and, if you like, dust it with a little cumin.

Serve as an appetizer or salad.

Fried Brains

2 sets calf's brains or 4 sets lamb's
   brains
3 teaspoons vinegar
Salt
White or black pepper
Flour

1 egg yolk, beaten
Fine dry breadcrumbs
Oil for deep-frying
2 tablespoons finely chopped
   parsley
Juice of ½ lemon (optional)

Soak the brains for 1 hour in water acidulated with 2 teaspoons of the vinegar. Remove the thin membranes in which they are encased and wash the brains under cold running water. Drop the brains into boiling salted water acidulated with the remaining teaspoon of vinegar, and simmer for about 3 minutes. Remove and drain thoroughly. Cut into smallish pieces. Roll the pieces first in seasoned flour, then in beaten egg yolk seasoned with a little salt and pepper, and lastly in breadcrumbs. Fry in deep, hot oil for a few minutes until golden brown, and drain on absorbent paper.

Serve hot or cold, garnished with chopped parsley and, if you like, sprinkled with lemon juice.

Brains Moroccan Style

2 sets calf's brains or 4 sets lamb's
  brains
Salt
Vinegar
3 cloves garlic, crushed
3 tablespoons oil
1 medium tin peeled tomatoes
1 small bunch of parsley, finely
  chopped

1 small bunch of fresh coriander,
  finely chopped
1 teaspoon paprika
A pinch of cayenne, to taste
1 teaspoon cumin
Juice of ½ lemon
½ preserved lemon (page 63),
  chopped up

Soak and clean the brains as described in the preceding recipe and cut them in 2 or 4. Fry the garlic in the oil in a large pan until the aroma rises. Add the peeled tomatoes and the rest of the ingredients (except the brains) and simmer for a few minutes. Then drop in the brains and cook gently a further 15 minutes.

As good cold as it is hot.

Tahina Cream Salad

Tahina in its various forms is a great Middle Eastern favourite. It is served as an appetizer with Arab bread (page 434), and invariably appears as an accompaniment to most cold, and some hot, main dishes.

Tahina itself is a paste made from sesame meal, and can be found in all Greek stores and a few delicatessens.

1–3 cloves garlic, to taste
Salt
150 ml (¼ pint) lemon juice or the
  juice of 2½ lemons, or more
150 ml (¼ pint) tahina paste

½–1 teaspoon ground cumin
  (optional)
6 tablespoons finely chopped
  parsley, or 2 only to garnish

Crush the garlic with salt. Mix it with a little of the lemon juice in a large bowl. Add the tahina paste and mix well. Then add the remaining lemon juice and enough cold water to achieve a light cream, beating vigorously. Season with salt and cumin, if liked;

taste and add more lemon juice, garlic or salt until the flavour is fairly strong and tart.

Tahina prepared in this way is most often served as it is, sprinkled with a little chopped parsley; but sometimes it is mixed with the larger amount of parsley given above, in which case it is called 'parsley salad'. As with all tahina-based salads and creams, the flavourings are combined to taste, and the cream must be tasted several times while adjusting the seasonings in order to achieve a good balance.

This mixture can be made very quickly and easily in an electric mixer or blender. In fact, the result will be smoother and creamier than mixing by hand.

Serve the tahina cream in a bowl or a plate and provide Arab or other bread to dip in it.

≈ An alternative seasoning is white wine vinegar. A few teaspoons of it can be used to replace a little of the lemon juice; or vinegar can be substituted for all the lemon juice. A little mustard is also added by some people.

≈ A usual garnish is to sprinkle with olive oil and lemon juice and to dust with cumin and chilli pepper or paprika.

Tahina Cream Salad with Yoghourt

This version has a very definite flavour of its own and is rather creamier than most. My mother discovered it in the Sudan, and has made it ever since.

2–3 cloves garlic	150 ml (¼ pint) yoghourt
Salt	Juice of 2½ lemons, or more
150 ml (¼ pint) tahina paste	Finely chopped parsley, to garnish

As in the first tahina cream salad recipe, crush the garlic with a little salt and mix it with the tahina paste. Add the yoghourt and lemon juice gradually, beating vigorously to make a smooth, thick cream. Taste and add more salt, lemon juice or garlic if necessary. (Here, again, an electric mixer or blender can be very useful.)

Serve in a bowl, garnished with finely chopped parsley, and provide Arab or other bread to dip into it.

Serve as an appetizer, or to accompany grilled or fried meat dishes and salads.

Teradot
Tahina with Walnuts

This is a Turkish variation of the tarator sauce on page 218, and is a speciality of Jehan in Southern Turkey.

120 g (4 oz) walnuts	3–4 tablespoons tahina paste
2 cloves garlic	Juice of 2 lemons
Salt	4 tablespoons chopped parsley

Pound the walnuts and garlic in a mortar with a little salt until the walnuts are almost, but not quite, ground to a paste. Add the tahina paste and lemon juice gradually, stirring well. Then mix in the chopped parsley.

An electric blender can be used. In this case, add the lemon juice and tahina paste at the same time as the walnuts and garlic, to allow them enough time to blend together without over-blending the walnuts, which might then lose their slightly rough texture. A few tablespoons of water are also necessary to achieve the right texture in a blender.

Serve with fried mussels, baked fish, or as an accompaniment to various salads and plainly cooked vegetables, such as steamed runner beans or cauliflower.

Hummus
Chick Peas

One of the best ways to use chick peas, so common in the Arab world that they could be a symbol of it, is puréed as a cream salad. Because it is so often combined with tahina, many use the name hummus for that combination.

250 g (8 oz) chick peas	50–90 ml (2–3 fl oz) fresh lemon
Salt and pepper, to taste	juice
2 teaspoons cumin	50 ml (2 fl oz) olive oil
2 large cloves garlic (crushed), or	A good pinch of cayenne
to taste	(optional)
	Parsley to garnish

Soak the chick peas for a few hours or overnight in cold water. Drain and simmer in fresh cold water until really soft, which usually takes more than an hour, adding salt towards the end of the cooking time. (A good pinch of bicarbonate of soda speeds up the softening but then you must throw away the cooking water, for it acquires a rather unpleasant taste.)

Cool a little and put in the liquidizer with the rest of the ingredients and enough of the cooking water to achieve a soft cream. You must add the flavourings gradually and taste often. It should be distinctly sharp. You can leave a few chick peas whole to use as garnish.

Serve in flat plates garnished with sprigs of parsley and a dribble of olive oil.

Accompany with warmed pitta bread to dip in.

≈ Dried beans can also be treated in this way very successfully.

Hummus bi Tahina
Chick Peas with Tahina

This tahina salad is the most widely known and appreciated of all outside the Middle East. It is the constant companion of shish kebab and *ta'amia* in Oriental restaurants.

It makes an excellent appetizer served as a dip with bread, fish, aubergines – practically anything – and can also be used as a salad with a main dish.

120–180 g (4–6 oz) chick peas, soaked overnight	2–3 cloves garlic
	Salt
Juice of 2–3 lemons, or to taste	150 ml (¼ pint) tahina paste

GARNISH

1 tablespoon olive oil	1 tablespoon finely chopped
1 teaspoon paprika	parsley

Boil the soaked chick peas in fresh water for about 1 hour, or until they are soft. The cooking time will depend on their age and quality. (½ teaspoon bicarbonate of soda in the soaking water will make them soft a little quicker.) Drain the chick peas, reserving the cooking water, and put aside a few whole ones to garnish the dish. Press the rest through a sieve or pound them in a mortar; or better still, use an electric mixer or blender to reduce them to a purée. In this case, you will have to pour the lemon juice and a little of the cooking water into the bowl or container first to provide enough liquid for the blending to be successful. Add the remaining ingredients and blend to a creamy paste, adding more water if necessary.

If you are blending by hand, crush the garlic cloves with salt, add them to the crushed chick peas and pound them together until well mixed. Add the tahina paste gradually, followed by the lemon juice, and mix vigorously. If the paste seems too thick, beat in a little water to thin it to the consistency of a creamy mayonnaise. Keep tasting and adjusting the seasoning, adding more lemon juice, garlic or salt if necessary.

This is one of the dishes which, for centuries, have been traditionally decorated in the same manner. Pour the cream into a flat serving dish and dribble a little red paprika mixed with olive oil over the surface. Sprinkle with chopped parsley and arrange a decorative pattern of whole chick peas on top.

Serve as a dip with Arab bread or pitta.

≈ An alternative, rather stronger cream is made by using a generous pinch of cayenne pepper instead of paprika. Some of it is mixed into the cream, the rest is sprinkled over the top together with a little ground cumin, in a star design of alternating red and brown.

≈ Pine nuts, toasted, or sautéed in a little butter, make a very special garnish, or you can sprinkle with ground *sumac* and a little chopped parsley.

Baba Ghanoush (also called Moutabal)
Aubergines with Tahina

This rich cream is a combination of two strong flavours: the smoky one of aubergines prepared as below, and the strong taste of tahina sharpened by lemon and garlic. It is exciting and vulgarly seductive. The ingredients are added almost entirely to taste, the harmony of flavours depending largely on the size and flavour of the aubergines used.

The quantities below give a fairly large amount, enough to be served as a dip at a party.

3 large aubergines
2–4 cloves garlic, or to taste
Salt
180 ml (¼ pint) tahina paste or less, depending on the size of the aubergines
Juice of 3 lemons, or more to taste

½ teaspoon ground cumin (optional)
2 tablespoons finely chopped parsley
A few black olives or 1 tomato, thinly sliced, to garnish

Cook the aubergines over charcoal or under a gas or electric grill (or roast them in a hot oven) as described in the recipe for aubergine purée (page 73), until the skin blackens and blisters. Peel and wash the aubergines, and squeeze out as much of the bitter juice as possible.

Crush the garlic cloves with salt. Mash the aubergines with a potato masher or fork, then add the crushed garlic and a little more salt, and pound to a smooth, creamy purée. Alternatively, use an electric blender to make the purée.

Add the tahina paste and lemon juice alternately, beating well or blending for a few seconds between each addition. Taste and add more salt, lemon juice, garlic or tahina if you think it necessary, and if you like, a little cumin.

Pour the cream into a bowl or a few smaller flat serving dishes. Garnish with finely chopped parsley and black olives, or with a few tomato slices. Serve as an appetizer with Arab or other bread, as a salad, or as a party dip.

Boiled Carrot Salad

This is a fiery Moroccan salad. Make it with old carrots, which taste better. Add the flavourings gradually, to taste. The colour is beautiful. Serve as a dip with bread or bits of raw vegetables.

500 g (1 lb) carrots
Salt and pepper
½–1 teaspoon harissa, or 1
    teaspoon paprika and a good
    pinch of cayenne
1–2 teaspoons cumin

3 tablespoons wine vinegar
4 tablespoons olive oil
2 cloves garlic, crushed
¼–½ teaspoon ginger
A few olives to garnish

Peel the carrots and boil in salted water until very soft. Drain and mash with a fork in a bowl and stir in the rest of the ingredients or, better still, turn to a smooth purée in a blender.

Serve cold garnished with a few green or black olives.

≈ Alternative additional flavourings are 2 tablespoons honey and 1 teaspoon cinnamon.

Ta'amia *or* Falafel
Bean Rissoles

This is one of Egypt's national dishes, welcome at all times, for breakfast, lunch or supper.

The Christian Copts, who are said to be pure representatives of the ancient Egyptians, claim this dish as their own, along with *melokhia* soup (page 161). Their claim is quite probably justified since these dishes, whose origins cannot be traced, are nevertheless believed to be extremely old. During Coptic religious festivals, and particularly during Lent, when they are not allowed to eat meat for many weeks, every Coptic family produces platefuls of *ta'amia* daily; it consumes large quantities itself and distributes the rest to non-Coptic friends.

Ta'amia (called *falafel* in Alexandria) are patties or rissoles made from dried, white broad beans (*ful nabed*), splendidly spiced and flavoured, and deep-fried in oil. They are delicious, and I have never known anyone who has not liked them instantly.

The best *ta'amia* I have eaten were in Alexandria, with my aunt and uncle. Every year they rented a flat there, the balcony of which was directly above a café which specialized in *ta'amia*. My relatives were both rather large, which was not surprising, since we always seemed to come upon them eating; and I could never visualize them eloping, gazelle-like, in their youth, which was the romantic legend related to us.

On each visit, we would sit with them for hours on their balcony overlooking the sea. Time and again, a basket would be lowered on a rope to the café below and pulled up again with a haul of fresh *ta'amia*, sometimes nestling in the pouch of warm, newly baked Arab bread. We would devour them avidly with pieces of the bread dipped in tahina salad, and then wait anxiously for the basket to be filled up again.

500 g (1 lb) dried white broad beans (ful nabed)	1 bunch parsley or fresh coriander, finely chopped
2 red or Spanish onions, very finely chopped or grated, or onions mixed with a bunch spring onions, finely chopped	1–2 teaspoons ground cumin
	1–2 teaspoons ground coriander
	½ teaspoon baking powder
2 large cloves garlic, crushed	Salt and cayenne pepper
	Oil for deep-frying

The dried white beans can be found in all Greek stores and in many delicatessens. Buy them already skinned if possible.

Soak the beans in cold water for 24 hours. Remove the skins if this has not been done. Drain, and mince or pound them, or put through a food processor. Mix with the rest of the ingredients and pound or blend to a paste. This must be very smooth if it is to hold together. Let it rest for at least ½ hour.

Take walnut-sized lumps and make flat, round shapes 2½–4 cm (1–1½ inches) in diameter. Let them rest for 15 minutes longer, then fry them in deep hot oil until they are a dark, rich golden brown.

Serve hot, accompanied by a tomato and cucumber salad and tahina cream salad (page 80). *Ta'amia* are delicious served as an appetizer, or as a main dish for a luncheon party, accompanied by a variety of salads and bread.

≈ If the paste does not hold together it usually means that it has not been properly mashed. You can remedy this a little by adding 2–3 tablespoons flour.

≈ 15 g (½ oz) fresh yeast or 7 g (¼ oz) dried yeast dissolved in a few tablespoons lukewarm water may be mixed in the paste which should then be allowed to rest for an hour. The result is lighter rissoles.

≈ A dry *falafel* 'ready mix' is now available in all Greek and Oriental shops. Add water as directed on the packet, allow the paste to rest for a while, then shape and fry in deep fat as above. This 'ready mix' is not nearly as good as the real thing, but you can use it for making appetizers if you are short of time. To improve the flavour, add a little finely chopped parsley, finely chopped spring onion, crushed garlic and the other seasonings to taste.

≈ In the countries of the Fertile Crescent – Syria, Lebanon and Jordan – *falafel* have been made with chick peas instead of white broad beans. Israelis have adopted this method for what has become their national dish. It is they who have popularized *falafel* in the West.

□ *Goha's Coat*

One day Goha was invited to a wedding. He had to rush there straight from work and did not have time to get changed. The hosts took one look at him and put him at the bottom of the table. Every time a dish was passed around he was the last one to be served. All the good bits had gone and he was served very little.

The next invitation he received for a wedding, he made sure he was well dressed and borrowed the grandest coat in the neighbourhood. The hosts treated him with joy and respect and he was offered the best place at the table. All the choice pieces were offered to him. One dish after another came first to him and his plate was piled high with delicacies. Instead of eating he started tugging at his own lapel saying, 'Eat! Eat!' His neighbour looked at him in surprise and after a while bent over and whispered, 'How can a coat eat?' Then Goha replied, 'It's all for him, not for me!'

Artichoke Hearts stewed in Oil

2 lemons
6 artichokes or a 14-oz tin
   artichoke hearts

4 tablespoons olive oil
2 cloves garlic
Salt and white pepper

Have ready a bowl of water to which you have added the juice of ½ lemon. Cut off the stems and the hard outer leaves of the artichokes, and slice off the remaining leaves to within ½ inch of the hearts. Scoop out the chokes. Rub each prepared artichoke with the squeezed lemon half and throw it into the bowl of acidulated water. This will prevent the artichokes from discolouring.

Bring ½ litre (¾ pint) water to the boil with the juice of the remaining 1½ lemons, olive oil, the 2 whole garlic cloves, and salt and pepper to taste. Throw in the artichoke hearts and simmer them, uncovered, for about 20 minutes, or until tender. Cool.

Serve cold, whole if small, halved or quartered if large, in their own liquid, which will have reduced considerably during the cooking.

If tinned artichokes are used, drain them well and let them simmer, covered, for about 15 minutes only in the lemon juice and olive oil, flavoured with garlic, salt and pepper. No water is necessary.

Koftit Ferakh
Fried Minced Chicken Balls

Here is one variety of minced chicken balls which is easily prepared from leftovers and which, rolled into shapes the size of small marbles, makes a good appetizer.

2 cooked chicken quarters, preferably breasts	Pinch of turmeric (optional)
	Salt and black pepper
2 large slices white bread	Flour
Milk	Oil for deep-frying
1 large egg	Juice of ½ lemon (optional)

Skin and bone the chicken, and remove any sinews and hard membranes. Mince the flesh, or chop it very finely if a mincer is not available. Remove the crusts from the bread. Soak the slices in a little milk and squeeze dry. In a bowl mix the chicken, bread, egg and seasonings. Knead well and shape into marble-sized balls. Roll them in flour and fry in deep hot oil until cooked and a dark golden colour.

Serve the balls hot or cold, with a few drops of lemon juice squeezed over them, if you like.

Dukkah

This is another dearly loved and old Egyptian speciality. It is a loose mixture of nuts and spices in a dry, crushed but not powdered form, usually eaten with bread dipped in olive oil. In Egypt it is served at breakfast time, as an appetizer, or as a snack in the evening. It is a very personal and individual mixture which varies from one family to another. Here are two mixtures, the first is my mother's.

500 g (1 lb) sesame seed	Salt and pepper to taste – try 1
250 g (8 oz) coriander seed	teaspoon salt and ½ teaspoon
120 g (4 oz) hazelnuts	black pepper
120 g (4 oz) ground cumin	

Roast or grill the ingredients separately. Pound them together until they are finely crushed but not pulverized. The crushing can be done in a mincer or an electric blender. In the last case run it for a very short time only, as otherwise the oil from the too finely ground seeds and nuts will form a paste with the pulverized ingredients. *Dukkah* should always be a crushed dry mixture, and definitely not a paste.

The quantities above make a good deal of *dukkah*, but it can be stored for many weeks in covered jars.

From a book published in 1860:

A meal is often made by those who cannot afford luxuries of bread and a mixture called *dukkah*, which is commonly composed of salt and pepper with *za'atar* or wild marjoram or mint or cumin-seed, and with one or more, or all, of the following ingredients – namely, coriander seed, cinnamon, sesame, and hummus (or chick peas). Each mouthful of bread is dipped in this mixture.*

Try mixing the ingredients to taste and improvise the proportions. Roast or grill the ingredients separately before pounding them. If you use chick peas, buy those sold pre-cooked, salted and dried, available in most Greek and Indian shops. They are tiny, white and very round.

≈ Another very humble preparation, a mixture of dried crushed mint, salt and pepper, is sold in the streets in little paper cornets as *dukkah* to sprinkle over bread.

Batarekh
French Boutargue

Known and favoured as a great delicacy since the time of the Pharaohs, and still considered so by Egyptians today, this is the salted, dried roe of the grey mullet. It is a deep, orangy, sienna-brown colour, rich and strongly flavoured.

In Egypt, we used to buy *batarekh* already dried and ready to eat. I was thrilled to eat a perfect one last year in Paris. It had been made by Mrs R. Telio, who now lives in Montreal and who had sent it, properly waxed and sealed, to her brother in Paris. Here is her recipe.

Grey mullet roes are sold in Canada from barrels, where they are kept frozen. They are held together by a thin skin and look like rather long sausages.

Although I have not found the roes in London, there is a chance that they will one day be sold here, and in the meantime you may like to experiment with fresh or smoked cod's roes instead.

Choose roes with skins which are intact, free from tears or holes. This is important to the success of the recipe. Roll the roes in kitchen salt and arrange them on a thick layer of absorbent paper. They will begin to lose their moisture. Keep changing the papers as they become saturated. Turn the roes over when you change the papers, and sprinkle with more salt. The secret of success lies in changing the papers frequently until they remain quite dry. This will take a few days.

* Lane, *Manners and Customs of the Modern Egyptians.*

At this stage, put the roes on a tray in front of an open window or hang them on a string in a very airy place such as an airing cupboard, to dry out still more. This part of the process will take about 8 days, longer for fresh cod's roes. The process can be speeded up by placing the roes occasionally in a turned-off warm oven, but care must be taken not to over-dry them, or they will be crumbly. When the roes are hard and rather dry, they are ready to eat.

Slice the *batarekh* very thinly and serve it with bread, either buttered or dipped in olive oil. If you like, squeeze a little lemon juice over it. The taste is an acquired one which can become a passion.

The dried *batarekh* can be preserved for months in a refrigerator. Each one must be individually wrapped in a polythene bag and sealed. If you wish to preserve them in a home deep-freezer, it will be necessary to expose them to the air for a little while after defrosting to dry out again before they can be eaten.

Mrs Telio, who usually travels with presents of *batarekh* to distribute to friends, covers them with wax to preserve them hermetically sealed on long journeys. Dipping them in melted wax also prevents over-drying.

I have dried *smoked* cod's roes by putting them occasionally in a turned-off warm oven and by hanging them in a very airy, dry place for a few days. The results were excellent, and were achieved with very little effort. So I can highly recommend this as a substitute for *batarekh*.

Taramasalata 1

This 'cream salad', well known in the West, is a Greek and Turkish speciality. *Tarama* is the dried, salted and pressed roe of the grey mullet, but you can use smoked cod's roe, which can easily be found at a fishmonger's or a delicatessen.

3 thick slices white bread	1–2 cloves garlic, crushed, or 2
Milk	tablespoons grated onion, or
90 g (3 oz) tarama or smoked cod's	both
roe	Juice of 1–2 lemons
	4 tablespoons olive oil
	Black olives, to garnish (optional)

Remove the crusts from the bread and soak the slices in a little milk. Skin the roes and pound them vigorously in a mortar to eliminate their gritty texture. Add the soaked bread, squeezed dry, the garlic and/or onion, and continue pounding until smooth. Gradually add lemon juice and olive oil, tasting until you get the flavour you like; more or less lemon, garlic or onion may be added to taste. Then work the mixture into a creamy, pale pink paste by vigorous beating.

Alternately, put all the ingredients in an electric mixer or food processor, and beat at a fairly high speed. Add a few tablespoons of water or milk if required.

Taramasalata is sometimes garnished with black olives, and usually served with thin toast.

≈ Numerous variations on taramasalata exist. Some people like to add a boiled, mashed potato or an egg yolk to bind the paste.

≈ With a food processor it is not necessary to skin the roes, but you must wash them. The blade will incorporate the skin into the cream giving it a lovely pink colour.

Taramasalata 2

Here is another recipe which gives a rather firmer cream with the texture of a stiff mayonnaise, and is, I feel, more successful than the first.

90 g (3 oz) smoked cod's roe
2 slices slightly dry, crustless
    white bread, soaked in water
    and squeezed dry
1 clove garlic, crushed

Generous pinch of cayenne
    pepper
Juice of 1–2 lemons
About 180 ml (6 fl oz) olive oil,
    nut or sunflower oil

Skin the roes and pound in a mortar or, preferably, beat in an electric mixer or food processor. Mix in the other ingredients as in the previous recipe. Add the lemon juice and oil gradually, as for a mayonnaise, mixing in first a little of one and then the other. Mix or beat vigorously all the time until you achieve a rich, smooth cream. Blend in 1 tablespoon hot water to finish the paste.

Blehat Samak
Miniature Fish Sticks

Prepare the recipe for fish sticks on page 212, but roll the mixture into smaller, marble-sized balls or tiny fingers and fry them in oil until golden brown. They will cook more quickly, being smaller. Serve hot or cold.

These little snacks can also be simmered in fish stock or the tomato sauce given with the main recipe, and served cold.

Cold Mussels Plaki

48 large mussels	2–3 cloves garlic
Salt	1 tablespoon caster sugar
2 medium onions, chopped	3 tomatoes, skinned and chopped
½ teacup olive oil	3 tablespoons chopped parsley
1 medium carrot, diced	2 tablespoons tomato concentrate
1 large potato, diced	Black pepper
1 medium celeriac, diced	

Wash and scrape the mussels clean. Open them by steaming in a covered saucepan with about 300 ml (½ pint) vigorously boiling water and a little salt for 5 to 7 minutes. Remove the mussels from their shells, and keep the cooking liquor.

Fry the onions in olive oil until soft and golden. Add the diced carrot and continue to fry gently for another 2 minutes. Then add the potato, celeriac, garlic cloves, sugar, tomatoes, parsley and tomato concentrate. Season with salt and pepper to taste, and moisten with the reserved mussel liquor. Stir gently and simmer over very low heat until all the vegetables are well cooked and the sauce is rich and reduced, adding a little more water if necessary. Be careful not to let the vegetables stick to the pan or burn. Finally, add the mussels and simmer for 5 minutes. Remove from the heat and allow to cool.

Serve cold as an hors d'œuvre or as a main luncheon dish.

Sardines in Vine Leaves

This is fiddly but, if you have the time, well worth trying.

12 large vine leaves (or 24 small ones)
12 plump sardines
A bunch of parsley, finely chopped
A bunch of coriander, finely chopped
3 cloves garlic, crushed
Salt and pepper
3 tablespoons olive oil
1 lemon

If you use fresh vine leaves, poach in boiling water for a few seconds until they change colour and become limp. If you use leaves in brine, soak them in water for about an hour and change the water twice to remove the salt.

Scale and behead the sardines if you like, cut open the belly and pull out the backbone (it is easily done if you flatten out the fish), then wash. Stuff with a mixture of herbs, garlic, salt and pepper moistened with olive oil. Roll each fish up in one or two vine leaves and put under the grill or over embers about 3 inches from the fire. Cook 5 minutes on both sides. Squeeze a little lemon juice over each and serve hot or cold. Everything is edible, leaves and all.

Tongue Salad

1 fresh or salted ox or calf's tongue (or two sheep's tongues)
1 large onion, cut in four
1 large carrot, cut into pieces
3 celery stalks and leaves
1 bay leaf
A few parsley stalks
salt and pepper

DRESSING

3–4 tablespoons olive oil
Juice of 1 lemon
1–2 cloves garlic, crushed
A few sprigs of parsley, finely chopped
Salt and pepper

Sheep's tongues are less easily available but they can be ordered from the butcher.

If the tongue is salted leave it to soak in cold water overnight, changing the water at least once. Otherwise scrub it well and put it in a large saucepan with the rest of the ingredients. Bring to the boil, remove the scum and simmer until it is tender. It will need about 50 minutes per 500 g (1 lb). Drain and allow it to cool just enough to handle it. If you let it get cold it will be difficult to skin.

Skin it and remove the roots and return to the pot to cool in the stock.

Cut into slices or small pieces and dress.

Cerkes Tavugu
Circassian Chicken

In Turkey during the period of the Ottoman Empire the women in the harems, the wives and concubines of the Sultans, were the widows and daughters captured at war. The Circassians amongst them were known for their beauty and their culinary skills. This classic is part of their legacy.

The following recipe is different from the one in the first edition, which was an old peasant version. This one was given by Luli Fevsi and comes from the kitchens of the Ottoman aristocracy. It is a cold dish which may be served as an hors d'œuvre or as part of a buffet table.

4 chicken breasts
4 chicken wings
1 onion stuck with 3 cloves
A few celery stalks
A sprig of tarragon or thyme
Salt and white pepper
2 thin slices dry white bread,
   crusts removed

250 g (8 oz) walnuts, coarsely
   minced or ground
1–2 cloves garlic, crushed
   (optional)
2 teaspoons paprika
2 teaspoons walnut or other oil

Put the breasts and wings (these are to enrich the stock) in a saucepan. Cover with water, bring to the boil and remove the scum. Add the onion and cloves, celery and herbs and season to taste with salt and pepper. Simmer for about 30 minutes until the breasts are tender.

In the meantime, prepare the sauce. Soak the bread in a little of the stock and turn it to a paste in a blender. Mix with the walnuts in a small saucepan and add enough stock to have the consistency of porridge. Cook, stirring, a few minutes until the sauce thickens. Add garlic if you like and a teaspoon of paprika and stir well.

Skin the chicken breasts and shred into small pieces. Mix well with two thirds of the sauce and spread on a serving dish. Cover with the rest of the sauce.

To garnish, mix the remaining paprika with the oil and dribble over the top. In Turkey, people use the oil squeezed out of walnuts but I have not been successful with this.

Serve cold.

Arais
Bread Stuffed with Meat

Pitta bread stuffed with spiced meat makes a good snack and, if cut up small, a very good appetizer.

6 pitta breads	½ teaspoon allspice
2 tablespoons oil	1 teaspoon cinnamon
1 large onion, finely chopped	2 teaspoons sumac or the juice of
600 g (1¼ lb) lean minced meat –	½ lemon
veal, beef or lamb	A good pinch of cayenne
1 small hot green pepper, finely	A small bunch of parsley, finely
chopped	chopped
Salt and pepper	2 tablespoons butter, melted

Cut each pitta on one side and open carefully without breaking the bread (warming it up makes it easier).

To make the filling, fry the onion in oil till golden, add the meat and fry, stirring, until it changes colour. Add the green pepper, season with salt and pepper and stir in the spices and parsley. Spread a sixth of the filling into each bread, then press it closed. Brush with melted butter and grill, turning over once, until both sides are lightly coloured. Cut in half and then into wedges and serve very hot with a piece of lemon and tahina if you like.

≈ You may stir 3 tablespoons fried pine nuts in with the meat.

Tabbouleh
Parsley and Mint Salad with Burghul (Cracked Wheat)

This very refreshing salad – all green herbs with buff-coloured wheat speckle – has become quite well-known in this country through the recently opened Lebanese restaurants. A mountain dish that became a national dish, it is now popular throughout the world.

This recipe is different from the one in the first edition of this book, which had more wheat and less herbs. That one had been brought back from Aleppo to Egypt by my father's family almost ninety years ago – a time when people needed to fill their stomachs.

Tabbouleh makes a wonderful first course and is always welcome on a buffet table.

250–310 g (8–10 oz) parsley (preferably flat-leafed), chopped

60–90 g (2–3 oz) fresh mint, chopped

60–120 g (2–4 oz) fine-ground burghul (cracked wheat)

Salt and pepper to taste

Juice of 2 lemons, or more to taste

100 ml (3 fl oz) olive oil

250 g (8 oz) spring onions or 1 large, mild onion, chopped

Young Cos lettuce leaves to garnish

3 medium tomatoes, diced

Wash the mint and parsley if necessary and dry well. Remove stems and chop (a food processor will do this well, but be careful that you do not turn them to a mush). Soak the burghul in cold water for 10 minutes, drain and press to remove excess water. Put it in a bowl and add salt and pepper and some of the lemon juice and the olive oil. Let it absorb the dressing for about ½ hour or until it is tender. Just before serving, add the burghul to the chopped parsley, a little at a time, just enough for a speckled effect. Add the spring onions, seasonings and more dressing to taste and mix well. The salad should be distinctly sharp with lavish quantities of lemon.

Serve on a large, flat plate or individual small ones, surrounded if you like by the pale crisp leaves from the heart of Cos lettuce to be used as a scoop. (In the mountain villages of Lebanon, freshly picked, sharp young vine leaves are passed around to pick up the salad.) Top with the chopped tomatoes.

Bazargan

This old recipe from Aleppo in Syria was rediscovered by my parents in Los Angeles. Quantities are enough for at least 15 people but the salad keeps well if you have some left over.

500 g (1 lb) burghul (cracked wheat)

2 large onions, grated or finely chopped

150 ml (¼ pint) olive oil (you may use sunflower oil)

250 g (8 oz) tomato concentrate

2 tablespoons oregano

60 g (2 oz) finely chopped parsley

120 g (4 oz) walnuts, coarsely chopped

3 tablespoons concentrated pomegranate juice or the juice of 2 lemons

2 teaspoons cumin

2 teaspoons coriander

1 teaspoon allspice

Salt and pepper to taste

Cayenne pepper to taste

Wash and soak the burghul in fresh cold water for 10 to 15 minutes. Drain well through a fine sieve. Soften the onions by frying in a little of the oil but do not brown.

Mix all the ingredients very thoroughly with a fork in a large bowl. Leave for a few hours, preferably overnight, in the refrigerator, for the burghul to absorb all the flavours and to become tender.

Salads

Salatat

Simple and unpretentious, rich and exotic, salads and cold vegetable dishes are present at practically every type of Middle Eastern meal. It is usual to present several at once as hors d'œuvres or as accompaniments to the rest of the meal. Almost anything can be made into a salad: fresh, raw vegetables, cooked vegetables, pulses, bread, cheese, cracked wheat (burghul) and meat (including brains and tongue) – see also the previous chapter. Chopped red Italian or Spanish onions, crushed garlic and chopped parsley are favourite ingredients. Great care is taken with the presentation, and colour plays an important part, as well as taste and texture.

As a general rule, boiled vegetables are usually dressed with olive oil and lemon, while raw vegetables can be dressed with olive oil and lemon or vinegar. The oil is used lavishly. Prepared commercially or by peasants, it ranges accordingly from a pure, pale golden colour to a coarser, brownish shade. People love it and sometimes drink it neat by the glass when they feel anaemic or tired. In the past, it was believed that olive oil would cure every illness except the one by which a person was destined to die.

It is related that Adam was suffering with pain and complained to God; Gabriel descended from heaven with an olive tree and presented it to Adam, and told him to plant it, to pick the fruit, to extract the oil and use it whenever he had pain, assuring him that it would be a cure for all ills . . .*

Beside its many other properties, olive oil is widely believed to have a powerful aphrodisiac effect. According to a recent report in a Greek newspaper, a man who had been accused of seducing a young woman cleared himself in court by swearing, and providing witnesses to testify, that he had eaten an extra large salad dressed particularly lavishly with olive oil.

If pure olive oil proves too expensive in this country, other salad oils will make an adequate substitute.

The ingredients of a salad should be as fresh as possible. Raw vegetables and lettuce must be unbruised, well washed, cold, crisp and dry. Cooked vegetables must *not* be overcooked, but rather firm. Pulses must be cooked carefully until they are tender but not too soft if they are to be kept whole, longer if they are to be puréed. These, as well as cooked vegetables, absorb their dressing better if dressed while still hot.

Salad Dressings

Middle Eastern dressings for salads are a mixture of olive oil and lemon juice or vinegar (preferably wine vinegar), used in much the same proportions as in the French vinaigrette sauce. Crushed garlic is often added with the salt and pepper. Sometimes, too, lemon dressings are sharper than in the West; more lemon is used in proportion to the oil. Occasionally, the Middle Eastern cook uses as much lemon as oil, or more, for instance in dressing dried vegetable salads.

* Donaldson, *The Wild Rue.*

Unless otherwise stated, the dressing for the salads which follow is made in the proportions below with the proviso that more oil and lemon juice or vinegar can always be added if you feel that the salad requires it:

1 tablespoon lemon juice or vinegar, or more	1–2 cloves garlic, crushed (optional)
3 tablespoons olive oil	Salt and black pepper

≈ Common additions are chopped parsley, fresh or dried mint, dill, fresh coriander, spring onions (usually mixed into the salad, but sometimes added with the dressing).

≈ To give a salad the distinctive flavours of the Maghreb add a pinch of cayenne, a teaspoon of paprika, cumin, coriander or cinnamon or a touch of *harissa* (page 65). Alternatively, you can perfume the dressing with drops of orange blossom or rose water or geranium essence and you may use bitter orange instead of lemon.

≈ Instead of adding raw crushed garlic, try boiling, grilling or roasting the cloves in their skins until they are soft, then peel and mash them into the dressing.

Na'na Mukhalal

A medieval recipe from al-Baghdadi for a vinegar dressing.

Take fresh large-leafed mint, and strip the leaf from the stalk, wash and dry in the shade: sprinkle with aromatic herbs. If desired, add celery leaves and quarters of peeled garlic. Put into a glass bottle and cover with good vinegar, coloured with a little saffron. Leave until the mint has absorbed the sourness of the vinegar so that the latter has lost its sharpness: then serve.

Tomato Salad

750 g (1½ lb) firm tomatoes, sliced	2 tablespoons finely chopped parsley
1 red Italian or large mild onion, or a few spring onions, chopped	½ teaspoon ground cumin (optional)
	Salad dressing (page 101)

It is not necessary to skin the tomatoes. Spring onions will do beautifully instead of an onion when they are in season.

Mix the tomatoes, onion, parsley, and cumin if used, in a bowl. Mix the dressing, pour it over the vegetables, and toss well. Or arrange the tomatoes in overlapping rows on a serving dish. Pour the mixed dressing over them, and sprinkle with the onions, chopped parsley and cumin.

Sweet Pepper Salad

.3 sweet green peppers
Salad dressing (page 101)

1 tablespoon finely chopped parsley

Cut the peppers in half and taste a small piece from each one in case it is too strong. Remove the seeds and grill the peppers under a low flame until their skins blister and darken, and their flesh becomes soft. Skin them, and cut them into long strips. Crisp and sharp when raw, they become mellow and sweet when grilled.

Put the peppers in a serving bowl. Mix the dressing ingredients together, using either salad oil or olive oil. Stir in parsley, pour over the peppers and mix well.

Salatit Khodar Meshakel
Mixed Fresh Vegetable Salad

This popular Arab salad is different from conventional Western salads in that all the ingredients are chopped and absorb the dressing and each other's flavours better. Do not prepare it too long before serving as the ingredients will wilt. Dress it just before putting it on the table. Ingredients can vary according to taste.

1 small Cos lettuce or ½ large one
2 small cucumbers or 1 long English one
3 tomatoes
1–2 red Italian onions if available, or 1 large mild onion, or 1 small bunch spring onions
6 radishes, thinly sliced (optional)

3–4 tablespoons finely chopped parsley
1 tablespoon finely chopped fresh dill or chervil (optional)
2 tablespoons finely chopped fresh mint or 1 teaspoon dried crushed mint (optional)

DRESSING

5 tablespoons olive oil
2 tablespoons lemon juice or wine vinegar

1 clove garlic, crushed with salt (optional)
Salt and black pepper

Carefully wash and dry the lettuce, cucumbers, tomatoes, spring onions and radishes, if used. Peel the onion or spring onions. Shred the lettuce; cut the cucumbers (peeled or unpeeled, as you wish) into small dice. Dice the tomatoes (remove the seeds and juice first), and chop the onions finely, using a sharp knife, or an Italian *mezzaluna* chopper if you have one. Put the prepared vegetables in a salad bowl and mix lightly with the radishes and herbs.

Mix the dressing ingredients thoroughly, sprinkle over the salad and toss well.

≈ An alternative dressing is the Jerusalem favourite, tahina – about 3 tablespoons – thinned with lemon juice to taste and a little water. Season with salt and pepper.

Salata Horiatiki
Greek Country Salad

This salad brings back for me the garland of islands floating in the deep blue sea, the plaintive sound of the bouzouki and the sugar-cake houses. It can serve as a meal.

1 Cos lettuce, cut into ribbons
2 large knobbly tomatoes, cut in wedges
1 cucumber, not necessarily peeled, split in half through its length and cut into thick slices
1 green pepper, cut in thin rings crosswise
1 large mild onion, thinly sliced and the rings separated, or a bunch of spring onions, thinly sliced

250 g (8 oz) Feta cheese, cut into small squares or broken with your fingers into coarse pieces
1 dozen or more black Kalamata olives
A good bunch of parsley, preferably the flat-leafed type, coarsely chopped

DRESSING
90 ml (6 tablespoons) olive oil
Juice of 1 lemon
Salt and pepper

Put all the salad ingredients together in a large bowl. Just before serving, mix the dressing to taste, beat well, pour over the salad and toss.

≈ Other usual additions are chopped dill or fennel, capers, sliced pickled gherkin, a sprinkling of oregano, a few sprigs of fresh mint, finely chopped.

White Radish Salad

The long white radishes, also called *mouli*, which could until recently only be seen in Greek and Indian stores can now be found much more easily. Slice them very thinly or grate them coarsely and dress with a lemon vinaigrette. A few drops of orange blossom water will give it a delicate perfume. Garnish with plenty of finely chopped parsley.

Cucumber Salad with Mint

The perfume of mint suits cucumber very well. Peel and slice it thin. Sprinkle with salt and let the juices drain for ½ hour. Dress with a vinaigrette. Sprinkle with finely chopped fresh mint or some dried mint. Wild thyme can also be used instead of mint and a teaspoon of orange blossom water added to the dressing gives it a very pleasant perfume.

Cacik
Cucumber and Yoghourt Salad

A Turkish salad makes an extremely popular *mezze* throughout the Middle East. It is sometimes served as a cold soup.

1 large cucumber or 2 small ones, peeled and diced	White pepper
Salt	1 tablespoon dried crushed mint or 3 tablespoons finely chopped fresh mint, or to taste
2–3 cloves garlic	
450 ml (¾ pint) yoghourt	Additional mint, to garnish

Sprinkle the diced cucumber with salt, and leave in a colander to drain for ½ hour. Crush the garlic with a little salt; use more than 3 cloves if you like. Mix a few tablespoons of the yoghourt with the garlic, then add the mixture to the rest of the yoghourt and mix well. Add more salt and pepper to taste. Finally add the mint, whose aroma and flavour make the salad deliciously refreshing. Drain the cucumbers and mix with the yoghourt.

Pour into a serving dish and decorate with more mint.

≈ For a sharper flavour you may stir in 2 tablespoons vinegar and 4 of olive oil.

≈ Another lovely alternative is to use a mixture of sour cream and yoghourt in equal quantities.

Salata Meshwiya

This salad is very popular all over North Africa, particularly in Tunisia. It is not unlike the French *salade niçoise*, so its origin might just as well be Nice as Tunis.

375 g (12 oz) firm tomatoes
2 large sweet peppers
1 mild onion or 6–7 spring onions
1 hot dried chilli pepper (optional)
A 100-g (3½-oz) tin of tuna fish

2 hard-boiled eggs, sliced
1 tablespoon capers
2 tablespoons finely chopped parsley

DRESSING

3 tablespoons lemon juice
4 tablespoons olive oil

Salt and black pepper

If you wish to skin the tomatoes, plunge them in boiling water for a minute or two first. Halve the sweet peppers and grill them skin side up until they are soft and mellow. Skin and seed them. Chop the onions and the chilli pepper finely. Slice off one end of the tomatoes, scoop out the seeds and juice, and slice them. Cut the sweet peppers into narrow ribbons.

Put all the vegetables in a large serving dish. Add the tuna fish, drained and crumbled, the sliced hard-boiled eggs and capers. Mix the dressing ingredients together, pour them over the salad and mix well. Serve sprinkled with finely chopped parsley.

≈ A very good local touch is to put 3 or 4 cloves garlic in their skins under the grill. When they are soft, mash the cream into the dressing – it will be sweet and mellow.

Cream Cheese and Celery Salad

250 g (8 oz) cream cheese
Juice of 1 lemon
2 tablespoons olive oil

150 ml (¼ pint) yoghourt
Salt and white pepper
1 head celery, finely chopped

With a fork, work the cream cheese with the lemon juice and olive oil until smooth. Add the yoghourt and salt and pepper to taste. Stir well. Lightly stir in the chopped celery and serve.

Michoteta
Cream Cheese and Cucumber Salad

This delightful Egyptian salad is usually made with salty Greek cream cheese, either Teleme or Feta. For an authentic salad, these can be found in most Greek stores, but good-quality cottage or curd cheese makes a good substitute.

250 g (8 oz) soft cheese (see above)
Juice of 1 lemon
2 tablespoons olive oil
1 red Italian or large mild onion, finely chopped

½ large cucumber, peeled and diced
Salt and black pepper

Crumble the cheese with a tablespoon of water, using a fork, and work in the lemon juice and olive oil. Mix in the onion and cucumber, and season with salt and pepper (Feta does not need salt).

This salad is wonderful as an appetizer or as an accompaniment to the dish of brown beans called *ful medames* (page 324).

Hamud Shami

Although *shami* means Syrian, this is an Egyptian salad, characterized by its definite taste of lemon and garlic. It is more like a chicken jelly than a salad.

600 ml (1 pint) chicken stock
1 tablespoon oil
2 large cloves garlic, crushed

4 tablespoons ground rice
Juice of 1 lemon, or a little more
½ teaspoon turmeric

Prepare a well-flavoured chicken stock.

Heat the oil in a saucepan and fry the crushed garlic until it turns golden and aromatic. Pour in a ladleful of the stock. Dissolve the ground rice in a little cold water and mix it with the garlic-flavoured stock. With the saucepan still over gentle heat, add the rest of the chicken stock gradually, stirring all the time. Continue cooking and stirring until the mixture becomes very thick. Add the lemon juice and turmeric, and bring the mixture gently to the boil, stirring vigorously. Pour into a serving dish.

Allow to cool fully, and chill if you wish. The mixture will become a delicate yellow jelly. It looks beautifully translucent in a transparent bowl.

This unusual salad is delicious served with cold chicken and plain hot rice. It is often served as an appetizer, with bread or vine leaves to dip into it.

Grated Carrot Salad

I discovered this refreshing salad on a kibbutz in Israel. It was introduced by a cook of Moroccan origin.

500 g (1 lb) carrots, coarsely grated
90–120 g (3–4 oz) raisins or
   sultanas
5 tablespoons olive oil
1–2 tablespoons honey

Juice of 1 lemon
½ teaspoon ginger
1 teaspoon cinnamon
Salt and pepper

Mix all the ingredients together in a bowl.

Three Moroccan Orange Salads

Orange Salad

Peel 3 large oranges, taking care to remove all the bitter white pith. Slice very thinly. Arrange on a plate. Sprinkle with orange blossom water and dust lightly with ground cinnamon.

Orange and Radish Salad

In this salad, a bunch of radishes is thinly sliced, and 1 or 2 oranges are peeled, sliced and divided into small pieces. The whole is seasoned lightly with salt and a little lemon juice.

Carrot and Orange Salad

Grate 750 g (1½ lb) of carrots, peel and cut an orange into small pieces and dress in a mixture of the juice of 2 oranges and 1 lemon and 2 tablespoons orange blossom or rose water. Stir in a bunch of chopped coriander leaves. This is very refreshing to serve with a hot spicy dish.

Turnip and Orange Salad

This salad is from Tunisia.

Wash 500 g (1 lb) young turnips and slice them very thin. Macerate for an hour in a mixture of 3 tablespoons olive oil, the juice of 1 bitter Seville orange or a grapefruit or a mixture of orange and lemon juice (it needs to be sharp) with a crushed clove of garlic, salt and pepper. A pinch of cayenne is optional.

Serve as it is with a few sprigs of parsley, or add a chopped-up orange.

Loubia bi Zeit
Green Beans in Olive Oil

750 g (1½ lb) green beans	4–5 tablespoons olive oil
1 large onion, coarsely chopped	Salt and pepper
4 cloves garlic, sliced	4 tomatoes, peeled and sliced

Top and tail, string and wash the beans and cut into 2 or 3 pieces. Fry the onion and garlic gently until they begin to colour. Add the beans and sauté briefly, stirring constantly. Cover with water, add salt and pepper and simmer until tender and the water is reduced. Add the tomatoes and stir gently until they have softened.

≈ Instead of using fresh tomatoes, you may stir 1 or 2 tablespoons tomato concentrate into the water.

Fennel, Celery and Cauliflower Salad

The vegetables may be used raw, but when boiled they make a rather unusual salad. Wash and cut them into pieces and florets. Boil in salted water until only slightly softened. Dress with plenty of olive oil, lemon juice, a little salt and pepper. The fennel has enough perfume of its own, but a little chopped, fresh mint is an agreeable addition.

Mixed Salad of Boiled Vegetables

Any vegetables available can go into this salad, but those listed below are the ones most commonly used.

2 potatoes
1 beetroot
2 courgettes
A few green or runner beans

½ small cauliflower
Salt
Salad dressing (page 101)

Peel the potatoes, scrub the beetroot and courgettes, string and rinse the runner beans, and wash the cauliflower. Boil the vegetables separately in salted water until just tender, or, preferably, steam them. Drain. Cube the potatoes and the peeled beetroot, slice the courgettes into rounds and the runner beans lengthwise, and separate the cauliflower into florets.

Arrange the vegetables in separate little groups on a large serving dish and sprinkle with well-mixed dressing.

Spinach Salad with Yoghourt

Spinach has a remarkable affinity with yoghourt, and it is delicious prepared in this particular manner.

500 g (1 lb) fresh spinach or 250 g
(8 oz) frozen leaf spinach
150 ml (¼ pint) yoghourt

1 clove garlic, crushed
Salt and black pepper

Wash the spinach carefully, snipping off any hard stems. Drain. Chop the leaves and stew them in their own juice in a large covered saucepan until tender, about 15 minutes. If using frozen spinach, de-frost it in a colander and simmer until cooked. Allow to cool.

Beat the yoghourt and garlic together, and add the mixture to the pan. Mix well and season to taste with salt and pepper.

Salq bi Loubia
Spinach with Black-eyed Beans

120 g (4 oz) black-eyed beans
500 g (1 lb) fresh spinach or 250 g
(8 oz) frozen leaf spinach

1 large onion, chopped
4 tablespoons olive oil
Salt and pepper

Simmer the black-eyed beans in water for about 20 minutes or until they are tender, adding salt when they have begun to soften. They do not usually need soaking and fall apart quite quickly if they are overcooked.

Wash the fresh spinach, removing the thick stems, and drain well. Frozen spinach must be completely thawed and all the water squeezed out of it.

Fry the onion in the olive oil until soft and transparent. Add the spinach and continue to fry, stirring constantly until well cooked. Add salt and pepper to taste, stir the drained beans into the spinach and warm through before allowing to cool.

Cooked Onion Salad

In the old days people used to put onions in their skins to cook very slowly in the ashes of a fire. They acquired a sweet, mellow taste which an hour in a low oven (160°C/325°F/Mark 3) will also give them. Put a few in while you are cooking something else. Let them cool, then peel and cut into slices or pieces and dress with a vinaigrette. Garnish, if you like, with capers or bits of parsley.

Eat this cold.

Sweet-and-Sour Onions

500 g (1 lb) little button onions	2 tablespoons sultanas
3–4 tablespoons olive oil	Salt and pepper
3 tablespoons wine vinegar	2 teaspoons dried mint (optional)
1 tablespoon sugar	

Peel the onions (one way is to plunge them for a few seconds in boiling water until the skins come off easily). Sauté in oil, shaking the pan to brown them all over. Add the rest of the ingredients and a little water and cook gently till soft, adding more water if necessary.

Courgettes with Raisins and Pine Nuts

Slice 500 g (1 lb) courgettes and fry quickly in 3–4 tablespoons olive oil with 2 tablespoons raisins or sultanas and 2 tablespoons pine nuts. Add 1 crushed clove garlic, salt and pepper, and 2 teaspoons dried mint (optional) and stir well. Squeeze the juice of ½ lemon, or more, over the salad and serve cold.

≈ Lately I have not fried the courgettes but macerated them in a lemon vinaigrette for at least an hour. It is healthier and delicious, but the courgettes must be very good and tasty. Toast the pine nuts and add them before serving. This is best without garlic.

Beetroot Salad

Beetroot is commonly served boiled and sliced, dressed with olive oil, lemon, salt and pepper, and sprinkled with chopped parsley. A more unusual way is to dress it with yoghourt, olive or corn oil, lemon juice and salt.

2 tablespoons lemon juice
2 tablespoons olive or corn oil
300 ml (½ pint) yoghourt
Salt

500 g (1 lb) boiled beetroot, diced
1 tablespoon finely chopped
   parsley, to garnish

Mix the lemon juice with the oil. Add the yoghourt, and salt to taste, and beat well. Fold in the diced beetroot and mix thoroughly. Pour into a serving dish and garnish with chopped parsley.

≈ An alternative dressing is olive oil and a little salt mixed with about 1 teaspoon of orange blossom water or rose water and a sprinkling of cinnamon.

Leek Salad

Use 500 g (1 lb) leeks. Split the green parts lengthwise and wash the leeks carefully, fanning them out in the water to remove all traces of soil between the leaves. Discard the tough outer leaves; trim the tops and roots. Cut the leeks into 3- to 5-cm (1- or 2-inch) lengths and boil them in lightly salted water until only just tender (about 15 to 20 minutes). Drain and cool.

Prepare a dressing with 3 tablespoons olive oil, the juice of ½ lemon or more, salt and pepper, 1 teaspoon dried mint, 1 or 2 crushed cloves garlic and ¼ teaspoon sugar. Pour over the leeks in a serving dish.

≈ A variation is to simmer the leeks very gently in the juice of ½ lemon, 3 tablespoons oil, and their own juice, seasoned with salt, black pepper and about ¾ teaspoon sugar. Cover and simmer until very soft, about 20 minutes.

Allow to cool in their liquid and serve cold, garnished with chopped parsley.

Leeks in a Yoghourt or Sour Cream Dressing

Wash, trim and boil leeks whole in salted water until only just tender. Roll in a sauce made by beating 2–3 tablespoons olive oil with the juice of 1 lemon, 4–5 tablespoons yoghourt thickened (see page 124) to the consistency of mayonnaise or sour cream, seasoned with salt and pepper. Allow to cool. Serve covered with sauce and a sprinkling of finely chopped parsley or coriander.

Turkish Tarator Sauce for Boiled Vegetables

Serve this in a bowl with plain boiled vegetables such as runner beans, courgettes or cauliflower.

2 thin slices bread, crusts removed	150 ml (¼ pint) olive oil
120 g (4 oz) walnuts or hazelnuts, ground	3–4 tablespoons wine vinegar
	1–2 cloves garlic, crushed
	Salt and black pepper

Dip the bread in water and squeeze dry. Crumble it, and add it to the ground nuts. Gradually add the olive oil, beating constantly. Stir in the vinegar and garlic, and season to taste with salt and pepper. The sauce should be very smooth and creamy. For an even smoother texture, blend the mixture in an electric blender.

Salade Rachèle

This salad was the speciality of a cook called Rachèle who helped to prepare many of the parties for our community in Cairo. In Egypt we used English pickles to make it. It is extremely simple, and always a great favourite because of its strong taste. It can also be served as an hors d'œuvre.

I have given amounts for rather a large quantity, enough for a party, or as a stock supply to be prepared and stored for future occasions. It keeps for many weeks in a jar if the surface is covered with a thin layer of oil.

1 kg (2 lb) aubergines
Salt
Oil
1 large onion, chopped

500 g (1 lb) tomatoes, skinned and sliced
1 medium jar mild or sweet mustard pickle

Slice the aubergines, sprinkle them with salt, and leave them in a colander for at least ½ hour to allow the bitter juices to drain away. Pat the slices dry and fry them in oil until soft and brown on both sides.

In a large pan fry the chopped onion until it is soft and lightly coloured. Add the tomatoes and stir until they are barely cooked. Mix in the aubergines and the pickles cut into small pieces.

Sweet-and-Sour Aubergine Salad

Broken pieces of toasted bread are sometimes placed at the bottom of the serving dish to become well moistened and soft with the juice of the vegetables.

750 g (1½ lb) aubergines trimmed and cubed
Salt
Olive oil
1 large Spanish onion, coarsely chopped
2 cloves garlic, crushed

1 × 400-g (14-oz) tin peeled tomatoes
4 tablespoons finely chopped parsley
1 tablespoon dried mint
3 tablespoons wine vinegar
1 tablespoon sugar
Pepper to taste

Sprinkle the aubergine cubes with salt and leave in a colander for about an hour for the juices to drain away.

Rinse and squeeze the water out from a few at a time with your hands.

Cover the bottom of a heavy pan with olive oil. Fry the onion in this until it is soft and golden. Add the garlic and fry, stirring until it begins to colour. Add the aubergines and stir and turn them for about 5 minutes. Add the tomatoes, cut into small pieces, with their juice, the parsley, mint, vinegar and sugar and the pepper. Cook over very low heat for about 20 minutes, until the aubergines are tender. Let it cool.

Bamia
Sweet-and-Sour Okra

A slight sweet-and-sour flavour is particularly good with cold dishes.

Cut off the stem ends and wash 500 g (1 lb) small young okra. Heat 2 tablespoons oil in a heavy pan. Add the okra and sauté gently for about 5 minutes. Turn each pod over, then stir in 1 tablespoon sugar, salt and pepper, and the juice of 1 small lemon. Add a little water to half-cover the okra.

Simmer, covered, for about 20 minutes or longer, adding a little water occasionally if necessary, and cook until tender. Allow to cool before serving.

Mushrooms in Olive Oil

A Greek Dish.

250 g (8 oz) small button
   mushrooms
3 tablespoons olive oil
1 tablespoon water
Salt and black pepper
Juice of ½–1 lemon

½ teaspoon dried thyme
   (optional)
1–2 cloves garlic, crushed
4 tablespoons finely chopped
   parsley

Wash and dry the mushrooms, or wipe them clean with a damp cloth. Cut them in half if they are a little large. Pour the oil and water into a deep frying pan. Stir in all the remaining ingredients except the mushrooms and bring to the boil. Finally, add the mushrooms and simmer gently for about 7 minutes, or until the mushrooms are tender, turning them over occasionally. Pour into a serving dish and allow to cool.

Taste and adjust the seasoning before serving as its intensity changes with the drop in temperature. Serve cold.

The mushrooms are sometimes not cooked. Instead they are left to marinate in the refrigerator in the same dressing as above (but without the water) for 24 hours.

Dried Vegetable Salads

Dried vegetables make rich, nourishing salads to accompany lighter main dishes. Their earthy texture is given excitement by a really sharp, lemony dressing flavoured with crushed garlic, sometimes with a little ground cumin or coriander, and always with finely chopped parsley or fresh coriander.

The vegetables are soaked overnight if necessary, then drained and brought to the boil in a fresh portion of unsalted water. They are simmered until tender but not completely soft, and salted just before the end of their cooking time. Finally, they are drained and dressed, preferably while still hot, mixed with herbs and allowed to cool.

These dried vegetable salads are also sometimes served puréed. In this case, they are simmered rather longer, drained well, seasoned and mashed with a fork; or they are made into a paste in an electric blender, using a little of the cooking liquor if necessary. They are then cooled and served garnished with chopped parsley, sprinklings of oil and paprika, and black olives.

The proportion of oil and lemon juice used in the seasoning is different from that of the vinaigrette type of dressing for fresh salads. Tastes vary, but usually more lemon is used, sometimes as much as, or more than, the oil.

Lentil Salad

250 g (8 oz) lentils
Salt

2–3 tablespoons finely chopped parsley

DRESSING

6–7 tablespoons olive or salad oil
Juice of 1½–2 lemons, or more
1–2 cloves garlic, crushed (optional)

Black pepper
½ teaspoon ground coriander or cumin (optional)

Use the large, dark brown lentils for this salad. Soak them for an hour, and boil them in a half-covered pan in fresh water until barely tender. This will take about ½ hour. Add salt only towards the end of cooking time. Drain well.

Mix the dressing ingredients and pour over the lentils while still quite hot. Stir in parsley, and arrange in a serving dish.

≈ One variation is to soften a finely chopped onion in about 6 tablespoons oil, add the soaked lentils, the juice of 1 lemon, a crushed clove of garlic and about a pint of water (but no salt). The mixture is simmered until tender (about ½ hour), water being added from time to time if necessary. Salt and black pepper are added near the end of the cooking time, together with 2 tablespoons chopped parsley and, if desired, a little ground cumin or coriander. The whole mixture is then cooked for just a few minutes more.

≈ The lentils can also be cooked as in the variation above, but for longer, until they are very soft. They are spiced in the same way, and are then mashed to a paste and served as a purée.

Lentil and Tomato Salad

250 g (8 oz) large brown lentils
1 large onion, chopped
4 tablespoons olive oil
3 tomatoes, peeled and cut into pieces

Salt and pepper
1 small bunch of parsley, finely chopped
2–3 tablespoons vinegar

Soak the lentils in water for a few hours. Fry the onion in oil until lightly coloured. Add the tomatoes and sauté for a minute. Add the drained lentils, cover with water and simmer gently for about ½ hour until they are tender, adding water as required, then season with salt and pepper, add parsley and vinegar and cook until the lentils are done and the liquid absorbed.

Taste and adjust the seasoning when it is cool. You may add a sprinkling of olive oil if you like.

Ful Nabed
Purée of Dried White Broad Beans

Choose the white broad beans to be found in all Greek shops and some delicatessens, usually skinned.

2 onions, finely chopped
6 tablespoons olive oil
250 g (8 oz) dried white broad beans, soaked overnight

Juice of 1 lemon
1 teaspoon caster sugar
Salt

DRESSING

2 tablespoons olive oil
Juice of ½ lemon
2–3 tablespoons finely chopped
  fresh dill or parsley

1 teaspoon paprika or a pinch of
  cayenne pepper (optional)

Fry the onions gently in oil in a large saucepan until they are only just soft and a very pale golden colour. Add about ½ litre (¾ pint) water and bring to the boil. Drain the beans of their soaking water, add them to the saucepan, and cook over low heat without any salt until they practically disintegrate. Add more water during the cooking time if necessary. This will take from 1 to 1½ hours, according to the quality of the beans.

When the beans are ready, there should be hardly any liquid left. Mash them to a paste. Season with the lemon juice, sugar and salt. For a very creamy consistency put the mixture through a sieve or in an electric blender.

Pour the purée into a serving bowl. When cold, decorate with a dribble of olive oil, lemon juice and chopped dill or parsley. Red paprika may be added to this mixture for colour, or cayenne pepper for strength.

Purée of Haricot Beans

250 g (8 oz) dried haricot beans,
  soaked overnight
4 tablespoons olive oil

Juice of 1 lemon, or more
Salt and black pepper
4 black olives (optional)

Boil the haricot beans until very soft. The time required will, as usual, depend on their quality and age. A pressure cooker can reduce it considerably.

Drain the beans thoroughly. Save a few whole beans for garnish, and mash, pound or blend the rest to a smooth paste in an electric blender. Add the olive oil and lemon juice, salt and pepper, beating with a wooden spoon to blend them into the purée. Thin with a little water if necessary.

Serve in a bowl, decorated with the whole beans and, if you like, a few black olives.

Piaz
Turkish Haricot Bean Salad

120 g (4 oz) dried haricot beans, soaked overnight	Salt and black pepper
4 tablespoons olive oil	2 hard-boiled eggs
Juice of ½ lemon, or more	4 black olives
	1 tomato, thinly sliced

Boil the beans until very tender and soft, bearing in mind their age and quality in assessing the cooking time. Take care not to overcook them if using a pressure cooker. They must be firm.

Drain the beans well. While still hot, add the olive oil, lemon juice, salt and pepper. Mix in the eggs cut into eighths, the black olives, pitted and halved, and thinly sliced tomato, taking care not to crumble or crush them, or the beans.

Fattoush
Bread Salad

This is a much-loved Syrian peasant salad in which pieces of soaked toasted bread provide an unusual texture.

½–1 flat pitta bread	2 tablespoons finely chopped fresh mint or 1 tablespoon dried crushed mint
Juice of 1–2 lemons, or to taste	
1 large English cucumber or 2 small ones, chopped	3 tablespoons chopped fresh coriander (optional)
3–4 firm tomatoes, chopped	2 cloves garlic, crushed (optional)
1 medium-sized mild onion or a bunch of spring onions, chopped	6–8 tablespoons olive oil
A bunch of parsley, finely chopped	Salt and black pepper

The ingredients and proportions of this salad vary with every family. Cos lettuce can be used instead of cucumber, and sometimes chopped sweet peppers are added.

Open out the pitta bread and put it in a hot oven or under the grill until it is crisp and brown, then crunch it in your hands to break it into little pieces.

Put the broken pieces of toast in a bowl. Moisten and soften with a little cold water or lemon juice. Mix with the remaining ingredients. Taste and adjust seasoning.

≈ In Lebanon today the fashion, as in Europe, is to mix the broken pieces of toasted bread in at the last minute so that they remain crisp and do not become soggy.

≈ Sprinkle with *sumac*, if you like, and with pomegranate seeds.

Rice Salad

375 g (12 oz) long-grain rice
Salt
2 firm tomatoes, chopped
1 large cucumber, cubed, sprinkled with salt and allowed to drain for ½ hour
½ hot dried chilli pepper, finely chopped
3 level tablespoons finely chopped parsley
3 level tablespoons finely chopped mint, or 1 teaspoon dried crushed mint

1 level tablespoon finely chopped fresh chives
5–6 spring onions or 1 large mild onion, finely chopped
6 tablespoons olive oil
Juice of 1 lemon
Black pepper, and salt if necessary
Pinch of cayenne pepper (optional)
Black olives and sliced cucumber, to garnish (optional)

Cook the rice according to one of the recipes for plain rice (pages 401–3), using oil instead of butter and salt to taste as directed. While it is still hot, add all the remaining ingredients and mix well.

This rather delicious salad can be garnished beautifully with black olives and pale green cucumber slices.

Nougada
Almond Salad

250 g (8 oz) ground almonds
Pinch of caster sugar
Salt and white pepper
1 clove garlic, crushed
Juice of 1½–2 lemons

100 ml (3 oz) olive or sunflower oil
2–3 tablespoons finely chopped parsley
Slivered or flaked almonds, to garnish

Put the ground almonds in a bowl. Add sugar and a very little salt and white pepper. Add garlic. Stir in the lemon juice and oil alternately, a little at a time, beating well with a fork. Pour into a serving bowl. Sprinkle the top with more oil and the parsley, and garnish with slivered or flaked almonds.

An excellent salad to serve with cold fish, cold chicken or *kibbeh* (page 277).

Yoghourt

In every Middle Eastern household, the making of yoghourt is a regular activity. With a little experience one learns the rhythm of preparation and the exact warmth required to turn milk into yoghourt. The actual preparation of yoghourt is extremely easy, but the right conditions are necessary for success. If these are fulfilled, the 'magic' cannot fail.

Yoghourt is an essential part of the Middle Eastern diet. In al-Baghdadi's medieval manual it was referred to as 'Persian milk'. In Iran today it is known as *mâst*, in Turkey as *yoğurt*. Syrians and Lebanese call it *laban*, Egyptians *laban zabadi*, while Armenians refer to it as *madzoon*.

In parts of the Middle East, as in the Balkans, yoghourt is believed by some people to have medicinal and therapeutic qualities – longevity and a strong constitution are sometimes attributed to the daily consumption of yoghourt.

In the past this was sometimes made by allowing milk to stand for 2 or 3 days until it turned sour and clabbered by itself.

More recently the Western world too has discovered the whole-some and diet-regulating qualities of yoghourt. But it is still unfortunately restricted to a minor role as a dessert, usually sweetened or synthetically flavoured. Yoghourt has yet to be allowed the freedom and versatility it enjoys throughout the Middle East, where it is, in turn, a hot or cold soup, a salad, a marinade for meat, or the basic liquid element in a meat and vegetable dish. The West has also still to discover the vast number of dishes which are refreshed, soothed and glorified when accompanied by yoghourt, and the splendid drink called *ayran* or *abdug* (see page 515), made with yoghourt and water.

To Make Yoghourt

If yoghourt is to be adopted as an important element in cookery, it is well worth learning to make it at home.

All sorts of equipment have been recommended as being needed: cake tins lined with padding, feather cushions, thermometers, different-sized bottles, jars, cork tops, to name but a few. Commercial firms sell rather expensive sets of equipment, but you can do perfectly well without them. All that is needed, at least for me, is a large earthenware or glass bowl, a plate to cover it entirely, and a small woollen blanket – I use two shawls.

The proportions are a tablespoon of starter or activator (culture of the bacteria *bulgaris*) or fresh, live yoghourt (I use ordinary, commercial *plain* yoghourt) to each ½ litre (¾ pint) of milk. If you increase the quantity of milk, increase that of the starter accordingly, but do not use too much of the latter, or the new batch of yoghourt will be excessively sour.

Bring the milk to the boil in a large pan. When the froth rises, lower the heat and let the milk barely simmer for about 2 minutes. Turn off the heat, and allow the milk to cool to the point where you can barely dip your finger in and leave it there while you count to ten. Although ten is the traditional count, the milk must, however, still be hot enough to sting – 41°–43°C (106°–109°F). If the milk is much cooler or hotter than this, the yoghourt is likely to fail.

Remove any skin that has formed on the surface of the milk.

Beat the activator or plain yoghourt in a large glass or earthenware bowl until it is quite liquid. Add a few tablespoons of the hot milk, one at a time, beating vigorously between each addition. Then add the rest of the milk slowly, beating constantly until thoroughly mixed.

Yoghourt

Cover the bowl with a large plate or with a sheet of polythene secured tightly with an elastic band. Wrap the whole bowl in a woollen blanket or shawl and leave it undisturbed in a warm place such as an airing cupboard, *free of draughts*, for at least 8 hours or overnight. It should then be ready, thick like a creamy custard. Do not leave the bowl in the warmth too long, or the yoghourt will become too sour.

As soon as the yoghourt is ready, you can cool it in the refrigerator. The yoghourt will keep for a week, but it is preferable to make a new batch every 4 days, using some of the previous one as an activator. This will ensure a constant supply of sweet, fresh-tasting yoghourt.

☐ *A Dish of Yoghourt for Two**

The Khoja and a friend of his bought some yoghourt to be eaten 'share and share alike'.

They were just beginning to eat it when his friend made a mark across the middle, saying, 'I am going to put sugar and salt on my half.'

'But this is liquid,' cried the Khoja, 'and part of it is sure to come over to my side. It won't be nice. If you do put it on, sprinkle it all over, and we shall know what we are eating.'

'I have very little sugar,' said the other, 'and I am not obliged to give you any.'

The Khoja got angry and, reaching out his hand to his knapsack, took out a bottle of salad oil and at once began to pour it on.

'What!' said the man. 'Salad oil! Who ever heard of putting salad oil into yoghourt!'

'What is it to do with you? I am going to pour it on my own half. I shall do as I please, and as for you, look after your own part.'

'But,' said the man, 'is it possible to put anything into a liquid which will not go from one side to the other?'

'Don't play the fool then!' said the Khoja. 'Put the sugar in the middle!'

* Barnham (trans.), *Tales of Nasr-ed-Din Khoja.*

To 'Stabilize' Yoghourt

Many Middle Eastern dishes call for yoghourt as a cooking liquid or sauce which needs to be cooked (boiled or simmered) rather than just heated. Salted goat's milk, which was used in these recipes in olden times, can be cooked without curdling, which explains why medieval recipes do not give any indication of ways of preventing yoghourt from curdling. Lengthy cooking, however, causes yoghourt made with cow's milk to curdle, and stabilizers such as cornflour or egg white are required to prevent this.

1 litre (1¾ pints) yoghourt ¾ teaspoon salt
1 egg white, lightly beaten, or 1
    tablespoon cornflour mixed
    with a little cold water or milk

Beat yoghourt in a large saucepan until liquid. Add the egg white, or the cornflour mixed to a light paste with water or milk, and a little salt. Stir well with a wooden spoon. Bring to the boil slowly, stirring constantly *in one direction only*, then reduce the heat to as low as possible and let the yoghourt barely simmer, uncovered, for about 10 minutes, or until it has acquired a thick, rich consistency. Do not cover the pan with a lid, since a drop of steam falling back into the yoghourt could ruin it.

After simmering, the yoghourt can be mixed and cooked with other ingredients such as meat or vegetables with no danger of curdling.

If carefully handled, this process can also be carried out successfully after the yoghourt has been mixed with other ingredients.

Labna
Cream Cheese

This delightful cream cheese is served as a snack, for breakfast or as a *mezze*. It is made by salting the yoghourt and adding from ½ to 1 teaspoon salt per 600 ml (1 pint) of yoghourt, according to taste. The yoghourt should be poured into a sieve or colander lined with damp muslin or fine cotton cloth. Allow it to drain overnight, or tie the corners of the cloth together and suspend the bundle over a bowl or the sink. The whey will drain away, leaving a very light, soft, creamy white curd cheese. Eat it as it is or stir in a little olive oil, salt and pepper or paprika, and if you like some chopped fresh mint or dill.

≈ In Syria they like to spread this on an opened-up piece of pitta bread and roll it up to eat it. They call it *arus*: the bride.

≈ You can also serve *labna* as a sweet with honey and a dusting of cinnamon.

≈ A lovely salad is made by mixing in a variety of raw and finely chopped vegetables such as celery, sweet or chilli peppers and spring onion.

≈ A very popular way of serving *labna* is rolled and shaped into little balls. For this you must let the cream cheese drain until it is quite firm. Sprinkle the balls with olive oil and paprika. You can also keep the balls preserved in oil in a glass jar.

Savoury Pastries

In his *Kanju'l Ishtiha* (Treasure of the Appetite) the fifteenth-century Persian poet of food, Abu Ishaq of Shiraz, wrote: 'We came into the kitchen for this purpose, that we might show the fried meat to the pastry.'

The Middle East has 'shown to the pastry' not only meat, but also chicken, brains, cheese, eggs, spinach, aubergines and all the nuts they have had available.

Savoury pastries are one of the most interesting features of Oriental food: *sambusak, börek, pasteles, bstilla, fila, brik, spanako-pitta, lahma bi ajeen* – a vast family of glorious little pastries, half-moon shapes, triangles, fingers, small pots, little parcels of all types, as well as medium-sized pies and enormous ones. Various doughs are used, each country and community favouring a particular type; and to make it more confusing, different names are given to the same pastries by different countries and communities, while sometimes the same name can apply to two very different pastries.

Pie pastry, flaky pastry, a paper-thin pastry called *fila* (somewhat thinner than strudel paste) and bread dough can all be used. Fillings for small pies can be any combination of cheese and egg, spinach and cheese, brains and parsley, minced meat and nuts, and fried aubergines. Large pies are filled with chicken, pigeon and meat stews thickened with eggs, as well as with the fillings used for the smaller ones.

For the smaller pastries, some regions favour a certain shape to which the people are touchingly attached, and from which they would never allow themselves to deviate. They require a certain amount of skill, but it is easily acquired; it is a skill well worth possessing, since the results are particularly delicious and never cease to provoke general admiration. It is indeed a pleasure to master the art of moulding perfect, dainty little pots, to make elegant, festoon-type edges, and to fold tidy little envelopes.

These savoury pastries make excellent appetizers and first courses, served hot or cold. They also make splendid buffet and party dishes, particularly in their smaller versions. Mountains of crisp, golden savouries are a familiar sight at parties. The larger pies such as the Moroccan *bstilla* (page 149) and the Tunisian *tagine mal-souka* (page 151) make a magnificent main dish and are practically a meal in themselves.

Quantities given for the smaller pastries are usually for making 30 or more pastries, and are appropriate for parties or buffet meals.

Raghîf Alsinîyyeh

An extraordinary pie or pastry is described by Abd al-Latif al-Baghdadi,* the versatile Arab scholar, scientist, historian, philosopher and traveller, in an account of conditions and events in Egypt in the early part of the thirteenth century, the *Kitab al-ifadah wa'l-l'tibar*.

One of the most singular foods made in Egypt is that called *raghîf alsinîyyeh*. This is how it is made: they take 30 *rotles* (Baghdad weight) of wheat flour. They knead it with 5½ *rotles* of sesame oil in the same way as they make the bread called *khoschinan*. They divide the whole into two parts, spreading one of the two parts in a round shape of a *rahgîf* (cake) in a copper plate made for this purpose of about 4 spans in diameter, and which has strong handles. After that they arrange on the dough three roasted lambs stuffed with chopped meats fried in sesame oil, crushed pistachios, various hot and aromatic spices like pepper, ginger, cloves, lentisk, coriander, caraway, cardamom, nuts and others. They sprinkle rose water, in which they have infused musk, over all. After that they put on the lambs and in the spaces left, a score of fowls, as many pullets, and fifty small birds, some roasted and stuffed with eggs, others stuffed with meat, others fried in the juice of sour grapes or lemon or some other similar liquor. They put above them pastry, and little boxes filled, some with the meat, some with sugar and sweet-meats. If one would add one lamb more, cut into morsels, it would not be out of place, and one could also add fried cheese.

When the whole is arranged in the form of a dome they again sprinkle rose water in which musk has been infused, or wood of aloes. They cover it again with the other part of the dough, to which they begin to give the shape of a broad cake. They are careful to join the two cakes of dough, as one makes pastry, so that no vapour escapes. After that they put the whole near the top of the oven until the pastry is solid and begins a degree of cooking. Then they lower the dish in the oven little by little, holding it by the handles, and leave it until the crust is well cooked and takes on a rose red colour. When it is at this point it is taken out and wiped with a sponge, and again sprinkled with rose and musk water, and then brought out to be eaten.

This dish is fit to be put before kings and wealthy persons when they go hunting far from home or take part in pleasures in far off places; for in this one dish is found a great variety. It is easy to transport, difficult to break, pleasing to the sight, satisfying to the taste, and keeps hot a very long time.†

---

* *Not* the al-Baghdadi from whom I have quoted extensively in this book (see page 522).
† Zand and Videan, *The Eastern Key*.

Savoury Fillings

Certain fillings are common to many savoury pastries. Here are a few.

For a dough made with 500 g (1 lb) flour:

Cheese Filling 1

500 g (1 lb) cheese, grated   White pepper
2 eggs, beaten

Use Greek Halumi, Gruyère, Cheddar, Wensleydale, Edam, Gouda or a mixture of any of these with a little Parmesan; try also Italian Mozzarella. Mix the grated cheese with beaten eggs and season to taste with pepper.

≈ I have of late been adding a pinch of nutmeg and a little dried crushed mint to this classic filling.

Cheese Filling 2

500 g (1 lb) crumbly white Greek Feta cheese or about equal quantities of Feta and cottage cheese

3–4 tablespoons finely chopped fresh parsley, dill, mint or chives
White pepper

Crumble the cheese with a fork. Do not use a cream cheese because it melts. Mix in chopped herbs and season to taste with white pepper, but do not add salt unless the cheese requires it. (Feta is very salty.) Work the ingredients into a paste.

Meat Filling

This is called a *tatbila*.

1 medium or large onion, finely chopped
2 tablespoons oil or butter
500 g (1 lb) lean lamb or beef, minced

2 tablespoons pine nuts
Salt and black pepper
1 teaspoon ground cinnamon or ½ teaspoon ground allspice (optional)

Gently fry the onion in 2 tablespoons oil or butter (I prefer to use oil) until soft and a pale golden colour. Add the meat and fry lightly until it changes colour. Stir in the pine nuts and fry for 2 minutes longer. The pine nuts can also be fried separately and added at the end.

Season to taste with salt and pepper, and if liked, cinnamon or allspice (these flavourings are particularly excellent). Some even add a little sugar. Moisten with about 5 tablespoons water. The meat will otherwise be too dry for a filling. Cook for a few minutes more until the water is absorbed and the meat tender.

≈ In some countries cumin and coriander are preferred as flavouring spices for this popular filling.

Brain Filling

500 g (1 lb) calf's or lamb's brains
Vinegar
Salt
2–3 tablespoons finely chopped
    parsley
White pepper
1 hard-boiled egg, chopped
    (optional)

Soak the brains in water with a tablespoon of vinegar for 1 hour. Drain and wash under cold running water, removing the thin outer membranes. Drop into boiling salted water acidulated with 1 tablespoon vinegar and simmer for about 10 minutes. Drain. Mash with a fork, adding parsley and a generous amount of salt and pepper, and mix well.

A rather good addition is to stir in a chopped hard-boiled egg.

Spinach Filling 1

500 g (1 lb) fresh spinach or 250 g
    (8 oz) frozen chopped or leaf
    spinach
1 tablespoon butter
120 g (4 oz) Gruyère, Cheddar or
    Wensleydale cheese, grated
1 egg
Black pepper
¼ teaspoon grated nutmeg
    (optional)

Trim stems of fresh spinach; wash carefully and chop the leaves finely. Put in a pan with a tablespoon of butter. Cover and let it cook in its own juice over very low heat, stirring occasionally, until tender. If using frozen spinach, de-frost it and squeeze all the water out.

Stir in the grated cheese, the lightly beaten egg, and black pepper to taste. Do not add salt unless necessary. Take into account the saltiness of the cheese melting into the spinach. Add a little nutmeg if you like, and mix well.

Spinach Filling 2

500 g (1 lb) fresh spinach or 250 g
(8 oz) frozen chopped or leaf
spinach
1 onion, finely chopped
Oil

2 tablespoons pine nuts or
chopped walnuts
1–2 tablespoons raisins
Salt and black pepper

Trim stems of fresh spinach. Wash, drain and chop finely. If using frozen spinach, de-frost it and make sure that the water drains away entirely.

Fry the onion gently in 2 tablespoons oil until soft. Add the spinach and stew it in its own juice until tender. Lightly fry the pine nuts or chopped walnuts separately in oil for 2 minutes. Drain, and add to the spinach with the raisins. Season to taste with salt and pepper, and mix well.

Spinach Filling 3

500 g (1 lb) fresh spinach or 250 g
(8 oz) frozen chopped or leaf
spinach

1 tablespoon butter
Salt and black pepper
250 g (8 oz) calf's brains

Trim stems of fresh spinach. Wash, drain and chop finely. If using frozen spinach, de-frost it and make sure that the water drains away entirely. Simmer the spinach in its own juice with a little butter until soft. Season to taste with salt and pepper.

Clean, wash and simmer the brains in acidulated water as described in the recipe for brain filling above. Mash with a fork and mix with the spinach. They will act as a rather creamy binder.

Khandrajo (Aubergine) Filling

This is a Sephardic Jewish filling similar to the French *ratatouille*.

500 g (1 lb) unpeeled aubergines,
cut into small cubes
Salt
Oil

1 large onion, finely chopped
3 tomatoes, skinned and chopped
Black pepper

Sprinkle cubed aubergines with salt and leave them in a colander for about ½ hour to allow the bitter juices to drain away. Rinse well and squeeze lightly.

Heat 2 tablespoons oil in a saucepan and fry the chopped onion to a dark golden colour. Add the aubergines and fry lightly until tender and a little coloured. Add the tomatoes and season generously with pepper. Add salt only if required, taking into account the aubergines, which are salty already. Simmer gently, covered, until the vegetables are very soft, then squash them lightly with a fork.

Chicken Filling

500 g (1 lb) cooked boned chicken
2 tablespoons butter
2 tablespoons flour
300 ml (½ pint) hot milk or
   chicken stock

Salt, white pepper and grated
   nutmeg
1 egg

Use left-over chicken, if you like, and cut it into small pieces.

Make a thick sauce. Melt the butter in a thick saucepan or preferably in the top of a double saucepan. Add flour and stir well. Cook gently over boiling water for 5 minutes, stirring constantly, until the flour is cooked through. Gradually add 150 ml (¼ pint) hot milk or stock, beating well between each addition, and cook until the sauce thickens. Add the rest of the milk or stock slowly, stirring vigorously until it begins to bubble and thicken again. Season to taste with salt, pepper and nutmeg, and simmer gently for 10 to 15 minutes.

Remove from the heat, break in an egg and beat well. Add the pieces of chicken and mix well.

Sanbusak

At a banquet given by the Caliph Mustakfi of Baghdad in the tenth century, a member of the company recited a poem by Ishāq ibn Ibrāhīm of Mosul describing *sanbūsaj* (*sanbusak*) as follows.

> *If thou woulds't know what food gives most delight,*
> *Best let me tell, for none hath subtler sight.*
> *Take first the finest meat, red, soft to touch,*
> *And mince it with the fat, not overmuch;*
> *Then add an onion, cut in circles clean,*
> *A cabbage, very fresh, exceeding green,*
> *And season well with cinnamon and rue;*

Of coriander add a handful, too,
And after that of cloves the very least,
Of finest ginger, and of pepper best,
A hand of cummin, murri just to taste,
Two handfuls of Palmyra salt; but haste,
Good master haste to grind them small and strong.
Then lay and light a blazing fire along;
Put all in the pot, and water pour
Upon it from above, and cover o'er.
But, when the water vanished is from sight
And when the burning flames have dried it quite,
Then, as thou wilt, in pastry wrap it round,
And fasten well the edges, firm and sound;
Or, if it please thee better, take some dough,
Conveniently soft, and rubbed just so,
Then with the rolling pin let it be spread
And with the nails its edges docketed.
Pour in the frying-pan the choicest oil
And in that liquor let it finely broil.
Last, ladle out into a thin tureen
Where appetizing mustard smeared hath been,
And eat with pleasure, mustarded about,
This tastiest food for hurried diner-out. *

Here is a modern recipe for *sanbusak*, popular in Syria, the Lebanon and Egypt. The recipe for the dough has for centuries been explained as 'one coffee cup of oil, one coffee cup of melted butter, one coffee cup of warm water, one teaspoon of salt. Add and work in as much flour as it takes.' Translated into English weights and measures, it is:

DOUGH

120 ml (4 fl oz) oil
120 g (4 oz) butter, melted
120 ml (4 fl oz) warm water
1 teaspoon salt
500 g (1 lb) plain flour, sifted

Cheese Filling 1 or Meat Filling
 (page 129)
1 egg, beaten
Sesame seeds (optional)
Clarified butter for shallow-frying
 or oil for deep-frying

To make the dough: put the oil and butter together in a small heatproof bowl, and heat over boiling water until the butter has

* From Mas'ūdī's *Meadows of Gold.* Translated by Professor A. J. Arberry in *Islamic Culture,* 1939.

melted. Mix with warm water and salt, and pour into a large mixing bowl.

Add flour gradually, stirring slowly with a knife and then your hand, until the dough forms a soft, rather greasy ball. A few table-spoons more flour may be required. The dough should be handled as little as possible, so stop mixing as soon as it holds together.

Traditionally, *sanbusak* are half-moon-shaped. Either roll the dough out thinly on a floured board and cut into rounds about 8 cm (3 inches) in diameter with a pastry cutter, or take walnut-sized lumps and flatten them out as thinly as possible between the palms of your hands.

Put a heaped teaspoonful of filling in the centre of one half of each circle. Fold the other half over to make a half-moon shape and seal by pinching the edges tightly. If you like, make the traditional festoon-type edge by pinching and folding over all along. Arrange on baking sheets, which need not be greased.

Brush the surface with beaten egg and, if you like, sprinkle lightly with sesame seeds. Bake in a preheated slow to moderate oven (160°–180°C/350°–375°F/Mark 3–4) until they are a pale golden colour, about 35 to 45 minutes. Alternatively, fry gently in clarified butter until golden and well cooked inside, which takes only a few minutes, or deep-fry in oil. In this case, do not brush with the egg and water mixture.

Serve hot or cold, but preferably just out of the oven, when they are at their best. Depending on the size of the *sanbusak*, this quantity makes about 30 pastries.

≈ Here is a similar alternative dough: Work the oil and creamed butter into the flour, and add milk instead of water gradually until the dough becomes a ball and leaves the sides of the bowl. In this case, too, do not work the dough longer than necessary.

Pasteles

These little pies are a Sephardic Jewish speciality, believed to have been brought by the Jews from Spain to Turkey; but both the dough and one of the traditional fillings are similar to those of the Oriental *sanbusak*.

Their shape is that of a little covered pot, like a tiny English meat pie. Two fillings are traditional: the meat filling on page 129, and the *khandrajo* (aubergine filling) on page 131.

Prepare the dough as in the recipe for *sanbusak*, using 500 g (1 lb) flour. Take walnut- or egg-sized balls and hollow them out with a finger. Shape them into little pots by pinching and smoothing up the sides. Fill the little pots with one of the fillings mentioned above, and cover with flat round lids of dough a little larger in diameter than the tops of the pots. Secure them firmly by pinching lid and pot edges together. Pinch and fold over the overlapping edges of each lid to make a festoon edge.

Paint the lids (and the sides as well if you like) with a mixture of egg beaten with 2 tablespoons water, and place on an ungreased baking tray. Bake in a preheated slow oven (160°C/325°F/Mark 3) for 30 to 45 minutes, until the dough is well cooked and the *pasteles* are a warm golden colour.

A modern labour-saving method for making *pasteles* is to use a bun tray or individual tart tins. Use deep shapes if possible. Line them with thinly rolled dough, fill with one of the fillings and cover each one with a lid, pressing it on firmly. Brush with an egg and water mixture, and bake as above.

The number of pastries varies according to their size, but will be about 30.

Turkish Savoury Börek

There are as many recipes for *börek* as there are people who make this Turkish version of *sanbusak*. They range from bread and pie doughs to flaky pastry.

1. Pie Dough

A very simple and particularly successful pie dough. Use any of the fillings described on pages 129–32.

500 g (1 lb) plain flour	About 4 tablespoons water
½ teaspoon salt	1 egg beaten with 1–2 tablespoons
250 g (8 oz) butter	water, to glaze
2 eggs	

Sift flour and salt into a large mixing bowl. Cream the cold butter and work it into the flour, first with your fingers, and then by rubbing the mixture lightly between the palms of your hands. Add 2 eggs and work them in lightly. Add enough water for the dough to stick together, working it in gently until it forms a soft ball. Stop kneading as soon as this happens. The dough is better for being worked as little as possible. Allow to rest in a cool place, covered with a damp cloth, for at least 1 hour.

Roll the dough out on a lightly floured board or marble top with a lightly floured rolling pin, or use a pastry cloth and a roller stocking. Roll as thinly as possible from the centre outwards, lifting up the roller and patching any tears as they occur. Cut out rounds about 8 cm (3 inches) in diameter with a pastry cutter. Alternatively, take walnut-sized lumps of dough, roll into a round ball and flatten out as thinly as possible between the palms of your hands.

Put a heaped teaspoonful of filling in the centre of each circle. Fold the pastry over to make a half-moon shape and pinch the edges together to seal them. Pinch and fold over all round the edges to make a festoon effect. Arrange on ungreased baking trays.

Brush the top with egg beaten with water, and bake in a preheated slow oven (160°C/325°F/Mark 3) for about 45 minutes, or until a warm golden colour.

Depending on the size of the pastries, this quantity makes about 30 *börek*.

2. Bread Dough

This is a rather more uncommon type of *börek* made with a bread dough, rather like a miniature stuffed pizza.

Prepare the dough as in the recipe for *lahma bi ajeen* (page 152). Prepare one of the cheese fillings or the meat fillings on page 129.

Take walnut-sized lumps of dough after it has been well kneaded and allowed to rise to twice its size. Flour the board and rolling pin, and roll the dough out, but not quite as thinly as for *lahma bi ajeen*. Put a tablespoon of filling on each round and fold over into a half-moon shape. Seal edges by wetting them with water and pressing them together.

Arrange on greased baking sheets and brush the tops with 1 egg beaten with 1 or 2 tablespoons water. Leave in a warm place to rise again, then bake in a preheated fairly hot oven (200°C/400°F/Mark 6) for about 10 minutes only. Makes about 30, but this again depends on the size of the pastries.

3. Flaky Pastry

The most delightful *börek* are made with flaky or puff pastry. One recipe is similar to the French *pâte feuilletée*. It requires much time and application, but the results are extremely good and worth the trouble.

One condition necessary for the pastry to be successful is that the ingredients, your hands, bowl and any working surface should be kept cold throughout the preparation. So this precludes attempting the pastry in hot weather unless a cooling fan is available.

500 g (1 lb) plain flour
1 teaspoon salt
Scant 300 ml (½ pint) iced water
500 g (1 lb) unsalted butter

1 egg beaten with 1–2 tablespoons water, to glaze
Fillings: see pages 129–32

Sift the flour into a large bowl, or on to a pastry board. Make a well in the centre. Dissolve the salt in the water and pour gradually into the well, working it into the flour as lightly and as quickly as possible. As soon as the dough forms a soft ball, stop mixing. Cover the bowl with a cloth and leave in the refrigerator for 15 minutes.

Work the butter with your hands to soften it, but dip it occasionally in cold water to prevent it from becoming warm.

Roll the dough out on a lightly floured board with a floured rolling pin into a neat rectangle three times as long as it is wide (about 20 cm/8 inches wide) and about ½ cm (¼ inch) thick. Shape the prepared butter into an oblong smaller than half the size of the rectangle of dough, so that when it is placed over one half of the dough, it is surrounded by a 3-cm (1-inch) margin of dough. Fold the other half of the dough over the butter and pinch the edges together.

Roll the dough out lengthwise very evenly, taking great care not to break it or allow the butter to ooze out. If there is a break, patch it quickly. Fold the pastry in three, overlapping the sections. Chill in the refrigerator for 15 minutes.

Now roll the dough out transversely (sideways) into a long strip. Fold in three once again and chill for 15 minutes. Repeat this process until you have rolled and folded the dough six times in all. The more times it is rolled and folded, the flakier the pastry will be. After the final folding, let the dough rest for about ½ hour. It will keep well for a few days if stored in the refrigerator, wrapped in silver foil, but it is preferable to use it on the same day.

Roll it out as thinly as possible and cut into round or square shapes (8 cm/3 inches or wider) with a sharp pastry cutter. Place a heaped teaspoonful of the chosen filling in the centre of each shape. Fold the rounds in half over the filling to make a half-moon shape. Seal the edges by pinching firmly with your fingers and fold them over to make a festoon effect. Bring the corners of the square shapes together over the filling like an envelope and seal by pinching together the edges nearest to each other. You will have about 30 pastries.

Place the *börek* on baking sheets which have been sprinkled with a little cold water. Brush the tops with a mixture of egg and water, being careful not to allow any of it to run on to the trays. Bake in a preheated very hot oven (240°C/475°F/Mark 9) for 5 minutes, then reduce the temperature to (180°C/350°F/Mark 4) and continue to bake for about ½ hour, or until the pastries are well done and golden.

These pastries are best eaten hot straight from the oven, when they are light, well puffed, crisp and golden; and they are good cold. They are also excellent deep-fried in hot oil.

4. Rough Puff Pastry

I was recently given a most ingenious and easy, if unconventional, way of preparing flaky pastry for *börek*. Margarine is used for its spreading quality.

120 g (4 oz) plus 250 g (8 oz) margarine	½ teaspoon salt
500 g (1 lb) plain flour, sifted	150 ml (¼ pint) iced water
	1 teaspoon lemon juice or vinegar

Rub 120 g (4 oz) softened but cold margarine into the flour. Sprinkle in salt. Mix the water with the lemon juice or vinegar, and add it to the flour gradually, working it in quickly and using only enough to bind the dough. Allow the pastry to rest overnight in a cool place, covered with a damp cloth.

Next day, roll the dough out as thinly as possible and spread the entire surface with the remaining 250 g (8 oz) margarine, softened but still cold. Roll up like a swiss roll and chill for about 1 hour. Then roll out as thinly as possible.

Use this pastry to make square or half-moon *börek* as described in the previous recipe, using any of the fillings given on pages 129–32. Arrange on ungreased baking trays. Bake in a moderate oven (180°C/350°F/Mark 4) for the first 10 minutes, then lower the heat to

(150°C/300°F Mark 2) and bake for 25 minutes longer, or until well done and lightly coloured.

5. Commercial Flaky or Puff Pastry

I have found the good quality, ready-made, commercial pastry makes very acceptable *börek*. Use any of the fillings described on pages 129–32, and shape in the usual way.

Fila Pastries

Fila is a fine, paper-thin dough extremely popular throughout the Middle East (*phyllo* to the Greeks, *yufka* to the Turks, *brik* or *malsouka* to the Tunisians). It lends itself to an infinite variety of uses. It is also cheap and extremely easy to work with.

The dough itself is easy enough to make, a mixture of flour and water kneaded to a fine, firm, elastic mass. But the achievement of paper-thin sheets is extremely difficult and requires much skill. Expert pastry cooks knead the dough vigorously for a long time until it is very elastic, then allow it to rest for 2 or 3 hours. Next, it is divided into fist-sized balls, which are again kneaded, and then pulled and stretched as much as the dough will endure (until it becomes almost transparent).

I have watched this being done at a small workshop in London. The dough was pulled out over large canvas sheets which had been stretched on a large square frame and served as a table. Two sources of heat, electric heaters, placed underneath the canvas 'set' the dough immediately. It was then cut into standard-sized sheets, 30 × 50 cm (12 × 20 inches), and quickly wrapped in polythene in weights of 250 and 500 g (8 oz and 1 lb) (500 g or 1 lb gives about 24 large sheets of pastry).

Fila is now readily available in London and can also be obtained in other towns in the UK. It comes in two forms: wrapped in polythene, the sheets can be used for up to two weeks; those sold in boxes are sealed in an airtight bag and last for many weeks. Both can be frozen for about three months – after that the ice that forms inside makes them soggy.

Once the packet has been unsealed, the sheets should be used as soon as possible because they become dry and brittle very quickly.

Fila sheets are used to make the casings for both large and small pies. They can also be folded into small triangles, cigar and snail shapes, envelopes and little nests – in fact, almost any shape you fancy.

Cut the sheets as required and put the pieces in a pile so that the air does not get to the ones underneath while you work. If you have to leave them for a few minutes, cover with a slightly damp cloth and wrap any left-over pieces in polythene to keep them.

Fila pies with any filling except one that is too moist can be very easily frozen and can be put straight from the freezer into the oven without thawing – but they will need a little more cooking time.

☐ *Börek in a Turkish Household.* *

We excelled in pastry, which we called börek. *Served at the beginning of a meal, as in my mother's family and at home, or at the end of a meal, as in some other houses, it was always stuffed either with cheese and herbs, or with spiced minced meat. The difference lay in the dough and the manner of its cooking. Börek was not among my own favourite dishes, and I do not remember all the varieties which were made with a dough which resembled the French* mille feuille. *I preferred such as were made of a paste rather like noodles, and which were boiled. Both the Tartar börek and the* piruhi *were made of thinly rolled-out dough. The former was cut into squares, stuffed with cream cheese and herbs and folded into triangles, boiled and eaten with yoghurt; with piruhi, the little squares were left open and minced meat was sprinkled between them. Browned butter was poured over it. The best börek of this kind is the* su börek, *or water börek, so named because it too is boiled. Afterwards the dough is spread in layers in a round flat börek dish made of silver, with a high edge, half of it being filled with cream cheese and the other half with minced meat or chicken. Browned in the oven it is a dish for kings.*

The undeniable king of all böreks is called, when rolled to look like a cigarette, sigara börek, *and when rolled into a ball the size of a*

---

* From Emine Foat Tugay, *Three Centuries.*

walnut, ceviz börek. *Very few cooks nowadays are able to make it as it should be and once was produced. I once saw it in the making. The kitchen at Moda, which was in the garden half-way between the harem and the selamlik, was out of bounds. None the less my brothers and I decided to see what it was like. We passed through the dining-room for the men-servants, into the large old-fashioned kitchen with its enormous range and adjoining larder. Thence we went on into the pastry-room. Wide marble-topped tables stood beneath the windows which overlooked the garden. Mustafa, his back to us, stood at one of the tables in front of an open window. He was rolling out an enormous sheet of dough. Suddenly he caught hold of two of its corners, swept the whole thing up into the air, twirled it several times above his white cap, and brought it down on the table without there being a rent in it. This procedure was repeated over and over again, whilst we watched spellbound. He furiously rolled the long, thin Turkish rolling-pin, then up would go the dough, kept upright by the swift rotation of his arms, and then down in one sweep. I was particularly impressed when looking at it, while it was in the air, to see that it was as transparent as gauze. Wrapped many times round minced meat in the sigara börek, or round grated kashar cheese in the ceviz börek, and cooked in deep fat, it is one of the superlative achievements of Turkish cooking.*

Small Savoury Fila Pastries

Light and delicate and delightful to eat, these splendid party and buffet savouries come in various traditional shapes and sizes. Use 12 sheets (about 250 g/8 oz) prepared *fila* and any of the fillings on pages 129–32.

The most common of the traditional shapes is the triangle. It is formed in the following manner.

Cut the standard sheets of *fila* lengthwise into 4 rectangular strips about 8 cm (3 inches) wide. Take one at a time and brush the whole length with melted butter. Put a teaspoon of filling near one end, about an inch from the short edge. Fold one corner over the filling, making a triangle, then fold the angle over again and again until the whole strip is folded. Tuck the loose end neatly into the triangular shape.

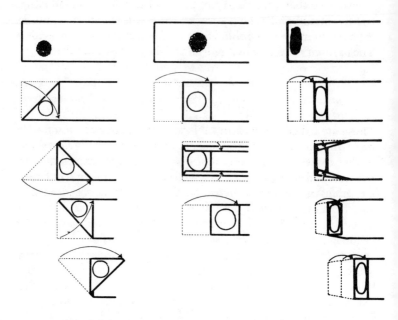

Repeat with the other strips of dough. Place the pastries on oiled baking sheets, brush them with melted butter and bake in a pre-heated slow oven (150°C/300°F/Mark 2) for 30 to 45 minutes, or until crisp and golden.

Another common shape is the square. This is made by putting a heaped teaspoon of filling at one end of a similar strip of pastry brushed with melted butter, folding the end over it, then the lower and upper edges and then folding the pastry with the filling inside over and over until you come to the end of the strip. Bake as described above.

A long, thin cigar shape is made with a strip about 10 cm (4 inches) wide and 25 cm (10 inches) long. A cheese filling (page 129) is commonly used. Place a heaped teaspoonful lengthwise about 1 cm (½ inch) from the shorter edge. Fold this nearest edge over it, then fold the two longer edges inwards a little over the filling to prevent it from oozing out. Roll the strip up like a cigar. Bake as above.

The traditional shape for spinach-filled pastries is a spiral (although triangular shapes are also used). Roll into long thin cigars as described above, then curl into snail-like spirals. Pack the pastries tightly on an oiled baking sheet to prevent them from unrolling. Brush with melted butter and bake as above until crisp and golden. The pastries will keep their shape once they have been baked.

Moroccan Cigars

These are called *briouats* in Morocco, where they are made with paper-thin pancakes called *ouarka*, but *fila* makes an easy and perfect substitute. They are elegant party fare that you can make by the hundred (perhaps with the help of your children) and keep uncooked in the freezer. In Morocco they are fried but it is much easier and just as good to bake them.

The most useful filling is meat. For 500 g (1 lb) fila, prepare the following minced meat filling:

1 medium onion, finely chopped
4 tablespoons oil
750 g (1½ lb) lean minced beef or lamb
2 teaspoons cinnamon
½ teaspoon allspice
¼ teaspoon ginger
Salt and pepper

Pinch of cayenne or, more optionally, a bunch of parsley, finely chopped, or a bunch of fresh coriander, finely chopped (or both)
5 eggs
180 g (6 oz) butter, melted

Soften the onion in the oil. Add the meat and crush it with a fork. Add seasonings and spices and cook, stirring with a wooden spoon, for 10 to 15 minutes until the meat is done. Add the herbs. Lightly beat the eggs in a bowl and pour them over the meat. Cook gently, stirring all the time, for a minute or so until the eggs have set to a creamy consistency. Let the filling cool. Add more spices and pepper if you like.

To roll the cigars: cut each sheet of *fila* into three rectangles and put them together in a pile so that they do not dry out.

Brush very lightly with melted butter.

Put a tablespoon of filling along one of the short edges, roll the *fila* over it, tuck the ends in to stop the filling falling out, then continue to roll up like a cigar. Place side by side on a greased tray, brush with melted butter and bake in a preheated slow oven (150°C/300°F/Mark 2) oven for ½ hour or until golden. Serve very hot.

≈ In Morocco they like dusting them with caster sugar or with cinnamon.

≈ If you want to fry a few for an instant snack (they are nice fried) do so in hot oil, turning over once, until browned, and drain on absorbent paper.

Seafood Filling for Cigars

Have a mixture of cooked prawns and mussels, shells removed, firm, flaked fish and crabmeat. Add fresh chopped coriander, parsley and mint to taste, a good amount of lemon juice, a little crushed garlic, a sprinkling of cumin, and paprika, a touch of cayenne or chilli peppers. Wrap it up as it is, or bind it together with a stiff Béchamel.

Chicken Filling for Cigars

This may be made as for the recipe for *bstilla* on page 149.

□ *The Hoca as Tamerlane's Tax Collector**

One day the Hoca chanced to be in Tamerlane's court when the despot's tax collector came to report on his receipts. The figures in impressive columns covered page after page of parchment, and the collector's voice droned endlessly through a recital of the sums. But, in the end, Tamerlane was not satisfied. It seems that first this account and then that one had been misrepresented. In short, the tax collector had revealed himself as a scamp and a cheat.

'So that is the way you manage your post as tax collector!' raged the testy ruler. 'Well, sir, I cannot swallow such outrageous lies. But' – and his eyes glinted – 'You will swallow them. Begin at once!'

'Begin what, sire!' questioned the tax collector, puzzled and frightened.

'Begin to swallow your own accounts. Quickly, now. I have other business at hand.' And the lordly Tamerlane watched with increasing amusement as the wretched collector choked and gagged on the sheets of parchment. At length he had chewed and swallowed them

* Barbara Walker, *Watermelons, Walnuts and the Wisdom of Allah and Other Tales of the Hoca.*

all, and his heroic effort was rewarded on the instant by Tamerlane, who declared him no longer tax collector.

'Instead,' declared Tamerlane, smiling broadly, 'I appoint you, Nasreddin Hoca, to be my tax collector.'

Appalled, the Hoca considered his sad plight. There was little doubt about the matter: no report could please Tamerlane. On the other hand, was it necessary to suffer such abuse for one's book-keeping, however faulty? Suddenly the Hoca had a fine idea. This business might be managed, after all ... Gravely he thanked Tamerlane for his fine evidence of trust in a simple hoca's judg-ment, and excused himself from the ruler's presence, to prepare himself for his new office.

Every morning during the following month, Nasreddin Hoca watched with tender concern as his wife rolled fine, fresh dough to paper thinness (yufka)* and baked it to form platelike pastries. Then he took the pastries to one side and on them he recorded the tax receipts of the preceding day. With painstaking care he stacked the pastries in a special cupboard where they would be protected from prying eye and tampering touch.

Finally came the day of reckoning. Taking a large wheelbarrow loaded with the precious pastries, the Hoca trundled off to Tamer-lane's court, and was admitted to the ruler's presence with his curious burden.

'Ah, there you are!' exclaimed Tamerlane, slapping his hands on his knees in great satisfaction. And, 'Yes, yes,' he murmured as he accepted the two large leather sacks containing the taxes collected. 'But where are your accounts?'

'Right here, sire,' replied the Hoca, gesturing towards the load in the wheelbarrow.

Tamerlane stared in disbelief. Then, 'Bring me one of those things,' he demanded.

Promptly the Hoca presented him with one of the pastries, covered from end to end with finely penned figures. As Tamerlane studied the inscriptions, a smile began to spread across his face. 'And what, may I ask, was your purpose in keeping your records on pastry?'

'Only, sire that either one of us might be able to swallow the reports of my labors,' answered the Hoca.

* *Fila.*

145

Brik à l'Œuf

This Tunisian version of *fila* savouries makes a brilliant and delightful snack. The pastry allows for much personal inventiveness and individual taste, since almost any ingredient can be wrapped up in a thin sheet of dough (or even a different filling in each little pastry), deep-fried and served immediately.

I feel that this dish would be a sure success for Western parties because of its versatility and the ease and rapidity with which it is made – a whole meal neatly wrapped in a delicate crisp casing, easily served and handled.

Filling for 1 Serving

2 tablespoons chopped onion, softened in oil or butter
3 tablespoons mashed tinned tuna

1 teaspoon finely chopped parsley
Salt and black pepper
1 egg

An Alternative Filling

3 tablespoons grated cheese
2–3 mushrooms, sliced and sautéed lightly in butter or oil

1 teaspoon finely chopped parsley
Salt and black pepper
1 egg

Spread one sheet of *fila* out on a large plate or flat surface. If the filling tends to be rather moist and you think that it may break the pastry, lay two sheets together one on top of the other.

Lay the filling ingredients (except the egg) at one end of the sheet. Break the egg over them. (Do not mix them together.) Fold the sheet over, rolling the filling up into a neat, firm packet, being careful not to squash the ingredients.

Drop the packet or '*brik*' into deep but not too hot oil. Turn it over as soon as it turns a light brown colour and fry the other side. Remove and drain on absorbent paper.

Serve hot immediately, or keep warm in the lowest of ovens until ready to serve.

≈ A ratatouille-type filling can be made with lightly fried, cubed aubergines, peppers and chopped tomatoes, seasoned with salt and pepper.

Large Pies

These larger versions of the small savouries, made with the same doughs and similar fillings, are far less time-consuming and make an excellent first course or main dish.

Spanakopitta 1

A Greek favourite, this spinach pie has been adopted by many countries throughout the Middle East.

1 kg (2 lb) fresh spinach
Butter, about 120 g (4 oz) in all
Salt and black pepper
¼ teaspoon grated nutmeg (optional)

120 g (4 oz) cheese (Gruyère, Parmesan, Cheddar or Feta), grated or mashed
8–10 sheets fila pastry

Wash spinach leaves and cut off any hard stems. Drain and chop. Stew gently with about 2 tablespoons butter, a sprinkling of salt and pepper, and grated nutmeg if liked, until tender. Drain off excess juice; add cheese and mix well.

Butter a large, deep, square or round baking tin or oven dish. Fit four or five sheets of pastry in it, one on top of the other, brushing each sheet with melted butter, and folding them up so that they overlap the sides of the dish. Spread the spinach and cheese mixture over this and cover with the remaining sheets of pastry, brushing melted butter between each layer as well as on top.

At this stage the pie is sometimes cut diagonally into lozenge shapes or squares with a sharp knife, but this is not really necessary. Put the pie into a preheated moderate oven (160°C/325°F/Mark 3) and bake for about ¾ hour. Then increase the heat to 220°C (425°F/Mark 7) for 5 to 10 minutes, or until the top of the pie is crisp and golden, and all the inner leaves are well cooked.

Spanakopitta 2

Bought puff pastry is a good substitute for sheets of *fila* pastry or bread dough rolled thin with which it is variously made.

1 kg (2 lb) fresh spinach
1 large onion, finely chopped
6 spring onions, finely chopped
60 ml (4 tablespoons) olive or a
    light vegetable oil
30 ml (2 tablespoons) dill or
    fennel leaves, finely chopped
250 g (8 oz) Feta or cottage cheese

4 eggs
Salt and pepper
A grating of nutmeg
A little oil to grease the pie dish
    and brush the top
500 g (1 lb) bought frozen puff
    pastry

Wash the spinach well in plenty of water and remove large stems. Drain and squeeze out the excess water. You do not need to chop the leaves.

Fry the onion and spring onions gently in the oil until soft and transparent but not coloured. Put the spinach in the pan with the dill or fennel leaves and let it cook in its own juice with no extra water. It will need turning with a wooden spoon so that all the leaves have a chance to simmer at the bottom of the pan. Cook for about 15 minutes or until the spinach has collapsed into a tender mass. Drain off the excess liquid.

When the spinach has cooled a little, add the cheese, mashed with a fork, and the lightly beaten eggs. Season with much black pepper and salt (hardly any salt if you are using the already salty Feta, more if it is cottage cheese) and ground nutmeg.

Cut the pastry in two, one piece slightly larger than the other. Roll the larger one thin and line a large lightly oiled tray, lifting the edges well over the sides of the tray. Spread the cooled spinach mixture evenly over this and cover with the rest of the pastry rolled out thin. Trim and seal the top and bottom edges together by making them moist with a little water and pressing them together. You can make a festoon-type edge by pinching and twisting the dough at close intervals. Brush the top with the remaining spoonful of oil and prick the crust with a fork so that the steam can escape.

Bake in a preheated moderate oven (180°C/350°F/Mark 4) for 45 minutes or until the crust is crisp and golden.

Serve hot or warm cut into squares.

Tyropitta

Another traditional Greek cheese pie made with Feta, the white Greek cheese available from most Greek stores. If you cannot find it, substitute your favourite English cheese.

For 8 to 10 sheets of *fila* pastry, prepare the following filling:

500 g (1 lb) Feta cheese	4 tablespoons finely chopped
2 eggs	fresh dill, chervil, chives or any
White pepper	other herb of your choice

Crumble and mash the cheese with a fork. Beat in the eggs, and season to taste with pepper. Stir in herbs and mix well.

Prepare the pie as in either version of the recipe for *spanakopitta* above. It is also excellent made with flaky pastry.

An Alternative Filling for Tyropitta

500 g (1 lb) white Feta cheese	150 ml (¼ pint) yoghourt
2 small onions, finely chopped	White pepper
and softened with salt	3 eggs, well beaten

Mash the cheese with a fork. Add the onions, which have been softened by being sprinkled with salt and allowed to drain, the yoghourt, white pepper and eggs. Mix well.

Kotopitta

This is a Greek chicken pie prepared with the chicken filling on page 132 and sheets of *fila* pastry or either of the flaky pastries on pages 137–9.

Large Meat Pie

A rather splendid large meat pie can be made with the meat filling on page 129 and *fila* or flaky pastry. For method see *spanakopitta* 1 and 2 (pages 146–7).

Bstilla

Pronounced 'pastilla', this is one of the Moroccan dishes said to have been brought back by the 'Moriscos' from Andalusia after the *Reconquista*.

'Food for the Gods', as it is described by Moroccans, this magnificent pigeon pie is baked on special occasions, such as when entertaining important guests. Its gentle harmony is achieved by contrasts – it is juicy and crisp, sweet and salty at the same time.

This pie is usually enormous and must be baked in a gigantic tray; even the very reduced quantities which I give below will feed 6 to 8 people generously. Traditionally, it is made with pigeons, but since English pigeons are of a different variety and taste, they would be inappropriate, and I suggest that you use poussins or a larger chicken instead.

The pastry for this pie is generally made at home in Morocco. The preparation of the dough requires much skill and an almost inherited experience. Bought sheets of *fila* make an excellent alternative.

FILLING

2 poussins or 1 large chicken	7–8 eggs
2 tablespoons butter	180 g (6 oz) butter, melted
1 large onion, finely chopped or grated	16 sheets fila
	1 tablespoon sugar
Salt and black pepper	¼ teaspoon ground cinnamon
½ teaspoon ground ginger	120 g (4 oz) almonds, chopped and sautéed in butter
¼ teaspoon powdered saffron (optional)	1 egg yolk, beaten, to glaze
½ teaspoon ground cinnamon	A little cinnamon and sugar, to garnish
½ teaspoon mixed spice or ground allspice	
3 tablespoons finely chopped parsley	

Wash the poussins or chicken. Quarter them, and simmer in a very little water with butter, onion, seasonings and parsley for about 2 hours, or until the flesh is so tender that it falls off the bones. Add a little more water as required. The giblets and liver may be simmered with the birds. When cooked, drain off the stock and reserve. Skin and bone the chicken, and cut the meat into smallish pieces.

Take about 150 ml (¼ pint) of the stock and beat it well with the eggs. Season to taste with salt and pepper, pour into a small pan and stir over low heat until the mixture is creamy and nearly set. The eggs and chicken constitute the filling of the pie.

Brush a large round (or square) pie tin or oven dish about 33 cm (13 inches) in diameter and 4 to 5 cm (1½ to 2 inches) deep with melted butter. Fit a sheet of *fila* in the dish so that the ends fold well up and overlap the edges. If this is not possible, use overlapping sheets of *fila*. Lay 6 sheets of pastry on top of each other, brushing melted butter evenly between each layer. Sprinkle the top layer with sugar, cinnamon and sautéed almonds. Spread more than half of the egg mixture over this, and sprinkle with a little of the remaining chicken stock. Cover with another 4 sheets of *fila*, each one brushed with melted butter. Lay the pieces of boned chicken neatly on top and cover with the rest of the egg mixture. Sprinkle with a little more chicken stock. Cover with the remaining *fila* sheets, brushing each layer with melted butter. Tuck the top *fila* sheets between the overlapping bottom sheets and the sides of the dish.

Paint the top with beaten egg yolk and bake in a slow to moderate oven (160°–180°C/325°–350°F/Mark 3–4) for the first 40 minutes. Then raise the temperature to 200°C (400°F/Mark 6) and bake for a further 15 minutes, or until the pastry is crisp and the top a deep golden colour.

Serve sprinkled with sugar mixed with cinnamon, and cut, if you like, in a criss-cross pattern of lozenges.

Tagine Malsouka
Tunisian Meat Pie

500 g (1 lb) lean lamb, cubed
2 tablespoons oil
120 g (4 oz) dried haricot beans, soaked overnight
Salt and black pepper
¼ teaspoon powdered saffron (optional)
½ teaspoon ground cinnamon
6 eggs
120 g (4 oz) butter, melted
12 sheets fila
Beaten egg yolk, to glaze

In a saucepan, brown the meat in 2 tablespoons oil. Add soaked and drained haricot beans, cover with water, and season to taste with pepper, saffron if used, and cinnamon. Bring to the boil and simmer slowly and gently, covered, for about 2 hours, or until the beans are soft, the meat tender and the liquid very much reduced. Add a little water while the stew is simmering if it evaporates too quickly and season with salt when the beans begin to soften. Break the eggs into the pan and stir well. Taste and adjust seasoning. Keep stirring over low heat until the eggs have thickened a little and are creamy.

Brush a large baking dish with melted butter and fit 4 sheets of *fila* pastry into the dish, one on top of the other, so that the edges fold up over the sides of the dish, brushing melted butter between each layer. Spread half of the meat stew evenly over the top and cover with another 4 sheets of pastry, again brushing each one with melted butter. Cover with the rest of the stew and the remaining sheets of pastry, each one brushed with melted butter. Brush the top with beaten egg yolk and bake in a slow to moderate oven (160°–180°C/325°–350°F/Mark 3–4) for the first 40 minutes. Then raise the heat to 200°–220°C (400°–425°F/Mark 6–7) and bake for 15 minutes longer, until the pastry is crisp and a deep golden colour, and the eggs in the stew have set firmly.

≈ A Sephardic Jewish dish for Passover makes use of sheets of matzos softened in water for a similar pie.

Lahma bi Ajeen

A brilliant dish – an Arab type of pizza with a meat filling. Delicious, dainty, elegant to serve at a party, these savouries are very easy to prepare with a simple bread dough.

A few years ago, my brother met a well-known ex-restaurateur from Alexandria in a cinema queue in Paris. He brought back from this encounter detailed instructions on how to make *lahma bi ajeen* – to our unanimous delight. My mother has made them on numerous occasions since, usually in large quantities. She uses a dough made with 1 kg (2 lb) flour to serve 20 people easily. I am giving smaller quantities to serve about 8 to 10.

DOUGH

15 g (½ oz) fresh yeast or 7 g (¼ oz) dried yeast	Pinch of sugar
	500 g (1 lb) plain flour
Scant 300 ml (½ pint) lukewarm water	1 teaspoon salt
	2 tablespoons oil

Dissolve the yeast with a pinch of sugar in about 150 ml (¼ pint) of the lukewarm water specified above. Leave aside in a warm place for about 10 minutes, or until the mixture begins to bubble.

In the meantime, sift the flour and salt into a large warmed mixing bowl. Make a well in the centre and add the oil and the yeast mixture. Work the dough vigorously, adding the remaining lukewarm water gradually to make a soft dough. Knead vigorously for about 15 minutes until the dough is pliable and elastic, and comes away from the sides of the bowl. Cover with a damp cloth and set aside in a warm, draught-free place for 2 to 3 hours, or until doubled in bulk. To prevent a dry crust forming on the surface, put a very little oil in the bottom of the bowl and roll the ball of dough in it to coat the entire surface before leaving it to rest.

While waiting for the dough to rise, prepare the filling:

500 g (1 lb) onions, finely chopped	1 teaspoon sugar
Oil	¾ teaspoon ground allspice
750 g (1½ lb) lean lamb or beef, minced	1–2 tablespoons lemon juice
	Salt and black pepper
500 g (1 lb) fresh tomatoes, skinned and chopped, or a 400-g (14-oz) tin skinned tomatoes	3 tablespoons finely chopped parsley (optional)
1 small tin tomato concentrate	Pinch of cayenne pepper (optional)

Soften the onions in a little warm oil until they are transparent and have lost their water, taking care not to let them colour. Mix the meat, tomatoes and tomato concentrate in a large bowl. If you are using fresh tomatoes, get rid of as much of their juice and seeds as possible, and crush them to a pulp. If you are using a tin of tomatoes, drain them well, as too much liquid will make the dough soggy. Add sugar, allspice and lemon juice, and season to taste with salt and pepper. Drain the onions of oil and add them to the meat mixture. Knead well by hand. Some people like to add chopped parsley and a little cayenne pepper as well.

The filling is sometimes varied by omitting the tomatoes altogether, and adding 60 g (2 oz) pine nuts and 2 to 3 tablespoons tamarind juice or 2 teaspoons paste (page 153) instead.

Knead the risen dough a few times and divide it into many walnut-sized balls. Allow to rest for a few minutes, then roll each piece on a lightly floured board with a lightly floured rolling pin into a round flat shape 12 to 15 cm (5 to 6 inches) in diameter. Alternatively, oil your hands lightly, take smaller lumps of dough, and flatten each piece as much as possible with the palm of your hand on an oiled plate.

Spread the prepared filling very generously over each piece, covering the entire surface (otherwise the filling will look meagre when the pastries are baked). Transfer each round to a lightly oiled baking sheet as you prepare it. Let them rest for 10 minutes.

Bake in a preheated very hot oven (230°–240°C/450°–475°F/Mark 8–9) for 8 to 10 minutes only. The pastries should be well done but still white and soft enough to roll up or fold in the hand to be eaten, as some people like to do.

Lahma bi ajeen can be reheated by putting them in a warm oven for a few minutes. They can also be warmed up in the top of a double saucepan. Serve with various salads: cucumber and yoghourt (page 104), *salade Rachèle* (page 112), or any other Arab salad.

≈ For people in a hurry an improvised *lahma bi ajeen* can be made with an opened out pitta bread instead of the dough.
≈ Delicious pies called *s'fiha* have yoghourt mixed with the meat instead of tomatoes.

Fatayer bi Sabanikh
Spinach Pies

Bread dough as for *lahma bi ajeen* (page 152), using 500 g (1 lb) flour.

FILLING

1 kg (2 lb) fresh spinach or 750 g (1½ lb) frozen leaf spinach	Seeds of 1 pomegranate or 3 tablespoons raisins (optional)
4 tablespoons olive oil	120 g (4 oz) walnuts, coarsely chopped (optional)
1 onion or 5 spring onions, finely chopped	Salt and pepper
Juice of 2 or more lemons	½–1 teaspoon allspice (optional)

If using fresh spinach, remove thick stems, wash and squeeze dry, then chop and shred. Heat the oil in a large saucepan and cook, stirring until the spinach crumples to a soft mass. Or de-frost frozen spinach, squeeze and chop. Mix in a bowl with the rest of the ingredients. The lemon should make the filling very sharp.

Divide the dough into about 30 small lumps and flatten into 8-cm (3-inch) rounds or roll out thinly on a floured board and cut into rounds with a pastry cutter. Put a tablespoon of filling in the centre and bring up 3 sides of the rounds to meet at the top. Pinch the edges closed to form a little 3-sided pyramid. You may also leave the pies partially open at the top to reveal the filling. Place on greased trays and bake in a preheated moderate oven (180°C/350°F/Mark 4) for 20 to 30 minutes until lightly browned.

Fatayer bi Jibn
Cheese Pies

Make as the preceding recipe, *fatayer bi sabanikh*, but replace the spinach filling with 500 g (1 lb) Feta cheese mashed with a fork, sprinkled with a little pepper and mixed with 3 tablespoons olive oil.

Fatayer bi Zahtar
Thyme and Sumac Pies

These are really spiced breads.

Bread dough as for *lahma bi ajeen* (page 152) with 500g (1 lb) flour	3 tablespoons powdered sumac
8 tablespoons dried thyme	8 tablespoons olive oil
	Salt to taste

Divide the dough into 20 small lumps and flatten out, or roll out thinly on a floured board, and cut into 8-cm (3-inch) rounds with a pastry cutter. Place on greased oven trays. Mix the spice and herb mixture (called *zahtar*) into a paste and spread with your hands over the top of each round. Bake for 15 to 20 minutes in a preheated medium oven (180°C/350°F/Mark 4). Place under the grill to brown the tops for ½ minute. Serve hot or cold.

Fatayer bi Hummus
Chick Pea Pie

A Lebanese lenten speciality.

Bread dough as for *lahma bi ajeen* (page 152)	250 g (8 oz) chick peas
	Salt

Soak the chick peas for a few hours. Boil in fresh water until tender, adding salt towards the end of the cooking. Drain and let them dry.

Divide the dough into 20 small lumps, flatten them out or roll out thinly on a floured board and cut into rounds with a pastry cutter. Place on greased trays, press a handful of chick peas in each and bake in a moderate oven (180°C/350°F/Mark 4) for 20 to 30 minutes until cooked and lightly coloured.

These breads should be eaten soon after they are baked – better still, warm from the oven.

Ataïf with Cheese

Ataïf (pancakes) are extremely popular served sweet, stuffed with nuts and soused with syrup (see page 480). A more uncommon but most excellent way of preparing them is to stuff them with cheese.

Prepare *ataïf*, following the recipe on page 481, and adding a little salt to the batter instead of sugar. Greek Halumi cheese is my favourite filling for savoury *ataïf*.

Fill with a small slice of Halumi cheese or Mozzarella; or make a filling with 250 g (8 oz) grated Gruyère, Wensleydale, Gouda, Edam or Canadian Cheddar, 1 whole egg and black pepper to taste. Mix the ingredients thoroughly with a fork.

Put a heaped teaspoon of filling in the centre of each little *ataïf* on the soft, unfried side. Fold the pancake over the filling to make a half-moon shape and seal the edges by pinching them together with your fingers. The soft, moist dough will stick together.

Deep-fry in hot oil until golden and drain on absorbent paper. Serve hot or cold, preferably hot.

≈ An alternative cheese filling is made with Feta, the white Greek cheese, crumbled with a fork, seasoned with white pepper, and mixed with a few finely chopped chives. Ordinary white cream cheeses will not do since they invariably melt and ooze out.

Soups

Shorbah

In the Middle East, soups are often eaten as a meal in themselves, accompanied by Arab bread or pitta for breakfast, lunch or supper. Vendors sell them in the street in the very early hours on winter mornings to catch those who want to fill themselves up before they get to work. Rich with vegetables, meat, pulses, cereals and rice, they are sometimes indistinguishable from stews, except for the fact that they have very much more liquid. They are often cooked for so long that you can no longer distinguish what is in the pot. Some of the richer soups play a part in the rituals of religious festivals, and are called 'festive' or 'wedding' soups. A few are Ramadan specials.

Calf's feet or sheep's feet are added for their gelatinous quality. Pulses – lentils, chick peas, yellow split peas, dried green peas and haricot and broad beans – lend themselves beautifully to make thick, creamy soups, delicately enhanced by spices, lemon, garlic and fresh herbs. There are infinite combinations of spinach and lentils, spinach and meat balls, yoghourt and barley, yoghourt and spinach, and so on. Chicken stocks are sometimes thickened with beaten egg yolks and lemon, and fish stocks with egg yolks and vinegar, while meat stocks are made richer with a marrow bone.

Some of these soups and stews were branded as 'servants' food' by the rich, Europeanized Egyptians, who preferred cosmopolitan food. Most of these families gave their servants a daily sum with which to buy themselves, say, 2 piastres worth of meat and 1 piastre worth of vegetables. These were put in a large pot and left to cook over a very low flame on a primus stove or *fatayel* on the roof-tops of the luxury blocks of flats, where the servants' quarters were usually situated. Sometimes all the servants of one block pooled their purchases or money to make one large, communal dish. The strong aromas enveloped the street below, drowning the limper, delicate perfumes of their masters' refined dishes.

The rich defended themselves from the accusation that they ate well while their servants had only cheap food, by saying that the latter *preferred* their own food. There was a great deal of truth in this, and I know many children of rich families who would sneak up to the roof terraces to share their servants' soups and stews.

I have discovered with some excitement that several of the soups I know are almost identical to dishes described in medieval texts. I am full of respect for the constancy of the people who continue to prepare them to this day, and for their dignified loyalty to their own past.

Hamud
Chicken Soup with Lemon

An Egyptian favourite, *hamud* has a versatile nature. Although generally served as a sauce for rice, it often appears twice in the same meal, first as a soup, and then again as the sauce. It is basically a chicken soup with celery, strongly flavoured with lemon and garlic, but other green vegetables find their place in it when they are at hand.

Carcass and giblets of 1 chicken	Salt and black pepper
3–4 stalks celery with leaves, sliced	Juice of 1–2 lemons
2 leeks, sliced (optional)	2–3 courgettes, sliced (optional)
2–3 cloves garlic, slivered	120 g (4 oz) rice, boiled (weight uncooked)

Collect a chicken carcass, giblets and bones to make a rich stock. The giblets must be very fresh, and the bones and carcass those of a chicken prepared the same day, otherwise any meat on them will be hard and dry, and the marrow in the bones very stale. Crack the bones slightly to release more flavour.

There are two ways of preparing this soup. The stock can be made beforehand and strained through a fine sieve, the vegetables then being cooked in the clear broth. However, I usually cook all the ingredients together in the following manner.

Put the carcass, bones and giblets in a large pan. Add the celery and, if you like, sliced leeks. (The basic recipe is made with celery only.) Add the slivered garlic and cover with about 2 litres (3½ pints) water. Bring to the boil and skim the scum off the surface. Season with salt and pepper, and squeeze the juice of 1 lemon into the pan. Simmer gently for about 1 hour. Remove the pan from the heat and discard all the bones, leaving only pieces of chicken in the broth. Add the courgettes, if using them, and cook for 15 minutes longer. Adjust seasoning, adding more lemon juice if necessary. The soup should have a distinctly lemony tang. It is this and the taste of garlic which give it an Oriental flavour.

Add cooked rice just before serving so as not to give it time to become sodden and mushy.

□ *Duck Soup**

A kinsman came to see Nasrudin from the country, and brought a duck. Nasrudin was grateful, had the bird cooked and shared it with his guest.

Presently another visitor arrived. He was a friend, as he said, 'of the man who gave you the duck'. Nasrudin fed him as well.

This happened several times. Nasrudin's home had become like a restaurant for out-of-town visitors. Everyone was a friend at some removes of the original donor of the duck.

* Idries Shah, *The Exploits of the Incomparable Mulla Nasrudin.*

Finally Nasrudin was exasperated. One day there was a knock at the door and a stranger appeared. 'I am the friend of the friend of the friend of the man who brought you the duck from the country,' he said.

'Come in,' said Nasrudin.

They seated themselves at the table, and Nasrudin asked his wife to bring the soup.

When the guest tasted it, it seemed to be nothing more than warm water. 'What sort of soup is this?' he asked the Mulla.

'That', said Nasrudin, 'is the soup of the soup of the soup of the duck.'

Souppa Avgolemone *or* Beid Bi Lamoun
Egg and Lemon Soup

This popular Middle Eastern soup is always made in Greece whenever chickens are boiled. Meat and fish stock are also used. The stock can be prepared in advance but the rest must be done at the last minute before serving.

STOCK

1 chicken, or a carcass and bones, or enough giblets for a good stock	2 celery stalks and leaves
	2 bay leaves
	Some parsley stalks
1 large onion, quartered	1 teaspoon thyme
2 carrots, cut into pieces	Salt and pepper
120 g (4 oz) long-grain rice, uncooked	3 large eggs
	Juice of 1 or 2 lemons

Put all the ingredients for the stock in a large saucepan. Cover with water, bring to the boil, remove any scum, then reduce the heat and simmer for an hour.

Ladle off any fat from the surface and strain through a fine sieve, then return to the pan, taste and adjust seasoning. There should be 1¾ litres (3 pints) of broth. Reduce by simmering further or add water if necessary.

Bring to the boil again, add the rice, well washed, and cook for about 15 minutes until it is tender.

When you are ready to serve, beat the eggs, add the lemon juice and continue to beat until the mixture is pale and frothy. Then add a ladleful of hot stock and beat with a fork. Add a little more, then pour the mixture into the remaining broth, stirring constantly and remove the pan from the heat quickly. The soup must not boil or the eggs will curdle. It must remain just below the boil. Taste and add lemon and seasonings if necessary. The soup must be sharp.

Serve immediately.

≈ As an alternative you can add vermicelli, pastina or tapioca instead of rice.

Melokhia

Melokhia is one of Egypt's national dishes. It is an ancient peasant soup, the making of which is believed to be portrayed in Pharaonic tomb paintings. The medieval *melokhia* seems to have been a little richer, incorporating fried minced meat and chicken balls. Today, only a few families add these.

This soup has all the qualities of the Egyptian peasant: his timelessness, his harmony with nature, the seasons and the soil. It seemed to us as children that the *fellah* was the same as he was when he first appeared in history. He wears the same clothes, uses the same tools, and daily repeats the same movements as did the peasants depicted in the Pharaonic tomb paintings and described in Coptic legends. In his present lies the past. The *fellah* gives himself entirely to the soil; in return, the soil yields to him his food. Every peasant, however poor, has a little patch of ground for his own use, and in summer this is reserved exclusively for the cultivation of the deep green *melokhia* leaf (*corchorus olitorius*). The leaves can be eaten fresh, or dried and stored for the winter.

Peasant women prepare this soup almost daily. Protein stock is too expensive, so they cook the leaves in water in which a few vegetables have been boiled. The leaves give the soup a glutinous texture. The women cook the soup in large pots, which they carry to the fields on their heads for the men to eat at midday. When the work is done and the men come home, they eat it again at dusk with equal pleasure.

Melokhia has recently acquired a symbolic and patriotic importance in Egypt, for it represents the national, popular taste as opposed to the more snobbish and cosmopolitan taste of the old régime. Most families have their own special way of preparing it, and the proportions vary according to the financial means, position and preferences of the people who make it.

Fresh leaves make occasional appearances in London but packets of dried *melokhia* can be found in Greek and Oriental shops.

2–2½ litres (3–4 pints) chicken, rabbit, goose, duck or meat stock (see method)	2–3 cloves garlic
	Salt
Salt and black pepper	2 tablespoons butter or oil
1 kg (2 lb) fresh melokhia or 120 g (4 oz) dried melokhia leaves	1 tablespoon ground coriander
	Cayenne pepper

To make the stock: boil a whole chicken or rabbit, half a goose, a duck, or a piece of lamb, beef or veal (I suggest knuckle of beef or veal) for 2 to 3 hours, removing scum from time to time. Season with salt and pepper.

Remove the bird or piece of meat, bone it if necessary, and discard the bones.

If you are using fresh leaves, cut off the stalks. Wash and drain the leaves, and spread them out on a cloth to dry. With a *mezzaluna* chopper or whatever chopping knife you are used to, chop the leaves on a board until almost reduced to a purée.

If you are using dried *melokhia*, crush the leaves with your hands into a large bowl, or use an electric blender. Throw a little hot water over them. Let them swell until doubled in bulk, sprinkling with a little more water if necessary. (If the leaves are not brittle enough to be crushed, try drying them out by putting them in a turned-off hot oven for 5 minutes, scattered over a large baking sheet.)

Strain the stock into a large saucepan and bring to the boil. Add the prepared *melokhia* leaves and stir well. Boil for 5 to 10 minutes if fresh, and 20 to 30 minutes if dried leaves have been used.

Prepare the *taklia* (garlic sauce). Crush the garlic with a little salt, using more or less garlic as you prefer. Fry it in butter or oil (in Egypt *samna*, a clarified butter, is used). When the garlic is golden brown, add the coriander and a good pinch of cayenne pepper. Mix thoroughly to a paste and fry a little longer.

Add this preparation to the soup, cover the pan tightly, and simmer for a further 2 minutes. Stir occasionally to prevent the leaves from falling to the bottom, and do not overcook for the same reason. The *melokhia* should stay suspended throughout the stock. Taste and adjust the seasoning.

This can be served on its own first, as a soup, then accompanied by plain rice (which can be cooked in some of the stock), and finally with pieces of the meat used for making the stock, cut into serving pieces and reheated.

≈ An embellishment if you like is to start off with a richer stock by adding 2 leeks, 2 turnips, 2 tomatoes, skinned and quartered, 1 onion and a clove of garlic at the beginning. When the stock has cooked for a few hours, remove the vegetables together with the meat, and proceed as described above.

Havuç Çorbasi
Turkish Carrot Soup

750 g (1½ lb) carrots	2 litres (3½ pints) chicken stock
4 tablespoons butter	2 tablespoons flour
Salt and black pepper	150 ml (¼ pint) milk
1 teaspoon sugar	3 egg yolks

Scrape, wash and chop the carrots into small pieces. Sauté until lightly coloured in 2 tablespoons butter, and add enough water to cover. Season to taste with salt, pepper and a teaspoon of sugar. Bring to the boil, cover the pan and simmer until the carrots are very soft. Drain and mash the carrots to a purée, or use an electric blender for a particularly smooth, creamy consistency. Combine the carrot purée and chicken stock in a saucepan. Bring to the boil and simmer gently for a little while until the purée has practically dissolved in the stock. (Alternatively, cook the chopped, sautéed carrots in the stock, and blend all together in an electric blender.)

Melt the remaining butter in a separate pan. Add the flour and blend well together, stirring for a few minutes over low heat. Gradually add the milk, stirring all the time, and cook until the mixture thickens. Remove from the heat. Add the egg yolks one by one, beating constantly. Then add to the soup a little at a time, mixing vigorously. Adjust the seasoning, bring almost to boiling point again, and remove from the heat at once so as not to allow the egg yolks to curdle. Serve immediately.

Pumpkin Soup

This delicate soup from Morocco also looks beautiful. It depends very much on the type of pumpkin you find. As it is difficult to tell what they are like, ask to taste a bit from an open one. You will know when it is not good.

2½ kg (5 lb) slice of pumpkin
¾ litre (1½ pints) chicken stock
¾ litre (1½ pints) milk

Salt and white pepper
120 g (4 oz) cooked rice, weighed
 uncooked (optional)

Remove the peel, seeds and fibre from the pumpkin and cut it into pieces. Put it in a large pan with the stock and the milk, season with salt and pepper and simmer for 15–20 minutes until it is tender. Lift the vegetable out and purée it in a blender or through a sieve and return to the pan. Bring to the boil, throw in the rice and simmer a minute more before serving.

≈ It is usual to flavour the soup with about a tablespoon of sugar. It is not to my taste but it may be to yours.

Ful Nabed Soup

This soup, made with the same broad white beans as *ta'amia* (page 86), is popular in Egypt, where sick and convalescing people are encouraged to eat it to regain their health. It is plain but delicate in flavour, and highly nutritious.

500 g (1 lb) white dried skinless
 beans (ful nabed)
2 tablespoons olive oil
Salt and white pepper

3 tablespoons finely chopped
 parsley
Juice of 1 lemon

Soak the beans overnight. Drain them and put them in a large saucepan with 2 to 2½ litres (3½ to 4 pints) water. Bring to the boil and simmer, covered, for 1 hour, or until they are very soft. Press the beans and liquid through a sieve, or blend in an electric blender. Alternatively, mash with a fork or potato masher.

Return the soup to the saucepan, add the oil, and season to taste with salt and pepper. Bring to the boil again and simmer for a few minutes, adding a little water if too thick.

Serve garnished with chopped parsley and squeeze a little lemon juice over each individual bowl. In Egypt, this soup is served with Arab bread to dip in it.

Lentil Soup

There are several versions of this favourite winter soup. Red, yellow, green or brown lentils can be used, but the tiny red lentils widely available here are best as they disintegrate very quickly.

The soup can be made with water, but a meat or bone stock will make it considerably richer and tastier.

3 tablespoons oil
1 large onion, chopped
1 stalk celery with leaves, chopped
1 carrot, chopped (optional)
375 g (12 oz) lentils, washed if necessary
2 litres (3½ pints) chicken or meat stock or water

1 marrow bone (optional)
Salt and black pepper
Juice of ½–1 lemon (optional)
1 teaspoon ground cumin (optional)
Small garlic-flavoured croûtons (see method) (optional)

Soften the onion, celery and carrot, if used, in oil in a large saucepan. Add the lentils, water or stock and the marrow bone which, if cracked, will release even more marrow; bring to the boil and skim if necessary. Simmer gently, covered, until the lentils are very soft. This will take 20 to 45 minutes – the cooking time varying according to the quality and age of the lentils.

When the lentils are cooked, season the soup with salt and pepper and, if you like, add a little lemon juice and cumin. Simmer for a few minutes longer, then remove the marrow bone. If the lentils do not disintegrate rub the soup through a sieve, put it in an electric blender, or squash with a potato masher to make a smooth purée (this is not necessary with red lentils). Return the soup to the saucepan, bring to the boil again and either add a little water if you want a lighter soup, or evaporate by simmering a little longer to reduce and thicken it.

Serve with small croûtons of bread fried in oil to which a clove or two of crushed garlic has been added just as they begin to turn golden brown. Garlic is not always used, but I feel that, fried and aromatic, it enhances the taste of the lentil cream.

≈ A good variation for a rather liquid soup is to add about 60 g (2 oz) washed rice and simmer for about 15 minutes, or until the rice is just tender. Or 60 g (2 oz) vermicelli may be added in the same way.

≈ An alternative flavouring to the cumin and lemon juice is to stir in, just before serving, a *taklia* (garlic) sauce, made with 2 or 3 cloves garlic, as described on page 162.

≈ A Turkish variation: to a similar lentil soup with the flavouring of cumin or coriander add a liaison of 2 tablespoons flour stirred into 2 tablespoons melted butter over low heat for 2 to 3 minutes. Add 300 ml (½ pint) warm milk gradually, stirring all the time until well blended. Cook gently for about 10 minutes, then add to the soup. Beat the yolks of 3 eggs. Beat in a ladleful of the hot soup, and pour back into the soup gradually, beating constantly. Reheat, but do not allow the soup to boil again. Bread sprinkled with grated cheese (Kephalotiri, Parmesan or Gruyère) and toasted in the oven makes an excellent accompaniment to this version.

☐ *The Alternative**

'I am a hospitable man,' said Nasrudin to a group of cronies at the teahouse.

'Very well, then – take us all home to supper,' said the greediest.

Nasrudin collected the whole crowd and started towards his house with them.

When he was almost there, he said:

'I'll go ahead and warn my wife: you just wait here.'

His wife cuffed him when he told her the news. 'There is no food in the house – turn them away.'

'I can't do that, my reputation for hospitality is at stake.'

'Very well, you go upstairs and I'll tell them that you are out.'

After nearly an hour the guests became restless and crowded around the door, shouting, 'Let us in, Nasrudin.'

The Mulla's wife went out to them.

'Nasrudin is out.'

'But we saw him go into the house, and we have been watching the door all the time.'

She was silent.

The Mulla, watching from an upstairs window, was unable to contain himself. Leaning out he shouted: 'I could have gone out by the back door, couldn't I?'

---

* Shah, *The Exploits of the Incomparable Mulla Nasrudin.*

Spinach and Lentil Soup

250 g (8 oz) large brown lentils
500 g (1 lb) fresh spinach or 250 g
   (8 oz) frozen leaf spinach
1 large onion, finely chopped
2–3 tablespoons oil

2 tablespoons tomato concentrate
   (optional)
Salt
Pinch of cayenne pepper

Put the lentils, cleaned and washed, in a large saucepan. Cover them with about 2 litres (3½ pints) water, bring to the boil and simmer for 20 to 40 minutes until they soften.

Meanwhile, wash fresh spinach carefully and drain well or defrost frozen spinach in a colander. Cut into pieces or ribbons. Fry the chopped onion to a russet colour in the oil. Add the prepared spinach and sauté over very low heat. It will release a considerable amount of juice. Let it stew in this liquor, covered, for a few minutes, then pour into the pan with the cooked lentils. Stir in the tomato concentrate, if used, season to taste with salt and cayenne pepper, and simmer until the flavours and colours have blended.

Add a little more water if the soup is too thick, season to your liking, and serve.

Turkish Spinach Soup

The traditional Turkish egg and lemon thickening gives this soup a creamy texture, and a delicate tang which is in harmony with the flavours of spinach, celery, dill and parsley.

2 litres (3½ pints) meat or
   chicken stock
Salt and black pepper
500 g (1 lb) fresh spinach or 250 g
   (8 oz) frozen leaf spinach
1 large carrot
1 stalk celery
A few celery leaves

2 tablespoons butter
2 tablespoons flour
3 egg yolks
Juice of 1 lemon
2 tablespoons finely chopped
   parsley
1 tablespoon finely chopped fresh
   dill (optional)

Prepare a meat or chicken stock. Stock cubes can be used. Season to taste with salt and pepper.

Wash the spinach leaves very thoroughly in several changes of water. If frozen spinach is used, let it de-frost thoroughly. Drain and chop the leaves finely. Wash and chop the carrot and celery stalk and leaves. For a prettier effect, cut the carrot into matchstick strips.

Cook the carrot and celery in the stock until nearly done. Add the spinach and continue to simmer for about 15 minutes longer, until all the vegetables are quite soft and cooked.

Make the thickening. Melt the butter, blend in the flour, and stir well over very low heat for a few minutes. Add a ladleful of the soup, beating constantly. Then pour the mixture back into the soup gradually, mixing thoroughly. Simmer over low heat for about 15 minutes. Mix the egg yolks and lemon juice, and beat vigorously. Add a ladleful of the soup and beat well. Pour back in the soup gradually, stirring constantly. Bring the soup to just below boiling point. Sprinkle with parsley, and dill if available, and serve.

Yellow Split Pea Soup

375–500 g (¾–1 lb) yellow split peas
1 stalk celery with leaves, finely chopped
2 litres (3½ pints) chicken or meat stock, or water
Salt and black pepper

1 teaspoon ground cumin (optional)
Juice of ½ lemon or more (optional)
2 tablespoons finely chopped parsley
Fried or toasted croûtons

Wash the split peas if necessary. It is sometimes recommended to soak the peas overnight, but I find this unnecessary. The larger amount of peas will give a thick, creamy soup, a favourite consistency in the Middle East.

Add the split peas and celery to the stock or water, bring to the boil, remove the scum and simmer gently, covered, until the peas are very soft and nearly disintegrating. The cooking time varies with the quality of the peas, where they were grown, and their age, but it should take from 1 to 1½ hours (after 25 minutes they are soft but still firm). Use a pressure cooker if one is available. In this case, 15 minutes should be sufficient.

When the peas are quite soft, season to taste with salt and pepper. A teaspoon of ground cumin and the juice of ½ lemon, or more, may also be added. Simmer for a few minutes longer to allow the peas to absorb the seasoning, then rub the soup through a sieve or blend in an electric blender to achieve a smooth cream. Return to the pan, bring to the boil again, and thin with a little water if necessary.

Garnish the soup with chopped parsley. Small croûtons are often served with it and sprinkled over each individual bowl.

Haricot Bean Soup

2 leeks
2 tablespoons butter or oil
375 g–500 g (¾–1 lb) dried haricot
  beans, soaked overnight

2 litres (3½ pints) meat stock or
  water
Salt and black pepper

Cut off and discard the green parts of the leeks and wash the rest well, particularly in between the leaves. Slice and sauté in butter or oil in a large saucepan until soft. Add the drained beans and stock or water. Bring to the boil, remove the scum, cover and simmer gently until the beans are very soft. Do not season until they are almost ready. This may take from 1 to 1½ hours or longer, according to the quality of the beans, but a pressure cooker will reduce the cooking time to about 30 minutes.

Season to taste with salt and pepper, and simmer for a few minutes longer. Rub the soup through a sieve or blend in an electric blender. (I also rather like it when the beans are left whole but practically disintegrating.) Return the purée to the saucepan and bring to the boil again. Add a little water if the soup is too thick, or reduce and thicken it by simmering a little longer, if it is too light. Adjust the seasoning and serve.

≈ Another version of this soup adds 2 skinned and chopped tomatoes and a tablespoon of tomato concentrate at the start of cooking. This colours the soup a gentle pink.

≈ The juice of 1 lemon is also sometimes added, and chopped parsley sprinkled as a garnish over each individual bowl.

Ab Ghooshte Fasl
Bean Soup

This nourishing soup makes a good winter meal. In Iran it is served with bread, bunches of fresh herbs such as cress, mint, coriander, and with spring onions, radishes and home-made pickles.

It is the type of soup you will find in the bazaar at the earliest hours of the morning, dished out for breakfast from huge cauldrons in which a sheep's head and feet have given their special richness and where all the vegetables in season find their place.

60 g (2 oz) dried white beans,
  soaked for a few hours
60 g (2 oz) yellow split peas
60 g (2 oz) black-eyed beans
60 g (2 oz) large brown lentils
500 g (1 lb) stewing lamb, cut into
  pieces
1 large onion, thickly sliced

Salt and pepper
1 teaspoon cinnamon
½ teaspoon turmeric
1 good bunch of parsley, chopped
4 tomatoes, skinned
1 large aubergine, cubed
2 green peppers, cut into pieces
4 small potatoes, peeled

Put the beans, peas and lentils in a large saucepan with the meat and onion and about 1¾ litres (3 pints) of water. Bring to the boil, remove the scum and simmer for an hour, adding salt, pepper and spices when the beans are already softened. Cook for an hour or more until the meat is very tender. Put in the vegetables and cook ½ hour or until the vegetables are done, adding water if necessary.

≈ You may add 120 g (4 oz) dried apricots or 120 g (4 oz) dried prunes at the same time as the meat, or you may scoop the contents of a pomegranate in when you put in the vegetables.

Harira
Moroccan Soup

During the thirty days of the fast of Ramadan, every household prepares its own version of this national soup. The smell permeates the streets of Morocco long before sunset, when it is time to break the fast. You may add some meat cut into cubes, and some bones, to this meatless version.

This makes enough for 15 to 20 people.

250 g (8 oz) chick peas
250 g (8 oz) haricot beans or other
  beans
250 g (8 oz) lentils
1 large tin peeled tomatoes
500 g (1 lb) onions, coarsely
  chopped
Salt and pepper to taste
1 tablespoon turmeric, or to taste

Juice of 1 large lemon, or more
3–4 tablespoons flour
1 small bunch fresh coriander,
  finely chopped
1 small bunch parsley, finely
  chopped
120 g (4 oz) cooked rice (optional)
1 teaspoon harissa (optional)

Wash and soak the chick peas, beans and lentils for a few hours or overnight. Drain. Bring the first two to the boil in fresh cold water in a large pan and simmer until tender. Add the lentils and continue to cook until these are just tender. Add the tomatoes, cutting them up into small pieces, the onions and more water. Season to taste with salt and pepper, add turmeric (some people use saffron instead) and lemon juice and simmer a further ½ hour.

In a small pan stir 600 ml (1 pint) cold water gradually into the flour, beating constantly so as not to have any lumps. Add some strained liquid from the hot soup and stir over low heat until it begins to boil. The flour gives the soup a velvety texture much loved in Morocco. Add the chopped coriander and parsley leaves and pour back into the soup.

Continue to cook until the pulses are soft and the taste is rich. Adjust the seasoning and add water if necessary. Add the rice just before serving and *harissa* if you like.

Yoghourt Soups

Milk, both fresh and sour, and particularly in the form of yoghourt, is a very ancient ingredient in the cooking of the Middle East in general. In certain soups, yoghourt is added at the end of the cooking and just allowed to become hot, without boiling. In this case there is little danger of it curdling. However when yoghourt is called for in the actual cooking, precautions must be taken to 'stabilize' it (see page 124).

It is good to prepare one's own yoghourt (see page 122), especially if making dishes which call for over a pint. Besides the quite different, fresher taste, the cost will be considerably reduced.

□ *A Tale of Goha*

Goha was found by a friend squatting on the edge of a lake with a spoon and a pot of yoghourt.

'What are you doing?' said the friend. Goha stirred a spoonful of thick yoghourt in the water and said:

'I am turning the lake into yoghourt.'

Ashe Mast va Khiar
Cold Yoghourt Soup

A refreshing summer soup from Iran.

900 ml (1½ pints) yoghourt
150 ml (¼ pint) sour cream
150 ml (¼ pint) water
Salt and pepper
1 cucumber, coarsely grated

4–5 spring onions, finely chopped
A few sprigs of fresh mint,
    chopped
4 tablespoons raisins or sultanas

Beat the yoghourt and sour cream with about 150 ml (¼ pint) water. Add salt and pepper, cucumber and spring onions and stir well. Just before serving, put in 6 ice cubes and sprinkle with mint and raisins or sultanas.

≈ A version of this recipe includes chopped hard-boiled eggs.

Labaneya
Spinach Soup with Yoghourt

An Egyptian soup traditionally made with the leaves of a plant of the spinach family called *silq* (beet); the French call it *blette*. The soup is equally delicious made with spinach, fresh if possible, but frozen leaf spinach will also do. (I often find *silq* in Greek stores.)

500 g (1 lb) silq (beet) or fresh
    spinach, or 250 g (8 oz) frozen
    leaf spinach
1 onion
About 2 tablespoons oil
1 leek or 3–4 spring onions, finely
    chopped

120g (4 oz) rice
Salt and black pepper
500 ml (¾ pint) yoghourt
1 clove garlic, or more, crushed
½ teaspoon turmeric (optional)

Wash the beets or fresh spinach leaves in a bowlful of water. Drain and cut into large pieces or ribbons, but do not chop them.

Chop the onion and sauté in oil in a large saucepan until faintly coloured and soft. Add the spinach, stir and sauté gently. A finely chopped leek or a few spring onions will add a delicate flavour to the soup. Add them to the saucepan, together with the washed and drained rice. Cover with 1 litre (2 pints) water, season with salt and pepper, bring to the boil and simmer gently until the rice and spinach are cooked. This will take about 15 minutes, and the rice should not be allowed to get too soft or mushy.

In the meantime, beat the yoghourt with one or more crushed cloves of garlic. When the rice and spinach are ready, add the yoghourt mixture to the soup and beat well. Heat but do not let the soup boil again, or it will curdle.

A pinch of turmeric added to the spinach and rice while they are cooking will give the soup a pale yellow, Oriental tinge.

Turkish Yoghourt Soups

Here are two more soups in which yoghourt is added at the end of the cooking. In the third one the yoghourt is cooked with the soup.

1.

A soup based on a meat stock which is thickened with a liaison of butter and flour.

½ litre (1 pint) meat stock
2 tablespoons butter
1½–2 tablespoons flour

Salt and white pepper
1 litre (1¾ pints) yoghourt
2 tablespoons dried crushed mint

Bring the stock to the boil in a large saucepan. Melt the butter in a small pan, add flour and blend it in well, stirring for about 5 minutes over very low heat. Pour in a ladleful of the stock and beat well. Pour this mixture back into the stock, stirring constantly, and bring back to the boil very slowly to avoid making lumps. Cook, stirring, for 15 to 20 minutes, until the soup thickens, is very smooth, and has lost the taste of flour. Season to taste with salt and pepper, and remove from the heat.

Beat the yoghourt in a bowl and pour it into the soup gradually, beating vigorously. Return the pan to the heat and bring the soup to just below boiling point. Do not allow it to boil, or it will curdle.

Serve garnished with crushed dried mint.

2.

A chicken and barley soup with yoghourt.

1 large onion, chopped
2 tablespoons butter
1 litre (1¾ pints) clear chicken stock
90 g (3 oz) pearl barley, soaked overnight

2 tablespoons finely chopped parsley
Salt and white pepper
1 litre (1¾ pints) yoghourt
2 tablespoons dried crushed mint

Fry the chopped onion in butter in a large saucepan until soft. Add the chicken stock (made with stock cubes if necessary) and bring to the boil.

Add the soaked and drained barley to the boiling stock and simmer over low heat for ¾ to 1 hour, or until the barley has swelled enormously and is soft. Add chopped parsley, and season to taste with salt and white pepper.

Beat the yoghourt. Add a little of the soup and beat vigorously. Pour the yoghourt mixture into the soup gradually, beating constantly, and heat to just below boiling point. Do not allow the soup to boil, or it will curdle.

Adjust the seasoning and serve, garnished with dried crushed mint.

3.

Chicken and yoghourt soup with rice.

1 litre (1¾ pints) chicken stock	1 tablespoon cornflour dissolved
Salt and white pepper	in ½ cup cold water
60 g (2 oz) rice, washed	3 egg yolks, lightly beaten
1 litre (1¾ pints) yoghourt	2 tablespoons dried crushed mint
	2 tablespoons butter

Bring the stock, seasoned to taste, to the boil. Add the rice, reduce the heat and let it simmer while you prepare the yoghourt. In another saucepan, beat the yoghourt well and add the cornflour dissolved in water. Stir well. This will stabilize it. Add the lightly beaten egg yolks and beat again. Put the pan on the heat and bring to the boil slowly, stirring constantly in one direction. When the mixture thickens, add it slowly to the chicken and rice soup, stirring constantly, and continue to simmer gently until the rice is soft. Adjust the seasoning.

Fry the mint gently in hot butter and pour a little over each individual bowl when serving.

Tutmaj
Armenian Yoghourt Soup

1 litre (1¾ pints) yoghourt
2 eggs, beaten
120 g (4 oz) flat noodles, or some
  other form of small pasta
Salt and white pepper

1 large onion, finely chopped
60 g (2 oz) butter
2–3 tablespoons dried crushed
  mint

Beat the yoghourt and eggs together in a large pan. Bring to the boil slowly, stirring constantly in the same direction. The eggs will prevent the yoghourt from curdling. Stir in 600 ml (1 pint) water and add the noodles. Season to taste with salt and pepper. Bring to the boil again and simmer gently for 10 minutes, or until the noodles are well done.

In the meantime, fry the onion very gently in butter until soft and a pale golden colour. Add the mint, stir well into the butter and fry for a minute longer.

Pour the hot onion and mint butter over each individual bowl of soup as you serve it.

Eshkeneh Shirazi
Persian Yoghourt Soup

A speciality of the city of Shiraz. This soup is given texture with chopped walnuts, and an unusual flavour from the herb fenugreek, called *shanbalileh* in Iran.

2 tablespoons butter
1–2 onions, finely chopped
2 tablespoons flour
60 g (2 oz) walnuts, chopped

A bunch of fenugreek, finely
  chopped
1 litre (1¾ pints) hot water
Salt and black pepper
600 ml (1 pint) yoghourt

Melt the butter in a large pan. Fry the onions in it until they are a pale golden colour. Add the flour and stir over very low heat for a few minutes until well blended. Add the walnuts and fenugreek. Pour in a ladleful of the hot water and beat vigorously, then add the rest of the water gradually, stirring constantly. Season to taste with salt and pepper, bring to the boil slowly and simmer, covered, for 15 to 20 minutes, until the soup thickens a little and has lost its floury taste.

Beat the yoghourt vigorously. Add a ladleful of the hot soup and beat well. Pour the mixture back into the soup gradually, stirring all the time. Leave over low heat until it comes to just below boiling point, but do not allow the soup to boil, or it will curdle. Serve immediately.

Meat Soups

There exists in the Middle East an infinite variety of soups so rich in meat, vegetables and pulses that one could almost call them stews. As with the repetitive and ornamental art of that part of the world, where motifs are taken and tried in every possible combination, so the ingredients for these soups are coupled, separated and recoupled in various new combinations.

Below, I give a few of the basic soups. These can be varied by using different vegetables or pulses.

Although, in the past, lamb or mutton was always used, beef and veal are used extensively today for their different qualities. The more expensive cuts would, of course, be wasted, and it is generally stewing meat, lean or fat according to taste, which is used.

Shoulder, leg, breast, saddle and shin of lamb will do beautifully. Topside or silverside of beef makes a marvellous soup, while shin gives a rich, gelatinous stock. If using veal, I recommend breast or shoulder, topside of leg, chump end of loin or knuckle for its gelatinous quality. Marrow bones are always added. They are removed before serving, but the marrow is slipped into the soup, to be eaten with a piece of bread.

The meat is either left whole and allowed to soften and break up during the long cooking, or it is cubed beforehand. Meat balls, well kneaded and smooth, are often dropped into the soup towards the end of cooking.

Pulses, rice and vegetables are added during the cooking, according to the time they require to become tender.

Chick peas, beans, lentils and whole wheat are soaked overnight and added to the soup at the start of cooking. Onions, leeks, tomatoes, celery, turnips and carrots are cooked at the same time as the meat and bones. Courgettes and aubergines, spinach and beets are added a short while before serving as they become tender very quickly and are not good overcooked.

Vermicelli and other pastas, and cereals such as rice which cook very quickly, are added just long enough before serving to give them time to soften. Small pastas and white rice take less than 20 minutes, but tapioca will take longer unless a quick-cooking variety is used.

These soups are sometimes seasoned very lightly with salt only; sometimes, depending on the region and the preference of the cook, they are seasoned gently or fiercely with allspice, cumin, coriander, ginger or cinnamon, and black pepper, paprika or cayenne. Some people add tomato concentrate, others prefer a little saffron. Garlic, lemon and vinegar are also used for flavouring. In my own experience, meat soups have always been rich in meat and vegetables but rather gentle in seasoning.

Make them as a complete meal for the family, or as a first course before a light main dish. They can be exciting and delicious served at a late party with Arab bread or pitta (page 434).

☐ *The Importance of Meat Broth**

With the exception of sweets, every kind of food was cooked in broth. Besides the meat used for consumption, meat for broth was provided in every palace and konak. At our house about ten pounds of beef and mutton were used every day for that purpose and then discarded. No one would have dreamt of cooking with plain water. In this connexion a story was told about a very able but equally parsimonious Grand Vezir. His son-in-law, who was a great gourmet and, according to the custom of the time, was living with his father-in-law, frequently complained about the meals, saying that he simply could not eat them. 'My son,' said the Grand Vezir, 'we eat to live but we do not live to eat.' The young man, hoping thus to improve matters, finally went to speak to the cook. 'Don't I know it,' cried the chef. 'What can you expect of food cooked with water from the tap?' When eventually the Grand Vezir's daughter and her husband were divorced, the quality of the food provided in her father's house was said to be the main reason for their separation.

* From Emine Foat Tugay, *Three Centuries*

Rich Meat and Vegetable Soup

This soup and other similar ones in which the meat and vegetables are fried before being boiled, are very rich and tasty, though heavier than they would be if they were only boiled.

500 g (1 lb) stewing beef, cubed
1–2 marrow bones, (optional)
1 large onion, thinly sliced
2 stalks celery, chopped
2 leeks, trimmed and thinly sliced
3 tomatoes, chopped
2 tablespoons oil or butter
Salt and black pepper

Pinch of cayenne pepper
  (optional)
1 large aubergine, chopped
  (optional)
2 courgettes, thinly sliced
  (optional)
2 tablespoons finely chopped
  parsley

Wash the meat and bones, put them in a large saucepan, and cover with 2 to 2½ litres (3½ to 4½ pints) cold water. Bring to the boil and remove the scum.

Fry the onion, celery, leeks and tomatoes lightly in oil or butter, adding the tomatoes last. Add the vegetables to the meat and bones. Season with salt and pepper and, if you like, a good pinch of cayenne; cover and simmer gently for about 2½ hours, or until the meat and vegetables are very soft. If you want to add the aubergine and courgettes, the former should first be sprinkled with salt and left to drain in a colander for at least ½ hour to get rid of its bitterness. Fry both the aubergine and courgettes gently, and add them to the soup about 20 minutes before serving. Simmer and adjust seasoning.

Add a little water to the soup if too thick. Crush the vegetables with a potato masher if you like them slightly mashed. Excess fat may be removed from the surface of the soup with absorbent paper or skimmed off with a spoon.

Remove the bones, garnish the soup with parsley and serve with Arab bread or pitta.

≈ An onion soup can be made in exactly the same way as above, substituting about 500 g (1 lb) onions for all the other vegetables.
≈ Another good combination consists of tomatoes, celery and potatoes.
≈ Yet another uses potatoes and marrow.

Beef and Puréed Vegetable Soup

500 g (1 lb) stewing beef
2 marrow bones, (optional)
2 stalks celery, chopped
2 carrots, chopped
3 leeks, trimmed and sliced
3 tomatoes, skinned and
    quartered
1 onion, chopped
Salt and black pepper

3 courgettes, sliced (optional)
1–2 aubergines, chopped, salted
    and drained for ½ hour
    (optional)
120 g (4 oz) rice, boiled (weight
    uncooked)
4 tablespoons finely chopped
    parsley

Wash the meat and bones, and put them in a large pan. Cover with 2 to 2½ litres (3½ to 4½ pints) water, bring to the boil over high heat and remove all the scum. Add all the vegetables except the courgettes and aubergines. Season with salt and pepper, and simmer, covered, for about 2 hours, until the meat is very tender. Add the courgettes and/or aubergines if used, and cook for about 15 minutes longer.

Remove the bones and drop the marrow into the soup. Put aside the meat. Ladle off any excess fat, or skim the surface of the soup with absorbent paper. Purée the soup and vegetables through a sieve or in an electric blender. Return the puréed soup to the saucepan and add the meat and cooked rice. Bring to the boil again, adjust seasoning and thin with a little water if necessary. (It is always better to start with less water than you need, since you can always add more later as it becomes reduced.)

Serve, giving a little meat to each portion, garnished with chopped parsley.

≈ For a spicier soup, add paprika and cayenne to taste, and any other favourite spices, such as ground cumin, coriander or cinnamon (about 1 teaspoon in all).

Meat Ball Soup

500 g (1 lb) stewing lamb or beef,
    cubed
2 marrow bones, (optional)
Salt and black pepper
Ground cinnamon (optional)
500 g (1 lb) minced lamb or beef

½ teaspoon ground allspice
2 tablespoons butter or oil
90–120 g (3–4 oz) rice, washed
3 tablespoons finely chopped
    parsley

Wash the stewing meat and bones, put them in a large pan and cover with 2 litres (3½ pints) cold water. Bring to boil, remove the scum, and season with salt and pepper. A little cinnamon is said by some to 'camouflage' the taste of the meat, by others to enhance it. I like to add ½ teaspoon. Simmer gently for about 2 hours, covered, until the meat is tender and the stock rich.

In the meantime, prepare little meat balls. Pound the minced meat to a paste with seasonings of allspice, salt and pepper, mincing it at least twice or kneading vigorously with your hands to achieve a smooth texture. Wash your hands and roll the mixture into marble-sized balls. Fry gently in butter or oil until lightly coloured all over.

Half an hour before the soup is ready, drop in the meat balls. A quarter of an hour before serving, add the raw rice, and simmer until tender. Alternatively, you can cook the rice separately, and add it to the soup just before serving.

Serve the soup sprinkled with chopped parsley and dusted with cinnamon.

≈ This soup can also be coloured lightly with one or two table-spoons of tomato concentrate.

Armenian Meat Soup with Burghul (Cracked Wheat)

750 g (1½ lb) knuckle of veal (with bone)
1 carrot
1 onion
1 teaspoon ground cinnamon (optional)

Salt and black pepper
120 g (4 oz) burghul
3 tablespoons finely chopped parsley

Wash the meat and bones, and bring them to the boil with 2 litres (3½ pints) cold water in a large saucepan. Remove the scum. Add the carrot and onion, both whole, and flavour with cinnamon if liked. Season with salt and pepper, and simmer gently, covered, for about 2 hours or until the meat is tender. Then remove the vegetables and bone, leaving the meat in the pan. Add the burghul and simmer for about 15 minutes longer until it is well cooked. Add more water if the mixture becomes too thick. The burghul will absorb a lot of liquid and expand considerably.

Adjust the seasoning and serve, garnished with parsley.

≈ This soup is sometimes made with whole wheat kernels. In this case, buy the variety already husked. Soak overnight and cook with the meat until very tender. The cooking time varies, depending on the quality and age of the grain, but it generally takes about 2 hours.

Harissa
Meat and Wheat Soup

Not to be confused with the fiery Moroccan *harissa* preserve (see page 65); this ancestral soup with the consistency of porridge symbolizes the diet of the mountain Kurds. It is back in fashion in Iraq, in the region north of Baghdad, as a breakfast dish. Those who cannot afford meat make it with wheat alone. The name means 'well cooked'. In Syria and Lebanon it is traditionally served on Assumption Day, *Id es Saidi*, or when a sheep is slaughtered for some special reason, in which case it is made with bone broth. It is also made with chicken and you can very well have it for supper instead of breakfast.

375 g (12 oz) whole wheat grain	Bones (optional)
250–500 g (½–1 lb) meat – traditionally lamb but chicken is also used	Salt and pepper
	½–1 teaspoon cinnamon
	2 tablespoons butter or oil

Soak the wheat grain in water overnight. Cover the meat and bones with water in a large saucepan. Bring to the boil and remove the scum. Drain and rinse the wheat and drop it into the boiling meat or chicken stock (there should be almost 1 litre (1¾ pints). Add salt and pepper and ½–1 teaspoon of cinnamon and simmer gently for at least 2 hours, stirring occasionally and adding water until it is very soft. Remove the bones and crush the meat with a fork. Some people put the stew in a blender so that you cannot recognize the meat. Serve hot in deep bowls, sprinkled if you like with sizzling hot butter or oil.

≈ In Iraq they sprinkle with sugar and cinnamon.
≈ A Lebanese version is further flavoured with a pinch of cumin and one of ground cloves. A chopped-up onion and peeled and chopped tomato may be added during the cooking.

☐ *Wedding Song**

Your father, oh beautiful one!
Has so often screamed and shouted,
And lowered the price of your dowry,
And said, 'My daughters are beautiful!'

Düğün Çorbasi
Turkish Wedding Soup

Mutton is traditionally used for this soup, but in England it is advisable to use lamb.

500 g (1 lb) lean lamb, cubed
Flour
1–2 tablespoons butter or oil
1–2 marrow bones
1 carrot
1 onion

Salt and black pepper
Pinch of cayenne pepper
   (optional)
3 eggs yolks
Juice of 1 lemon

GARNISH

2 tablespoons melted butter
1 tablespoon paprika

½ teaspoon ground cinnamon
   (optional)

Roll the cubed meat in flour and turn it in hot butter or oil in a large saucepan until lightly coloured all over. Add 2 litres (3½ pints) water and the marrow bones and bring to the boil. Skim off the scum and add the carrot, onion and salt and pepper to taste. Add a pinch of cayenne as well if you like. Simmer gently, covered, for about 2 hours, or until the meat is very tender and the soup rich and full of flavour. Remove the bones and vegetables. The carrot may be sliced into thin sticks and used as a garnish.

Just before serving, beat the egg yolks. Add the lemon juice and beat again. Beat in a ladleful of hot soup and pour back into the soup slowly, beating constantly. Do not allow the soup to boil again, or it will curdle.

Decorate in the Turkish manner by dribbling melted butter with paprika over the top of the soup tureen or individual soup bowls. Add the reserved carrot sticks, dust with cinnamon if liked, and serve immediately.

* From Maspéro, *Chansons populaires*.

Shorbet el Fata
Bread Soup

An Egyptian feast-day soup, traditionally eaten seventy days after Ramadan. It is made of the left-over meat and bones of a sacrificial lamb. The custom is to slay the lamb in the name of God, and to distribute the meat among the poor. However, the family of the donor must eat some of the lamb in order to benefit from the sacrifice; this soup is a good way of doing so.

500 g (1 lb) lean leg of lamb, cubed
A few lamb bones, cracked
Salt and black pepper
60 g (2 oz) rice, washed and drained
3 rounds Arab bread or 6 slices white bread, toasted

2 or more cloves garlic, crushed
3 tablespoons butter
3–4 tablespoons vinegar
2 tablespoons finely chopped parsley

Make a rich stock by boiling the meat and bones in 2–2½ litres (3½ to 4 pints) water. Bring to the boil, remove the scum, season with salt and pepper, and simmer until the meat is tender, about 2 hours.

Add the rice and continue to simmer for a further 15 minutes, until it is cooked but not mushy.

Arrange the toasted bread slices in the bottom of a large soup tureen. Fry the crushed garlic in hot butter until lightly coloured and aromatic. Sprinkle with vinegar, bring to the boil, and pour over the toasted bread. Allow the toast to become well soaked; then pour the soup over it and serve, garnished with chopped parsley.

This method of serving soup over toasted and seasoned bread is a familiar one in the Middle East, and can also be used with stews. The toast swells and becomes imbued with the rich juices.

Shorbet el Samak
Fish Soup

Several Turkish fish soups recorded by Sidqi Effendi in the last century are on the following theme: a fish stock coloured with saffron, flavoured with vinegar, lemon, mint and cinnamon, and thickened with egg yolks. Unfortunately, quantities are all given in piastres' worth and difficult to follow. However, here is a modern Turkish recipe with almost identical ingredients.

2 large onions, finely chopped
3 tablespoons olive oil
Several fish heads, bones and tails*
3–4 tablespoons wine vinegar
2 tablespoons finely chopped parsley
Salt and black pepper
1–2 cloves garlic, crushed
¼ teaspoon saffron or 1 teaspoon turmeric (optional)
500 g (1 lb) white fish: slices of cod, haddock, halibut, etc., skinned if necessary
3 egg yolks
Juice of 1 lemon, or more
½ teaspoon ground cinnamon

Soften the onions in olive oil in a large saucepan. Add as many fish heads, bones and tails as are available to make a good broth. Pour in 2 to 2½ litres (3½ to 4 pints) water and add vinegar, chopped parsley, salt and pepper to taste, the garlic, and if you like, a little powdered saffron or turmeric. Bring to the boil and simmer for about 1 hour, until a good rich broth is obtained. Strain through a fine sieve and return the clear stock to the pan. Bring to the boil again and poach the pieces of fish for about 5 to 10 minutes, until the flesh flakes easily with a fork.

Beat the egg yolks. Add lemon juice and beat again. Beat in a ladleful of the fish stock and return the mixture to the soup, beating vigorously. Heat the soup again to just below boiling point, but do not let it boil, or it will curdle.

If you prefer to keep the fish slices whole, remove them while you beat in the egg and lemon mixture, and return them to the pan later.

Serve hot or cold, dusted with cinnamon.

* If you manage to get very large fish heads, you may find that they are so meaty that you do not need additional fish.

Egg Dishes

Beid

Egg dishes are very popular throughout the Middle East. *Beid*, as they are called, receive the full Oriental treatment. Hard-boiled and coloured yellow or brown, flavoured with cumin, coriander or cinnamon, they are sold in the streets with little cornets of rolled-up newspaper filled with a thimbleful of seasoning to dip them in. Fried or scrambled, they are enhanced with flavourings of garlic, onions and tomatoes, lemon, vinegar or yoghourt.

The Arab omelette, called *eggah*, is more like a cake. Thick and rich, with an infinite variety of vegetables, it is not unlike the Spanish *tortilla* to which it is undoubtedly related through the Moorish conquerors of Spain. Did the Moriscos introduce the omelette to Spain, or did they bring it back to North Africa after the *Reconquista*? It does not appear in early Arab culinary literature, so its origin is still a matter for speculation.

From very early times, however, eggs were used poached, hard-boiled or long-cooked in the *hamine* fashion (page 187), as a garnish

185

for various types of dishes, especially stews. This custom has been continued to the present day. Eggs are still added in their shells (duly scrubbed) at the start of the lengthy cooking of a stew so that all the flavours and aromas of the other ingredients can penetrate the shells. They are usually peeled and returned to the pan before serving. They can also be opened over the stew just before serving to be 'poached' in the sauce. This type of egg 'garnish' was a feature of al-Baghdadi's medieval cooking, and it is still a feature of Moroccan cooking today.

Besides the thick *eggah*-type omelettes, which make an excellent first course or main dish, a new type of light omelette, inspired by the French one, has recently been adopted in many Middle Eastern countries. It has, however, been adapted to local taste and acquired a Middle Eastern touch.

Hard-boiled Eggs

During the numerous festivals, such as the *Mûlid el Nabi*, which celebrates the birth of the Prophet, the pilgrimage to the sacred well of Zemzem, or the *Cham el Nessim*, a festival in honour of nature originating in Ancient Egypt and signifying 'breathing the new fresh air', people were in the habit of filling baskets with picnic food and spending the days and nights in public gardens or on pilgrimages to sacred places and the tombs of the saints. There, they would settle down to enjoy the contents of their baskets while they listened to reciters of romances recounting the tales of *Abou-Zeyd*, *El Zahir* and *Alf leyleh wa-leyleh* (*A Thousand and One Nights*), and watched the antics of conjurers, buffoons and dancers. Hard-boiled eggs have since time immemorial taken pride of place in these picnic baskets – beautifully flavoured and sometimes coloured.

In North Africa, ordinary hard-boiled eggs are sometimes peeled, then gently simmered in water in which a little saffron and salt have been dissolved. This gives them a brilliant yellow colour. They make a good substitute for *hamine* eggs.

☐ *'When it has been proved that the evil eye has been given, steps may be taken to detect the guilty person. A common expedient is to hold an egg between the two palms and to press upon it as the name of each suspect is spoken. At the name of the guilty one the egg will* *break.'** – *One of a large variety of beliefs and practices connected with the 'evil eye'.*

Beid Masluq
Hard-boiled Eggs with Cumin

Prepare hard-boiled eggs in the usual way. Peel them. Cut in half and sprinkle with salt and ground cumin; or serve whole, accompanied by a small bowl of salt mixed with about twice as much cumin, to dip the eggs in. Serve as an appetizer.

In Morocco, vendors sell these eggs in the streets, sprinkled with the same seasoning.

Baid Mutajjan
Fried Hard-boiled Eggs

A medieval recipe from al-Baghdadi advises hard-boiling the eggs, then peeling them, frying them in oil, and sprinkling them with, or dipping them in, a mixture of dried ground coriander (1 teaspoon), cinnamon (½ teaspoon), cumin (1 teaspoon), and salt to taste. This type of egg is still sold in the streets in Egypt and Morocco today, and many families prepare these eggs (without the strong seasoning) as a garnish for meat and potato dishes.

Beid Hamine
Hamine Eggs

Great favourites of ancient origin.

Put the eggs and skins from several onions in a very large saucepan. Fill the pan with water, cover and simmer very gently over the lowest heat possible for at least 6 hours, even overnight. A layer of oil poured over the surface is a good way of preventing the water from evaporating too quickly. This lengthy cooking produces deliciously creamy eggs. The whites acquire a soft beige colour from the onion skins, and the yolks are very creamy and pale yellow. The

* Donaldson, *The Wild Rue.*

flavour is delicate and excitingly different from eggs cooked in any other way.

Some people add ground coffee to the water, to obtain a slightly darker colour.

My mother sometimes uses a pressure cooker to prepare *hamine* eggs in a hurry. In this case, it is advisable to hard-boil the eggs first, and then cook them under pressure with the onion skins. They will be ready after about 1½ hours. Although this method produces reasonable results, the traditional way still provides better, creamier eggs.

Serve *hamine* eggs as an appetizer over a dish of *ful medames* (page 324), or as a garnish for meat stews.

Deep-fried Eggs

A fine way of preparing eggs is deep-fried in hot oil, garnished with a sprinkling of finely chopped fresh mint, dried *rigani* (wild marjoram) or oregano, and whole spring onions.

Scrambled Eggs with Vinegar

Fry 1 or 2 cloves of crushed garlic slowly in plenty of butter until just golden, using a non-stick frying pan if possible. Beat 6 eggs very thoroughly, and season with salt and black pepper. Pour into the pan and cook over gentle heat, stirring constantly. As the eggs begin to thicken, add 3 tablespoons vinegar, one at a time, and keep stirring to a creamy consistency.

Beid bi Tom
Fried Eggs with Garlic and Lemon

2 cloves garlic	2 tablespoons butter
Salt	6 eggs
Juice of ½ lemon, or 1 teaspoon sumac	Dried crushed mint, to garnish

Crush the garlic cloves with salt. Melt the butter in a large frying pan, or use two smaller ones. Add the garlic and lemon or *sumac*. As the garlic begins to colour, slide in the eggs, previously broken into a bowl, and continue to fry gently. Rub some dried mint in the palm of your hand, letting it sprinkle over the eggs. When the whites are set, remove the pan from the heat, sprinkle lightly with salt, and serve.

Beid bi Tamatem
Eggs with Tomatoes

1 large onion, finely chopped	5 tomatoes, skinned and sliced
2 tablespoons butter or oil	Salt and black pepper
1–2 cloves garlic, crushed	6 eggs

Soften the chopped onion in butter or oil in a large frying pan. Add the crushed garlic. When it turns golden, add the tomato slices, season with salt and pepper, and continue to cook gently until they are soft, turning the slices once with a spatula.

Break the eggs carefully into a bowl and slip them unbeaten into the frying pan. Cook until set, season if necessary, and serve immediately with pitta (page 434) or other bread.

The eggs can also be stirred gently until creamy and thickened, but I prefer to leave them whole.

Beid bi Gebna Maqlia
Fried Eggs with Cheese

This dish is traditionally prepared in individual portions in two-handled frying pans and served in the same pans straight from the fire. You can, of course, use one large frying pan, or as many as are convenient.

In the Middle East, the hard, dry Greek cheeses Kashkaval, Kephalotiri or Kasseri are used for frying, or Halumi, which is white and firm. The white cheese for which I have given a recipe on page 74 can also be fried once it has become dry and firm enough. As alternatives, Gouda, Cheddar and especially Gruyère lend themselves well to frying.

PER PORTION

1 thick slice cheese	1 egg
Flour (optional)	Salt and pepper
1 tablespoon butter or oil	

Some people dip the slice of cheese in flour before frying it, but this is not really necessary.

Fry the cheese in hot butter or oil in a small frying pan just large enough to hold it. When it begins to melt and bubble, open the egg over it and continue to cook until the white has set. Sprinkle lightly with salt and pepper, and serve piping hot.

Fried Eggs with Chicken Livers

250 g (8 oz) chicken livers
2 tablespoons butter or oil
Salt and black pepper
½ teaspoon ground cinnamon

6 eggs
tablespoon finely chopped
  parsley

Toss the chicken livers in hot butter or oil in a large frying pan. Season with salt, pepper and cinnamon. Do not overcook the livers: their merit lies in their juiciness.

Break the eggs over the livers and fry until set. Season lightly with salt and black pepper, sprinkle with finely chopped parsley and serve immediately.

Chakchouka

This is a dish of Tunisian origin which today is eaten in most Middle Eastern countries. A Turkish version is called *menemen*.

1–3 green peppers, depending on
  size
2 onions
8 small tomatoes

Butter or olive oil
Salt and black pepper
6 eggs

Cut the peppers open and remove the cores and seeds. Cut them into strips. Slice the onions and cut the tomatoes in half.

Fry the onions and peppers in butter or oil in a large frying pan. Season to taste with salt and pepper, and let them stew gently in their own juices. When the peppers are soft, add the halved tomatoes and continue cooking until they, too, are soft. Taste the mixture, adding more seasoning if necessary. Drop the eggs in whole, and cook until set. Season again if necessary, and serve.

In some versions, the eggs are not left whole but stirred and blended with the vegetables to achieve a creamy texture.

Variations

1. Fry 4 sliced courgettes or 1 cubed aubergine at the same time as the onions and peppers.
2. Add 3 medium-sized cooked potatoes, cut into pieces.
3. Add 3 or 4 sliced *mergez* (spicy sausages).
4. For alternative flavourings fry 2 crushed cloves garlic with 2 tablespoons dried mint. Add a sprinkling of paprika or make it fiery with a teaspoon of *harissa* (page 65) or a good pinch of cayenne.

Çilbir
Turkish Poached Eggs with Yoghourt

6 eggs	300–450 ml (½–¾ pint) yoghourt
1 tablespoon vinegar	3 tablespoons butter
Salt	1 tablespoon paprika

Use fresh eggs. Poach them in the usual way.

A good method for poaching eggs is to dip them, still in their shells, in boiling water for a few seconds so as to set a thin layer of the white nearest the shell. This will prevent the egg white from spreading too much. Break each egg into a cup and slide into another pan of boiling water to which a tablespoon of vinegar and some salt have been added. Remove the pan from the heat and leave it, covered, for 4 minutes. Then remove the eggs with a perforated spoon. Do not attempt to poach more than 2 eggs at a time.

Arrange the poached eggs on a hot serving dish.

Beat the yoghourt with salt to taste and pour some over each egg. Melt the butter and stir in the paprika. Dribble over the yoghourt and serve.

Eggah

I have classed the *eggah* as an egg dish or omelette, but this is misleading unless one describes its character further. The idea of an omelette, influenced by the image of the French version, implies extreme lightness, softness, creaminess and a slight fluidity in texture. If one looked for these qualities in an Arab *eggah*, one could well feel disappointed.

An *eggah* is firm and sound, rather like an egg cake. It is usually 2 cm (1 inch) or more thick, and generally bursting with a filling of vegetables, or meat, or chicken and noodles, suspended like currants in a cake. The egg is used as a binding for the filling, rather than the filling being an adornment of the egg. For serving, the *eggah* is turned out on to a serving dish and cut into slices, as one would cut a cake. It is sometimes cooked in a rectangular dish, especially if baked in the oven. In this case, it is usually served cut into rectangular or square pieces.

These extremely popular dishes are used for several purposes. They are cut into very small pieces as hors d'œuvre or into larger ones as first courses, and they are also used as side dishes to accompany grills and meat balls. Some are so rich with meat or chicken and noodles that they are a main dish in themselves, often served with yoghourt and a salad.

An *eggah* can be eaten cold as well as hot, which makes it a good luncheon or party piece. It is a great favourite for picnics and pilgrimages during national holidays. The fact that a very large one can be prepared to serve several people, cooked in advance and warmed up or eaten cold, gives it a great advantage over the French type of omelette, which must be small, and eaten immediately it is prepared to be successful.

As far as the pan is concerned, any large heavy frying pan which will assure an even distribution of heat can be used. One with its own lid, or any lid or plate which fits it tightly, is useful. If the dish is to be baked in the oven, any ovenproof dish will do, provided it has a lid.

When the dish is cooked on top of the stove, it requires from 15 to 30 minutes over very gentle heat, according to the number of eggs used and the type of filling, and depending on whether the filling has been cooked beforehand. It is usually cooked covered.

If it is cooked in the oven, the tray or dish must first be greased with butter. The cooking time in a 160°C (325°F/Mark 3) oven varies from ½ hour to 1 hour, again depending on the size of the dish and the type of filling. The dish may be covered to begin with, and then uncovered towards the end to allow the top to brown. When cooked, the *eggah* should be firm, even in the centre.

I prefer the first method over heat.

Butter or *samna* (clarified butter) is commonly used to cook these omelettes but oil will also do.

In Persia, the *eggah* is called a *kuku*, and plays a particularly impressive role in the cuisine. It is served on almost all occasions, as an appetizer, a first course or a side dish.

Most of the omelettes in the chapter on egg dishes can be turned into small fritters (tiny *eggahs*) by dropping the egg mixture by the tablespoon into a little hot oil in a frying pan and turning them over to brown on the other side. They are usually as good hot as they are cold and make tasty party finger foods.

Eggah bi Eish wa Kousa
Bread and Courgette Eggah

250 g (8 oz) courgettes	6 eggs
Salt	3 slices bread, crusts removed,
1 medium-sized onion, finely	soaked in a little milk
chopped	3 tablespoons chopped parsley
2 tablespoons butter	Black pepper

Wash the courgettes and cut them into ½-cm- (¼-inch-) thick slices. Sprinkle with salt and allow the water to drain off in a colander for about ½ hour. Pat dry with a clean cloth or kitchen paper.

Fry the chopped onion in hot butter until soft and just golden. Add the courgette slices, and sauté until soft and lightly coloured all over.

Beat the eggs. Add the soaked bread, squeezed dry, crumbling it in your hand. Then add the onion and courgettes, and the chopped parsley, and season lightly with salt and pepper. Mix well.

Pour the mixture on to sizzling butter in a frying pan and cook gently over very low heat until the eggs are set, about 20 minutes. Dry and brown the top lightly under a hot grill; or invert the omelette on to a plate of the same size and carefully slip it back into the frying pan for a few minutes longer.

If you wish to bake this *eggah*, pour the mixture into a buttered ovenproof dish and cook in a preheated slow oven (160°C/325°F/ Mark 3) for 45 to 60 minutes, or until well done. Cover the dish for the first 30 minutes, then remove it to allow the omelette to brown for the final 10 to 15 minutes.

Serve as a main dish with salads and yoghourt.

Eggah bi Ful Akhdar
Fresh Broad Bean Eggah

375 g (12 oz) fresh or frozen broad
    beans
6 eggs

Salt and black pepper
Butter
2 tablespoons chopped parsley

Boil the beans until they are tender, and drain them thoroughly. Beat the eggs and add the cooked beans. Mix well and season to taste with salt and pepper. Cook as above, in a frying pan or in the oven.

Turn out on to a heated serving dish and sprinkle with chopped parsley. Serve cut in wedges like a cake.

Eggah bi Betingan
Aubergine Eggah

2 aubergines
Salt
1 onion, finely chopped
Oil

1–2 cloves garlic, crushed
6 eggs
Black pepper

Wash the aubergines and cube them. Sprinkle them with salt and leave in a colander for about 1 hour for their bitter juices to drain off. Squeeze, wash and dry them lightly.

Fry the chopped onion in a little oil until soft and yellow. Add the crushed garlic. When it begins to colour and smells sweet, add the aubergines. Sauté with the garlic until cooked and gently coloured all over. Then add the eggs, lightly beaten and seasoned with salt and pepper, and stir well. Cook over very low heat until the eggs are set, about 20 minutes. Dry and brown the top of the omelette under the grill, or turn it over on to a plate and slip it back into the frying pan to cook the underside.

≈ It is good to add a small tin of peeled tomatoes to the aubergines once these are browned and cook for 10 minutes longer.

Eggah bi Korrat
Leek Eggah

750 g (1½ lb) leeks
Butter
½ teaspoon sugar

Juice of ½ lemon
Salt and black pepper
6 eggs

Wash the leeks, trimming off the roots and removing the outer leaves. Cut off the tough tops of the leaves and wash the leeks again carefully. Cut into thinnish slices. Sauté in a little butter, then season with the sugar, lemon juice, and salt and pepper to taste. Let the leeks stew in their own juices until soft and lightly coloured.

Alternatively, the leeks can be washed and trimmed as above, then boiled in salted water until just soft, drained and chopped.

Beat the eggs lightly in a large bowl. Add the leek mixture, mix again and adjust seasoning. Cook as usual, in a frying pan or in the oven, and serve cut in slices.

Eggah bi Sabaneh
Spinach Eggah

500 g (1 lb) fresh spinach or 250 g (8 oz) frozen leaf spinach
6 eggs

Salt and black pepper
Pinch of nutmeg
Butter

Wash spinach thoroughly, if fresh. Stew it in its own juice until tender. Drain well and chop. If you are using frozen spinach, allow to de-frost, then drain it thoroughly and simmer in its own juice until tender.

Beat the eggs and add the chopped spinach. Mix well, and season with salt, pepper and nutmeg. Cook as usual, in a frying pan or in the oven.

Turn out on to a heated serving dish, and serve cut in slices like a cake. Accompany with yoghourt and a salad if serving it as a main dish.

Tiny Courgette Eggahs

This makes good finger food.

1 onion, grated
Oil for frying
1 clove garlic, crushed
6 small courgettes
5 eggs

A small bunch of parsley, finely chopped
Salt and pepper
Pinch of nutmeg or allspice

Fry the onion in 2 tablespoons oil until golden, add the garlic and fry until the aroma rises. Wash and trim the courgettes and boil in salted water. Drain and mash to a pulp. Beat the eggs lightly and mix with all the ingredients. Drop by the tablespoon in a little hot oil in a frying pan and turn over to brown the other side. Serve hot or cold.

Tiny Herb Eggahs

Perfect for a buffet party – this makes more than 30.

6 eggs
1 large mild onion, or 6 spring onions, finely chopped
A good bunch of parsley or coriander, finely chopped

A few sprigs of fresh mint, finely chopped, or 2 tablespoons dried mint
Salt and pepper
Oil for frying

Lightly beat the eggs until they are just blended and stir in the rest of the ingredients. Pour a spoonful at a time into hot oil (you can have a few in the frying pan at the same time). Turn as soon as the bottom has set firmly and brown the other side. They can be reheated in the oven before serving on a large platter, or you can eat them cold.

Eggah bi Lahma
Meat Eggah

1 large potato (optional)
1 large onion, chopped
Oil
500 g (1 lb) lean minced beef
Salt and pepper to taste

½ teaspoon allspice
1 teaspoon cumin
3 tablespoons finely chopped parsley
6 eggs

Peel the potato and chop or grate it coarsely.

Fry the onion in 2 tablespoons oil until it is golden. Add the minced meat, crush and stir it until it changes colour. Add the salt and pepper, spices and parsley and remove from the fire.

Beat the eggs lightly with a fork in a bowl. Add the fried meat and onion, draining off any fat through a sieve. Add the grated potato (if used) and beat well. Taste and add salt and pepper and spices if necessary.

Heat 2 tablespoons oil in the cleaned frying pan, turning to cover the bottom well. Pour in the egg mixture. Reduce the heat as low as possible and cover the pan with a lid. Cook for about 20 minutes until the eggs have set and only the top is still runny. Place a plate over the pan, invert the omelette on to it and slip it back carefully into the pan to cook and brown the other side.

Alternatively, put the frying pan under a hot grill to set and brown the top of the omelette. Turn out on a plate. Serve hot or cold, cut into wedges like a cake.

≈ You may use a boiled and mashed potato instead, or have no potato.

Eggah bi Ferakh wa Rishta
Chicken and Noodle Eggah

This magnificent *eggah* will do equally well as a first course or as a main dish. The cardamom gives a delicate and distinctively Arab flavour.

375 g (12 oz) chicken, cooked and boned
375–500 g (¾–1 lb) tagliatelle or flat noodles
Chicken stock, for cooking tagliatelle

4 eggs
2–3 cardamom pods, cracked
Salt and black pepper
Butter
2 tablespoons chopped parsley

Cut the cooked chicken into small pieces. Boil the tagliatelle or flat noodles in stock until just soft but not overdone. Use chicken stock left over from cooking the chicken, or one made by boiling the chicken bones for some time. A commercial stock cube will also do, though not as well.

Drain the noodles in a colander, leaving behind any which have stuck to the pan.

Beat the eggs in a large bowl. Add the chicken, noodles, cardamom pods, and salt and pepper to taste, and mix well. The eggs will act more as a binding medium than as the main feature.

Heat a little butter in a large frying pan. Add the egg mixture and cook over very low heat for about ½ hour, or until quite set. Dry and brown the top under a hot grill. Unmould on to a heated serving dish, decorate with chopped parsley and serve.

Ojja bil Mergaz
Tunisian Eggah with Sausages

3–4 tablespoons olive oil
4 medium potatoes, cubed or diced
1–2 tablespoons tomato concentrate
1 teaspoon–1 tablespoon harissa

3–4 cloves garlic
2 teaspoons crushed caraway seed
2 teaspoons paprika
6 small, spicy sausages, sliced
6 eggs
Salt

Heat the olive oil in a large thick frying pan. Add the potatoes and sauté lightly. Add tomato concentrate, *harissa* diluted in a little water, the garlic and caraway seed, and the paprika. Pour in just enough water to cover and cook over low heat for about ¾ hour. Add sausages and cook for a further 15 minutes.

Beat the eggs and pour them into the pan gradually, stirring constantly, until they set to a firm but creamy consistency. Season to taste with salt and serve immediately.

Eggah bi Mokh
Eggah with Brains

2 sets calf's brains or 4 sets lamb's brains
Vinegar
Salt

6 eggs
Black pepper
2 tablespoons butter

Soak the brains for about 1 hour in water to which you have added a tablespoon of vinegar. Remove the membranes under running water. Throw the brains into boiling salted water acidulated with a teaspoon of vinegar, and simmer for about 10 minutes, until cooked. Cut into slices.

Beat the eggs, and season to taste with salt and pepper. Take two frying pans and heat a tablespoon of butter in each. Pour half of the egg mixture into each pan and drop the sliced brains on top, spreading them evenly over the surface and letting them sink in. Cook over gentle heat until the eggs are just set, about 20 minutes. Then finish the cooking under a hot grill; or, as usual, invert each *eggah* on to a plate, slip it back into its frying pan, and cook for a few minutes longer.

Kukuye Sabsi

The Persian *eggah*-type omelettes called *kuku* are generally baked in the oven. *Kukuye sabsi* is particularly Persian in flavour and texture. It is made with fresh green herbs and green vegetables, and sometimes with chopped walnuts and raisins.

This is a traditional Iranian New Year's Day dish. Its greenness is believed to be a symbol of fruitfulness in the coming year, bringing prosperity and happiness.

Any favoured herbs may be used in addition to the usual parsley, spring onions, spinach and leeks. (One may use either or both of the last two.) Dill, chervil, tarragon, chives and fresh coriander are others. A few chopped walnuts may be included to add to the quality of the texture and flavour.

2 leeks
120 g (4 oz) spinach
4–5 spring onions
6–8 eggs
2–3 tablespoons chopped parsley
3 tablespoons mixed chopped
    fresh herbs

2 tablespoons walnuts, chopped
    (optional)
2 tablespoons raisins (optional)
Salt and black pepper
2 tablespoons softened butter

Wash the vegetables, dry them and chop them very finely. Beat the eggs in a large bowl, add the chopped vegetables, parsley and mixed herbs, and a few chopped walnuts or raisins if liked. Season to taste with salt and pepper, and mix well.

Butter an ovenproof dish and pour in the egg mixture. Bake in a slow oven (160°C/325°F/Mark 3) for 45 minutes, covering the dish for the first 30 minutes. The vegetables should be tender and the eggs set, with a golden crust on top. Alternatively, cook the *kuku* in a large frying pan like an *eggah*. When the eggs have almost set, brown the *kuku* under a hot grill or turn out on a plate and slip back into the pan to colour the underside.

Serve hot or cold as an appetizer or side dish, accompanied by yoghourt.

Kuku Sibzamini
Persian Potato Omelette

2 medium-sized potatoes	Salt and black pepper
2 tablespoons butter	2 tablespoons finely chopped
6 eggs	parsley
4–5 spring onions, chopped, or	
1 bunch chives, chopped	

Peel and boil the potatoes, and mash them to a smooth purée. Mix with about 2 tablespoons butter. Beat the eggs and add them to the potato purée gradually, beating all the time to achieve a smooth texture. Add onions or chives, and season to taste with salt and pepper.

Pour into a buttered baking dish and bake in a slow oven (160°C/325°F/Mark 3) for about ¾ hour, or until set and coloured. Alternatively, pour over hot butter in a large frying pan and cook over very low heat until the eggs have almost set, about 20 minutes. Then turn out on to a large plate and slip back into the pan to dry and colour the underside.

Turn out on to a heated serving dish, garnish with finely chopped parsley and serve cut in slices like a cake.

≈ Another Middle Eastern potato omelette is made with thinly sliced potatoes, onions and tomatoes. These ingredients are first sautéed in butter for 15 to 20 minutes. The beaten eggs are then poured over them and cooked over very low heat, until they have set.

Omelettes

A new type of omelette, inspired by the French example, has recently been adopted by many in the Middle East. It is nevertheless Middle Eastern in flavour, adapted to local taste by the addition of favourite regional fillings.

Make a plain French omelette, using not more than 4 eggs. Beat the eggs lightly in a bowl, and season only very mildly, to allow for the seasoning of the filling. Heat the frying pan. Add a tablespoon of butter and shake the pan to allow it to run all over the base. When it starts to sizzle, but before it has had a chance to brown, pour in the eggs, stir a little, and when they start to set on the bottom, lift the edge up with a fork and tip the pan to allow the liquid from the top to run underneath. As soon as the eggs are no longer liquid but still very moist on top remove the pan from the heat. Pour the prepared filling in a line across the centre (only a little is required so as not to unbalance the omelette) and fold in three with a palette knife or fork. Slip the folded omelette on to a heated serving dish and garnish with a little of the filling.

The filling must always be prepared in advance.

Fillings for a 4-egg Omelette

1. Chicken Livers

Chop 3 chicken livers finely, and cook gently in a little butter for 2 or 3 minutes. Season to taste with salt, black pepper and a pinch of ground cinnamon.

2. Onions and Tomatoes

Soften 2 tablespoons finely chopped onion in a little butter. Add ½ clove crushed garlic. When it is golden, add 2 skinned, chopped tomatoes. Season to taste with salt and black pepper, and cook gently until the tomatoes are almost reduced to a pulp.

3. Spinach

Frozen spinach, either chopped or puréed, will do. De-frost 60 g (2 oz) spinach and simmer it with a small knob of butter. Season with salt and black pepper. If you like, you can add a pinch of ground coriander fried in a little oil with ½ clove crushed garlic.

Fish

◆━━◆▸◆◂◆━━◆

Samak

☐ 'A remedy for a man who is "tied" by his enemies, and made impotent. He must go to a quack, who will say: "There is something written against you that has been eaten by a fish in the sea. I can release you from your trouble by obtaining the fish for a fee!" The quack finds a fish, writes a curse, perhaps on a piece of bread, puts it in the mouth of the fish and delivers it to the patient. The latter will be cured.'*

* From an ancient book of Egyptian folk medicine.

In some parts of the Middle East fish is still believed to have magical properties. Tunisians in particular believe it to be highly beneficial. The day after their wedding, couples are encouraged to step over a large fish as an assurance of happiness and a protection from evil. Today, the shape of a fish has become a symbol. Embroidered on material and carved in metal, it is believed to ward off the evil eye. In Egypt, one felt compelled to eat fish for the first meal in a new home. In Persia, fish is eaten on New Year's Eve to cleanse the people from evil, while Jews display the head alone in the centre of the New Year table in the hope that Jews will always be at the 'head'.

The medieval cookery manual of al-Baghdadi gives a few recipes for fish, both fresh and salted, but without specifying any varieties. Even today, recipes for fish can often be applied to any of a number of varieties. When asking which fish should be used for *cousbareia*, *sayyadiah* or *blehat samak*, I was inevitably told 'any fish you like' or 'any fish will do'. Nevertheless, certain fish are more suitable for a particular dish, if only because of their size and oiliness. Their distinctive flavours and affinities also make them natural favourites for certain methods of preparation; but it is always possible to substitute a similar one if a particular kind is unobtainable.

These recipes were, of course, originally evolved for fish from the Mediterranean and neighbouring seas. Most popular are the red mullet, called *barbunya* by the Turks and *Sultan Ibrahim* by the Arabs; the grey mullet; a fish called *morgan* or *arous*, which is the French *daurade*, and whose closest English equivalent is the sea bream; the sea bass, called *loukoz*; and the sole, called *samak Moussa* after Moses (because of its thinness it is said to have been cut in half when Moses separated the Red Sea). Turbot, cod, sardines, tuna, John Dory, gurnard and swordfish abound in the seas of the region.

Of the freshwater fish, a type of trout called *chaboute* is fished in the Tigris and Euphrates rivers. It is usually smoked over a fire to make *masgouf*, a popular Iraqi speciality. Carp is a Turkish freshwater favourite, and shad is a popular fish found in the rivers of North Africa. However, fish from the Nile are considered hardly fit to eat as they are impregnated with the strong taste and smell of the Nile mud.

Ever since ancient times, salted and dried fish has been known in all parts of the Middle East. This was originally done to preserve the fish so that it could be stored and taken on long journeys, or sent to regions far away from the coast. Today, it is prepared in this way primarily because people like it so much. Methods vary in detail but are basically the same. The fish is washed and cleaned and split open. It is salted inside and out and left to dry in the hot sun, or else it is buried in the hot sand or mud for a few days to 'mature'. The result is called *fessih*.

Chermoula
A Moroccan Marinade for Fish

Every town, even every family, has a special combination for this marinade in which every type of fish, big or small, whole, filleted or cut in chunks, is left to absorb the flavours. Different herbs are used – parsley instead of coriander, spices in varying proportions, onion instead of garlic – so you may feel free to use the following list of ingredients as a guide and suit your taste.

It is marvellous and I strongly recommend it, but not for a fish with a delicate flavour.

The following measures make a rather large quantity but it keeps well for several days if covered by a thin layer of oil.

1 large bunch fresh coriander, very finely chopped	1 tablespoon paprika
1 large bunch parsley, very finely chopped	1 very good pinch cayenne
6 large cloves garlic, crushed	Juice of 1 or 2 lemons, or 150 ml (¼ pint) vinegar
1 tablespoon cumin	300 ml (½ pint) olive or other oil
1 teaspoon coriander	

Beat all the ingredients well together. Scale, gut and clean the fish if necessary and marinate for at least an hour (you may leave it overnight). If the fish is large, put some of the marinade inside as well.

For Grilled Fish (see page 205)

Brush the marinade on as the fish is on the grill. Serve with lemon wedges.

For Fried Fish (see page 208)

Roll the marinated fish in flour, fry in clarified butter (page 64) or in deep hot oil until browned. Serve with lemon wedges.

For a Baked Fish (see page 216)

Put it in the oven in an earthenware dish, pour the marinade over it and bake slowly, covered with a lid or foil (they like it a little overcooked in Morocco).

≈ You may add a variety of vegetables, one or two or more at a time such as sliced or whole tomatoes, turnips or carrots, celery or boiled fresh broad beans and chopped, preserved lemon (page 63).
≈ It is also very good to cook the fish with olives. Use 250 g (8 oz) of green ones. Boil them in plenty of water for 5 to 10 minutes to remove the bitterness, drain and throw them over the fish or stuff the fish with them.
≈ You may serve any remaining *chermoula* as a sauce. Heat it up if the fish is hot but do not boil as this would cause the loss of the fresh taste of the herbs.

Samak Meshwi
Charcoal-grilled Fish

One of the most excellent ways of eating fish is grilled over a charcoal fire. Swordfish is popular *alla shish* or on skewers but other firm fish can also be used. The fish is cubed, marinated in oil, lemon juice, salt and pepper, and threaded on to skewers together with slices of onion and tomato. It is then grilled over charcoal with frequent turning and basting with the marinade.

All types of fish, small, medium and large, can be cooked over a fire. Large ones are usually sliced or filleted or fixed whole to the spit with a thin wire, and turned and basted continuously. For small or flat fish, fillets and slices, it is useful to have a double grill in which the two parts fold over each other, securing the fish in between so that it can be turned without breaking its flesh or skin. The grill must be well oiled and preferably hot before the fish is placed on it, to prevent it from sticking. It should be placed about 5 cm (2 inches) from the heat.

Washed, cleaned and scaled fish need only be sprinkled with salt and brushed with oil before grilling, but marinating enhances the flavour considerably. Marinades vary. The basic mixture includes oil and lemon or vinegar (preferably lemon), well mixed and seasoned with salt and pepper. Sometimes crushed chopped onions (pieces of onion squeezed in a garlic press to extract juice) and bay leaves are added, together with favourite herbs. Marjoram, oregano, basil, tarragon, rosemary, fennel, thyme and sage perfume the fish beautifully. The fish can also be slit open and stuffed with herbs for a more penetrating flavour. The skin should be slit in a few places to prevent it from breaking during grilling. Judge from the thickness of the fish how near it should be to the heat so that it does not dry out too quickly. Vary the distance from the fire if you like (and if possible) to achieve a soft, juicy interior and a crisp, brown skin.

Most of the fish available in Britain can be treated in this manner. Trout, sole, salmon, plaice, red and grey mullet, sea bream and sea bass, herring and mackerel are all very suitable. Sole should be skinned before grilling. Red mullet is particularly good grilled wrapped in silver foil together with its seasoning. Turks have a marvellous way of grilling sardines wrapped in vine leaves. Try this with other fish, but be careful not to let the leaves burn.

Finally, when it is not possible to grill over charcoal, an electric or gas grill will also gives excellent results, but make sure in this case, too, that the grid is well oiled.

Samak Masgūf

This could be called the Iraqi national dish. The recipe is from *Recipes from Baghdad* (see page 527).

In the summer when the moon is full the banks of the river Tigris are dotted with the flames of brushwood fires against which are silhouetted the roasting fish.

When the heat of the day is over, picnic parties set out in high-powered boats or *ballams* with a pile of brushwood in the bow, a good supply of bread, fruit and chilled beverages and the fish which are towed behind by strings tied through the gills. The *ballamchis* or boatmen are expert at preparing the fish. When it is finally lifted from the embers and laid before one, the lateness of the hour and the innumerable biting insects are forgotten and, with a round of Arab bread for a plate and fingers instead of forks, one falls to it with zest.

1 *shabbūt* 2 feet in length or 1
   large freshwater fish
A large bundle of dry brushwood
   (fine twigs without leaves)
2 or 3 pointed stakes 30–38 cm
   (12–15 inches) long
3 onions

9 tomatoes
2 tablespoons Worcester sauce
1–3 tablespoons curry powder
2 tablespoons butter
½ glass water
Salt and pepper

Cut the fish down the back at the side of the backbone, gut it and wipe with a clean cloth. Rub with salt.

Make a fire about 2 feet in diameter. Insert 2 or 3 sharp pointed stakes into the ground at about 35 cm (14 inches) from the fire and slightly curved in order to be equidistant from it. Hold the fish with the cut surface towards the fire and force it on to the pointed ends of the sticks so that they penetrate the skin and the fish hangs in front of the sticks with the cut surface towards the fire and the skin surface towards any breeze. It is advisable to make the fire in as sheltered a place as possible.

Make a second smaller fire. Chop the tomatoes roughly into a large frying pan. Add sliced onion, water and butter and cook for about five minutes. Add curry powder (1–3 tablespoons according to taste). Continue cooking for another 10 minutes.

By this time the fish should be fairly well cooked, the fire having been adjusted to provide continuous heat without burning or smoking it. Spread out the embers of the fire to about 5 cm (2 inches) in depth and allow them to become slightly black on top. Quickly remove the fish from the stakes and lay it skin side down on the embers. Leave for about 10 to 15 minutes till it is well cooked. Meanwhile add the Worcester sauce to the tomato mixture and heat to scalding. Spread this over the surface of the fish after adding any further seasoning if desired. Prick here and there with a pointed stick or fork to allow the sauce to penetrate and serve on a tray or large dish.

Masqūf may be served without the sauce. It may be served with the tomato mixture but without the Worcester sauce or it may be done in the oven, the fish first being rubbed generously inside and out with butter, but the flavour is never so good.

Samak Maqli
Fried Fish

A popular way of preparing fish in the Middle East is to deep-fry them and serve them accompanied by a sauce or simply with lemon wedges.

Wash, clean and scale the fish if necessary. Leave small fish whole (very small fish like whitebait do not need gutting) but cut larger ones into thick slices. Pat dry with a cloth or kitchen paper and dredge with flour.

Fry in olive oil if possible (nut oil will also do) deep enough to cover the fish entirely. The oil must be very hot. Do not put too many pieces of fish in at a time, or the temperature will drop considerably and the fish will be soggy instead of crisp. As soon as the fish is in, turn the heat up to maximum for a short time to make up for the heat lost.

The pieces of fish take from 5 to 10 minutes' frying. Shake the pan occasionally to prevent them from sticking. Drain, sprinkle with salt, and garnish with chopped parsley and lemon wedges. Serve accompanied by one of the sauces for fried fish below, and a salad such as *baba ghanoush* (page 84) or thinly sliced aubergines or courgettes deep-fried until crisp (page 353).

≈ Medium fish or slices are often cooked in *samna* (clarified butter). Season and dip in flour. Fry on both sides till the flesh begins to flake. Garnish with chopped parsley and serve with lemon wedges and any of the sauces given.

Fried Fish with Cousbareia Sauce

This is an Egyptian regional speciality. Any fish that can be fried will do (small fish left whole, larger ones thickly sliced). Red mullet is often prepared in this way.

A fish weighing about 1 kg (2 lb)
Olive oil for deep-frying
2 onions, thinly sliced
2 tablespoons oil
250 g (8 oz) tomatoes, sliced

120 g (4 oz) hazelnuts, chopped
60 g (2 oz) pine nuts
2–3 tablespoons finely chopped parsley
Salt and black pepper

Fry the fish as directed in the preceding recipe.

In a separate deep frying pan or sauté dish, fry the onions in oil until soft and just golden. Add the hazelnuts and pine nuts, and fry for only 2 minutes longer. Add the tomatoes and sauté gently until soft. Add just enough water to cover, stir in parsley, and season to taste with salt and pepper. Simmer for a few minutes longer.

Lower the pieces of fried fish in carefully and simmer again for about 15 minutes. Alternatively, put the pieces of fish in an oven-proof dish, cover with the sauce and bake for 15 minutes in a moderately hot oven (190°C/375°F/Mark 5).

Beid bi Lamoun (Avgolemono Sauce) for Fried Fish

450 ml (¾ pint) fish stock (see method)	1 tablespoon cornflour or flour
	2–3 egg yolks
Salt and black pepper	Juice of 1 lemon, or more

Strain the fish stock (made by boiling the discarded heads and tails of the fish with perhaps a celery stalk and a carrot) into a thick-bottomed pan. Season to taste with salt and pepper. Mix the cornflour or flour (I much prefer the former) with a little cold water, and introduce the paste gradually into the hot stock, mixing vigorously to avoid lumps. Cook gently, stirring constantly, until the sauce thickens and no longer tastes floury, about 15 to 20 minutes.

Beat the egg yolks in a bowl. Add the lemon juice and stir well. Add a little of the hot sauce, beating well, then return the mixture to the pan with the sauce gradually, stirring with a wooden spoon over low heat until the sauce thickens to a smooth, custard-like consistency. Do not let it come to the boil, or it will curdle. If you use cornflour, the result will be more jelly-like and translucent.

Serve hot or cold, poured over the fish or in a separate bowl. This sauce is also delicious with poached or baked fish.

Khall wa-Kardal

A medieval almond and vinegar sauce from al-Baghdadi which makes an excellent accompaniment to fried fish. Echoes of this sauce are found in the modern fish *tarator* (page 218) and Turkish walnut *tarator* sauce (page 112).

'Take sweet almonds, peel, and chop up fine: then moisten with sour vinegar until making a thin paste. Grind mustard fine, and mix in as required . . .'

Sardines in the Algerian Manner

1 kg (2 lb) fresh sardines	Salt
3 teaspoons ground cumin	2 eggs, beaten
2–3 cloves garlic, crushed	Flour or fine dry breadcrumbs
½ teaspoon cayenne pepper	Oil for deep-frying

Wash the sardines and remove heads and tails. Slit them open down one side only, and remove their backbones. Dip the sardines, open side down, in a mixture of ground cumin, garlic, cayenne pepper and salt. Stick the open sardines together in pairs, trapping the seasonings between them.

Dip the pairs in beaten egg, then in flour or breadcrumbs. Deep-fry in hot oil, being very careful not to allow the pairs to separate.

I suppose a good alternative method would be simply to deep-fry the fish individually and not in pairs after they have been slit down one side, relieved of their back bones, flattened out and dipped in seasonings, then closed again.

You can try this recipe with other small fish available in Britain, such as sprats, smelts or pilchards. The dish also makes an excellent *mezze*.

≈ A Moroccan version of this has a stuffing of mashed potatoes trapped between two sardines which have been split open and flattened out and had their spines removed.

Mash 500 g (1 lb) of potatoes and mix with 1 bunch of parsley and 1 of fresh coriander, both finely chopped, 3 beaten eggs and season to taste with salt and pepper, 1 teaspoon cumin or 1 teaspoon cinnamon if you like, 1 tablespoon paprika and a pinch of cayenne. Take a lump the size of a small egg. Roll it into a long oblong shape and press between two sardines. Dip in flour and deep fry.

Small Red Mullet with Garlic

A street vendor in Cairo used to sell these small red fish garnished with parsley and lemon wedges and wrapped in newspaper, to be eaten on the spot or carried home.

They were rubbed with crushed garlic, salt and pepper, stuffed with finely chopped parsley mixed with a little crushed garlic, then lightly floured and deep-fried in very hot oil.

Tarator bi Tahina
Tahina Sauce for Fish

The most popular Arab sauce for fish is one made with tahina. It is used as an alternative to the more expensive *tarator* (pages 217–18), made with pine nuts. You can serve it with fried and grilled fish as well as with a cold fish.

300 ml (½ pint) tahina
150 ml (¼ pint) lemon juice, or more

50–90 ml (2–3 fl oz) water
Salt
2 cloves garlic, crushed

Beat the lemon juice and then the water into the tahina. It will stiffen at first and then become smooth. Add only enough water for a light cream. Season to taste with salt and beat in the garlic.

Pour over cold fish or serve in a separate bowl.

Qras Samak
Fish Cake with Burghul

This type of *kibbeh* (page 277) is a delightful way of making fish go a long way.

250 g (8 oz) fine or medium burghul (cracked wheat)
500 g (1 lb) raw minced fish, such as cod, haddock or halibut
1 small onion, grated or finely chopped

Juice of ½ lemon
Salt and pepper
1 good bunch fresh coriander or parsley, finely chopped

Wash the burghul and let it soak in cold water for 15 minutes, then drain it. Either pound all the ingredients to a soft paste in a mortar or knead vigorously with your hands. A food processor makes the operation of chopping, mincing and reducing everything to a dough-like paste very quick and simple. Take smallish lumps, shape into flat cakes and fry in hot oil, turning over once until lightly browned on both sides.

Serve hot or cold with salad and tahina (page 80).

≈ You may use the fish paste in a different way. Spread it in a flat oven dish or tray on a bed of lightly fried chopped onion. Flatten well and cut diagonally into lozenge shapes. Sprinkle with a tablespoon or two of melted butter or oil and bake in a moderately hot oven (180°C/350°F/Mark 4) for about 20 minutes. Allow to cool a little before separating the pieces.

Blehat Samak 1
Fish Sticks 1

These make an excellent cold buffet dish or hors d'œuvre. They are also good served hot in a tomato sauce, accompanied by rice.

A few fish heads, tails and bones	2 cloves garlic
500 g (1 lb) fish: cod, haddock, halibut, sea bream, sea bass, or a mixture of any of these	2 tablespoons finely chopped parsley
2 small onions	1 teaspoon ground coriander
2 bay leaves	1 teaspoon ground cumin
1 stalk celery	1 egg
Salt and black pepper	Flour
180 g (6 oz) white bread or 120 g (4 oz) dry white breadcrumbs	Butter or oil
	Juice of ½ lemon, or more
	Chopped parsley, to decorate

Ask the fishmonger to give you some heads, tails and bones to make a stock.

Skin, bone and mince the fish. Alternatively, boil whole pieces of fish until soft and mash them to a paste with a fork.

Boil the fish trimmings in about 1 litre (1¾ pints) water with a whole onion, the bay leaves, celery, and salt and pepper to taste. Simmer gently for about ½ hour; strain and reserve.

Slice the bread and remove the crusts. Soak in water and squeeze dry. Or if using dry breadcrumbs, moisten them with water. Crush the garlic cloves with a little salt. Chop the remaining onion finely. Put all these in a large bowl with the minced (or mashed cooked) fish. Add the finely chopped parsley, coriander, cumin and egg, and salt and pepper to taste. Mix and knead thoroughly by hand. Take walnut-sized lumps of the mixture and roll them into small finger shapes. Roll them in flour. Fry them in butter or deep-fry in oil until golden brown. Drain thoroughly; arrange in a large pan.

Pour in enough of the prepared fish stock to cover. Add lemon juice, bring to the boil and simmer gently for 20 minutes. Turn the fish into a large serving dish and cover with the sauce. Allow to cool. The sauce will become a jelly when cold. Serve sprinkled with parsley.

≈ Some people like to colour the *blehat* yellow by adding ½ teaspoon turmeric to the stock.

≈ A variation to this dish is to poach the fingers in a tomato sauce. Fry 1 onion, finely chopped, in a little oil. When it is golden brown, add a small tin of tomato concentrate diluted with about 300 ml (½ pint) water. Throw in a bay leaf and season to taste with salt and pepper. Bring to the boil and simmer for 20 minutes. Add the fish sticks, previously fried in butter or oil as above, and simmer for a further 20 minutes. Serve cold sprinkled with a little chopped parsley.

≈ In a speciality of Jedda in Saudi Arabia called *kabab samak*, the fish sticks are cooked in an onion sauce: fry 2 or 3 chopped onions until they are very dark, add a little water and blend to a cream in a liquidizer.

Blehat Samak 2
Fish Sticks 2

There are innumerable versions of this popular fish dish varying in flavouring and consistency. This one is to Egyptian tastes.

1 kg (2 lb) fish – cod or haddock or a mixture of your choice	2 cloves garlic, crushed
4 medium slices wholemeal bread, crusts removed	2 teaspoons cumin
4 medium eggs	Salt and pepper
	Oil for frying

Poach the fish for 5 minutes, drain, remove any skin or bones and flake with a fork. Soak the bread in water, then squeeze dry and crumble. Combine all the ingredients in a large bowl. Mix well and knead with your hands to a smooth paste, then shape into 2½-cm (1-inch) balls.

Sauté in hot oil until brown, then drain on absorbent paper. You can use a food processor instead of kneading but then the paste becomes too soft to shape and you will have to drop it in the oil by the tablespoon.

Serve hot or cold.

≈ You may add 1 teaspoon ground coriander, a touch of ginger and cayenne pepper, as well as a bunch of chopped parsley or coriander.

Fish in Olive Oil (served cold)

A Turkish speciality, popular throughout most of the Middle East. This makes a good first course or cold buffet dish. Sliced swordfish is generally used, but most fish available in Britain are also excellent cooked in this manner.

1 kg (2 lb) fish: whole red mullet or mackerel, or a piece of a larger fish, sliced
Olive oil
2 large onions, sliced
2 green peppers, seeded and sliced
2 cloves garlic, crushed

500 g (1 lb) tomatoes, skinned and sliced, or a 400-g (14-oz) tin skinned tomatoes, drained and sliced
A bunch of parsley, finely chopped
1 tablespoon tomato concentrate
Salt and black pepper
About a dozen green or black olives, stoned (optional)

Scale and clean the fish. Fry it gently in a few tablespoons olive oil until lightly coloured. Remove to a plate and reserve.

Fry the onions in the same oil until soft and golden. Add the sliced green peppers and fry until soft and sweet. Add the crushed garlic and fry for only about a minute more. Finally add the tomatoes, chopped parsley, and tomato concentrate diluted in about a small teacup of water. Season to taste with salt and pepper, stir well, bring to the boil and simmer for 10 minutes.

Lay the fish in the sauce carefully, making sure that the pieces are completely covered, and cook for a further 10 to 15 minutes until done, adding a little water if necessary. A few olives that have been blanched in boiling water to remove excess salt can also be added to the dish towards the end of the cooking.

Arrange the fish in a serving dish and pour the sauce over it. Serve cold.

Fish Plaki

– or *poisson à la grecque*, as we used to call it in Egypt. Most fish can be cooked in this way: large fish such as grey mullet, sea bream, sea bass and John Dory, as well as halibut, cod or haddock.

1 kg (2 lb) fish, cut into thickish slices
Olive oil
2 large onions, sliced
2–3 cloves garlic

500 g (1 lb) tomatoes, skinned and quartered, or a 400-g (14-oz) tin peeled tomatoes
Juice of ½ lemon
A bunch of parsley, finely chopped
Salt and black pepper

Fry the fish slices quickly in olive oil in a frying pan until they are a pale golden brown colour. Transfer to an ovenproof baking dish.

Fry sliced onions and whole garlic cloves until soft and golden. Add the tomatoes, lemon juice and parsley, and season to taste with salt and pepper. Stir well and simmer for about 10 minutes. Dilute the sauce with a little water if too thick and pour it over the fish slices.

Bake in a slow oven (160°C/325°F/Mark 3) for about 20 minutes, or until the fish is opaque and easily pierced with a fork.

≈ The fish can also be left whole, in which case simply bake in a similar oven (160°C/325°F/Mark 3) for 30 to 45 minutes.

≈ The flavour of this dish can be made richer by adding a teaspoon of dried oregano (or *rigani*, the Greek variety) and a bay leaf or two to the sauce.

Boiled or Poached Fish

Put the fish, whole or cut into steaks, in cold salted water. Bring to the boil slowly and simmer gently until it is cooked and its flesh flakes easily with a fork, about 10 minutes per 500 g (1 lb) if whole. To avoid breaking a large fish when lifting it out of the pan, cook it wrapped tightly in a thin muslin cloth. Use a baking tin large enough to hold it comfortably.

Alternatively, poach the fish in a *court-bouillon* – a stock made by boiling 1 litre (1¾ pints) water with 150 ml (¼ pint) wine vinegar, a finely chopped onion, salt, a few peppercorns, a bay leaf, 3 table-spoons chopped parsley and the juice of ½ lemon. Boil for 10 minutes before adding the fish.

Serve the fish hot or cold, garnished with lemon wedges and accompanied by 'rice to accompany fish' (page 224) and a sauce: *avgolemono* sauce (page 209), one of the *tarator* sauces (pages 112 and 218) or the medieval *khall wa-kardal* (page 209).

Fish Baked in the Oven

Almost any fish can be baked in the oven, medium or large, whole or cut into thick slices, either in an open dish or wrapped in foil. Red mullet is a Middle Eastern favourite, but most other fish are treated in the same way.

Scale, clean and wash the fish. Rub it generously with salt, pepper and olive oil or *samna* (melted clarified butter – see page 64). The flavour of the fish can be enhanced by marinating for a few hours in a mixture of oil, lemon juice, onion juice (extracted by squeezing pieces of onion in a garlic press) and any favourite fresh herbs: bay leaves, oregano, marjoram, tarragon and basil give a pleasant perfume. For those who like it, crushed garlic may be added for a faint aroma.

A few incisions should be made in the skin of the fish to prevent it from curling and, particularly if the skin is tough, to allow the heat to penetrate better.

The cooking time depends not only on the weight of the fish but also on its shape and whether it is whole or in pieces. The fish should be tested for doneness after the minimum cooking time specified. If done, its flesh should flake easily with a fork and no longer be translucent. Bake a 1- to 1½-kg (2- to 3-lb) fish in a preheated slow oven (150°C/300°F/Mark 2) for 20 to 45 minutes, or until done, basting frequently with the oil.

≈ A rather better way, to my taste, is to bake the fish in foil. Place the seasoned or marinated and well-oiled fish on a large piece of oiled foil. Wrap up and seal the edges of the foil firmly. Bake in a rather warmer oven (160°C/325°F/Mark 3) and test for doneness after about 30 to 45 minutes.

The baked fish is often smothered in a sauce at the end of cooking or when it is half-done. It can also be served more simply, accompanied by a sauce which is handed separately or poured over the fish just before serving.

Tajin Samak bi Tahina
Fish Baked in Tahina Sauce

Olive oil
2 large onions, sliced
300 ml (½ pint) tahina
150 ml (¼ pint) lemon juice

150 ml (¼ pint) water
Salt
1 fish weighing between 1–2 kg
(2–4 lb)

Sauté the onions in olive oil until soft and slightly coloured. Beat lemon juice and enough water into the tahina to achieve a light cream sauce (it will stiffen at first before becoming smooth). Add salt to taste. Spread two thirds of the onions at the bottom of an oven dish, lay the fish on top and sprinkle with the remaining onions. Pour the sauce over the fish and bake at 160°C (325°F/Mark 3) for 30 to 45 minutes or until the flesh flakes easily.

Serve hot with rice or salads.

≈ Some people like to let the fish become a little crisp in the oven before pouring on the sauce.
≈ Instead of baking, you may sauté fillets or slices briefly in oil in a frying pan, add the sauce and continue to cook a few minutes.

Samak Tarator
Fish with Tarator Sauce

This is a great gala dish, particularly popular in Egypt, Syria and the Lebanon. It is usually served lavishly decorated in a variety of brilliant colours and traditional designs according to local taste. Today it is sometimes replaced on special occasions by the French *poisson à la mayonnaise*, or decorated in a more European manner.

Choose a large fish such as sea bass, bream or John Dory. Clean and wash it. Leave the head on, but remove the eyes. Rub all over with salt, pepper and olive oil, and bake in an oiled baking dish or wrapped in foil as described above.

Serve the fish cold on a large dish on a bed of parsley or lettuce. Decorate it with lemon slices, sliced green pickles, black olives, radishes, fried pine nuts or almonds, and pieces of pimento. Make an Oriental design, for example a criss-cross pattern.

Accompany with bowls of *tarator* sauce made as follows:

2 slices white bread, crusts
  removed

250 g (8 oz) pine nuts (ground
  almonds will do if these are
  unobtainable or too expensive)

1–2 cloves garlic, crushed with
  salt

Juice of 1–2 lemons, or more

Fish stock left over in baking dish
  or foil, or water

Soak the bread in water and squeeze it dry. Pound the pine nuts. Add the bread and pound them together. Add crushed garlic, lemon juice and enough fish stock or water to make a firm paste. Beat well and put through a sieve, or blend in an electric blender to a smooth creamy paste.

≈ A delightful version of this dish is boned fish *tarator*. Prepare the fish and bake it in foil. Allow to cool. Cut off the head and tail neatly and set aside.

Skin the body of the fish and bone the flesh. Season to taste with salt and pepper. Place the boned fish on a large serving dish, patting it back into its original shape. Place the head and tail at each end and mask the whole body of the fish with *tarator* sauce.

Serve decorated with whole pine nuts or almonds, lightly fried, pickles, olives, and whatever else you like.

This method of boning and reassembling the fish is particularly useful if dealing with a very large fish that does not fit into the oven. It can be cut into manageable pieces instead, and then baked in foil as usual.

Samak Harra
Hot Spicy Fish

This is a hot sauce for a whole fish such as bass or bream or any large white firm fish. It is good to bake the fish with the sauce, but you may prefer to serve the sauce separately as it is very strong and garlicky.

A fish weighing about 1½–2 kg
  (3–4 lb)

375 g (12 oz) walnuts, coarsely
  chopped

A bunch of coriander, finely
  chopped

7–10 cloves garlic, crushed (some
  put up to 15)

6 tablespoons olive oil

Juice of 2 or 3 lemons

Salt

1 teaspoon cinnamon

½–1 teaspoon cayenne or chilli (I
  find this too much)

Clean, wash and salt the fish and place in a baking dish. Mix well or blend the rest of the ingredients, adding a little water to achieve the consistency of a sauce. Put some inside the fish and pour the rest on top. Bake in a medium oven (180°C/350°F/Mark 4) for 30 to 40 minutes, until the fish is done.

Serve hot or cold.

≈ A sprinkling of *sumac* (page 63) or water in which it has soaked can replace the sharpness of the lemon.

≈ When pomegranates are about, scoop out the seeds and discard the pith from half a fruit and stir them into the sauce.

Fish with Onions and Raisins

A good recipe for sea bass or bream which will do well with other fish too.

A fish weighing 1–1½ kg (2–3 lb)
150 g (5 oz) onions, finely chopped
3–4 tablespoons oil (sunflower or olive)
Salt and pepper

250 g (8 oz) raisins or sultanas
1 teaspoon cinnamon
½ teaspoon ginger
Pinch of nutmeg
A bunch of parsley

Scale, gut and wash the fish. Slash the skin diagonally in the thicker parts. Soften the onions in 2 tablespoons of the oil with a little salt. Blanch and drain the raisins or sultanas. Rub the fish with the rest of the oil and the seasonings and spices and place it in an oven dish on top of the bunch of parsley. Cover it with a mixture of onions and raisins. Add a few tablespoons of water to the dish and bake in a preheated slow oven (160°C/325°F/Mark 3) for 30 to 45 minutes by which time the raisins and onions will have turned into a golden crust.

Uskumru Dolmasu
Stuffed Mackerel

A Turkish delicacy. A humble fish for a regal occasion. The skin of the fish is stuffed with its own flesh mixed with a rich filling. It is rolled in beaten egg, then in flour and breadcrumbs, and deep-fried in olive or nut oil. It is delicious eaten hot or cold as an entrée or as a main dish.

6 small mackerel
2 eggs, lightly beaten

Fine dry breadcrumbs
Oil

STUFFING

250 g (8 oz) onions, finely chopped
Olive oil
120 g (4 oz) shelled walnuts,
   ground or pounded
60 g (2 oz) shelled hazelnuts,
   ground or pounded
60 g (2 oz) seedless raisins

2 teaspoons mixed spices (a
   mixture of allspice, cinnamon,
   nutmeg, cloves and black
   pepper)
Salt
A bunch each of parsley and fresh
   dill or chervil, finely chopped

Clean the fish and cut off their heads. Snap the backbones off near the tail. Rub the skins to loosen them and to soften the flesh. Then, using your hands, rub and squeeze the fish, starting from the tail, forcing the flesh and bones out of the loosened skin as though emptying a tube of paste. This is quite easily done as the skin is very strong. Any tears in the skin can be mended by sewing them up with a needle and thread. Another good method of emptying the fish skins is to loosen them as above, then, holding the backbone firmly where it shows at the head, to pull the skin down, turning it inside out. Proceed as above. Remove the bones carefully and use the flesh for the stuffing.

Prepare the stuffing. Fry the onions until soft and golden in 2 tablespoons oil. Add the nuts, raisins, spices, and salt to taste, and mix well. Add the boned fish and fry for 5 minutes longer. Stir in the chopped parsley and dill or chervil, and remove from the heat.

Fill the fish skins tightly with this mixture, closing the openings by sewing them up carefully. Dip in beaten egg and then in breadcrumbs. Fry in hot oil until golden brown and cooked through. Serve hot or cold.

Sayyadiah
Fish with Rice

A popular Arab dish. Sea bass, bream, turbot, haddock, cod or halibut can be used.

1 kg (2 lb) fish (see above)
Oil
4–5 large onions, finely chopped
Salt

1 teaspoon ground cumin or
   allspice
500 g (1 lb) long-grain rice,
   washed (weight uncooked)
Juice of ½–1 lemon

Wash the fish and cut it into pieces. Heat 2 or 3 tablespoons oil in a large saucepan, and fry the onions gently until soft and transparent but still white. If you let them get dark brown you will have a brown *sayyadiah*, a good alternative. Add about 1 litre (1½ pints) of water and simmer until the onions have nearly melted. You can leave the onions as they are or, if you like, reduce them to a pulp with a little of the liquid in an electric blender, or rub them through a sieve.

Return them to the pan, season with salt and cumin or allspice. Add the fish and simmer for about 15 minutes until well cooked but still firm. Skim off the scum as it rises to the surface.

Remove the fish and keep hot. Retain about the same volume of stock in the pan as that of the rice to be used (550 ml/18 fl oz or a scant pint). Pour the remaining stock into another pan and add lemon juice to taste to make a well-flavoured sauce. Simmer to reduce it until richly flavoured.

Throw the washed and drained rice into the first portion of boiling stock. Let it boil vigorously for a minute, then reduce the heat, cover the pan and simmer gently, undisturbed, until the rice is tender, about 15 to 20 minutes. Allow to 'rest' for 10 minutes.

Serve the rice heaped in a mound on a large heated serving dish. Arrange the pieces of fish over or around it, and pour the hot, lemony sauce over the whole dish.

≈ For an elegant presentation press the fish, then the rice over it, in an oiled mould and turn out carefully. Garnish with lightly fried pine nuts or halved blanched almonds.

≈ Here is an Egyptian variation. Colour and soften the onions, then fry the fish with the onions. Make a stock with the bones, head and trimmings of the fish, simmered with 1 stalk celery, 1 onion and 1 carrot. Strain through a fine sieve. Cook the rice as above, in its own volume of stock. Mix the cooked rice with the fish and onions in a baking dish. Garnish with lightly fried pine nuts and moisten with a little of the stock, considerably reduced. Bake in a slow oven (150°C/300°F/Mark 2) for about 20 minutes.

≈ Another way of preparing this dish is to make a fish stew and then cook the rice in it. Slice the onions into half-moon shapes and fry until golden. Add the pieces of fish and fry until coloured all over. Cover with water and season to taste with salt, pepper and ¼ teaspoon powdered saffron. This will give the dish a lovely pale golden colour and a subtle aroma. Simmer until the fish is nearly done, then break it up into smallish pieces with a fork. Add the washed and drained rice to the pan, and extra boiling water to cover if the stock has reduced too much. Cover and simmer gently, undisturbed, until the rice is tender, about 15 to 20 minutes. Add a little more water if the mixture becomes dry before the rice is soft. Serve with a light salad.

Moroccan Shad Stuffed with Dates

This freshwater fish, found in the Sebou river, is popular in Morocco. It is fat but rather full of bones, and its delicate flesh is said to be at its best soon after spawning up-river. Shad is found in British rivers but rarely reaches the fishmonger's slab. However, other oily fish such as mackerel can be prepared in the same way.

The dish requires rather lengthy preparation, which can be enjoyable from time to time. Dates are stuffed with rice and blanched almonds, and they, in turn, provide the stuffing for the fish.

A 2- to 2½-kg (3- to 4-lb) shad
250 g (8 oz) fresh dates (dried ones will do, but choose soft, juicy ones)
60 g (2 oz) almonds, blanched and finely chopped
2–3 tablespoons cooked rice
1 teaspoon sugar
½ teaspoon ground cinnamon

Black pepper
Ground ginger
1–2 tablespoons butter
Oil
Salt
½ onion, finely chopped
¼ teaspoon ground cinnamon, to garnish (optional)

Wash and clean the fish. Slit its belly open and remove as many of the bones as you can. If there are roes, leave them in for they are a delicacy.

Stone the dates and stuff them with a mixture of chopped almonds, rice, sugar, cinnamon and a pinch each of pepper and ginger, kneaded with a little butter to hold it together.

Rub the fish all over with oil, salt, pepper and a little ground ginger. Fill it with the stuffed dates. Place the fish on a large, well-oiled sheet of foil and sprinkle with the finely chopped onion. Wrap the fish up neatly and seal the edges of the foil firmly. (The foil allows you to omit the sewing up of the fish.) Lay the parcel on a large baking tray.

Bake in a preheated slow oven (160°C/325°F/Mark 3), allowing about 15 minutes per 500 g (1 lb). Then unwrap the foil and allow the fish to become crisply golden. Serve dusted with cinnamon if you like.

Ritza*
Sea Urchins

Hunting for *ritza* is a favourite pastime in Alexandria. It is a pleasure to swim out to the rocks, dive into the sea and discover hosts of dark purple and black, spiky, jewel-like balls clinging fast to the rocks, a triumph to wrench them away, and a delight to cut a piece off the top, squeeze a little lemon over the soft, salmon-coloured flesh, scoop it out with some bread, and savour the subtle iodized taste, lulled by the rhythm of the sea.

Prawns with Rice

1 kg (2¼ lb) prawns, shelled, fresh or frozen
1 onion, sliced into half-moon shapes
2 leeks, thinly sliced
1 celery stalk, thinly sliced
2–3 tomatoes, skinned and chopped
1 clove garlic, slivered
60 g (2 oz) butter or 3 tablespoons oil
1 medium tin tomato concentrate, or less
½ teaspoon sugar (optional)
Salt and black pepper
3 tablespoons finely chopped parsley
500 g (1 lb) long-grain rice
2 tablespoons butter

Shell, clean and wash the prawns carefully. If using frozen ones, de-frost them slowly and thoroughly.

Soften the vegetables in butter or oil. Add tomato concentrate and season to taste with sugar, salt and pepper. Add parsley and cover with about 600 ml (1 to 1½) pints water (some people like to use white wine instead of water, though this is uncommon). Bring to the boil, reduce the heat and simmer gently, covered, until the sauce is reduced and rich, about 45 minutes. Add the prawns and simmer for 5 to 8 minutes longer (frozen prawns need less time).

Pour this sauce into the centre and over the crest of a ring of plain rice, prepared according to one of the recipes on pages 402–4,

* After the Greek name.

pressed into a mould and kept hot until ready to turn out into a hot dish.

Deep-fried Prawns

Use cooked or uncooked prawns. Shell them. Roll in flour or dip first in lightly beaten egg and then roll in flour.

Deep-fry in hot oil until golden. Remove and drain on absorbent paper.

Serve garnished with lemon wedges and accompanied by a *tarator* sauce made with pine nuts or almonds (page 218), or with walnuts (page 112).

Spicy Prawns

A Moroccan speciality.

500 g (1 lb) large, unpeeled and uncooked prawns	1 teaspoon cumin
	½ teaspoon ginger
3 large cloves garlic, crushed	A good pinch of cayenne
4 tablespoons oil	A bunch of fresh coriander or
Salt	parsley, finely chopped
1 teaspoon paprika	

Large prawns can easily be found frozen. They are cheapest in Chinese supermarkets. A few have skins that are too tough to eat and should be peeled. De-frost if necessary, remove heads, limbs and tails and de-vein. Fry the garlic in the oil until the aroma rises. Add seasoning and spices, stir, then throw in the prawns. Fry quickly, stirring until they turn pink. Add the coriander or parsley, and keep on the fire a minute more.

Rice to Accompany Fish

Most Middle Eastern fish dishes are accompanied by rice. The traditional Arab rice for fish is cooked with pine nuts and coloured pale yellow with saffron.

Oil
¼–½ teaspoon saffron
500 g (1 lb) long-grain rice
Salt and black pepper

60 g (2 oz) pine nuts
2 onions, sliced into half-moon
  shapes

Heat 2 tablespoons oil in a heavy saucepan. Stir in the saffron and throw in the washed and thoroughly drained rice. Sprinkle with salt and pepper and stir well over high heat until the rice acquires a yellow, transparent glow. Add boiling water equal to the volume of rice used (550 ml/18 fl oz or a scant pint). Bring to a vigorous boil, cover the pan and simmer very gently, undisturbed, until the rice is tender and fluffy, and the water has been absorbed, about 20 minutes.

In the meantime, fry the pine nuts in a little oil for about 2 minutes until golden. Remove them and fry the onions in the same oil until very soft, and brown rather than golden.

Serve the rice in a mound, garnished with fried pine nuts and onions.

≈ Turmeric, which is called 'Oriental saffron', often replaces the expensive saffron pistils in this dish.

Poultry

Touyour

In the villages of most Middle Eastern countries, where it requires an *eid el kibir* or very important feast to kill a lamb, poultry is the usual festive dish. Geese, ducks, hens or fat chickens are the festival queens.

Often they are boiled first to provide the legendary wedding or other festive soups, and in Egypt, the *melokhia* (see page 161). Sometimes they are filled with rich stuffings before they are boiled. At all times they are served beautifully decorated and flavoured in an extraordinary variety of ways.

In his *Kitab al-ifadah wa'l-l'tibar*, written in 1204 after a visit to Egypt, Abd al Latif al-Baghdadi gives a description of the food of the time:

As for the stews of the Egyptians, those which are sour or ordinary having nothing in particular, or very little different from those used elsewhere, but on the contrary, their sweet stews are of a singular kind, for they cook a chicken with all sorts of sweet substances. Here is how they prepare the food: they boil a fowl, then put it in a julep, place under it crushed hazelnuts or pistachio nuts, poppy seeds or purslane seeds, or rose hips, and cook the whole until it thickens. Then they add spices and remove it from the fire.

These stews are surnamed *fistakiyyeh* (pistachio), *bondokiyyeh* (hazelnut), *khashkhaschiyyeh* (poppy) or *wardiyeh* (rose hip) or *sitt alnoubeh* (purslane, called 'Nubian woman' because of its black colour). There are many skilful ways of preparing this kind of food which would entail too great detail to describe. *

Maxime Rodinson, in his description of the manuscript of the *kitab al Wusla il al Habib*, which is believed to have been written in the thirteenth century, notes over 500 recipes for chicken of which he has unfortunately fully translated and explained only a few. Among them are:

Minced chicken and lamb rissoles

Stuffed boned chicken

Chicken with vinegar

Chicken boiled with crushed chick peas

Chicken with lemon or pomegranate sauce

Chicken with rhubarb or quinces

Chicken with hard-boiled egg yolks and herbs

Chicken with pistachio nuts; with hazelnuts, walnuts, almonds or poppy seeds; with parsley, oranges or rose jam; with plum jelly, yoghourt or mulberries

Chicken with chick peas, onions and cinnamon, or spiced rice

Chicken with pistachios, perfumed with rose water and musk

A loaf of bread stuffed with chicken.

Luscious ingredients for recipes which are echoed in the dishes of today – in the fruit stews of Morocco, the walnut and hazelnut sauces of Turkey and Syria, and the chick peas, onions and lemons of Egypt.

---

* Zand and Videan, *The Eastern Key*.

Every day, the trams and buses coming into the towns from the villages are crowded with peasants carrying crates of live, cackling poultry. The chickens are killed and plucked at the market or poultry shops. In Egypt, it is common practice for peasants and shopkeepers to push a large handful of corn down the birds' throats before killing them so that they weigh more.

☐ *A Tale of Goha*
He was stopped at the gates of the town by the Turkish police, who asked what he fed his chickens. 'Wheat,' said Goha. The police then demanded to see his receipt for the taxes paid on the wheat he had used. Not having heard of, nor paid, any taxes on wheat, Goha was dragged off to the qadi *(magistrate) and forced to pay a fine of five piastres, more than half of what he expected to get for his chickens.*

The next time he journeyed to the soukh, *he declared that he had fed the chickens on barley, to escape the fine. It turned out that barley, too, was taxable and he was fined again.*

The incident was repeated several times. Goha tried chick peas, millet and beans, but it turned out that all of these were taxable. Finally, in desperation, having been stopped yet again by the police and asked what his chickens had been fed on, he replied, 'Oh! I just give each one a maleem *(farthing) a day and tell him to buy what he likes!'*

Although many of the following recipes are for chicken 'stews' and a boiling chicken could be used, I have found that boiling fowls are tough and rubbery even after many hours of cooking. I therefore suggest using roasting chickens for all dishes.

Grilled Chicken

My favourite way of preparing chicken is to grill it over charcoal. It can also be grilled under an oven grill, but then the delicious aroma of the charcoal is lost.

Only young chickens or poussins should be treated in this way. Cut into serving pieces and marinate for at least 1 hour (Iranians always marinate overnight) in the following marinade:

MARINADE

Juice of 1 lemon
½ onion, chopped and crushed to extract juices

1–2 cloves garlic, crushed (optional)
2–3 tablespoons olive oil
Salt and black pepper

Place the marinated chicken pieces on an oiled grill over a charcoal fire that is already very hot and glowing, and no longer smoking. Grill until the pieces are golden brown all over but still pale and tender inside, basting with marinade and turning once.

≈ Turks like to flavour the chicken with a little cinnamon instead of the garlic and lemon.
≈ Brushing with melted butter instead of the marinade produces a very succulent result.
≈ A delicious variation is to marinate the chicken pieces for as long as possible in yoghourt flavoured with crushed garlic, salt and pepper. Sometimes dried crushed mint is added, and a little paprika is mixed with the yoghourt to give the chicken an appetizing red colour. Yoghourt used in this way does not contribute very much to the flavour, but serves to soften the flesh of the chicken, rather like the Indian manner of preparing *tandoori* chicken which has become so popular in this country. Serve sprinkled with chopped parsley.

Chicken Awsat
Chicken in a Bread Loaf

This is a medieval recipe from the *Kitab al Wusla il al Habib*, where it is also called 'Egyptian chicken'. It is a loaf of bread from which the soft inside has been removed to make room for a stuffing of boned chicken meat and livers.

I am giving my own interpretation and quantities of ingredients as I have prepared them.

1 medium loaf with an attractive shape (rectangular or cottage)
1 medium chicken, boiled or sofrito (see next recipe)
250 g (8 oz) chicken livers
Oil (originally sesame oil, but corn or nut will do well)
Chicken stock
¼ teaspoon ground allspice
Salt and black pepper

30–60 g (1–2 oz) pistachio nuts, chopped
3 tablespoons finely chopped parsley
1 teaspoon dried crushed mint
Juice of ½ lemon
½ teaspoon rose water (optional)
Sprigs of parsley and other fresh herbs

Cut a slice off the top of the loaf and put it aside to serve as a lid. Carefully remove all the pith from the loaf, leaving the crust intact.

Bone and chop the cooked chicken. Clean the chicken livers and sauté gently in a little oil for 3 to 4 minutes. Add about ½ teacup of the stock in which the chicken was cooked, and season to taste with allspice, salt and pepper. (A little brandy or sherry could be used instead of chicken stock, but this does not, of course, appear in the original recipe.) Mash or pound the livers to a smooth paste, using an electric blender if you have one.

Mix the liver pâté with the chopped chicken in a large bowl. Add pistachio nuts, parsley, mint and lemon juice. Mix well and taste for seasoning, adding more salt and pepper if necessary. Knead the mixture vigorously until well blended, and add a little more stock if too dry.

Moisten the bread shell with stock to make it soft and easy to cut. The original recipe recommends sprinkling with a few drops of rose water, but I do not care for its perfume in this particular dish. Fill the shell with the chicken and liver mixture, packing it tightly. Cover with the lid, which has also been sprinkled with stock to soften it.

Chill in the refrigerator until ready to serve.

This is a rather beautiful dish. Decorate it with sprigs of parsley and other fresh herbs. Serve cut in slices and accompanied by a light salad.

Cold Chicken Sofrito

1 large roasting chicken
2 tablespoons sunflower oil
Juice of ½–1 lemon

½ teaspoon turmeric
Salt and white pepper
1 cardamom pod, cracked

Wash the chicken and wipe it dry.

In a large saucepan or flameproof casserole put the oil, lemon juice, a coffee cup of water, turmeric, salt and white pepper, and the cardamom pod. Bring to the boil, then place the chicken in the pan. Cover and cook over very low heat, turning the chicken over frequently and adding another coffee cup of water as the juices are absorbed. Continue cooking until the chicken is very soft and tender. Adjust the seasoning. Remove the pan from the heat and allow to cool.

Divide the chicken into joints, removing the larger bones, skin and arrange in a deep serving dish. Pour the sauce over it and allow it to become quite cold. On cooling, it will become a pale, lemony jelly and the chicken will be a very delicate off-white. If you prefer an absolutely clear jelly, simply skim any fat off the surface before pouring it over the chicken. Use absorbent paper to remove the last traces.

This is a very simple and delicate way of cooking chicken. Serve as part of a cold buffet, or for a family meal in summer, accompanied by salads. The ground almond salad on page 119 will do particularly well.

Chicken with Melokhia Sauce

The famous *melokhia* soup of Egypt is served as a sauce for chicken and rice in Syria and Lebanon. Make it with chicken as described in the recipe on page 162 but using twice as many *melokhia* leaves, fresh or dried, so that it is really thick. Remove the chicken before adding the *melokhia*. Bone it and cut it into pieces, and keep it moist with a little stock.

Prepare toasted croûtons (page 434) with 2 or 3 pittas to serve as a side dish.

Another accompaniment is onion marinated in lemon juice or vinegar. Chop 1 or 2 large mild onions very small, put them in a small bowl and cover with lemon juice or vinegar.

Add the juice of 1 lemon to the *melokhia* before presenting chicken, rice and sauce, all very hot, in separate dishes, accompanied by a plate of croûtons and the bowl of onions.

The usual way to eat this is in a soup bowl. Put a layer of toasted bread first, then some rice, then chicken. Cover with *melokhia* sauce and sprinkle with the chopped onion.

Chicken with Chick Peas

A Middle Eastern dish which is particularly popular in Morocco.

1 large roasting chicken	Juice of 1 lemon, or more
2 tablespoons oil	2–4 cloves garlic, crushed
1 onion, finely chopped	Salt
1 teaspoon turmeric	Black pepper or a pinch of
250 g (8 oz) chick peas, soaked overnight	cayenne

Heat the oil in a saucepan or deep flameproof casserole (large enough to hold the chicken). Fry the chopped onion in the oil until soft and golden. Sprinkle with turmeric and mix well. Add the chicken and sauté gently, turning it until it is a dark yellow colour all over. Add 600 ml (1 pint) of water, the soaked and drained chick peas, lemon juice and garlic, and season with salt and pepper. Bring to the boil and simmer gently, covered, for 1 hour or longer, until the chicken is very tender, the chick peas soft, yellow and lemony, and the liquid very much reduced. Adjust seasoning and serve, cut up into joints.

Moroccan Tagine T'Faia

It is said in Morocco that this dish was brought back from Andalusia by the Moriscos after the *Reconquista*.

1 roasting chicken, jointed	2 onions, finely chopped
Butter or oil	3 tablespoons finely chopped parsley
Salt and black pepper	6 hard-boiled eggs
½ teaspoon ground ginger	120 g (4 oz) blanched almonds, or more
About ¼ teaspoon saffron (optional)	

Put the chicken in a large pan with 2 tablespoons butter or oil, salt, pepper, ginger, saffron if used, onions and parsley. Cover with water, bring to the boil and simmer gently, half-covered, for 1 hour, or until the chicken has absorbed the taste of the ginger and saffron and is well cooked, and the sauce is reduced.

Heat a little water to which you have added a pinch of saffron. Shell the hard boiled eggs and roll them in the saffron water to colour them all over. Fry the blanched almonds in butter.

Turn the chicken into a deep serving dish and pour the sauce over it. Arrange the eggs on top, placing them between the pieces of chicken, and garnish the dish with fried almonds.

≈ A similar dish can be made using lamb instead of chicken.

□ *Geese at Akshehir Have Only One Leg**

One day the Khoja cooked a goose and took it as a present to Tamerlane. On the road he could not restrain his appetite and ate one of the legs. On arrival at the palace he presented his offering in due form, but Tamerlane noticed that there was one leg short and asked him where it was. The Khoja replied, as cool as a cucumber, that all the geese at Akshehir had only one leg. 'If you don't believe me, look at those geese standing over there by the fountain!'

It was quite true. The geese were all standing on one leg, sound asleep in the sunshine, the other leg tucked up and their heads sunk in their breasts.

Tamerlane looked out of the window and saw that they really had only one leg.

Now, it chanced to be the moment for changing the palace guard. The band struck up. The roll of the big drum and skirl of pipes made the welkin ring. The geese soon found their second legs and ran off helter-skelter, trying to escape. Tamerlane saw them and at once called the Khoja to the window saying, 'You are a liar. You see they all have two feet.'

'Yes,' replied the Khoja, 'and if you had the noise of those drum-sticks ringing in your ears you would grow four legs.'

Treya
Chicken with Pasta

A filling dish described to me by an aunt in Paris, the origin of which I was thrilled to discover in al-Baghdadi's medieval cookery manual. In Egypt, spaghettini, which are thinner than spaghetti but not quite as thin as vermicelli, were used to prepare this dish, but spaghetti, tagliatelle or other pasta can also be used.

---

* Barnham (trans.), *Tales of Nasr-ed-Din Khoja.*

1 large roasting chicken, cooked
(see method)
Salt and black pepper
1 cardamom pod
Juice of ½ lemon

500 g (1 lb) spaghettini or other
pasta
Sunflower oil
1 teaspoon ground cinnamon

Prepare the chicken according to the recipe for *sofrito* on page 230, seasoning it with salt and pepper, and flavouring with 1 cardamom pod (cracked to release the flavour from the seeds) and lemon juice. Simmer gently, covered, in a little oil and about 1 teacup water until very tender, turning it over occasionally. When cooked, bone the chicken, discarding the skin and tendons, and cut the meat into medium sized pieces.

While the chicken is cooking, boil the spaghettini for about 7 minutes until almost but not quite tender. Drain in a colander.

Heat about 3 mm (⅛ inch) sunflower oil in a large ovenproof pan or sauté dish until very hot. Throw in the well-drained spaghettini and sauté for a few minutes, stirring and tossing with a fork. Remove half the spaghettini and spread the remainder over the bottom of the pan. Arrange the chicken pieces in a layer over them, sprinkle with cinnamon and cover with the remaining spaghettini. Pour over the sauce in which the chicken was cooked and cover the pan with a lid.

Bake in a moderate oven (180°C/350°F/Mark 4) for 20 to 30 minutes. Unmould on to a serving dish and serve either hot or cold.

≈ Alternatively, make extra sauce by adding a little more water to the chicken while it is cooking. Remove the chicken when cooked; skin, bone and chop it, and put the pieces back in the sauce. Boil the spaghettini until only half cooked as before; drain and add to the chicken. Continue to simmer the mixture until the spaghettini are well done and have absorbed the sauce, sprinkling with the cinnamon during cooking. They acquire a particularly delicious flavour.

≈ *Mishmisheya* (a rich apricot sauce) is traditionally served with this dish: soak 250 g (8 oz) dried apricots overnight and simmer until soft in water or stock left over from cooking the chicken. Add a little sugar, and the juice of ½ lemon if you prefer a sharper taste. When the apricots are soft, crush them with a fork and continue to simmer until reduced to a soft purée. Serve cold in a separate bowl.

Ferique

A delicious Egyptian chicken dish with young whole wheat and hard-boiled eggs. A few medieval recipes from al-Baghdadi are for dishes of chicken or meat cooked with whole wheat in a similar manner.

1 large roasting chicken	1–2 teaspoons turmeric
1 calf's foot	2–3 tablespoons oil
6 eggs in their shells	Salt and black pepper
250 g (8 oz) husked whole wheat kernels, soaked overnight	

Wash the chicken. Scrape the calf's foot and blanch it in boiling water to clean it. Scrub the egg-shells well.

Put all the ingredients in a large saucepan and cover with water. Bring to the boil and simmer gently for 3 to 4 hours, or until the chicken is practically falling apart, the calf's foot very tender, and the wheat well cooked.

Remove the eggs, shell them and return them to the pan. The lengthy cooking will have given them a creamy texture and they will be coloured pale yellow by the turmeric. Cook for a further 10 minutes. Taste and adjust seasoning.

Serve in deep bowls.

Moroccan Lemon Chicken

Preserved lemons, for which there is a recipe on page 63, give a delicious flavour to chicken. They are usually coupled with green olives but I prefer to have them alone as in this recipe. You may leave them whole (slit for preserving) or chop them up in the sauce.

1 large chicken	½ teaspoon cinnamon
2 tablespoons oil	Salt and pepper
1 onion, grated or very finely chopped	A good bunch of coriander leaves, finely chopped
½ teaspoon saffron, or 1 teaspoon turmeric	A good bunch of parsley, finely chopped
½ teaspoon ginger	1–2 preserved lemons, chopped

Put the chicken in a large saucepan with all the ingredients except the preserved lemons. The saffron is an expensive ingredient in a dish where its flavour is masked by that of the lemon. It can be replaced for colour by turmeric, otherwise you may use the cheaper quality of pistils. Crush them with salt with a spoon in a teacup so that they yield more.

Half cover the chicken with water and simmer gently, turning it over a few times until it is so tender that the flesh can pull off the bone (about 1½ hours) and the liquid is much reduced. Throw the lemons into the sauce and cook a few minutes longer.

Chicken with Olives

This excellent Middle Eastern dish is a particularly Moroccan speciality.

1 large roasting chicken	1 teaspoon paprika
2 tablespoons oil	1 onion, finely chopped
2 onions, sliced	250 g (8 oz) green olives
Salt and black pepper	Juice of ½ lemon, or more
¼–½ teaspoon ground ginger	

Heat the oil in a large saucepan. Add onion slices, sprinkle with salt, pepper, ginger and paprika, then add about 1 teacup water very gradually, stirring vigorously, and lay the chicken on top. Cook over low heat, covered, for 1 hour, turning the chicken frequently. Add a little more salt if necessary, and the finely chopped onion, and cook for ½ hour longer.

Stone the olives. Put them in a pan, cover with cold water, bring to the boil and leave for 1 minute. Drain off the water and repeat the process. This will remove excess salt. Add the olives to the pan and cook with the chicken for a few minutes only.

Just before serving, squeeze a little lemon juice over the dish. Sometimes a few pickled lemon slices (page 63) are added just before serving. Serve with plain boiled rice or couscous (page 335).

☐ *Riddle: Our negress servant is green. Her children are born white and then grow black. Who is she?*
Answer: An olive tree.

Moroccan Chicken Qdra

This is a stew we made in Egypt which came to us from Morocco.

1 large roasting chicken, quartered	Salt and black pepper
2 tablespoons butter	250 g (8 oz) chick peas, soaked overnight
375–500 g (¾–1 lb) onions	120 g (4 oz) almonds, blanched and peeled
¼ teaspoon powdered saffron (optional)	A bunch of parsley, finely chopped
1 teaspoon ground cinnamon, or more	Juice of ½ lemon

As so often in Moroccan cooking, one onion is cooked first with the meat or chicken, and when these are nearly done, the remaining onions are added. This is because of the prolonged cooking. The first onion is used to add flavour to the meat, and it practically melts and disappears into the sauce. The onions added later keep their shape and add body to the sauce.

Put the chicken, butter and 1 onion, finely chopped, in a large pan, and cover with water. Add a little saffron for colour if liked, and season to taste with cinnamon, salt and pepper. Bring to the boil, add the soaked chick peas, and simmer for about 1½ hours, until the chick peas are soft and the chicken well cooked, adding more water if necessary. The chicken should be jointed as soon as it is tender enough to take to pieces.

Add the rest of the onions, finely chopped, the almonds and parsley, and simmer until the onions are soft and the sauce considerably reduced.

Arrange the chicken pieces on a serving dish and cover with chick peas and almonds. Squeeze ½ lemon over the dish and serve.

≈ Dried black-eyed beans or haricot beans can be substituted for the chick peas, or all three can be cooked together. However, where dried beans are used, salt should not be added until they are soft, since it tends to keep them hard.

Tagine with Prunes

In the *Kitab al Wusla il al Habib*, a medieval manuscript, there is a dish of chicken with prunes. Moroccans today cook a similar dish. Here is the recipe.

1 large or 2 small chickens
1 onion, sliced
¼ teaspoon powdered saffron
¼–½ teaspoon ground ginger

Salt
2 onions, finely chopped or grated
500 g (1 lb) prunes, soaked
overnight

Wash the chicken and put it in a large pan with the sliced onion. Sprinkle with saffron, ginger and salt to taste, cover with water and simmer gently, covered, until the chicken is tender and the stock is very much reduced. After about the first ¾ hour of cooking, add the finely chopped onions.

When the chicken is tender, add the prunes and continue cooking with the pan uncovered for about ½ hour longer, or until the prunes are soft and the sauce is considerably reduced.

Serve the chicken cut into pieces and covered with the sauce and prunes. Accompany with plain rice or couscous (page 335).

Moroccan Fruit Tagine

1 large roasting chicken, jointed
2 onions, finely chopped
3 tablespoons finely chopped
parsley
2–3 tablespoons butter

¼ teaspoon ground ginger
(optional)
Salt and black pepper
500 g (1 lb) cooking or sharp
eating apples, peeled, cored and
sliced

Put the chicken joints, chopped onions and parsley in a large saucepan. Cover with water, add butter, and the ginger if liked, and season with salt and pepper. Bring to the boil and simmer, covered, until the chicken is very tender and the onions have practically disintegrated, about 1 hour. The sauce should be reduced.

Add the sliced apples and continue to simmer until they are only just tender. The apples must not be allowed to disintegrate; eating apples will keep their shape better than cooking ones.

Serve with rice, couscous (page 335), or Arab bread to dip into the sauce.

≈ Similar *touajen* can be made with pears, quinces, fresh dates, raisins or prunes.

Stuffed Chicken

1 large roasting chicken
Salt and black pepper

Butter

STUFFING

500 g (1 lb) beef or lamb, minced
3 tablespoons oil
Salt and black pepper
120 g (4 oz) blanched almonds,
  halved

60 g (2 oz) pine nuts
120 g (4 oz) rice, cooked (weight
  uncooked)

Clean the chicken, burning off any stray feathers over a flame if necessary. Wash and wipe dry. Simmer in seasoned water for about ¾ hour, or until nearly tender, skimming away scum to begin with. Allow to cool a little.

Prepare the stuffing. Fry the minced meat in 2 tablespoons oil until browned and season to taste with salt and pepper. In a separate pan, heat the remaining tablespoon of oil or butter and fry the almonds and pine nuts for 2 or 3 minutes only. Mix the meat, almonds and pine nuts with the cooked rice, and taste for seasoning. Stuff the chicken tightly with this mixture and skewer the openings. (If there is any stuffing left over, warm it up again later and serve with the chicken.)

Roast the stuffed chicken, brushed with butter, in a preheated slow oven (160°C/325°F/Mark 3) for 20 minutes, or until it is a beautiful golden colour.

≈ If you prefer, you can stuff the chicken raw and roast it in the usual manner, surrounded with butter shavings and wrapped in foil, in a fairly hot oven (200°C/400°F/Mark 6) until tender, allowing about 20 minutes per 500 g (1 lb). Or cook it uncovered, placed on a rack in an oven preheated to 220°C (425°F/Mark 7) and then reduced at once to 160°C (325°F/Mark 3) for about 20 minutes per 500 g (1 lb).
≈ One or two peeled and chopped tomatoes can be included in the stuffing, which can also be flavoured with ½ teaspoon ground cinnamon.

☐ *The Roast Chicken**

The Khoja sat under a tree eating some roast chicken.

* Barnham (trans.), *Tales of Nasr-ed-Din Khoja.*

A man came up to him and said, 'How nice! I should like some of that. Please give me a bit.'

'I am very sorry, brother,' answered the Khoja. 'It isn't mine. It is my wife's chicken.'

'But you are eating it,' said the man.

'Of course,' said the Khoja. 'What else can I do! When she gave it to me she said, "Eat it."'

Boned Stuffed Chicken

A splendid party dish, similar to those featured in medieval manuals.

1 large roasting chicken	60–90 g (2–3 oz) pistachio nuts,
Oil	coarsely chopped
Salt and black pepper	Juice of ½ lemon
750 g (1½ lb) veal, minced	

Clean and wash the chicken, and cut off the wing tips and leg ends to make the removal of the skin possible. Singe the chicken over a flame to 'loosen' it and burn away any feathers. Loosen the skin from the flesh. Carefully pull the skin right off as though undressing the chicken, taking care not to tear it, starting from the neck and pulling it off the legs last. It will come right off with the occasional help of a pointed knife. Wash the skin, turn it right side out and put it aside.

Quarter the skinned chicken, put it in a saucepan and cover with water. Add 2 tablespoons oil, season to taste with salt and pepper, bring to the boil and simmer gently until the chicken is very tender. Remove from the heat and let it cool in the stock. Drain and keep the stock.

Bone the chicken, discarding nerves and tendons, and mince or chop the meat finely. Put it in a large bowl and mix with the minced veal. Use extra veal if the chicken is not very meaty. Knead well. Add the pistachio nuts and knead them in. Season the mixture to taste with salt and pepper.

Using a needle and strong thread, sew up all but the largest vent in the chicken skin and 'darn' any holes. Stuff the skin carefully with the chicken and veal mixture, and re-form as nearly as possible in its original shape. Sew the opening tightly.

Turn the stuffed chicken over in about 2 tablespoons warm oil in a pan until the skin is golden. Add the lemon juice and about half a ladleful of left-over stock and simmer gently, covered, for about 1 hour, adding more stock or water, half a ladleful at a time, if it becomes dry. At the end of cooking time, the veal should be well cooked and almost blended with the chicken, and the sauce much reduced. Remove from the heat and allow to cool overnight in its own sauce.

Traditionally, the chicken should be served in thick slices, but I think it looks rather beautiful with its subdued boneless shape, served whole and sliced at table.

≈ A variation of this dish, said to be for lazy cooks, is just as delicious though not as dramatic. Cook the chicken as in the recipe for *sofrito* (page 230), adding just a pinch of turmeric or none at all. When cool, skin it and remove the bones and tendons. Mince or chop the flesh and mix it with the minced veal, 1 egg and a handful of chopped pistachios. Knead thoroughly and shape or roll into a thick sausage. Sauté in 2 tablespoons hot oil until golden all over. Add water, a little at a time, as it becomes absorbed, and simmer gently, covered, until well cooked. Allow to cool in its sauce for several hours before serving. Serve cut in slices.

□ *Arab saying: 'Eat and praise your host.'*

Persian Chicken Stuffed with Dried Fruits

1 large roasting chicken	60 g (2 oz) seedless raisins
1 onion, finely chopped	2 apples, peeled, cored and
Butter	chopped
250 g (8 oz) prunes, soaked, stoned	Salt and black pepper
and chopped	1 teaspoon ground cinnamon
250 g (8 oz) dried apricots, soaked	
and chopped	

Clean and wash the chicken, and wipe it dry. Fry the chopped onion in 2 tablespoons hot butter until soft and golden. Add the chopped fruits and raisins and sauté gently for a few minutes. Season to taste with salt, pepper and cinnamon.

Stuff the chicken with this mixture. Rub it with salt and pepper, truss and place in a baking tin. Roast in a preheated slow oven (160°C/325°F/Mark 3), allowing about 20 minutes per 500 g (1 lb). Baste frequently with melted butter.

Alternatively, cover the chicken with butter shavings and wrap in foil before putting it in a hotter oven. It will be more tender and juicy. Place any left-over stuffing in the foil with the bird.

Serve the chicken surrounded with the extra stuffing and plain rice.

Faisinjan
Duck or Chicken in Pomegranate Sauce

This sweet-and-sour Iranian sauce for wild duck or pheasant is also good with chicken but a little too rich for an ordinary duck. Make it in the autumn when fresh pomegranates are in season, or use the thick dark brown bottled pomegranate syrup. Be sure that the walnuts are not stale.

1 duck or chicken, cut into quarters	1 medium onion, coarsely chopped
2–3 tablespoons light vegetable oil	250 g (8 oz) chopped or pounded walnuts

4 pomegranates
Juice of 2 lemons
1 tablespoon sugar   *or*   3 tablespoons concentrated
150 ml (¼ pint) water   pomegranate syrup
Salt and pepper   450 ml (¾ pint) water

Brown the duck quickly in hot oil in a large heavy pan. Remove the pieces and fry the onion in the same oil until it is a rich brown, stirring occasionally. Add the walnuts which should not be too finely ground (you should be able to feel them) and cook gently, stirring often, for about 2 minutes.

To extract the juice from the pomegrantes, cut in half, scoop out the seeds (discarding the pith) into a blender or processor and blend a few seconds, enough to break the delicate skin surrounding the seeds. Pour into a bowl through a strainer, squeezing out all the juice. There should be at least 300 ml (½ pint). Pour into the pan and add lemon, sugar, water, salt and pepper. Bring to the simmer, stir and add the duck or chicken pieces and cook gently for 1 to 1½ hours until they are very tender. Taste and adjust the delicate balance between sweet and sour by adding more lemon or more sugar. If it is duck that you are using, remove as much fat as you can from the surface with a spoon. The sauce may be thinned with a little more water.

If you are using pomegranate syrup, stir it into the walnuts and onions in the pan and add 450 ml (¾ pint) water.

Koftit Ferakh 1
Chicken Balls 1

This recipe for leftovers is inspired by the medieval *Kitab al Wusla il al Habib*. For 3 or 4 people.

250 g (8 oz) cooked boned chicken
120 g (4 oz) white bread, crusts removed
60 g (2 oz) pistachio nuts, finely chopped

1 tablespoon olive or salad oil
Juice of ½ lemon
Salt and white pepper

Mince or chop the chicken finely. Soak the bread in water, squeeze dry and crumble. Mix the chicken with the crumbled bread, pistachios, oil, lemon juice, and salt and pepper to taste, and knead vigorously. Shape and roll into marble-sized balls.

These can either be served as they are, as a cold dish with salad; or they can be rolled in flour and fried, or poached in a chicken soup, and served hot.

Koftit Ferakh 2
Chicken Balls 2

Here is a modern version of the same dish. Yet another recipe is given on page 88.

250 g (8 oz) cooked boned chicken (preferably white meat)
1 slice white bread
250 g (8 oz) minced veal
2 tablespoons finely chopped parsley

1 egg
Salt and black pepper
About 2 tablespoons butter or oil
½ teaspoon turmeric (optional)
Juice of ½ lemon

Mince the chicken. Trim the bread of crusts, soak in water and squeeze dry. In a large bowl, mix the minced chicken, crumbled bread, veal, parsley and egg, and season to taste with salt and pepper. Knead well and roll into marble-sized balls.

Melt butter or oil in a large, deep frying pan, and fry the chicken balls, shaking the pan, until they are gently browned all over. Add a little turmeric if liked, sprinkle with lemon juice and a pinch of salt and pepper. Half-cover with water and simmer gently, uncovered, for about 20 minutes, until the *koftit* are very tender and well cooked.

≈ Artichoke hearts are often stewed with the *koftit*. If fresh ones are not available, tinned artichoke hearts make an excellent substitute. Add them 10 minutes before the dish is ready.

≈ In another variation, the fried chicken balls are simmered in a tomato sauce made with a small tin of tomato concentrate, diluted with water and seasoned with salt, pepper and a little lemon juice. Ten minutes before the end of cooking time, throw in 500 g (1 lb) fried potatoes cut into squares, and let them absorb the sauce.

Stuffed Turkey

In the Middle East, turkeys range very freely and are small and tough, more like game birds. So they are usually stewed rather than roasted. This makes the flesh very juicy, and helps it to absorb the flavours of the stuffing as well as the seasonings in the stock. A very large pan is required to hold the bird.

A 5- to 6-kg (10- to 12-lb) oven-ready turkey
Lemon juice
Oil or butter
1 kg (2 lb) beef, lamb or veal, minced
250 g (8 oz) chopped mixed nuts: blanced almonds, walnuts, pistachio nuts and pine nuts
375 g (12 oz) long-grain rice
60 g (2 oz) raisins (optional)
Salt and black pepper
1 teaspoon ground cinnamon
¼ teaspoon ground allspice

Wash the turkey thoroughly and rub it both inside and out with a little lemon juice.

Prepare the stuffing. In a saucepan heat 2 tablespoons butter or oil and fry the meat until it changes colour, mixing with a fork. Stir in the nuts and fry for 2 to 3 minutes longer. Add the washed and drained rice, and fry for another minute or so until well coated with fat. Add raisins if used. Season to taste with salt, pepper, cinnamon and allspice. Mix well.

Stuff the turkey loosely with this mixture to allow the rice to expand, and sew the openings tightly with strong thread. Truss the bird.

Heat 2 tablespoons butter or oil in a pan large enough to hold the turkey and brown it well, turning it to colour it all over. Add enough water to cover and season to taste with salt and pepper. Bring to the boil and simmer gently, removing the scum to begin with, until the turkey is very tender. This will take 2 to 2½ hours, depending on the size of the bird.

The turkey may either be served whole, or cut into pieces and arranged over the stuffing in a large platter.

≈ The turkey can also be boned before stuffing: cut the skin and flesh of the bird along the spine all the way down from the neck. Starting from the neck, strip and cut away the flesh from the carcass as close to it as possible, using a very sharp knife, taking care not to damage the skin, and pushing the flesh back as you cut. Break the shoulder and leg joints. Carefully remove the carcass all in one piece. Pack with stuffing and sew up neatly, re-forming the bird as far as possible in its original shape. In this way it will take more stuffing and can be served in slices. The legs and wings remain unboned and help to keep the shape of the turkey firm.

≈ If a large enough pan is not available, roast the turkey in the oven, but you must use already cooked rice for your stuffing. Rub with either butter or oil, wrap in foil and baste frequently. Begin roasting in an oven preheated to 220°C (425°F/Mark 7) and as soon as the bird is brown, reduce the heat to 160°C (325°F/Mark 3). Allow 25 minutes to the 500 g (1 lb) and 25 minutes over. If roasting in foil, roast for the same time but keep the oven heat at a constant 190°C (375°F/Mark 5).

Browned Duck

This is a Turkish recipe from Sidqi Effendi's nineteenth-century cookery manual.

A 2½- to 3-kg (5- to 6-lb) oven-ready duck	Liver and heart of the duck
300 ml (½ pint) yoghourt	Black pepper
Salt	60 g (2 oz) mixed chopped almonds and pine nuts
2 medium-sized onions, chopped	60 g (2 oz) raisins
Oil or butter	500 g (1 lb) long-grain rice, washed

Clean and wash the duck, and cut it in serving pieces. Marinate for several hours in yoghourt seasoned with a little salt.

In a large pan, fry the onions in 2 tablespoons oil or butter until soft and golden. Add the well-drained pieces of duck and brown all over. Cover with a little water, season to taste with salt, bring to the boil and simmer gently, covered, for about 20 minutes, or until tender. Drain, reserving stock.

Cut the duck liver, heart, and other duck giblets if you like into small pieces. Fry these in oil or butter until soft, using another large saucepan, and season to taste with salt and pepper. Add the nuts, raisins and rice, and mix well. Pour in the same volume of duck stock, made up with water if necessary, as that of rice (½ litre or a scant pint), cover and cook very gently, undisturbed, until the rice is tender and has absorbed the liquid. Taste for seasoning and adjust if necessary.

Serve very hot on a large, heated serving dish, alternating layers of the rice mixture and duck.

Grilled Quail

Every year, a type of migrating quail not found in Britain flies over Alexandria. Hundreds of the small birds fall, exhausted, on the dunes of the beaches of Agami, to be caught in large nets and collected in baskets. They are plucked and cleaned and marinated in a rich sauce flavoured with cumin and coriander, and grilled on the beaches over numerous little fires.

The flesh of these birds is not as gamey as that of British quail, and the nearest equivalent available here is a poussin or tiny spring chicken.

Clean and wash the birds. Rub the following sauce into them, and marinate for at least 1 hour before grilling over charcoal or under a hot grill.

4 tablespoons olive oil	1 onion, cut in half and crushed in
Salt	a garlic press to extract juices
1 teaspoon ground cumin	2 tablespoons finely chopped
1 teaspoon ground coriander	parsley
	Pinch of cayenne pepper

Saman bil Roz
Quails in Rice

500 g (1 lb) rice, cooked in any
way (page 401)
6 quails
1 large onion, chopped
90 g (3 oz) butter

1 clove garlic, crushed
1 teaspoon cinnamon
Salt and pepper
A squeeze of lemon juice
300 ml (½ pint) water

Clean the birds. In a large pot soften the onion in butter until slightly coloured. Put in the birds with the garlic and sauté, turning them to brown them all over. Sprinkle with cinnamon, salt and pepper and a little lemon juice, add the water and cook for about 15 to 20 minutes, turning the birds over occasionally and adding more water if necessary until the quails are done.

Make a pyramid of the steaming hot rice. Press the quails on top of it and pour the pan juices over them.

Saman bil Einab
Quails with Grapes

This is a Moroccan recipe, which I have adapted from René R. Khawam's *La Cuisine Arabe*.

6 quails
60 g (2 oz) butter
1 tablespoon ginger juice*
Salt and pepper

500 g (1 lb) fresh large white
grapes
A squeeze of lemon juice

Clean, singe and wash the quails. Sauté briskly in butter in a large pot for about 6 minutes, turning them to colour them all over. Season with ginger and salt and pepper. Add the grapes and lemon juice and cook gently for another 10 minutes until the quails are done and the grapes have softened.

Serve with rice or burghul pilav (page 332).

□ *The Quails†*

The Khoja shot a large number of quails, which he dressed and put on to stew. He clapped the lid on the saucepan and went out to

---

* Squeeze fresh root ginger in a garlic press.
† Barnham (trans.), *Tales of Nasr-ed-Din Khoja*.

invite his friends to dinner, wishing to give some of them who were always questioning his skill an agreeable proof of it.

While he was out, another man came and carried off the cooked quails, putting live quails in their place.

The Khoja's friends arrived, the saucepan was brought out, and the Khoja proudly took the cover off; the quails flew out with a flutter and disappeared. The Khoja stared in amazement, and then ejaculated:

'Oh Lord! granted that Thou hast restored the quails to life and made the dear little creatures happy again, how about my butter, salt, pepper, herbs, cooking expenses, and all my hard work? Who is going to pay for them?'

Hamam Meshwi
Grilled Pigeons

One of the happiest and most popular outings of my childhood in Cairo was to go for the day, in the company of several uncles, aunts and cousins, to an old restaurant called Le Café des Pigeons, on the way to the Pyramids. There we would feast on charcoal-grilled pigeons shot in the neighbourhood.

I cannot recollect a more delicious meal. Huge dishes piled high with halved pigeons, sprinkled with lemon juice and chopped chervil or parsley, were brought to us in the ancient gardens of the restaurant, overgrown with jasmine and bougainvillaea. We ate them all, even their small soft bones.

To my dismay, I found that, as with quail, the pigeons available in Britain are of a totally different variety. Again, the nearest in flavour that I can suggest (though still very far removed) is spring chicken. Our pigeons were often just grilled over charcoal and sprinkled with salt, but if spring chickens are used, I suggest that you marinate them first in oil and lemon with salt and pepper to tenderize their flesh and enhance their flavour. Serve sprinkled with chopped fresh chervil or parsley.

Pigeons Sucrés aux Dattes

This comes from Fettouma Benkirane's *La Nouvelle Cuisine Maro-caine*. Lamb is often cooked with dates in the same manner, but it suits these birds best.

In a large pot put:

6 pigeons, cleaned and washed	Salt
3 onions, finely chopped	¾ teaspoon ginger
1–2 cloves garlic, crushed	A good pinch of saffron
120 g (4 oz) butter	¾ litre (15 fl oz) water

Simmer 30 minutes, then add:

750 g (1½ lb) fresh dates, pitted	2–3 tablespoons clear honey
1 teaspoon cinnamon	

Cook 10–15 minutes longer, or until done.

Arrange the pigeons in a ring on a serving dish with the dates in the centre and pour the sauce over. Sprinkle with 60 g (2 oz) lightly toasted sesame seeds.

Meat Dishes

———◆·◆———

Louhoumat

In Arabic literature and folklore, meat dishes have always been labelled the food of the rich and aristocratic, in contrast to the filling dishes of beans, lentils and wheat which are the diet of the lowly poor. Many stories and proverbs illustrate this distinction. Here is an old Egyptian tale of the Mamluk period by Ahmad ibn al Hajjar, in which the various foods are personified and their status is defined:

☐ *A Book about the Pleasant War Between*
*Mutton and the Refreshments of the Market**
King Mutton reigns over a large and powerful people, comprising

* From the French translation by M. Rodinson.

mainly meats. He hears of the power of a rival, King Honey, who has been crowned by the poor, and who reigns over vegetables, fruits, sweets, fish, milk dishes, and particularly the refreshments of the market. King Mutton sends his ambassador, Mutton's Tail (alya), to King Honey, demanding that he surrender his kingdom and pay tribute. King Honey refuses and calls his troops together, but the ambassador has taken advantage of his stay in the kingdom to debauch and corrupt the officers of rank, in particular, the Sugar, the Syrup, the Clarified Fat and others, to whom he has promised important positions at the court of his master. Thus, because of their treachery, the battle between the two armies is easily won by the troops of King Mutton, and even the reinforcements of fruits sent to help the broken army of King Honey are of no avail.

Most Middle Eastern meat recipes, both the medieval ones and more recent versions, simply state 'meat' – meat with lentils, meat with yoghourt, and so on – without specifying what kind of meat or any particular cut. This is because, in the past, only mutton and lamb were eaten, apart from an occasional gazelle, kid or camel. Cattle were seldom bred, except for a type of buffalo mainly used to work in the fields. Those brought from elsewhere had to travel a long way, across whole countries, to reach the Middle East, and by the time they got to their destination, their flesh was tough and inedible unless minced.

Today, however, beef and veal are gradually becoming more popular. Although mutton and lamb remain, from habit, the most widely used and favoured, beef and veal quite often replace them, the recipes themselves remaining unchanged.

It is common in the Middle East for people to buy a live sheep at the market, and to keep it for a few days in their kitchen before killing it. A tale of Goha illustrates this custom.

□ *One day, Goha took his small son to the market with him to buy a sheep. Now it is well known that the value of a sheep depends on the amount of fat which it stores in its tail. At the soukh (market), Goha proceeded to feel, and weigh in his hands, the tails of the sheep one after another, until his son asked:*

'Father, why do you do that?'

'I must do so before I decide which sheep to buy,' Goha replied.

A few days later, while sitting waiting for the evening meal, the little boy turned to his father and said:

'Father, our neighbour was here today. I think he wants to buy my mother!'

In the Middle East, as elsewhere, grilling, frying, mincing and stewing are common ways of dealing with meats. For all grilled dishes, such as the shish kebabs well known in the West, buy the best and most tender cuts of meat: leg or loin of lamb, and fillet of beef or veal. Cut the meat preferably across the grain for extra tenderness. Clean it well, trim off the fat and remove any tendons, tough membranes and ligaments. Marinate for as long as possible (anything from 2 to 24 hours) to tenderize and flavour it.

Meshwi (Grills)

The word *meshwi* in Arabic covers all types of meat, whether large joints or smaller pieces, which are grilled or roasted over a fire. In North Africa, people light small fires in their courtyards and sit around them while a leg or other joint of lamb is turned on a spit, helping themselves to slices of the meat as it becomes deliciously brown.

In Turkey, *döner kebab* is a great favourite. Slices of tender lamb 3 cm (1 inch) thick and 10 to 12 cm (4 to 5 inches) wide, marinated for several hours in a mixture of oil, salt, pepper and onion juice with parsley, *rigani** and sometimes mint, are threaded and packed tightly, with a few pieces of fat squeezed between them, on to a rotating vertical spit. The spit turns automatically and slowly over a hot charcoal fire. Gas and electric heat are sometimes used. Slices are cut off as the meat acquires a warm brown glow. In restaurants this is often done in full view of the diners.

The ubiquitous *döner* (called *shawarma* in Arabic) which have now deluged Britain are a sad version of the real thing with their poor meat, excessive fat and uninspired flavouring.

Rotisserie spits which are available in this country as an attachment to oven cookers, or on their own, give excellent results.

Leg of lamb is ideal for spit-roasting. Marinate it for 2 hours in any one of the marinades given below for shish kebab. Then set it over a charcoal fire which has stopped smoking. If gas or electric heat is

* The Greek variety of wild marjoram, to be found in Greek and Cypriot stores. If not available, use dried oregano or thyme.

used, preheat the grill very thoroughly. Turn the leg, basting or brushing with marinade occasionally. The cooking time will depend on the size and age of the meat. A small leg of young lamb should provide some cooked slices within 35 to 45 minutes, older meat in 1 hour. When these are cut off, the inside meat continues to cook, providing more slices within 10 to 15 minutes.

Lamb cutlets, loin and chump chops lend themselves beautifully to the *meshwi* treatment. They should be placed on a hot oiled grid over an open fire which has stopped smoking, or under a thoroughly well-heated grill.

Serve with plain rice, salads, both fresh and puréed or creamed, and pitta or Arab bread (page 434).

Lahma Mashwi/Shish Kebab
Grilled Meat on Skewers

Also called *shashlik*, this is probably the most famous Turkish dish, and it undoubtedly lives up to its reputation. It is said by Turks to have been created during the splendid, conquering era of the Ottoman Empire, when Turkish soldiers, forced to camp out in tents for months on end, discovered the pleasure of eating meat grilled out of doors on open fires of charcoal or dry wood.

The meat grilled on its own is delicious with only salt and pepper. An added refinement is to marinate it first, and to perfume the flames over which it is grilled with herbs. In Greece and Turkey, quartered raw tomatoes and pieces of onion and sweet pepper are threaded on to the skewers in between the cubes of meat.

The kebabs may be served in a flat, hollow Arab bread or pitta, which is often placed under them to catch the juices when they are grilled *under* the heat. These 'hollow cups' can be served topped with a salad of finely chopped raw tomato and raw onion.

Alternatively, serve the skewers on a bed of parsley or chervil accompanied by various salads or, as is traditional in some countries, on a bed of plain white rice. In Persia, the rice is garnished with an egg yolk, presented on the half-shell. The yolk is then stirred into the rice at table.

Here are three popular marinades for seasoning the meat, enough for 1 kg (2 lb) leg of lamb or fillet of beef, cut into medium sized cubes about 2 cm (¾ inch) square.

Marinade 1

150 ml (¼ pint) olive oil	2 teaspoons dried rigani
Juice of 1 lemon	Pulp of 2 tomatoes, sieved
2 onions, chopped and crushed to extract juices*	(optional) Salt and black pepper
2 bay leaves, cut into small pieces	

This is a particular favourite in Greece, where the distinctive flavour of *rigani* (see footnote on page 252) is much appreciated.

Mix all the ingredients together in a large bowl. Marinate the cubed meat for at least 2 to 3 hours, longer if possible. Iranian cooks marinate it for at least 12 hours, which makes it beautifully tender.

The method of cooking the meat for shish kebab is much the same, whichever marinade is used.

Drain the cubes and thread them on to skewers, preferably the four-sided type. Grill over charcoal or wood, or under a preheated gas or electric grill, turning and basting them from time to time, or brushing them with the marinade. Make sure that the fire has stopped smoking before grilling. Cook the meat until the cubes are a rich brown colour on the outside, but still pink and juicy within. This takes from 7 to 10 minutes, but the time depends on the type and degree of heat, how far the skewers are from the heat source, and the size of the cubes.

Marinade 2

from Sidqi Effendi's Turkish cookery manual.

150 ml (¼ pint) olive oil	1 teaspoon ground cinnamon
Juice of 2 onions	Salt and black pepper

Prepare the marinade and proceed as above.

Marinade 3

300 ml (½ pint) yoghourt	Salt and black pepper
Juice of 1 onion	

Marinate the meat cubes for at least 3 hours in the well-mixed marinade ingredients. Serve sprinkled with a little ground cinnamon if you like.

* Can be done in a garlic press or an electric blender.

□ *By reason of the sweet smiles of the salt cellar of her mouth,*
blood flows from the heart as from a salted kebab.*

Kofta Meshweya
Grilled Minced Meat on Skewers

Each country and each area in the Middle East has its favourite
flavourings for *kofta*. Here is a basic recipe, giving a few simple
alternative seasonings. Use fat meat to keep it moist and juicy.

1 kg (2 lb) lamb, beef or a mixture of both, minced 2 onions, grated Salt and black pepper	Optional seasonings: 1 teaspoon ground cinnamon, or 1 teaspoon allspice, or 1 teaspoon ground cumin and 1 teaspoon ground coriander.

Put the meat through the mincer two or three times, then mix
together with the remaining ingredients in a bowl, and pound or
knead until very, very smooth. The art of making this delicious
meat dish lies in achieving an extremely soft and pasty texture.

Take smallish lumps of the mixture and pat them into sausage
shapes around skewers (preferably the four-sided type). If grilling
over a barbecue, wait until the charcoal has stopped smoking and
glows dull red before you place the skewers over it. Try not to let the
meat touch the metal, and make sure the grid is well oiled to prevent
the meat from sticking to it. Turn the skewers until the *kofta* are
cooked and browned all over.

Serve nestling in warm Arab bread or pitta to catch the juices, or
with plain rice, and accompanied by salad.

≈ A very special version of this *kofta* is made with a few pine nuts
worked into the meat. It is usually shaped in small ovals around the
skewer.

≈ In Turkey they serve *kofta kebab* on a bed of yoghourt beaten
with a sprinkling of salt, pepper, chopped parsley and mint topped
with chopped tomatoes.

≈ You can also spoon a little of the yoghourt on to the meat and
garnish with chopped spring onion. This is called *yoğurtlu kebab*.

≈ Grill rows of shish kebab (above) and *kofta* together. Serve them

* From the *Kanju'l Ishtiha (The Treasure of the Appetite)* by Abu Ishaq of Shiraz, the
sixteenth-century Persian poet of food.

on a bed of parsley or chervil, sprinkled with finely chopped onions. This is often served in Egyptian cafés as *kofta wa kebab*.

Moroccan Brochettes

Moroccans call their diminutive *kofta*, *brochettes*, in the French manner. The streets of Fez are dotted with little braziers of glowing charcoal over which turn many small skewers heavy with tiny pieces of meat, liver or *kofta*, irresistibly enveloping passers-by with their enticing aroma.

More than any other Middle Eastern people, Moroccans have adopted and become intoxicated with every spice that has come their way en route to Europe from the Far East. But they use them so discreetly that one should only just be able to guess what has gone into the rich combination. Moroccan *kofta* are sometimes rich with every spice sold in the *attarin* or market. Here is one of many variations.

1 kg (2 lb) beef or lamb, finely minced	¼ teaspoon ground cumin
2 onions, grated	¼ teaspoon ground coriander
4 tablespoons finely chopped parsley	½ teaspoon harissa or ras el hanout (see page 65)
½ teaspoon dried sweet marjoram or oregano	Salt and black pepper
	¼ teaspoon cayenne pepper (optional)

Mix finely minced meat with onions, herbs and seasonings, and pound or knead vigorously until very smooth and pasty. Shape small lumps of the mixture round skewers, and grill as in the preceding recipe.

≈ If the meat is lean it is good to pour a sauce of melted butter with salt and a squeeze of lemon juice on the brochettes.
≈ Another favourite brochette is made up of grilled pieces of lamb's liver sprinkled with salt, cayenne pepper and cumin.

☐ *Riddle: It is red like blood:*
       It burns like fire.
       What is it?
 Answer: Red pimento.

Whole Roast Lamb on a Spit

Whole roast lamb or sheep is a festive, ceremonial repast in the Middle East, prepared for parties, festivals and family gatherings. Although the poor can rarely afford meat, there is one day at least when all are assured of eating it. This is at the *Eid-el-Kurban* (sometimes called *Eid-el-Kibir* in Egypt), on the tenth day of the last month of the Muhammadan year, a festival in commemoration of Abraham's sacrifice of Isma'il.*

By ancient custom, well-to-do families sacrifice a sheep or lamb on this day. The victim must be fat, young and unblemished. The eyes of the animal are blackened, a piece of confectionery is placed in its mouth and its head is turned towards Mecca. The words, 'In the name of God', are spoken as the animal is slain. It is then usually roasted on a spit, and the meat is distributed to the poor. These offerings are also made after a death, a birth, and on other important occasions such as moving house, the start or end of a long journey, or the arrival of an important guest.

In Cairo, our balcony overlooked a street where, on several occasions, I watched the roasting of a 'ceremonial' lamb, accompanied by wailing and singing. The smell penetrated my bedclothes and wardrobe, and remained with me through the night.

A recipe written by Sidqi Effendi in the nineteenth century gives instructions for roasting a lamb in the open, a fabulous piece for a summer party in the garden.

Buy a baby lamb (see the recipe for baby lamb on page 259) or a young lamb. Ask the butcher to clean it and remove the entrails. (You can keep the heart and liver to cook separately.) The head may be left on, but have the eyes removed.

Rinse the lamb inside and out, and wipe it dry. Rub it well with salt and black pepper, and sprinkle it with onion juice, made by squeezing a few onions in a garlic press or puréeing them in an electric blender. Push a wooden or metal rod right through the lamb from breast to hindquarters, and truss its legs together.

If you do not have a large enough barbecue, it is not difficult to make one. In his recipe, Sidqi Effendi describes the fire and the spit used in his day – a hole dug in the ground and filled with charcoal – a rather primitive method which, I suspect, would not be entirely successful in a British climate and on damp soil.

* In Islamic lore, he offered Isma'il, not Isaac.

In their booklet *Profitable Catering with New Zealand Lamb*, the New Zealand Meat Producers' Board gives a rather more detailed and accurate explanation for building a turnspit and fire:

An outdoor fire must be red hot when starting to roast. The building of an efficient turnspit involves some considerations. The spit must be set on a level which turns the meat at the right distance from the fire. Air vents to the ash pit, dripping trays set low enough to prevent the drippings from being burnt, a fender barrier to prevent live pieces from the fire falling into the drippings – all these need close and careful attention.

The fire is best raised on old furnace bars or a piece of an old iron fence placed at least 30 cm (1 ft) off the ground, and the fire built up on this at least 60 cm (2 ft) high so that the heat is radiated on to the carcass as it slowly revolves. A back brick wall and wings are needed – 1·2 to 1·4 m (4 to 4½ ft) in height and supported by buttresses at the back and sides. The spit can consist of a long galvanized pipe about 4 cm (1½ in) in diameter with a sturdy old cart wheel fixed to it for turning. This is then set in grooves on top of the side walls at not more than 90 cm (3 ft) above the basting pans. The lamb carcass is then impaled on the pipe and rotated backwards and forwards by an operator standing on one side of the fire out of the direct line of the heat.

Before a barbecue occasion, the fire should be lit and a complete test made of the arrangements for shielding the wind, the type of fuel being used, the efficiency of the turning wheel, and so on. The fire should be started early enough in the day to allow it to get well burnt through, so that an even flow of heat is available along the full length of the turnspit. Later, as the lamb is being roasted, the heat must be reduced at the forequarter end, or it will be done before the thicker hindquarter is cooked.

The essential of good spit-roasting is constant basting. Use ladles or basting spoons firmly fastened to long poles for this purpose. The use of a shield with eye holes is also an advantage when basting a carcass.

After 3 or 4 hours' roasting allow the carcass to rest for 20 to 30 minutes to enable top heat to escape, and for the meat to settle for clean carving. Serve from the spit or remove to a large tray.

Allow at least 3 hours to roast a 13- to 16-kg (29- to 35-lb) lamb. Increase this to at least 4 hours for a lamb up to 23 kg (50 lb) in weight. With the carved lamb serve mounds of rice cooked with pine nuts or almonds and raisins, and scented with spices (see the stuffing in the next recipe), and a selection of salads. Alternatively serve with Arab bread, which can be used to hold the meat and salads.

If a deep-frozen lamb is used, it must first be allowed to defrost for at least 24 hours before being prepared. Rub with salt, black pepper and onion juice, and proceed as above.

A medieval cookery manual gives a method of barbecuing adopted from the Crusaders. It was pierced with a rod and held between two poles. Fires were lit on either side, with the result (it was said) that roasting was quicker and more even.

Qouzi Mahshi aw Kharouf Mahshi
Roast Stuffed Kid or Baby Milk-fed Lamb

This is a Saudi Arabian speciality. It appears at every feast, be it royal or humble, served on a huge tray, surrounded by mountains of rice and decorated with hard-boiled eggs. Kid is traditionally used, but baby lamb is often substituted. The lamb is stuffed, then roasted outdoors over charcoal as in the preceding recipe. It can also be roasted in the oven if there is room for it.

Baby lambs of 7 to 8 kg (15- to 18-pounders) are hard to come by in this country for various reasons, chiefly the system of government subsidies. These milk-fed lambs can, however, be bought either from a specialist butcher or possibly from a farmer. They are most likely to be available in spring. At other times of the year they must be ordered in advance and are more expensive.

What is generally sold as young lamb, and readily available, is already weaned, usually weighing at least 11 kg (24 lb).

A 7- to 8-kg (15- to 18-lb) baby lamb
2 tablespoons ground coriander
1 teaspoon ground ginger
Salt and black pepper
Juice of 1–2 onions

STUFFING

1 kg (2 lb) long-grain rice
¼–½ teaspoon saffron (optional)
2 onions, chopped
2 tablespoons oil
120 g (4 oz) almonds, chopped
120 g (4 oz) pistachio nuts, chopped
120 g (4 oz) walnuts, chopped
120–250 g (4–8 oz) seedless raisins
Salt and black pepper

GARNISH

Sprigs of parsley
2–3 hard-boiled eggs, sliced
2 large onions, thinly sliced

Ask the butcher to prepare the lamb as in the preceding recipe.

Rinse the meat inside and out, and wipe it dry with a clean cloth.

Rub inside and out with the seasonings and onion juice, and set aside while you prepare the stuffing.

To make the stuffing: boil the rice until tender, adding a little saffron if you like. Drain well. Sauté the chopped onions in the oil until transparent. Add them to the cooked rice and mix well with the nuts and raisins. Season to taste with salt and pepper.

Stuff the lamb tightly and sew the openings with strong thread. Put it in a large baking tray in an oven preheated to 220°C (425°F/ Mark 7), then reduce the heat to 150°–160°C (300°–325°F/Mark 2–3). Roast the lamb, basting it occasionally with its own juices and turning it over once or twice if possible. Alternatively, you can wrap it in foil and roast it in a moderate oven (180°C/350°F/Mark 4), uncovering it for the last ½ hour of cooking. Roast for approximately 2 hours for well-done meat, and 1½ hours if you prefer it slightly pink.

If using an 11-kg (24-lb) lamb, prepare in the same manner, using about half as much again stuffing, and roast for about 4 hours, or until done to your liking.

Serve on a large tray or platter, lavishly decorated with parsley, sliced hard-boiled eggs and sliced onions. Surround with a ring of rice prepared in the same way as the stuffing.

This magnificent dish serves 15 to 18 people, if you prepare the smaller lamb.

≈ The lamb can also be boned before it is stuffed. I have seen baby lambs served at weddings, made to look like miniature camels, their boneless backs shaped into a hump.

□ *Arab saying: 'One's eating shows one's love.'*

Whole Roast Leg of Lamb

Here is another traditional dish which, in the past, would probably have been sent to the local baker's oven for cooking.

1 large leg of lamb	2 large onions, sliced
3–4 cloves garlic, slivered	500 g (1 lb) tomatoes, sliced
Salt and black pepper	1 teaspoon dried rigani* or
750 g (1½ lb) potatoes, thickly	oregano (optional)
sliced	1–2 aubergines, sliced (optional)

* See footnote on page 252.

Wipe the leg of lamb clean. Pierce it all over with the point of a sharp knife and insert the slivers of garlic at different depths. Rub generously with salt and pepper.

Put the prepared lamb, fat side up, in a large baking tin, and surround it with the sliced potatoes, onions and tomatoes. Sprinkle if you like with a little *rigani* or oregano. If aubergines are to be used, sprinkle the slices with salt and leave them in a sieve or colander for at least ½ hour to allow the bitter juices to drain away. Do not add them at this stage.

Have the oven preheated to 220°C (425°F/Mark 7). Put in the leg of lamb, reduce the heat to 160°C (325°F/Mark 3) and roast for about 2½ hours, or until done to your liking – only about 1½ hours if you prefer the meat very rare. Baste occasionally with the pan juices.

Squeeze the moisture from the aubergine slices and add them after the first ¾ hour. Turn the vegetables over once during the cooking so that they cook evenly in the juices from the joint, and pour off excess fat.

The joint should be very tender, juicy and sweet, and the vegetables quite soft. I like them practically disintegrating, but if you prefer them to be rather more firm, add them to the joint after about 1 hour's cooking, when it has already released some fat. Baste the vegetables when you baste the meat, and moisten occasionally with a little water if necessary.

≈ You can of course cook the leg of lamb without the vegetables. Here is a sauce which you can pour on each serving as you hand it out: Sauté a handful of blanched, slivered almonds, add the juices from the pan and a little water and stir in 2 tablespoons raisins or sultanas.

Leg of Lamb Sofrito

An alternative way of cooking a leg of lamb is by the method called *sofrito*. Page 265 gives detailed directions for this cooking method, under the recipe for veal *sofrito*. Briefly, it consists of cooking the meat, seasoned and flavoured to taste, in a large, covered pan over very low heat, with only about 150 ml (¼ pint) water and a few tablespoons of oil or other fat. The meat simmers gently and is turned occasionally, with a few more tablespoons of water added as necessary. It is cooked until almost falling apart. This takes about 3 hours for an average-sized leg of lamb of, say, 2 to 3 kg (4½ to 6 lb).

Thickly sliced potatoes, tomatoes and onions are sometimes added to the pan in the same way as in the preceding recipe for roast leg of lamb. Aubergines may also be included, added about ½ hour before the end of cooking time.

Dala' Mahshi
Stuffed Breast of Lamb

This is an extremely cheap dish. It is exquisite served with vegetables or accompanied by a pyramid of extra stuffing, and a great favourite in our family.

This is one of the Middle Eastern fruit and meat dishes, possibly inspired by ancient Persia. A quince sauce, stewed apples, black cherry jam or cranberry sauce may be substituted for the apricots in this recipe.

2 whole large breasts of lamb	250 g (8 oz) dried apricots – a
Oil	sharp kind
Salt and black pepper	1 tablespoon sugar

STUFFING

500 g (1 lb) long-grain rice	Salt and black pepper
2 medium-sized onions, chopped	120 g (4 oz) pine nuts or chopped
2–3 tablespoons oil	walnuts
250 g (8 oz) beef, minced	120 g (4 oz) small seedless raisins
3 tablespoons finely chopped	(optional)
parsley	

Ask the butcher to chine the meat and to cut a pouch between the skin and the ribs – or do the latter yourself with a long, sharp knife. Wipe clean with a damp cloth.

Prepare the stuffing. Wash the rice first in very hot and then in cold water, then drain well in a colander. Fry the chopped onions in oil until golden brown, using a large saucepan. Add the minced beef and fry until browned. Add the rice and continue to fry for a few minutes until well coated. Sprinkle with parsley and pour in an equal volume of boiling water as you have of rice (i.e. for 2 cups of raw rice add 2 cups water). Season to taste with salt and pepper, cover the pan tightly and simmer undisturbed over low heat for 20 minutes, or until the water has been absorbed and the rice is tender but still firm. Remove from the heat and, when cool, add the nuts and, if you wish, raisins. Sometimes the stuffing is coloured with ½ teaspoon saffron or turmeric, or perfumed with a tablespoon of orange blossom water, but I do not personally care for these additions.

Stuff the pouches with the rice mixture. Rub the joints with oil, salt and pepper, and roast, uncovered, in an oven preheated to 220°C (425°F/Mark 7), then reduced to 160°C (325°F/Mark 3). Roast for about 1 hour, or until the meat is well cooked and browned on the outside.

Put the apricots in a small saucepan with 1 tablespoon sugar and their soaking water. Bring to the boil and simmer, uncovered, for about 20 minutes. By this time the apricots will be soft and the liquid reduced.

A few minutes before serving, pour off the excess fat from the roasting tin. Turn the oven up to 230°C (450°F/Mark 8). Pour the apricot sauce over the lamb and glaze in the oven for 5 to 7 minutes. Do not leave in the oven too long, as the apricots burn easily.

≈ Instead of being roasted, the lamb may be braised on top of the stove. It is first seared in hot fat to brown it all over, then simmered until quite tender. The apricots and their water are added after searing, and the lamb simmers with them gently for about ¾ to 1 hour. In this method, there is no need to simmer the apricots separately first. They need only be soaked.

Kuzu Kapama
Turkish Lamb with Spring Onions and Herbs

1 tender leg of lamb	1 large onion, quartered
2 large bunches spring onions, chopped	1 teacup water
	2 tablespoons oil
1 bunch fresh dill or chervil, finely chopped	Salt and black pepper

Clean the leg of lamb and remove excess fat. Put it in a saucepan or casserole with the spring onions, herbs and onion. Add water and oil, and season with salt and pepper. Cover and simmer gently for 2 to 3 hours, or until very tender, turning the joint over occasionally, and adding a little more water when necessary.

Choua
Moroccan Steamed Lamb

Besides favouring rich stews, Moroccans also appreciate tender steamed meat, gently flavoured with cumin alone. The Turks also eat steamed lamb, not usually alone as in the recipe below, but accompanied by vegetables such as tomatoes, shallots and sliced aubergines (the last sprinkled with salt and allowed to drain before being added), and flavoured with a little tomato concentrate and a sprinkling of sage.

1 kg (2 lb) leg or shoulder of lamb	1 teaspoon ground cumin
Salt	

Cut the meat into 2-cm (¾-inch) cubes. Sprinkle lightly with salt and cumin. Steam over boiling water for about 2 hours, or until the meat is tender and juicy. In the past, steaming was done in a pot sealed with paste, but today a hermetically sealed double steamer can be used instead.

Serve with plain rice or couscous (page 335).

Arni Tou Hartiou
Lamb with Vine Leaves Baked in Fila Packets

This is a not-so-common version of a Greek dish of lamb baked in parchment packets. It is very presentable and you can eat everything. (See *fila* page 139).

24 vine leaves, fresh or preserved in brine	Pepper
	2 cloves garlic, crushed
1 small leg of lamb	2 teaspoons oregano or marjoram
4–5 tablespoons olive oil	2 tablespoons butter, melted
Juice of ½ lemon	6 sheets fila pastry
Bottom of a bottle of red wine	Salt

If you are using fresh vine leaves, blanch them for a few seconds in boiling water until they become limp and their colour changes. If you are using leaves preserved in brine, soak them in boiling water for at least 1 hour to remove their saltiness, changing the water once. Drain well.

Cut the meat into six fat slices.

In a bowl mix the oil, lemon juice, wine, pepper, garlic and oregano or marjoram and turn the pieces of meat in this marinade. Leave in a cool place for ½ to 1 hour, or longer.

When you are ready to cook, brush each sheet of *fila* very lightly with melted butter. Place two vine leaves side by side towards the middle of a long edge. Lay a piece of meat over them and sprinkle with very little salt, and cover with two more vine leaves.

Fold the *fila* over and over the meat and leaves making a well-closed packet. Repeat with the rest of the *fila*, meat and leaves. Brush the top lightly with melted butter and place all the packets on an oven rack.

Bake in a preheated oven (160°C/325°F/Mark 3) for about 20 minutes by which time the meat should be done and the *fila* lightly coloured. You will have to cut into one piece to make sure that it is done as you like it.

Serve the packets as they are, crisp and hot.

≈ A variation is to sprinkle the meat with 250 g (8 oz) grated cheese. Kefalotiri is used in Greece, but mature Cheddar is an acceptable alternative.

Veal Sofrito

Sofrito, the name our community in Egypt used to describe a method of cooking halfway between roasting and stewing in oil with very little water, is, predictably, a Spanish name. For a *sofrito* of lamb, see page 261.

The cooking fat in this method varies according to the country and the community in which it is practised. Butter *can* be used, but I prefer sunflower oil.

A 1- to 1½-kg (2- to 3-lb) joint of veal, leg or loin	Salt and black pepper
	Juice of ½ lemon
3 tablespoons oil	1 teaspoon powdered turmeric

Turn the meat in hot oil in a large pan until it is browned all over. Sprinkle with salt and pepper, lemon juice and turmeric, and moisten with a coffee cup of water. Cover the pan and cook over very low heat for about 2 hours, turning it over once, or until the meat is very tender. It will cook in its own juices, released by the salt, so add only very little more water at a time, about a teacup in all, as it becomes absorbed.

Serve hot with potatoes or rice, or cold with salad.

Yoğurtlu Kebab
Kebabs with Yoghourt

A Turkish meat and yoghourt dish with bread.

750 g (1½ lb) lean tender lamb or beef
Oil
Butter
Salt and black pepper

6 thick slices bread
4 tomatoes, skinned and chopped
300–450 ml (½–¾ pint) yoghourt
1 tablespoon paprika

Cut the meat into 3-cm (1-inch) cubes and sauté gently in oil or butter until tender but juicy. Season to taste with salt and pepper. (Some people like to marinate the cubes first in a mixture of oil, onion juice, salt and pepper, or in seasoned yoghourt, for at least an hour to tenderize them.)

Remove the crusts from the bread and cut the slices into 3-cm (1-inch) squares. Toast lightly or fry in butter. Arrange at the bottom of a shallow serving dish.

Sauté tomatoes in a very little butter until they are very soft, and season to taste with salt and pepper. Beat the yoghourt and season to taste.

Just before serving, spread the puréed tomatoes over the squares of toast, pour the yoghourt over the tomatoes, arrange the meat cubes on top, and dribble 2 tablespoons butter mixed with the paprika over the entire dish.

Serve immediately.

≈ A rather good party snack is made keeping the bread slices whole. Fry or toast them and arrange them in individual plates. Then cover them just before serving with the respective layers of puréed tomatoes, yoghurt and fried kebabs, and decorate with paprika butter.

Lamb or Veal Chops in Tomato Sauce

6–8 large lamb or veal chops
About 2 tablespoons butter
1 large onion, sliced
2–3 whole cloves garlic
250 g (8 oz) ripe tomatoes, skinned and chopped, or a 225-g (7-oz) tin skinned tomatoes, drained and chopped

Salt and black pepper
2 tablespoons chopped parsley
½ teaspoon ground cinnamon (optional)

Trim as much fat from the chops as possible and flatten them lightly. Sauté in hot butter for a few minutes on both sides until just coloured. Remove them from the frying pan and arrange in a large pan. Keep hot.

Fry the onion and garlic cloves in the same butter until they are golden and the garlic is sweet and aromatic. Add the tomatoes, season to taste with salt and pepper, and sprinkle with parsley and cinnamon if liked. Cook for a few minutes longer, then add about 150 ml (¼ pint) water. Mix well and pour the sauce over the chops. Simmer gently, uncovered, until the chops are tender and the sauce is rich and aromatic, adding more water if necessary. Taste and adjust seasoning, and serve on plain rice (pages 401–4) or burghul pilav (page 332), or with sautéed or mashed potatoes.

The garlic may be removed at the end of cooking time, and the sauce sieved or put through an electric blender. I prefer to leave it as it is.

Minced Meat Dishes

Behind the seemingly inexhaustible range of subtly varying and intriguing minced meat balls, one can discern the creative spirit responsible for the luscious designs which decorate Arab pottery, carpets and minarets. It inspired in cookery a rhythmic and prolific repetition as it did the floral and geometric patterns, endless variations on a theme. Each district and each town has striven to offer its own particular speciality for a meat ball.

One thing they all have in common is a perfectly smooth texture. To achieve this, the meat is usually minced two or three times, then pounded, sometimes with a little grated onion, until it becomes extremely soft and pasty. A food processor reduces meat to a paste in minutes. First blend the chopped onion until practically liquefied, then add the meat, egg or eggs (if used) and seasonings, and blend at high speed until pasty. Other ingredients should then be added and blended for a short time until thoroughly mixed. It is also possible to knead the meat to a paste with your hands.

Use minced lamb, beef or veal, or a combination of lamb and beef, according to your taste – beef and lamb give a rich, strongly flavoured dish, veal a paler, more delicate one. Always pound or knead it for as long as possible. The delightful smoothness of the texture is well worth the effort.

Seasonings vary within the Middle East from gentle cinnamon to allspice, cumin, coriander and, of course, salt and either mild or strong pepper. Season mildly to begin with and keep on adding spices, salt and pepper until you achieve the flavour you desire.

Kofta bil Roz
Minced Meat Fingers with Ground Rice

1 kg (2 lb) lean beef, minced
2 heaped tablespoons ground rice
3 tablespoons finely chopped
  parsley

2 onions, finely chopped
2 cloves garlic, crushed (optional)
Salt and black pepper
Oil or butter

Put the meat through the mincer two or three times if possible. Turn it into a large bowl. Add the ground rice, chopped parsley, onions and garlic (if used). Work to a fine smooth paste by squashing with a wooden spoon and kneading vigorously by hand. If you have a food processor, use it as described above. Season to taste with salt and pepper.

Take large, walnut-sized lumps and shape them into long fingers. Fry them gently in oil or butter, turning them until they are brown all over and well cooked inside. This should take about 10 minutes.

≈ Quite often, Middle Eastern cooks drop the lightly fried fingers into a tomato sauce similar to the one suggested for *koukla* below.

Koukla

From the Greek word for doll.

3 slices white bread, crusts
  removed
1 kg (2 lb) lamb or beef, a mixture
  of these, or veal
3 eggs

¾ teaspoon ground allspice or 1
  teaspoon ground cinnamon
Salt and black pepper
Oil for deep-frying

Soak the bread in water; squeeze dry and crumble. Mince the meat two or three times if possible, then add the soaked bread, eggs, and allspice or cinnamon. Knead vigorously to work the mixture to a smooth paste. If you have a food processor, drop in the eggs first and beat for 10 seconds; add the bread and beat for another 10 seconds. Add the meat and seasonings gradually, beating between each addition. This gives a beautiful paste. Season to taste with salt and pepper.

Roll the mixture into marble-sized balls and deep-fry in hot oil for a few minutes until cooked through and a rich brown colour.

≈ Alternatively, you can stew the *koukla* in a tomato sauce made by blending 1 tablespoon flour with 1 tablespoon melted butter in a large pan, and stirring for a few minutes over low heat. Gradually add a medium tin of tomato concentrate diluted in about ½ litre (¾ pint) water, stirring constantly. Bring to the boil and season generously with salt and pepper. Drop in the meat balls and simmer them for about ½ hour, or until they are well done and the rich sauce is thick and reduced. (In this case the frying of the meat balls is best omitted, since the sauce would otherwise become very rich indeed.)

Kadin Budu *or 'Lady's Thighs'*
(Turkish Meat Balls)

This interesting recipe with the enticing name reverses the usual procedure of frying the meat balls before simmering them in sauce. Its virtue lies in producing a juicy, tender combination, and then trapping it in a crisp, dry shell.

500 g (1 lb) lamb or beef, minced	1 teaspoon finely chopped parsley
1 tablespoon uncooked rice	1 teaspoon finely chopped fresh
3 eggs	dill (if available)
1 teaspoon olive or other cooking oil	Salt and black pepper
	Flour
1 small onion, grated	2 tablespoons butter

Work the meat to a smooth paste (see the recipe for *koukla* above). Put it in a bowl with the rice, 2 eggs, the oil, grated onion, parsley and dill if available, and season with salt and pepper. Mix well and knead to a smooth paste. Take walnut-sized lumps and roll into the shape of a chicken thigh, rinsing your hands with water to prevent the meat from sticking to them, and arrange them in a pan with a little water to cover them. Cover and simmer gently for about 20 minutes, or until the water has been absorbed and the meat and rice are cooked. Drain the meat balls and cool them.

Beat the remaining egg. Dip the meat balls in the beaten egg and roll them in flour. Melt the butter in a frying pan. When it is sizzling, add the meat balls and fry them until crisp and golden brown all over.

Terbiyeli Köfte

Here is a Turkish way of cooking meat balls also popular in Greece.

Prepare the meat mixture for either *kofta bil roz* or *koukla* (page 268), and shape it into marble-sized balls. Poach them in lightly salted water for about 20 minutes until soft and tender.

Prepare the following sauce. Beat 3 egg yolks until light. Add the juice of 1 or 2 lemons (2 for a strong, lemony flavour) and a teacup of water, and continue beating until well blended. Season to taste with salt and pepper. Heat very gently over water, using a double saucepan if you have one, to just below boiling point. Do not on any account let the mixture boil, or the eggs will curdle.

Lift the meat balls out of the poaching water, using a slotted spoon. Drain them well. Then drop them into the egg and lemon sauce and heat them through.

This is delicious served with plain rice.

Kofta fil Sania
Minced Meat Loaf in a Tray

1 kg (2 lb) lamb, beef or veal, minced	Oil or butter
2 onions, grated	1 small tin tomato concentrate
Salt and black pepper	4 tablespoons finely chopped parsley
1 teaspoon ground cinnamon or allspice	

Have the meat minced two or three times if possible. Add the grated onions and work them together to a very smooth, soft paste, as for all *kofta* mixtures. Season to taste with salt, pepper and cinnamon or allspice, and mix these spices in thoroughly.

Spread the meat mixture evenly over the bottom of a large oiled or buttered baking tray, flattening it out with a wooden spoon. The meat should be 2 to 3 cm (¾ to 1 inch) thick. Dot with butter shavings and bake in a moderate oven (180°C/350°F/Mark 4) until the surface of the meat is browned and gives off a roasted aroma – about 40 minutes to 1 hour.

Mix the tomato concentrate with 300 ml (½ pint) water and pour it over the meat. Return the loaf to the oven, and continue to bake for about 10 minutes, or until the tomato sauce has become absorbed and the meat is well cooked. It will shrink away from the sides of the tray.

Turn the loaf out on to a large serving dish and cut it into squares or lozenges; or, if you are using a round baking tray, cut it into wedges like a cake. Garnish with chopped parsley, and serve with mashed or roast potatoes or a selection of salads.

≈ Some people prefer to flavour the meat with a teaspoon each of ground cumin and coriander instead of cinnamon or allspice.

≈ A version of this is very popular in Israel where it is simply called *sania* after the tray in which it is cooked. For this, add 3–4 tablespoons tahina to the tomato concentrate and beat in enough water to form a very light cream.

Armenian Kofta

500 g (1 lb) potatoes, boiled and mashed	30–60 g (1–2 oz) pine nuts
	Butter
750 g (1½ lb) lean lamb or veal, minced	30–60 g (1–2 oz) small seedless raisins
1 egg, beaten	Flour
Salt and black pepper	Oil for deep-frying

Mix the potatoes and minced meat together in a bowl. Add beaten egg, and salt and pepper to taste, and knead vigorously by hand until the mixture is very smooth and soft. Fry the pine nuts in butter for a minute or two to colour them lightly. Drain and knead them into the meat and potato mixture, together with the raisins.

Shape into walnut-sized balls. Roll them in flour and deep-fry in hot oil until crisp and brown on the outside and well done inside.

Blehat Lahma bi Beid
Meat Rolls Stuffed with Hard-boiled Eggs

1 kg (2 lb) lean beef or lamb, minced
3 slices white bread, crusts removed
1 onion, finely chopped
2 egg whites
1 teaspoon ground cinnamon
½ teaspoon grated nutmeg
Salt and black pepper

2 tablespoons finely chopped parsley (optional)
4 hard-boiled eggs, shelled
Flour
Butter or oil
1 small tin tomato concentrate
1 bay leaf
1 celery stalk with leaves

Mince the meat two or three times if possible, then work it to a very smooth paste with your hands. Soak the bread in water, squeeze it dry and crumble it into the meat. Add the onion, egg whites, spices, salt and pepper to taste, and chopped parsley if used. Mix well to a light paste.

Divide the mixture into four equal parts and shape each portion round a hard-boiled egg, making four oval rolls. Pat and press the meat firmly round the eggs so that the rolls do not come apart during cooking. Alternatively, you can make one fat, long roll and stuff it with all four eggs.

Flour the rolls and fry in hot butter or oil until coloured all over.

Make a sauce with the tomato concentrate, bay leaf, celery, about 300 ml (½ pint) water and salt and pepper. Bring it to the boil and simmer for a few minutes. Drop in the meat rolls and simmer them gently until they are well done, and the sauce has reduced and thickened.

Lift the rolls out very carefully. Serve them hot with the sauce, accompanied by rice or sautéed potatoes; or serve them cold, also in their sauce. Thinly sliced, they make a fine appetizer or a cold main course.

≈Persians vary this dish by adding about 60 g (2 oz), yellow split peas, boiled until soft, to the minced meat mixture, and embedding a few soaked and stoned prunes next to the hard-boiled eggs. It is a delight to encounter them, sweet and soft, in the midst of the beautifully spiced and flavoured meat. A splendid variation.

Daoud Pasha
Meat Balls with Pine Nuts and Tomato Sauce

1 kg (2 lb) lamb, beef or veal,
  minced
Salt and black pepper
Seasonings: 1 teaspoon ground
  cinnamon or allspice, or ¾
  teaspoon each ground cumin
  and coriander*

2 largish onions, cut in half-moon
  slices
Oil or butter
60 g (2 oz) pine nuts
1 medium tin tomato concentrate
Juice of ½ lemon
2 tablespoons finely chopped
  parsley

Mince, pound or knead the meat to a smooth paste as described in the preceding recipes. Add salt, pepper and seasoning (I prefer cinnamon for this dish). Knead well and roll into marble-sized balls.

In a saucepan or deep frying-pan, fry the onion slices gently in a little oil or butter until golden and transparent. Add the meat balls and sauté over low heat, shaking the pan and rolling the balls about almost constantly to colour them all over. Add the pine nuts and fry gently for 2 minutes longer. Mix the tomato concentrate with a little water and add it to the pan. Add more water, enough to cover the balls; flavour with lemon juice and season with salt and pepper. Stir well and simmer over low heat until the balls are well done and the sauce is reduced; add more water from time to time if the sauce reduces too quickly.

A few minutes before serving, adjust the seasoning and sprinkle the dish with finely chopped parsley.

≈ An attractive way of serving this dish is to fry extra pine nuts in butter for about 2 minutes until lightly coloured. When the meat balls are cooked, decorate each one by sticking a pine nut into the top. Serve with plain white rice.

≈ A popular variation is to knead the same quantity of pine nuts into the meat ball mixture instead of having them in the sauce.

---

* These quantities will give a rather highly flavoured dish – reduce them for a more delicate aroma.

Kofta Mabrouma
Meat Rolls with Pine Nuts

This is a speciality of Aleppo in Syria, where it is traditionally baked in a round tray and served on a round dish, with the rolls arranged in diminishing circles.

2 medium-sized onions
2 eggs
1 kg (2 lb) lean lamb or beef, minced
Salt and black pepper

4 tablespoons pine nuts
3 tablespoons butter or margarine
Chopped parsley and slices of lemon, to garnish

Peel and grate the onions. Beat the eggs with a fork. Have the meat minced two or three times if possible, and mix it with the grated onions and eggs. Season with salt and pepper, and mix well. Knead vigorously by hand, in the old Middle Eastern style – or use a food processor to make the mixture very soft and pasty.

Flatten the meat mixture on a board or large plate into six thin rectangular shapes. Put a row of pine nuts about ½ cm (¼ inch) in from one of the longer sides of each rectangle and roll up into a fat sausage shape, starting from the edge lined with pine nuts.

Take an oven tray or dish, square or round, which will just hold the six rolls, and arrange them in it side by side. Dot with butter or margarine shavings, or melt the butter and brush it over each roll. Sprinkle with about 3 tablespoons water and bake in a moderate oven (180°C/350°F/Mark 4) for about ¾ hour or longer, depending on the thickness of the rolls, until cooked and well browned.

Turn out on to a hot serving dish, garnish with chopped parsley and slices of lemon, and serve hot with rice or sautéed potatoes.

Meat Balls with Raisins and Walnuts

These make lovely buffet and party finger foods.

1 kg (2 lb) lamb with quite a bit of fat, minced
Salt and pepper to taste
1 teaspoon ground allspice
½ teaspoon cumin

½ teaspoon coriander
1 large onion, grated or finely chopped
3 tablespoons raisins or sultanas
60 g (2 oz) chopped walnuts

The meat should be minced twice if possible, or turned to a paste in a food processor. Mix all the ingredients together and knead well with your hands to a soft, pasty texture. Roll into small walnut-sized balls. Fry in oil, in a few batches, turning them so that they are well browned all over but still moist and juicy.

Serve hot or cold.

≈ 2 lightly beaten eggs added to the meat paste will serve to bind it better if you have not worked the meat to a pasty texture.

≈ A few sharp dried apricots (such as those which come from Iran) soaked, drained and chopped may be used instead of raisins or sultanas.

Meat Balls in Tomato Sauce

This is a Moroccan version of an everyday Middle Eastern dish. Serve it with rice.

MEAT BALLS

1 kg (2 lb) minced lamb or beef	1 teaspoon cumin
2 medium onions, finely chopped	1 teaspoon cinnamon
2 cloves garlic, crushed	½ teaspoon ginger
1 bunch of parsley, finely chopped	Salt and pepper
1 bunch of fresh coriander, finely chopped	

SAUCE

750 g (1½ lb) tomatoes, peeled and chopped, or 1 large tin peeled tomatoes	A small bunch of parsley, chopped
2 tablespoons oil	½ teaspoon cumin
3 small fiery peppers, chopped	½ teaspoon cinnamon
	1 teaspoon cayenne, or more (or to taste)

Put all the ingredients for the meat balls together in a bowl and work to a smooth paste. Roll into small balls the size of large marbles.

To make the sauce, soften the fresh tomatoes in the oil and add the rest of the ingredients. Drop in the meat balls, add enough water to cover and simmer gently for about 20 to 30 minutes until they are done and the water reduced.

≈ In Morocco the cooking is finished in a shallow earthenware *tagine* which goes on top of the fire. Often eggs are cracked open and dropped into the sauce, one for each person, and cooking continues until they set.

Courgette or Aubergine Meat Balls

This dish is a speciality of Smyrna.

1 kg (2 lb) courgettes or peeled aubergines	60 g (2 oz) Parmesan or Cheddar cheese, grated
Salt	2 large eggs, beaten
Oil	Black pepper
2 onions, chopped	Flour
500 g (1 lb) beef, lamb or veal, minced	

Slice courgettes or aubergines. Sprinkle with salt and leave to drain in a colander for at least ½ hour. If courgettes are used, boil them until tender. Otherwise, fry the aubergines in a little oil until soft, and drain on absorbent paper. Fry the chopped onions until soft and golden.

Chop the courgettes or aubergines finely, and mix with the meat, which has been squashed with a wooden spoon and kneaded or blended to a smooth paste. Add the cheese, onions and beaten eggs, and season to taste with salt and pepper. Mix well.

Shape the mixture into walnut-sized balls. Roll them in flour and fry or sauté them gently over very low heat so that they are well cooked inside before they become too brown on the surface.

These vegetable meat balls can be eaten hot with potatoes or rice, or cold with salad. Both ways are delicious.

≈ A variation given to me by an Egyptian uses 500 g (1 lb) chopped artichoke hearts mixed with 600 g (1¼ lb) minced meat which has been worked to a paste.

Leek Meat Balls

1 kg (2 lb) leeks	Black pepper
Salt	Oil
500 g (1 lb) beef, minced	Juice of 2 lemons
60 g (2 oz) dry white breadcrumbs	1 tablespoon butter
2–3 eggs	

Wash the leeks very carefully. Remove their tough outer leaves and trim both ends. Boil in lightly salted water until just tender. Drain and mince or chop very finely.

Turn the meat into a very smooth paste in the usual way. Mix it with the minced leeks, breadcrumbs and eggs, and season with salt and pepper. Mix well. Shape into walnut-sized balls and fry in oil until coloured all over.

Put the lemon juice, butter and a little water (about 1 teacup) in a large pan. Sprinkle with salt and pepper, and bring to the boil. Drop in the meat balls and simmer, covered, for 15 to 20 minutes, or until they are soft and well cooked, and the lemony sauce has been absorbed, shaking the pan occasionally and adding a little more water if the sauce reduces too quickly. The combination of leek and lemon with meat is unusual and delicious.

≈ An excellent version of these vegetable and meat balls is made with spinach. Substitute 750 g (1½ lb) fresh spinach for the leeks. Wash the leaves carefully and stew them for a few minutes without additional water. Put through a mincer or chop finely and add to the meat mixture.

Kibbeh

Kibbeh is the great love of the inhabitants of the Fertile Crescent. It is the national dish of Syria and Lebanon, and Iraq boasts of dozens of *koubba*. There are innumerable versions of this family of dishes which epitomize the food of the area. *Kibbeh* is said to have been mentioned in ancient Assyrian and Sumerian writings and to have been served by King Ashur Nassir Bal II. Today the daily life of the people revolves around its preparation, a dramatic ritual. The pounding of the meat and wheat in a stone or metal mortar with a heavy metal pestle is a sound that wakens one in the morning and lulls one to sleep in the afternoon, a sound instantly provoked by the arrival of an unexpected guest or a ring of the door-bell.

I know of no other dish whose preparation is enveloped by such a mystique. Some women are known to have a special 'hand' or 'finger' for making *kibbeh*. This knack is envied by other women and especially by their husbands. One is said to be favoured by the gods if one is born with a long finger, which makes the shaping of *kibbeh* easier.

Today, one can use a very fine mincer to save some of the pounding (or an electric blender as suggested for meat ball mixtures) and a machine has recently been developed in the Lebanon which takes care of the whole process.

There are countless variations of *kibbeh*, some widely known throughout the Middle East, others less common or belonging to one particular community. I shall give as many as I know, for I think that they are really worth trying.

The most common *kibbeh* is a mixture of fine cracked wheat or burghul, grated onion and minced lamb pounded to a paste. Eaten raw, it is called *kibbeh nayé*. The same paste can be fried or grilled. In *kibbeh bil sanieh*, a layer of minced meat filling is sandwiched between two layers of *kibbeh* and baked in the oven. Stuffed *kibbeh* are hollow, oval or long torpedo-shaped shells of the same paste, filled with a minced meat mixture and deep-fried. This last type has innumerable variations: the outer *kibbeh* shell is sometimes made with seasoned cracked wheat alone. Jews have a variation made with matzo meal (called *massa* by Sephardic Jews), evolved for Passover but prepared throughout the year because of its particular lightness. Another *kibbeh*, popular in Egypt, is made with ground rice instead of cracked wheat and is stewed in a lemony stock or *hamud*. We called it *kibbeh hamda* (page 283).

Small *kibbeh* are often added to aubergine and other vegetable stews, or are cooked in yoghourt, pomegranate juice, or sesame meal mixed with orange juice.

Kibbeh Nayé
Raw Kibbeh

500 g (1 lb) lean tender lamb (leg is good)	Black pepper
Salt	120 g (4 oz) fine burghul (cracked wheat)
1 large onion	

Pound the meat rhythmically and vigorously with a little salt in a stone mortar until it is smooth and pasty. Alternatively, if a mincer is available, put the meat through it several times. Grate and pound the onion with salt and pepper, or mince it a few times. Mix the onion and meat together and mince or pound again, adding 1 or 2 tablespoons cold water or 1 or 2 ice cubes to achieve a soft and smooth texture.

Rinse the burghul in a sieve and quickly squeeze out the excess moisture. Add to the meat and onion mixture, and knead vigorously by hand. Adjust seasoning and pound in the mortar for as long as possible, about ½ hour; or mince together several times, then pound and knead again until soft and smooth. Now that food processors have come in there is no need for all that pounding. If you have one, blend the burghul separately and turn the meat to a paste, then blend the two together.

This dish is traditionally served on a decorative glass or china plate, accompanied by a bowl of young Cos lettuce leaves. It is passed round as an appetizer or at the start of a meal. Each guest selects a lettuce leaf, and using it as a spoon, scoops up a small portion of *kibbeh* which is eaten together with the lettuce. Some people also like a squeeze of lemon and a dribble of olive oil.

≈ Another way of serving *kibbeh nayé* is to roll the meat mixture into small thin fingers, pile them on a bed of lettuce leaves and accompany them with a bowlful of young lettuce. Cos lettuce is used in the Middle East. Sprinkle with olive oil and lemon juice or tamarind and garnish with spring onions and a dusting of cayenne.
≈ Proportions of meat and wheat can be varied and quantities reversed.
≈ You may like to spice the meat mixture with 2 teaspoons cumin, 1 teaspoon allspice and a good pinch of cayenne. I have become very fond of that.

Keema
Sauce for Kibbeh Nayé

Another popular way of serving raw *kibbeh* is accompanied by a minced meat sauce – in this case, veal is a favourite.

500 g (1 lb) onions, finely chopped	60 g (2 oz) pine nuts
2 tablespoons butter or oil	Salt and black pepper
500 g (1 lb) lean veal, minced	Juice of 1 lemon

Fry the onions in butter or oil until golden. Add the minced veal and continue to fry until the meat changes colour. Add the pine nuts. Season to taste with salt and pepper, and add water to cover. Bring to the boil and simmer gently until the meat is well cooked and soft, and the sauce is reduced. Some people prefer to fry the pine nuts lightly on their own, and add them just before serving. Sprinkle with lemon juice and serve in a separate bowl with the *kibbeh nayé*.

Grilled or Fried Kibbeh

500 g (1 lb) lean tender lamb, cubed	Black pepper
Salt	250 g (8 oz) fine burghul (cracked wheat)
1 large onion, finely grated	Oil

Prepare the basic mixture as in the recipe for *kibbeh nayé* (page 278) but using double the quantity of burghul, as given above. Pat into round, flat, biscuit shapes. Grill over charcoal or under a grill, or fry in hot oil until crisp and golden. Grilled *kibbeh* are dry and people like to dip them in hot fat.

Kibbeh bil Sanieh
Kibbeh in a Tray

This is the easiest stuffed *kibbeh*. Prepare *kibbeh* mixture using 500 g (1 lb) meat to 250 g (8 oz) burghul, and following the method described for *kibbeh nayé* (page 278).

FILLING

1 medium-sized onion, finely chopped	Salt and black pepper
2 tablespoons oil	½ teaspoon ground cinnamon
250 g (8 oz) lamb, veal or beef, minced	½ teaspoon allspice
60 g (2 oz) pine nuts	A few tablespoons stock
	Butter

Fry the onion in hot oil until golden and soft. Add the meat and pine nuts, and continue to cook until the meat has changed colour. Add a few tablespoons of water to soften the meat, season and add the cinnamon and allspice.

Butter a baking tray and smooth half of the *kibbeh* mixture over the bottom. Spread the filling over this evenly and cover with a second layer of *kibbeh* mixture. Press down well. Cut diagonal lines over the top to make lozenge shapes.

Melt about 3 tablespoons butter and pour this all over the top of the *kibbeh*. Bake in a moderate oven (180°C/350°F/Mark 4) for ¾ to 1 hour. It should be well done, and beautifully brown and crisp on top. Basting occasionally with a few tablespoons of stock makes the inside moist and even better.

This is equally delicious hot or cold. Serve with yoghourt and salads.

≈ An Iraqi version includes 2 tablespoons each of raisins and chopped walnuts.

≈ A simple and very good *kibbeh bil sanieh* can be made with a crust of burghul without meat and the same meat filling. For the crust, soak 250 g (8 oz) burghul in water for 5 minutes, drain then put in the processor with an onion, 1 teaspoon cumin, 1 teaspoon coriander, salt and pepper. Press two layers in the tray with the filling in between.

Syrian Stuffed Kibbeh

This is the most popular as well as the most intriguing of *kibbeh*. The preparation of these small *kibbeh* requires all the talent of *kibbeh*-making. Syrian women measure their art and make their reputations by their craftsmanship and finesse when making this dish. The art lies in making the outer shells as long (at least that is what we thought in Egypt, for I realize now that the Lebanese prefer a small, oval, stocky shape), as thin and as even as possible. The crisp, light, tasty shells should crack to divulge a juicy, aromatic meat filling.

Prepare the *kibbeh* meat mixture as for raw *kibbeh* on page 278, using 500 g (1 lb) meat to 250 g (8 oz) burghul, and the filling as for *kibbeh bil sanieh* (opposite).

Wet your hands with cold water. Take a small lump of *kibbeh* mixture the size of an egg. Holding it in your left hand, make a hole in it with a finger of the right hand and use the left hand to pat the paste round the finger and work it into a long, slim, oval shape, pressing it up the finger, widening it and slipping it round and round. This is rather reminiscent of pottery-making. If the paste cracks, dip a finger in cold water and use it to stick the shell together again. There must be no holes in the shell. British soldiers in the Middle East during the Second World War used to call these *kibbeh* 'Syrian torpedoes', and I think that this describes their shape rather well.

Fill the shell with about a tablespoon of filling. Close the opening by wetting the rim with cold water and sticking the edges together.

Pat and smooth into a thin end to achieve a slim, oval shape. If you find all this too difficult, make a small round or oval shape. This seems easier to achieve.

Deep-fry the 'torpedoes' in oil to a rich, dark brown colour. Drain. Serve hot or cold with a selection of salads: ground almond (page 119), a tahina cream salad (page 80) or a mixed fresh vegetable salad.

These *kibbeh* can be prepared ahead and fried just before serving, or fried and warmed up again in a covered dish in the oven.

≈ Smaller versions get thrown into aubergine, courgette and meat stews.

≈ These *kibbeh* may also be baked. Put them on a tray, brush with oil, and bake in a hot oven (230°C/450°F/Mark 8) for a few minutes, turning over once, until well browned.

Plain Burghul Kibbeh

This variation of the preceding *kibbeh* is a much easier one which does not require the long preparation of mincing and pounding. It is equally delicious and rather lighter, although the shell has a tendency to break as it is handled, and must be carefully patched if it does.

KIBBEH SHELL

750 g (12 oz) fine burghul (cracked wheat)
120 g (4 oz) plain flour

1 tablespoon oil
Salt and pepper

FILLING

As for kibbeh bil sanieh (page 280)
Oil for deep-frying

Make the shell. Wash the burghul in a fine-meshed sieve and squeeze it dry. Put it in a large bowl with the other shell ingredients and knead vigorously for at least 15 minutes to achieve a smooth paste, adding a little water if necessary.

Shape and fill the shells as in the preceding recipe. Deep-fry and serve with salads.

≈ Some people like to add 4 tablespoons tomato concentrate and 1 teaspoon cumin to give the colour of meat and also more flavour.

Stuffed Kibbeh in Yoghourt

Prepare stuffed *kibbeh*, using burghul and meat (Syrian stuffed *kibbeh*) (page 281), or burghul alone (opposite).

YOGHOURT SAUCE

1 litre (1¾ pints) yoghourt	3–4 cloves garlic, crushed
1 tablespoon cornflour or 1 egg white	2 tablespoons dried crushed mint
Salt	3 tablespoons butter

Stabilize the yoghourt with cornflour or egg white and salt to taste as described on page 124, to allow it to be cooked without curdling. Add the *kibbeh* uncooked and continue to simmer for about 20 minutes. (You may also deep-fry the *kibbeh* first, and then cook them in the yoghourt for a few minutes only.)

Fry the crushed garlic and dried crushed mint in hot butter with salt to taste. Pour this over the yoghourt and stir well.

Alternatively, add the crushed garlic raw to the yoghourt and garnish the dish with dried crushed mint.

Serve hot or cold, with plain rice.

≈ Cooked rice is sometimes added to the yoghourt in the pan and simmered for a few minutes before serving.

Kibbeh Hamda
Kibbeh of Ground Rice Cooked in Hamud

This is my mother's recipe for an unusual *kibbeh*. It is very easy to prepare and does not require so much time. This dish is always served in a *hamud* sauce (page 423) or soup as an accompaniment to rice.

FILLING

90 g (3 oz) lamb or beef, minced	2 tablespoons finely chopped parsley
30 g (1 oz) fat (from the meat), finely chopped	Pinch of ground allspice
	Salt and black pepper

KIBBEH SHELL

180 g (6 oz) lamb or beef, minced	Salt and black pepper
250 g (8 oz) ground rice	

Oil
1 recipe hamud (page 423)

Mix the filling ingredients well together in their raw state.

Make the *kibbeh* shell. Pound the minced meat and ground rice with a little seasoning. Gradually add a little water (a few tablespoons should be enough) and knead to a smooth paste. You can either pound the mixture in a mortar or use an electric blender to achieve a soft, homogeneous paste.

Put a little oil on your hands to prevent the paste from sticking to them and roll the mixture into walnut-sized balls. Hollow each ball with your finger, and fill with about a teaspoon of filling. Close the openings by pinching them together firmly.

Drop the balls into boiling *hamud* (page 423) and simmer gently for about 1 hour.

≈ These little *kibbeh* can also be fried in hot oil and then cooked in an aubergine, broad bean, artichoke or plain meat stew. They are quite delightful.

Potato Kibbeh in the Tray

This is a bit like an Oriental shepherd's pie. For a grander presentation people make potato croquettes with the ingredients using the minced meat and nuts as a filling and sometimes dipping in beaten egg and flour before deep frying. But it is far simpler and just as good to make it in the tray.

SHELL

375 g (12 oz) coarse burghul	A shake of nutmeg
750 g (1½ lb) potatoes	½ teaspoon allspice
60–90 g (2–3 oz) butter, melted	Salt and pepper
3 eggs	

FILLING

1 large onion, chopped	2–3 tablespoons pine nuts or
3 tablespoons oil	chopped walnuts
750 g (1½ lb) minced meat – lamb or beef	1 teaspoon cinnamon
	Salt and pepper
2–3 tablespoons raisins or sultanas	

Soak the burghul in cold water for an hour, then drain and squeeze out the excess water. Peel and boil the potatoes in salted water till soft, then drain and mash well. Mix both together in a bowl, add melted butter and eggs, spices, salt and pepper and beat well.

To make the filling, fry the onion in oil till golden. Add the meat and continue to fry, stirring, until it changes colour. Add raisins or sultanas, nuts, cinnamon, salt and pepper and 3–4 tablespoons of water. Cook gently for a little while longer until the meat is soft and most of the water absorbed.

Spread half the potato mixture on the bottom of a baking dish. Cover with the meat mixture and top with the remaining potato. Bake in a medium oven (190°C/375°F/Mark 5) for about 35 minutes or until the top is slightly browned.

Koubba Helwa
Minced Meat Dumplings in a Sauce

This Iraqi speciality is part of the *kibbeh* family. It takes quite some time to make but it is very good.

SHELL

Salt

500 g (1 lb) semolina

Flour

FILLING

500 g (1 lb) lean minced beef

1 large onion, grated

2 dried limes (noumi basra, page 63)

Salt and pepper

SAUCE

1 large onion, chopped

2 tablespoons oil

2 cloves garlic, crushed

90 g (3 oz) tomato concentrate

A few celery leaves

3 tablespoons chopped parsley or coriander leaves

Juice of ½ lemon, or more

Salt and pepper to taste

500 g (1 lb) courgettes, thinly sliced

or 500 g (1 lb) tender young okra

To make the shell stir ½ teaspoon salt into the semolina and moisten with just enough cold water to make a paste, working it in your hands until it is doughy and elastic.

For the filling, mix the minced beef with the onion, salted first and allowed to disgorge its juice in a sieve, and dried limes (these give the dish its distinctive taste), pounded in a mortar or pulverized in a blender. Season to taste with salt and a good amount of pepper and work well with your hands to a smooth paste.

Wash your hands and, dusting them with flour so that they do not stick to the semolina paste, take a walnut-sized lump of semolina, roll it into a ball and flatten it thinly in the palm of your hand. Place a tablespoon of the meat filling in the centre. Bring the semolina up over the filling, pinching well to close tightly and pat into a ball shape. Roll in a little flour so that the dumplings do not stick together while waiting to be cooked.

Make the sauce in a very large saucepan. Fry the onion in oil until golden, add the crushed garlic and, when the aroma rises, add the tomato concentrate and the rest of the ingredients and enough water to cover the dumplings eventually. Bring to the boil, reduce the heat, then drop the dumplings in very gently. The sauce should be barely quivering and should cover the dumplings, which remain submerged until they are cooked and then begin to float. Cook until the semolina is soft – about 25 minutes.

Serve hot, with rice. Release any dumplings which may get stuck to the bottom and sides of the pan very gently.

Shish Barak
Meat Dumplings in Yoghourt Sauce

A speciality from Syria and Lebanon. This is a dish that takes time.

DOUGH

250 g (8 oz) flour
1 teaspoon salt

Water

FILLING

1 onion, chopped
2 tablespoons oil
3 tablespoons pine nuts or
   chopped walnuts

500 g (1 lb) minced lamb
Salt and pepper
1 teaspoon cinnamon or ½
   teaspoon allspice

SAUCE

2½ litres (4½ pints) yoghourt
1 tablespoon cornflour
1 egg
Salt

1 tablespoon dried mint
2 cloves garlic, crushed
2 tablespoons butter

To make the dough, stir the salt into the flour and add water by the tablespoon, about 50 ml (2 fl oz), just enough for the dough to hold together in a ball. Let it rest for ½ hour.

For the filling, fry the onion in oil till soft, add nuts (let the pine nuts brown), then add the meat and seasonings and cook, stirring until the meat changes colour.

Roll out the dough thinly on a floured board and cut into small rounds about 4–5 cm (1½–2 inches) in diameter with a pastry cutter. Place a teaspoon of filling on each round and fold the pastry over it into a half-moon shape. Press the edges together firmly so that they stick, then bring the ends together in the shape of little hats.

To stabilize the yoghourt so that it does not curdle, beat in the cornflour mixed with a few tablespoons of water and the egg, add salt if desired and bring it to the boil slowly in a saucepan, stirring all the time, until it thickens. Drop in the dumplings and simmer for 20 minutes or until they are done. Before serving, fry the mint and garlic in butter and pour over the dumplings. You may accompany with rice.

Meat and Vegetable Stews

For most people in the Middle East the main dish of the day is a rich vegetable stew with a little meat, accompanied by rice in the towns and by wheat, pulses or bread in the villages. *Yakhnie* to the Syrians and Lebanese, *touagen* to the North Africans and *abgusht* to the Persians, stews are one of the finest features of Middle Eastern food. In his *Işret Nāme*, the sixteenth-century Turkish poet Revani describes a stew as 'a saint who makes his prayer rug float upon the water', comparing the pieces of meat floating in the rich sauce to the prayer rugs on which the saints of old were wont to traverse rivers.

The earliest recipes that have been found, written in Baghdad in the year 1226, were for the most part descriptions of stews, dishes otherwise known only by name – extraordinary and breathtaking dishes in which the art of blending flavours, of balancing and composing textures and aromas is manifested in wonderful array. In many ways, it is similar to the art of the painter who builds up his canvas, knowing when one stroke of his brush demands another one, sharper or more subtle, larger or smaller; feeling his way towards a harmony of shapes and surfaces, colour and tension; trying to achieve a balance between a small, sharp, acid yellow and a large, soft, pastel mauve; supporting the one with a cooler, sweeter red and piercing the other with an orange dart.

It is this subtle, sensuous feeling for the balance of ingredients, the harmony of flavours and aromas (sometimes achieved by a sharp contrast), which produced the recipes recorded by Muhammad ibn Hasan ibn Muhammad ibn al-Karim al-Katib al-Baghdadi, who 'loved eating above all pleasures'. The same talent is responsible for the stews of today, some originating in and extraordinarily similar to the ancient ones using the same contrasts of sweet and sour, spicy and sweet, or the peace of equals. Some stews are earthy and simple, others are complicated and intoxicating, using fascinating combinations of meat with fruits, nuts and vegetables. Persians have brought this luxurious cooking to its peak, as their recipes below will show. It is interesting to note the influence of the rich period of the Persian Empire on the food of all the Middle East, stretching as far as the North African Maghreb.

These stews can be served as party and family dishes alike, and they can always be extended for the unexpected guest simply by adding water. Nineteenth-century cookery manuals often remark that the amounts given will serve a certain number of people, but that you can add water if a friend should arrive.

The usual accompaniment is couscous (page 335), plain rice or burghul, but some people prefer to eat the stew simply with large quantities of bread, breaking pieces from it and dipping them into the sauce.

Finally, to those who are afraid of trying new symphonies and harmonies of taste, may I remind them that not so long ago discordant colours such as pinks and oranges, blues and greens, were painful to Western eyes. The taste for them having been acquired, they have revolutionized design and fashion; and wherever colours are used today, it is the discords that stimulate, excite and give the greatest pleasure.

When making these stews, use lean or fat meat, as you wish. Cheaper cuts are good enough, as the lengthy cooking ensures that the meat becomes tender. Clean the meat carefully, removing membranes, tendons, etc. Cut into cubes 2 to 3 cm (¾ to 1 inch) square. Then sear the meat in oil or butter until lightly coloured before stewing it. This adds richness and a deeper colour to the dish, and keeps the meat juices within the meat. If you want a pale, light stew, simmer the meat in water without frying it first, removing any scum as it comes to the surface.

Marrow bones are often added to Middle Eastern stews for richness; they are cracked to allow as much of the marrow to escape as possible.

Use very small amounts of spices to begin with, and then add more to your taste after the stew has been cooking for some time. Add herbs, onions, garlic, celery and spring onions for flavouring. Introduce vegetables to enrich and vary the flavour, and yellow split peas, beans, lentils or chick peas to give weight, to bind, or to create extra texture. Use saffron to colour the dish yellow, tomatoes to make it red, and pomegranate sauce to give it a brown colour. Pour in a little wine vinegar where you would usually add wine, and balance it with sugar for a sweet-and-sour sauce. Use chopped or ground almonds, walnuts, pistachios or hazelnuts to thicken the sauce, and raisins and fresh or dried fruits to sweeten it.

In the Middle East, stews are cooked for several hours over very low heat; quite often they are sent to the local communal oven to be cooked. Cook a stew gently for several hours on top of the stove, with a lid on the pan. Alternatively, you *can* put it in a slow oven (150°C/300°F/Mark 2) in a covered dish; but in this case, you should use less liquid – only half that suggested in the following recipes.

Meat Stew with Aubergines

3 small aubergines or 2 medium ones
Salt
1 large onion, finely chopped
Oil
750 g (1½ lb) lean or fat lamb, or veal, cut into cubes
2–3 tomatoes, skinned and quartered
1 tablespoon tomato concentrate
Juice of ½ lemon
1 teaspoon ground cumin
½ teaspoon ground allspice (optional)

Slice the aubergines and sprinkle them with salt. Allow them to drain in a colander for at least ½ hour.

Fry the onion in about 2 tablespoons oil until soft and golden. Add the meat and brown it well. Add the tomatoes and squash them with a fork. Stir in the tomato concentrate and lemon juice thoroughly. Season to taste with salt, pepper and cumin, and if you like, allspice. Cover with water, bring to the boil and simmer gently, covered, for about 1½ hours.

Wash the aubergine slices and pat them dry. Fry them in hot oil for a few minutes to colour them all over. Drain and add them to the stew, and simmer, covered, for a further ½ hour.

Turkish Meat Balls with Aubergine Purée

4–6 aubergines, depending on size
1 kg (2 lb) beef, minced
2 eggs
3 tablespoons dry white breadcrumbs
1 teaspoon ground cumin
1 teaspoon ground allspice
Salt and black pepper
Flour
About 3 tablespoons oil
1 large onion, sliced
2 tablespoons tomato concentrate

Grill the aubergines under a hot grill or over a flame until the skins are blackened and blister away from the flesh. Cool, and rub the skins off under cold running water, taking care to remove every charred particle. Squeeze out as much of the bitter juices as possible; drain well and mash the flesh with a fork.

Mince the beef two or three times if possible, and knead by hand to a very smooth, soft paste (or use a food processor as suggested on page 267). Add the eggs, breadcrumbs and seasonings (less if you want a blander mixture – this is rather strong). Knead again. Shape the mixture into small balls, roll them in flour and fry in oil over fairly gentle heat until they are cooked through and coloured all over. Remove and drain.

In the same oil, fry the sliced onion until soft and golden; add the aubergine purée and tomato concentrate, season to taste with salt and pepper, and cook gently for another 10 minutes. Drop in the meat balls and simmer for a final 10 minutes.

Serve with plain rice or bread, and with one or two salads.

Mefarka

A great delicacy of ancient origin, *mefarka* was always prepared by my paternal grandmother and several of my aunts on Jewish feast days for the men to relish on their return from the synagogue. It is a very unusual *cold* dish of minced meat, fresh broad beans and eggs, lightly perfumed with thyme and spices.

Oil

1 kg (2 lb) fresh broad beans,
  shelled, or 500 g (1 lb) shelled
  frozen broad beans

Salt and black pepper

½ teaspoon dried thyme, or more

750 g (1½ lb) lean beef, minced

1½ teaspoons mixed spices:
  nutmeg, cinnamon, cayenne
  pepper, ground cloves

3 eggs

Juice of ½ lemon (optional)

Mix 3 tablespoons oil with a little water (about 1 small teacup) in a saucepan. Add broad beans, sprinkle with salt and pepper to taste, and perfume with a little thyme. Simmer gently until the beans are tender, adding water, a little at a time, as it becomes absorbed.

In the meantime prepare the meat mixture, called *tatbila*. Heat 2 tablespoons oil in a deep frying pan or heavy, flameproof casserole. Add the minced beef when it is just warm – if the oil is too hot, the meat will dry up. Add also the mixed spices, salt and pepper to taste, and just enough water to cover. Simmer the whole until the meat is well cooked, soft and moist, and has absorbed the water as well as the aroma of the spices.

Add the meat mixture to the beans and stir well, crushing lightly with a fork. Break the eggs into the pan and stir. Cook, stirring constantly, until they set. Turn out on to a serving dish and allow to cool. Taste and correct seasoning – the balance and degree of flavouring alters with the change in temperature.

Serve cold, sprinkled with a little lemon juice.

Lahma bi Ma'Ala
Meat in the Frying Pan

1 kg (2 lb) best stewing beef,
  topside or top rump

2–3 tablespoons oil

500 g (1 lb) onions, coarsely
  chopped

Salt and black pepper

1 teaspoon ground allspice (or
  more for a spicy dish)

60 g (2 oz) parsley, chopped

500 g (1 lb) tomatoes, skinned and
  chopped, or a 400-g (14-oz) tin
  skinned tomatoes

1 small tin tomato concentrate

Cut the beef into cubes. Fry in hot oil in a large frying pan, stirring and shaking the pan to brown the cubes all over. Remove from the pan. In the same oil, fry the onions to a dark golden colour. Return the meat and add salt, pepper, allspice, parsley, tomatoes and tomato concentrate, and about 4 tablespoons water. Simmer gently for 2 hours, uncovered. Add a very little water from time to time, but only if necessary. If using tinned tomatoes, the liquid should be enough and no water need be added, except at the start.

The large quantity of onions and parsley and the allspice give this dish a distinctively Middle Eastern flavour.

Serve with rice or sautéed potatoes.

≈ A similar Moroccan *tagine*, a speciality of Fez, varies in that the ingredients are not fried first but covered with cold water and simmered gently for 2½ hours with a little oil and a variety of seasonings: cumin, ginger, allspice, salt, black pepper, paprika and cayenne are all used, though with a light hand, so that the effect is gentle rather than fiery. This *tagine* is sometimes coloured with ¼ teaspoon turmeric.

≈ Another similar stew is the Tunisian *mirmiz*, which includes a sliced sweet green pepper, and possibly a hot dried chilli pod or two.

≈ Chick peas or haricot beans, soaked overnight, are sometimes added at the start of cooking as well.

Runner Bean and Meat Stew

This is a popular family meal in Egypt, Syria and the Lebanon.

1 kg (2 lb) fresh runner beans	2–3 tablespoons tomato
2 large onions, finely chopped	concentrate
3 tablespoons oil	Salt and black pepper
1 kg (2 lb) stewing lamb or beef, cubed	

Wash, string and cut the runner beans in half. Fry the onions in oil in a large, thick-bottomed saucepan until transparent and golden. Add the meat and brown it all over to seal it. Add the beans and fry very gently until slightly softened. Stir in the tomato concentrate, blending it well into the fat. Cover with water, season with salt and pepper, and bring to the boil. Cover the pan and simmer gently for about 1½ hours, or until the meat and vegetables are very tender and the sauce is quite thick. Add more water if necessary during the cooking time. Adjust seasoning and serve.

≈ This dish can also be flavoured with ¼ teaspoon grated nutmeg, ½ teaspoon ground cinnamon and the juice of 1 lemon. You may use green or French beans.

☐ *The Steam from a Meat Stew**

A poor man at Akshehir found a crust of dry bread and was thinking how he could find something to give it a relish when he passed by a cook's shop and saw a saucepan of meat sizzling and boiling on the fire. It gave out a delicious odour.

He went up to the saucepan and began breaking off little bits of bread, holding them in the steam until they became quite soft, and then he ate them.

The Cook looked on with astonishment at this very odd way of making a meal, and for some time said nothing, but no sooner had the poor man finished, than he caught hold of him and demanded payment.

The man protested that he had really had nothing from the Cook, and refused.

It happened that our Khoja was Cadi† of Akshehir at the time, and when the Cook brought the man before him he heard the charge in the ordinary course. Taking two coins from his pocket, he said to him, 'Now listen to this,' and he began to shake the coins and make them rattle. 'All the satisfaction you get will be the sound of these coins.'

The Cook cried out in amazement, 'But, your Honour, what a way to treat me!'

'No!' said the Khoja. 'It is a perfectly just settlement of the claim. A man who is so mean as to ask for payment for the steam of his meat will get the sound of these coins and nothing more.'

Mozaat
Shin of Veal Stew

The particular quality of this dish (which I used to hate as a child) lies in its texture. The connective tissue of the shin softens in the cooking process and turns into gelatine, while the meat becomes extremely tender and soft.

1 kg (2 lb) shin of veal in large pieces	Salt and black pepper
6 potatoes, peeled and sliced	½ teaspoon turmeric (optional)
2–3 tablespoons oil	Juice of ½ lemon

* Barnham (trans.), *Tales of Nasr-ed-Din Khoja*.
† Judge.

In a large pan, sauté the meat and sliced potatoes gently in hot oil, turning them to brown them all over. Season with salt and pepper, and add the turmeric if you wish to give the stew a yellowish colour. Half-cover with water. Simmer, covered, for about 2 hours, or until the meat is very soft and the sauce reduced, adding a little more water during this time if necessary, and turning the meat over occasionally. Adjust the seasoning and squeeze a little lemon juice over the pan just before serving.

≈ This dish is particularly delicious if about a dozen little *kibbeh hamda* (page 283) are simmered in it instead of some of the potatoes.

≈ In other variations, about 6 artichoke hearts or 2 sliced, salted and drained aubergines are added. In this case one again uses fewer potatoes; and, if using aubergines, one omits the turmeric.

□ *Arab proverb: 'God loveth those who are content.'*

Jellied Shin of Veal

1 kg (2 lb) shin of veal and 1 shin bone, cracked	6 hard-boiled eggs, shelled and quartered
2–3 tablespoons oil	2 tablespoons boiled green peas
Salt and black pepper	1 boiled carrot, cut into thin sticks
½ teaspoon turmeric (optional)	A little chopped parsley
Juice of ½ lemon	Thin slices of lemon

Sauté the meat and bone (well scrubbed and cracked to release the marrow) in hot oil in a large pan until coloured all over. Season with salt and pepper, and sprinkle with turmeric if used. (This gives a fine taste and a delicate colour.) Cover with water. Bring to the boil and simmer gently, covered, for about 2½ hours. The meat will be quite soft and the sauce rich and gelatinous. Remove any excess fat by drawing absorbent paper across the surface. Stir in the lemon juice and adjust the seasoning.

Remove the bone and cut up any largish pieces of meat. Rinse out a large mould and arrange the meat and hard-boiled eggs in it in a decorative pattern. Boiled green peas, thin sticks of cooked carrot and chopped parsley can be used to brighten the dish. Strain the pan juices into the mould through a fine sieve, and leave the dish in the bottom of the refrigerator for a few hours or overnight until the liquid has set to a jelly. To serve, heat the sides of the mould by dipping it in hot water.

Turn out on to a large serving dish and decorate with thin slices of lemon.

≈ The addition of a calf's foot at the start of the preparation or 1 teaspoon softened gelatine at the end will give a much firmer jelly.

Lissan al Assfour
Birds' Tongues

This is a lamb stew made with pasta, and I am assured that it only tastes right if small Italian *pastine* called *graniamo* (which look like tiny birds' tongues or largish grains of rice) are used. During the last war, when this Italian import was not available, families who loved the dish used to make the pasta themselves with flour and water, rolling it into the correct, tiny thin ovals between their fingers. A friend recalls spending hours with her brother every Sunday as a small child, rolling the little bits of dough.

2–3 onions, sliced
3 tablespoons oil
1 kg (2 lb) lean lamb (e.g. leg), cubed
Salt and black pepper
1 teaspoon ground cinnamon (optional)

½ litre (1 pint) meat stock or water
250–500 g (½–1 lb) graniamo pasta
Grated Parmesan cheese

Fry the sliced onions in oil until soft and golden, using a large pan. Add the cubed meat and brown it on all sides. Season with salt, pepper and a little cinnamon if liked; cover the pan, and let the onions and meat cook very slowly in their own juice until nearly ready, about 1½ hours. Pour in the stock or water, and simmer for ½ hour longer.

Add the pasta and cook for a further 20 minutes, or until the meat is very tender and the pasta has swelled to double its bulk. Add more water if and as required. Some sauce must be left at the end of cooking time. Taste and adjust seasoning.

Serve with grated Parmesan cheese – a recent innovation in Egypt, due to the Italian influence of the last century.

Meat Balls with Spinach and Chick Peas

One of the dishes inspired by the ancient Persian tradition.

750 g (1½ lb) beef, lamb or veal, minced
1 onion, finely chopped
Salt and black pepper
Oil
120 g (4 oz) chick peas, soaked overnight

500 g (1 lb) fresh spinach
1 tablespoon butter
2 cloves garlic, crushed
1 teaspoon ground coriander

Make small meat balls in the usual way (see page 267) with the minced meat, onion and a little salt and pepper. Fry them lightly in oil until brown all over.

Boil the soaked and drained chick peas in water until soft. Wash the spinach leaves thoroughly, removing any thick stems. Drain well and chop the leaves finely on a board. Stew them in their own juice and the butter until tender. Add the drained, cooked chick peas and the meat balls, cover and continue simmering for a further ½ hour, or until the meat balls are well done, adding a little water if necessary.

The particular refinement of this dish comes from a fried mixture called *taklia*, a great Arab favourite for flavouring stews and soups. It is made by crushing the 2 cloves of garlic with a little salt, then frying them in oil with the ground coriander until the mixture smells sweetly. This should be added to the other ingredients at the end of the cooking and stirred in well.

Serve with rice.

≈ A rather delicious Turkish way of eating this dish is to smother it in yoghourt mixed with crushed garlic, seasoned with salt, pepper and dried crushed mint. The whole is decorated with a sprinkling of scarlet paprika. In this case, omit the *taklia*.

≈ Another interesting variation from modern Persia is *khoresh sak*, a spinach and orange sauce served with rice. The juice of 1 lemon and 2 oranges is mixed with 1 tablespoon flour and cooked with the meat and spinach for the last ½ hour. In this case, add only crushed garlic fried in butter instead of the complete *taklia*.

☐ *A Tale of Goha**

Goha hadn't eaten meat for several weeks and had worked up a great desire for it, so he sold an old pair of shoes and a hat and gave the money to his wife saying: 'Today I want a good stew with meat. Put whatever vegetable you like in, but there must be meat. Here's ten piastres, go and buy a rotl of mutton.' He went off to work, happy with the thought of the marvellous stew. On her way to the butcher the wife stopped at the spice merchant and could not resist buying some perfume with the money she had in her pocket. When Goha came home beaming all over, she put the pot of stew in front of him and served him a large plateful. He ate it all, finding beans, lentils, chick peas, potatoes, macaroni, rice, aubergines and bamia, but no meat. He served himself again, fished around in the pot but still found no meat. He asked his wife: 'Where's the meat?' 'Oh!' she said, 'I went to the neighbour's to borrow some spices and when I came back the cat had eaten the meat.'

Goha got up, looked around the flat, saw the cat, took hold of him, tied him up and put him on the scales. He weighed just over a rotl. 'If this is the cat where's the meat, and if this is the meat where's the cat?'

Meat and Okra (Bamia) Stew

This is a great Egyptian favourite. Lamb was always used in the past, but today many families prefer to make it with beef or veal.

1 kg (2 lb) fresh okra (bamia or ladies' fingers)
2 large onions, finely chopped
2 large cloves garlic
60 g (2 oz) butter or 3 tablespoons oil
1 kg (2 lb) stewing beef, lamb or veal, cubed

500 g (8 oz) ripe tomatoes, sliced
1–2 tablespoons tomato concentrate
Salt and black pepper
Juice of 1 lemon (optional)
1 teaspoon ground coriander (optional)

Wash fresh okra and cut off the stems. Fry the chopped onions and whole garlic cloves in butter or oil until both are golden and the garlic is aromatic. Add the cubed meat and brown all over. Then add the prepared okra and fry gently for a little while longer. Add the

---

* Told by a troubadour in the South of France.

tomatoes, continue to cook for a few more minutes, and cover with water in which you have diluted the tomato concentrate. Season with salt and pepper, and stir well. Bring to the boil and simmer over low heat for 1½ hours or more, until the meat and vegetables are very tender and the rich sauce is reduced, adding a little more water if necessary. Taste and adjust seasoning.

The juice of a lemon may be added to the sauce, and a teaspoon of ground coriander can be fried with the garlic and onion before adding the meat, for those who like its distinctive taste.

Beef Stew with Fresh Broad Beans

1 kg (2 lb) lean stewing beef, cubed
3 tablespoons oil
500 g (1 lb) fresh or frozen green broad beans
2 whole cloves garlic
1 teaspoon ground coriander
Salt and black pepper

Sauté the meat in hot oil in a large pan until well browned. Add the remaining ingredients and cover with water. (If frozen beans are used, they should be de-frosted and added only about ½ hour before the end of cooking time.) Bring to the boil and simmer gently, covered, for about 2 hours, or until the meat is very tender.

Meat with Courgettes and Chick Peas

Another Egyptian favourite. A large English marrow, peeled and cubed, may be used if courgettes are not available.

2 onions, chopped
2 whole cloves garlic (optional)
60 g (2 oz) butter or 3 tablespoons oil
1 kg (2 lb) lean stewing lamb or beef, cubed
2–3 tablespoons tomato concentrate
60 g (2 oz) chick peas, soaked for 1 hour
Black pepper
1 teaspoon ground allspice (optional)
1 kg (2 lb) courgettes, washed and sliced
Salt

Fry the chopped onions and whole garlic cloves, if used, in hot butter or oil until golden. Add the meat cubes and brown them all over to seal in the juice. Stir in the tomato concentrate, add the soaked and drained chick peas, and cover with water. Season to taste with pepper and ground allspice if liked. Bring to the boil, stir well and cover the pan. Simmer gently for about 1½ hours. Add the courgettes (or marrow) and salt and simmer for a further ½ hour, or until the meat, chick peas and vegetables are very tender and the liquid has been absorbed, adding a little more water during cooking if necessary. Adjust seasoning and serve.

Khashkhashiya

A medieval recipe from al-Baghdadi, of doubtful ingredients (*khash-khash* is the poppy from which an intoxicating drug is made) not to be recommended. I am including it only as a curiosity.

Cut red meat into small slices: melt fresh tail and throw the meat in to fry lightly. Drop in half a *dirham*; and the same quantity of brayed (ground) dried coriander. Then cover with lukewarm water, boil and skim. Add fine-chipped cinnamon-bark and a little fine ground ginger. Make a broth with 1½ *rotls* of hot water, and add 150 *dirhams* of sugar and honey. When the sugar is dissolved, sprinkle in a handful of poppy-flour. Stir well until cooked and set. Then throw in 30 *dirhams* of fresh poppy: or, if this be not procurable, of dry poppy soaked and ground. Stir until well mixed. Colour with saffron and spray with a little rose-water. Wipe the sides of the saucepan with a clean rag, and leave to settle over a slow fire for an hour; then remove.

Tagine of Kofta and Eggs

A Moroccan dish which may have been inspired by the medieval ones of meat and eggs described by al-Baghdadi.

750 g (1½ lb) lamb or beef, minced	½ teaspoon ground allspice
3 tablespoons finely chopped parsley	½ teaspoon ground cumin
	¼ teaspoon paprika
1 tablespoon finely chopped fresh mint or 1 teaspoon dried crushed mint	Pinch of cayenne pepper
	Salt
	2 tablespoons butter
½ teaspoon dried sweet marjoram	6 eggs

Combine the meat with the herbs and spices, add salt to taste and knead well to a smooth paste. Roll into marble-sized balls. Sauté in butter in a large, deep frying pan, shaking the pan to colour them all over. Cover them with water, add a pinch of salt, and simmer for about 20 minutes, or until the meat balls are very tender and the liquid reduced.

Break the eggs carefully into the pan over the mixture and cook over low heat until set. Leave them whole or scramble them lightly with a fork. Serve with plain boiled rice or mashed potatoes.

Meat Stews with Fruit

I have found many Moroccan *touajen* (the plural form of *tagine*) incredibly like al-Baghdadi's medieval stews – a mysterious culinary bond between ancient Persia and modern Morocco.

Many Moroccans originate from the regions of the Yemen, Iraq and Saudi Arabia. They came there at different times: first in the pre-Christian era, then with the Arab Islamic invasion in the seventh century, and then again in the twelfth, thirteenth and fourteenth centuries. I suspect that the Arabs of the Abbassid period (the time of al-Baghdadi) brought these dishes with them. They were then adopted and perpetuated through the ephemeral Almovarid dynasty, the brilliant Moroccan period of the dynasty of the Almohads which diffused Moorish civilization throughout a vast empire, and again during the Sharifian dynasty of the descendants of Fatima, daughter of the Prophet, who came from Arabia at the end of the fourteenth century.

The same fruits – apples, prunes, quinces and currants – and to a large extent the same spices, are used by Moroccans today as were used by the ancient Persians and the Arabs of the Abbassid period. Al-Baghdadi's recipes recommend mashing the fruits to a pulp, but Moroccans leave them whole or sliced, and add them towards the end of cooking, to prevent them disintegrating. Fasis (inhabitants of Fez) stew their ingredients, as al-Baghdadi did, without preliminary frying, as they consider that frying would add heaviness to otherwise delicate dishes.

Every Moroccan family prizes its own very special *touajen* which generations of their cooks have prepared for them, keeping the recipes fiercely secret, and I realize that I have been able to include only a few from a vast culinary treasury.

Persian stews (*khoreshtha*), included in the chapter on rice, as they are intended as sauces for rice, have a lot in common with these stews.

Mishmishiya

A splendid meat and apricot dish which derives its name from the Arabic word for the fruit, *mishmish*. Lamb seems to have a special affinity for apricots, and a similar dish was a great favourite in our family.

From al-Baghdadi's thirteenth-century cookery manual.

Cut fat meat small, put into the saucepan with a little salt, and cover with water. Boil and remove the scum. Cut up onions, wash, and throw in on top of the meat. Add seasonings, coriander, cummin, mastic, cinnamon, pepper and ginger, well ground. Take dry apricots, soak in hot water, then wash and put in a separate saucepan, and boil lightly: take out, wipe in the hands, and strain through a sieve. Take the juice, and add it to the saucepan to form a broth. Take sweet almonds, grind fine, moisten with a little apricot juice and throw in. Some colour with a trifle of saffron. Spray the saucepan with a little rose-water, wipe its sides with a clean rag, and leave to settle over the fire: then remove.

SUGGESTED QUANTITIES

1 kg (2 lb) lean lamb, cubed	Black pepper
Salt	¼ teaspoon ground ginger
1–2 onions, finely chopped	250 g (8 oz) dried apricots, soaked
½–1 teaspoon ground coriander	and passed through a food mill
½–1 teaspoon ground cumin	60 g (2 oz) ground almonds
¼ teaspoon pulverized mastic	¼ teaspoon saffron (optional)
¼–½ teaspoon ground cinnamon	1 teaspoon rose water

This is one of the dishes in which the meat is not fried before stewing. It may seem dull at first, but the apricot sauce thickened with the ground almonds gives it a particular richness which makes frying superfluous. The apricots must be of a sharp (not sweet) variety.

The stew requires about 2 hours of gentle cooking, preferably on an asbestos mat. Leave out the mastic and saffron if you wish – I do not think they are at all necessary.

≈ A modern Persian version consists of a lamb and apricot pilav, or *polo* as it is called in Persia. I have included it in the rice chapter (page 410).

☐ *Song to a Girl**

Goodnight, oh watermelon, oh red wheat waiting in a sack,
I have waited beneath your window for the past four nights
Without food or drink, listening for the sound of your voice.
Goodnight, oh fresh ripening apricot,
I want you for my wife, yet I am too shy to say it.

Moroccan Tagine with Quince

1 kg (2 lb) fat or lean stewing lamb, cubed
2 onions, finely chopped
Salt and pepper (black, cayenne and paprika)†
1 bunch fresh coriander or parsley, finely chopped
¼ teaspoon powdered saffron (optional)
½ teaspoon ground ginger
250–750 g (½–1½ lb) quinces, cut in half and cored but not peeled‡
60 g (2 oz) butter (optional)

Put the cubed meat and 1 chopped onion in a large saucepan. Cover with water and season to taste with salt and pepper. (Moroccans use a variety of peppers, including paprika and cayenne, adding them with a light hand.) Add fresh coriander or parsley, saffron if used and ginger, bring to the boil and simmer gently, covered, until the meat is tender and the onion has practically disintegrated in the sauce. This takes about 1 hour.

Now add the other chopped onion and cook until soft. Half an hour before serving, add the quinces and cook until only just tender. The quinces may be sautéed in butter first for a richer flavour.

≈ Pears or apples (peeled and cored), dates and raisins or prunes (soaked overnight) may be used instead of the quinces, sometimes in combinations. They all make rather luxurious dishes.
≈ Chicken is also delicious cooked in this way.

---

* Maspéro, *Chansons populaires.*
† Use in moderation, to taste.
‡ You may prefer to use less fruit the first time you try this dish. Increase the amount once you have become accustomed to the taste of the meat flavoured with the sweet aromas of the fruit, and the sharp shock of quince with ginger. Some people prefer to soften the taste of quince with a little sugar.

Lahma bil Karaz
Meat Balls with Cherries

1 kg (2 lb) lean lamb or veal, minced
Salt and black pepper
½ teaspoon grated nutmeg
½ teaspoon ground cloves
½ teaspoon ground cinnamon

Oil
500 g (1 lb) sour or morello cherries, pitted
Sugar and/or lemon juice
Rounds of Arab bread or slices of white bread

Mince the meat two or three times, then squash with a wooden spoon or knead vigorously by hand to achieve a smooth, pasty texture. Season with the salt, pepper and spices, and knead again. Form marble-sized balls with the mixture and fry them gently in oil, shaking the pan to colour them all over.

Fresh, pitted sour cherries or dried ones should be used for this dish if possible. If these are not available, use tinned ones. Stew the fresh cherries in a large pan with a very little water, adding sugar and/or lemon juice to taste according to the sweetness or acidity of the fruit. Soak dried cherries overnight. If using tinned fruit, add only lemon as they will be sweet enough already. Add the sautéed meat balls, and simmer gently until cooked through, crushing the cherries with a fork when they become soft enough. Let the sugar in the sauce become caramelized a little, but add more water if this happens before the meat balls are cooked and the fruit is soft.

This dish is traditionally served on pieces of Arab bread, soft side up. If this is not available, cut thinnish slices of white bread, remove the crusts and arrange the slices on a large serving dish. Cover each slice with several meat balls and some cherry sauce. Served in this manner, they can be picked up and eaten like an open sandwich.

≈ A richer variation involves preparing a tomato sauce with a chopped onion fried with a clove of garlic, some skinned and chopped tomatoes, a little tomato concentrate and water. The cherries and meat balls are added to this sauce and simmered in it until tender.

□ *Arab proverb: 'A guest is the captive of the whole quarter.'*
(Said to a guest who declines the invitation of his host's friends.)

Persian Lamb with Apples and Cherries

1 kg (2 lb) lean lamb, cubed	500 g (1 lb) sour or morello
2 tablespoons butter or oil	cherries, pitted*
120 g (4 oz) yellow split peas	1 apple, peeled, cored and diced
Salt and black pepper	Lemon juice (optional)

Turn the meat in hot butter or oil in a large saucepan until lightly coloured all over. Add the split peas and water to cover, and season to taste with salt and black pepper. Bring to the boil and skim off any scum. Cover the pan and simmer for about 2 hours, or until the meat is very tender.

Add the cherries, diced apple, lemon juice (if the fruits are not sharp) and a little more water if necessary. Adjust seasoning. Cook for a further ½ hour.

This stew is usually served as a sauce with plain rice.

Moroccan Tagine with Fruit and Honey

This fragrant dish, a speciality of Fez, can be prepared with various fruits – apples, pears or quinces, for example. Below is a version using prunes, a local favourite, particularly good as a winter dish. Honey is used in this dish in rather an unexpected way, its sweetness sometimes threatened with a little ginger and much pepper. Saffron is traditionally added, but its taste is almost lost among the rich flavours and its high cost therefore makes it, in my opinion, optional.

1 kg (2 lb) lean lamb, preferably	1 onion, finely chopped
leg, cubed	250 g (8 oz) prunes, soaked
2–3 tablespoons oil	overnight
¼ teaspoon ground ginger	1–2 tablespoons honey, or to taste
¼ teaspoon saffron (optional)	1 teaspoon orange blossom water
Salt and black pepper	Roasted or grilled sesame seeds,
½ teaspoon ground coriander	to garnish (optional)
1 teaspoon ground cinnamon	

In this recipe the meat is not fried first. Put the meat in a large saucepan, cover with water and add oil, ginger, saffron if used, salt

---

* Fresh or tinned. You may prefer to use less fruit the first time you try this dish. Increase the amount once you have become accustomed to the combination of meat and fruit.

and pepper to taste, coriander, cinnamon and the finely chopped onion. Bring to the boil, cover the pan and simmer very gently until the meat is tender and the water has become a rich sauce. This will take about 2 hours.

Add the prunes and simmer for 20 minutes longer. Stir the honey into the sauce, blending it in well, and cook for a further 15 minutes. Sprinkle with orange blossom water. The dish is sometimes served garnished with roasted or grilled sesame seeds.

≈ This dish is similar to a modern Persian prune sauce or *khoresh*, made with prunes, meat and spinach. I have given the recipe on page 427, in the rice chapter.

Rutabiya

A regal medieval dish of meat balls stuffed with almonds and garnished with dates, *rutab* being the Arabic word for dates. From al-Baghdadi.

Cut red meat into small, long, thin slices: melt fresh tail, and throw out the sediment, then put the meat into the oil, adding half a *dirham* of salt and the same quantity of fine brayed (ground) dry coriander. Stir until browned. Then cover with lukewarm water, and when boiling, skim. Put in a handful of almonds and pistachios, peeled and ground coarsely, and colour with a little saffron. Throw in fine-ground cummin, coriander, cinnamon and mastic, about 2½ *dirhams* in all. Take red meat as required, mince fine, and make into long cabobs (meat rolls), placing inside each a peeled, sweet almond: put into the saucepan. Take sugar candy dates, or Medina dates, as required: extract the stone from the bottom with a needle, and put in its place a peeled sweet almond. When the meat is cooked and the liquor all evaporated so that only the oils remain, garnish with these dates. Sprinkle with about ten *dirhams* of scented sugar, and a *danaq* of camphor: spray with a little rose water. Wipe the sides of the saucepan with a clean rag, and leave to settle over the fire for an hour: then remove.

□ *Cooking by Candle**

Nasrudin made a wager that he could spend a night on a nearby mountain and survive, in spite of ice and snow. Several wags in the teahouse agreed to adjudicate.

* Shah, *The Exploits of the Incomparable Mulla Nasrudin.*

Nasrudin took a book and a candle and sat through the coldest night he had ever known. In the morning, half-dead, he claimed his money.

'Did you have nothing at all to keep you warm?' asked the villagers.

'Nothing.'

'Not even a candle?'

'Yes, I had a candle.'

'Then the bet is off.'

Nasrudin did not argue.

Some months later he invited the same people to a feast at his house. They sat down in his reception room, waiting for the food. Hours passed.

They started to mutter about food.

'Let's go and see how it is getting on,' said Nasrudin.

Everyone trooped into the kitchen. They found an enormous pot of water, under which a candle was burning. The water was not even tepid.

'It is not ready yet,' said the Mulla. 'I don't know why – it has been there since yesterday.'

Dfeena

A very rich and filling Egyptian speciality. It was particularly popular as a Sabbath meal in Jewish circles, since it could be left cooking gently from early on Friday.

1 kg (2 lb) lean or fat stewing beef
1 calf's foot (optional)
6 small potatoes
6 eggs in their shells
2 large onions, finely chopped
Oil

250–500 g (½–1 lb) chick peas or haricot beans, soaked overnight
2 cloves garlic, crushed
1 teaspoon ground allspice
Salt and black pepper

Cut the meat into cubes. Blanch the calf's foot in boiling water. Peel the potatoes, and scrub the egg-shells thoroughly. Fry the chopped onions in oil until soft and golden.

Put all these ingredients together with the drained chick peas or haricot beans (less commonly used for this dish than chick peas) in a large ovenproof pot or casserole with a tight-fitting lid. Cover with water and add the garlic and seasonings. If using haricot beans, it is preferable to add salt only after they have become tender as it seems to prevent them softening. Cover the pot and bake in a moderate oven (180°C/350°F/Mark 4) for 1 hour, then lower the temperature to the lowest setting and continue to simmer for several hours longer or overnight. Alternatively you can leave the stew *barely* simmering over extremely low heat for several hours.

The meat will be extremely tender and practically falling apart, and the chick peas or haricot beans will be very soft and impregnated with the rich calf's foot stock. The eggs will have become creamy, like the *hamine* eggs described on page 187.

≈ A variation is to boil about 375 g (12 oz) long-grain rice, washed first, until just tender, then lower it into the casserole tied up in a muslin bag. This will allow it to absorb the rich sauce without being lost among the other ingredients. Serve with the *dfeena*. It will make it easier for everyone if you shell the eggs and return them to the pan a few minutes before serving.

Immos – *meaning 'his mother's milk'*

Recipes for meat cooked in milk or yoghourt abound in early cookery manuals. Today, they are still a great favourite throughout most of the Middle East, as well as in the Balkans and India.

The name of this particular version, a Lebanese one, implies that the meat of a young animal is cooked in his own mother's milk, a vivid and rather tragic image which, of course, makes this and other similar dishes prohibited by Jewish dietary law: 'Thou shalt not cook the lamb in his mother's milk.'

1 kg (2 lb) lean lamb, preferably leg, cubed	1 egg white or 1 tablespoon cornflour
2 medium onions, sliced	1 teaspoon salt
Salt and black pepper	2 cloves garlic, crushed
½ litre (1 pint) yoghourt	1 teaspoon ground coriander
	2 tablespoons butter

Steam the meat with the onions, and salt and pepper to taste, for about 1½ hours. Alternatively, boil it or cook it under pressure with very little water. It should be extremely soft and tender. Reduce the liquid if necessary by boiling vigorously, uncovered, for the last few minutes.

Prepare the yoghourt with egg white or cornflour dissolved in water and salt, according to the directions for stabilizing yoghourt on page 124, to prevent it from curdling during cooking. Add it to the cooked meat, and simmer gently for 10 to 15 minutes longer.

Fry the crushed garlic and coriander in butter until the garlic just turns golden. Pour the mixture over the meat and yoghourt, and serve accompanied by plain or saffron rice (pages 401–4).

Liver, Kidneys, etc.

Albanian-style Liver

1 kg (2 lb) calf's or lamb's liver, sliced
1½ tablespoons paprika
Flour
Olive or other oil
Salt
2–3 tablespoons finely chopped parsley
½ onion, thinly sliced

Wash the liver and cut it into small pieces about 2½ cm (1 inch) square, removing any tough pieces or skin. Drain and dry on absorbent paper. Sprinkle with 1 tablespoon paprika and toss well, then roll in flour, shaking to separate each piece of liver.

Heat some oil in a frying pan and fry the liver, stirring and turning the pieces until well browned all over. They should be pink and juicy inside. Remove from the pan and drain well. Sprinkle with a little salt.

Mix the remaining ½ tablespoon paprika with a little of the frying oil and dribble over the liver. Serve garnished with chopped parsley, and slices of onion which have been sprinkled with salt and left for at least an hour to soften and become mellow.

Calf's or Lamb's Liver with Vinegar 1, 2

Here are two equally delicious recipes for liver, both using vinegar. This is often substituted for wine which is, of course, taboo to Muslims; as it happens vinegar is better than wine in this case. For both recipes, the liver is tenderized and enhanced if marinated first in a mixture of oil, vinegar, salt and pepper. Seasoned milk is sometimes used, though not by Jews. Drain well on absorbent paper before cooking.

1.

A dish called *higado con vinagre* by some in our Sephardic community.

60–90 g (2–3 oz) dry white
  breadcrumbs
2–3 cloves garlic, crushed
2–3 tablespoons oil
150 ml (¼ pint) wine vinegar
Salt and black pepper

½ teaspoon sugar
750 g (1½ lb) calf's or lamb's liver,
  sliced
2 tablespoons finely chopped
  parsley

Fry the breadcrumbs and crushed garlic in hot oil until they are slightly coloured, and the garlic becomes aromatic and sweet. Add vinegar, salt and pepper to taste, and sugar, and bring to the boil.

Poach the slices of liver in this mixture, simmering gently for 5 to 10 minutes, until just cooked. They must not be overdone.

Serve garnished with chopped parsley.

2.

This is a Lebanese recipe flavoured with mint, a favourite Lebanese herb. *Samna* or clarified butter is generally used for frying in the Lebanon, but butter is a perfectly adequate alternative.

750 g (1½ lb) calf's or lamb's liver,
  sliced
Salt and black pepper
2 tablespoons butter
1 large onion, finely chopped

2–3 cloves garlic, crushed
1 tablespoon dried crushed mint
1 teaspoon flour
150 ml (¼ pint) wine vinegar

Sprinkle the liver with salt and pepper. Brown it lightly and quickly on both sides in butter; remove from the pan, and put aside.

Fry the onions gently in the same pan until golden and soft. Add crushed garlic, mint and flour, and blend well into the hot butter. Stir in vinegar and a little water, and season with salt and pepper. Bring to the boil slowly, stirring, and cook for 5 minutes. Add the fried liver and a little more water if necessary to cover. Simmer gently until the liver is just cooked but not overdone, about 5 minutes.

≈ A different sort of sharpness can be obtained by using 1 tablespoon ground *sumac* mixed with 150 ml (¼ pint) water instead of vinegar.

Kidneys with Lemon

750 g (1½ lb) calf's or lamb's
   kidneys
1–2 tablespoons wine vinegar
2 tablespoons butter

Salt and black pepper
Juice of 1 lemon, or more
3–4 tablespoons finely chopped
   parsley

Wash the kidneys. Remove the outer skins and cut out the fat cores. Soak them for 1 hour in water acidulated with a little vinegar and, if you like, blanch them for 2 to 3 minutes in a fresh portion of acidulated water.

Drain the kidneys and slice them in half lengthwise. Sauté in hot butter for a few minutes until firm and coloured all over but tender inside. Season to taste with salt and pepper, sprinkle with lemon juice, and serve garnished with chopped parsley.

Kidneys in Tomato Sauce

2 onions, sliced
1 clove garlic, finely chopped
2–3 tablespoons oil or butter
6 calf's kidneys or 12 lamb's
   kidneys

1–2 tablespoons wine vinegar
   (optional)
2 tomatoes, skinned and chopped
1 small tin tomato concentrate
Salt and black pepper

Fry the onions and garlic in hot oil or butter until soft and golden. Wash the kidneys, remove the outer skins and fat cores and, if you like, soak and blanch them in acidulated water as described in the preceding recipe.

Drain the kidneys and slice them in half lengthwise. Add them to the onions and garlic, and sauté until coloured all over. Add the tomatoes and the tomato concentrate, season to taste with salt and pepper, and moisten with 2 to 3 tablespoons water. Cover and cook gently for about 20 minutes, taking care not to overcook the kidneys, as they will become tough and hard if you do.

Yoğurtlu Paça
Sheep's Feet with Yoghourt

A delicious Turkish dish. The earthy richness of the meat is matched with the coolness of the yoghourt.

6 sheep's feet (or 2 calf's feet)	6 thin slices bread, crusts
Rind of ½ lemon	removed
2 large cloves garlic	Butter
Salt and black pepper	

GARNISH

½ litre (¾ pint) yoghourt	Salt and white pepper
Stock	3 tablespoons butter
2 cloves garlic, crushed	1 teaspoon paprika

Scrub the feet thoroughly, blanch them in boiling water for 5 minutes and drain. Cover with fresh water in a saucepan, and add lemon rind, garlic, and salt and pepper to taste. Bring to the boil and simmer for 3 to 4 hours, or 1 hour in a pressure cooker.

Fry the slices of bread in butter until very brown and crisp or toast them. Lay the slices in one layer in a large, shallow, ovenproof dish and moisten well with stock from the meat. Drain the feet and bone them, arranging the meat on top of the bread slices. Sprinkle with more stock if the dish seems too dry, cover it and keep it warm in a low oven.

Prepare the garnish. Beat the yoghourt with a few tablespoons of stock, the crushed garlic, and salt and white pepper to taste. Melt the butter in a small saucepan and colour it bright red with paprika.

Serve the meat on the bread, smothered with the yoghourt mixture and decorated with a trickle of red paprika butter.

Brains Sofrito

3 sets calf's brains or 6 sets lamb's	½ teaspoon turmeric
brains	Juice of ½ lemon, or more
1 tablespoon wine vinegar	Salt and black pepper
2–3 tablespoons oil	3 tablespoons finely chopped
2 cloves garlic, crushed or halved	parsley
1 stalk celery, thinly sliced	
(optional)	

Soak the brains in water acidulated with a little vinegar for 1 hour. Remove the thin outer membranes and wash under cold running water. Drain well. Separate each brain into two or four parts, depending on whether calf's or lamb's brains are used.

In a pan, heat the oil with ½ teacup water, the garlic, sliced celery if used, turmeric and lemon juice. Add salt and pepper to taste. Simmer for a few minutes – for about 15 minutes if celery is used, to allow it to soften, but otherwise for only 2 to 3 minutes.

Poach the brains gently in this barely simmering mixture for 10 to 15 minutes, taking care not to break them. They will be tinged a beautiful yellow by the turmeric. Add a little water if the sauce evaporates too quickly.

Serve the brains in their sauce, sprinkled with finely chopped parsley, and if you like accompanied by artichoke hearts stewed in oil (good quality tinned ones will do) and rice.

≈ A variation is to add 1 teaspoon ground cumin to the sauce.

Kawareh bi Hummus
Calf's Feet and Chick Peas

This dish is loved all over the Middle East, in the Balkans, and in Spain and Portugal. Non-Muslims, and Muslims who are lax about their prohibitions, sometimes use pig's trotters instead of calf's feet. The dish is sometimes served as a soup, prepared with only 1 calf's foot, and more water.

2 calf's feet	250 g (8 oz) chick peas, soaked
3 tablespoons oil	overnight
Salt and black pepper	2 hard-boiled eggs, sliced
1 teaspoon turmeric	(optional)

Wash and scrape the feet thoroughly. Blanch them in boiling water until a scum has formed. Throw out the water. Heat the oil in a large saucepan and fry the feet in it for a few minutes until coloured all over. Add salt and pepper to taste, turmeric, and the soaked and drained chick peas. Cover with water, bring to the boil and simmer gently until the meat is practically falling off the bones, about 4 hours. The time can be reduced to about ¾ hour with a pressure cooker. Bone the feet if you wish and return the meat to the pan.

Serve with a light salad and, if you like, garnished with hard-boiled eggs.

≈ A variation to this dish uses cubed or thickly sliced potatoes instead of the chick peas. They should be added only about 20 minutes before the end of cooking time, as prolonged cooking would make them disintegrate.

≈ *Hergma*, a Moroccan variation, is spiced with ½ teaspoon ground ginger, 1 teaspoon paprika and ½ teaspoon cayenne, instead of turmeric, and 1 cup cooked rice is added at the end of the cooking time.

≈ It is customary to cook eggs in their shells (well scrubbed) in the stew, adding them with the beans. They will become creamy and brown inside (see *hamine* eggs on page 187).

≈ A Turkish version called *fasulyeli paça* is made with haricot beans instead of chick peas. Turmeric is not used.

Substantial Dishes
including Grains, Pulses and Pasta

Since ancient times, dishes based on chick peas, beans, lentils and cereals have been looked down on as the food of the poor. In literature, proverbs and songs they are constantly referred to as 'the food of the poor' or 'the food of the mean'. They have even been included as such in the *Kitab al Buhala* (*Book of Misers*).*

Regardless of this stigma, these dishes are nevertheless loved by rich and poor alike. Numerous jokes are told about Arab dignitaries who, when served with French *haute cuisine* or cosmopolitan food in hotels or at banquets, long for the *ful medames* (page 324) or chick peas and spinach which they can tell that the servants are eating from the aromas wafting up from the kitchens.

* By Jahiz, Damascus, 1938.

A little dull at times, but more often rich and splendidly vulgar, seasoned with spices, garlic, onions and herbs, or used in exciting combinations with other ingredients, pulses are also important for their nutritive value. By themselves, they can be eaten cold as salads or hot as vegetables. Cooked with meat, vegetables, rice and pasta, they add body and texture to many dishes.

Generally, pulses have to be washed and picked clean of impurities, although the majority of the packaged varieties available in Britain are already prepared and quite clean. Most, however, need soaking in cold water for a number of hours, except for the small yellow and red lentils, which cook and disintegrate very quickly. The soaking helps to tenderize the dried vegetables and shorten their cooking time. With brown and green lentils and yellow split peas, soaking helps to shorten this time only slightly. Haricot beans and dried broad white or brown beans require lengthy soaking, but again, some varieties are pre-treated and need only be cooked. When soaking pulses, cover them with a large quantity of cold water since they will quickly swell and absorb a great deal of it.

The time required to cook each variety varies widely according to the soil in which they were grown and their age since drying. However, varieties are constantly being improved and it seems that each new season's production requires less cooking time than the last.

Always cook in fresh, cold water. Generally, brown and green lentils take between 20 and 40 minutes to become tender. Haricot beans may take any time between 1½ and 3 hours. Black-eyed beans can take as little as 20 minutes. Egyptian brown beans require longer soaking than the others and very long, slow simmering.

Haricot beans, broad white and brown beans must not be salted at the start of cooking, or they will never become soft. They must be seasoned only when already tender.

Dried vegetables can also be pressure-cooked but there is always the danger of over-cooking since the exact time is so often a matter of guesswork, and you may end up with a purée – except in the case of chick peas and yellow split peas, which never disintegrate. Unless pressed for time, therefore, it is preferable not to use this method. It is far better to cook them in advance to ensure that they are ready when needed, since they keep and reheat well.

Beside pulses, other substantial dishes are those based on burghul (cracked wheat), called *bulgur* by the Turks and *pourgouri* by

Greeks, and whole wheat kernels. These earthy peasant dishes are particularly popular among the Armenian communities scattered all over the world. *Couscous*, a cracked, uncooked wheat resembling semolina, makes the superb North African dishes which, together with the magnificent stews and broths over which the couscous is steamed, make ideal substantial one-course meals.

I have also included in this chapter dishes made with *rishta*, which is similar to Italian pasta. In the last century, Italian pasta dishes have become increasingly popular throughout the Middle East. Spaghetti and tagliatelle *alla bolognese, al aglio e olio* and *al pomidoro* as well as *maccheroni al forno con besciamella*, are common, everyday dishes in Turkey, Syria, the Lebanon, Egypt and North Africa. I have been told that these dishes are often prepared in Cairo today by people wishing to impress their village or Bedouin friends visiting town – they are Oriental enough to please and yet have a foreign snob value.

Rishta, however, is of ancient Oriental origin. It was known in ancient Persia and is featured in medieval cookery manuals. Like rice, it has escaped the stigma of being a filling dish for the poor. Instead, it is considered rather grand, and is served on special occasions.

The preparation of the *rishta* dough is identical to that of any Italian pasta dough, and the cheese-filled pasta called *calsones* by the Jews is very similar to cheese ravioli. I have included these pasta dishes here since they are truly Oriental and do not owe their inspiration to Italian dishes, although they may sometimes share a certain flavour.

Recipes for dried vegetables served cold with olive oil are to be found in the chapters on *mezze* and salads. Recipes for stews with dried vegetables are given in the meat chapter.

□ *The Young Girl's Song**

By my father's life! By my father's life!
I will not have the poor man!
He wakes me in the morning and says,
He wakes me in the morning and says,
'Pound the lentils early!'

* Maspéro, *Chansons populaires*.

Substantial Dishes

By my father's life! By my father's life!
I will have the rich man!
He wakes me in the morning and says,
He wakes me in the morning and says,
'Pound the pastry with fat!'

Lentils in Butter

375 g (12 oz) brown lentils
1 onion, finely chopped
1 clove garlic
3 tablespoons butter

Salt and black pepper
1 teaspoon ground cumin
Juice of ½ lemon (optional)

Clean and wash the lentils, and soak them in cold water for a few hours if possible. Drain well.

In a large saucepan fry the onion and garlic in 2 tablespoons hot butter until the onion is soft and golden. Add the lentils and stir with the butter in the pan for a minute or two. Pour in about 300 ml (1 pint) of water, bring to the boil and remove scum. Season to taste with salt and pepper, and a teaspoon of ground cumin. Cover the pan and simmer gently for about ½ hour, adding more water as it becomes absorbed, until the lentils are tender but not too soft.

Serve with the remaining butter stirred in until melted, and a squeeze of lemon if you like.

This is particularly good as a partner to omelettes or little spicy fried sausages, and any lean meat dish. Served with fried aubergine slices and boiled *rishta*, it also makes an excellent dish.

Lentils with Peppers and Tomatoes

500 g (1 lb) brown or green lentils
3–4 tablespoons oil
1 large onion, chopped
1 green pepper, chopped
1–2 chillis, finely chopped

5 tomatoes, peeled and sliced
Salt and pepper
A bunch of parsley or coriander,
  finely chopped

Soak the lentils in cold water for at least an hour. Drain and boil in fresh water for about 20 minutes until tender. Fry the onion in the oil in a large saucepan until golden. Add the pepper and chillis and sauté until softened. Add the drained lentils and tomatoes, salt and pepper and cook gently for about 15 minutes, adding the chopped herbs towards the end of the cooking.

≈ You may serve this cold, in which case it would be nice to use olive oil. If tomatoes are without flavour, it is just as well to use peeled tomatoes. A medium-sized tin will do.

Lentil and Vegetable Stew

250 g (8 oz) lentils, soaked overnight if necessary
2 medium potatoes, peeled and coarsely diced
250 g (8 oz) courgettes or marrow, sliced or cubed
250 g (8 oz) leeks, trimmed and sliced
1 stalk celery, sliced
Salt and black pepper
1 onion, finely chopped
Oil
2 cloves garlic, crushed
2 tablespoons finely chopped parsley
Juice of 2 lemons

Drain soaked lentils and simmer in a large pan in 1 pint water for about 20 minutes, or until nearly soft. Add the potatoes, courgettes, leeks and celery, season to taste with salt and pepper, and continue cooking for 15 to 20 minutes longer, or until the vegetables are cooked, adding more water if necessary. Only a little liquid should be left at the end of cooking.

Fry the onion in oil until soft and golden. Add garlic and fry for a minute or two longer until coloured. Drain and add to the lentils and vegetables, together with parsley and lemon juice. Simmer for a few minutes longer, adjust seasoning and serve hot or cold.

□ *A Tale of Goha*

Goha invited a friend to his house. No sooner had he placed a plate piled high with food before him than the man had eaten it all up. Several times he rushed to fetch more beans, more rice and more chick peas, which he had prepared for his own lunch and for next day's as well. Each time the man emptied the plate and waited for more. Finally, there was nothing left in the house to eat. Then the man remarked that he was on his way to the doctor because he was suffering from loss of appetite. Appalled, Goha begged him to stay away when he had recovered it!

Shula Kalambar

A lentil and spinach dish prepared in medieval Persia to heal the sick. For the cure to be effective, the ingredients, so it was said, had to be bought with money begged in the streets.

250 g (8 oz) large brown lentils, soaked if required
500 g (1 lb) fresh spinach or 250 g (8 oz) frozen leaf spinach
½ teaspoon ground coriander
½ teaspoon ground cumin
1 clove garlic, crushed
Salt and black pepper
1–2 tablespoons butter

Boil the lentils until very tender, between 20 and 30 minutes. Wash the spinach carefully. If using frozen spinach, de-frost and drain well. Chop spinach leaves finely and stew gently in their own juices until tender. Drain the cooked lentils and add them to the spinach. Season with coriander, cumin and garlic, and salt and pepper to taste. Stir well.

Add butter, let it melt into the vegetables and serve.

Lentil Purée

An idea from Egypt which can be used as a bed for a variety of foods.

2 tablespoons oil
1 large onion, chopped
2–3 cloves garlic, crushed
500 g (1 lb) tiny red lentils
1½ teaspoons powdered cumin
1½ teaspoons powdered coriander
Salt and pepper to taste
Pinch of cayenne (optional)

Fry the onion in the oil in a large, thick-bottomed saucepan. When it is golden, add the garlic and stir until it has begun to colour. Add the lentils and cover with water. Add cumin and coriander, stir well and cover. Cook on a very low flame, adding salt and pepper when the lentils begin to disintegrate and more water as required, being careful not to let the bottom burn. The lentils disintegrate to a purée without any need of mashing.

Serve as a side dish or press some pieces of cooked meat or boiling sausage into it, or pour a stew over it.

Lentils with Rishta (Noodles)

250–375 g (8–12 oz) brown or green lentils	1 teaspoon ground coriander
Salt	Black pepper
2 onions, finely chopped	375 g (12 oz) rishta (page 326), noodles or tagliatelle
Oil	2 tablespoons butter
2–3 cloves garlic, crushed	

Soak lentils and drain. Boil in a fresh portion of salted water to cover (about 300 ml or 1 pint) for between 20 to 30 minutes or until the lentils are soft and the water has been absorbed. Use a large pan which will accommodate the noodles as well. Drain the cooked lentils thoroughly.

Fry the onions in 2 tablespoons oil until soft and golden. Add the garlic and coriander, and continue to fry gently for about 2 minutes, until golden. Add this mixture to the cooked lentils, and season to taste with salt and pepper. Throw the noodles into boiling salted water and cook until just tender (about 10 minutes if using the dried commercial variety). Drain well and add to the lentils. Stir in butter and mix well.

Serve very hot.

≈ You may also use red lentils for this dish and let them disintegrate to a purée.

Hummus
Chick Peas

These hard, round, corn-coloured peas, earthy in flavour and aesthetically attractive, lend themselves, as do most ingredients in the hands of Middle Eastern cooks, to an infinite variety of dishes. Mashed and smoothly puréed, they make an excellent base for a tahina cream or a meat soup. Whole, they combine deliciously with chicken, meat and calf's feet. Mixed with rice and vermicelli or in a stew destined for couscous (page 335), they provide excitement in texture and flavour.

In the past, chick peas had to be soaked for hours in cold water with a pinch of bicarbonate of soda, and then required prolonged cooking. In addition, it was often necessary to remove their tough outer skins, a long and tedious operation, especially when a large quantity was required. The chick peas sold today are of a superior quality. It is necessary only to soak them in plain cold water overnight – the bicarbonate of soda used to leave a peculiar taste – and they are usually tender after 1–1½ hours' cooking in boiling unsalted water. However, this cooking time, although generally short, does vary according to the quality of the chick peas, their place of origin and their age.

To cook them 'dry', as a Moroccan friend calls them when they are cooked alone, as opposed to in a stew, put a chilli pepper in the cooking water, season with salt and pepper when soft, and add a bunch of coriander leaves, chopped, when almost done.

Fatta

A number of Arab dishes go under the name of fatta, which describes the manner of breaking crisp bread into pieces with your hands. They all have a bed of toasted bread soaked in flavoursome stock and a topping of yoghourt with a variety of fillings. The most common filling is chick peas. A special favourite is made with chicken, minced meat and rice, another is with aubergines and one is made with *melokhia* sauce.

All are part of the repertoire which is considered family food because it is filling, and they are not usually given to guests, but in reality they are much more popular than most party dishes.

Pitta bread is opened out, left for a few minutes in a very hot oven or turned under the grill to become crisp and brown, then crumpled into bits in the hand.

Yoghourt is thickened to the consistency of mayonnaise by draining it through muslin in a colander. The usual garnish is fried pine nuts.

Fattet Hummus
Chick Peas with Yoghourt and Toasted Bread

90–120 g (3–4 oz) chick peas
1 teaspoon bicarbonate of soda (optional)
Salt
½ litre (1 pint) yoghourt
3 cloves garlic, crushed
Pepper

2 pitta breads
Oil for frying (optional)
1–2 tablespoons dried mint leaves
3 tablespoons pine nuts or slivered almonds
1 tablespoon butter (or clarified butter)

Soak the chick peas overnight in cold water and with 1 teaspoon bicarbonate of soda if you like. Drain and simmer in fresh water to cover until they are very tender, usually well over an hour, adding salt only when they are nearly done. Drain the yoghourt, which should be at room temperature, in a muslin cloth placed in a sieve until it is the thickness of mayonnaise – this usually takes about ¾ hour – then pour into a bowl and beat in the garlic and pepper to taste. Open out the bread and toast it in a very hot oven until it is crisp and brown. Then break it up into the bottom of the serving dish. Alternatively, you may cut the bread into triangles and deep fry in hot oil, then drain them on absorbent paper. Pour the chick peas and some of their water over the bread, soaking it thoroughly, keeping a few to decorate the dish. Pour the yoghourt mixture over the chick peas. Crush the mint leaves over the top.

To garnish, fry the pine nuts or almonds in sizzling butter until they are a light brown and sprinkle over the yoghourt with the extra chick peas. Serve at once with the chick peas hot and the rest lukewarm.

≈ This is often served for breakfast with tea, accompanied by whole spring onions and green peppers cut into strips. Some people like to sprinkle it with hot red chilli pepper or cayenne.

≈ A Damascus version called *tasseia* has the chick peas crushed with a pestle and mortar and mixed with 4 or 5 tablespoons tahina, the juice of ½ lemon and 1 crushed clove garlic. You can put it in a blender with a little of the cooking liquor. Squeeze a little lemon juice in the chick pea water before sprinkling over the bread, spread the mashed chick pea cream over the top and cover with yoghourt, then garnish as before.

Fattet Jaj
Fatta with Chicken

This makes a large quantity.

1 litre (1¾ pints) yoghourt
4 cloves garlic, crushed
1 large chicken
Juice of 3 lemons
2 cardamom pods, ground to a powder
Salt and pepper
1 large onion, finely chopped
4 tablespoons butter

500 g (1 lb) lean minced beef
250 g (8 oz) basmati rice, washed and drained
1 teaspoon ground cinnamon
1 teaspoon allspice
3 pitta breads
Vegetable oil for frying
60 g (2 oz) pine nuts

Let the yoghourt, which should be at room temperature, drain through a fine muslin placed in a sieve for about ¾ hour or until it is as thick as a mayonnaise. Pour into a bowl, add the garlic and beat well.

Put the cleaned chicken in a large pot and cover with water. Bring to the boil, remove any scum, then simmer gently. Add the lemon juice and cardamom, salt and pepper and cook until the chicken is very tender and almost falls off the bones.

In the meantime, make what is the common *hashwa* or filling: fry the onion in 3 tablespoons of butter until it is golden brown, stirring occasionally. Add the minced meat, crushing and stirring it until it has changed colour, then add the rice and continue to stir. Add cinnamon and allspice, salt and pepper, and just cover with water. Cover the pan and reduce the heat to a minimum. Cook gently until the rice is done.

Cut the bread into triangles. Deep fry in a light vegetable oil until crisp and brown and drain on absorbent paper; or you may prefer, as I do, to toast the bread in the oven or under the grill. Spread at the bottom of a large bowl. Cover with the rice and meat *hashwa*. Lay over this pieces of chicken, skinned and boned, and pour over enough of the flavoursome stock to soak the bread thoroughly. Cover entirely with the thickened yoghourt and sprinkle the top with the pine nuts lightly fried in the remaining tablespoon of butter.

Serve at once.

≈ Most people do not feel that this dish need be eaten piping hot, but if you prefer it that way you may serve it in an ovenproof dish and put it in a medium oven for a few minutes if you cannot arrange the layers quickly enough while they are still hot.

Fattet Betingan
Fatta with Aubergines

500 g (1 lb) lean lamb, cubed	1 pitta bread
625 g (1¼ lb) aubergines, cut into cubes	300 ml (½ pint) yoghourt at room temperature
Oil for frying	1 teaspoon tahina
Salt and pepper	½ clove garlic, crushed (optional)
½–1 teaspoon allspice	

Cover the lamb with water and simmer until it is very tender, adding more water to keep the meat covered. Fry the aubergines in hot oil until coloured all over, drain on absorbent paper and put them in with the lamb. Season with salt, pepper and allspice and continue to cook for about 5 minutes until they are done.

Open out the pitta bread and cut it into pieces. Either toast it or fry it in hot oil until crisp and brown and then drain. Beat the yoghourt with the tahina and the garlic if you like.

Just before serving, spread the crisp bread at the bottom of a serving dish. Cover with a layer of meat and aubergines and pour the sauce over to soak into the bread. Top with the yoghourt mixture.

≈ One way of presenting this is with 1 tablespoon finely chopped parsley or mint mixed in 2 tablespoons melted butter.

Ful Medames
Egyptian Brown Beans

An Egyptian dish which has become 'the' national dish. *Ful medames* is pre-Ottoman and pre-Islamic, claimed by the Copts and probably as old as the Pharaohs. According to an Arab saying: 'Beans have satisfied even the Pharaohs.'

Although basically a peasant dish, the rich and the middle classes also delight in these small dark beans.

Ful medames is eaten in the fields and in village mud houses, in luxury restaurants and on town terraces by masters and servants alike. It is sold in the streets, sometimes buried in Arab bread, garnished with tahina salad and accompanied by a tomato and onion salad. It is the usual substantial breakfast traditionally cooked overnight in an earthen vessel buried up to the neck in ashes or left on the lowest flame of a primus stove.

The small brown beans can be bought in all Greek stores and some delicatessens. Ready-cooked, tinned beans can also be found.

1 kg (2 lb) ful medames, soaked overnight	Olive oil
	Quartered lemons
2–4 cloves garlic, crushed (optional)	Salt and freshly ground black pepper
Finely chopped parsley	1 teaspoon cumin (optional)

Boil the soaked beans in a fresh portion of unsalted water in a large saucepan until tender. In the past this took at least 7 hours but the qualities available now are soft after 2 to 2½ hours of gentle simmering. A pressure cooker will reduce the time considerably – to 30 or 45 minutes – but care must be taken not to overcook the beans.

When the beans are soft and the liquid reduced, drain them and add crushed garlic to taste, or instead pass some round with the other garnishes for people to take as much as they want.

Serve in soup bowls and sprinkle with chopped parsley. Pass round olive oil, quartered lemons, salt, black pepper and cumin for each person to season as he wishes.

≈ A pleasant way of thickening the sauce is to throw a handful of red lentils into the water at the start of the cooking.

≈ In Iraq large brown beans are used instead of the small Egyptian ones in a dish called *badkila*, which also serves for breakfast in the street.

≈ It is common to serve *hamine* eggs (page 187). Put one of these, or a hard-boiled egg, on top of the beans.

≈ Another way of serving *ful medames* is to smother it in a tomato sauce flavoured with garlic (see page 397).

≈ Yet another is to top it with a chopped mixed salad and thinly sliced onions or spring onions.

☐ *Egyptian proverb: The man of good breeding eats beans and returns to his breeding.*

☐ *Riddle: It is divided into two equal parts and covered by a strong skin. Praised be God who made it! And how do Arabs call it?*
Answer: El ful.

Haricot Beans with Onions and Tomatoes

375 g (12 oz) haricot beans, soaked
   overnight
2 onions, sliced
2 tablespoons oil
2 cloves garlic, sliced
2 tomatoes, skinned and chopped
3 tablespoons tomato concentrate
Salt
1 teaspoon paprika
Pinch of cayenne
1 bay leaf
2 tablespoons finely chopped
   parsley (optional)

Drain the soaked beans and boil them in a fresh portion of unsalted water to cover until almost tender. The time will vary from 1 to 2 hours, depending on their age and quality.

Fry the sliced onions in oil until soft and golden. Add garlic and fry for 2 minutes longer. Then add tomatoes and sauté gently until well cooked and almost reduced to a pulp. Stir in tomato concentrate and add the beans, together with some of their cooking water (about 150 ml or ¼ pint). Season to taste with salt, paprika and cayenne. Add a bay leaf and a little chopped parsley if liked.

Mix well and simmer for 15 to 20 minutes longer, until the beans are very soft and coloured a faint salmon pink. Serve hot or cold.

Haricot Bean Stew with Meat

500 g (1 lb) haricot beans, soaked overnight	750 g (1½ lb) stewing beef or lamb, lean or fat, cubed
2 onions, finely chopped	2 tomatoes, skinned and chopped
60 g (2 oz) butter	2–4 tablespoons tomato concentrate
2–3 cloves garlic	Salt and strong pepper

Drain the beans and boil them in a fresh portion of unsalted water to cover for ½ hour. Drain and reserve.

In a large saucepan fry the onions in butter until soft and golden. Add the garlic cloves and fry until lightly coloured. Add meat and brown all over. Add tomatoes and sauté gently. Stir in tomato concentrate, pepper and the drained haricot beans, and cover with water. Bring to the boil and simmer gently until the meat is very tender, and the beans are soft and well flavoured with the tomato sauce, adding salt only when they have begun to soften.

☐ *To dream of eating beans forbodes quarrelling and discord.* *

Rishta
Fresh Noodles

Recipes for *rishta*, an Italian-type pasta, appeared in the early Arab manuscripts. The word itself means 'thread' in Persian. Today pastas of all kinds are becoming increasingly popular all over the Middle East.

---

* From the *Egyptian Dream Book*, 1231.

Here is the basic recipe for plain *rishta*.

500 g (1 lb) plain flour	1 teaspoon salt
2 large eggs, beaten	4–5 tablespoons water

Sift the flour on to a large board or marble slab and make a little well in the centre to hold the beaten eggs, salt and 4 tablespoons water. Bury these in the flour. Mix well and knead vigorously until all the ingredients are thoroughly blended, adding the remaining tablespoon of water only if necessary. The dough should be firm and not sticky. Work it well for about 10 minutes until smooth and elastic, sprinkling a little flour over the board and your hands occasionally to prevent the dough from sticking. Divide the dough into 2 or 3 pieces.

Roll each piece out as thinly as possible, working from the centre and sprinkling both the surface it is rolled on and the rolling pin with flour to prevent the dough from sticking or tearing. Continue until it is extremely thin, like a very fine, elastic cloth. Lay the sheet aside and roll out the remaining pieces of dough in the same way. Let the pastry sheets rest and dry out for 40 minutes.

Roll each sheet up tightly like a swiss roll and cut into thin slices, making ribbons of pastry. Spread these out on a floured cloth and leave them to rest for a little while longer.

Five minutes before they are to be served, throw them into boiling salted water and simmer for about 5 minutes, stirring occasionally to prevent them from sticking to the pan.

Drain and serve immediately with salt, pepper and a generous amount of butter.

This pasta is similar to Italian tagliatelle, but commercial dried varieties will require longer cooking, usually at least 10 minutes.

In all the following recipes, the amounts of fresh and dried pasta required are the same, but double the cooking time given if using dried pasta of any kind.

Rishta with Meat and Tomato Sauce

This dish can be made equally well with Italian spaghetti, macaroni or tagliatelle. The sauce is rich enough to make a main dish and has a particularly Arab flavour.

2 onions, finely chopped
1 clove garlic
Oil
750 g (12 oz) lean stewing lamb,
    cut into small cubes
Salt and black pepper
¾ teaspoon ground allspice
500 g (1 lb) ripe tomatoes,
    skinned, or a 400-g (14-oz) tin
    skinned tomatoes

1 small tin tomato concentrate
½ teaspoon ground cumin
    (optional)
750 g (1½ lb) rishta, spaghetti,
    tagliatelle or macaroni
Grated Parmesan or Gruyère
    (optional)

Fry the onions then the garlic in 2 tablespoons oil in a saucepan until golden. Add meat and brown it all over. Season with salt, pepper and allspice. Add tomatoes and tomato concentrate, stir well and simmer gently in the tomato juice, covered, adding a little water if necessary. Cook for 1½ hours, or longer, until the meat is very tender and the sauce rich in texture and aromatic, adding water if necessary. Adjust seasoning. Some people like to flavour the sauce with a little ground cumin as well as the allspice.

Boil the *rishta* vigorously in a large pan of salted water for about 5 minutes, or until tender but not too soft – *al dente*. Drain and turn into a serving bowl. Pour the meat sauce over the pasta and serve, sprinkled with grated cheese if you like.

≈ An attractive and particularly Oriental variation is to serve the pasta with its sauce in a casing of *fila* pastry (see pages 139–40).

Prepare the sauce as above but let it reduce rather more. Boil 500 g (1 lb) pasta until just tender. Line a large buttered oven dish or tray with a sheet of *fila* pastry and brush it with melted butter. Lay another sheet on top and brush again with butter. Repeat with three more sheets, arranging them so that they overlap the sides of the dish, folding them back neatly where necessary. Fill this pastry shell with the pasta and sauce mixed together, and sprinkle very generously with grated cheese. Cover with 5 sheets of *fila*, each one brushed with melted butter, including the top one. Fold the edges of the sheets neatly, tucking them down the sides of the dish.

Bake in a hot oven (220°C/425°F/Mark 7) for 15 minutes, then reduce the heat to 150°C (300°F/Mark 2) and continue to bake for about 30 minutes longer, until all the sheets of *fila* are well cooked and the top is crisp and golden.

Serve in the dish, or unmould and turn over on to a serving platter so that the golden side is on top. Serve cut in slices like a cake.

Baked Rishta (Noodles) with Aubergines 1

3 large aubergines, sliced
Salt
1 onion, finely chopped
Oil
A 400-g (14-oz) tin skinned
   tomatoes
1 teaspoon dried oregano
Black pepper
750 g (1½ lb) rishta or spaghetti
Butter
4 hard-boiled eggs, thinly sliced
60 g (2 oz) grated Parmesan

Sprinkle the aubergine slices with salt and leave them in a colander for at least ½ hour to allow the bitter juices to drain away.

Prepare a tomato sauce in the following manner. Fry the onion in 2 tablespoons oil until soft and golden. Add tomatoes and oregano, and season to taste with salt and pepper. Moisten with a little water and simmer, covered, for at least ½ hour.

Drain the aubergine slices and pat them dry. Fry them in a little oil until very tender, turning them once. Drain on absorbent paper.

Cook the pasta in vigorously boiling, salted water until *al dente* – just tender. Drain; mix with the tomato sauce and 2 tablespoons butter.

Butter a large oven tray or dish. Spread a layer of pasta and sauce over the bottom of the dish; cover with a layer of fried aubergines and one of thinly sliced hard-boiled eggs, and sprinkle with a quarter of the grated Parmesan. Repeat all the layers twice more, so that there are three sets of layers in all. Cover with a thin layer of pasta and sprinkle with the remaining cheese.

Bake in a moderate oven (180°C/350°F/Mark 4) for about 30 minutes, or until a warm golden colour on top.

This dish can be prepared a day ahead and baked just before serving.

Baked Rishta (Noodles) with Aubergines 2

750 g (1½ lb) aubergines, sliced
Salt
750 g (1½ lb) rishta, spaghetti or
   tagliatelle
1 large onion, chopped
1 clove garlic
Oil
2 tomatoes, skinned and chopped
2 tablespoons tomato concentrate
½ teaspoon ground cinnamon
¼ teaspoon grated nutmeg
Cayenne pepper
Butter
Grated Parmesan or Gruyère
   (optional)

Sprinkle aubergine slices with salt and leave them in a colander for at least ½ hour to allow the bitter juices to drain away. Squeeze the slices and wash them in cold water. Pat dry with a clean cloth or kitchen paper.

Boil the noodles in salted water until still slightly underdone. Drain and keep warm.

Fry onion and garlic in 3 tablespoons oil until soft and golden. Add aubergine slices and fry until lightly coloured on both sides, using a little more oil if necessary. Stir in chopped tomatoes and tomato concentrate, and season to taste with spices, salt and a generous amount of cayenne. Moisten with a little water and simmer gently until the aubergines are soft and the sauce is reduced.

Butter a large baking dish. Fill it with alternating layers of pasta and the aubergine mixture, starting and finishing with a layer of pasta. End by pouring all the sauce from the aubergines over the entire dish. Sometimes grated cheese is sprinkled over the top.

Bake in a moderate oven (180°C/350°F/Mark 4) for about 30 minutes.

≈ As a variation, fried kidneys and chicken livers can be added to the aubergine and tomato sauce.

Calsones

This is a Sephardic pasta similar to cheese ravioli.

Prepare the *rishta* dough on page 327. Roll it out into very thin, long sheets, but do not cut it into ribbons. Along one of the longer edges and about 3 cm (1 inch) from the edge, put a row of little mounds of filling made as follows.

Mix 120 g (4 oz) grated Parmesan or Greek Kashkaval with 375 g (12 oz) grated Greek Halumi, Gruyère or mild Cheddar, and work it into a paste with 3 egg yolks, beaten, and a little salt and white pepper.

Alternatively, make a filling with the home-made curd cheese on page 74. I also use Italian Ricotta, available in all Italian groceries. Crumble 375 g (12 oz) cheese with a fork. Add 2 to 3 tablespoons cold milk, 120 g (4 oz) grated Parmesan, 2 tablespoons finely chopped parsley, a pinch of nutmeg and a little pepper if you like, and mix well.

Set the mounds of filling about 3 cm (1 inch) apart on the sheet of dough, and continue with rows of mounds until nearly half of the sheet is covered. Fold the other half of the sheet over to cover the mounds of filling and press gently with your finger between each one to seal it completely. Then cut little squares out with a sharp knife. Continue with the remaining dough and filling until all are used up.

Throw the *calsones* into boiling water and boil gently for about 10 to 15 minutes, or until well cooked.

Drain and serve with a generous amount of butter.

≈ The boiled and drained *calsones* can also be put in a lightly buttered baking dish, dotted with butter, sprinkled with grated cheese, and baked in a moderate oven (180°C/350°F/Mark 4) until the top is faintly golden, about 15 minutes.

Megadarra

Here is a modern version of a medieval dish called *mujadarra*, described by al-Baghdadi as a dish of the poor, and still known today as Esau's favourite. In fact, it is such a great favourite that although said to be for misers, it is a compliment to serve it.

An aunt of mine used to present it regularly to guests with the comment: 'Excuse the food of the poor!' – to which the unanimous reply always was: 'Keep your food of kings and give us *megadarra* every day!'

The proportions of lentils and rice vary with every family. The caramelized onions are the main feature. With the olive oil they are also the main flavouring. In the Lebanon they call it *mudardara*.

250 g (8 oz) large brown lentils
2 onions, finely chopped
125 ml (4 fl oz) olive oil
Salt and black pepper

250 g (8 oz) long-grain rice, washed
2–3 onions, sliced into half-moon shapes

Wash and drain the lentils. Boil in a fresh portion of water to cover for about 25 minutes or until only just tender. Fry the chopped onions in 2 to 3 tablespoons oil until they are brown. Add it to the lentils and season to taste with salt and pepper. Mix well and add rice, together with enough water to make the liquid in the pan up to the volume of rice. Season again and simmer gently, covered, for about 20 minutes until the rice is soft and well cooked, adding a little more water if it becomes absorbed too quickly.

Fry the sliced onions in the rest of the very hot oil until they are dark brown and sweet, almost caramelized.

Serve the rice and lentils on a large shallow dish, garnished with fried onion slices, with the oil poured over.

This dish is delicious served either warm or cold, and accompanied by yoghourt.

≈ A tip: you may find it easier to cook rice and lentils separately and to mix them together when they are both done.

≈ For different flavours add 1 teaspoon cumin and 1 teaspoon coriander in the cooking water or 2 teaspoons dried mint.

≈ In another dish of rice and lentils called *masafi*, the lentils are turned to a purée. Red lentils, which disintegrate easily, can be used for this.

Burghul Pilav
Cracked Wheat Pilav

This easy dish is an ideal and delicious alternative to rice, pasta or potatoes. A version featured in the early edition is heavier with a lot of butter and the initial frying of the cracked wheat. You may well want to adopt this one as an instant health food which will do as an accompaniment to stews, grills and indeed to all foods that are usually coupled with rice. Of course, it is better when stock is used, but water will do.

500 g (1 lb) coarse burghul	Salt and pepper
Water or stock	60–90 g (2–3 oz) butter

Note the volume of the burghul (about ½ litre/1 pint), rinse it in a sieve, then put it in a pan with 1½ times the volume of water or stock. Season with salt and pepper and cook covered over low heat for 10 to 15 minutes until it is tender and all the liquid is absorbed. Add a little water if it becomes too dry. Stir in the butter and leave off the heat or over the lowest possible one for about 20 minutes to allow the wheat to swell and become tender (it was usual in the past to stretch a cloth under the lid to absorb the excess steam).

If you are against butter, you may substitute 2 tablespoons oil.

Burghul is as versatile as rice and there are many excellent and simple variations. For these, stir into the burghul in the saucepan from the start any of the following:

≈ 2–3 tablespoons toasted pine nuts or slivered almonds and 2 tablespoons raisins or sultanas.

≈ Fried aubergine cubes or slices.

≈ About 250 g (8 oz) vermicelli previously toasted or fried in butter.

≈ Cubes of cheese such as Halumi, Gruyère or mature Cheddar at the end of the cooking and allow to melt.

≈ Boiled chick peas.

Burghul bi Dfeen

A Lebanese dish.

120 g (4 oz) chick peas
2 medium onions, sliced, or 6 tiny
   ones
Butter or clarified butter or oil
500 g (1 lb) lean lamb, cut in cubes
Pepper

1½ teaspoon allspice
Salt
375 g (12 oz) coarse burghul
   (cracked wheat)
½ teaspoon cinnamon

Soak the chick peas overnight. Fry the onions in 2–3 tablespoons fat until brown. Add the meat and fry until it changes colour. Cover with water and add the drained chick peas. Season with pepper and allspice and simmer, covered, until the meat and chick peas are very tender – about 1 hour – adding salt only when the chick peas have softened. Rinse and add the burghul last and cook stirring until it is tender, adding water if it is too dry.

It is usual to pour 60–90 g (2–3 oz) melted clarified butter into the pan before serving but you may leave this out. Sprinkle with cinnamon. Accompany with yoghourt.

≈ *Roz bi dfeen* is a similar dish made with rice instead of burghul (see page 405).

Imjadra
Lentils and Burghul

A simple vegetarian dish from the Lebanon.

250 g (8 oz) brown or green lentils
250 g (8 oz) coarse burghul
   (cracked wheat)
Salt and pepper

2 large onions, coarsely chopped
   or thinly sliced
6 tablespoons oil

Soak the lentils in water for about an hour, drain and boil in fresh water for about 20 minutes until tender. There needs to be about 450 ml (¾ pint) of liquid left. Add the burghul, season with salt and pepper and cook very gently for about 15 minutes longer, adding a little water if it becomes too dry, until the burghul is tender but not mushy. Fry the onion in plenty of oil until it is very brown – almost caramelized.

To serve, pour the oil over the lentils and wheat in the serving dish and sprinkle the onions on top. It is very good to eat with a salad and yoghourt.

≈ People also like to melt great dollops of butter into the lentils and burghul. In that case they use a little less oil.

Burghul Pilav with Lamb

A Turkish dish.

2–3 onions, finely chopped
180 g (6 oz) butter
750 g (1½ lb) lean stewing lamb, cubed
Salt and black pepper

3 tomatoes, skinned and chopped
1 small tin tomato concentrate
500 g (1 lb) burghul (cracked wheat)

Fry onions in a saucepan in about 60 g (2 oz) butter until soft and a pale golden colour. Add the meat and turn it over moderate heat for a few minutes to colour the cubes all over. Season to taste with salt and pepper. Add the tomatoes and tomato concentrate, cover with water and simmer gently for about 2 hours, or until the meat is tender, adding more water as required.

In another pan, fry the burghul in about 60 g (2 oz) butter for 2 minutes, stirring constantly. Add salt to taste, then pour in the meat mixture together with its sauce, which should measure about 1 litre (1¾ pint). Stir well and cover. Simmer gently for 10 minutes, or until all the liquid has been absorbed. Then steam for a further ½ hour on an asbestos mat over very low heat, with a cloth stretched under the lid to absorb the steam. The burghul should be plump and soft.

Stir in the remaining butter. There is a lot of butter in this dish so you can leave out the last 60 g (2 oz) without spoiling it.

≈ Burghul pilav with chicken can be made simply by substituting jointed chicken for lamb. Cook for about 30 minutes, depending on the size of the joints.

Couscous

Couscous is the national dish of the Maghreb, the North African countries of Morocco, Tunisia and Algeria. Of Berber origin, this is a truly local dish. A couscous has been adopted by other Arab countries, who call it *maghrebia*, but this is very different from the one eaten in North Africa.

Couscous itself is a type of fine semolina made from wheat grain. Until very recently, every family would send its wheat (bought at the market) to the local mill to be ground to the degree of fineness they preferred. Back home, the grain went through a process of rubbing with fine flour. It was put in a large wooden bowl. Gradually, flour was sprinkled over it, while the women rolled it into the couscous with their hands so as to coat each grain with a fine film of flour. This was in order to keep each grain separate when it was steamed. Today, most people buy their couscous ready-made for the sake of expediency.

There are infinite regional and family variations of this dish. Every time it is made it is different, the women putting all their expertise into varying it and yet keeping to the traditional form.

The basic process for the preparation of couscous is the steaming of the grain over a stew or broth. This is generally made with meat, usually lamb or chicken, and a variety of vegetables. Chick peas are usually added, and sometimes raisins as well. The broth is often coloured red with tomato purée or yellow with saffron. Many spices are used but so sparingly that one can hardly define each individual aroma. Often a sauce is prepared separately with some of the broth and made strong and fiery with cayenne or chilli pepper and a concentrate of red pimento called *harissa* (see page 65). This sauce is served beside the couscous for those who wish to be 'inflamed and intoxicated'.

In the Moroccan city of Fez, the stews or broths are generally lighter. The ingredients are boiled and delicately blended and perfumed.

In Tunisia and Algeria, they are richer and heavier. The meat, and sometimes the vegetables as well, are first braised in oil. Tunisians seem to prefer the stronger, spicier broths with cayenne and chilli. Algerians like to add tomato purée, while Moroccans prefer the aroma and colour given by a pinch of saffron.

A strong French influence on Algerian food has led to the adoption by the younger generation of more European vegetables such as runner beans, peas and carrots, for their stews.

The actual process of cooking the couscous is very simple, but calls for a subtle handling of the grain. The aim is to make it swell and become extremely light, each grain soft, delicate, velvety, and separate from its neighbour. Bad handling of the grain will result in a lumpy and rather stodgy couscous. The grain must never cook *in* the broth or sauce, but only in the steam. It must not even touch the broth throughout the steaming. The *couscousier*, the pot traditionally used, is in two parts, made from glazed earthenware or copper, and, more recently, aluminium. The bottom part is a large round pan in which the stew is cooked. The top consists of a sieve with widish holes. This holds the couscous. If you cannot get hold of an authentic *couscousier*, you can improvise with a double steamer or a metal sieve which fits exactly over a large pan.

The treatment of the grain is always the same, whatever the sauce. Moisten the couscous slightly with a little cold water, working it in with the fingers to prevent lumps from forming. Turn it into the sieve part of the *couscousier*. This should be done after the stew below has already been cooking for some time and the ingredients are nearly ready. Rake the grains with your fingers to air them and help them to swell better. Do not cover the sieve. Steam over the simmering sauce for 30 minutes.

Now turn the couscous into a large bowl. Sprinkle generously with cold water and stir well with a wooden spoon to break up any lumps and to separate and air the grains. Add a little salt at this point if you like. The water will make the grains swell very much. (A tablespoon of oil is sometimes added at the same time.) Return to the top container and steam for a further 30 minutes.

Some people like to steam the couscous over boiling water, and then serve it with a stew prepared separately.

Important note: It is difficult at the moment in the UK to find any couscous other than the precooked variety which requires only moistening with water and heating through either in a pan or, better, over steam.

About 20 minutes before you want to serve, when the stew is ready, put the couscous in a large bowl and add water gradually – ¾–1 litre (1½–1¾ pints) for 1 kg (2 lb) grain. (This is double the quantity of that in the recipe. It is for hungry people and because the precooked grain is easier to handle.) Let it swell, stirring occasionally for 15 minutes until it is tender. It is always easier to add water, so start with less to ensure that the result is not lumpy or soggy. Heat up the couscous with 3–4 tablespoons oil or butter in a large saucepan or steam it over the stew or over water, stirring until the steam comes through.

☐ *From Couscous to Loaf**

A man one day brought home some meat to his wife for dinner. She took semolina and began to make couscous. Only . . . she put so much water in that the grain grew to the size of mhammas.† *Her husband watched her in silence.*

'My dear, wouldn't you rather have some good mhammas?' *she asked him.*

'Why not?' he replied.

Quickly she added more water to the grains, so they got sticky and formed a dough. The man watched her without saying a word.

'My dear, wouldn't you prefer bread?'

'Why not?'

Quickly she kneaded the dough . . . and made a fine loaf. When she put it in front of him he shouted:

'By my forebears! if you don't immediately change this loaf into couscous, you won't spend one more night under this roof!'

And he repudiated her.

---

* Nacer Khemir, Stories from *Oum el Kir – contes d'une mère*.
† *Mhammas* is a soft pasta-like grain.

Moroccan Couscous

Here is a basic Moroccan couscous around which you can improvise.

1 kg (2 lb) lean stewing lamb or 500 g (1 lb) lamb, 250 g (8 oz) beef and ½ chicken
2 onions, chopped
60 g (2 oz) chick peas, soaked overnight
2 turnips, quartered
2 large carrots, sliced
2 tablespoons olive oil
Salt and black pepper
¼ teaspoon ground ginger (optional)
¼ teaspoon saffron (optional)

500 g (1 lb) or more couscous
60–120 g (2–4 oz) raisins
3 courgettes, sliced, or ½ marrow, cut in pieces
120 g (4 oz) fresh shelled or frozen broad beans
2 tomatoes
A bunch parsley, finely chopped
A bunch coriander, finely chopped
Cayenne or chilli pepper
1 teaspoon paprika
2 tablespoons butter

Use a *couscousier*, or improvise one as described above.

Put the meat, chicken if used, onions, chick peas, turnips and carrots – all the ingredients which require longer cooking – in the bottom part of the pan. Cover with water, add the oil, pepper, and ginger and saffron if you like, bring to the boil and simmer for about 1 hour. Add salt only when the chick peas have softened.

Now moisten the couscous as described in the introduction, put it in the top part of the *couscousier* or whatever you are using, and steam for ½ hour. Remove the sieve. Moisten the grain and treat it as described. Before fitting the sieve over the pan again, add raisins, courgettes or marrow, broad beans, tomatoes, parsley and coriander to the simmering stew. Cook for a further ½ hour.

Take a good cupful of sauce from the stew and stir in cayenne or chilli pepper, enough to make it very strong and fiery, and a little paprika.

To serve, pile the couscous on to a large dish, preferably a wooden or earthenware one. Add butter and work it into the grains as it melts. Arrange the meat and vegetables over the couscous and pour the broth over it. Pass the hot, peppery sauce round separately in a little bowl.

Alternatively, serve the couscous, the meat and vegetables, the broth and the peppery sauce in separate bowls.

≈ This dish can be varied indefinitely. Fry the meat and chopped onions in oil before adding the other ingredients if you like. Add baby onions, sliced green peppers and a slice of pumpkin, small shredded white cabbage, a few pitted dates, or, as Algerians sometimes do, runner beans and peas. Colour the stew with tomato concentrate and paprika, and make it fiery with cayenne or *harissa* (see page 65). Or add a little cinnamon and rose water to the butter when you melt it into the couscous.

Couscous with Fish

A couscous favoured by Tunisians. Any type of fish can be used, but generally red or grey mullet are preferred.

120 g (4 oz) chick peas, soaked overnight
Fish tails and heads to make a rich stock
3 carrots, sliced
3 turnips, quartered
1 onion, quartered, or a few baby onions
1 sweet green pepper, seeded, cored and sliced

Salt and black pepper
Cayenne pepper
¼ teaspoon saffron
500–750 g (1–1½lb) couscous
750 g–1 kg (1½–2 lb) fish (see above)
2–3 quinces, peeled, cored and sliced

In a large pan, make a rich fish soup. Boil the fish tails and heads with all the vegetables, salt, black and cayenne pepper and saffron in 1–1½ litres (2–3 pints) water. Remove the scum as it rises to the surface. Simmer for an hour until the stock is rich and the vegetables are soft.

Prepare the couscous as described on page 336. Put it in the sieve and steam it over the simmering fish stock for 30 minutes. Remove the couscous and treat it as previously described.

Remove the fish tails and heads from the stock, and if you like strain through a fine sieve, then return the vegetables to the stock. Lower in the whole fish, sliced if too large. Add the sliced quinces. Return the couscous to the sieve and steam it over the simmering fish for a further 30 minutes, less if the pieces of fish are not large. Adjust the seasoning of the reduced fish stock.

Serve the fish and its sauce over the couscous in a large dish, or in separate dishes. The strong-tasting quinces give this dish a very distinctive flavour.

Couscous with Yoghourt

A couscous served with yoghourt is steamed over water, seasoned with salt and pepper, allowed to cool and thoroughly mixed with yoghourt. It is eaten cold.

Sweet Couscous

In Algeria, a sweet couscous is served an an entrée. It is steamed over water and served with butter, sugar and a few raisins. Milk is drunk at the same time. Some people like to pour milk over the couscous as well.

Vegetables

Khodar

Vegetables in the Middle East do not play second fiddle as do the 'two veg' to meat in England. They hold a dignified, sometimes splendid position in the hierarchy of food. They are, in turn, *mezze*, pickles and salads. They can be stuffed and ranked as a main dish, an adornment to meat in a stew, or deep-fried, sautéed or steamed. In cooking, their nature is taken into account, and their flavour, texture and colour are treated with respect. They are expected to give of their best.

They do not come in polythene bags or packed tight in little boxes, synthetically remote from their buyers. They are hunted, eyed covetously, handled and smelt, chosen and bargained for, and at last brought home in triumph.

Early in the morning, people leave their houses to do their shopping at the market stalls spilling over with vegetables and fruits fresh from the villages. Men often do this pleasant task before going to work or on the way home.

To look for aubergines for one's *Imam Bayildi* or for courgettes for one's *kousa bi gebna* is a pleasure. Will the courgettes be good for stuffing? Or will they be too small? Will the aubergines be round today, or thin and long? Which stall will have the best tomatoes, and at what price? It is a challenge and a triumph to find a truly good, unblemished vegetable at a good price. There is also the pleasure of bargaining, an ancient ritual. How dull it would be to have fixed prices and not to indulge in this game which daily sharpens the wits and brings shopping to a personal, human level.

Practically all the vegetables used in the Middle East are available almost anywhere in Great Britain. They are certainly abundant in London, where they can be found in supermarkets as well as in specialist Greek and Indian shops. Some of these vegetables, such as courgettes, are now grown here. Others are still imported and have only a short season, so it is as well to buy them as soon as they appear in the shops. A good number are available frozen or in tins, and although these cannot equal fresh vegetables, they are a possible alternative.

The basic vegetables, such as tomatoes, lemons, cucumbers, garlic, broad beans, courgettes or marrow, celery, onions, sweet peppers, leeks and spinach are common British vegetables.

COURGETTES When buying courgettes, choose medium-sized or largish ones for stuffing, small or very large ones for slicing and deep-frying, or for use in omelettes, stews, etc. Marrows can be used in all the recipes for courgettes except those that call for stuffing or deep-fried cooking.

AUBERGINES Often called 'poor man's meat' and, in one form, 'poor man's caviar', the aubergine is one of the staple foods of the Middle East. It is extremely versatile.

There are different types of aubergine: small and round, large and round, long and thin, and small and thin. The colour varies from mauve with sparks of violet, to blue-black, and one variety is opaline white. All should be shiny and firm.

The type of aubergine often determines the dish that can be made with it. Pick the smaller ones, preferably the longer type, for stuffing. The larger ones can be sliced or cubed, and deep-fried, sautéed or stewed.

CUCUMBERS The variety to be found in the Middle East is small and stubby in appearance, rather like a gherkin. It is sweeter than the larger variety usually sold here, and has fewer seeds. I have sometimes found them in Greek shops in London.

Vegetables

TOMATOES are usually large and knobbly, and are very flavourful.

SWEET PEPPERS are similar to those sold in Britain, varying in colour from olive, pale or dark green, to bright green, like a card table felt, or vivid yellow or red. When buying them, pick an odd scarlet one to place among the green ones and bring out their brilliance.

Peppers have a sweet, piquant flavour, but their seeds are usually very strong and should be removed. One in forty will be truly fiery, so it is advisable to taste a small piece from every pepper before using it.

ONIONS are usually very pale-skinned and white-fleshed. Many of the ones available here are, in fact, imported from the Middle East. Another favourite variety in the Middle East is the Italian onion, which has a cherry-red skin and a mauve-tinged, sweet, mild flesh, excellent raw in salads. Spanish onions are a good alternative.

GARLIC in the Middle East is of a variety with large cloves, rather like those sold in Britain. Where a clove of garlic is indicated in a recipe, a largish one or 2 or 3 very small ones should be used.

LEMONS are small and round, with very thin skins and sharp, generous juice. This type can be found in most Indian and Greek food shops, but the usual variety available in Britain will do.

LETTUCE in the Middle East, is the long, crisp, Cos variety. It is grown abundantly and is a great favourite. In Egypt, discarded leaves are found scattered about all the public gardens at the end of festival days.

ARTICHOKES occur in several varieties, both large and small. All are generally very tender. They have a short season in Britain, and are usually expensive; but the better qualities of tinned artichokes keep their flavour and make a passable substitute.

PARSLEY is the flat-leafed Continental type which has a much stronger flavour.

OKRA, or *bamia* as it is called in Arabic, is also called 'ladies' fingers' in Britain, a very evocative name for this long, green, pointed vegetable. It is now widely available in supermarkets.

Middle Eastern SPINACH is of a different variety from the one available here. The small tender leaves are attached in bunches growing out of one root.

BEETS (*blette* in French) are a type of spinach with rather longer leaves.

SWEET POTATOES can now be found everywhere. Bake them in their jackets like ordinary potatoes, but for rather longer. Cut open and eat with butter but no salt, or peel and mash them. They are deliciously sweet.

Plain and Mixed Vegetable Dishes

Potatoes with Chick Peas and Tomatoes

This dish is eaten cold in the Middle East. The hot version is the same, except that it uses butter or *samna* (clarified butter) instead of oil.

1 kg (2 lb) potatoes	500 g (1 lb) tomatoes, skinned and
3 onions, thickly sliced	chopped
4–5 tablespoons oil	2 tablespoons tomato concentrate
60 g (2 oz) cooked chick peas	Salt and black pepper
2–3 cloves garlic	

Peel and slice the potatoes thickly. Fry the onions in oil until golden, using a large saucepan. Add the chick peas and the whole garlic cloves, and fry until coloured. Add the potato slices and turn them until they too are slightly coloured. Add tomatoes, and water to cover mixed with tomato concentrate. Season to taste with salt and pepper.

Bring to the boil and simmer gently until the potatoes are done. Serve cold.

Aubergines or Courgettes with Tomatoes

This dish can be prepared with either one kind of vegetable or both; in the second case, reduce the quantity of each vegetable.

750 g (1½ lb) aubergines or
  courgettes
Salt
1 clove garlic, crushed
4–6 tablespoons oil (use olive oil
  if serving cold)

375 g (12 oz) tomatoes, skinned
  and chopped
2 tablespoons chopped parsley
Salt and black pepper

Cut the aubergines or courgettes into moderately thick rounds. Sprinkle them with salt and leave them to drain in a colander for at least ½ hour. Squeeze aubergines dry.

Sauté gently with the crushed garlic in olive oil, turning the slices over once, until they are soft. Add the tomatoes and squash them gently in the pan. Sprinkle with parsley, season to taste with salt and pepper, and simmer until the vegetables are well done.

Serve hot to accompany meat dishes, or cold as an hors d'œuvre.

≈ A delicious version of this dish has a sweet-and-sour flavour. Add 1 or 2 tablespoons wine vinegar and 1 teaspoon sugar, or more.
≈ For a more substantial dish add 250 g (8 oz) cooked chick peas.

Okra (Bamia) with Tomatoes and Onions

This popular dish is often flavoured with garlic and coriander, a favourite Arab combination. It is customarily served cold, and for this reason it is cooked in oil. However, it is equally delicious hot, served with rice or as a side dish with meat or chicken.

1 kg (2 lb) fresh young okra
375 g (12 oz) tiny white button
  onions or large onions
4–5 tablespoons olive oil
2–3 cloves garlic, halved

500 g (1 lb) tomatoes, skinned and
  sliced
Salt and black pepper
Juice of 1 lemon

Wash and scrub the fresh okra. Cut off any hard stems and dry them thoroughly. Peel the button onions but leave them whole. If using large onions, slice them thickly.

Heat the oil in a large saucepan and fry the onions with the halved garlic cloves until slightly soft, transparent and golden. Add okra and continue to fry until slightly softened. Add the sliced tomatoes and sauté for a few minutes longer. Season to taste with salt and pepper. Cover with water, bring to the boil and simmer until the okra are very tender, ½ to 1 hour. Squeeze in the lemon juice and cook for a further 15 minutes. (Tinned okra require a much shorter time.)

Serve hot or cold. If to be served cold, allow to cool in the saucepan before turning out into a serving dish.

≈ If you wish to flavour the dish with coriander, add 1 teaspoon of ground coriander together with the garlic cloves, which should in this case be crushed and not halved.

Betingan
Aubergines

It is said that there are a hundred ways of cooking aubergines but the most common is simply to fry them. Slice and sprinkle with salt and leave for an hour in a colander for their bitter juices to drain away. This also makes them absorb less oil. Rinse if there is too much salt and squeeze several slices together to rid them of all their juices. Fry in hot, shallow oil, turning over once, until lightly coloured on both sides. Drain on absorbent paper. Serve with chopped parsley and, if you like, a sprinkling of vinegar.

Some people like to fry slices of garlic, usually plenty of them, at the same time.

Aubergines, Tomatoes and Green Peppers in Oil

This dish, similar to the French *ratatouille*, is usually served cold, although it is also good hot. It makes a splendid hors d'œuvre.

2 aubergines, sliced	1–2 green peppers, sliced, seeded
Salt	and cored
1 onion, sliced	4 tomatoes, skinned and sliced
1 teacup olive oil	Black pepper

Sprinkle the aubergine slices with salt and let them drain in a colander for at least ½ hour to get rid of their bitter juices, squeeze, wash and dry the slices.

Fry the onion in olive oil until soft and a pale golden colour. Add the sliced peppers and aubergines, and fry gently for 10 minutes longer. Add the tomatoes and season to taste with salt and pepper. As they cook, the vegetables will give out a great deal of water.

Simmer for 30 minutes until they are tender and the liquid in the pan is considerably reduced. Allow to cool in the pan.

≈ Turks serve this with beaten yoghourt, sometimes flavoured with crushed garlic and salt, and poured over the entire dish.

Turlu
Turkish Mixed Vegetables in Olive Oil

1 onion, sliced
1 teacup olive oil
250 g (8 oz) white haricot beans, soaked overnight
2 small potatoes, peeled and sliced
1 medium celeriac, peeled and sliced

1 large carrot, scraped and sliced
5 spring onions, chopped
2–4 large cloves garlic, or more
Salt and black pepper
1 teaspoon caster sugar
3 tablespoons finely chopped parsley

Fry the onion in half the oil until soft and a pale golden colour, using a large saucepan. Add the drained beans and about 600 ml (1 pint) of water, but no salt. Bring to the boil and simmer for 1 to 2 hours, according to quality, until the beans are practically tender. A pressure cooker will reduce this time considerably.

Add remaining vegetables and garlic, and more water if necessary. Simmer until all the vegetables and the beans are well cooked. Season to taste with salt and pepper, add sugar and the remaining olive oil, and cook for a further 10 minutes.

Serve hot, garnished with chopped parsley.

Aubergines in Turkey

Emine Foat Tugay says in her family chronicles *Three Centuries* that in Turkey the egg-plant (aubergine) is the 'king of vegetables'. She gives a description of ways of cooking them beginning with those which are cooked in oil and eaten cold.

(i) *Egg-plant salad.* The egg-plants are cooked on a hot baking tin, then peeled and mashed with yoghurt. Olive oil, lemon juice, and salt are added. The purée, which should be fairly firm, is served garnished with halved black olives and thin slices of sweet pepper. It is also delicious as hors d'œuvres.

(ii) With its skin peeled in strips, and sliced to the thickness of a little finger, the egg-plant is fried in deep oil and left to drip. It is eaten with a sauce of yoghurt beaten smooth.

(iii) The egg-plant is slit up lengthwise, stuffed with thinly-sliced onions, white pistachios, and black currants, and covered with a slice of tomato, then cooked in broth and oil.

(iv) *Yalanci dolma.* Hollowed out and stuffed with fried rice, white pistachios, and black currants, the egg-plant is cooked in broth and oil.

(v) Forming the basis of a mixed vegetable dish, called the *türlü* variety, it can be cooked with oil and eaten cold in the summer.

(vi) *Türlü proper.* The same mixture is cooked with butter and flavoured with small pieces of meat and sliced tomatoes. It is arranged in the shape of a mound, in a pattern, the dark colour of the egg-plant being relieved by the lighter shades of accompanying vegetables.

(vii) The egg-plant is cut into small squares and cooked plain with broth and flavoured with sliced tomatoes.

(viii) *Musakka.* The egg-plant is cut up into largish pieces, fried, and then cooked with minced meat sprinkled over it.

(ix) *Dolma.* With its two ends cut off, the egg-plant is hollowed out, and stuffed with spiced minced meat, herbs, and rice.

(x) *Karniyarik* (literally 'split belly'). As the name indicates, the egg-plant cooked in this way is cut open lengthwise and stuffed with spiced minced meat, black currants, and white pistachios.

(xi) *Oturtma,* meaning 'made to sit down', is a variation of the *karniyarik,* except that the egg-plant is here cut into thick round slices, hollowed and filled with the same stuffing as above. It is eaten with plain pilav (rice).

Moussaka

A splendid meal in itself, this dish is a favourite throughout the Middle East. Although it is claimed by the Greeks as their own, its name is an Arabic one. It is possible, however, that the Turks adopted the dish from the Greeks and gave it its present name. Numerous variations exist.

3 aubergines	1 tomato, skinned and chopped
Salt	2–3 tablespoons tomato
Oil	concentrate
1–2 onions, thinly sliced or chopped	2–3 tablespoons chopped parsley
750 g (1½ lb) lamb or beef, minced	4 tablespoons butter
Black pepper	4 tablespoons flour
½ teaspoon ground allspice or 1 teaspoon ground cinnamon (optional)	600 ml (1 pint) hot milk
	Pinch of grated nutmeg
	2 eggs

Slice the aubergines thinly. Sprinkle the slices generously with salt and allow their bitter juices to drain away in a colander for at least ½ hour. Squeeze, wash in cold water and pat dry. Fry quickly in oil, turning the slices once. Remove and drain on absorbent paper.

Fry the onions in 2 tablespoons oil until pale golden. Add the minced meat and fry until well browned. Season to taste with salt and pepper, and flavour with allspice or cinnamon if you like. Add the chopped tomato, tomato concentrate and parsley. Stir well, moisten with a few tablespoons of water and simmer for about 15 minutes, or until the meat is well cooked and the water is absorbed.

Put alternate layers of aubergine slices and meat and onion mixture in a deep baking dish, starting and ending with a layer of aubergines.

Prepare a white sauce: melt butter in a saucepan. Add flour and stir over low heat for a few minutes until well blended. Add the hot milk gradually, stirring until it boils, taking care not to allow lumps to form. Season to taste with salt, pepper and a pinch of nutmeg. Simmer until the sauce thickens. Beat the eggs, stir in a little of the sauce and beat well. Pour back into the pan slowly, stirring constantly. Do not allow the sauce to boil again.

Pour the sauce over the minced meat and aubergines and bake, uncovered, in a preheated moderate oven (180°C/350°F/Mark 4) for about 45 minutes, until a brown crust has formed on the top and the layers have fused and blended. This looks interesting and attractive in a transparent baking dish.

Serve hot, straight from the dish. Moussaka makes a splendid party or family dish served with salad and yoghourt. It can also be cooked in small individual bowls, the layers repeated in exactly the same way.

≈ A variation popular in Britain makes use of seasoned mashed potatoes. A layer is spread over the top of the dish and covered with the sauce. Potatoes can also be sliced and sautéed and arranged on top before the sauce is poured over the whole.

≈ Courgettes are sometimes used instead of, or at the same time as, aubergines.

≈ A very rich moussaka can be made by sprinkling grated Kephalo-tiri or Parmesan cheese (or by adding layers of thinly sliced Gruyère) over each layer of aubergines.

≈ An Arab variation is made with 300 ml (½ pint) of yoghourt poured over the top instead of the white sauce.

Kousa bi Gebna
Courgettes or Marrow with Cheese

A perfect vegetable dish. Although courgettes are traditionally used, marrow does very well. Use a good melting cheese such as Gruyère or Cheddar, mixed with a little Parmesan.

1 large onion, chopped	3 eggs
2 tablespoons butter or oil	250 g (8 oz) grated cheese
1 kg (2 lb) courgettes or marrow	White pepper
Salt	

Soften the onion in butter or oil. Wash the courgettes or marrow. Scrape skins lightly if necessary. Trim the courgette ends and cut into 1-cm (½-inch) slices. Cut the marrow into 3-cm (1-inch) cubes. Poach in salted water for a few minutes until tender, or steam if you prefer. Drain well. Put into an ovenproof dish and mix with the onions.

Beat the eggs, add the grated cheese and pepper to taste, and mix well. Pour over the vegetables.

Bake in a preheated moderate oven (180°C/350°F/Mark 4) for about 20 minutes. Allow the top to colour delicately.

Excellent served with yoghourt.

≈ Lately I have been adding a little grated nutmeg to the beaten eggs and found it very nice.

Hünkâr Beğendi
Sultan's Delight

Emine Foat Tugay writes about this delicious egg-plant (aubergine) cream in her book *Three Centuries*. '*Sultan's Pleasure*,' she says,

is a purée of egg-plant, with small pieces of meat cooked in butter and tomato juice placed in the centre. As in the salad, the egg-plant is cooked on a hot baking tin, peeled, and mashed. A little melted butter is poured over it just before serving. The dish derives its name from a legend. Once upon a time a sultan went out hunting. Whilst pursuing his quarry, he penetrated into a large forest, and soon lost sight of both the game and his attendants. He wandered about till nightfall, getting farther and farther into unknown country until, hungry and exhausted, he at last saw a light in the distance. Filled with hope, the sultan urged his weary horse towards it till he came to the house whence the light had proceeded. Here he was hospitably received, and his host immediately sent word to the cook to prepare a meal. It was late, dinner was over long since, and all that remained in the kitchen were some scraps of meat and a few egg-plants. The cook, being a resourceful man, cut up the meat and put it in a pot, the vegetables he threw on the hot cooking range, and mashed them. The result was a steaming dish, of which the sultan ate every morsel. Replete and rested he sent a purse filled with gold to the cook and asked the name of the dish, never having eaten it before. He was told that the cook had invented it on the spot, whereupon the sultan declared that henceforth it should be called Sultan's Pleasure.

This dish is pale and delicate, with the distinctive flavour of *grilled* aubergines.

1 kg (2 lb) aubergines	Salt
1 tablespoon lemon juice	60 g (2 oz) grated Parmesan or dry
4 tablespoons butter	Cheddar
4 tablespoons flour	Finely chopped parsley
½ litre (1 pint) hot milk	

Grill the aubergines over a naked flame or under a grill until their skins are black and blistered all over. Peel carefully, removing all charred particles.

Leave them covered with water acidulated with 1 tablespoon lemon juice for 15 minutes. This will keep them white.

Melt the butter in a saucepan. Add the flour and stir over very low heat for about 2 minutes until well blended. Remove from the heat. Add the milk gradually, beating vigorously all the time. Season to taste with salt. Cook until the mixture thickens and the taste of flour has disappeared, about 15 minutes.

Drain the aubergines and squeeze out as much of the water and juices as possible. Mash well, add to the milk sauce, and beat vigorously or use a liquidizer until well blended. Return to the heat. Add the grated cheese, stir until melted and turn into a serving dish. Sprinkle with finely chopped parsley.

Serve with steamed kebabs, stewed meat or chicken cooked in a tomato sauce. The aubergine cream serves as a bed for the meat or chicken.

Artichoke Hearts and Broad Beans in Oil

The Copts observe a long and arduous fast during Lent (*El Soum el Kibir*), when they abstain from every kind of animal food, such as meat, eggs, milk, butter and cheese, and eat only bread and vegetables (chiefly beans), and *dukkah* (see page 89).

Here is a favourite Lenten dish, also popular with the Greeks of Egypt, and a general favourite throughout the Middle East.

6 artichokes (or good-quality tinned artichoke hearts)*	1 teaspoon sugar
Juice of 1 lemon, or more	500 g (1 lb) fresh shelled or frozen broad beans
2–3 tablespoons olive oil	Salt and black pepper
1 clove garlic, crushed, or more	1 tablespoon flour or cornflour

Buy young artichokes. Remove the leaves, stems and chokes, and use only the hearts. Rub with lemon juice and drop in 150 ml (¼ pint) water acidulated with lemon to prevent discoloration.

Put the olive oil, garlic, sugar and the acidulated water in a large pan with the artichoke hearts. Add the broad beans, and season to taste with salt and pepper. Add more water to cover if necessary. Simmer gently over low heat for about ¾ hour, until the artichoke hearts and beans are very tender and the liquid is considerably reduced.

Mix the flour or cornflour to a smooth paste with a little cold water. Add a little of the hot liquid and stir well. Then add this to the pan gradually, stirring constantly. Simmer gently, stirring occasionally, until the sauce thickens and has lost the taste of flour (about 15 minutes). Pour into a dish.

Serve hot to accompany main dishes, or cold as an hors d'œuvre. The sauce will be gelatinous if cornflour is used.

Tartoufa
Jerusalem Artichokes

Peel and wash them. Simmer in salted water, chicken or meat stock to cover for just under ½ hour, adding more liquid if necessary. They should be tender and the liquid practically all absorbed. Finish with a tablespoon of butter or the juice of 1 lemon.

* If tinned artichokes and frozen beans are used, the cooking time will, of course, be much shorter.

Tartoufa in Tomato Sauce

1 kg (2¼ lb) Jerusalem artichokes
1 onion, finely chopped
1 clove garlic, halved
3 tablespoons olive oil
3 tomatoes, skinned and chopped

2 tablespoons tomato concentrate
2 tablespoons finely chopped
  parsley
Salt and black pepper
Juice of ½ lemon (optional)

Wash and peel the artichokes. Fry the onion and garlic in olive oil until soft and golden. Add the artichokes and roll them in the oil by shaking the pan. Add the tomatoes and squash them into the oil. Add tomato concentrate, parsley, seasoning, and lemon juice if used. Stir well and cover with water. Simmer gently for ½ hour, or until the artichokes are tender and the sauce is rich and reduced. Add more water during cooking if necessary.

Celeriac in Olive Oil

2 large celeriacs
3–4 tablespoons olive oil

Juice of 1 lemon, or more
Salt and black pepper

Peel the celeriacs and cut into 2-cm (¾-inch) cubes. Fry gently in olive oil until lightly coloured. Add a little water to cover, lemon juice to taste, and salt and pepper. Simmer until the vegetables are tender and the liquid is considerably reduced, about ½ hour.

Eat hot or cold.

≈ 1 tablespoon tamarind syrup or paste with 1 of sugar instead of the lemon will lend an unusual sweet-and-sour flavour.

Deep-fried Aubergines or Courgettes

Thinly slice the vegetables, lengthwise or crosswise. Sprinkle them with salt and leave them to drain in a colander for at least ½ hour. A plate with a weight on top will help to squeeze the juices out. Or squeeze with your hands after they have been left for some time. This will get rid of their bitterness and will also make them lose their capacity for drinking oil.

Pat the slices dry and deep-fry a few at a time for 2 to 3 minutes in very hot oil. Remove and drain when golden brown.

Alternatively, you may roll the aubergine slices in flour or dip them in a light batter. This is made by gradually adding 150 ml

(¼ pint) water to 120 g (4 oz) plain flour mixed with 3 tablespoons oil, leaving it to rest for 2 hours, and folding in a stiffly beaten egg white just before use. Another batter is made by beating the flour and water mixture with 1 whole egg. Fry as above, turning over once, remove with a perforated spoon and drain.

Garnish with roughly chopped parsley, deep-fried in the same oil. Serve with lemon wedges as an appetizer or side dish.

Deep-fried Cauliflower

Wash the cauliflower and separate into florets. Boil in salted water until only just tender. Drain and allow to dry well.

Roll the florets in beaten egg, and then in flour or bread-crumbs. Deep-fry in very hot oil until crisp and golden. Drain on absorbent paper.

Alternatively, dip in one of the batter mixtures given in the preceding recipe, and deep-fry until golden, turning over once. Drain well.

Serve with yoghourt or Turkish walnut *tarator* sauce (page 112).

Egyptian Cauliflower

Wash, boil and deep-fry a cauliflower as directed above. Both the egg and flour and the batter methods are equally suitable.

Prepare a tomato sauce in a large saucepan. Fry 2 cloves garlic in about 2 tablespoons oil until golden. Add 3 to 4 tablespoons tomato concentrate diluted in 150 ml (¼ pint) water, 3 tablespoons chopped parsley, and salt and black pepper to taste. Simmer for 10 to 15 minutes.

Drain the deep-fried florets, and drop them into the tomato sauce. Simmer for about ½ hour until the cauliflower is very tender and the sauce is reduced and rich.

Cauliflower with Lemon Juice

Wash, and boil or steam a young white cauliflower for about 10 to 15 minutes, until just tender. Acidulating the salted water in which it is boiled with a little lemon juice helps to keep it white.

Drain the tender head well. Break into florets. Heat 1 tablespoon butter with 1 tablespoon or more olive oil in a pan, add the juice of 1 lemon, and sprinkle with a little salt and pepper. Roll the cauliflower in this and keep over very low heat until it is heated through and has absorbed the lemon juice. Some people also like to add a little crushed garlic.

Grilled Corn Cobs

Walking along the *corniche* or waterfront in Alexandria, one is irresistibly lured by the smell of corn grilled over charcoal. Vendors sit at the braziers, fanning the flames vigorously, or letting the sea breeze do it for them.

Remove the leaves or husks from the corn cobs. Place the cobs on a charcoal grill, not too close to the fire. Turn them constantly. They will become flecked with black, charred spots, but inside they will be soft and milky.

☐ *Riddle: Beaded, her head is high and she sleeps in a shawl. Guess who she is.*
☐ *Answer: A corn cob.*

Spinach with Almonds

1 kg (2 lb) spinach	Salt and pepper
1 onion, coarsely chopped	4 tomatoes, peeled and sliced
2 tablespoons oil	60 g (2 oz) blanched almonds

Wash the spinach, remove hard stems and shred if the leaves are large. Sauté the onion in oil until soft, then add the spinach and cook gently, stirring, until it crumples. Add salt and pepper and the tomatoes and cook until they have softened only slightly. Toast the almonds and stir them in just before serving.

Aloo Sfenaj
Spinach and Prunes with Beans

A Persian combination.

120 g (4 oz) black-eyed beans or
   dried red beans
1 large onion, coarsely chopped
2–3 tablespoons oil
120 g (4 oz) pitted prunes

½ teaspoon turmeric
1 teaspoon cinnamon
Pepper
Salt
1 kg (2 lb) spinach

Soak the beans in water for an hour. Fry the onion in oil until golden in a large saucepan. Add the prunes and the drained beans, cover with water, add spices and pepper and cook until the beans are tender (from ½ to 1 hour) and the water much reduced, adding salt when the beans have softened. Wash the spinach and remove thick stems. Put it in the pan and cook, turning it over and stirring, for about 10 minutes until the spinach is done.

Fistuqia
Broad Beans with Yoghourt

This recipe is inspired by one in *Recipes from Baghdad*.

½ kg (1 lb) fresh shelled broad
   beans or frozen ones
600 ml (1 pint) yoghourt
1 small egg

3–4 tablespoons cooked rice, or
   more
2 cloves garlic, crushed
Salt and pepper
2 teaspoons dried mint (optional)

Boil the beans in salted water until tender, and drain. Beat the egg into the yoghourt so that it does not curdle when it is cooked, and pour it into the pan with the beans. Add rice, garlic, salt and pepper and simmer gently, stirring, for 10 minutes.

    Serve hot or cold, sprinkled with mint if you like.

Battata Harra
Hot Spicy Potatoes

A Lebanese recipe.

500 g (1 lb) new potatoes, diced
   raw
3–4 tablespoons olive oil
2–3 hot chillis, chopped

Salt
3 cloves garlic, crushed
A bunch of fresh coriander,
   chopped

Fry the diced potatoes in olive oil until crisply cooked. Add the chillis, salt and garlic and cook for a minute or two. Add the coriander and cook gently, stirring until it wilts.

Another Recipe for Spiced Potatoes

Here the potatoes are left whole.

For 1 kg (2 lb) of new potatoes mix in a saucepan: 4–5 tablespoons vegetable oil, 4–5 crushed cloves garlic (or to taste), salt, black pepper, 2 teaspoons paprika and, if you like, a good pinch of cayenne. Put in the potatoes and only just cover with water. Simmer gently until they are tender but still firm.

You may also add a bunch of chopped coriander leaves and 1 teaspoon each of ground cumin and coriander.

Spiced Mashed Potatoes

This flavoursome purée comes from Algeria, where it is more usually shaped into cakes, dipped in beaten eggs and deep-fried till brown. It is simpler and just as good to leave it as it is in a bowl. Mix 1 kg (2 lb) mashed potatoes with 3 large eggs, season with salt and pepper, 2 teaspoons cumin, 1 tablespoon paprika and, if you want, 1 of cayenne. Stir in a bunch of parsley or coriander, finely chopped.

Mashed Potatoes with Pine Nuts

1 kg (2 lb) potatoes	Salt and pepper
2 tablespoons oil	1 teaspoon cinnamon
1 large onion, coarsely chopped	A good pinch of nutmeg
3 tablespoons pine nuts	A good pinch of chilli pepper
90 g (3 oz) butter	1 tablespoon finely chopped
90 ml (3 fl oz) milk	parsley

Wash and boil the potatoes. Fry the onion in oil till golden, add the pine nuts and let them brown. Peel and mash the potatoes, beat in butter and milk and season with salt and pepper and spices. Serve with the onion and pine nuts on top and a sprinkling of parsley.

Sweet Potatoes

Peel 1 kg (2 lb) of sweet potatoes and cut them into pieces. Boil in salted water with a handful of sultanas, about 150 g (5 oz) or more, until they are very soft. Drain and mash with a fork. Add butter, about 120 g (4 oz) and season with pepper, extra salt if necessary, a pinch of ginger and 1 teaspoon cinnamon.

Sweet Turnips

Cooked vegetables have not much importance in Iraq, where they only find a place in a pot to go with meat, but turnips are treated with special respect.

Young turnips are usually peeled and boiled in salted water, then pressed under a weight to squeeze out some of the water, and served with a dusting of sugar.

A special flavour is obtained when a little date syrup called *dibbis* (see page 64) is stirred into the cooking water. Instead of the syrup you can put a few dried dates in the water and mash them with a fork when they are soft.

Lately, I have tried sautéing sliced turnips with fresh dates, 4–6 for 500 g (1 lb), pitted and halved, in a little butter with only a sprinkling of salt and pepper, and found it very pleasant to serve as a side dish with meat, chicken or fish.

☐ *Turnips are Harder**

The Mulla one day decided to take the King some fine turnips which he had grown.

On the way he met a friend, who advised him to present something more refined, such as figs or olives.

He bought some figs, and the King, who was in a good humour, accepted them and rewarded him.

Next week he bought some huge oranges and took them to the palace. But the King was in a bad temper, and threw them at Nasrudin, bruising him.

As he picked himself up, the Mulla realized the truth. 'Now I understand,' he said; 'people take smaller things rather than heavy

* Shah, *The Exploits of the Incomparable Mulla Nasrudin.*

ones because when you are pelted it does not hurt so much. If it had been those turnips, I would have been killed.'

Mahshi Khodar
Stuffed Vegetables

Dolma to the Turks, *dolmathes* to the Greeks, *dolmeh* to the Iranians, and *mahshi* to the Arabs, stuffed vegetables are the great family favourites, the party pieces and festive dishes of the Turks, the Uzbeks, the Azerbaijanis, Armenians, Greeks, Egyptians, Iranians, Syrians, Lebanese, Saudi Arabians and North Africans. Adopted by all, each country has developed its own variations.

Their origin is not certain, though both the Turks and the Greeks claim them as their creation. They do not appear in the very early Persian and Arab manuscripts, but seem to have been known at the time of the Ottoman Empire, and were served at the lavish banquets of the Sultans. Perhaps they were developed at this time; but they may equally well have been adopted from the vanquished Greeks, who claim a rich culinary tradition stemming from their early civilization.

However, stuffed vegetables were obviously developed as a 'court cuisine', invented and prepared for a rich and powerful leisured class to excite their curiosity and titillate their palates, as well as to satisfy their desire for ostentation. The long, elaborate preparation required for these dishes, and the experienced and delicate handiwork that goes into the making of them are proof of the number of dedicated cooks employed in the huge kitchens, while the subtle harmony of the vegetables and their fillings demonstrates the refined taste and deep culinary knowledge of their masters.

Today, poorer people can usually afford vine leaves, courgettes, onions and aubergines; and although they have had to make the fillings simpler and cheaper, they count their own time as cheap as their masters deemed it, and spend it lavishly on rolling and filling their beloved *mahshi*.

As well as the love for different, subtle flavours, for the exciting fusion of vegetables and their fillings, the traditional wish to take pains and give of oneself is satisfied by the trouble one takes in making these dishes. So is the wish to impress by one's culinary expertise. And how the guest loves to be surprised by an intriguing parcel, the contents of which are always slightly unpredictable!

In the past, Arabs have been – and in certain places still are – obsessed by their belief in the existence of numerous spirits or *djinns*, several *djinns* per person in fact, who inhabit both things and people whenever they get a chance. Their tales give a fascinating picture of vegetables inhabited by *djinns* – rice *djinns*, meat *djinns*, chick pea *djinns* – seasoned and spiced, and given piquant, naughty or gentle personalities, like the *djinns* who inhabit humans.

A very common filling for any stuffed vegetable is a mixture of chopped onion, minced meat, rice and chopped parsley, sometimes with chopped tomatoes as well, seasoned with salt and pepper. Sometimes raisins, pine nuts and chopped walnuts are added to the mixture. Iranians favour the addition of well-cooked yellow split peas. An Armenian filling is made with burghul (cracked wheat) flavoured with aniseed and garlic.

In the past, stuffed vegetables were customarily fried gently in oil or *samna* (clarified butter) before being stewed. Today, since the tendency is to make dishes lighter and less rich, this step, though an enhancement to the flavour of the dish, is omitted.

Almost any vegetable can be, and is, stuffed.

☐ *A man carried seven eggs in the fold (pocket) of his robe.*

He met another man in the street and said to him:

'If you can guess what I have in the fold of my robe, I will give you these eggs, and if you can tell me how many there are, I will give you all seven.' The other thought for a while and said:

'I don't understand, give me another clue.'

The man said:

'It is white with yellow in the middle.'

'Now I understand,' exclaimed the other. 'It is a white radish that has been hollowed and stuffed with a carrot!'

A man told this anecdote to a group of people. When he had finished, one of his audience asked, 'But tell us, what was there in the fold of his robe?'[*]

What is more natural than a white radish stuffed with a carrot?

* Christensen, *Contes persans*.

Fillings for Vegetables

From the great variety of fillings, I am giving the ones which are most widely used and the general favourites. They can also be flavoured with different spices and herbs. The quantities given are enough to stuff about 1 kg (2 lb) vegetables, but this varies a little according to the size of the vegetables to be filled, and the amount of pulp scooped out of them.

Filling 1

Sheikh el Mahshi filling, also called *tatbila*. The word 'sheikh' implies that it is the grandest, since it is all meat.

2 tablespoons butter or oil	Salt and black pepper
1 medium-sized onion, finely chopped	½ teaspoon ground cinnamon or ¼ teaspoon ground allspice
275 g (12 oz) lean lamb or beef, minced	60 g (2 oz) pine nuts (optional)

Heat the butter or oil in a frying pan. Add the onion and fry gently until soft and transparent. Add the meat and fry it, tossing it and squashing with a fork, until it changes colour. Season to taste with salt and pepper, sprinkle with spices and stir in pine nuts if used. Moisten with a few tablespoons of water, and cook gently, covered, until the meat is very tender.

Filling 2

Meat and rice filling (the most common one).

250 g (8 oz) lean lamb or beef, minced	2 tablespoons finely chopped parsley (optional)
90 g (3 oz) short- or medium-grain rice, washed and drained	Salt and black pepper
1 tomato, skinned and chopped (optional)	½ teaspoon ground cinnamon or ¼ teaspoon ground allspice

Put all the ingredients together in a bowl. Knead well by hand until thoroughly blended.

Do not fill the vegetables more than three-quarters full, to allow for the expansion of the rice.

≈ If you will be baking a vegetable in the oven rather than simmering it in a saucepan this filling should be cooked before the vegetable is stuffed: Fry the onion in 2 tablespoons oil, add the minced meat and fry gently until it changes colour. Then add the rest of the ingredients, mix well, barely cover with water and simmer for 15 minutes or until the rice is done.

≈ In North Africa they like to add 2 eggs to bind the filling ingredients.

≈ 1 or 2 tablespoons raisins and/or pine nuts may be added to this filling, an agreeable though uncommon variation.

≈ An alternative flavouring is ½ teaspoon dried basil or marjoram.

Filling 3

A Persian filling of meat and rice with yellow split peas.

60–90 g (2–3 oz) yellow split peas
1 medium-sized onion, finely chopped
2 tablespoons butter or oil
250 g (8 oz) lean lamb or beef, minced
60 g (2 oz) rice, cooked (weight uncooked)

3 tablespoons finely chopped parsley
2–3 spring onions, finely chopped (optional)
Salt and black pepper
½ teaspoon ground cinnamon
Pinch of grated nutmeg

Cook the yellow split peas in unsalted water for about 25 minutes, or until soft. Soften the onion in butter or oil. Put all the ingredients together in a bowl, including the split peas and onions. Mix well and knead by hand until thoroughly blended.

Filling 4

A rice filling for vegetables to be eaten cold.

180 g (6 oz) short- or medium-grain rice, washed and drained
180 g (6 oz) tomatoes, skinned, seeded and finely chopped
1 large onion, finely chopped

A small bunch of parsley, finely chopped
Salt and black pepper
½ teaspoon ground cinnamon or ¼ teaspoon ground allspice (optional)

Mix all the ingredients together in a bowl, kneading well by hand until thoroughly blended.

When filling the vegetables, allow room for the rice to expand. Use cooked rice and pack the vegetables tightly if they are to be baked.

≈ This filling is sometimes flavoured with about 2 teaspoons finely chopped fresh dill or mint – 1 teaspoon only if dried.

Filling 5

A rice and chick pea filling for vegetables to be eaten cold.

60 g (2 oz) chick peas, cooked
120 g (4 oz) short- or medium-
  grain rice, washed and drained
180 g (6 oz) tomatoes, skinned,
  seeded and finely chopped

1 large onion, finely chopped
Salt and black pepper
½ teaspoon ground cinnamon or
  ¼ teaspoon ground allspice
  (optional)

Prepare and use as above.

Filling 6

For vegetables prepared *à la Imam Bayildi*, to be eaten cold, and sometimes called *yalangi dolma* or 'false dolma', because of the lack of meat. A very popular filling in Turkey.

375 g (12 oz) onions
3–4 tablespoons olive oil
2–3 large cloves garlic, crushed
A bunch of parsley, finely
  chopped

375 g (12 oz) tomatoes, skinned,
  seeded and chopped
Salt

Slice the onions thinly. Soften them gently in olive oil, but do not let them colour. Add garlic and stir for a minute or two until aromatic. Remove from the heat and stir in parsley and tomatoes. Season to taste with salt, and mix well.

Filling 7

A Turkish filling for aubergines.

2 small onions, finely chopped
2 tablespoons oil
250 g (8 oz) lamb or beef, minced
Salt and black pepper

2 tomatoes, skinned and chopped
120 g (4 oz) Gruyère or hard
  Cheddar, grated

Sauté the onions in oil until soft and a pale golden colour. Add the minced meat and fry, squashing well with a fork, until it changes colour. Season to taste with salt and pepper, add the tomatoes, and moisten with a few tablespoons of water. Cook until the tomatoes are reduced to a purée. Stir in the grated cheese and remove from the heat.

☐ A True Artist in the Kitchen*

Our chef, who had already served my mother before she was married, was very old and wished to retire and settle in his village. His second assistant, a young man named Mustafa, who had been with the old man ever since he began as a scullery-boy, asked to be kept on in the house. My father had already noticed him as being intelligent and singularly gifted as a cook. He therefore gave him the chance to show his mettle and promoted him to be head chef. Mustafa was an apt pupil, and as my father had himself explained to him the finer points of preparing both Turkish and European food, he soon excelled in both. He remained with my parents for many years, till his abominable temper, which apparently grew worse in the same ratio as his cooking approached the summit of culinary perfection, forced them to dismiss him in 1909. He used to vent his ill-humour on the cooking of the servants' food, which finally became quite uneatable, and in the end neither complaints nor his master's sharp reprimands had any lasting effect.

He was still with us when in 1908 we went for part of the summer to Ostend, and was summoned to cook for us there. The family spent a few days at Brussels and accordingly Mustafa was put on the Brussels coach of the Orient Express at Istanbul. We were rather anxious about him since he had never been abroad and spoke nothing but Turkish. However, he arrived safely and was met at the station by my mother's French and Turkish maids. Having acquired a smattering of each other's languages, each was capable of understanding what the other said. They took him to a pension where he was to spend a night before going with us to Ostend, and told him about the hours of meals and how to ask for anything he might need. The next morning, when the French maid went to fetch Mustafa, the proprietor of the pension met her in the hall and said that having abruptly left his seat at dinner, Mustafa had hurriedly gone to his room and locked his door. He had not answered when the proprietor went up to ask whether anything was wrong, nor had he come out for breakfast. The maid knocked at Mustafa's door

* From Emine Fort Tugay, *Three Centuries*

until he cautiously opened it to ascertain who she was, and admitted her. Asked whether anything was the matter, he exploded and shouted that they had given him HAM at dinner. Horrified by the sight of 'unclean' meat, he had sought the sanctuary of his room, where at least he was spared from further abominations. The only thing he wanted was to leave this house of perdition as soon as possible. The maid soothed him as best she could and took him to our hotel. The shock of this experience lasted all through our sojourn at Ostend, and during the whole time he was there he never ate or drank anything outside our house.

In his kitchen Mustafa was a true artist, and even invented a form of dolma which I have never eaten since he left. He lightly boiled leeks, carrots, and celery, just enough to soften them, and peeled them into thin layers. These he cut into squares, placed some spiced minced meat in the centre, and folded each piece into a small triangle. He then neatly arranged the different vegetables in layers in a cooking pot with a rounded bottom, and cooked them in broth. Before serving up he would reverse the pot on to a round dish, where the little dolmas formed an appetizing mound. He was the only cook I ever met who had the skill and patience for this work.

In those days every vegetable was skilfully laid out in a cooking pot, with a few pieces of meat cut small, and sliced tomatoes at the bottom, if cooked with butter, or a whole onion when with oil, and then the finished product served reversed in a dish. The appearance of the little shapes thus turned out was most attractive. No self-respecting chef would ever have served up his vegetables in any other form. Owing to the great expenditure of time which was required for the preparation of such dishes, this kind of elaboration is no longer practised.

Stuffed Aubergines

Aubergines are available in abundance throughout the year all over the Middle East, either home-grown or imported from a neighbouring country where the seasonal crop comes at a different time.

The appearance of the vegetable, shiny, at times subtle and gentle in colour, but more often fierce and blue-black, has stirred the imagination of the people, who have given it, in turn, gentle virtues and malicious magical powers. It is recommended in some parts not to grow aubergines in one's garden in case an evil one might spring up bearing the curse of female infertility. This same dark and shiny aspect, however, makes the aubergine a particularly attractive vegetable to serve.

Aubergines can be stuffed in an infinite variety of ways, but two slightly awkward characteristics must be dealt with before they can be cooked successfully. The first is their bitter juice, which is sometimes unpleasant in flavour; the second is their amazing power of absorbing large quantities of oil when frying. Both these disadvantages are corrected by sprinkling the peeled flesh with salt and placing the slit, sliced, chopped or emptied-out aubergines in a colander to drain until much of the juices are lost. This takes at least ½ hour, occasionally much longer. A weighted plate can be placed over the vegetables to speed the process; or you can squeeze them gently by hand.

Another way of removing the bitter juice from the aubergines is to soak them, scooped out or sliced, in salted water for about 1 hour. The vegetables, thus lightened of their juices, are softer and ready to use. They should then be rinsed in cold water and lightly patted dry with a towel or absorbent paper or squeezed gently in your hands.

Various methods are used to prepare the aubergines for filling. Here are a few of the more common ones.

Method 1

Cut a slice off the stem end of the aubergines just below the hull, which may be removed. Keep the slices to use as 'corks'. Scoop out the pulp with a small knife or a pointed spoon, taking care not to break their skins, and reserve the pulp for a stew or salad. Sprinkle the inside of each shell with salt, and leave them inverted in a colander for at least ½ hour to allow the bitter juices to drain away.

Rinse the softened shells and stuff them with the prepared filling. Close them with the reserved 'corks', and place them upright in a large saucepan or deep oven dish with the corked ends facing upwards. Pack them tightly if they are small. If they are medium-sized, they can be laid sideways, but again closely packed to prevent the filling from falling out.

Method 2

Leave about 1 cm (½ inch) of the stalks on, but remove the hulls. Peel off 1-cm- (½-inch) wide strips lengthwise, leaving alternating strips of bare flesh and shiny peel. This ensures that the aubergines keep their shape, while the peeled strips allow the bitter juices to escape. Sprinkle them with salt and leave them in a colander for ½ hour. Rinse and pat dry.

Make a slash along the centre, right through the aubergine, to within 1 cm (½ inch) of each end. Press the filling well into this slash.

Method 3

Cut the aubergines in half lengthwise. They may be peeled or not, as you prefer. Scoop out the centres. Sprinkle the hollowed-out vegetables with salt, and leave to drain for at least ½ hour. Then rinse with cold water and pat dry.

Fill each hollowed-out half with filling and proceed according to the recipe.

☐ *Syrian saying: 'The woman killed herself with work, yet the feast lasted only one day.'*

Imam Bayildi
'The Imam *fainted'*

This is a Turkish speciality. Widely conflicting stories are told about the origins of its name. Some say that the dish acquired it when an *imam* or Turkish priest fainted with pleasure on being served these stuffed aubergines by his wife. Others believe that the *imam* fainted when he heard how expensive the ingredients were, and how much olive oil had gone into the making of the dish.

The dish is delightful and, in fact, not very expensive. It makes a splendid first course.

6 long medium-sized aubergines	1 teaspoon sugar, or more
Filling 6 (page 363)	Salt
150 ml (¼ pint) olive oil	Juice of 1 lemon

Prepare the aubergines for filling by any of the methods described on Page 366. Stuff them with Filling 6.

Arrange the aubergines side by side in a large pan. Pour over them the oil and enough water to cover (about 150 ml/¼ pint) mixed with a little sugar, salt to taste, and the lemon juice.

Cover the pan and simmer gently until the aubergines are very soft, about 1 hour. Remove from the heat and allow to cool. Turn into a serving dish. Serve cold.

≈ Substituting the water with tomato juice for cooking and adding 2 crushed cloves garlic adds to the taste.

Sheikh el Mahshi Betingan
Aubergines Stuffed with Meat and Pine Nuts

12 small long aubergines or 6 medium-sized ones	2–3 tablespoons tomato concentrate
Butter or oil	Juice of 1 lemon (optional)
Filling 1 (page 361)	Salt and black pepper

Prepare the aubergines for filling according to Method 1 or 2 (pages 366–7). Everyone has a favourite way of softening aubergines before stuffing. It was usual to deep fry – and this is still done, but now people feel it is healthier to steam or to poach the vegetables.

Stuff them with the prepared filling and place them in an oven-proof dish.

Mix the tomato concentrate with enough water to come halfway up the aubergines in the dish. Pour into the dish with about 4 tablespoons oil (omit the oil if the vegetables have been fried), lemon juice, and a little salt and pepper. Bake for 15 minutes in a hot oven (220°C/425°F/Mark 7), then reduce the heat to 150°C (300°F/Mark 2) and bake until well done, about 45 minutes.

Alternatively, arrange the stuffed uncooked aubergines in a large saucepan with the flavourings and water to cover, and simmer gently for about ¾ hour or until cooked, adding more water if necessary.

Serve hot with plain rice.

≈ Another version is to stew the stuffed aubergines in a little water until they are soft. Then transfer them to a baking dish, and pour over them a Béchamel sauce (about ½ litre/¾ pint). Put the dish in a hot oven (200°C/400°F/Mark 6) until the top is browned.

Aubergines Stuffed with Rice and Meat

12 small long aubergines or 6
   medium-sized ones.
Filling 2 or 3 (pages 361–2)
60 g (2 oz) pine nuts or chopped
   walnuts (optional)

4 tablespoons olive oil
Salt and black pepper
Juice of 1 lemon

Prepare the aubergines for filling according to Method 1.

Prepare Filling 2 or 3 in a bowl. Add the nuts if you wish, lightly fried for 1 or 2 minutes beforehand.

Stuff the aubergine shells three-quarters full with the filling, to allow room for the rice to expand. Close them with the reserved 'corks'.

Heat the olive oil in a large saucepan. Place the aubergines in it, arranged close to each other, and add enough water to come halfway up them. Season with salt and pepper, and squeeze a whole lemon over them. Cover and cook over very gentle heat for ¾ to 1 hour, adding more water if necessary. By the end of the cooking, the water should be almost completely absorbed.

≈ A delicious variation and an attractive way of serving this dish is to cook a few stuffed aubergines in an aubergine stew. Take the aubergine centres and about 500 g (1 lb) sliced or cubed additional aubergines, sprinkle with salt, and let them drain in a colander for 1 hour. Squeeze them as dry as possible, then fry them in hot oil in a large saucepan, together with 2 large onions, sliced, until soft and golden. Add 4 or 5 tomatoes, skinned and sliced, 3 or 4 whole cloves garlic, and salt and pepper. Simmer, covered, over low heat until half-cooked, adding a little water if necessary. Place the stuffed aubergines in the stew and simmer gently, covered, for ½ to ¾ hour longer, until the aubergines are soft and the rice is well cooked, adding a little water if the whole becomes too dry.

≈ In an unusual Persian variation using Filling 3, the aubergines are cooked in a sweet-and-sour sauce made with vinegar and sugar and coloured with a little saffron. Half-cover the aubergines with water to which you have added 3 to 4 tablespoons oil, and simmer gently, covered, for about ½ hour. Mix 150 ml (¼ pint) wine vinegar with about 90 g (3 oz) sugar and ¼ teaspoon powdered saffron. Pour over the vegetables and continue to cook gently, covered, for another ½ hour. Serve hot with plain rice.

☐ *Nasrudin and a friend went to an eating-house and decided, for the sake of economy, to share a plate of aubergines.*

They argued violently as to whether they should be stuffed or fried.

Tired and hungry, Nasrudin yielded and the order was given for stuffed aubergines.

His companion suddenly collapsed as they were waiting, and seemed in a bad way. Nasrudin jumped up.

'Are you going for a doctor?' asked someone at the next table.

*'No, you fool,' shouted Nasrudin. 'I am going to see whether it is too late to change the order.'**

Aubergines Stuffed with Rice – served cold

12 small long aubergines
Filling 4 or 5 (pages 362–3)
60 g (2 oz) chopped walnuts
  (optional)

½ teacup olive oil
250 g (8 oz) tomatoes, thinly
  sliced

Prepare the aubergines for filling according to Method 1.

Prepare Filling 4 or 5. If using Filling 5, the chick peas may be replaced by chopped walnuts.

Stuff the aubergines only three-quarters full, to allow the rice to expand. Close the openings with the reserved 'corks'.

Heat the olive oil in a large saucepan. Cover the bottom of the pan with a layer of sliced tomatoes and arrange the stuffed aubergines in layers on top. Cover with another layer of tomato slices and pour the remaining olive oil over. Add water to cover the vegetables and simmer over very low heat, covered, for 30 to 45 minutes, or until the aubergines and their filling are cooked through, adding a little more water if necessary. The liquid should be very much reduced by the end of cooking time.

* Shah, *The Exploits of the Incomparable Mulla Nasrudin.*

Allow to cool in the saucepan and turn out on to a serving dish. Serve cold. This dish makes an excellent first course. Use the leftover centres for a stew or salad.

Aubergines Medias

A Jewish dish.

6 aubergines
2 eggs
250 g (8 oz) cheese, grated (Greek Halumi, Parmesan or Cheddar)

Oil for deep-frying
Pepper

TOMATO SAUCE (optional)

2–3 tablespoons tomato concentrate
About 300 ml (½ pint) water

Salt and black pepper
Pinch of sugar (optional)

Prepare the aubergines for filling according to Method 3 (page 367).

Beat the eggs and mix well with the grated cheese. Fill each hollowed-out aubergine half with the egg and cheese mixture. Then lower each half, cheese side up, into very hot, deep oil, one at a time. Fry for only a few minutes, until slightly browned. Remove from the oil and drain on absorbent paper.

Place the aubergines side by side in a saucepan, add just enough water to come halfway up them, sprinkle with pepper, bring to the boil and simmer gently, covered, for ½ hour, or until well cooked. Add a little more water during the cooking time if necessary.

Serve hot with yoghourt and cucumber salad.

≈ A popular variation is to cook the aubergines in a tomato sauce instead of water. Dilute the tomato concentrate with water, add a little salt, pepper and sugar, if desired, pour into the saucepan, and continue cooking as above.

Stuffed Courgettes

As with aubergines, there is an infinite number of variations for stuffed courgettes, all slightly different, each preferred by a certain region or town. I have chosen some of the more popular ones. The recipe below was given to me by a Syrian lady. It will serve 6 people generously.

24 small courgettes or 18 medium-sized ones	1–2 tomatoes, sliced
	2 tablespoons tomato concentrate
Salt	Juice of 1½ lemons
Filling 2 (page 361)	2–4 cloves garlic
3–4 tablespoons butter (optional)	1 teaspoon dried crushed mint

Wash the courgettes well and slice off the stem end. Using a narrow apple corer, make a hole at the stem end of each courgette and scoop out the pulp, being careful not to break the skin. The other end must remain closed. Keep the pulp for a stew or salad.

Prepare the filling in a bowl. Make a larger quantity if the size and weight of the vegetables require it. Fill each courgette half-full only, to allow room for the rice to swell. There is no need to block the openings.

In the past, it was customary to fry the stuffed courgettes in butter until lightly coloured before stewing them, but the tendency today is for lighter food, and many people prefer to omit the preliminary frying. However, if you wish to make the dish richer, fry the stuffed courgettes lightly in the butter.

Lay a few thin slices of tomato in the bottom of a large, deep saucepan. Place the stuffed courgettes side by side in layers on top of the tomatoes. In a small saucepan, mix the tomato concentrate with 300 ml (½ pint) water and the juice of 1 lemon. Bring to the boil and simmer for a little while. Pour the tomato sauce over the courgettes, cover the saucepan and simmer very gently for about 1 hour, or until the courgettes are soft and the filling cooked, adding a little more water if necessary.

Crush the garlic cloves with a little salt. Mix with the mint and the remaining lemon juice, sprinkle over the courgettes and continue cooking for a few minutes longer. The mint is added at the end, since prolonged cooking tends to spoil its taste.

≈ Iranians favour Filling 3 with yellow split peas (page 362), and serve the dish topped with yoghourt.

≈ The tomato sauce can be made differently: Fry 1 large chopped onion in 2 tablespoons butter or oil until soft and golden. Add 2 cloves crushed garlic, and fry until golden and aromatic. Add 500 g (1 lb) tomatoes, skinned and finely sliced, and sauté gently. Add a little water, season to taste with salt and pepper, and simmer gently until soft. Finally, add about 12 small stuffed courgettes and water to cover, and simmer until well done.

Stuffed Courgettes in Yoghourt

This is a marvellous variation.

Stuff 18 small courgettes as described in the previous recipe. Arrange them in a saucepan and pour in about 600 ml (1 pint) water, or enough to cover. Bring to the boil and simmer gently, covered, for about 35 minutes, until the water is absorbed and the courgettes are nearly done. Add a little more water during the cooking time if necessary.

Prepare about 1 litre (1¾ pints) yoghourt for cooking (page 124). Pour this over the courgettes and simmer, covered, for about 20 minutes longer, or until the courgettes are very tender.

Crush 3 garlic cloves with a little salt. Add about 1 teaspoon dried crushed mint, and mix well. Fry this mixture in 1 tablespoon butter for a minute or two, and mix with the yoghourt. Stir and taste, adding more salt if necessary.

Serve hot with plain rice or *roz bil shaghria* (page 404).

Stuffed Courgettes with Apricots

Although a family favourite, this is not an Egyptian dish. It may have drawn its inspiration from medieval Persian dishes in which apricots were cooked together with meat and vegetables. However, Iranians today do not seem to know this most excellent variation of stuffed courgettes.

Soak 250 to 375 g (8–12 oz) dried apricots (sharp ones) in cold water to cover overnight.

Prepare and stuff the same number of courgettes as in the basic recipe on page 372, using Filling 2 (page 361).

Drain the apricots, reserving the soaking water. Cut them open without separating the halves completely. Arrange a layer of fruit halves over the bottom of a large saucepan. Place a layer of stuffed courgettes side by side over the apricots, and cover them with a second layer of apricots. Continue with alternate layers of vegetables and fruit, ending with a layer of fruit.

Mix the water in which the apricots have been soaked with 3 tablespoons olive oil, and pour into the pan. Squeeze the juice of 2 lemons over the whole. Cook, covered, over very low heat for about 1 hour, until the stuffed courgettes are soft; add water, a ladleful at a time, as the liquid in the pan becomes absorbed.

Mock Stuffed Courgettes or Aubergines

This recipe, contributed by a Turkish lady, is a modern one supposedly devised to save time, which it does not. It is nevertheless a delightful dish.

3 courgettes or small thin aubergines	1 egg
Salt	Black pepper
Oil for deep-frying	¾ teaspoon ground cinnamon (optional)
500 g (1 lb) beef, minced	2 tablespoons olive oil
1 slice bread, crusts removed	

Slice the vegetables lengthwise into very thin slices. Sprinkle the slices with salt and leave them in a colander to drain for at least ½ hour. Wash in cold water and pat dry. Fry in deep, hot oil until soft and a little bronzed. Remove and drain on absorbent paper.

Mix the minced beef, the bread soaked in water and squeezed dry, the egg, salt, pepper and cinnamon if used, and knead thoroughly. Shape into walnut-sized balls and deep-fry until slightly brown. Remove and drain on absorbent paper.

Roll the courgette or aubergine slices round the little meat balls and secure them with toothpicks. Put 2 tablespoons olive oil and about 150 ml (¼ pint) water in a large pan. Add the 'stuffed' vegetables, sprinkle with salt, and cook over very gentle heat until they are soft and well done. The liquid should all be absorbed by the end of cooking time, but add more water if the pan becomes dry too soon.

≈ These vegetable rolls can also be simmered in a tomato sauce made with 2 to 3 tablespoons tomato concentrate diluted with a little water and seasoned with salt and pepper.

Courgettes Imam Bayildi

A courgette version of the famous Turkish aubergine dish on page 367.

Filling 6 (page 363)	Olive oil
1 kg (2 lb) courgettes	1 teaspoon sugar, or more
2 tomatoes, sliced	Salt

Prepare the filling.

Prepare the courgettes for stuffing as described on page 372. Scoop out their centres from the stem end, using an apple corer, and taking care not to pierce them right through.

Stuff the courgettes tightly with the onion and tomato filling. Lay them in layers side by side in a large pan on a bed of tomato slices, and pour over them about 150 ml (¼ pint) olive oil mixed with 300 ml (½ pint) water, a teaspoon of sugar and a little salt. Cover the pan tightly and simmer gently over low heat for about 1 hour, or until soft, adding a little water if necessary. Serve cold as a first course or buffet dish.

Whole Stuffed Onions

6 large onions or 12 smaller ones   Filling 2 (page 361)

Skin the onions and boil them in water for 15 minutes until they are fairly tender. Drain and cool. Cut a thin slice off the root ends and carefully scoop out the centres, leaving a thick shell.

Prepare the filling. Stuff the onions with this mixture, only three-quarters full to allow room for the rice to expand. Place side by side, open ends upwards, in a large pan. Pour in water to half-cover them. Cover the pan and cook gently for about ¾ hour, or until the onions and the filling are well cooked. Add more water during cooking time if necessary.

≈ An alternative is to pour the following tomato sauce over the onions instead of water.

TOMATO SAUCE

1 tablespoon butter	Salt and black pepper
1 tablespoon flour	300 ml (½ pint) water
2–3 tablespoons tomato concentrate	

Melt the butter in a pan and blend in the flour. Add the tomato concentrate and stir well. Gradually add 300 ml (½ pint) water, stirring constantly, and season to taste with salt and pepper. Bring to the boil and simmer for a few minutes. Pour over the onions and continue as above, adding water if necessary.

□ *An ancient Persian remedy: 'A cold may be cured by throwing an onion on a neighbour's house – the neighbour will get the cold.'*

It was also believed that 'A person must not eat a raw onion on Friday, or the angels will not remain with him.' Nevertheless, 'He who eats onions for forty-one days will become a hadji, or pilgrim, to Mecca.'*

Saudi Arabian Stuffed Onions

2 large onions	2 tablespoons oil
Filling 2 (page 361)	1–2 tablespoons vinegar

Peel the onions. With a sharp knife, make a cut from top to bottom on one side of each onion through to the centre. Throw into boiling water and cook until the onions are soft and start to open so that each layer can be detached (about 10 to 15 minutes). Drain and cool. Separate each layer carefully.

Make the filling. Put a tablespoon in each hollow onion layer and roll up tightly. Pack closely in a wide, shallow pan. Pour in water to cover, sprinkle with oil and vinegar, and continue to cook, covered, over gentle heat until well done – about ¾–1 hour.

Finishing them in the oven in a baking tray dries them out a little and gives them a nice wrinkly look.

Onions Stuffed with Meat

3 large onions	1½ teaspoons cinnamon
750 g (1½ lb) minced beef	½ teaspoon allspice
A few sprigs of parsley, finely chopped	1–2 tablespoons tamarind paste
Salt and pepper	1 tablespoon sugar
	3 tablespoons oil

Peel the onions and cut off the ends. With a sharp knife make a cut from top to bottom on one side of each onion through to the centre. Throw into boiling water and cook until the onions soften and start to open so that each layer can be detached (about 15 minutes). Drain and cool and separate each layer carefully.

Make the filling by working the minced meat with the parsley, salt and pepper, cinnamon and allspice. Put a small lump into each onion layer and roll up tightly.

* Donaldson, *The Wild Rue*.

Line the bottom of a heavy pan with the discarded bits of onion. Pack the stuffed onion rolls closely over them.

Cover with water (about 150 ml/¼ pint) in which you have dissolved the tamarind paste and sugar and added the oil. Place a small plate on top and simmer gently, adding a little water if necessary, until they are very tender and the water mainly absorbed. Serve hot or cold.

≈ You may like to arrange the onions on a heatproof dish after cooking, sprinkle with a little extra sugar and let them caramelize under the grill.

Stuffed Pumpkin

Choose a round pumpkin of any colour which feels heavy, has no soft patches and does not sound hollow when you tap it.

The amount of stuffing you need depends on the size of the pumpkin. You may like to make it without meat. In that case, increase the quantity of rice.

1 pumpkin about 25 cm (10 inches) in diameter	120 g (4 oz) short- or medium-grain cooked rice
1 medium onion, finely chopped	2–3 tablespoons pine nuts
2 tablespoons oil	2–3 tablespoons raisins or sultanas
250 g (8 oz) minced meat – lamb, beef or veal	Salt and pepper
	1 teaspoon cinnamon or allspice

Wash the pumpkin and cut a slice from the stalk end to use as a lid. Remove the seeds and fibre.

To make the filling, or *hashwa*, first soften the onion in oil, then add the meat and continue to cook, crushing it with a spoon and stirring until it changes colour. Add the rest of the ingredients (the pine nuts are improved by frying separately till lightly coloured) and fill the pumpkin. Put the lid on, place it on an oven tray and bake for at least an hour in a moderate oven (190°C/375°F/Mark 5) until the flesh is really soft.

Bring it to the table as it is and to serve cut into generous slices and top each with the stuffing.

≈ An alternative is to replace the rice with a burghul pilav (page 332).
≈ You may like to sprinkle a little sugar inside to sweeten the flesh before filling the pumpkin.

Sweet-and-Sour Stuffed Cabbage

This is a Persian recipe which is sometimes also made with lettuce leaves.

1 medium white cabbage	Salt and pepper
250 g (8 oz) rice	1 tablespoon tomato concentrate
120 g (4 oz) yellow split peas	A small bunch parsley, finely
1 large onion, finely chopped	chopped
Oil	150 ml (¼ pint) vinegar
500 g (1 lb) minced beef	2 tablespoons sugar
1 teaspoon turmeric	

Separate the cabbage leaves and put them in a large saucepan with a little water – about two fingers – and steam them for a few minutes until they soften. Drain. Wash the rice and cook in boiling water until it is just tender – about 10 minutes – then drain quickly. Boil the split peas separately. Fry the onion in 3 tablespoons oil until soft and transparent. Add the meat and turmeric and season to taste with salt and pepper. Cook, stirring until the meat changes colour, then remove from the heat and add the rice and split peas, tomato concentrate and parsley, and more salt and pepper. Mix well.

If the cabbage leaves are very large, cut them in half and cut out the thick rib. Put a heaped tablespoon of the mixture at the bottom of each leaf, bring the edges up over it and roll up into a bundle. Put a little oil at the bottom of a heavy pan, cover with a few broken leaves to protect the others from burning, then put over them rows and layers of stuffed leaves. Mix the vinegar with an equal quantity of water, stir in 2 tablespoons sugar and pour over the leaves. Put a plate over them, cover the pan and cook gently on a very low flame until very tender and the liquid has been absorbed, adding water if necessary.

Serve hot or cold.

Stuffed Cabbage Leaves

1 medium-sized head white	Filling 2 (page 361)
cabbage	Black pepper
Salt	Juice of 1 lemon

Carefully strip off the leaves from the cabbage and wash them. Dip them in boiling salted water, a few at a time, until they become wilted and pliable. Trim the hard central veins flat. Cut very large leaves in half, but leave small ones whole.

Prepare the filling. Put a tablespoon of filling at one end of each cabbage leaf. Fold the sides of the leaf towards the centre and roll up, making a neat little finger shape. Continue until all the filling is used up.

Line a large saucepan with torn or unused leaves to prevent the stuffed leaves from sticking to the bottom. Lay the stuffed leaves on top of them in layers, packing them tightly. Cover with water and lemon juice mixed with a little salt and pepper. Cover the pan and cook very gently for about 1 hour. Serve hot.

≈ In some parts of the Middle East as many as 6 or 7 whole cloves of garlic are tucked in between the stuffed leaves to give a very strong aroma.

≈ In the Lebanon, dried mint (about 1 teaspoon) or chopped fresh dill (1 tablespoon) is often added to the sauce towards the end of cooking time.

≈ A good variation to this dish is made by cooking the stuffed leaves in a rich tomato sauce. Prepare and stuff the leaves as above, and pack them in a cabbage-lined saucepan. Then dilute 4 table-spoons tomato concentrate in some water and pour this over the stuffed vegetables. Add the lemon juice, salt and pepper. Continue cooking as above.

≈ A modern, labour-saving variation is to prepare the same filling, but to make a sort of tart or pie with the cabbage leaves instead of rolling them into individual parcels. First separate and soften the leaves as described above. Then arrange alternate layers of leaves and seasoned meat filling in a deep oven dish, starting and ending with cabbage leaves. Mix 4 tablespoons tomato concentrate with about 150 ml (¼ pint) water. Add a little salt and pepper. Pour this sauce over the dish. Bake in a moderate oven (180°C/350°F/Mark 4) for about 1 hour, or until the leaves are very soft and the filling is well cooked. Add water during the cooking if the dish dries out too quickly.

Stuffed Potatoes

12 largish potatoes	3 tablespoons tomato concentrate
3 tablespoons butter	Salt and black pepper
Filling 1 (page 361), including pine nuts and, if you like, raisins	5 tablespoons oil

Choose a type of potato which does not disintegrate easily. Peel the potatoes and hollow them out with an apple corer or a small pointed knife. Turn them in hot butter for a few minutes until they are slightly coloured.

Prepare the filling. Stuff the potatoes with it and pack them tightly side by side in a large oven dish. Dilute the tomato concentrate with enough water to half-cover the potatoes. Season to taste with salt and pepper, add oil and mix well. Pour over the potatoes.

Bake, uncovered, in a preheated moderate oven (180°C/350°F/Mark 4) until the potatoes have browned a little. Then cover with a lid or a large piece of foil, and continue to bake for ¾ hour longer, or until the potatoes are soft but do not fall apart, and most of the sauce has been absorbed.

Iraqi Stuffed Potato Cakes

1 kg (2 lb) potatoes	Filling 1 (page 361)
3 large eggs	Fine dry breadcrumbs or flour
2 tablespoons flour	Oil for deep- or shallow-frying, or
Salt and black pepper	butter

Peel, boil, drain and mash the potatoes, keeping them as dry as possible. Add 1 egg, 2 tablespoons flour, and salt and pepper to taste; knead thoroughly until well blended.

Prepare the filling.

Take lumps of the mashed potato mixture the size of a small egg. Shape into balls. Hollow them out with your finger and stuff with the filling. Close the openings over the filling and pat into ball shapes again, then flatten slightly into a cake, dip in the 2 remaining beaten eggs, then in breadcrumbs or flour. Deep-fry, one at a time, or fry in shallow oil or hot butter, turning the cakes to brown them all over. Keep them hot in a warm oven until they are all prepared.

≈ For a different filling add a handful of raisins and 1 of chopped walnuts.

Stuffed Sweet Peppers and Tomatoes

A dish popular throughout the Middle East and along the Mediterranean, where peppers and tomatoes are often cooked and served together. They seem to achieve a harmony and balance, both in colour and flavour. So, although you can serve each vegetable separately, the two combined (perhaps with a few other stuffed vegetables such as courgettes and aubergines) will make a more perfect dish.

6 medium-sized sweet green peppers (add a red one if you like)	Filling 2 if to be served hot, or Filling 4 if to be served cold (pages 361–2)
6 large firm tomatoes	Oil (olive oil is desirable if serving cold)
	Salt and black pepper

Wash the peppers and tomatoes. Cut a thin slice off the stem end of each vegetable and reserve. Remove the cores and seeds from the peppers. Scoop out the tomato pulp and reserve.

Prepare the ingredients for either filling. They can be used raw; but one should preferably cook them to avoid them still being a little uncooked when the vegetable shells are already very soft.

For Filling 2, fry the onion in 2 tablespoons oil until soft. Add the minced meat and fry gently until it changes colour. Then add the rest of the ingredients (pine nuts and raisins may be included if liked). Moisten with water, using the same volume of water as that of rice. Bring to the boil, cover and simmer gently for 10 minutes.

If using Filling 4, fry the onion in 2 tablespoons olive oil, add the rice and the other ingredients, and cover with the same volume of water as that of rice. Cook gently, covered, for 10 minutes.

Stuff the vegetables with either filling, moistening with a little extra olive oil. Cover with the reserved tops. Arrange the stuffed vegetables in one layer in a wide baking dish into which you have poured a few tablespoons of oil. Chop the tomato pulp, add about 150 ml (¼ pint) water, season with a little salt and pepper, and pour over the vegetables. Add enough extra water to come halfway up.

Cover the dish with a lid or a sheet of foil, and bake in a preheated moderate oven (180°C/350°/Mark 4) for 30 minutes; then uncover, add a little more water if it has all been absorbed, and bake for a further 15 minutes, or until the vegetables are coloured and well done.

Serve hot or cold as a first course, or hot as a main dish, accompanied by various salads and rice.

≈ In the past, it was usual to deep-fry or sauté the peppers before stewing them gently in a sauce or baking them in a slow oven. Today, this is still done by some cooks who prefer the richer taste.

≈ You can also cook the vegetables on top of the stove. Arrange them in a large heavy pan, half-cover with water mixed with a few tablespoons of oil, and simmer, covered, for about 1 hour over very low heat, adding water if necessary, a little at a time. Sprinkle with a little lemon juice towards the end of cooking. In this case, the filling need not be pre-cooked, but do not fill the vegetables too tightly to allow room for the rice to expand.

Stuffed Tomatoes

12 large firm tomatoes	4 tablespoons oil
Filling 1 (page 361) with pine nuts if available	2 tablespoons tomato concentrate
	Salt and black pepper

Wash the tomatoes. Cut a thin slice off the tops; scoop out the pulp and reserve.

Prepare Filling 1, preferably with pine nuts. Raisins, too, may be added for an unusual flavour, as well as some of the tomato pulp. Stuff the tomatoes and cover with their own tops. Arrange the stuffed vegetables close to each other in a baking tin to which you have added a thin layer of oil.

Dilute the tomato concentrate with about 150 ml (¼ pint) water. Season to taste with salt and pepper, and add the sieved tomato pulp. Pour over the stuffed tomatoes.

Bake in a preheated moderate oven (180°C/350°F/Mark 4) until the tomatoes are very soft, ½ hour or longer.

Serve as a first course or a main dish, accompanied by plain rice, *roz bil shaghria* (page 404), or burghul pilav (page 332) and yoghourt.

Stuffed Leeks with Tamarind

1 kg (2 lb) large fat leeks	1 tablespoon finely chopped parsley
Salt	Oil
Filling 2 (page 361) omitting tomatoes, and using only 30–60 g (1–2 oz) rice	2–3 tablespoons tamarind syrup or 2 tablespoons tamarind paste

Cut off the hard green part of the leek leaves and trim off the root ends. Throw the leeks into boiling salted water and poach until only just softened.

Cut a slice off the root end, thus freeing the layers from each other. Make a slit very carefully with a sharp knife along one side of each leek, through to the centre. You will have wide, rectangular leaves. Separate them from each other.

Add parsley and 2 tablespoons oil to the filling. Mix well.

Put a little of the filling in the centre of each leaf (about 1 tablespoon). Roll up tightly like a cigarette. When you come to the narrow leaves, lay two together, side by side and overlapping, to achieve a roll as with the bigger ones. The ends of the rolls are open but the filling will not spill out as it has been placed in the centre.

Arrange in a wide, heavy pan in which you have heated ½ teacup oil. Sauté gently in this oil for a few minutes. Then pour water in which you have diluted some tamarind syrup or tamarind paste over the vegetables to cover.

Cover the pan and cook on a very low heat for about 1 hour, adding water as it becomes absorbed, until the leeks are very tender.

Stuffed Artichokes

The winning recipe in the 1964 'National Queen of the Kitchen' contest, held in Israel. It was submitted by Mrs Abla Mazawie, a well-known restaurant owner in Nazareth. It is also an old Arab dish.

1½ kg (3 lb) artichokes	2 large onions
½ lemon	60 g (2 oz) pine nuts
375 g (12 oz) margarine	1 tablespoon salt
500 g (1 lb) lamb, plus a piece of lamb's tail or other lamb fat	1 teaspoon black pepper
	1 teaspoon ground cinnamon
250 g (8 oz) beef, minced	

Peel the artichokes to the hearts. Pierce and remove the chokes. Soak the artichokes in cold water acidulated with the juice of ½ a lemon.

Melt the margarine in a frying pan and fry the artichokes on all sides. Remove to a baking tray.

Mince the meat and onions together. Fry in the margarine in

which the artichokes were fried. Add the pine nuts, salt, pepper and cinnamon.

Fill the artichokes with the meat mixture. Add water to cover and simmer on top of the stove or in a moderate oven (180°C/350°F/ Mark 4) for 1 hour.

Serve hot as a first course or main dish. If the latter, accompany with rice with *hamud* (page 423).

Stuffed Artichoke Hearts

If fresh artichokes are out of season, try this recipe with good-quality tinned artichoke hearts. These are not like the fresh ones, but nevertheless acceptable.

12 artichokes	½–1 teaspoon dried thyme
Salt	¼–½ teaspoon grated nutmeg
2 lemons	Oil for deep-frying
500 g (1 lb) lean beef, minced	1 tablespoon olive oil
1 egg	½ teaspoon turmeric
2 slices bread, crusts removed	1 bay leaf
Black pepper	

Remove the stems, leaves and chokes of the artichokes, leaving only the hearts. Dip them in a little salted water acidulated with the juice of 1 lemon, to prevent them from discolouring.

Mix the minced beef, egg, bread soaked in water and squeezed dry, salt and pepper, thyme and grated nutmeg, and knead well.

Fill the artichoke hearts, shaping the mixture into a mound. Deep-fry one at a time in hot oil, using a perforated spoon to lower them in and lift them out again. Take care the filling does not become dislodged. Remove and drain on absorbent paper.

Place the fried artichoke hearts in a large saucepan. Mix olive oil with about 150 ml (¼ pint) water, the turmeric, salt and pepper, and the juice of the remaining lemon. Pour over the artichoke hearts and bury a bay leaf between them.

Bring to the boil and simmer over very low heat for about 1 hour, until the artichokes are tender, adding water when necessary.

Sweet-and-Sour Dishes

Reading quite recently about ancient pre-Islamic Persia of the Sassanid period and its Zoroastrian dualist religion, which is based on the confrontation of the two enemy forces of good and evil, I was struck by the similarity between the early philosophy of the Persians and principles of harmony which they apply to their food.

The Zoroastrian belief is that their god Ahouramazda created the world. The spirit of creation which pulled matter out of nothing awoke a force of resistance, giving birth to a spirit of evil, Angromainyous, whose creative and malicious urge was to destroy the harmony of the universe. In this religion, creation could only exist in the equilibrium of the opposing forces which it had aroused.

It is this same equilibrium, poised between the vinegar and the sugar, the quince and the meat, which the Persians of the Sassanid period reflected in their dishes. Both ancient and modern Persian dishes blend opposite flavours and textures, coupling sweet with sour or spicy, strong with mild. These dishes were adopted by the Caliphs of Baghdad, and some were taken further afield to Morocco. (Other Middle Eastern countries have not, however, adopted the more markedly sweet-and-sour-dishes, although welcoming most others.)

During the same period, parts of India adopted a version of the Zoroastrian religion – the Parsees of today, but with one god of creation, and without a necessary enemy or evil force. North Indian food is not unlike Persian food, but, strangely enough, it seems to lack the particular harmony through opposites which the Persian dishes have.

It is also interesting to compare the Middle Eastern 'sweet and sour' with that of China. The Chinese have a predilection for sweet and sour, and harmony through opposites, and their early religion was one also based on opposing forces of good and evil.

Leeks with Lemon and Sugar

This is a particularly delicious sweet-and-sour way of preparing leeks.

1 kg (2 lb) leeks	3–4 tablespoons sunflower oil
2–3 cloves garlic, crushed	Juice of 1–2 lemons
1 tablespoon sugar	

Wash the leeks carefully, removing any soil nestling between the leaves. Cut off the tough green part of the leaves. Cut the rest into medium pieces.

Fry the garlic and sugar in hot oil until the sugar becomes slightly caramelized. Add the leeks and turn them a little over moderate heat to colour them lightly. Sprinkle with lemon juice. Stew gently, covered, in this and the vegetables' own juices over very low heat until tender.

Serve hot or cold.

Dolmeh Sib
Persian Stuffed Apples

Persians have produced two dishes (and maybe more) of fruit stuffed with meat, one of apples and the other of quinces, which are exciting and very pleasing.

Either cooking or eating apples do equally well for this dish, although there is less danger that eating apples will disintegrate.

12 large tart apples	Butter

FILLING

60–90 g (2–3 oz) yellow split peas	500 g (1 lb) beef, minced
1 onion, finely chopped	Salt and black pepper
2 tablespoons oil	½ teaspoon ground cinnamon

SAUCE

150 ml (¼ pint) water	1–2 tablespoons sugar
5–6 tablespoons wine vinegar	

Make the filling. Boil the yellow split peas for about ½ hour until soft. Drain. Fry the chopped onion in oil until soft and only just golden. Add the meat and fry gently until it changes colour. Season to taste with salt, pepper and the cinnamon, and mix in the cooked split peas.

Wash the apples. Core them with an apple corer to within 1 cm (½ inch) of the bottoms, and remove some of the pulp to make room for the filling. Chop the pulp and reserve.

Stuff the apples with the split pea mixture and arrange them side by side in a large baking dish, on a bed of chopped apple pulp. It will disintegrate and form a sauce. (Alternatively, mix the chopped pulp with the prepared filling.) Put a shaving of butter on top of each apple and pour ½ litre (¾ pint) of water into the dish. Bake in a preheated moderate oven (180°C/350°F/Mark 4), covered, for about ½ hour, or until the apples are almost done.

Boil the water, vinegar and sugar together, and pour a little into each apple. Return to the oven and cook for a further 15 minutes, or until done. The apples must be tender but not mushy, and their skins should not be broken.

Serve two per person: alone as a first course, or as part of a main dish.

Persian Stuffed Quince

This dish is similar to that of stuffed apples above, but the strong aroma of the fruit demands a slightly different flavouring. Serve one quince per person, two if they are very small.

Core and prepare the fruit as in the preceding recipe. Prepare the same filling, omitting the cinnamon. Pack it into the quinces. Arrange them side by side to fit tightly in a pan (or two pans if one is not large enough). Pour in water to come halfway up the fruits. Add a few butter shavings and a pinch of sugar. Cover the pan and simmer gently for about 30 minutes, until the fruits are tender.

This can be served on its own as a first course, or with grilled or plain steamed meat and a rice dish, or with a selection of salads.

Pickles

Mekhalel

Food preservation is a particularly important problem in hot countries, especially in isolated, non-agricultural areas. The processes used today by Middle Eastern families, grocers and street vendors are those inherited from their ancestors of the ancient Oriental and classical civilizations, who had an even greater need for careful preservation in the days before easy transport, refrigerators and tins.

Pickles

Although pickling was originally devised as a method of preservation, the result is so delicious that pickles are now prepared for their own sake – for their flavour and texture – to be served as *mezze* or to accompany many main dishes. They are prepared in large quantities in their season, and often throughout the year, since even when the vegetables are not in season in one area, it is now generally possible to import them from a neighbouring country. Every home has its *martaban* or jars filled with various pickles, ready to be eaten at all times of the day.

My father has told me that when he was a child visiting relatives in Syria he remembers that the women of the family devoted their time to pickling and to making jams and syrups whenever they had no parties, feasts or other household activities to occupy them. Large glass jars were filled with turnips, onions, cucumbers, lemons, cauliflowers, aubergines and peppers. The family could hardly wait to start eating them, and often did so before the pickles were quite ready. A visit to the cellar or store cupboard to see how they were maturing and mellowing to soft pinks, saffrons, mauves and pale greens, was a mouth-watering expedition.

Grocers in the Middle East prepare their own pickles. It was customary in the past, and still is today in many places, for them to offer customers a taste of their newly mellowed pickles as well as a sample of their cheeses and jams. This custom may, of course, have been motivated by the hope that, having tasted them, the customer would not be able to resist the urge to take some home; but any ulterior motive was well concealed behind a heart-warming affability and generosity. Some Greek or *'Roumi'* grocers in Egypt would even insist on offering a second helping regardless of whether there appeared to be any intention on the customer's part to buy.

A relative of my father's was known to go from one grocer to another, tasting here and there, a little of everything, dipping a large finger into a new batch of jam or honey, until he had satisfied his appetite. No shopkeeper ever begrudged him, since they all regarded 'tasting' as a traditional and obligatory duty. They may even have been secretly flattered that this fat man visited them so often.

Restaurants like to display a vividly colourful assortment of pickles, sometimes placing them on their window-sills to lure customers in. Pickle jars are also a colourful feature of Middle Eastern streets. Squatting on the pavements of busy streets, vendors sell home-made pickled turnips swimming in a pink solution, or aubergines looking fiercely black and shiny in the enormous jars. Passers-by dip their hands in the liquor, searching for the tastiest and largest pieces, and savour them with Arab bread provided by the vendor, soaking it in the pink salt and vinegar solution or seasoned oil. The poor can only afford to dip their bread in the pickling liquor. They sit in the sun, rapturously savouring this modest treat. And when the pickles are finished, the vendor sometimes sells the precious, flavoursome liquor as a sauce for rice.

Methods of Pickling

The Middle Eastern method of pickling is simple. Raw or lightly poached vegetables are left to soak in a salty acidulated solution (usually vinegar) in a warm place for a certain length of time, depending on their age and quality. The salt draws the moisture from the vegetables, preventing the growth of the micro-organisms which cause decay. The salt and acid bath allows the vegetables to ferment and mature to mellowness, and also stops micro-organisms entering the jar, as well as preventing the growth of those already in it. For pickling to be successful, it is most important to keep out the air in which micro-organisms flourish. In ancient times, jars were filled, sealed with a flour-and-water paste and buried in the earth. Today, people drive away the air bubbles trapped between the vegetables by prodding them with a skewer or fork. Then they fill the jars with liquid, covering the vegetables entirely, and seal them tightly.

Choose very fresh, unblemished vegetables. Clean and wash them carefully, and peel or scrub them if they need it. Use perfectly clean or sterilized glass jars with tightly fitting glass tops. Quarter or slice the vegetables, or leave them whole, and pack them tightly in the jars. Mix the pickling salt and vinegar solution in a clean glass or china container, pour it over the vegetables, filling the jars to the top; cover and seal tightly.

The proportion of salt to water and vinegar can vary slightly according to personal taste. More or less salt can be used, but the quantities are generally near enough to 3 tablespoons salt for every ½ litre (whole pint) water. Too little salt will cause the vegetables to decay, too much would be unpleasant.

The proportion of vinegar to water varies more widely. Some

people use as much vinegar as water, some pickle in vinegar alone. Others recommend half as much vinegar as water, while others again pickle in a salt and water brine, leaving out vinegar altogether. To my taste, the most successful combination to use is approximately three parts salted water to one part vinegar. This is what our family uses.

It is possible to adjust the degree of concentration during and after the process of pickling by adding more water, salt or vinegar, thus changing the balance if it is not agreeable.

The solution can also be flavoured according to individual taste with garlic, celery leaves, small hot dried chilli pepper pods and dill. To satisfy the Middle Eastern passion for colour, they are tinted pink or red with raw beetroot, or purple with red cabbage.

In Egypt, the solution is usually poured warm or cold over the tightly packed vegetables in the jar, but in some countries, such as the Lebanon, it is more common to use it boiling hot.

The U S Government advises Americans to boil bottled pickles for at least ½ hour. To my knowledge this has never been done in the Middle East, and although pickles are not generally made to last, and are usually opened as soon as they are ready, certain types, such as those pickled in vinegar only or in oil, can safely be kept for over a year. Olive, sesame and cotton seed oil are generally used in the Middle East, but any good vegetable oil will do.

Torshi Left
Pickled Turnips

These are great favourites. They have a very distinctive taste which is enjoyed by most people even when first encountered. The turnips are traditionally coloured pink by adding sliced raw beetroot. The rich, cherry-coloured juices penetrate the white turnips, colouring them bright red or soft pink, according to how much is used, and giving them a delicious taste.

Huge jars of these *torshi* adorn the streets and decorate the windows and counters of most cafés and restaurants.

1 kg (2 lb) small white turnips	4–5 level tablespoons (about 90 g
A few celery leaves	(3 oz)) salt
2–4 cloves garlic (optional)	1 scant litre (1½ pints) water
1 raw beetroot, peeled and sliced	300 ml (½ pint) white wine
or cut into medium-sized pieces	vinegar

Choose small white turnips. Peel and wash them, and cut them in halves or quarters, depending on their size. Pack the pieces in a clean glass jar with celery leaves and garlic cloves if liked, placing pieces of raw beetroot between the layers at regular intervals.

Dissolve salt in water and stir in vinegar. Cover the vegetables with this solution and seal the jar tightly with a glass top if possible.

Store in a warm place. The turnips should mellow and be ready in about 10 days. Then transfer the jar to a cool spot.

This pickle should be eaten within a month to 6 weeks of making. We eat it long before.

≈ A medieval recipe for *lift mukhalal muhalla* (turnips in vinegar, sweetened) from al-Baghdadi gives directions for turnips pickled in vinegar, sweetened with honey, perfumed with aromatic herbs and tinted with saffron.

☐ *Lebanese saying: 'Her face is whiter than the inside of a turnip.'*

Torshi Arnabeet wa Koromb
Pickled Cauliflower and Red Cabbage

A popular pickle, stained deep purple by red cabbage. If using white cabbage, colour the pickle with a few slices of raw beetroot.

1 young white cauliflower	300 ml (½ pint) white wine
½ red or white cabbage	vinegar
4–5 level tablespoons (about 90 g (3 oz)) salt	1 small dried chilli pepper pod (optional)
1 scant litre (1½ pints) water	

Wash the cauliflower and separate it into florets. Cut the cabbage into thick slices in one direction, and then again thickly in the other direction. Leave it in chunks; do not shred it or take the leaves apart. Pack into a large glass jar, arranging alternate layers of cauliflower and cabbage chunks.

Mix salt, water and vinegar in a glass or china container. Pour the liquid over the vegetables, and bury a chilli pepper pod in the jar if you like. Close tightly with a glass top if possible, and store in a warm place for about 10 days, by which time the vegetables will be mellow and ready to eat.

This pickle, like the first, should be eaten within a month or 6 weeks of making.

Torshi Basal
Pickled Onions

Choose small, perfect button onions. Peel them and poach them for about 3 minutes in boiling white wine vinegar seasoned to taste with a little salt and sugar. Pack the slightly softened onions in a glass jar and cover with the poaching vinegar. Close tightly. Leave for about 10 days before using.

This pickle will keep indefinitely.

Torshi Felfel
Pickled Sweet Peppers

1 kg (2 lb) sweet peppers
1 small dried chilli pepper pod (optional)
4–5 level tablespoons (about 90 g/3 oz) salt

1 scant litre (1½ pints) water
300 ml (½ pint) white wine vinegar

Rinse the sweet peppers and cut off the stems. The peppers can either be sliced or cut into large pieces or, if small, left whole. If slicing or cutting them, discard the cores and seeds. If leaving them whole, make small holes all over to allow the pickling solution to penetrate to their hollow centres and bathe them entirely.

Pack tightly in a large glass jar, with a chilli pepper pod buried in the middle if you like. Cover with the salt, water and vinegar solution, mixed in a china or glass container, and make sure that no air is left trapped inside the peppers or between the layers. Seal the jar tightly with a glass top if possible, and store in a warm place for about 2 weeks. By this time the peppers will be soft and mellow.

Do not keep this pickle longer than 2 months, unless stored under refrigeration.

Torshi Khiar
Pickled Cucumbers

1 kg (2 lb) small pickling cucumbers
4 cloves garlic
A few celery leaves, or a few sprigs fresh dill, or 1 teaspoon dill seed
3–4 black peppercorns

3–4 whole coriander seeds
4–5 level tablespoons (about 90 g/3 oz) salt
1 scant litre (1½ pints) water
150 ml (¼ pint) white wine vinegar

Scrub the cucumbers well and pack them in a large glass jar with the whole garlic cloves, celery leaves, sprigs of dill or dill seed, peppercorns, and coriander seeds distributed at regular intervals.

Mix the salt, water and vinegar solution in a glass or china container, and pour over the vegetables. Close the jar tightly with a glass top if possible, and leave in a warm place to soften and mellow. The pickle should be ready in 10 days to 2 weeks.

Do not keep for longer than about 6 weeks unless stored under refrigeration.

☐ Selling Pickles*

Once the Khoja started to sell pickles. He bought the entire stock-in-trade of a man, including his donkey. He started on his rounds, crying, 'Pickles for sale!' but when they came to the crowded part of the town and to the house of a former customer, the donkey would begin to bray so loudly that the Khoja could not make himself heard, and was obliged to hold his tongue.

One day in a crowded thoroughfare the Khoja was just preparing to cry, 'Pickles!' when the donkey got the start of him and began to bray. Then he lost his temper and said, 'Look here, mate, are you selling them, or am I?'

Torshi Betingan
Pickled Aubergines

There is a superstitious belief in some Middle Eastern countries that certain types of aubergine bring on one the curse of infertility. Women are sometimes afraid to use a particularly black one or an oddly mauve one. On the other hand, a walk through a field of aubergines is sometimes prescribed as a cure for female sterility. For many years the head gardener at the Ezbekieh Gardens in Cairo derived a small income from a patch of aubergines by charging women a fee to walk through it.

1 kg (2 lb) very small, long, thin aubergines	A few celery leaves and stalks, finely chopped
Salt	600 ml (1 pint) water
4 cloves garlic, finely chopped	3 level tablespoons salt
1–2 small dried chilli pepper pods, finely chopped	300–475 ml (½–¾ pint) white wine vinegar

* Barnham (trans.), *Tales of Nasr-ed-Din Khoja.*

394

Wash the aubergines. Do not peel them, but make a small incision in each one. Poach them in boiling, salted water for 5 to 10 minutes until just slightly softened. Drain well. This will make them lose their bitterness.

Mix the chopped garlic, pepper pods and celery. Stuff the aubergines with this mixture through the incisions. Arrange them in layers in a glass jar. Mix the water, salt and vinegar solution in a glass or china bowl as usual, and pour it over the aubergines. Close the jar tightly with a glass top if possible, and leave it for about 4 days before using.

Do not keep this pickle longer than 6 weeks to 2 months unless it is stored under refrigeration.

□ *Arab saying: 'Give what is in your pocket. God will give you what is absent.'*

Marinated Aubergines

1 kg (2 lb) aubergines
Salt
300 ml (½ pint) white wine
   vinegar

4–6 cloves garlic, crushed
1 tablespoon dried crushed
   oregano
Olive, nut or sunflower oil

Peel and slice the aubergines. Arrange them in a sieve or colander, sprinkling each layer with salt. Leave them for 2 to 4 hours, shaking them occasionally, to allow the bitter juices to drain away. Poach the slices for 5 minutes in vinegar and a little water to cover.

Drain well and arrange the aubergine slices in layers in a large glass jar, putting a little crushed garlic and oregano between each layer. Fill the jar with oil and close it tightly.

The aubergines will be mellowed after about a week, but they will keep indefinitely. An excellent pickle.

Lamoun Makbouss
Pickled Lemons

A delicacy which is also good made with fresh limes.

Scrub lemons well and slice them. Sprinkle the slices generously with salt and leave for at least 24 hours on a large plate set at an angle, or in a colander. They will become soft and limp, and lose their bitterness. Arrange the slices in layers in a glass jar, sprinkling a little paprika between each layer. Cover with olive, nut, or a light vegetable oil.

Close the jar tightly. After about 3 weeks the lemons should be ready to eat – soft, mellow and a beautiful orange colour.

My mother accidentally discovered a way of speeding the process when left with dozens of lemon wedges which had been used to garnish a large party dish. She put them in the freezing compartment of her refrigerator to keep them until she was ready to pickle them. When she sprinkled the frozen lemons with salt, she found that they shed a large quantity of water and softened in just over an hour. They were ready for eating after only a few days in oil and paprika.

Pickled Artichoke Hearts

3–4 lemons	12 artichokes
Salt	Olive or nut oil

Squeeze the lemons into a bowl and add salt to taste. Prepare the artichokes by removing the tough outer leaves and chokes, trimming the leaves close to the hearts. Cut them in half if they are large. As each one is prepared, rub it with a squeezed-out lemon half and drop it into the salted lemon juice.

When all the artichokes have been prepared, arrange them in a large glass jar. Add oil to the remaining lemon juice and beat well with a wooden spoon. Pour over the artichoke hearts, adding more oil if necessary to cover them completely. Seal the jar tightly.

The artichokes will be ready in about 4 weeks, and will last for months.

Torshi Meshakel
Mixed Pickles

250 g (8 oz) small, whole pickling cucumbers
2 large carrots, thickly sliced
1 small cauliflower, separated into florets
1 sweet green pepper, thickly sliced, seeded and cored
250 g (8 oz) small white turnips, peeled and quartered
½ raw beetroot, peeled and cut into medium-sized pieces (optional)

A few raw green beans, if available, cut in pieces
3 cloves garlic
1 small dried chilli pepper pod
A few sprigs fresh dill and 2 teaspoons dill seed
4–5 level tablespoons (about 90 g/3 oz) salt
1 scant litre (1½ pints) water
300 ml (½ pint) white wine vinegar

Wash and prepare the vegetables and pack them tightly in glass jars together with the garlic cloves, a hot pepper pod divided between them and dill.

Mix the water, vinegar and salt solution in a glass or china bowl, and pour over the vegetables. Prepare and add more liquid if this is not enough. Seal tightly and store in a warm place. The pickle should be ready in about 2 weeks. The vegetables will be soft and mellow, and tinted pink by the beetroot. However, the beetroot can be omitted if you prefer the vegetables in their natural colours.

Do not keep longer than 2 months unless stored under refrigeration.

Tomato Sauce

Although this is not a pickle, I am including the recipe in this chapter since it is a very useful sauce to have at hand when required, and it can be prepared in advance and stored in jars.

1 kg (2 lb) tomatoes
Olive oil
1 large onion, finely chopped
4 cloves garlic
Salt and black pepper

1 teaspoon sugar (optional)
2 tablespoons finely chopped parsley
2 teaspoons dried crushed oregano

Skin the tomatoes by throwing them into boiling water for a minute or two to loosen their skins. Alternatively, hold them on a fork over an open flame until the skin bursts and blisters. They can then be skinned easily. Quarter them.

Heat 3 tablespoons oil in a large saucepan. Fry the chopped onion until soft and golden. Add the whole garlic cloves and fry for a few minutes longer until lightly coloured. Add the tomatoes. Season to taste with salt and pepper, and a teaspoon of sugar if you like. Sprinkle with parsley and oregano, and sauté gently, squashing the tomatoes lightly with a wooden spoon, until softened. Then cover the pan and simmer very gently for at least an hour. The tomatoes should be stewed in their own juice as far as possible, and a little water should be added only if really necessary.

Remove the garlic cloves and pour the sauce into a glass jar. Pour a thin layer of oil over the surface, cover the jar tightly and store in a cool place until required. This sauce keeps for many months if the surface remains completely covered with a film of oil.

Batingas Makbus bi Zeit
Stuffed Aubergine Pickle in Oil

1 kg (2 lb) small, thin, long aubergines	1 small chilli, finely chopped
Salt	2 cloves garlic, crushed
120 g (4 oz) walnuts, finely chopped	Olive oil

Cut the stem off the aubergines and pierce the skin in a few places with a sharp knife. Poach in salted water for 20 minutes (keep the aubergines down with a small, heavy lid) until soft. Drain, and when they are cool very gently squeeze to get rid of the bitter juices.

Mix the walnuts with the chilli and garlic and add a little salt. Cut a slit down the middle of the aubergines but not right through, and leave the ends so as to have a pocket. Stuff with the walnut mixture, put in a jar and cover with oil.

Rice

Roz

While wheat is the staple of the rural parts of the Middle East, rice is the everyday food of the cities. It was introduced in the marshlands of the area through Persia from India. It is often the main part of the meal, with small amounts of meat and vegetables acting as garnish or accompaniment. It is *roz* to the Arabs, *pirinç*, or pilav when cooked with other ingredients, to the Turks. Iranians call it *chilau* when it is plain, and *polo* when cooked with other ingredients. In the Arabian gulf they have taken to an Indian way of making it called *birian*.

Cooked plainly with water, salt and a little oil or butter, it serves as an accompaniment to stews or grilled meats and salads, or is itself accompanied by rich sauces. It can also be cooked together with other ingredients, added to the sauce of a meat stew when the meat is already tender, or partially cooked and added to other cooked ingredients to finish cooking together. In this form it is known in the West as pilav.

Rice is sometimes coloured yellow with saffron or turmeric, or red with tomatoes. It is moulded into various shapes, the favourite one being a ring, and often garnished with nuts and sauces.

399

Following Middle Eastern tradition, it is served at the same time as all the other dishes, to be chosen first or last to each individual's taste. Some people claim that they cannot taste anything without eating rice at the same time as a sort of background and basic measure of taste. In families where the Western style of serving three courses has been adopted, rice is often served at the end of the meal, accompanied by a special sauce or by part of the main dish which has been set aside to be savoured with it.

An Egyptian riddle describes this manner of serving:

☐ *Question: Why is rice like a* chaouiche *(policeman)?*
Answer: It is brilliantly white like the chaouiche's *uniform in the summer, and it arrives at the end like the* chaouiche *when everything (i.e. the trouble) is over.*

How to Cook Rice

Throughout the Middle East, the preparation of rice is enveloped by a certain ritual mystique. Although an extremely simple dish, various ways of cooking it exist. Each family cherishes a particular method and is sceptical about all others, refusing to believe that it is possible to achieve successful results in any way other than their own. Generally speaking however, each country seems to prefer one method above all others. I have given those most commonly followed.

Long-grain rice is used except for stuffing vegetables, when short- or medium-grain rice is preferred because it sticks together. The particular qualities of the longer grain lie in its fluffiness, and its ability to remain firm and separate. If well cooked, it is tender but firm, not too soft, and never mushy. Varieties of long-grain rice available in Britain include *basmati* and *patna* rice from India, and the American 'Uncle Ben'.

Basically, plain rice is cooked in water with salt and some fat – usually butter, clarified butter, oil or margarine. The quantity of water necessary and the cooking times vary. Each batch of rice is different and so, as households buy it by the large sackful, the first dish made from the opened sack ascertains the amount of water and the time required for cooking the rest. Generally the same volume of water as that of dry raw rice is needed, but if the rice is a year old more water must be used. It also depends on the type of grain.

The rice is almost always cooked in a pan with a tightly fitting lid, but a few people prefer to leave the lid only half on. In this case, more water must be used to make up for the rapid evaporation.

When rice comes in hessian sacks it has to be cleaned of stones and roughage (and sometimes small insects too) and washed many times before it is ready for cooking. The pre-packed rice available is perfectly clean and needs only to be rid of the starchy powder which causes it to be less separate and slightly sticky when cooked. Some people do not object to this and find the result of rice cooked without preliminary washing very acceptable, maintaining that the zeal of excessive washing is a hangover from the 'hessian sack' era.

A special word about Persian rice. As with her art of miniature painting and poetry, Persia has carried the preparation of rice to extraordinary heights of refinement. It is a base or accompaniment for practically every dish and it is said that no other Middle Eastern country prepares rice in the same perfectionist manner. Its preparation is often started a day before it is to be eaten.

At least six different qualities of rice are cultivated in Persia. The best, 'royal' rice, called *domsiah*, grows in rare conditions and is very expensive. The next best is *darbori* rice; then come *sadri* and *champâ*. These are not available in Britain. *Basmati* rice, now found in most supermarkets as well as in specialist shops, is the nearest to the third quality of rice and the best substitute to use.

Ways of Cooking Plain Rice

By some Middle Eastern standards 500 g (1 lb) of rice is needed to feed 2 people, but by European ones it is usually enough for 6. In my own family it satisfies 4.

It is more convenient to measure rice in teacupfuls because it is the accurate volume rather than the weight that is important in measuring the liquid for cooking. You will find that a large teacup, 225 ml (8 fl oz), holds about 250 g (8 oz) of rice.

In a few countries, though not all, it is considered preferable to cook the rice in stock. A chicken or meat stock left over from a soup or stew, used instead of water, will make a magnificent rice.

1. A Syrian Way

2 teacups long-grain rice	Salt
2 teacups water	60–90 g (2–3 oz) butter

To wash the rice, pour boiling water over it in a bowl and stir well for a few seconds. Pour into a sieve or a small-holed colander and rinse under cold running water until the water runs clear. Drain well.

Bring 2 cups water to the boil in a pan with a little salt to taste. Throw in the drained rice, bring to the boil again, and boil vigorously for 2 minutes. Cover the pan with a tight-fitting lid and simmer very gently, undisturbed, for about 20 minutes, until the water has been absorbed and the rice is cooked. It should be tender and separate, with little holes all over the surface. Turn off the heat, and allow the rice to rest for about 10 minutes.

Melt the butter (by today's standards this is rather a large quantity which you may prefer to reduce) in a saucepan and put it evenly all over the rice. Let it rest again, covered, for 3 minutes longer, until the melted fat has been absorbed by the rice.

2. A Lebanese Way

The ingredients and quantities are the same as above (although some people use half as much water).

Wash the rice as above and drain well. Put the 2 teacups water, salt and butter or margarine in a saucepan, and bring to the boil. Throw in the rice and boil vigorously for 2 minutes. Cover the pan tightly and simmer very gently, undisturbed, for about 20 minutes, until the rice is tender and fluffy, and little holes have appeared all over the surface. Turn off the heat and allow to rest for 10 minutes before serving.

3. An Egyptian Way

The ingredients and quantities are the same as in the first recipe, although Jewish households like my own used oil instead of butter.

Wash and drain the rice as above. Allow the rice grains to dry out as much as possible. (In this method the rice can be left unwashed if you wish.)

Heat the butter or oil in a saucepan. Throw in the rice and fry it gently for a minute or so, until the grains are translucent and well coated with fat. Add the water and salt to taste. Bring to the boil vigorously for 2 minutes, then simmer gently, tightly covered and undisturbed, for about 20 minutes, until the rice is tender and the characteristic little holes have appeared on the surface. Never stir while it is cooking. Allow to rest for 10 minutes before serving.

4. A Persian Way
and a particularly excellent one – *Chilau* or Steamed Rice

Use *basmati* rice. Wash well in a colander then put it in a bowl with 2 tablespoons salt and lukewarm water to cover. Stir and let it soak overnight if you can, or for at least an hour. The longer the better.

Fill a large saucepan with plenty of water, add 2 tablespoons salt and bring to the boil. Sprinkle the drained rice in gradually and let it boil vigorously for about 4 to 8 minutes. The cooking time varies from one batch of rice to another and depends mainly on when it has been harvested. Test a grain of rice by biting it. When it is just a little underdone – it must be slightly harder than you would like to eat it – drain quickly and rinse in lukewarm water.

Put 2 tablespoons butter and let it melt at the bottom of the pan, then put in all the rice and stir. Cover with 2 more tablespoons butter. Stretch a clean dishcloth across the top of the pan, put the lid on top and lift the corners of the cloth up over it. (In Iran the lid, made of raffia and covered by a removable and washable cloth, is called a *damkoni*.)

Then leave the rice to steam over a very low flame for 20 to 30 minutes. It should be cooked and separate. The cloth will absorb the excess steam. The crisp, brown, golden crust that forms at the bottom is considered a delicacy to be offered first to guests. It is called *dig*. Remove it with a spatula and serve separately.

Some people like to put thin slices of fried bread or raw potato at the bottom of a pan when steaming with rice, and serve them in the same way as the crisp rice.

Although this preparation may sound complicated, it is not so, and the result is so exquisite that it is well worth trying. You will understand the importance of rice in Persian life and the national pride in making it to perfection.

Chilau is accompanied by various sauces or *khoreshta* (see page 426) – aromatic and textural symphonies, the result of centuries of traditional harmonizing, creating and enjoying.

Served without a sauce, for example as an accompaniment to shish kebab, it is eaten with a generous lump of butter and, traditionally, with a raw egg yolk served in an egg-shell. The yolk is poured over each individual portion of rice and then stirred into it, making a glistening, creamy sauce.

Bowls of *sumac* are put on the table for people to help themselves.

Saffron Rice

Prepare rice according to the Egyptian way (see page 402), adding ¼ to ½ teaspoon saffron to the rice as it is frying.

The cooked rice will become a beautiful yellow.

In the Middle East it is prepared in this manner for its delicate flavour, and its decorative quality, and in the hope that its yellow colour will bring joy and happiness.

You can substitute ¾ teaspoon turmeric (sometimes called 'Oriental saffron') for a cheaper version.

Roz bil Shaghria
Rice with Vermicelli

A rice and vermicelli dish, eaten in many countries on the second night of the New Year 'so that one's employment may be prolonged and multiplied' like the vermicelli, or, as some say 'so that one may be prolific and beget many children'. Chick peas are not usually included but they make an interesting addition.

1½ cups (375 g/12 oz) long-grain rice
120 g (4 oz) chick peas, soaked (optional)
1 onion, finely chopped
90 g (3 oz) butter
2 tablespoons oil
180–250 g (6–8 oz) vermicelli, broken into smallish pieces
Water: a little more than the volume of rice
Salt

Wash the rice in boiling water, then rinse in cold water and drain well. Boil the soaked chick peas in a fresh portion of water until very tender (about 1 hour or more, according to their age and quality).

Fry the onion in butter mixed with oil (or in 60 g (2 oz) clarified butter), using a large, heavy saucepan. When the onion is golden and transparent, add the vermicelli and fry until lightly coloured. Add the rice, previously washed and drained, and stir over moderate heat until the grains are transparent and well coated with fat. Add water and salt to taste. Bring to the boil and simmer gently, tightly covered, until the water has been absorbed and the rice is cooked and fluffy, about 20 minutes.

Mix in the cooked and drained chick peas, and heat again until all the ingredients are very hot.

Serve with yoghourt and cucumber salad.

Roz bi Dfeen
Rice with Meat and Chick Peas

500 g (1 lb) lean beef or lamb, cubed (optional)
90–120 g (3–4 oz) butter
500 g (1 lb) button onions
60 g (2 oz) chick peas, soaked overnight

Salt and black pepper
1 teaspoon ground cumin or cinnamon
2 teacups (500 g/1 lb) long-grain rice, washed and drained

If you are using meat, brown it in hot butter in a large heavy saucepan at the same time as the onions. Let the onions become golden and the meat a rich brown colour all over. Add the soaked and drained chick peas, and cover with water. Add pepper to taste, cumin or cinnamon, and simmer gently, covered, until the meat is very tender and the chick peas are soft, about 2 hours, adding salt when the chick peas have begun to soften.

If there is less than 2 cups liquid left in the pan, make it up to this amount with a little water. If there is more, reduce it by cooking uncovered, or pour some out. Bring to the boil again, throw in the rice, mix well and simmer, covered and undisturbed, for about 20 minutes. Add a little water and cook further if the rice seems undercooked. Turn off the heat and allow to rest for a few minutes before serving.

≈ If you are not using meat, fry the onions and then cook with the chick peas in a meat stock. When the chick peas are tender, make the liquid up to 2 cups with water, add rice and continue cooking as above.

Rice with Meat, Pine Nuts and Almonds

Here is a most delicious and attractive way of presenting rice at a party.

2 teacups (500 g/1 lb) long-grain rice, cooked (see method)
250 g (8 oz) lamb, beef or veal, minced
60 g (2 oz) pine nuts
60 g (2 oz) almonds, peeled and chopped

Oil or butter
Salt and black pepper
½ teaspoon ground cinnamon or ¼ teaspoon ground allspice (optional)
30–60 g (1–2 oz) seedless raisins (optional)

Prepare 500 g (1 lb) long-grain rice as described in one of the recipes for plain rice on page 400.

Fry the meat and the mixed nuts separately in oil or butter. The nuts require only 2 or 3 minutes' frying. Cook the meat longer, adding a few tablespoons water and crushing it with a fork until it has changed colour and become soft, light and crumbly. Mix the meat with the nuts; season to taste with salt and pepper, and other spices if you like. An exquisite variation is to add a few seedless raisins to the meat and nut mixture.

Pat or mould the hot rice into a pyramid or ring shape in a heated serving dish, and crown with the meat and nut mixture. Alternatively, spread half of the meat and nuts over the bottom of an oiled ring mould. Press the rice over it tightly to fill the mould and turn out on to a heated serving dish. Put the rest of the meat and nuts in the hollow in the centre.

☐ *'Honour to rice; let burghul go hang itself!' – an old Lebanese saying originating from the time when rice was a delicacy and was rapidly eclipsing burghul, until then considered the staple food of the Lebanon.*

Rice with Broad Beans

Nut oil
1 large onion, finely chopped
500 g (1 lb) fresh shelled or frozen broad beans
Salt and black pepper

2 cloves garlic, crushed
½–1 teaspoon ground coriander
2 teacups (500 g/1 lb) long-grain rice, washed and drained

Heat 2 tablespoons oil in a large, heavy pan and fry the onion until soft and golden. Add the broad beans and sauté a little, turning them over and stirring. Cover with a little water and season to taste with salt and pepper. Simmer until the beans are tender.

Fry the garlic and coriander in 2 tablespoons oil in a large frying pan. Add the washed and drained rice, and fry until transparent but not browned. Add all this to the cooked broad beans together with enough water to make the liquid in the pan up to 2 teacups. Bring to the boil and simmer very gently, covered and undisturbed, for about 20 minutes, or until the rice is tender.

Serve hot as an accompaniment to meat, or cold with yoghourt and a salad.

≈ Sometimes the rice is cooked separately as in one of the recipes for plain rice (page 400). The fried garlic and coriander are added to the broad bean stew. Just before serving, the beans and rice are mixed together.

Rice with Fresh Herbs

Iranians have a predilection for fresh herbs. A traditional New Year's dish consists of rice cooked with a variety of fresh herbs; their greenness is believed to ensure a happy and 'green' year ahead.

The herbs are chosen according to individual taste and mood, and to what is available at that time of year. Favourite Iranian herbs include *tare* (tarragon), chives, parsley and dill, and others, including fresh fenugreek and *gishnise*, which I have not found in Britain. Use whichever you prefer, but try to use fresh ones.

Wash and chop the herbs finely. Prepare 500 g (1 lb) *basmati* rice according to the recipe for *chilau* (page 403). Boil it vigorously, and when it is nearly cooked, throw in the herbs. As soon as the rice is tender but not too soft – after 8 to 10 minutes – drain in a sieve or colander. The herbs will cling to the rice. Steam with oil or butter as directed in the basic recipe, with a cloth stretched under the lid to absorb vapour.

A splendid rice dish, often served with fried fish.

Rice with Pine Nuts, Pistachios and Almonds

This is a rather elegant and highly decorative way of serving rice, a perfect party dish.

Prepare plain or saffron rice, or cook it in a chicken stock, following one of the recipes at the beginning of this chapter.

Chop 60 g (2 oz) mixed pistachios and almonds coarsely, and fry them with the same quantity of pine nuts in a little oil until just golden. (Use only one or two kinds of nuts if you like.)

Just before serving, spread the nuts evenly over the bottom of an oiled ring mould large enough to hold all the rice. Press the rice over the nuts tightly and turn out on to a heated serving dish. This traditional round shape is particularly attractive for serving rice. In this case, it will be crowned by the assortment of fried nuts.

If more convenient, you can pack the rice and nuts into the oiled mould in advance and keep it warm in a low oven, ready to be unmoulded just before serving.

Turkish Aubergine Pilav – served cold

500 g (1 lb) aubergines	2 teacups (500 g/1 lb) long-grain
Salt	rice
About 1 teacup olive oil	

Cut the aubergines into smallish chunks and put them in a large sieve or colander. Sprinkle with salt and leave to drain for at least 30 minutes to rid them of their bitter juices. Squeeze out as much of the juices as possible, rinse in cold water and pat dry with a clean cloth or kitchen paper.

Fry the aubergine pieces gently in half the oil until coloured and tender; they do not require any additional salt.

Prepare plain rice according to one of the recipes on pages 400–403, using the rest of the oil instead of butter, and salt to taste. Let the rice cook for 15 minutes, then bury the aubergines in it. Steam for 20 minutes over low heat as directed for *chilau* (page 403), stretching a cloth under the lid to absorb the steam.

Serve cold with yoghourt.

☐ *Arab saying: 'Rather than eat rice with aubergines, buy some-thing to cover your hind part.' (Until very recently rice was consi-*

dered an expensive dish and only for the rich. A poor man buying rice and aubergines too was therefore thought to be unnecessarily extravagant.)

Tomato Pilav

250 g (8 oz) onions, chopped
3 tablespoons nut or olive oil
1 clove garlic (optional)
750 g–1 kg (1½–2 lb) ripe
tomatoes, skinned, or a 850-g
(30-oz) tin skinned tomatoes
Salt and black pepper

1 teaspoon sugar (optional)
1 bay leaf (optional)
1 teaspoon dried oregano
(optional)
2 teacups (500 g/1 lb) long-grain
rice, washed and drained

In a large, heavy saucepan, fry the onions in hot oil until soft and golden. A whole clove of garlic may be added to the onions if liked. Add the tomatoes and season to taste with salt, pepper, and a little sugar if needed. Sauté lightly, squashing the tomatoes a little with a fork, until they acquire a 'fried' taste. Cover with water and allow to simmer gently for about ¾ hour. This sauce may be perfumed with a bay leaf or oregano, but it is also good plain. Add more water while cooking if required.

When the sauce has become rich in flavour and texture, throw in the rice. Add a little water to the pan to make up the liquid to about the same volume as that of the rice. Bring to the boil and simmer gently, covered and undisturbed, for about 20 minutes, until the rice is tender. It will have acquired a pale, salmon pink colour and will be impregnated with the flavour of the tomatoes.

≈ Sometimes small pieces of left-over meat or a little minced raw meat are cooked with the tomatoes for a richer dish.

Kuzu Pilav
Turkish Lamb Pilav

1 large onion, finely chopped
3 tablespoons butter or oil
375–500 g (¾–1 lb) lean lamb, cut
into small pieces
Salt and black pepper
1 teaspoon ground cinnamon

2–3 tablespoons tomato
concentrate
3 tablespoons finely chopped
parsley
2 teacups (500 g/1 lb) long-grain
rice, washed and drained

In a large, heavy saucepan, fry the onion in hot butter or oil until soft and golden. Add meat and brown it gently all over. Season to taste with salt, pepper and cinnamon. Cover the pan, and cook the meat and onions in their own juices for about 10 minutes. Dilute the tomato concentrate in a little cold water, pour into the meat mixture and stir well. Add more water to cover, sprinkle with finely chopped parsley, bring to the boil and simmer gently for 1–1½ hours until the meat is very tender and the sauce thick and reduced.

Make the liquid left in the stew up to about the volume of the dry rice (about 2 teacups) with water. Add the rice, bring to a vigorous boil, then simmer gently, covered and undisturbed, for about 20 minutes, or until rice is soft, adding more water if necessary.

≈ An exquisite variation is to add about a tablespoon each of pine nuts and raisins to the simmering stew.

≈ Another is to cook a sliced sweet pepper and 2 ripe tomatoes, skinned and cut into pieces, in the stew.

≈ A pinch of saffron may be added to give a subtle colouring (in this case the tomato concentrate is left out). Alternatively, chopped parsley and celery leaves can be used.

In each case, the rice is added and the cooking completed in the same way as described in the main recipe.

Persian Lamb and Apricot Polo

The apricot has a special affinity for lamb. But it must be of the sharp variety. The early Arab Abbassid dynasty, centred in Persia, greatly favoured the combination and created a series of dishes on this theme which they called *mishmishiya* (see page 301), *mishmish* being the Arab word for apricot. It is still a great favourite as a partner to lamb in modern Iran. The rest of the Middle East has adopted it to a much lesser degree.

120 g (4 oz) butter	2 tablespoons seedless raisins
1 onion, finely chopped	120 g (4 oz) sharp dried apricots
500 g (1 lb) lean lamb, cubed	2 teacups (500 g/1 lb) long-grain
Salt and black pepper	rice
½ teaspoon ground cinnamon	

Heat 60 g (2 oz) butter in a large, heavy saucepan and fry the onion until soft and golden. Add the meat and fry gently, turning the pieces to brown them all over. Season with salt, pepper and cinnamon. Add raisins and halved apricots, and sauté lightly. Cover with water and simmer gently, covered, for about 1½ hours, until the meat is very tender and has absorbed the sweet and acid flavours of the fruit. If the stew is still rather liquid by the end of cooking time, reduce it by fast boiling.

Cook the rice as in the recipe for *chilau* (page 403) or plain rice (page 400), using the remaining 60 g (2 oz) butter. If using the *chilau* method, boil the rice but do not steam it. If using the recipe for plain rice, simmer the rice until half cooked, i.e. for 10 to 15 minutes only.

Arrange alternate layers of rice and meat with sauce in a large heavy saucepan, starting and ending with a layer of rice. Cover and steam gently for 20 minutes longer, until the rice is tender and has absorbed some of the sauce. A cloth stretched underneath the lid will absorb the steam and make the rice lighter.

Seleq
Lamb with Rice Cooked in Milk

Rice cooked in milk for very long, until it is a soft cream, is a speciality of Saudi Arabia. It serves as a bed for lamb, often a whole animal, presented on a tray with melted clarified butter trickled on top. It is known that in the city of Taif they make it better than in Jedda or Medina.

Here is a popular Saudi Arabian speciality which is similar to a medieval al-Baghdadi dish.

This makes rather a large quantity suitable for a party. Reduce it by half to serve 6 people.

1 large leg of lamb	4 teacups milk
2 onions, finely chopped	4 teacups long-grain rice, washed
Salt and black pepper	180–250 g (6–8 oz) butter, melted

Simmer the joint whole or cut into pieces for 2 hours, or until tender, together with the chopped onions in water to cover, seasoned to taste with salt and pepper. When cooked, remove the meat and keep warm. Add water if necessary to make the volume of stock up to 6 teacups. Add the milk and bring to the boil. Then throw in the rice and cook very gently, covered, until it is so soft it is almost a purée. Adjust seasoning.

Serve in a large tray with melted butter poured over the rice and the pieces of meat arranged on top. This dish is served with a cucumber, lettuce and tomato salad. Some people like to accompany it with clear, pure honey, to be stirred into each portion separately.

≈ This is a Moroccan way of cooking rice in milk: Boil 500 g (1 lb) rice in plenty of salted water for 10 minutes and drain. Then cook in 1.4 litres (2½ pints) milk to which have been added 3 cinnamon sticks, 1–2 grains mastic (pulverized), 2 tablespoons orange blossom water and salt to taste. Simmer gently until all the liquid has been absorbed. Serve in a large dish with a meat stew on top.

Labnieh
Rice with Yoghourt

A recipe exists for cooking rice in yoghourt which has been stabilized (page 124), but it is simpler and also more appealing to simply pour yoghourt over plain rice. Everyone likes to do this and Arab doctors prescribe it for people with stomach troubles.

Beat ½ litre (1 pint) yoghourt in a bowl with 1 tablespoon dried mint, 2 crushed cloves garlic, and salt and white pepper to taste. Let the flavours infuse for at least ½ hour before you serve.

☐ *The Feast of Tantalus**

One of the notables invited the Khoja to Iftar.† He went to ask him quite early in the day, then took him round from one mosque to another until he became desperately hungry.

As they entered the dining-room he saw stuffed turkey, baklawa, and cakes on the sideboard and felt that he could hold out no longer. As they took their places his mouth began to water.

First some excellent tripe soup was served, and the host with great ceremony proceeded to taste it.

'Drat the man!' he cried. 'Kiaya!‡ come here at once! How often

---

* Barnham (trans.), *Tales of Nasr-ed-Din Khoja.*
† *Iftar* is the breaking of the month's fast on the eve of the Bairam. It is also applied to the breaking of the fast every evening.
‡ *Kiaya:* head servant, butler, or major-domo.

have I bid you tell the cook not to put garlic into the soup? Take it away at once!'

The Khoja looked after it wistfully and gently tightened his belt.

Then turning to him his host remarked, 'It is quite impossible to make these cooks understand. They will do as they like, whatever you say to them.'

A chorus of voices answered, 'They will indeed.'

At this moment the turkey was put on the table. It was done to a turn and smelt delicious. The stuffing was made of raisins, rice, and pistachios, and there was so much of it that it went all over the dish.

The host took a small piece, but he had no sooner done so than he cried out furiously, 'Aga, come here! Did I not tell you the other day to see that the rascal does not use spice? Do you do this on purpose? Thirty years you have been in my service and yet you allow this to go on! God pay you out for this! Take it away!'

Out went the turkey, and the poor Khoja heaved a deep sigh as he saw his sheet-anchor disappear.

Then a eunuch brought in the baklawa, but the host scowled at him and said, 'You stupid Arab! Do hungry people begin with sweets? Away with it!'

As the whip fell on his shoulders, the poor fellow let the dish fall and bolted from the room.

The Khoja, seeing all these tempting dishes carried out one after the other, took his spoon and catching hold of a dish of pilaff which was on a side-table, began to devour it.

'Hullo! what are you doing there, Khoja?' cried the host.

'Oh! sir,' said the Khoja, 'do give me a chance before you condemn it to the same fate as the others. Let me have a little talk with my old friend the Pilaff – ask how he is and find out what he has inside him! Never mind me!'

At this the guests began to roar with laughter. The dishes were then brought in again, they set to work in earnest and made a merry meal.

Tavuklu Pilav
Plain Turkish Chicken Pilav

1 large roasting chicken	1 teaspoon dried herbs
2 tablespoons oil	2 teacups (500 g/1 lb) long-grain
Salt and black pepper	rice, washed and drained

Clean and wash a large fat chicken. Colour it gently in hot oil, turning it so that it becomes golden all over. Add water to cover, and season to taste with salt, pepper and a teaspoon of your favourite herbs. Bring to the boil and simmer until the chicken is very tender (usually about 1 hour). Let the chicken cool a little before taking it out of the stock.

When it is cool enough to handle, cut the large pieces into serving pieces and keep warm in a little of the stock to prevent them from becoming dry. Cut the rest of the meat into small pieces. Measure the stock. If there is more stock than the volume of dry rice, reduce by vigorous boiling. Return the small chicken pieces to the stock. Throw in the rice, stir and bring to the boil, then reduce the heat and simmer gently, covered and undisturbed, for about 20 minutes until the rice is tender.

Heap the rice on a large, flat serving dish. Arrange the reserved chicken pieces over it and serve.

Roz bi Jaj
Chicken and Rice

In a Lebanese version of the above chicken pilav the chicken stock is perfumed with a teaspoon of ground cinnamon. The rice is cooked in the broth with small pieces of chicken, as described above. 60 g (2 oz) blanched almonds and about 30 g (1 oz) pine nuts are lightly fried in butter and arranged at the bottom of an oiled mould. The cooked rice is pressed over them, then the mould is turned out on to a heated serving dish and garnished with portions of chicken.

For an elegant presentation sprinkle the mould with nuts then line with the boned chicken and pack the rice over the meat. Inverted, this looks very attractive.

Persian Chicken Polo

Two of the most delicious chicken dishes are versions of Persian *morg polo*. Both are meant, understandably, for great occasions such as the New Year, weddings and saints' days.

2 teacups (500 g/1 lb) basmati rice
1 onion, finely chopped
5 tablespoons butter or oil
1 large roasting chicken, jointed
Salt and black pepper

1 tablespoon raisins, or more
120–180 g (4–6 oz) sharp dried
   apricots, chopped
½–1 teaspoon ground cinnamon

Fry the onion gently in 3 tablespoons butter or oil until golden, using a saucepan or a deep frying pan. Add the chicken pieces and brown on all sides. Season to taste with salt and pepper, add raisins and apricots, and continue to cook for a minute or two longer, turning the fruit in the fat. Sprinkle with cinnamon, cover with water and simmer gently, covered, until the chicken is very tender and the sauce reduced. Bone the chicken if you like.

Wash and boil the rice according to the recipe for *chilau* (page 403), but do not steam it. Alternatively, half-cook according to one of the recipes for plain rice on page 400.

Put 2 tablespoons melted butter or oil at the bottom of a large, heavy saucepan. Spread half of the partly cooked rice over this, cover with the chicken pieces, pour the rich, fruity sauce over them and cover with remaining rice. Cover the pan with a cloth, put the lid on tightly, and steam over very low heat for 20 to 30 minutes. The cloth will capture the steam rising from the rice and help to make it fluffy. Serve all mixed together.

Teheran Zeresk

This wonderful chicken *polo* is given extra quality and excitement by the barberries, sour little red berries called *zeresk* in Persian.

1 large roasting chicken, jointed
4 tablespoons butter or oil
300 ml (½ pint) yoghurt
1 egg, lightly beaten
¼ teaspoon powdered saffron or
   ½ teaspoon pistils

Salt and black pepper
2 teacups (500 g/1 lb) basmati rice
30–60 g (1–2 oz) dried barberries,
   washed

Sauté chicken pieces in 2 tablespoons butter or oil in a large saucepan until coloured all over. Add water to cover and simmer gently until very tender. Allow to cool. Bone the chicken pieces. In a large bowl mix yoghourt and egg with saffron mixed with a little water (pistils should be crushed with a little salt), and salt and pepper to taste. Beat well. Add the boned pieces of chicken and turn them so that they are well coated with the mixture.

Wash and boil the rice according to the recipe for *chilau* (page 403). No other method would give such a good result.

When you are ready to steam the rice, put 2 tablespoons melted butter or oil at the bottom of a large, heavy saucepan (as in the original recipe). Spread half of the rice over the bottom of the pan and cover with the chicken and yoghourt mixture. Throw the barberries over this. (They must only be washed – soaking will make them lose their colour.)

Add the rest of the rice. Steam, covered, for 30 minutes, with a cloth stretched across the pan underneath the lid to absorb the steam.

Tachin
Moulded Rice

Tachin is a version of the above. The lady who wrote out this recipe for me fifteen years ago also noted that it was the most famous and traditional of Iranian dishes. The quantity of rice is large by British standards. It could be halved. The chicken could be roasted, boiled or sautéed.

4 teacups (1 kg/2 lb) basmati rice	1 teaspoon saffron
1 large cooked chicken	1 teaspoon granulated sugar
500 g (1 lb) yoghourt	2 tablespoons oil
2 eggs	60 g (2 oz) zereshk (barberries)
Salt and pepper	

Prepare the rice according to the recipe for *chilau* (page 403). Skin and bone the chicken and cut it into pieces. Mix the yoghourt and beaten eggs together (the eggs prevent the yoghourt from curdling) and add salt and pepper. Put the saffron pistils and sugar in a cup and grind them together with the back of a spoon, then add a few drops of boiling water and grind the saffron again to extract the maximum flavour and colour. Stir this into the yoghourt mixture, put the chicken pieces in and lift them out again on to a plate. Mix half the rice with the yoghourt mixture.

Put the oil at the bottom of a saucepan (preferably a heavy-bottomed, non-stick one which is just large enough to contain all the ingredients). Cover the bottom and sides with the rice and yoghourt mixture. Put a layer of chicken pieces in this mould, sprinkle with a few washed barberries and cover with a layer of plain rice. Repeat one, two or three times, making sure that there is always the yoghourt and rice mixture on the sides, until the ingredients are finished.

Put a piece of grease-proof paper or cling film on top and press gently down all over, then throw it away. Put the lid on and cook for about 45 minutes on a very low flame. Turn it out on a round serving dish. The outside should be crisp and brown, and the beautiful yellow and white layered inside crumbly. If you are not using a non-stick pan, dipping the bottom into cold water will help you to turn it out. Alternatively you can cook it in a pot in the oven for about an hour.

Shirini Polo

90–120 g (3–4 oz) candied tangerine or orange peel (see method)
Sugar
1 large roasting chicken, jointed
Salt and black pepper
½ teaspoon powdered saffron

120 g (4 oz) blanched almonds or pistachio nuts, chopped
2 teacups (500 g/1 lb) long-grain rice, preferably basmati, washed and drained
Butter or oil

To prepare the candied peel: use peel with as much of the white pith removed as possible. Slice it into thin strips and make a note of the weight. Simmer without sugar in about ½ teacup water until soft. Then add sugar equal to the original weight and cook until the water is reduced and the strips of peel are sweet. Bitter peel is particularly good prepared in this manner. (The candied peel available in shops can also be used.)

Boil the chicken joints in water to cover with salt and pepper to taste and ¼ teaspoon saffron until the chicken is tender and the stock greatly reduced. Bone the chicken and cut the flesh into small pieces. Return the pieces to the pan with the remaining stock, add the peel and almonds or pistachios, and continue to simmer for 15 to 20 minutes, uncovered only if the sauce needs reducing to suit the rice.

Wash and boil the rice according to the recipe for *chilau* (page 403), adding the remaining ¼ teaspoon saffron. Do not steam it yet. First, melt 1 to 2 tablespoons butter or oil in the bottom of a large, heavy saucepan. Put alternate layers of rice and chicken with peel and nuts in the pan, starting and ending with a layer of rice.

Now, stretch a clean cloth over the top of the pan, put on the lid and steam over very low heat for 20 to 30 minutes, until the sweet juices of the chicken sauce have penetrated the rice. The cloth will absorb the steam and help the rice to retain its fluffiness.

Cherry Polo

This recipe is inspired by a Persian one in *Recipes from Baghdad*. It is best made with sour cherries.

2 teacups (500 g/1 lb) rice	250 g (8 oz) sugar (optional)
Salt	4 tablespoons butter
500 g (1 lb) sour cherries	

Pour boiling water over the rice, add 1 tablespoon salt, stir and let it soak for several hours or overnight.

Stew the cherries in water to cover and sugar if you like until just tender. Remove the stones when cool enough.

Rinse and drain the rice and drop into vigorously boiling water. Let it cook for about 4 minutes until it is still underdone and drain quickly. In a heavy pan, preferably a non-stick one (you can use the same for boiling), melt 2 tablespoons butter, then spread alternate layers of rice and fruit starting with rice. Dot with the remaining butter and cover with a tight-fitting lid. Put on a very low flame for ½ hour for the rice to steam and become tender but separate.

Serve with lamb, chicken or duck.

Turn out carefully just before serving, without upsetting the layers.

Addas Polo

A Persian lentil and rice dish.

500 g (1 lb) lamb, cut into cubes	5–6 pitted dates, split in half or chopped
120–180 g (4–6 oz) butter	
Salt and pepper	180 g (6 oz) brown or green lentils
150 g (5 oz) raisins or sultanas	2 teacups (500 g/1 lb) basmati or long-grain rice

Sauté the lamb in 2 tablespoons butter and brown all over. Cover with water, add salt and pepper and simmer until it is tender and the liquid absorbed. Stir in the dried fruits.

Wash and boil the lentils for about 20 minutes until done (they do not need soaking), adding salt only when they start to soften, then drain.

Wash, soak and boil the rice as in the recipe for *chilau* (page 403) and drain it quickly when it is only just tender. Arrange layers of rice, lentils and meat mixture in a heavy pan. Melt the butter and pour all over. Cook, covered, on very low heat for 20 to 30 minutes.

This is usually served with yoghourt or cherry jam.

≈ You may use chicken pieces instead of lamb and red kidney beans instead of lentils and you may flavour the meat with 1 teaspoon cinnamon and ¼ teaspoon allspice.

Kalam Polo
Rice with Cabbage

A homely Persian dish.

1 kg (2 lb) white cabbage	1 teaspoon turmeric
Oil	1 teaspoon cinnamon (optional)
1 large onion, finely chopped	2 tablespoons tomato concentrate
500 g (1 lb) lean stewing lamb or beef, cubed	2 teacups (500 g/1 lb) basmati or long-grain rice
Salt and pepper	

Cut the cabbage into small pieces and sauté in a large pan in a few tablespoons oil till soft and lightly coloured. Fry the onion till golden in about 2 tablespoons oil in another pan. Add the meat and brown it all over, then turn into the first pan. Season with salt and pepper and spices. Cover with water and cook until the meat is tender, adding water when necessary. Stir in the tomato concentrate and cook further until the liquid is absorbed. Wash, soak and boil the rice as for the recipe for *chilau* (page 403) and drain before it is quite tender.

Put a little oil at the bottom of a large saucepan, then a layer of rice. Cover with some cabbage and meat mixture and repeat with alternate layers of rice and cabbage and meat, finishing with a layer of rice. Let it cook by steaming over a very low flame, covered, with a cloth stretched across the pan under the lid to absorb excess steam, for about 30 minutes.

Havij Polo
Rice with Carrots

This is an excellent sweet Persian *polo*, usually served with minced lamb meat balls, or as an accompaniment to a whole leg of lamb which has been rubbed with salt, pepper and paprika, and roasted in the oven (see page 260).

1 onion, finely chopped	½ teaspoon ground cinnamon
Butter or oil	(optional)
500–750 g (1–1½ lb) carrots, coarsely grated	2 teacups (500 g/1 lb) long-grain rice
1–2 tablespoons sugar, or more (optional)	Salt
	1 tablespoon rose water

Fry the onion in 2 to 3 tablespoons butter or oil until soft and golden. Add the grated carrots and sauté gently for 10 minutes. Sugar and cinnamon may be added at this stage if desired.

Wash and boil plain rice separately, preferably according to the recipe for Persian *chilau* (page 403). Before steaming, put a little butter or oil at the bottom of a large, heavy pan, then spread alternate layers of rice and sautéed carrots in the pan, starting and ending with a layer of rice. Sprinkle rose water over the top and cook over very low heat for about 30 minutes, with a cloth stretched over the top of the pan underneath the lid. The rose water, a relic of early medieval times, gives a subtle perfume to the dish.

Surround a roast joint of lamb with the rice mixture. If you prefer meat balls instead, knead 750 g to 1 kg (1½ to 2 lb) minced lean lamb until smooth and pasty, and season to taste with salt, pepper and 1 teaspoon of ground cinnamon. Shape into marble-sized balls. Fry them lightly in oil or butter until cooked through and coloured all over, and bury them in the middle of the rice and carrots before steaming.

□ *A Tale of Goha*
One day Goha went to the market. He stopped to gaze into the window of a restaurant where pilavs, stews, chickens, fish and

other appetizing dishes were displayed. As he stood there enjoying the delicious aromas which reached him through the open door, the head cook hailed him:

'Come in, Sir, and make yourself at home!'

Believing that he was being invited as a guest, Goha accepted. He sat down and ate as much as he could of all the dishes, filling his pockets with pilav to take home to his son. But as he got up to leave, the head cook called out:

'Pay me! You have eaten 10 piastres' worth of food!'

'But I haven't any money,' Goha replied. 'I thought I was your guest.'

The head cook dragged Goha before the Emir, who ordered him to be driven through the streets sitting backwards on a donkey as a punishment. As he proceeded through the town in this manner, followed by a train of jeering onlookers, some of them even playing music on pipes and drums, a friend saw him and exclaimed:

'What are you doing, Goha? Why are they treating you in this manner?'

'I was served good pilav for nothing, with extra thrown in for my son,' replied Goha. 'And now I am having a free donkey ride with free music as well!'

Rice with Dates and Almonds

An Arab dish, said to be of Bedouin origin.

2 teacups (500 g/1 lb) long-grain rice	120 g (4 oz) butter
Salt	60 g (2 oz) raisins
120 g (4 oz) blanched almonds, halved	120 g (4 oz) dates, chopped (dried dates will do, if soft and juicy)

Wash and boil the rice until not quite tender, following the recipe for *chilau* (page 403). Drain and keep warm.

Fry the almonds in 60 g (2 oz) butter until just golden. Add raisins and dates, and stir gently over moderate heat for a few minutes longer. Add about ¾ teacup water and simmer gently for a further 15 minutes until the dates are soft and the water has been absorbed.

Melt a tablespoon of butter in a large, heavy saucepan. Add half of the rice and spread evenly with the date and almond mixture. Cover with the remaining rice and dot the top with butter shavings. Cover with a clean cloth and a tight-fitting lid, and steam over very low heat for about 30 minutes.

Makloub 1
Vegetable and Rice Mould

Many dishes in which the rice is cooked over meat and vegetables in a large saucepan and then turned out without disturbing the layers are Palestinian favourites. I have received many recipes using a variety of different vegetables and have chosen two. The first arrived in a letter.

2 large onions, chopped	2 medium aubergines
Oil	500 g (1 lb) tomatoes (optional)
500 g (1 lb) lamb, cubed	1 teaspoon allspice
Salt and pepper	1 teaspoon cinnamon
1 large cauliflower	2 teacups (500 g/1 lb) rice, washed

Fry the onions in 3 tablespoons oil until soft, add the meat and brown all over. Cover with water, add seasoning and cook till the meat is tender (½ to 1 hour). Separate the cauliflower into florets. Cut the aubergines into slices, sprinkle with salt and let the juices run for about an hour. Peel the tomatoes (pouring boiling water over them first) and cut into four. Fry each of the vegetables separately, add seasonings and arrange in layers on top of the meat, starting with the cauliflower. Pour in the rice, with a little salt on top; do not stir. Add enough water to just cover the rice (about 2½ teacups liquid in all). Bring to the simmer then cook covered on the lowest possible heat for about an hour until the rice is done and the liquid absorbed. To serve, carefully turn upside down on to a flat round serving plate and tap the bottom of the pan so that the contents come out undisturbed.

Makloub 2

This *makloub*, which comes from *Recipes from Baghdad*, is an uncommon one with chestnuts.

2 teacups (500 g/1 lb) rice	2 tablespoons oil
500 g (1 lb) chestnuts	Salt and pepper
500 g (1 lb) mutton or lamb, cubed	

Soak the rice in boiling water. Make two cross-cut gashes in the skin of each chestnut on the flat side and simmer in boiling water for 15 to 25 minutes. Drain and remove shells and skins as soon as they are cool enough to handle.

Fry the meat in the oil until it is brown all over, cover with 3 teacups water, add salt and pepper and simmer till it is tender. Add the chestnuts and then pour the rice, washed and drained, on top, without stirring. Let it cook, covered, very gently undisturbed until it is done, adding a little water if necessary, then leave a further ½ hour to rest over the slightest flame. Turn out carefully just before serving.

Roz ou Hamud
Rice with Hamud Sauce

An Egyptian speciality and a great favourite. This is rice served with a rich, lemony chicken soup or sauce called *hamud*. For the soup version, see the recipe on page 158.

Prepare 2 teacups (500 g/1 lb) long-grain rice according to one of the recipes for plain rice at the beginning of this chapter, but do not start until the *hamud* is ready.

Use chicken giblets or left-over chicken bones and a carcass to make a rich stock. The stock left over from boiling a chicken would be ideal; it is also possible to use stock cubes but, although acceptable, they are not as good.

Chicken giblets, bones, etc., or 2 chicken stock cubes
1 turnip, cut into pieces
1 large potato, cut into pieces
2 stalks celery with leaves, chopped
2 leeks, thinly sliced
2–3 courgettes, thinly sliced
2 tablespoons finely chopped parsley
2–4 cloves garlic
Juice of 1–2 lemons, or to taste
Salt and black pepper

Put all the ingredients in a large saucepan and cover with about 1 litre (1¾ pints) water. Bring to the boil and boil vigorously at first, removing the scum as it rises to the surface. Then lower the heat and simmer gently for 1 hour or more, until the meat comes away from the bones, the potato has practically disintegrated, the other vegetables are extremely soft, and the stock is rich and full of flavour. Add water if necessary to bring the volume of sauce up to about 1 litre (1¾ pints). Remove all the bones but leave the pieces of chicken and vegetables in the sauce. It will be gently flavoured with the leeks, celery and garlic, and will have a sharp, lemony tang.

Serve the sauce and rice in separate bowls, and pour the sauce over each portion of rice with a soup ladle, as an accompaniment to chicken dishes.

Almond Sauce for Rice

This is an exquisite alternative to *hamud* (above), a speciality of Damascus.

60 g (2 oz) ground almonds, or more for a thicker sauce
600 ml (1 pint) chicken stock
Salt and white pepper
1 clove garlic, crushed

2 tablespoons finely chopped parsley
½ teaspoon sugar
Juice of 1 lemon, or more
Pinch of turmeric (optional)
Finely chopped parsley, to garnish

Mix the almonds and cold stock together in a saucepan. Bring to the boil, season to taste, and add all the other ingredients. A pinch of turmeric may be used to give the sauce an attractive pale yellow colour. Simmer gently, stirring occasionally, for 20 to 30 minutes, until the mixture thickens and the ingredients have blended to give a rich, flavoursome sauce.

Serve garnished with chopped parsley as an accompaniment to plain rice (pages 401–4), with chicken dishes.

≈ If you have some left-over chicken available, cut it into small pieces and add to the sauce with the other ingredients. One or two tablespoons of pine nuts can also be added 10 minutes before the end of cooking time.

Rice with Beid bi Lamoun

Beid bi lamoun is the Greek *avgolemono* sauce, made with eggs and lemon juice, and popular all over the Middle East.

The quantities and ingredients are the same as for *avgolemono* sauce for fish (see page 209), except that a rich chicken stock is used instead of the fish stock.

Serve hot as an accompaniment to plain rice, cooked according to one of the methods described at the beginning of this chapter.

İç Pilav
Goose Liver Pilav

A rich and delightful Turkish speciality. Chicken livers can be used instead of goose livers.

2 teacups (500 g/1 lb) long-grain rice
120 g (4 oz) butter
375 g (12 oz) goose livers, cleaned and sliced
Salt and black pepper
1 teaspoon ground allspice (optional)
8 spring onions, finely chopped

1 medium-sized onion, finely chopped
1 tablespoon pine nuts
1 tablespoon raisins
1 teaspoon sugar
2 tablespoons tomato concentrate or 1 large ripe tomato, skinned and chopped
3 tablespoons finely chopped fresh dill or parsley

Wash the rice as described on page 400. Heat 2 tablespoons of the butter in a frying pan. Fry the livers until just coloured and remove. Season them to taste with salt, pepper, and a little ground allspice if liked. Toss well and reserve. In the same fat, fry the spring onions lightly for a few minutes to soften them.

Put the rest of the butter in a large, heavy saucepan. Heat until melted and fry the onion until golden. Add pine nuts and prepared rice, and stir well over moderate heat. When the grains are well coated with fat, add the same volume of water as that of dry rice. Stir in raisins, sugar and tomato concentrate (or the skinned and chopped fresh tomato), and season to taste with salt and pepper. Use a wooden spoon for stirring to avoid breaking the grains. Bring to the boil, cover and simmer for 15 minutes until the rice is just cooked and has absorbed all the water.

Now return the fried goose livers to the pan with the spring onions. Add freshly chopped dill or parsley, mix well and stir lightly into the cooked rice. Cover the top of the pan with a clean cloth, put on the lid and leave over very low heat for 20 minutes.

Rice with Quail

This delicious dish can also be made successfully with pigeons.

6 small quail	2 teacups (500 g/1 lb) long-grain
120 g (4 oz) butter	rice, washed and drained
Salt and black pepper	Pinch of grated nutmeg
1 onion, finely chopped	

Clean, wash and wipe the quail. Sauté in hot butter in a large pan until coloured all over. Remove to another pan. Cover with water and season to taste with salt and pepper. Bring to the boil, remove the scum and simmer gently, covered, until tender (about 6 to 10 minutes). Drain and keep warm. Reserve the stock.

Now fry the onion in the same butter until soft and golden. Add the washed and well-drained rice, and sauté in the hot butter until all the grains are coated and transparent. Pour over it 2 teacups of the stock left over from cooking the quail. Add a pinch of nutmeg. Bring to a vigorous boil, then reduce the heat and simmer very gently, covered and undisturbed, until tender, about 20 minutes.

Serve on a large tray, the quail embedded in the rice.

Persian Khoreshtha or Sauces

Of all the favourite Persian dishes, the most common are the sauces or *khoreshtha* or, since they are always intended to be served over rice, *chilau khoreshtha*. They are common only in so far as they are eaten daily and sometimes twice a day. Otherwise they deserve all the culinary superlatives. It is in these dishes, most of all, that the refined knowledge and experience of centuries have crystallized to give the exquisite Persian combinations of meat and poultry with vegetables, fruits, nuts, herbs and spices; combinations which are never overpowering, but in which all the ingredients retain their dignity, enhanced and complemented by each other.

Khoreshtha are, by English standards, stews rather than sauces.[*] An infinite variety of ingredients is used to make them. Meat and poultry are usually cubed or cut into smallish pieces. Vegetables are diced, sliced, or left in larger pieces. Fruits are sliced and cut, nuts

[*] *Faisinjan* (see page 242) – duck or chicken with pomegranate sauce – is also eaten as a *khoresh*.

chopped, and beans soaked beforehand. Fresh herbs are used if possible.

Delicate spices are used in small quantities – the sauces are never hot, peppery or strong. Occasionally, a drop of rose water is added; sweet-and-sour pomegranate juice or sauce is also a favourite flavouring. Sometimes the sauces are coloured brick-red with tomatoes, sometimes rich brown with the pomegranate sauce, green with spinach and herbs, or golden with saffron.

The ingredients are usually sautéed in butter or oil. Then water is added, never very much, and they are left to cook slowly and gently for a long time until the juices and flavours blend and fuse. The sauces are also good prepared a day in advance.

These *khoreshtha* vary slightly from family to family and according to which ingredients are in season. Generally, people are faithful to what they know and what has been passed to them by tradition. In the summer, all the local vegetables find their way into the *khoreshtha*. As they become more scarce, apples and quinces appear, and when they, too, disappear in the winter, their place is taken by nuts and dried fruits.

Since *khoreshtha* contain both meat and vegetables, they can be served at our Western tables as a meal in themselves, accompanied only by plain rice, preferably steamed in the Persian manner (page 403). In modern Iran they are often preceded by an egg dish or *kuku* (the Arab *eggah*) – see pages 199–200.

Spinach and Prune Khoresh

Meat and fruit dishes have recently become popular in the West, particularly in America. In the Middle East, they are a very ancient tradition. Moroccans and Persians excel in the art of those splendid combinations, each family daily repeating the dishes of the past with its own particular and individual variations.

1 onion, finely chopped	Salt and black pepper
Butter or oil	Juice of 1 lemon, or more
500 g (1 lb) lean stewing beef or lamb, cubed	250 g (8 oz) prunes, soaked overnight
½–1 teaspoon ground cinnamon	250 g (8 oz) fresh spinach, washed and chopped
¼ teaspoon grated nutmeg	

In a large saucepan, sauté the onion gently in 2 to 3 tablespoons hot butter or oil until soft and golden. Add the meat and brown all over. Sprinkle with cinnamon and nutmeg, and season to taste with salt and pepper. Add about 600 ml (1 pint) water to cover, and the lemon juice. Bring to the boil, remove any scum and simmer over a low heat for about 1½ hours, or until the meat is nearly tender. Throw in the drained prunes and spinach, and cook for a further 15 to 20 minutes. Add more water if necessary. This should be rather more liquid than a stew. Adjust seasoning and serve with plain cooked rice.

≈ An apple and prune *khoresh* substitutes yellow split peas and apples for the spinach. Add about 60 g (2 oz) split peas to the meat together with the water, and simmer until the peas are soft and the meat is tender. Peel 1 or 2 tart apples. Slice and sauté in butter, then add them to the stew at the same time as the prunes. (You will need fewer prunes for this version, only 90–120 g (3 or 4 oz).) The flavourings are, again, lemon, cinnamon and nutmeg, in about the same quantities.

Apple Khoresh

1 onion, finely chopped	1 teaspoon ground cinnamon
4–5 tablespoons butter or oil	3 tart apples (cooking or eating
500 g (1 lb) lean stewing lamb,	ones)
cubed	Juice of 1 lemon, or more
Salt and black pepper	

Sauté the onion in 2 tablespoons butter or oil in a large saucepan until soft and golden. Add the meat and brown all over. Season to taste with salt and pepper, and sprinkle with cinnamon. Cover with about 600 ml (1 pint) of water. Bring to the boil, remove any scum and simmer gently for 1½ to 2 hours, or until the meat is tender. Add more water during the cooking time if necessary.

Peel, core and slice or chop the apples into largish pieces. Sauté gently in the remainder of the butter or oil until lightly coloured all over. Add to the meat stew with the lemon juice. Cook for a further 5 minutes, or until soft. Do not allow the apples to disintegrate unless you prefer to mash them to a purée with a fork.

Serve with plain rice.

≈ Yellow split peas can be added to the meat stew at the start of cooking for a richer texture, and chicken can be used instead of meat. Bone it before adding the fruit.

Peach Khoresh

Prepare the sauce as in the preceding recipe, using either meat or chicken, and substituting 4 peaches, preferably not quite ripe ones, for the apples. Peel them, remove the stones, and slice them or cut them into largish pieces. Fry in butter and add them to the sauce. Simmer for a further 15 to 20 minutes. Here again, lemon juice and cinnamon are a pleasant flavouring. Some people also like to add about 1 tablespoon sugar.

Rhubarb Khoresh

Butter	¾ teaspoon ground cinnamon or
1 onion, finely chopped	allspice
500 g (1 lb) lean stewing beef,	500 g (1 lb) fresh rhubarb stalks
cubed	Juice of ½ lemon
Salt and black pepper	

Heat 2 tablespoons butter in a large saucepan, and fry the onion until soft and golden. Add the meat and sauté until well browned. Cover with water, season to taste with salt and pepper and add cinnamon or allspice. Bring to the boil and simmer for 1½ to 2 hours, until the meat is very tender.

Trim the rhubarb stalks and cut them into 5-cm (2-inch) lengths. Sauté in 2 tablespoons butter for a few minutes, then sprinkle with lemon juice and cook for a few minutes longer. Add to the meat sauce and simmer for 10 minutes.

Serve with plain white rice.

Aubergine Khoresh

Chicken may be used for this sauce instead of lamb or beef. A courgette sauce is prepared in the same way, using 500 g (1 lb) *whole* courgettes.

2 aubergines, sliced
Salt
1 large onion
Butter or oil
500 g (1 lb) lean stewing beef or
  lamb, cubed
60 g (2 oz) brown lentils or yellow
  split peas, soaked for a few
  hours

Black pepper
½–1 teaspoon turmeric (optional)
½ teaspoon ground cinnamon
  (optional)
¼ teaspoon grated nutmeg
  (optional)
2 tablespoons dried crushed mint
1–2 cloves garlic, crushed

Sprinkle aubergine slices with salt and leave them to drain in a colander for at least 30 minutes to rid them of their bitter juices.

Chop the onion finely and set aside 1 tablespoon to use as a garnish. Fry the remainder in 2 tablespoons butter or oil until soft and golden. Add the meat and brown the cubes on all sides. Add the drained lentils, and cover with water (about 600 ml/1 pint). Season to taste with salt and pepper, and simmer gently for 1½ to 2 hours, until the meat is tender and the lentils are soft. A teaspoon of turmeric may be added if you like for colour, and a little cinnamon and nutmeg may be included for a mild aroma.

Wash the salt off the aubergine slices, pat them dry and sauté in about 2 tablespoons butter or oil until soft and golden. Add them to the stew and cook for 15 minutes longer.

A traditional and very tasty garnish is made by frying the reserved chopped onion in a little butter or oil until soft and golden, then adding dried mint and garlic, and frying for only 1 minute longer.

Serve the sauce in a bowl, garnished with this mixture, as an accompaniment to a large dish of plain, fluffy white rice.

≈ A variation is to add 1 dried lime or the juice of 1 lemon and 250 g (8 oz) skinned and chopped tomatoes or 3–4 tablespoons tomato concentrate.

Khoresh Torsh
Meat and Vegetable Sauce with Dried Fruit

1 large onion, coarsely chopped
3–4 tablespoons oil
500 g (1 lb) lamb, cut into pieces
1 aubergine, cubed
3 tomatoes, skinned and sliced
90 g (3 oz) yellow split peas
2 dried limes, or the juice of ½ lemon
½ teaspoon ginger
1 teaspoon cinnamon
½ teaspoon allspice
¼ teaspoon nutmeg
¼ teaspoon turmeric
Salt and pepper
120–250 g (4–8 oz) dried prunes, apricots (sharp ones) or sour cherries or the scooped out seeds of a pomegranate

Soften the onion in oil, then add the meat and aubergines and fry, stirring, until they colour. Add the rest of the ingredients, cover with water and simmer gently with the lid on for 1 or 2 hours until the meat is very tender.

Breads

❧ ✦ ❧

Khubz

In the Middle East, as in the rest of the world, bread is the staff of life. There are many types of bread, leavened and unleavened, thick and paper-thin, which are normally baked over a metal dome on an open fire or in a charcoal oven. The most common is round, flat and only slightly leavened, with a hollow like an empty pocket running right through it. It is made with various qualities of wheat flour: a coarse flour makes an earthy, dark bread, a refined white one results in a delicate white bread. It is soft. Even the outer crust is not crisp but soft, while the inside is chewy, and good for absorbing sauces.

The religious and superstitious feeling attached to bread is stronger in some Middle Eastern countries than others. To some it is, more than any other food, a direct gift from God. A hungry man will kiss a piece of bread given to him as alms. An invocation to God is murmured before kneading the dough, another before placing it in the oven. A piece of bread found lying on the floor is immediately picked up and respectfully placed on the table.

Although bread is available everywhere in towns, many people still prefer to make their own and send it to be baked in the oven of the local bakery, as is done in the villages. Children rushing through the streets balancing a large wooden tray or a flat wicker basket on their heads are a common daily sight. The trays hold rounds of flattened dough laid on a cloth, and covered by another cloth. At the bakery, the children stand close to the big oven, watching where their bread is put down so as not to lose it among the other loaves. People often mark their loaves with a pinch or brand it with a sign drawn with a stick in order to be able to recognize and claim their own when it comes out of the oven.

Bread is eaten with every meal. Sometimes people break off a piece and double it over to enclose and pick up a morsel of meat or vegetable, or dip it in a sauce or cream salad, holding it delicately between the thumb and the first two fingers. Sometimes it is cut in half and the pocket is filled with hot shish kebab and salads or *ful medames* (page 324). It can also be toasted, or broken into pieces and used as a base for various dishes such as *fata* soup (page 183), *fattoush* salad (page 118), and a few stews. Some people, my father among them, claim that they cannot truly savour sauces or juices, or anything in fact, without a piece of bread.

Many shops and supermarkets in Britain now sell pitta bread and these are available in different shapes (round and oval) and sizes, and with different flours at specialist bakeries.

The bread becomes dry and hard very quickly but it is easy to resuscitate. To do so, moisten slightly with a sprinkling of water and warm up under the grill or in the oven. To keep many loaves hot, put them in the oven packed together in silver foil. Pitta freezes very well. Put loaves in the freezer as fresh as you can get them and transfer them straight from there to the oven or the grill.

Toasted Croûtons and Fried Bread

To make toasted croûtons, open out flat Arab breads (pitta) and put them straight on to the shelves of the hottest oven for about 10 minutes until crisp and brown. Break into small pieces by crumpling in your hands.

Serve in a pile to accompany soup or line the bottom of a salad bowl to absorb the dressing (in which case it becomes pleasantly soft and soggy).

Many dishes called *fatta* (page 321), after the manner of breaking the bread, make use of these croûtons.

Deep-fried pitta bread is as tasty as it is rich. Cut the bread into triangles, open them out and drop into very hot oil. Use this to garnish salads and cold vegetable dishes.

Khubz (Eish Shami)

This is more commonly known in the West as Pitta bread.

15 g (½ oz) fresh yeast or 7 g (¼ oz) dried yeast	500 g (1 lb) strong flour
About 300 ml (½ pint) tepid water	½ teaspoon salt
Sugar	Oil

Dissolve the yeast in about 100 ml (3 fl oz) of the total amount of tepid water. Add a pinch of sugar and leave in a warm place for about 10 minutes, or until it becomes frothy and bubbly.

Sift flour and salt into a warmed mixing bowl. Make a well in the centre and pour in the yeast mixture. Knead well by hand, adding enough of the remaining water to make a firm, soft dough. Knead the dough vigorously in the bowl, or on a floured board or pastry cloth, for about 15 minutes, until it is smooth and elastic, and no longer sticks to your fingers. Knead in 1 or 2 tablespoons oil for a softer bread. Sprinkle the bottom of the bowl with a little oil and roll the ball of dough round and round to grease it all over. This will prevent the surface from becoming dry and crusty. Cover with a dampened cloth and leave in a warm place free of draughts for at least 2 hours, until nearly doubled in size.

Punch the dough down and knead again for a few minutes. Take lumps of dough the size of a large potato or smaller (according to the size of bread you wish to have). Flatten them on a lightly floured board with a dry rolling pin sprinkled with flour, or with the palm of your hand, until about ½ cm (¼ inch) thick. Dust with flour and lay the rounds on a cloth sprinkled with flour. Place them a good distance apart so that they do not touch as they grow considerably. Cover with another lightly floured cloth, and allow to rise again in a warm place.

Preheat the oven set at the maximum temperature for at least 20 minutes, and leave the oiled baking sheets in it for the last 10 minutes to make them as hot as possible. Take care that the oil does not burn.

When the bread has risen again, slip the rounds on to the hot baking sheets, dampen them lightly with cold water to prevent them from browning, and bake for 6 to 10 minutes, by which time the strong yeasty aroma escaping from the oven will be replaced by the rich, earthy aroma characteristic of baking bread – a sign that it is nearly ready.

Do not open the oven during this time.

Remove from the baking sheets as soon as the bread comes out of the oven and cool on wire racks. The bread should be soft and white with a pouch inside.

If your oven does not get hot enough to make a good pouch, make the bread under the grill: put it low enough underneath so that it does not touch the grill (and burn) when it puffs up. Turn as soon as it does and leave only a minute longer.

Put the breads, while still warm, in a plastic bag to keep them soft and pliable until ready to serve.

≈ A very good bread can also be made by replacing ⅓ of the strong flour with wholewheat flour. It is called *baladi* bread.

≈ You can make a savoury bread with the same dough. Brush with olive oil mixed with a few drops of lemon juice and sprinkle with plenty of *zahtar* (page 65) (this is called *mnaquish bi zahtar*), or with sesame seeds or chopped walnuts. Or you may simply like to colour the oil with paprika.

≈ An excellent snack can be made by making a depression in the flattened dough and breaking an egg into it before it goes in the oven. Sprinkle with salt and pepper. The egg will set firm as the bread bakes.

≈ To make olive bread, press black olives, pitted if you like, into the dough.

Khubz Abbas

In Iraq minced meat is mixed into the bread dough before it is baked.

A note in *Recipes from Baghdad* says: 'A vow to make *khubz Abbas* as a thanks offering on the fulfilment of one's wish is generally taken at the time of acute anxiety, such as the illness of a beloved relative. In the event of recovery this savoury bread is prepared in vast quantities. Hot melted butter is also poured over rounds of plain *khubz* which are then sprinkled with sugar. The rounds of bread are arranged in great piles and are distributed in hundreds to the poor.'

Kahk
Savoury Bracelets

Three recipes for '*ka'ak*' are given in the medieval *Kittab al Wusla il al Habib*. Here is a modern recipe. It makes rather a large quantity but they keep for a long time in a box.

1 kg (2 lb) strong flour
60 g (2 oz) fresh yeast or 30 g (1 oz) dried yeast
About 1 teacup tepid water
Pinch of sugar
250 g (8 oz) margarine

1–1½ tablespoons salt (or less)
½–1 tablespoon ground cumin
½–1 tablespoon ground coriander
1 egg, lightly beaten
Sesame seeds

Sift the flour into a large mixing bowl. Dissolve the yeast in a little of the tepid water, add a small pinch of sugar and let it stand in a warm place for about 10 minutes until it begins to bubble. Melt the margarine (used instead of butter as it does not become rancid) and let it cool.

Season the flour with salt, cumin and coriander to taste – I prefer the larger quantity given – mixing them in well. Work in the melted margarine and the yeast mixture. Add enough water, gradually, to make a stiff dough, kneading vigorously. Continue to knead for about 10 minutes.

Take walnut-sized lumps of dough and roll them into thin cigarette shapes about 10 cm (4 inches) long. Bring the ends together and press them firmly against each other to make little bracelets. Paint their tops with lightly beaten egg mixed with 2 tablespoons water, using a pastry brush or a piece of cotton wool. Dip the

436

egg-coated surface in a plate containing sesame seeds. Some will stick.

Place the bracelets on an oiled baking sheet and allow them to rest and rise in a warm place for about 2 hours. Some people allow the dough to rise once in a large bowl covered with a damp cloth before shaping the little bracelets, and then allow it to rise again. Both ways work equally well.

I am told that a good way of knowing when the bracelets are ready for the oven is to put a small lump of dough in a glass of water when it is first made. It will sink to the bottom, but then it will slowly rise again. When this happens, the rest of the dough is ready for baking. (I hasten to add that for some mysterious reason this method does not always work for me, although others swear by it.)

Bake the bracelets in a preheated moderate oven (180°C/350°F/ Mark 4) for 20 minutes, then lower the heat to 150°C (300°F/Mark 2) and bake for 1 hour longer.

Leave to dry out for up to 2 or 3 hours in a slow oven (100°C/225°F/ Mark ¼) until the bracelets are firm and crisp right through and a pale golden colour. Let them cool before you put them in a box.

≈ We sometimes vary our *kahk* by sprinkling with *mahlab* as well as sesame seeds.

≈ Moroccan friends add ½ teaspoon allspice and a pinch of chilli to the dough.

Semit
Bread Rings Covered with Sesame Seeds

Cairo vendors sell these bread rings covered with sesame seeds from large baskets, or sometimes threaded on to long wooden poles. In summer, they cry their wares at the entrances of open-air cinemas, or carry them round the tables and across the rows of chairs, chanting '*Semit! Semit!*' The audience eagerly collect provisions to last them through the performance: rings of *semit*, cheese, salted, grilled melon seeds or *leb*, peanuts and Coca-Colas. They while away the time as they wait for darkness to fall and the film to start by eating and chatting; or they watch the children running up and down the aisles, and dancing on the cinema stage to popular Arab and Greek tunes.

One can make excellent *semit* at home. Make an ordinary bread dough. After its first rising, knead and shape it into large rings about 18 cm (7 inches) in diameter and 2 cm (¾ inch) thick. Brush them with an egg beaten with 2 tablespoons water, and dip them in a bowl of sesame seeds. Arrange on oiled baking sheets. Leave to rise in a warm place until nearly doubled in bulk again. Bake in a preheated hot oven (220°C/425°F/Mark 7) for the first 10 minutes, then reduce the heat to 160°C (325°F/Mark 3), and bake for a further 15 to 20 minutes, or until the rings are golden and sound hollow when tapped.

≈ Other more unusual and more refined types of *semit* are made with a rich dough containing butter, oil and eggs.

≈ *Semit* are often sold with *zahtar* (page 65).

Fatayer bi Semsem
Sweet Sesame Rolls

Bread dough, as for *lahma bi ajeen* (page 152) with 500 g (1 lb) flour
120 g (4 oz) sesame seeds

120 g (4 oz) sugar
8–10 tablespoons light vegetable oil

Divide the dough into 20 small lumps and flatten them out, or roll out thinly on to a floured board and cut into 8-cm (3-inch) rounds with a pastry cutter. Place on greased oven sheets or trays. Mix the rest of the ingredients into a paste and spread over the top of the rounds. Bake in a moderate oven (180°C/350°F/Mark 4) for 15 to 20 minutes or until done.

Tsoureki
Greek Sweet Easter Bread

There are many feast days in the Greek Orthodox Calendar which are felt in the kitchen. Easter is the most important. The date is movable, fixed on the first Sunday following the full moon of the Spring equinox, but generally falling within the first half of April.

Houses are whitewashed and decorated with lilac, clothes are made and new shoes are bought. There is much activity in the kitchen, for the feast also marks the breaking of forty days' Lenten fast and a complete fast on Good Friday. Solemn candle-lit processions are followed by national rejoicing to celebrate the Resurrection. Paschal Lambs are roasted on spits in gardens and open spaces and the innards are used for *mayeritsa* soup which is finished with the favourite egg and lemon mixture. Hard-boiled eggs are dyed red, a colour supposed to have protective powers, and polished with olive oil, and a sweet braided bread is adorned with them.

The following quantities give 3 large breads. You may decorate them with split blanched almonds and sesame or caraway seeds. If you like, place dyed eggs in the braided dough before it is left to rise. To make them, hard-boil for 10 minutes, then leave them in a bright-red food dye until the intensity of the colour is strong enough. Drain, and when they are dry, make them shine by gentle rubbing with a lightly oiled cloth.

30 g (1 oz) dry yeast, equivalent to 60 g (2 oz) fresh yeast	1.5 kg (3.31 lb) flour
	Oil
125 ml (4 fl oz) warm water	1 egg yolk
150 g (5 oz) sugar	Sesame seeds (optional)
250 g (8 oz) butter	Split almonds (optional)
5 eggs	Hard boiled eggs (optional)
425 ml (14 fl oz) warm milk	

Dissolve the yeast in the warm water, adding 1 teaspoon of sugar and leave in a warm place for 10 minutes until it bubbles.

In a large mixing bowl beat sugar and butter to a light cream then beat in the eggs, one at a time. Slowly pour in the warm milk and the yeast mixture, beating well. Add the flour gradually, a little at a time and mixing well, enough to form a soft dough. Knead the dough until it is smooth and elastic (at least 10 minutes by hand), adding flour if it is sticky. Oil the top with your hands, cover with a damp cloth and leave in a warm place. Let it rise for at least an hour until it has doubled in bulk.

Punch it down, knead again, oil the top and let it rise once more. When it has risen a second time, punch down again and divide in nine equal parts. Roll each part into a long strand, pulling to stretch it further. Join three strands together and braid. Do the same with the other strands. Place the braided loaves on well-oiled baking sheets. Brush the loaves with the egg yolk mixed with 1 tablespoon water. Sprinkle with sesame seeds, press in a few split almonds, and push 1 or 2 eggs in the braiding in each loaf if you like.

Set aside to rise in a warm place for 40 minutes.

Meanwhile, preheat the oven to a moderate 190°C (375°F/Mark 5) and bake about 50 minutes or until the loaves are lightly browned and sound hollow when tapped.

Place on a rack to cool.

Puddings, Cakes and Sweets

Halawiyat

In the Middle East the usual conclusion to a meal is a bowl of fruit. The sweet pastries, desserts, jams and preserves which have given the region its reputation for a sweet tooth are made to mark special occasions and for entertaining guests. They are symbols of generosity and friendship, happiness, rejoicing and success. Quantities are made regularly and stored away, ready for the casual caller and the unexpected friend, who by Middle Eastern convention, expects and enjoys a warm, enthusiastic welcome at any time of the day. He will invariably be received, even at an awkward time, with the famous Oriental hospitality, the ingrained courtesy and decorum which have been rooted deeply by centuries of custom. Pastries, jams and preserves will be pressed upon him with a Turkish coffee.

Besides spontaneous calls, there are special occasions when visiting is obligatory. A new arrival in town, a return home from a trip, a sickness, a death, a birth, a circumcision, a wedding, and the innumerable Muslim festivals, the *mûlids*, all set the cake- and pastry-making and eating rituals in motion. Certain occasions call for a particular sweet. Pastries, jams and preserves, sweet-scented creams and delicately fragrant fruit salads are made days in advance and served to commemorate or celebrate an event, as symbols of joy or sadness. They are often beautifully coloured and decorated.

Muslim festivals always seem to be in progress. They sometimes last for as long as ten days – ten days of continuous merry-making. Nearly every week brings some excitement and has some saint to be honoured, some memory to be cherished or some rite to be performed. The first ten days of the sacred Moharram, the opening month of the year, are holy. The passion play of Hasan and Hoseyn follows, performed in reverence to the memory of the martyr Hoseyn. In the second month, caravans of pilgrims returning from Mecca are welcomed with a picnic celebration. In the third month comes the Rabi el Awal or Mûlid el Nabi, the festival of the Prophet's birth. Then come the Mûlid el Bulak, the feast of the Lady Zeinab and the feast of the 'miraculous ascent', the visit to Paradise. After the great fast of Ramadan follow the Id es-Saghir and the visiting of cemeteries. Then there is the procession of Kisweh, of the Holy Carpet, and that of the Mahmal, the Ark of the Covenant.

In Egypt, many of the festivals are not based on either the Muhammadan or the Coptic religions, but derive from ancient Egyptian pagan rites and customs. People want to enjoy themselves and any occasion is a pretext for fun, for laughter and merry-making, for dancing and singing in the streets, for glass- and fire-eating, for *kara Guz* (the Egyptian Punch and Judy), and for tying coloured papers to bicycle spokes. It is a time for putting on dresses in fabulous *baladi* colours – sugar pinks and oranges, mauves, purples, lilacs, limes, acid greens and scarlets – and for wearing Western pyjamas in the streets. It is also a time for buying, from the street vendors, brilliantly coloured violet, pink and pale green syrups, and sweet pastries made with nuts, honey and sugar, and coloured yellow, pink and green, the colours of joy and happiness.

At one particular festival, the day of the sacrifice of the bride of the Nile (the Bent el Nil), we used to buy a large sugar doll painted in many different colours, with red lips and pink cheeks, and dressed in frilled and pleated multi-coloured tissue and silver papers. To my mother's horror, I once ate the whole doll, licking and chewing it for a month, undressing it and dressing it again after every repast.

For me, sweets are particularly associated with feelings of well-being, warmth and welcome, of giving and receiving, of crowds of people smiling, kissing, hugging and showering hospitality. I remember how hard it was to refuse, when visiting our many relatives and friends, the delicacies and pastries that were literally forced upon us, after our mother had impressed on us that we should not take more than three stuffed vine leaves, two *kahk* and two *ma'amoul* because it was discourteous to be too eager and it would appear that we were not properly fed at home. We learnt to say 'No' a few times before we accepted and even today, after many years in Europe, I find it hard to say 'Yes' the first time when offered a drink or something to eat, and then sadly regret the loss of a longed-for tea or pastry.

Many of the pastries are sold in shops which are famous for their specialities. They are also made at home. Every housewife prides herself on making a perfect *konafa* or the lightest *fila*, and will rarely divulge her secrets of success to anyone but her daughter. Or she *may* give the recipe under pressure, but with one deliberate mistake, so as to ensure failure when a competitor attempts it.

It is customary during periods of general festivity for every house-wife to prepare mountains of assorted pastries on large trays, to be sent to all her sisters and relatives. She duly receives as many in return. On family occasions, relatives and friends come to help the hostess prepare a great variety of dishes days before the party. Sometimes a specialist is called in, a cook who comes to make one or two dishes for which she is famous, and then moves on to another house to make the same dish again. We always knew beforehand if we were to be served Rachèle's *ataïf* or Nabiha's *karabij* or *konafa à la crème*, and we could rejoice for a few days in advance at the thought.

Ever since my parents joined us in Europe, we have been making these specialities ourselves, and we have found them extremely easy to prepare. I am sure that everybody who tries will be able to make them easily and successfully, so I have included them in this chapter with all the old, traditional family sweets.

Fruit

Fruit is plentiful and varied. The market stalls glow with the brilliant colours of bananas, peaches, sweet lemons, mangoes, melons, figs, watermelons, pomegranates, grapes and apricots.

When fruits are in season they are served both at lunch and dinner, piled high on plates or, when it is hot, in large bowls surrounded by ice. Each person dips his fruit in an individual finger bowl of ice-cold water.

Fruits are sometimes served in the Persian manner, grated and mixed with crushed ice and scented water. They are also stewed and sometimes stuffed.

When fresh fruits are not available, jams and compotes, prepared while they were plentiful, are served, as well as stewed or macerated dried fruits. As with all dishes, people have their favourite combinations. Some families put extra apricots or nuts in their dried fruit compote; others prefer scented water to syrup. I have given below the quantities and varieties which are best known. Adapt them to your own taste.

Stuffed Melon

1 large melon	2–3 tablespoons caster sugar
2 ripe peaches, pears or mangoes	1–2 tablespoons lemon juice
A few grapes or stoned cherries, if available	1 tablespoon rose or orange blossom water

Cut a slice off the top of the melon and set aside to use as a lid. Remove the seeds and scoop out as much of the flesh as you can, being careful not to bruise the outer skin. Scoop melon balls out with a rounded scooper, or use a spoon and then cut the chunks into small pieces.

Put the scooped-out melon in a bowl with the peaches, pears or mangoes, peeled and sliced, and the grapes or stoned cherries. Add sugar and lemon juice to taste, sprinkle with rose water or orange blossom water, and mix well.

Return the fruits and juice to the melon shell. Cover with the top slice and chill for about 2 hours before serving. Serve from the melon shell, which can be decorated with flowers stuck into little holes made with a knitting needle, or tied with a bow like an Easter egg.

≈ Another version makes an especially elegant presentation. Pour a fruit jelly into the stuffed melon. Make it with real fresh fruit juice such as orange – dissolve 15 g (½ oz) gelatine in 150 ml (¼ pint) water and add 450 ml (¾ pint) orange juice, beating well; or use a bought jelly. Refrigerate, and when it has set inside the melon you can cut it into slices to serve.

☐ *Arab saying: 'He who fills his stomach with melons is like him who fills it with light – there is* baraka *(a blessing) in them.'*

Grated Apples

In an *Egyptian Dream Book* translated into English by 'a Lady' in 1231, it is said that 'to dream of looking at apples betokens a wedding. To dream of eating apples is a sign of mourning, unless they are very sweet, then it is a sign of a great deal of prosperity in the marriage state.'

Here is a typically Persian way of serving apples or other fruit. It is ideal for a hot summer's day.

6 eating apples
Juice of 1 lemon
3–6 heaped tablespoons icing
   sugar

2 tablespoons rose or orange
   blossom water
3–4 ice cubes, crushed
6 thin slices lemon

Peel and grate the apples into a glass bowl. Squeeze the lemon juice over them to prevent them from discolouring. Add sugar to taste, sprinkle with rose or orange blossom water, and mix lightly. Chill for a few hours.

Just before serving, add the crushed ice. The ice can either be crushed in an electric blender or in a mortar. Decorate with thin slices of lemon and serve.

Turkish Fruit Komposto

A dish of one kind of stewed fruit is always certain to be on the menu of even the humblest café, usually spelled *kompot* in a Frenchified manner. It is the 'bread and butter' dessert, made with fresh fruits when they are in season, dried fruit in the winter.

Although I call them 'stewed', in actual fact fresh fruits, especially, should only be poached, dropped in a very little boiling water or syrup, then simmered gently until they are just tender. They should not be overcooked.

Apples should be simmered in water, with a little sugar added to taste when they are nearly tender. Apricots, plums, cherries and grapes are best simmered in a boiling syrup made of one part sugar to two parts water. Soft fruits such as strawberries, figs, peaches and pears, are simmered in a thicker syrup made of equal volumes of sugar and water.

When making a dried fruit *kompot*, wash the fruits only if necessary. Soak overnight if required. Bring to the boil in the same water and simmer until tender. Add sugar if you must. Dried apricots, prunes, apples, cherries, raisins and figs can all be used. The *kompot* can be flavoured with a stick of cinnamon, a little lemon juice, rose water or orange blossom water. Serve hot or cold, on its own, or accompanied by fresh cream or yoghourt.

Fresh Fruit Compote

This compote can be made with any fresh fruits that are in season, and in various combinations to suit individual taste. I have listed more fruits than are needed for 6 portions. They will not all be in season at the same time, so use those that are available.

2 cooking apples	4 apricots
2 pears	A handful of strawberries or
2 peaches	cherries
4 plums	

SYRUP

Water	Lemon juice
Sugar	

Make a syrup by boiling water with half its volume of sugar and lemon juice to taste, allowing it to simmer for about 10 minutes.

Wash, peel, core and slice all the fruit, and remove stones where necessary. Put the sliced fruit in a large pan with the syrup, bring to the boil gently and simmer for about 15 minutes, or until they are all soft. Chill and serve cold, with thick cream or strained yoghourt.

Quince Compote

1 kg (2 lb) quinces	½ litre (¾ pint) water
250 g (8 oz) sugar	Juice of ½ lemon

Peel and core the quinces, and cut them into thick slices. Put the peels and cores into a thin syrup made by simmering the sugar and water with lemon juice. Cook for 30 minutes, by which time the syrup will have acquired a jelly-like quality. Strain the syrup and return it to the pan. Bring it to the boil again and poach the slices of quince until soft.

Serve hot or cold with thick double cream, whipped cream or yoghourt. This compote is excellent mixed with an apple compote, cooked separately.

Mixed Dried Fruit in Syrup

This dessert is particularly favoured during Ramadan, the month-long fast during which Muslims fast all day and eat only after sunset. All through the hot day the people, hungry and listless, are hardly able to work, and dream of what they would like to eat. At nightfall, when the sky is a cherry red, the cannons boom through the cities to signal the end of the fast and the muezzins sing it out from all the minarets. The silent city suddenly trembles and comes alive with the clatter of spoons and plates, glasses and jugs, and with the sound of relieved hunger and laughter, of music and merry-making.

The longed-for dishes wait on tables, trays and on the floor, piled high with *ful medames*, *falafel* and *bamia*, meat balls, kebabs and stewed fruit.

120 g (4 oz) each of: dried apricots, figs, peaches, prunes and cherries
60 g (2 oz) seedless raisins

60 g (2 oz) each of: blanched almonds, pistachio nuts and pine nuts
Sugar

Wash and soak the dried fruits overnight if necessary. Use a larger proportion of the fruits which you like best. (I use 250 g (8 oz) apricots and no figs.) Put them in a large pan with blanched almonds and, if they are available, pistachios and pine nuts. If using only one kind of nuts, raise the amount to 120 g (4 oz). Cover with water, sweeten to taste, and bring to the boil slowly. Simmer gently until all the fruits are well cooked, at least ½ hour or longer depending on their quality.

Khoshaf
Dried Fruit Salad

A great Middle Eastern favourite in which the fruit is not stewed but macerated. A superb dessert. Various dried fruits may be used, but purists feel that only apricots and raisins should go into this classic dish, together with the nuts and almonds.

500 g (1 lb) dried apricots	60 g (2 oz) pistachio nuts or pine
250 g (8 oz) prunes	nuts
120 g (4 oz) raisins	Sugar
120 g (4 oz) blanched almonds,	1 tablespoon rose water
halved	1 tablespoon orange blossom
	water

Wash the fruits if necessary and put them all in a large bowl. Mix with the nuts and cover with water. Add sugar to taste (from 120 to 250 g/¼ to ½ lb is usual but you need not add any at all), and sprinkle with rose water and orange blossom water. Let the fruits soak for at least 48 hours. The syrup becomes rich with the juices of the fruit and acquires a beautiful golden colour.

≈ A less common variation is to add 120 g (4 oz) each of dried figs and peaches, and a few fresh pomegranate seeds when these are available. Their luminosity brings out the rich orange, mauve and brown of the fruit, and the white and green of the nuts.

≈ Some people dissolve *amardine* (sheets of dried compressed apricot) in the water to thicken and enrich it. 3 soaked apricots put through the food processor with a little water will achieve the same effect.

Apricot Pudding

The use of gelatine is a recent innovation in the Middle East, but this pudding, which was an aunt's speciality, is a favourite of mine and so I feel compelled to include it.

1½ kg (3 lb) dessert apricots or 2	20 g (¾ oz) gelatine (2
large tins (820 g/1 lb 13 oz each)	tablespoons)
apricots, drained	150 ml (¼ pint) hot water or juice
Juice of 2 oranges (150 ml/¼ pint	from the tinned apricots
juice)	Whipped double cream (optional)
Juice of ½ lemon	A few halved apricots and
Caster sugar	chopped almonds or pistachio
	nuts, to decorate

Choose sweet ripe apricots. Remove the stones and turn the apricots into a purée either by rubbing them through a sieve or by putting them in a food processor with the orange and lemon juice. Add caster sugar if required, depending on the sweetness of the fruit, and the gelatine, which has been stirred in a little hot water or fruit juice until completely dissolved. Sieve the mixture and whisk it, or put it in the food processor again and blend until smooth and creamy. Pour into a wetted mould and chill for 3 to 4 hours. It should set very firmly.

To unmould, dip the mould for a few seconds in very hot water and turn out immediately on to a cold serving dish.

Decorate with whipped double cream if you like, and with a few halved apricots and a sprinkling of chopped almonds or pistachios.

Orange Jelly

This is another modern, European-inspired dessert which is nevertheless Oriental.

20 g (¾ oz) gelatine (2 tablespoons)
300 ml (½ pint) water
6 large juicy oranges
1 lemon

2 tablespoons orange blossom water
Caster sugar
2 eating apples, thinly sliced (optional)
A few pistachio nuts, chopped

Stir the gelatine in the water over low heat until it dissolves. Then add the juice of 4 oranges and the lemon, and the orange blossom water. Sweeten to taste.

Peel the remaining 2 oranges, removing as much pith as possible. Slice thinly and halve. Place the half-slices decoratively along the sides of a moistened mould, with a few in the centre to hold them in place. Slices of apple can also be arranged in the centre of the mould at the same time as the orange slices.

Pour the liquid into the mould and chill until firmly set. Turn out on to a serving dish and decorate with little mounds of chopped pistachio nuts.

☐ *Riddle: She is the beautiful daughter of a handsome man. Her beauty is that of the moon. Her children are in her bosom, and her dwelling is high. Who is she?*
Answer: An orange.

Prunes with Cream

This is a popular dessert in which alcohol was sometimes added by Jewish households.

500 g (1 lb) prunes
Boiling tea
1 liqueur glass Cointreau or
   Kirsch
300 ml (½ pint) double cream
   mixed with 150 ml (¼ pint)
   single cream

3 tablespoons caster sugar
   (optional)
A few drops of vanilla essence or a
   packet of vanilla sugar

Wash the prunes if necessary and put them in a bowl. Pour boiling hot tea through a strainer over them to cover and let them soak overnight. They will swell and become very tender. Drain and place them in a serving bowl. Sprinkle with liqueur. (No sugar is required.)

Whip the cream until stiff, and stir in sugar to taste and vanilla. Smother the prunes with cream and chill for a few hours before serving.

≈ Another simple alternative is to simmer the unsoaked prunes in sweet red wine until they are tender.

Prunes Stuffed with Walnuts

Making this dessert of ancient origin was once an arduous task. Soaking the prunes in tea was supposed to make pitting easier but in reality helped only a little. Now that pitted prunes are available the dish becomes really worth doing.

500 g (1 lb) pitted prunes
Same number of walnut halves
300 ml (½ pint), water, or 150 ml
   (¼ pint) each water and red
   wine, or more

300 ml (½ pint) double cream
2 tablespoons caster sugar
1 tablespoon rose water

Make the hole in the prunes a little wider with your finger and stuff each with half a walnut. Put them to simmer in a pan with water or a mixture of water and wine for about ½ hour – adding more if they become too dry – until they are soft. Turn them into a serving bowl and let them cool.

Whip the cream until it thickens and add sugar and rose water.

Pour all over the prunes and chill together before serving. This is even better a day after.

Amardine Cream

This exquisite pudding is traditionally made in Egypt during the period of Ramadan. The sheets of dried and compressed apricots called *amardine* can be found in most Greek and oriental grocers.

Put about 500 g (1 lb) sheets of *amardine* in a bowl and cover with about 1 litre (1¾ pints) water. Let the sheets soak for a few hours, then bring to the boil in the same water and simmer until they are very soft and have practically dissolved. Add sugar to taste if you wish, and cook gently until the mixture thickens into a rich cream. Stir occasionally with a wooden spoon and take care not to let the cream burn. Add a few halved blanched almonds, mix well and pour into a serving bowl. Serve chilled, with whipped cream if you like.

I have found that a delicious cream, similar to the one above, can be made with ordinary dried apricots which are more readily available and much cheaper. Use about 500 g (1 lb) good quality apricots. Soak them overnight in about 600 ml (1 pint) water. The following day, simmer them in the same water until soft. Turn them into a purée either by rubbing them through a sieve or blending them with their cooking water in a food processor. Return to the pan, add sugar to taste and simmer gently, stirring occasionally with a wooden spoon, until thick. Stir in a few slivered almonds, pour into a bowl and serve chilled.

You may also top with a dollop of whipped cream.

Stuffed Apricots

18 fresh dessert or cooking
  apricots
Juice of ½ lemon, or more
250 g (8 oz) sugar, or less if
  apricots are sweet

120 g (4 oz) ground almonds
60 g (2 oz) caster sugar
2 tablespoons rose water

Make a slit in each apricot and remove the stone, taking care not to break the fruit in half. Put the apricots in a large pan with the lemon juice and sugar. Warm the pan slowly, covered, and let the apricots simmer gently in their own juice, turning them and stirring from time to time, and moistening with a few tablespoons of water if necessary. Cook until the apricots are soft and have released their juice to form a syrup with the sugar. Allow to cool.

Make a paste with the ground almonds, caster sugar and rose water, and knead well. Fill the apricots with this paste and serve them cold in individual bowls, with the syrup poured over them. The apricots can also be served warm, in which case they should be returned to the pan and heated gently in the syrup.

≈ A variation is to stuff each apricot with a whole blanched almond instead of the ground almond paste.

Belila

This fragrant dish of whole grain cooked in syrup is given to nursing mothers to enrich their milk. It is generally served to commemorate happy occasions and in the Sephardic community it was offered to visitors to celebrate a baby's first tooth. You can make it with young wheat or with barley. The addition of nuts makes it a grander offering.

500 g (1 lb) wheat or barley, soaked overnight
250 g (8 oz) sugar
A squeeze of lemon

2–3 tablespoons orange blossom or rose water
60 g (2 oz) pistachios, chopped
120 g (4 oz) flaked almonds
30 g (1 oz) pine nuts

Simmer the wheat or barley in plenty of fresh water until it is very tender and the skin begins to open – about 1 hour. Drain. Make a syrup by putting the sugar in a pan with 150 ml (¼ pint) water and the lemon and simmering for about 10 minutes until it thickens enough to coat a spoon. Stir in the flower water then pour over the grain in a serving bowl. Let it cool and garnish with the nuts.

A Few Cream Puddings

The Middle East possesses a wide range of desserts made with ground rice, cornflour or semolina, each with a subtle difference in texture and flavouring. The addition of such delicate flavourings as orange blossom water, rose water, mastic or cinnamon, the incorporation of ground almonds, raisins and nuts, and traditional decorations transform these humble ingredients into exquisitely fragrant Oriental desserts. (It was simpler to give these recipes in teacups because this is how they are measured: the proportion is more important than the exact measure.)

Balouza

1 teacup cornflour
8 teacups water
1–2 teacups sugar, or to taste
½ teacup orange blossom or rose water

½ teacup or more chopped blanched almonds or pistachio nuts

Mix the cornflour to a smooth paste with a little of the water in a large pan. Add the rest of the water and the sugar, and stir vigorously with a wooden spoon until dissolved. Bring to the boil slowly, stirring. Lower the heat and simmer gently, stirring constantly, until the mixture thickens. An asbestos mat will help prevent the pudding from burning. To test if it is ready, dip a spoon in the hot mixture and see if it clings and coats the spoon. Another test is to drop a quarter-teaspoonful on to a cold plate – if it remains a solid little ball and does not flatten out, it is ready.

Stir in orange blossom or rose water and continue to cook for 2 or 3 minutes longer. Add the chopped nuts, stir well and pour into a glass bowl. Chill.

This pudding is like white opaline encrusted with little stones. When it is served it trembles like a jelly. It is customary for an admiring audience to compliment a belly dancer by comparing her tummy to a *balouza*.

Balouza Muhallabia

This is a creamier, less firm version of the plain *balouza* above, made with milk instead of water and without the nuts, which are used as a garnish instead.

Chill the pudding in a large glass bowl or in individual dishes and decorate with chopped blanched almonds or pistachios, or both, making decorative patterns all over the top of the pudding.

≈ This *balouza* is also sometimes flavoured with ½ teaspoon mastic, pounded to a powder with sugar or pulverized in a blender.

☐ *'When I go to my house after a day of labour, the food tastes good to me though it be cheap. Does, then, the richest merchant in the city enjoy his quail and duck and partridges more than I enjoy my bread and dates? And can man be happier than I with my wife, for if there be not love, what pleasure has a man in a woman?'* – Arab wisdom.

Balta *or* Hetalia

A beautiful and delicate dessert, like white blossoms and brown leaves floating in a pure scented stream.

1 recipe balouza

SYRUP

About 1 litre (1½–2 pints) cold water	1 teacup raisins
1 teacup sugar, or more to taste	1 teacup blanched halved almonds
2–3 tablespoons orange blossom or rose water	½ teacup chopped pistachio nuts, if available

Prepare the *balouza* and pour it into a large, moistened, square tray or mould. This will give you a wide thin sheet of *balouza*. Cool and chill in the refrigerator. When it has set firmly cut it into 3-cm (1-inch) squares with a knife.

Prepare the syrup in a very large mixing bowl or two smaller bowls. Pour in water and add sugar and a little orange blossom or rose water. Stir until the sugar has dissolved. (This syrup is not cooked.) Taste again and add sugar if it is not sweet enough, or water if it is too sweet. Stir in raisins, washed if necessary, almonds, and chopped pistachio nuts if available.

Unmould the squares of *balouza* and drop them into the syrup. Stir gently and serve. Serves 10 to 12 people.

Meghlie
Ceremonial Rice Pudding with Aniseed

This pudding is traditionally served to visitors and well-wishers on the birth of a son. It is said that a family will serve it on the birth of a daughter only if they are truly pleased to have one after a succession of four sons. Large amounts are made in expectation of many visitors.

This is a highly aromatic pudding. I recommend it to those who like the flavour of aniseed. As it is strong, serve small portions only.

120 g (4 oz) ground rice
1.3 litres (2¼ pints) water
8 tablespoons sugar
1 teaspoon caraway seed
1 teaspoon fennel seed
1 teaspoon aniseed

Pinch of ground ginger
To decorate: chopped blanched almonds, pistachios, toasted pine nuts, hazelnuts, whichever are available

Mix the ground rice to a smooth paste with some of the cold water. Add sugar, caraway seed, fennel seed and aniseed, and mix well. (The spices can be used in powdered form if more convenient.) Bring the remaining water to the boil in a large saucepan with a pinch of ginger. Add the ground rice paste gradually, stirring vigorously with a wooden spoon. Bring to the boil again, then allow to simmer, stirring occasionally. Cook until it thickens, about 1 hour. Pour into individual serving bowls or a large glass bowl, allow to cool and chill until ready to serve.

Serve decorated generously with patterns of chopped blanched almonds, toasted pine nuts, chopped pistachio nuts and hazelnuts. Use all or any that are available.

□ *Lullaby for a Son**

*After the heat and after the bitterness, and after the sixth of the
   month,*
*After our enemies had rejoiced at her pain and said, 'There is a
   stone in her tummy!'*
The stone is in their heads! And this overwhelms them.
*Go! Oh bearer of the news! Kiss them and tell them, 'She has borne
   a son!'*

* From Maspéro, *Chansons populaires*.

☐ *Lullaby for a New-born Girl**

When they said, 'It's a girl!' – that was a horrible moment.
The honey pudding turned to ashes and the dates became
  scorpions.
When they said, 'It's a girl!', the corner stone of the house crumbled,
And they brought me eggs in their shells and instead
  of butter, water.
The midwife who receives a son deserves a gold coin to make
  earrings.
The midwife who receives a son deserves a gold coin to
  make a ring for her nose.
But you! Oh midwife! Deserve thirty strokes of the stick!
Oh! You who announce a little girl when the censorious are here!

Sholezard
Persian Yellow Rice Pudding

This excellent dish is traditionally served on the anniversary of the death of a member of the Prophet Muhammad's family. Saffron gives it its elegant colour and distinctive taste.

120–150 g (4–5 oz) short-grain pudding rice	60 g (2 oz) blanched almonds, chopped (optional)
¼ teaspoon powdered saffron	1 teaspoon ground cinnamon (optional)
250 g (8 oz) sugar	
1 teaspoon lemon juice	

Wash the rice well. Bring it to the boil in a generous litre (2 pints) water in which you have dissolved the saffron. Simmer gently for about ¾ hour until the rice is soft and swollen. Add a hot syrup made by simmering together the sugar, lemon juice and 150 ml (¼ pint) water. Cook all together for about ½ hour, until much of the liquid has been absorbed.

If you like, stir in some chopped blanched almonds. Allow to cool a little and pour into a glass serving bowl. Chill and serve dusted with a little cinnamon if you wish.

* From Maspéro, *Chansons populaires.*

Muhallabia

This most common of Middle Eastern desserts can be quite regal when properly made. It is a milk cream thickened by cornflour or ground rice (in the old days this was pulverized with pestle and mortar). I have used a mixture of both. If you like your pudding firmer increase the quantity of starch.

2–3 tablespoons cornflour
60 g (2 oz) ground rice
A generous litre (2 pints) milk
90 g (3 oz) sugar, or to taste

2–3 tablespoons orange blossom
or rose water, or a mixture of
the two
Chopped almonds and pistachio
nuts, to decorate

Mix the cornflour and ground rice to a smooth paste with a little of the cold milk. Bring the rest of the milk to the boil with sugar and add the paste gradually, stirring constantly with a wooden spoon. Simmer the mixture gently, stirring constantly but being careful not to scrape the bottom of the pan (the milk may burn slightly at the bottom and if it is scraped it will give a burnt taste to the whole pudding). When you feel a slight resistance to the spoon while stirring, and the mixture coats the back of the spoon, continue to cook and when it thickens a little more add orange blossom or rose water, stir and cook for a further 2 minutes. Remove the pan from the heat, allow to cool slightly, then pour the pudding into a large glass bowl or individual dishes. Chill and serve, decorated with a pattern of chopped almonds and pistachios.

≈ Some people pour a syrup made of honey boiled with water and scented with a little orange blossom water over the cold *muhallabia*.

≈ It can also be decorated with crystallized rose petals or violets, available in many Soho shops.

≈ An unusual and pleasant texture is given by stirring in 120 g (4 oz) ground almonds.

≈ For a stiffer cream increase the amount of ground rice to up to 120 g (4 oz), pour into oiled moulds and turn out just before serving, then decorate with nuts.

≈ When a bowl of *muhallabia* is garnished with little mounds of chopped nuts of different kinds (which can be done in gorgeous patterns) it is so rich that it is called, ironically, 'the dish of the poor' – *keshk el fu'ara*.

☐ *Turkish Sweets**

Of the sweets, some, like the talash tatlisi, a brittle hollow roll which melted in the mouth and was garnished with kaymak, the Turkish cream, have now disappeared entirely. The hurma tatlisi (date sweet), so-called because it had the shape of a ripe date, and both crisp and melting, is also hardly ever seen nowadays. The sweets which are easier to make still survive. Among the desserts made with milk, the most deceptive under its bland appearance is the tavuk gögsü, or breast of chicken. The white flesh of chicken wings was beaten to an absolutely smooth pulp. Not one little solid piece was allowed to remain. The pulp was then cooked with milk, sugar, and a little powdered sahleb root, till it became a thick mass. Poured into a dessert dish, its surface was garnished with powdered cinnamon. Tavuk gögsü had a delicious flavour and when it was properly made the presence of meat was quite imperceptible. My parents sometimes had it served when they had foreign guests. They always liked it and could hardly believe that they had been eating camouflaged chicken. This dish is also dying out for lack of chefs who can make it. There are of course several simpler milk puddings, which it would take too long to describe in detail. My favourite dessert boasted the name of keshkül-ü-fukara, or bowl of the pauper. Long ago dervishes and holy men, who called themselves 'the paupers of God', went begging food from house to house. Everyone gave a little piece of what they had, until finally the bowl was filled with many different kinds of food. The name was applied to the dessert, which is made from the juice and flesh of coconuts and milk of almonds, because its surface was covered with little mounds of different kinds of very finely chopped nuts. Walnuts, hazel-nuts, almonds, green pistachios, and the snow-white flesh of the coconut formed a pleasing pattern, satisfying both to the eye and to the palate.

Roz bi Haleeb
Rice Pudding

90 g (3 oz) short-grain rice	120 g (4 oz) sugar or to taste
300 ml (½ pint) cold water	1–2 tablespoons orange blossom
¾ litre (1½ pints) milk	or rose water

* From Emine Foat Tugay, *Three Centuries.*

Wash the rice and boil in water for 15 minutes until tender. Add the milk and simmer gently on very low heat for about 45 minutes, stirring constantly to make sure that the bottom does not burn. When it is soft and creamy, add sugar and stir well. Add orange blossom or rose water and cook for 2 minutes longer.

Pour into individual bowls and serve hot or cold.

≈ You may give this pudding a special flavour by stirring in a ¼ teaspoon mastic, pulverized by pounding with sugar.

≈ Garnish if you like with chopped nuts or top with fruits in syrup.

☐ *Riddle: A sparkling sabre, so sweet to pull out. The kings of the East and the kings of the West cannot put it back into its sheath. What is it?*
Answer: Milk.

Ma'mounia
Semolina Porridge

A similar medieval dish made with rice was probably called by this name after the Caliph Ma'moun, who reigned in the tenth century. *Ma'mounia* is now made with semolina and it is eaten for breakfast in Syria. It once oozed with butter but the trend now is to use much less. Make it according to taste – more or less sweet, more or less thick, with water or with milk or with a mixture of both. Measuring in teacups is easier.

90 g (3 oz) butter	1 teacup water
1 teacup semolina	1 teacup sugar
2 teacups milk	Cinnamon

Melt the butter in a large saucepan and stir in the semolina. Bring the milk and water to the boil with sugar and pour gradually over the semolina, stirring constantly over a very low flame. Cook for a few minutes until the mixture has thickened to a cream. Turn off and let it rest for 15 minutes before serving in small bowls sprinkled with cinnamon.

≈ You may serve with thick double or clotted cream and garnish with toasted pine nuts and chopped almonds, hazelnuts and walnuts if you want to make a pudding of this.

Basbousa bil Laban Zabadi
Basbousa with Yoghourt

Unsalted butter
½ teacup blanched almonds
150 ml (¼ pint) yoghourt
1 teacup sugar
1½ teacups semolina

1 teaspoon baking powder
1 tablespoon vanilla sugar or a
  few drops of vanilla essence
Eishta (page 462), clotted cream
  or whipped double cream
  (optional)

SYRUP

1½ teacups sugar
½ teacup water

Juice of ½ lemon

Make a thick syrup by boiling the sugar, water and lemon juice together and simmering until it thickens. Allow to cool, and chill.

Melt 120 g (4 oz) butter. Toast the blanched almonds and chop them finely. Beat the yoghourt with the sugar in a large mixing bowl. Add the butter and all remaining ingredients except the cream, and beat well until thoroughly mixed. Pour into a large, rectangular, buttered baking tray and bake in a fairly hot oven (190°C/375°F/Mark 5) for ½ hour.

Pour the cold syrup over the hot *basbousa* as soon as it comes out of the oven. Cut into lozenge shapes and return to the oven for a further 3 minutes.

Serve soused with the remaining hot melted butter and spread with *eishta*, thick clotted cream or whipped double cream if you like.

Basbousa bil Goz el Hind
Basbousa with Coconut

120 g (4 oz) unsalted butter
2 teacups semolina
1 teacup caster sugar
¾ teacup desiccated coconut

½ teacup plain flour
⅔ teacup milk
1 teaspoon baking powder
A few drops of vanilla essence

SYRUP

1½ teacups sugar
½ teacup water

1 tablespoon lemon juice

Prepare the syrup first by dissolving the sugar in the water and lemon juice and simmering until it is thick enough to coat a spoon (about 7 minutes). Allow to cool, and chill.

Melt the butter in a large saucepan. Add the remaining ingredients and beat well with a wooden spoon until thoroughly mixed. Pour the mixture into a large buttered oven dish or baking tray, making a thin layer. Flatten out as much as possible. Bake in a moderate oven (180°C/350°F/Mark 4) for about ½ hour. Look at it after 20 minutes to see if it has cooked enough. It should be crisp and a rich golden ochre.

Cut into squares or lozenge shapes as soon as it comes out of the oven, and pour the cold syrup over the hot *basbousa*.

Serve hot or cold.

Basbousa is also called *helwa*, which means sweet.

□ *The National Dish Helwa**

One day he was chatting with some friends, when the conversation turned upon the national dish, helwa.

'Some years ago,' said the Khoja, 'I wanted to make some helwa flavoured with almonds, but I could never manage to do it.'

'That is very odd. It is not difficult at all. Why couldn't you make it?' they asked.

'Well,' said he, 'when there was flour in the larder there was no butter, and when there was butter there was no flour.'

'Oh, nonsense, Khoja! Do you mean to say that all that time you could not find both?'

'Ah, yes,' he answered, 'it did happen once, but then you see I was not there to make it.'

Basbousa bil Loz
Basbousa with Almonds

3 teacups water
2 teacups sugar
1 teaspoon lemon juice
1 teacup blanched almonds
⅔ teacup butter

1 teacup semolina
Whole blanched almonds, *eishta* (over) or clotted or whipped double cream

---

* Barnham (trans.), *Tales of Nasr-ed-Din Khoja.*

Bring water, sugar and lemon juice to the boil in a pan. Simmer for a few minutes. Chop the almonds finely and fry them in hot butter together with the semolina until they are a beautiful golden colour. Add the hot syrup slowly, stirring constantly over low heat until the mixture thickens. Remove from the heat and cover the pan. Let it cool a little.

Pour into individual greased moulds and flatten out on top. Unmould and serve warm. Decorate each portion with an almond or a dollop of cream.

Date and Banana Dessert

4–5 bananas
250 g (8 oz) stoned dates, fresh or
dried

300 ml (½ pint) single cream

Arrange alternate layers of thinly sliced bananas and halved dates in a serving bowl. Pour cream all over and chill for a few hours before serving. The cream will soak into the fruit and give it a soft, slightly sticky texture. A delightful way of eating dates.

Eishta
Thick Cream or Middle Eastern Clotted Cream

The rich *gamoussa* (buffaloes' milk) in the Middle East yields, when it is boiled, a thick cream which can be cut with a knife. Every family collects layers of this cream whenever the milk is boiled, to eat with honey or jam or with various pastries. A substitute, though not as splendid, can be made with double cream and milk.

Stir 1 litre (1¾ pints) milk with 300 ml (½ pint) double cream. Pour into a wide, shallow tray. Use the widest available to give the cream the greatest possible surface. Bring to the boil slowly. Simmer gently over very low heat so that it barely trembles for about 1½ hours. Turn off the heat and let stand for 7 hours before putting in the refrigerator. Chill overnight before using. A thick layer of cream will have formed on the surface of the milk. Using a sharp-pointed knife, detach the edges of the cream from the pan and transfer to a flat surface or a large plate. Cut into squares.

Lay the cream flat on pastries or curl it into little rolls.

Ordinary thick clotted cream or whipped double cream is a good substitute for *eishta*.

Atr
Sugar Syrup

A traditional and constant feature of Middle Eastern sweets and pastries is the sugar syrup which is used to make, bathe, soak or sprinkle most of them.

It appears almost everywhere, either thin and liquid, or thick and treacly, scented with rose water or orange blossom water, or both. These distilled essences can be obtained from every Greek and Oriental store.

It is extremely easy to make by boiling water and sugar together with a little lemon juice to prevent it crystallizing.

The usual proportions for a syrup are:

500 g (1 lb) sugar	1–2 tablespoons or more rose
300 ml (½ pint) water	water or orange blossom water,
½–1 tablespoon lemon juice	or both

Bring sugar, water and lemon juice to the boil, remove any scum, lower the heat and simmer gently for 5 to 10 minutes until it has thickened.

Quantities of sugar and water can be varied according to the degree of thickness required for a particular recipe. However, one can also determine the thickness by the length of the cooking time. The longer it is simmered, the more it is reduced, and the thicker it will be. If a syrup is not thick enough, it may be thickened by further cooking and reduction. If it is too thick, it may be thinned by adding a little water, stirring, and simmering a little while longer.

The usual test to determine if a syrup has thickened is to see if it coats a spoon (a metal one). For a greater degree of thickness, one usually feels a slight (but only slight) resistance to the spoon as the syrup is stirred.

It is only when the syrup has cooled that one can know its true degree of thickness (since it always appears thin when hot). If this is not correct, it can be remedied as described above.

The flavourings of rose water or orange blossom water are stirred in at the end of the cooking and simmered for only a minute or two, as prolonged cooking impairs their aroma.

If used heavy-handedly, this syrup will give pastries the rather sweet sickly stickiness which characterizes badly made pastries in pastry shops.

When syrup is used for making pastries, it must be added only when they are already baked, fried or cooked. It is added *very cold* to the *hot* pastries. (The opposite view, that the syrup must be poured hot, has many adherents but we always held firmly to our own.) It is either poured over them as they come out of the oven; or the pastries themselves (such as *luqmat el qadi*) are dropped in for a few minutes, then lifted out, richly saturated. If this condition is not fulfilled, the result will be a failure.

Syrup can be made in advance and stored for many weeks in a glass jar, ready to be used.

Ice Cream

Italian and French ice creams such as *sfogliatella*, *cassata* and the *café liégeois* were made in masterly fashion in Egypt, but specialists excelled in particularly Middle Eastern ice creams – *dondurma kaymakli*, a milk ice cream, and various granitas and fruit ices.

Ice creams were served in every café in Cairo and Alexandria. Groppi's, the café Paradis, the Sans Souci, Cecil's and the Beau Rivage were famous all over the world for their ices. These were made in large, barrel-shaped cylinders with hollow centres filled with a mixture of ice and salt. A rotating pole turned continually, stirring the ice cream so that it froze with a creamy soft texture. Water ices did not need stirring and were only made to freeze.

I have many happy childhood memories of long, hot afternoons spent eating ice creams. In the evenings, for a special family treat, we were taken before or after, or instead of, the cinema to sample ice creams in an open-air café. There, we almost invariably met numerous relatives, friends and acquaintances. Tables were joined together and grew to swallow up the whole café. The fragrance of the ice creams, made with ripe fruit, fresh eggs, butter and thick cream, mingled with the scent of necklaces of threaded fresh jasmine which the fathers and husbands were compelled to buy for their women when the vendors came round the tables, their arms heavy with rows and rows of the little white flowers.

Dondurma Kaymakli
Ice Cream

A brilliantly white milk ice cream made with the starch of a root called *sahlab* (sold under the name of *saleb* in Britain), and flavoured with mastic and orange blossom water. Its creamy, slightly elastic texture comes from the mastic, a hard resin which, when softened with ordinary candle wax, becomes the Middle Eastern chewing gum.

3 tablespoons powdered sahlab or 3 tablespoons cornflour	¼ teaspoon mastic
900 ml (1½ pints) milk	1 tablespoon orange blossom water
300 ml (½ pint) double cream	Chopped pistachio nuts, to decorate
250 g (8 oz) sugar	

Dissolve the powdered *sahlab* or cornflour in a little of the cold milk. Put the rest of the milk in a saucepan together with the cream and sugar, and bring to the boil. Add the cold milk and starch mixture gradually, stirring all the time with a wooden spoon. Crush and pulverize the mastic by pounding with a little granulated sugar, and stir into the milk mixture. If lumpy, a liquidizer will give a smoother texture. Simmer very gently over low heat for about 15 minutes, stirring occasionally.

Add orange blossom water, remove from the heat and beat well with a wooden spoon. Pour into refrigerator trays, cover with foil and freeze in the freezing compartment of the refrigerator, set at the lowest setting. Beat the mixture well by hand three or four times at intervals to break up the ice crystals. Transfer to the non-freezing part of the refrigerator for about 20 minutes before serving. The ice cream should be perfectly smooth and free of crystals. Serve in little bowls, sprinkled with chopped pistachios.

□ *Chewing Mastic Gum**

The Khoja had been invited out, and sat with the guests chatting and chewing mastic gum, when a servant came in to say that dinner was ready.

As the guests rose to go into the dining-room the Khoja took the mastic out of his mouth and stuck it on the tip of his nose.

* Barnham (trans.), *Tales of Nasr-ed-Din Khoja.*

When they asked him why he did it, he answered, 'Poor people should always keep an eye on their property.'

Lemon Granita
A Sorbet

900 ml (1½ pints) water
250 g (8 oz) sugar

1 tablespoon orange blossom
   water
300 ml (½ pint) lemon juice

Boil water and sugar together for a few minutes, stirring until the sugar has dissolved. Cool and add orange blossom water and lemon juice. Stir well and pour into a mould or refrigerator trays. Cover with foil and place in the freezing compartment of the refrigerator, set at the lowest setting. As the ice freezes a little, beat lightly with a fork without removing it from the trays to reduce the size of the crystals. Repeat a few times at ½-hour intervals. Transfer from the freezer to another part of the refrigerator about 20 minutes before serving. Serve, if you like, in scooped-out lemon halves.

Orange Granita
A Sorbet

600 ml (1 pint) orange juice or 475
   ml (¾ pint) orange juice and
   125 ml (¼ pint) lemon juice
900 ml (1½ pints) water

375 g (12 oz) sugar
1 tablespoon orange blossom
   water

Strain the orange juice if you wish – I prefer not to. Add lemon juice if you prefer a slightly acid tang.

Boil water and sugar together for 5 minutes. Remove from the heat and when cool stir in juice and orange blossom water.

Freeze in the same way as the lemon granita above.

A decorative way of serving the ice is to pack it into the scooped-out shells of small oranges.

Pastries

Baklava and Konafa (Kadaif)

Baklava and *konafa*, the grandest of Middle Eastern pastries, are the best known abroad. Unfortunately, they are known at their worst because, as with all food prepared commercially in a foreign country, they are invariably degraded. The cooking fats used are the cheapest, peanuts are sometimes used instead of pistachios and walnuts, and of course few people are in a position to judge if the pastries are well made.

Baklava and *konafa* prepared at home can be entirely different from those found in shops and restaurants. They should be light, crisp and delicate. They may look elaborate but they are so easy and cheap to prepare, and they make an excellent dessert as well as pastries for tea.

Both can be prepared days ahead, stored in the refrigerator and baked on the day they are to be served. They also keep for several days after they have been baked.

Fila pastry, used to make *baklava*, and *konafa*, a shredded dough, can be bought at a few Greek bakeries and shops. I have described *fila* in greater detail on pages 139–41. In the old days in the Middle East, people used to make the pastry doughs at home, but today they are generally bought ready-made.

All over the Middle East, these pastries are present at every party and served at every occasion. No bakery or café could be without them. They even go in donkey carts on those national day-long picnics to the cemeteries, filling the huge baskets alongside the pickles, bread, lettuce and *falafel* (page 86). They are part of the celebrations, the rejoicing with the dead, tokens of love for the departed, who are believed to come out from the tombs to play on the see-saws and swings, and to enjoy the merry dancers, musicians, jugglers and *gala-gala* men with their relatives. *Baklava* and *konafa* are always brought to be shared in these happy reunions.

The pastries are not mentioned in medieval Persian or Arab works, and seem to have made their appearance in the region during the time of the Ottoman Empire.

☐ The 'Poisoned' Dish of Baklawa*

In view of the high character and learning of the Khoja, the notables of Akshehir were anxious that their boys should profit by his instruction and appointed him head master of the town school.

One of the notables whose boy attended the school examined him on the lessons he was preparing. The boy answered his questions so well that his father was highly delighted and, calling a servant, bade him take the Khoja a present of a tray of baklawa.

It came just when lessons were going on, and the Khoja wondered how he could prevent the boys getting hold of it. He himself had been called away suddenly to attend a funeral, so, as he could do nothing with it till he came back, he called up the head boys and said to them, 'I am putting this tray on the shelf here. Be careful you don't touch it. I don't quite trust the man who sent it, for we were once on very bad terms. Most likely there is something poisonous in it, and if so, it is not a mere practical joke, but a crime he has committed. Mind, it is your own look-out; but if you all die of poison, I shall be held responsible, and you will cause me to be thrown into prison and rot there.'

When the Khoja had gone, the head boy, who happened to be his nephew and knew that this was only humbug, took the tray down from the shelf, sent for his particular chums, and tried to persuade them to join him in eating it.

The boys cried, 'No! It is poisoned. The Khoja said so. We won't touch it. We don't want to die.'

'It is a trick, boys. Just see me eat it! Now you can't say anything after that,' said he, as he took some.

'All right,' said the others; 'but what answer are we to give the Khoja?'

'You leave that to me,' said he. 'I have got an answer ready that will quiet him. Now then, let us polish off the baklawa.'

Feeling more at ease, the boys at once set to work and made a clean sweep of it, shouting and laughing as they did so.

That rascal of a nephew must have made his plans ever since the baklawa arrived, for no sooner had they finished eating it than he ran into the Khoja's room, caught hold of a penknife on the inkstand and broke it. At that moment the Khoja came in, and seeing the penknife, asked angrily who had broken it.

* Barnham (trans.), *Tales of Nasr-ed-Din Khoja.*

The boys all pointed to his nephew as the culprit.

'What did you do this for?' he demanded. 'Do you want me to break your bones for you?'

The boy pretended to cry and said, 'My pen broke. I tried to mend it with your penknife and broke the knife. Then I said to myself, "How ever can I look Uncle in the face? What answer can I give him? If he comes in now, he is sure to give me such a thrashing that he will break every bone in my body. It were far better to die than bear such torture," said I. Then I began to think what was the best way to kill myself. I did not think it nice to throw myself down the well, because it would make it smell. Then I suddenly remembered the baklawa on the shelf which you told us was poisoned. I took down the tray, and first I repeated the words of our Creed, "There is no God but God, and Mahomet is his prophet"; then I said good-bye to my schoolfellows and sent word to my father and sister and to my poor mother who had been angry with me. I begged them all to forgive me, and then saying "Bismillah!"† I shut my eyes and swallowed the baklawa. I did not forget to clean up the tray with my fingers, but . . . I am sorry to say . . . such is my unhappy lot . . . I did not die . . . I could not die!'

The poor Khoja, though exasperated at the loss of his favourite dish and the breaking of the penknife, which had been a present from his father, could not help exclaiming, 'My lad, I am amazed that at your age you should have thought of such a clever plan. I am always ready with an answer whatever I am asked, but you will soon be able to give me points. It is quite clear that this is hereditary in our family.'

Baklava

500 g (1 lb) fila (about 24 sheets)
180 g (6 oz) unsalted butter,
  melted

375 g (12 oz) pistachio nuts,
  walnuts or almonds, ground
  or finely chopped

SYRUP

500 g (1 lb) sugar
300 ml (½ pint) water
2 tablespoons lemon juice

2 tablespoons orange blossom
  water

† In the name of God.

Buy fila ready-made in paper-thin sheets (see pages 139–41). You will need a large deep baking dish, round or square, and a pastry brush. Paint the dish (the sides as well) with melted butter. Fit half the number of pastry sheets in the dish one at a time, brushing each sheet with melted butter and overlapping or folding the sides over where necessary.

Spread the nuts of your choice evenly over the sheets of pastry in the dish. Cover with the remaining sheets of pastry, fitting layer after layer, folding the sides where necessary and brushing each sheet, including the top one, with melted butter. Cut diagonally into lozenge shapes with a sharp knife.

Prepare the syrup, unless you have made it earlier. Dissolve the sugar in water and lemon juice and simmer until it thickens enough to coat a spoon. Add orange blossom water and simmer for another 2 minutes. Allow to cool, and chill lightly in the refrigerator.

Bake the *baklava* for ¾ hour in a preheated slow to moderate oven (160°C/325°F/Mark 3), then raise the heat to 220°C (425°F/Mark 7) and bake for 15 minutes longer. The *baklava* should be puffed and a very light golden colour. Remove from the oven and quickly pour the *very cold* syrup over the *hot baklava*.

Important note: this is a rather large quantity of syrup and you may not want to pour all of it on. I sometimes use only half. Leave to cool.

When cold and ready to serve, cut the pieces of pastry out again and place them separately on a serving dish; or turn the whole dish out (by turning it upside down on to a large plate and then turning it over again on the serving dish) and cut out again along the original lines.

≈ A variation called *kul-wa-shkur* ('eat and thank') is filled with coarsely ground almonds mixed with half their weight in sugar. The syrup provides extra sweetness.
≈ In Iraq 1 or 2 teaspoons cinnamon or a cardamom pod, pounded or pulverized in a blender, are added to the chopped nuts.
≈ In Greece they stir a spoonful or two of honey into the syrup.

□ *The Khoja's Feigned Assault on His Wife**

Behold the Khoja in a violent passion with a big stick in his hand rushing after his wife and shouting, 'I have had enough of you! I'll

---

* Barnham (trans.), *Tales of Nasr-ed-Din Khoja.*

give you a good thrashing and pay you for all the annoyance you have caused me these thirty years! Then go and complain to anyone you wish!'

His wife ran along screaming, 'Help! Good people of Mohammed! This fellow has gone mad again. Save, oh, save me!'

There happened to be a wedding at a house close by, and the guests, hearing the cries, rushed out into the street and carried the Khoja's wife into the harem for safety. They then turned to the Khoja and begged him to be quiet, saying, 'We all know how foolish women can be; but is this a nice thing for you to do? – for you are a man of culture and you would be the first to find fault with us if we were to do it.'

While they were trying to pacify him, the owner of the house came forward and said, 'My dear Khoja, let me profit by this unpleasant business to ask you a favour. Of course I was rude not to have invited you to our party. It was partly because it was for young people and I was afraid you might find it tiresome, but I am so delighted to have this opportunity. Please do us the honour of joining us for a while and let us hear what it was all about.'

Though these words served to calm the Khoja to a certain extent, he was still growling with indignation when he entered the house.

As the wedding breakfast was ready, the guests took their places. The Khoja at once began to describe how the quarrel had arisen and kept them all in a roar of laughter.

Just then some baklawa was brought in. The Khoja ate from the dish which was placed before him with the greatest relish, while he continued his description of the quarrel, and then wound up by saying, 'Lucky woman! Lucky rascal! So she took refuge here, did she? If I could have got hold of her I would have given her ear a twist like this,' said he, twirling the dish of baklawa round towards himself, which made the people laugh again.

'Ha! ha!' they said, 'you can't help joking even when you are angry!'

After trying a variety of delicacies, the guests left the table and coffee was served.

The Khoja then made a humorous speech to those present. He said, 'Our good neighbour here gave a wedding party, but did not invite us. As I found out that he was going to have some nice things to eat and especially my favourite dish baklawa, my wife and I thought the matter over and we got up this little pantomime so as to get our share. As for my little wife, I am really very fond of her. God bless her! Would you mind sending someone into the harem to let her know that I am waiting! We must be off, but I hope you will go on enjoying yourselves.'

He left them marvelling at this very ingenious trick he had played them.

Om Ali

This homely Egyptian dessert has become very popular in the last thirty years. People in Cairo say it arrived from the villages of Upper Egypt; but there it is said to be from Cairo. (One theory is that it is a bread pudding introduced by a Miss O'Malley, an Irish mistress of the Khedive Ismail.) People find all sorts of ways of making it – with pancakes, with thinly rolled-out pastry and, more easily, with pieces of bread. I have found that *fila* pastry (page 139) gives the required effect and it is healthier to bake it first rather than fry it in butter as is usual in Egypt.

5–6 sheets of fila (about 90 g/ 3 oz)	1 litre (1¾ pints) milk
120 g (4 oz) raisins or sultanas	300 ml (½ pint) double cream
120–175 g (4–6 oz) mixed flaked almonds, chopped hazelnuts and pistachios	90–120 g (3–4 oz) sugar
	1–2 teaspoons cinnamon (optional)

Put the sheets of *fila* loosely in a slow oven (150°C/300°F/Mark 2) for about 15 minutes or until crisp and brown. Crumple into a baking dish, sprinkling raisins and nuts in between the layers.

Bring the milk and cream to the boil in a saucepan with the sugar and pour over the pastry. Sprinkle with cinnamon and return to the oven. Raise the heat to 240°C (475°F/Mark 9) and bake for about 20 minutes or until the top is browned. Serve very hot.

≈ You may prepare the pudding in individual bowls as they do in Egypt.
≈ A Moroccan version has the boiling milk and cream poured on to crisp, paper-thin pastry broken small and eaten like a cereal with nuts and raisins without further baking.

Konafa
Called Kadaif by Greeks and Turks

The dough for this pastry can also be bought ready-made in Greek shops. It is made of flour and water mixed into a liquid batter and thrown through a sieve on to a hot metal sheet over a small fire. The dough sets in strands which are swept off the sheet very quickly and remain soft. They look like vermicelli or shredded wheat, only soft, white and uncooked.

You can make *konafa* with different fillings. A cream filling, one of walnuts or pistachios and a simple one with a soft cheese are the most common.

500 g (1 lb) konafa pastry	250 g (8 oz) unsalted butter, melted

SYRUP

500 g (1 lb) sugar	2 tablespoons lemon juice
300 ml (½ pint) water	2 tablespoons orange blossom water

CREAM FILLING

6 tablespoons ground rice	1 litre (1¾ pints) milk
4 tablespoons sugar	150 ml (¼ pint) double cream

or WALNUT OR PISTACHIO FILLING

375 g (12 oz) pistachios or walnuts, coarsely chopped	1 teaspoon cinnamon (optional)

or CHEESE FILLING

1 kg (2 lb) Ricotta

The quantities for the syrup make a rather large amount. If you do not like your pastries too sweet you can halve them. Prepare the syrup by stirring the sugar, water and lemon juice over moderate heat, then simmering until it thickens and coats a spoon. Stir in orange blossom water and cook for 2 minutes longer. Cool and chill lightly in the refrigerator. Prepare either of the following fillings.

Cream filling: mix ground rice and sugar to a smooth paste with ½ cup milk. Boil the rest of the milk and add the ground rice paste slowly, stirring vigorously. Simmer, stirring, until very thick. Then allow to cool, add cream and mix well.

Walnut or pistachio filling: mix the chopped nuts with the cinnamon.

Cheese filling: work the cheese with a fork or with your hands.

Put the *konafa* pastry in a large bowl. Pull out and separate the strands as much as possible with your fingers so that they do not stick together too much. Pour melted butter over them and work it in very thoroughly with your fingers, pulling the shreds and mixing so that each one is entirely coated with butter. Put half the pastry in a large, deep oven dish. Spread the filling over it evenly and cover with the rest of the pastry, evening it out and flattening it with the palm of your hand.

Bake in a preheated slow to moderate oven (160°C/325°F/Mark 3) for 1 hour, then in a hot oven (220°C/425°F/Mark 7) for only 10 to 15 minutes longer, until it is a light golden colour. Remove from the oven and immediately pour the *cold* syrup over the *hot konafa*.

Serve hot or cold.

≈ *Konafa* can also be made into small, individual rolled pastries. This is the form in which they are most commonly sold in pastry shops. The threads of dough are wrapped around a filling of chopped or ground walnuts, chopped pistachios or ground almonds to which a little sugar and some rose water have been added. One way of making them is to lay a flat bundle of threads of dough moistened with melted butter on a clean surface. Lay a flat stick or a wide skewer along it diagonally. Arrange the filling over the stick or skewer, then roll or flap the threads of dough tightly round the stick. Slip the stick out carefully, leaving the filling inside the roll. Arrange the rolls on baking trays and bake as described above. Then pour cold syrup over them as they come out of the oven. Cut into individual portions and serve, preferably cold. One traditional way of baking the rolls is to arrange them in a spiral in a round baking tin.

≈ I have recently heard that in Saudi Arabia *konafa* is filled with sliced bananas.

Ma'amoul
Stuffed Tartlets

Ma'amoul are glorious little stuffed pastries that can have many different shapes and fillings. It is always a thrill to bite into them and to find walnuts, pistachios, almonds or dates. They are an Easter speciality.

An uncle told us of a baking competition organized by a dignitary in Aleppo many years ago. The maker of the best *ma'amoul* would get a prize, the equivalent of about £2, to be paid by the dignitary. Hundreds of *ma'amoul* poured into his house, certainly more than £2 worth, and enough to keep him eating happily for months.

This recipe makes about 40 *ma'amoul*.

500 g (1 lb) plain flour	4–5 tablespoons milk or water
250 g (8 oz) unsalted butter	Date or Nut Filling (below)
2–3 tablespoons orange blossom or rose water	Sifted icing sugar

Sift the flour into a large mixing bowl. Work butter into the flour and mix thoroughly by hand. Add orange blossom or rose water, followed by milk or water – just enough for the dough to hold together – and work until it is soft, malleable and easy to shape.

Take a walnut-sized lump of dough. Roll it into a ball and hollow it out with your thumb. Pinch the sides up to make a pot shape. Fill with either of the two fillings below, then press and pinch the dough back over the filling, making a little ball shape. Place the pastries on a large oven tray. Decorate the tops of the pastries with tweezers or make little dents with a fork. (This will help the icing sugar to cling when they are baked.) Bake in a preheated slow oven (160°C/325°F/ Mark 3) for 20 to 25 minutes. Do not let the pastries become brown. They will become hard and their taste will be spoiled. While they are still warm, they will appear soft and uncooked, but on cooling they will become firm.

When cold, roll them in icing sugar. They will keep for a long time in a tightly closed tin.

A simpler version of this is the *ma'amoul* date roll. For this use only the date filling below. Divide the dough into four parts. Roll out and flatten each part into a rectangle 5 cm (2 inches) wide. Spread the filling over each rectangle thinly and roll up lengthwise into thick sausage shapes. Cut diagonally into 3-cm (1¼-inch) sections. Pinch tops or decorate with a fork so that they will hold the sugar better. Bake as above and, when cold, roll in icing sugar.

Fillings for Ma'amoul

1. Date Filling

Chop 500 g (1 lb) stoneless dates. Put them in a saucepan with about

½ teacup water. Cook over low heat, stirring, until the dates have softened into a practically homogeneous mass. Allow to cool.

2. Nut Filling

375 g (12 oz) walnuts, almonds or
   pistachio nuts, finely chopped
1 teaspoon sugar

1 tablespoon rose water or 1
   teaspoon ground cinnamon

Mix the chopped nuts with sugar. Add rose water if you are using almonds or pistachios, cinnamon if you are using walnuts. Mix well.

Karabij

This sweet consists of small round *ma'amoul* pastries bathed in a brilliant white cream with a very distinctive flavour, called *naatiffe*.

1 recipe Ma'amoul Dough

1 recipe Nut Filling

NAATIFFE CREAM

60–90 g (2–3 oz) Bois de Panama
   (erh halawa or 'soul of the
   sweet', see page 61)
250 g (8 oz) sugar

1 tablespoon lemon juice
1 tablespoon orange blossom
   water
Whites of 3 large eggs

Prepare the *ma'amoul* dough exactly as described in the basic recipe, but leave out rose or orange blossom water, and use water rather than milk to bind. Shape the *ma'amoul* and fill them with nut filling. Do not decorate their tops. Bake as directed and cool.

Prepare the cream. Pulverize or grind the dried white branch of Bois de Panama. Soak it for several hours in ¼ pint water. Transfer to a *large* saucepan together with the soaking water, and boil until the mixture has thickened and is reduced to about a quarter of the original volume. Take care while doing this as the mixture foams and rises considerably. Strain through fine muslin. You will be left with about ¼ small coffee cup.

Heat the sugar with 8 tablespoons (just under 150 ml/¼ pint) water until dissolved. Bring to the boil and add lemon juice. Simmer until thickened. Add the orange blossom water, and remove from the heat. Add the hot solution of Bois de Panama (off the heat, as otherwise it will foam up and overflow), stirring vigorously with a fork. Leave to cool.

Beat the egg whites until very stiff. Add the heavy cold syrup mixture gradually as you would add oil to a mayonnaise, beating vigorously all the time. It will froth and expand.

Dip each *ma'amoul* in this thick, brilliantly white cream, making sure it is well coated. Arrange them in a pyramid in a serving dish and pour the rest of the cream over them.

≈ The following is a cream that a cousin resorts to when Bois de Panama cannot be found: Boil 300 g (10 oz) sugar in 225 ml (8 fl oz) water with 2 tablespoons lemon juice until it has thickened enough to coat a spoon and add 1 tablespoon rose water. Beat an egg white very stiff, stir it into the cold syrup and refrigerate.

Sanbusak bil Loz
Almond Rissoles

These are prepared with the dough given under savoury *sanbusak* on page 133, using a little sugar instead of salt, and a filling of 250 g (8 oz) ground almonds mixed with 175 g (6 oz) caster sugar and 2 tablespoons orange blossom water.

Roll the dough out thinly and cut into rounds with a tumbler. Put a teaspoon of filling in the centre of each round. Fold in half, making a half-moon shape, and pinch and fold the edges firmly in a sort of festoon.

Deep-fry the pastries in hot oil until golden brown, and drain on absorbent paper. Alternatively, paint their tops with lightly beaten egg yolk and bake in a preheated moderate oven (180°C/350°F/Mark 4) for ½ hour until a pale golden colour.

Ghorayebah

These are charming, plain pastries that appear to melt in the mouth and are very simple to make

500 g (1 lb) unsalted butter	Blanched almonds or pistachio
250 g (8 oz) caster sugar	nuts, to decorate
625 g (1¼ lb) plain flour, sifted	

Cream the butter and beat it until it becomes white. Add the sugar gradually, beating constantly for about 5 minutes, or until it is a smooth cream. Stir in flour slowly and knead by hand. Although no liquid is added, this makes a very soft dough. If the dough is too soft, add a little more flour.

There are two traditional shapes for *ghorayebah*. Make walnut-sized balls, flatten one side of them on a baking tray and stick a blanched almond on top of each one. Alternatively, roll the dough into 10-cm- (4-inch-) long sausage shapes about 1 cm (½ inch) thick, and bring the ends together to make bracelets. Decorate the tops with chopped almonds or pistachio nuts. Place the bracelets on baking trays, a little apart as they will spread slightly.

Bake in a slow oven (160°C/325°F/Mark 3) for 20 to 30 minutes. Do not let the *ghorayebah* overcook or go even slightly brown. They must remain very white, and they taste quite differently if they are even slightly browned.

Serve these delicate, light cakes with tea or coffee.

≈ An exquisite variation is to replace 120 g (4 oz) of the flour with 120 g (4 oz) ground hazelnuts.

≈ You may also flavour *ghorayebah* with a grate of nutmeg or a teaspoon of cinnamon or with the seeds of a cardamom pod. I prefer it plain.

Assabih bi Loz
Almond Fingers

These pastries are extremely easy to make and delightfully light. They feature in medieval manuscripts as *lauzinaj*, which were fried and sprinkled with syrup, rose water and chopped pistachios.

250 g (8 oz) fila pastry sheets (see page 139)
90 g (3 oz) unsalted butter, melted
250 g (8 oz) ground almonds

120 g (4 oz) granulated sugar, or to taste
3 tablespoons orange blossom water
Icing sugar, to decorate

Cut the sheets of *fila* into four rectangles and pile together so they do not dry out (see page 140). Brush the centre of each rectangle with melted butter.

Prepare a filling of ground almonds mixed with sugar and orange blossom water.

Put 1 heaped teaspoon filling at one end of each rectangle. Roll up into a cigar shape and fold the longer sides slightly over the filling midway. Place on a buttered baking tray and bake in a preheated slow to moderate oven (160°–180°C/325°–350°F/Mark 3–4) for 20 to 30 minutes, or until slightly coloured.

Serve cold, sprinkled with icing sugar.

≈ You may deep-fry the pastries instead of baking them, in not very hot oil and for only a very short time, until lightly coloured. Drain on absorbent paper and dust with icing sugar. Serve hot or cold.
≈ Other delicious fillings are chopped pistachios flavoured in the same way with sugar and orange blossom water and chopped walnuts mixed with sugar and a tablespoon of ground cinnamon.

Trovados

A Sephardic variation of the Arab *sanbusak bil loz* on page 477. The dough is made with sweet red wine, which gives the pastries an unusual colour and flavour. Like the Arab version, these pastries are stuffed with a mixture of ground almonds and sugar, perfumed with rose and orange blossom water.

DOUGH

625 g (1¼ lb) plain flour
1 tablespoon sugar
250 g (8 oz) unsalted butter or margarine

About 250 ml (½ pint) sweet red wine

FILLING

375 g (12 oz) ground almonds
250 g (8 oz) caster sugar

2 tablespoons rose water

Sift the flour into a bowl. Add sugar and work in butter or margarine. Add wine gradually, working it in quickly, and only enough for the dough to have the consistency of wet sand. Allow to rest for 15 minutes. Mix the filling ingredients together in a bowl.

Roll the dough out thinly and prepare the pastries as in the recipe for *sanbusak*, but only 5 cm (2 inches) wide, putting a teaspoon of filling in each one. Bake in a preheated slow to moderate oven (160°–180°C/325°–350°F/Mark 3–4) for about ½ hour, or until the *trovados* are done and lightly coloured. They will be a soft pink colour and have a faint taste of wine. This recipe makes about 40 *trovados*.

Serve on a wide, shallow dish, sprinkled with syrup – 150 ml (¼ pint) water and a little lemon juice to 250 g (8 oz) sugar).

Ataïf
Arab Pancakes

Ataïf is a sweet dearly loved all over the Middle East, a medieval dish which has remained unchanged to this day. It was particularly favoured by the Caliph Mustakfi of Baghdad in the tenth century, to whom a poem, written by a certain Mahmud ibn Husain al-Kushâjim about the merits of the sweet, was recited at a lavish banquet in honour of the Caliph.

Ataïf are basically pancakes dipped in syrup. Sometimes they are sprinkled with pistachios and eaten with thick cream, sometimes piled high on a platter in a pyramid of alternate layers of *ataïf* and cream. Or they may also be stuffed with chopped walnuts, sugar and cinnamon.

They are eaten as often as possible during festivals and on happy occasions. *Ataïf* is a special sweet of the Id es-Saghir after the fast of Ramadan. It is also a wedding sweet. In Egypt, on the day of betrothal, a string of camels or donkeys brings the bride's furniture and belongings to the house of the bridegroom, while he gives a farewell 'stag' banquet complete with dancers and singers. The young bride has a ritual bath and is then conducted to her new home by a colourful procession headed by buffoons and musicians, dancers, jugglers, sword-swallowers and fire-eaters, and followed by numerous, lavishly decorated donkey carts. The first cart carries a coffee-maker with pots and cups and a fire, making coffee for well-wishers. The second carries makers of *ma'amoul* and trays covered with these pastries to distribute. The third carries pancake-makers, handing out *ataïf* to passers-by.

When the bride arrives at the house, she sits down with her guests to a feast where hundreds of *ataïf* are gleefully consumed.

This was common in the past and is still done in some parts today.

Families nowadays usually buy their *ataïf* ready-made from bakeries, and then stuff them and dip them in syrup. But the batter is easy enough to make at home. Several people I know always make it themselves. None have weights, nor do they measure quantities. They just look at the batter and add more water or more flour if they think it requires it. An aunt who lives in California and who has never ceased to cook in the Oriental manner uses a well-known pancake mix called 'Aunt Jemima', which is very acceptable.

BATTER

15 g (½ oz) fresh yeast or 7 g (¼ oz) dried yeast
1 teaspoon sugar

Scant 2 teacups lukewarm water
2 teacups plain flour

SYRUP

500 g (1 lb) sugar
300 ml (½ pint) water

1 tablespoon lemon juice
1–2 tablespoons orange blossom water

Oil
Whipped double cream or clotted cream

Chopped pistachio nuts or almonds

Dissolve the yeast with 1 teaspoon sugar in ½ teacup of the water. Allow it to stand in a warm place for 10 minutes, or until it begins to bubble. Sift the flour into a large bowl. Add the yeast mixture and work it into the flour. Add the remaining water gradually, stirring constantly, until the batter is smooth. Leave the bowl in a warm place, covered with a cloth, for about 1 hour. The soft, almost liquid batter will rise and become bubbly and a little elastic.

Make a syrup by dissolving the sugar in water with lemon juice and simmering it until it is thick enough to coat the back of a spoon. Stir in orange blossom water and simmer for 2 minutes longer. Allow it to cool, then chill in the refrigerator.

When the batter is ready, dip a piece of cotton wool in oil and rub a heavy frying pan with it so as to grease it with a very thin film of oil. Heat the pan until it is very hot, then reduce the heat and keep it at medium.

Pour half a ladleful of batter into the pan, tilting the pan a little to allow it to spread. It will not spread out too much and will remain in a small, round, fattish shape. (Do not try to spread it out too much.) When the pancake loses its whiteness, becomes bubbly and comes away from the pan easily, lift it out with a palette knife. *Fry one side of the pancake only if you are making stuffed pancakes.* Otherwise, flip it over and cook the other side.

Put the pancakes aside in a pile on a plate. They should be a little thicker and spongier than English pancakes.

The *ataïf* can be eaten flat, as they are. Dip each one in the cold syrup and spread with thick cream. In the Middle East a cream made from buffaloes' milk called *eishta* is used (see page 462). You may, instead, use whipped double cream or clotted cream. Sprinkle chopped pistachios or almonds over the cream. A popular idea for weddings is to spread a teaspoonful of rose petal jam over the cream.

≈ A beautiful way of serving *ataïf* at a party is to make the plain *ataïf*, fry them on both sides, and dip them in syrup as above. Put a layer of *ataïf* on a round serving dish, spread it with *eishta* (no other cream will do) and sprinkle with chopped pistachios or almonds. Repeat several times, making a pyramid, and ending with a layer of cream and nuts.

Stuffed Ataïf

To my taste, the stuffed *ataïf* are the most exquisite ones. When making these, remember to fry one side of the pancakes only (the other side must remain moist so that its edges can be stuck together). Pile them up on a plate as you make them.

1. Ataïf Stuffed with Eishta

Put a tablespoon of *eishta* (page 462) on the unfried side of each pancake. Clotted cream and whipped cream are not suitable in this case, as they would melt and ooze out when fried. An unsalted cheese such as Ricotta, Mozzarella, and even a slightly salted Halumi may be used. Fold it in half and pinch the edges together firmly to seal them, making a half-moon shape and trapping the filling.

Drop each pancake in very hot oil and deep-fry for 2 to 3 minutes until a pale golden colour. Remove with a perforated spoon. Drain well on absorbent paper. Dip the hot pancakes in syrup and serve hot or cold. If you have a very sweet tooth, serve them with the syrup poured over them.

2. Ataïf Stuffed with Nuts

Make a filling of 250 g (8 oz) walnuts, chopped, 3 to 4 tablespoons sugar and 2 teaspoons ground cinnamon. Stuff and deep-fry the pancakes as above and serve in the same syrup.

□ *Arab saying condemning an ostentatious wedding: 'The bride is a frog but the wedding is a cyclone.'*

Eish es Seray *or* Ekmek Kadaif
Palace Bread

A popular sweet of Turkish origin. Some bakeries and cafés always have a tray full of the rich, translucent, golden-ochre bread soaked in honey and syrup. Numerous recipes exist, and of course the quality and taste of the dish depend on the bread and honey used.

Make a thick syrup by boiling 750 g (1½ lb) sugar in 300 ml (½ pint) water and 1 tablespoon lemon juice, and simmering until it thickens. Add between 150 and 300 ml (¼ and ½ pint) honey, preferably a delicate one (Hymettus or acacia), and one or two tablespoons of rose water. Stir well and simmer for 2 minutes longer.

Use a large round white or preferably wholemeal loaf. Cut a round of bread horizontally through the widest part so that after all the crusts are removed it is 1½ to 2 cm (½ to ¾ inch) thick. Dry out in a very low oven until lightly browned. Moisten with water. Pour the syrup into a wide, shallow pan which will hold the whole bread. You can darken the syrup to a deep rich brown (the traditional colour for this sweet) by melting 2 tablespoons sugar in another pan until it is a dark brown caramel and stirring it into the syrup. Bring the syrup to the boil. Place the bread in it and simmer very gently, squashing and pressing it down with a wooden spoon to help it to absorb the syrup better. Cook for about ¾ hour, adding water if it becomes too sticky, until the bread is entirely soaked through and is soft, rich and heavy.

Turn out on to a round serving platter and allow to cool.

Serve spread with a very thick layer of clotted cream or whipped double cream and sprinkled with chopped pistachios. In the Middle East they use the cream called *eishta* (page 462), which is thick enough to be cut with a knife.

Individual square slices of bread can be used in the same way as the large round and simmered until soaked through.

Serve very small portions as *eish es seray* is extremely rich and nobody can eat too much of it.

≈ In the Lebanon the syrup is also scented with the grated zest of an orange.

Siphnopitta

This honey and cheese pie is a Greek Easter-time speciality. They make it in most islands but it is especially renowned in the island of Siphnos. Mizithra, a soft, fresh, unsalted cheese made from sheep's milk, is used there, but a bland, unsalted curd or cream cheese with little fat may be substituted.

250 g (8 oz) butter	4 eggs
250 g (8 oz) flour	125–150 ml (4–5 fl oz) honey
½ teaspoon salt	2 teaspoons cinnamon
500 g (1 lb) curd or cream cheese	

To prepare the crust, work the chilled butter into the flour mixed with salt very lightly with your hands or a pastry blender and gradually add 3–4 tablespoons of water, just enough to make the dough hold together in a soft ball. Handle it no further and chill for about 30 minutes.

Line a deep 25-cm (10-inch) pie pan with the dough. It is easier to pat it in with the palm of your hand. Bake in a preheated medium oven (180°C/350°F/Mark 4) for 10 minutes.

In the meantime make the filling. Mix together cheese, eggs, honey (add less and taste before you add more) and 1 teaspoon cinnamon, and blend well.

Cool the empty baked shell before filling or it will disintegrate. Pour the cheese mixture gently all over the pastry base and return to a preheated moderate oven (190°C/375°F/Mark 5) for about 35 minutes until it is firm and the top golden.

Dust with cinnamon and let it cool before serving.

Sweet Turkish Börek

Ancient recipes call these little pastries *taratir-at-turkman* or 'bonnets of the Turks'. The quantities below make a large number of pastries.

5 egg yolks	5 tablespoons yoghourt
½ teaspoon salt	500 g (1 lb) self-raising flour
3 tablespoons caster sugar	Oil for deep-frying
2 tablespoons brandy	Icing sugar

Place the egg yolks in a large mixing bowl, add salt and beat until thick and lemon-coloured. Add the sugar and brandy, and continue beating. Add the yoghourt and mix well. Sift in the flour, stirring with a wooden spoon to begin with, and then working the dough by hand. Knead on a floured board until the dough blisters, then roll out as thinly as possible with a floured rolling pin. Cut into ribbons about 2 cm (¾ inch) wide, then divide into 8-cm (3-inch) strips. Make a 2-cm- (1-inch-) long slit down the centre of each strip and pull one end through – or tie the strips in knots, which is rather easier.

Fry in deep oil which is not too hot until the pastries are puffed and just golden, turning once. Lift out with a perforated spoon. Drain on absorbent paper and sprinkle with caster sugar.

Sephardic Cakes

Amongst the minority dishes of the Middle East, there are some which are particularly Sephardic Jewish in origin. Besides peculiarities due to their religious dietary laws, such as the use of oil and vegetable cooking fats instead of butter or *samna* (clarified butter), the Jews brought with them their favourite dishes from previous homelands. The main feature of Sephardic cooking as distinct from Middle Eastern cooking is the evidence of Spanish and Portuguese influence.

During the fourteenth and fifteenth centuries, the time of the Inquisition, thousands of Jews left Spain and Portugal after a thousand years of life in the Peninsula. Many headed towards the countries of the Middle East. The local Arab Jews, overwhelmed by their superior intellect, high rank and refined social manners, copied and adopted their language, manners and customs, as well as their dishes. These dishes, similar to those prepared in Spain today – some still bearing Spanish names – are still faithfully prepared by Middle Eastern Jews. Among them are cakes baked specially for the Jewish Passover, made with ground almonds instead of flour. During Passover dried breadcrumbs are not used, nor is the baking tin floured. Instead, fine matzo meal is substituted for both.

These cakes, which are half pudding, half cake, can never fail. If they are undercooked they make a fine dessert with cream. They are too moist ever to be overcooked or to dry up.

Orange and Almond Cake

2 large oranges	250 g (8 oz) sugar
6 eggs	1 teaspoon baking powder
250 g (8 oz) ground almonds	Butter and flour, for cake tin

Wash and boil the oranges (unpeeled) in a little water for nearly 2 hours (or ½ hour in a pressure cooker). Let them cool, then cut them open and remove the pips. Turn the oranges into a pulp by rubbing them through a sieve or by putting them in an electric blender.

Beat the eggs in a large bowl. Add all the other ingredients, mix thoroughly and pour into a buttered and floured cake tin with a removable base if possible. Bake in a preheated moderately hot oven (190°C/375°F/Mark 5) for about 1 hour. If it is still very wet, leave it in the oven for a little longer. Cool in the tin before turning out. This is a very moist cake that may serve as a dessert.

Another Orange and Almond Cake

5 eggs	1 tablespoon grated orange rind
1 teacup sugar	1 tablespoon orange blossom
¾ teacup ground almonds	water
¼ teacup matzo meal or fine dry white breadcrumbs	Butter and flour, for cake tin

Beat the eggs well in a large bowl. Add the remaining ingredients and mix thoroughly. Pour the mixture into a buttered and floured cake tin and bake in a preheated moderate oven (180°C/350°F/Mark 4) for about ¾ hour. Cool in the tin, then turn out.

Chocolate Cake

250 g (8 oz) bitter or plain chocolate	6 eggs, separated
2 tablespoons milk	Butter
120 g (4 oz) ground almonds	Flour
6 tablespoons sugar	Caster sugar, to decorate

Melt the chocolate with the milk in the top of a double saucepan over boiling water. Mix the melted chocolate with the ground almonds, sugar and egg yolks, and beat well. Fold in the stiffly beaten egg whites and pour into a buttered and floured cake tin, preferably one with a removable base. Bake in a preheated moderate oven (180°C/350°F/Mark 4) for about ¾ to 1 hour.

When the cake is cool, turn out and sprinkle the top with caster sugar.

≈ Similar cakes are made with matzo meal or Farina potato flour instead of ground almonds, used in the same proportions.
≈ 60 g (2 oz) coarsely chopped walnuts folded in with the egg whites makes a good variation.

Coconut Cake

6 eggs, separated	1 tablespoon orange blossom or
6 tablespoons sugar	rose water or a few drops of
120 g (4 oz) desiccated coconut	vanilla essence
	Butter
	Flour

FILLING

120 g (4 oz) desiccated coconut	1 tablespoon orange blossom
120 g (4 oz) sugar	water
A drop of lemon juice	300 ml (½ pint) double cream

Beat the egg yolks with sugar until thick and lemon-coloured. Add coconut and flavouring, and mix well. Fold in the stiffly beaten egg whites and pour into a buttered and floured cake tin. Bake in a preheated moderate oven (180°C/350°F/Mark 4) for about 45 minutes. Allow to cool and cut in two layers.

Prepare the filling. Sprinkle the coconut with cold water to moisten it thoroughly. Make a syrup by dissolving the sugar in about 90 ml (3 fl oz) water and a drop of lemon juice. Simmer for about 5 minutes. Add the coconut and simmer for a few minutes longer. The coconut will swell and become creamy. Stir in orange blossom water. This is really a coconut jam.

Whip the cream. Spread half the coconut on the bottom layer of cake and pour all the syrup over it. Put the layers together again and spread the thick whipped cream over the top of the cake. Finish with the rest of the partially drained coconut jam spread over the top.

Hojuelos de Haman

A Sephardic Jewish speciality commemorating the defeat of Haman by Esther and Mordechai. The pastries symbolize Haman's ears and are usually prepared for the feast of Purim. The pastry itself, though authentic, is not particularly exciting, but its shape is. For a tastier pastry I suggest that you try the one given for Turkish sweet *börek* (page 484) instead.

3 eggs	Oil for deep-frying
½ teaspoon salt	Cinnamon sugar or clear honey or
2 tablespoons caster sugar	sugar syrup (page 463)
Just under 375 g (12 oz) plain flour	

Beat the eggs until pale and thick. Add salt, sugar and 3 tablespoons water, and beat well. Sift in enough flour to make a rather soft dough which does not stick to the fingers. Knead until smooth.

Roll the dough out thinly on a lightly floured board. Cut it in half-moon shapes with a pastry cutter. Pinch the centres of the shapes like bow ties and fold the two leaf-like ends up to make 'ears'.

Deep-fry in hot oil until golden, turning the pastries over once. Serve hot or cold, dusted with a mixture of cinnamon and sugar or sprinkled with clear honey diluted with a little water or sugar syrup (page 463).

≈ A variation is to replace 1 or 2 tablespoons water with the same quantity of rose water or orange blossom water, or to replace all three with sweet white or red wine. One or two tablespoons of melted butter may be added to the dough. In this case, use only 1 egg.

Petits Fours

Among Middle Eastern pastries there are some very small delicacies which are easy to prepare in large quantities, and which make excellent *petits fours* to serve at large parties or after dinner with coffee. Several are made with ground almonds and sugar. There are also apricot drops, dates and walnuts stuffed with ground almonds, caramelized hazelnuts, pistachios and walnuts.

Various recipes exist for almond paste. Some date back to medieval times. All are still very popular today. Many are traditionally cut into lozenge shapes: in fact, it is believed that the etymology of the word 'lozenge' is derived from these Arab sweets made with almonds, the word for which is *loz* in Arabic.

On a recent visit to Portugal, I was surprised to find these same little sweets in every bakery and pastry shop, where they are said to be a national speciality. Their Spanish names, such as *mogados* and *maronchinos*, are still used in Middle Eastern Sephardic circles today. The Spanish Sephardic saying, '*A los asnos maronchinos?*' (Does one give *maronchinos* to donkeys?) denotes the high esteem in which these delicacies are held.

Tamr bi Loz
Stuffed Dates

These little delicacies have been part of the European confectionery trade for a long, long time. Could they have come from the Arab world in the Middle Ages?

180 g (6 oz) ground almonds
90 g (3 oz) caster sugar
3–4 tablespoons rose water or
   orange blossom water

500 g (1 lb) dried dates (the
   slightly moist California ones
   are good)

Mix the ground almonds and sugar in a bowl, add just enough rose or orange blossom water to bind them into a firm paste. Put less than you seem to require, for once you start kneading with your hands the oil from the almonds will act as an extra bind. You can always add more as required. Make a slit on one side of each date with a sharp knife and pull out the stone. Press in a small lump of ground almond paste and close the date slightly so as to reveal the filling well.

☐ *Arab proverb: 'A year in which there are plenty of almonds and dates increases prosperity and life.'*

Halawa Tamr
Date Drops

Chop and pound to a paste or put through a food processor an equal quantity of stoned, dried dates (of the moist variety) and shelled walnuts. Roll into small balls and turn to cover in icing sugar.

☐ *The Date-Stones**

The Khoja was eating dates, and his wife noticed that he did not take out the stones.

'It seems to me that you are not taking out the stones,' said she.

'Of course not,' said he. 'When I bought them the greengrocer did not allow for the stones when he weighed the dates. Had he thrown them away, he could not have sold his dates; and as I paid cash down, do you think I am going to throw them into the street? Not I! Whoever told you I was so wasteful? I paid for them, have eaten them and found them very good, so that is enough!'

Orass bi Loz
Almond Drops

These are the simplest to make, and my favourites.

1 teacup ground almonds	Additional icing sugar and halved
1 teacup sifted icing sugar	almonds or pistachio nuts, to
4–6 tablespoons orange blossom	decorate
water	

Mix the ground almonds, icing sugar and enough orange blossom water to make a stiff paste; knead by hand until smooth. Let the paste rest for a few minutes. Wash and dry your hands, and shape the paste into little balls the size of large marbles. Roll them in icing sugar. Decorate if you like with halved almonds or pistachio nuts embedded in the top of the balls. Serve in individual little paper cases.

≈ A variation is to stuff the almond balls with chopped pistachios. This is really superb. Make a little hole in each almond ball with your finger and fill it with chopped pistachios mixed with granulated sugar. Close the hole over the pistachios and shape into a ball again. Roll the balls in icing sugar and place them in small paper cases. Decorate the top of each ball with a whole or half-pistachio which has been stripped of its thin skin to make its greenness apparent.

≈ In Iraq almond paste, coloured yellow with saffron, is flattened in a tray, cut into lozenges and covered with gold paper. Thus adorned

---

* Barnham (trans.), *Tales of Nasr-ed-Din Khoja*.

it is sent to friends by a bride's family to celebrate her wedding. The name *lowzinage* reveals the etymology of the word lozenge.

Kahk bi Loz
Almond Bracelets

Use a paste similar to that given for almond drops above. To 500 g (1 lb) ground almonds mixed with 250 g (8 oz) icing sugar add the white of 1 *small* egg, stiffly beaten (for a paste made with 250 g (8 oz) ground almonds, only half the amount of egg white is necessary. Do not be tempted to add more) and just enough orange blossom water to make a firm, dryish paste.

Knead the paste well, and roll into thin cigarette shapes. Bring the ends together and flatten them, making bracelets the size of small serviette rings. Decorate, if you like, with a few blanched almonds. Alternatively, make little round, flattened ball shapes and stick a blanched almond in the middle. Arrange on well-buttered baking trays on parchment paper.

Bake in a preheated moderate oven (200°C/400°F/Mark 6) for about 10 minutes. The bracelets must not be allowed to colour. They will be soft while hot, but become firm on cooling. Lift carefully.

These almond bracelets are favourites at engagement and wedding parties. They are also traditionally served at the ritual bath of a young bride. My mother went through this ceremony on her wedding day, but today, although it is still common in rural districts, the custom is fast disappearing from modern town weddings.

The bride goes to the public bath accompanied by her female relatives and friends. She walks with a woman at each side, under a canopy of silk borne by four men. Married ladies head the procession, followed by young, unmarried girls. The bride walks behind.

At the bath, she washes in scented water, watched by all the women and girls. A feast follows. While the guests are entertained by female singers, large trays piled high with pastries are passed round. No feast of this type could be without the traditional *kahk bi loz*.

Among the songs sung at the bath, one goes as follows:

'Shimmering, shimmering, little lettuce heart, shimmering!
Oh my little brother, she is white, and her whiteness is tinted
*   with pomegranate!*
Oh my little brother, she is white, and her whiteness is seductive!'

On such occasions the relatives try to assess if the girl will make a good wife and if she will be able to bear children easily. Remarks abound on the width of her hips and the size of her breasts.

☐ *A Persian Tale**

A peasant went into town. As he walked through the bazaar, he came across a confectionery shop with all sorts of brightly coloured confectionery displayed on the street. The owner of the shop sat on the door-step.

The peasant went up to him, pointed two fingers at his eyes and said:

'Hou!'

The confectioner asked him why he had done that.

'I thought you were blind and could not see me!' came the reply.

'But I am not blind!' said the confectioner.

'Then how,' asked the peasant, 'if you can see, can you resist eating your sweets?'

Stuffed Walnuts

120 g (4 oz) ground almonds	20 shelled walnuts
120 g (4 oz) caster sugar	120 g (4 oz) granulated sugar
3 tablespoons or more orange blossom water	

Make a firm paste by mixing the ground almonds, caster sugar and orange blossom water together thoroughly. Add more orange blossom water if necessary, to bind the paste. Squeeze about 1 teaspoon of the paste between two walnut halves. Place these on a cold oiled surface.

Make a little caramel by heating and stirring the granulated sugar until it melts and turns a light brown colour. Pour a little over each

* Christensen, *Contes persans.*

walnut. When it is cold and hard, it will hold the walnut halves together.

Place in little paper cases to serve.

Glazed Nut Clusters

Caramelized almonds, hazelnuts and pistachio nuts were among the range of confectionery sold on the beaches of Alexandria when I was a child. Young vendors paced the sands carrying confections and sweetmeats in large, flat wicker baskets, chanting *'Fresca!'* – a name probably originating from the Italian, meaning 'fresh'. They balanced the baskets on their heads, resting them on a coiled piece of soft cloth, and sometimes carried a second basket perched on one hip and held at the other side by an outstretched hand. Their chant was echoed by that of other vendors singing: *'Casquette, baranet, pantofla, pastillia, chocolat!'* (caps, hats, slippers, pastilles, chocolate), or *'Gazouza, gazouza!'* (lemonade). Some sold salted roasted peanuts and pistachios as well as confectionery, and they gambled for these in games of odds-and-evens with their customers.

To make nut clusters, put about 500 g (1 lb) hazelnuts, almonds or pistachio nuts together in little heaps on an oiled marble slab or on a large oiled plate. Melt 500 g (1 lb) or more granulated sugar over very low heat, stirring constantly. Allow the caramel to become light brown, then pour it over the nut clusters. As it cools, the caramel will harden and hold the nuts together.

Alternatively, and perhaps more simply though less attractively, the nuts or almonds can be thrown into the hot, light brown caramel and stirred until they are all well coated. Pour the whole on to an oiled slab or plate. When it has hardened, crack it into pieces.

A less common variation is to simmer the nuts in honey instead of caramel for ¾ hour until it thickens.

Sesame seeds are also sometimes used in this manner.

Apricotina
Apricot Drops

500 g (8 oz) sharp dried apricots   A few pistachio nuts (optional)
Icing sugar

Wipe the apricots with a damp cloth. Do not soak or wash them as this would make them too moist. Mince or chop them very finely. Add a few tablespoons icing sugar to taste, and knead thoroughly by hand, wetting your hands from time to time to make a smooth, soft, slightly moist paste. Shape into marble-sized balls. Roll them in icing sugar and let them dry overnight. You can dig half a bright green pistachio nut on top to offset the rich orange of the apricots.

≈ A splendid variation is stuffed *apricotina*. Use 1 tablespoon ground almonds or finely chopped pistachios mixed with 1 heaped teaspoon granulated sugar. Make a small hole in the centre of each *apricotina*. Put in a little of the filling, close the hole again and roll in icing sugar.

Rahat Lokum
Turkish Delight

This little sweet epitomizes luxury, pleasure and leisure. No harem film scene could be without it. Most Middle Eastern homes have platefuls lying on little tables in the living room, and in the past these were largely responsible for the extra weight put on by the ladies of the leisured classes.

Luscious *lokum*, some stuffed with fresh cream, others with nuts of various kinds, are made by specialized confectioners famous throughout the Middle East. Unfortunately, their recipes are closely guarded family secrets.

Here is a basic recipe which gives a rather large quantity. Although easy, it does require a certain expertise.

500 g (1 lb) glucose
2½ kg (5½ lb) granulated sugar
375 g (12 oz) cornflour
Juice of 1 lemon
1 teaspoon pulverized mastic
A few drops cochineal or other
   food colouring if desired

3 tablespoons orange blossom
   water or rose water
90–120 g (3–4 oz) almonds or
   pistachios, chopped
Cornflour to dust tray
Icing sugar

Put the glucose and the granulated sugar into a large pan with 600 ml (1 pint) of water. Stir well and bring to the boil, stirring occasionally.

Put the cornflour into another large pan. Add 1½ litres (2½ pints) water gradually, stirring until well mixed. Bring to the boil slowly, stirring all the time, until you have a smooth, creamy white paste. Add this slowly to the hot sugar and water syrup, stirring vigorously so as not to allow lumps to form.

Bring to the boil again and cook, uncovered, over a constant low flame for 3 hours, stirring as often as possible with a wooden spoon. (In the commercial preparation, a mechanical stirrer operates continuously.) If the flame is too high, the bottom of the mixture will tend to caramelize.

The mixture must be cooked until it reaches the right consistency. This takes about 3 hours, and on this depends the success of the recipe. To test if the consistency is right, squeeze a small blob of the mixture between two fingers. *Only when it clings to both fingers as they are drawn apart, making gummed threads, is it ready.* It may then have acquired a warm golden glow.

Add the lemon juice and the flavourings. The mastic should be ground with a little granulated sugar to be successfully pulverized. Add colouring if you wish. Stir vigorously and cook for a few minutes longer. Add the chopped nuts and mix well.

Pour the hot mixture out about 2 cm (1 inch) deep into trays which have been dusted with cornflour to prevent sticking. Flatten it with a knife and leave it to set for at least 24 hours. Then cut into squares with a sharp knife, and roll in sifted icing sugar.

The *lokum* will keep for a long time packed in a box.

≈ For a richer flavour, grape juice is substituted for some of the water.

≈ This is how confectioners make their long *lokums* stuffed with walnuts: 500 g (1 lb) walnut halves are threaded on to 4-foot lengths of strong button thread, the first and the last walnuts tied securely at each end to hold them all firmly. This is dipped into a *lokum* mixture and coated thoroughly. It is then removed, and allowed to cool and set. The process is repeated at least three times with a fresh mixture until the walnuts are well covered. They are then hung up to dry for a few days, and finally rolled in icing sugar.

Jams and Preserves

Murabbiyat

Like the pastries, jams remind me vividly of my childhood, of visiting relatives, of sitting on low sofas surrounded with bright silk cushions, of being enveloped by perfumes, faint and delicate or rich and overpowering.

My father's sisters, whom we visited regularly, were always fragrant with their favourite home-made soaps perfumed with violets, rose water, orange blossom and jasmine. Their homes were intoxicating with the frankincense which they used in every room – *bakhoor el barr*, benzoin or aloes-wood – with musk and ambergris, and the jasmine, orange blossom and rose petals which were left soaking in water in little china or crystal bowls.

Candied orange peel, quince paste, coconut, fig, date, rose, tangerine and strawberry jams would be brought in as soon as we arrived, together with pyramids of little pastries, and accompanied by the tinkling of tiny silver spoons, trembling on their stands like drops on a chandelier. Delicately engraved and inlaid silver trays carried small crystal or silver bowls filled with the shiny jams: orange, brilliantly white, mauve, rich brown, deep rose or sienna red. They were arranged around the spoon stand, next to which was placed a glass of water, ornate with white or gold arabesques.

The trays were brought round to each of us in turn as the coffee was served, for us to savour a spoonful of each jam, or more of our favourite one, with one of the little spoons, which was then dropped discreetly into the glass of water.

At our beautiful Aunt Régine's we would be served the best date jam in existence, our favourite rose jam was made by our gentle Aunt Rahèle, and Camille made an inimitable *wishna. Harosset* and coconut jam were traditionally made for our Passover celebrations by my mother. We ate them all the more rapturously because they appeared so rarely.

Although they can be eaten with bread, these jams and preserves are at their best savoured on their own with black coffee or a glass of ice-cold water, or as a dessert with thick cream.

Tangerine Jam

This magnificent jam makes a delicious dessert if served with thick cream.

1 kg (2 lb) tangerines	1 kg (2 lb) sugar

Cut the tangerines in half and squeeze out the juice. Pour into a bowl and set aside. Remove the thin skins which separate the segments inside the peel. Then simmer the peel in water until soft, say 7 to 10 minutes. Drain well, cover with a fresh portion of cold water and soak for 12 hours or overnight, changing the water once or twice if possible to get rid of all the bitterness.

Drain the peel and put it through the coarse blade of a mincer, or chop it roughly, using a *mezzaluna* chopper if you have one.

Pour the reserved tangerine juice into a large saucepan. Add the sugar and minced or chopped peel; simmer until the syrup is slightly thickened and the juice forms a firm jelly when a drop is left on a cold plate. It takes 15 to 30 minutes. Let the jam cool slightly, then pour it into clean warmed jars and seal tightly.

Clementine Preserve

This must be done with the very tiny clementines. Wash them well and cover with cold water overnight. This gets rid of some of the bitterness of the skin.

Make a syrup by boiling 1 kg (2 lb) sugar and 1 litre (1¾ pints) water. Drain the fruit and prick each all over with a needle (making around 6 holes in each). Drop them into the syrup and simmer for about an hour. Lift them out and when they are cool enough transfer to a clean glass jar. Reduce the syrup very much until it is thick enough to coat a spoon. Let it cool before you pour it over the fruit.

Strawberry Jam

1 kg (2 lb) strawberries, preferably wild ones

1 kg (2 lb) sugar
Juice of ½ lemon (optional)

Hull the strawberries. Wash them only if necessary. Layer strawberries and sugar in a large glass or earthenware bowl, or in a deep china dish. Leave them to macerate for 12 hours or overnight.

Transfer the strawberries and their juice to a large pan and add a little lemon juice if you like. Bring to the boil very slowly, stirring gently with a wooden spoon or shaking the pan lightly, and skimming off the white froth as it rises to the surface. Simmer for 10 to 15 minutes, depending on the ripeness of the fruit. Wild strawberries will require only 5 minutes, sometimes even less.

When the strawberries are soft, lift them out gently with a flat, perforated spoon and pack them into cleaned, heated glass jars. Let the syrup simmer for a little while longer until it has thickened enough to coat the back of a spoon or sets when tested on a cold plate. Pour over the strawberries and, when cool, close the jars tightly as usual.

Naring
Bitter Orange Peel in Syrup

An exquisite preserve which is particularly good made with bitter orange peel. As orange peel keeps well in any tightly closed container in the refrigerator, you can collect it gradually. Choose thin-skinned oranges. Rub lightly with a grater to remove some of their bitterness, then peel in six strips.

1 kg (2 lb) orange peel	1 litre (1¾ pints) water
1 kg (2 lb) sugar	Juice of ½ lemon

Boil the peel in water for about ½ hour, until soft. Drain well and soak in a fresh portion of cold water for a day if using the peel of ordinary oranges, changing the water once or twice if possible. If using bitter orange peel, it should be left to soak for 4 days and the water should be changed twice a day.

If the peel is very pithy, scrape some of the white pith away with a soup spoon, to make it less pasty. Roll the strips of peel up one by one, and thread them on to a thick thread like a necklace to prevent them unrolling. Drop the necklace into a syrup, made by boiling the sugar with water and lemon juice, and simmer for about 1 hour, until the peel has absorbed the syrup thoroughly. Lift out, remove the thread, and drop the peel rolls into a clean glass jar.

If the syrup is not thick enough, boil vigorously to reduce it until it coats the back of a spoon. Cool slightly and pour over the orange peel to cover it completely. Close the jar tightly.

Serve the rolls of peel either with some of their syrup, or rolled in granulated sugar syrup like crystallized fruits.

Dates in Syrup

This preserve must be made with fresh dates – the red or yellow varieties which occasionally appear in Greek shops. They are hard and sour and are called *zaghlouli*. Treated in the following manner, they are totally different from the dried dates with which people in the West are so familiar.

1 kg (2 lb) fresh dates	Juice of ½ lemon
750 g (1½ lb) sugar (or the weight of stoned dates)	3–4 cloves

Peel the dates carefully. Boil them in enough water to cover for about 1 hour, or until they are very soft. Drain them, reserving the water, and remove the stones.

Measure the date liquor and make up to 900 ml (1½ pints) with cold water. Add sugar and lemon juice, and bring to the boil. Simmer for a few minutes, then drop in the dates and cook for a further 20 minutes. Lift the dates out carefully with a flat perforated spoon and put them in a clean glass jar, burying the cloves among them.

Thicken the syrup by allowing it to boil until it coats the back of a spoon or sets when tested on a cold plate. Pour over the dates and close as usual.

≈ These dates are also delicious stuffed with about 90 g (3 oz) chopped, candied orange peel or with 120 g (4 oz) halved blanched almonds. They should be filled as they are stoned, before cooking in the syrup.

Apricot Jam

1 kg (2 lb) fresh cooking apricots	750 g (1½ lb) sugar, or the weight in sugar of stoned apricots

Wash and stone the apricots. Layer them with sugar in a large glass or earthenware bowl and leave overnight to macerate. The following day, pour the contents of the bowl into a large saucepan. Bring to the boil very slowly and simmer gently for about 40 minutes, until the apricots are soft and translucent, and the juice has thickened enough to set when tested on a cold plate. Stir occasionally to prevent the fruit sticking to the bottom of the pan and burning.

Let the jam cool in the pan, then pour into clean glass jars and close as usual.

Apricots in Syrup

Use the same proportions of apricots to sugar as above. Wash and stone the apricots. Bring sugar to the boil with 600 ml (1 pint) water and the juice of ½ lemon, and simmer for a few minutes. Drop in the apricots and cook gently until soft, about 40 minutes. Lift them out carefully with a flat perforated spoon and put them in clean, heated glass jars.

Thicken the syrup considerably by boiling it down until it falls in heavy drops from a spoon. Cool slightly and pour over the fruit, covering it entirely. Close as usual.

Green Walnut Preserve

A delicacy which should be attempted whenever green walnuts are available.

500 g (1 lb) fresh green walnuts, shelled	450 ml (¾ pint) water
	1 tablespoon lemon juice
500 g (1 lb) sugar	2–3 cloves

Skin the walnuts carefully, trying not to break them. Soak them in cold water for 5 to 6 days, changing the water twice a day to remove any bitterness.

Make a syrup by boiling the sugar and water with lemon juice until thickened enough to fall in heavy drops from a spoon. Let the syrup cool, then add the well-drained walnuts. Bring to the boil gently and simmer for ½ hour. Remove the pan from the heat and leave the walnuts submerged in the syrup overnight.

The following day, bring to the boil again and simmer for a further ½ hour. Add cloves, and pour the walnuts and syrup into a large, clean, warmed glass jar. Allow to cool and close as usual.

Pumpkin Slices in Syrup

This Kurdish preserve makes a ready sweet and spoon jam.

1½ kg (3 lb) pumpkin	120 g (4 oz) chopped walnuts or
750 g (1½ lb) sugar	almonds or spooning of clotted
½ litre (¾ pint) water	cream (to garnish)
A squeeze of lemon	

Peel the pumpkin and remove seeds and fibres and cut the flesh into slices. Bring the sugar and water with the lemon juice to a boil in a large saucepan. Drop in the pumpkin and cook for 15 to 20 minutes or until it is tender. Cool before serving garnished with nuts or cream.

The preserve keeps very well in a jar, covered with syrup.

Green Figs in Syrup

1 kg (2 lb) young green figs
875 g (1¾ lb) sugar
600 ml (1 pint) water
Juice of ½ lemon

1 tablespoon orange flower water
or a few drops of vanilla essence
(optional)

Choose small, unblemished, slightly underripe figs. Wash them carefully. You can leave them unpeeled if they have perfect skins. Trim their stems, leaving only a little part.

Boil the sugar and water together with the lemon juice for a few minutes until slightly thickened. Soak the figs in this syrup overnight. The following day, bring to the boil and simmer until the figs are soft. Lift them out with a flat perforated spoon and put them in a clean glass jar. If the syrup is a little thin, reduce it by simmering for a few minutes longer until it is thick enough to coat the back of a spoon. When it is ready it can, if you like, be flavoured with a little orange flower water or vanilla. Pour the syrup over the figs and close as usual.

Dried Fig Jam

1 kg (2 lb) dried figs
750 g (1½ lb) sugar, or to taste
750 ml (1¼ pints) water
Juice of ½ lemon
1 teaspoon ground aniseed

3 tablespoons pine nuts
120 g (4 oz) walnuts, coarsely
chopped
¼ teaspoon pulverized mastic
(optional)

Chop the figs roughly. Boil the sugar and water with the lemon juice for a few minutes, then add the figs and simmer gently until they are soft and impregnated with the syrup, which should have thickened enough to coat the back of a spoon. Stir constantly to avoid burning. Add the aniseed, pine nuts and walnuts, and simmer gently, stirring, for a few minutes longer. Remove from the heat and stir the mastic in very thoroughly. (To be properly pulverized, it must have been pounded with sugar.) Pour into clean, warmed glass jars and close as usual.

Wishna
Sour Black Cherry Jam

A magnificent jam and a great Middle Eastern favourite. Serve as a dessert with thick cream, or plunge a tablespoonful into a glass of iced water, then drink the syrupy water and eat the fruit left at the bottom.

1 kg (2 lb) pitted sour or morello cherries (pitted weight)	1–1.2 kg (2–2½ lb) sugar, or to taste Juice of ½ lemon (optional)

Layer the pitted cherries and sugar in a large glass or earthenware bowl, and leave them to macerate overnight. The following day, pour the cherries and juice into a large pan and bring to the boil very slowly, stirring frequently to prevent them burning. Let the cherries simmer in their own juice for about ½ hour, or until very soft, adding a little water only if necessary. If the syrup is still too thin at the end of the cooking time, remove the cherries carefully to glass jars with a flat perforated spoon and simmer the syrup for a few minutes longer until it coats the back of a spoon. The juice of ½ lemon is sometimes added during the cooking.

Pour into clean, heated glass jars and close as usual.

≈ If sour cherries are not available, you can make a very good, though not, to my taste, as wonderful, jam with ordinary sweet cherries. Prepare them as directed above, using more lemon and less sugar.

≈ Dried sour cherries, available in some Greek and Oriental groceries, also make an excellent jam. Soak them in enough cold water to cover for at least 24 hours. Drain and pit them. Then drop them into a boiling syrup made by simmering 1 kg (2 lb) sugar with 900 ml (1½ pints) water and a little lemon juice for a few minutes. Simmer gently until the cherries are soft, stirring frequently with a wooden spoon to prevent them burning. Lift the cherries out of the syrup with a flat perforated spoon and pack them into clean, heated glass jars. Cover with the syrup, which should be simmered for a while longer until it thickens. Close up as usual.

Harosset

This is my mother's recipe for a traditional Jewish Passover date and raisin paste which, according to tradition, symbolizes the cement used for building and the hope that Jews will continue to build. To the Jews of Egypt, the colour and texture of *harosset* are reminiscent of the rich, red Nile silt.

250 g (8 oz) pitted dates
250 g (8 oz) large sultanas
120 ml (4 fl oz) sweet red Passover
  wine

60 g (2 oz) walnuts, chopped, to
  garnish

Finely chop the dates and raisins. Put them in a bowl with about 1 tumbler water or enough to cover, and leave them to soak overnight. The following day bring them to the boil in the same water and simmer over very low heat, stirring constantly with a wooden spoon to prevent the fruit burning, and squashing it to a smooth, thick paste against the sides of the pan. No sugar is required as the fruit is already sweet enough. You can make the paste even smoother by puréeing it in a food processor. Allow the paste to cool.

Just before serving, add the wine and stir well. Serve in a glass bowl, garnished with chopped walnuts.

≈ If you wish to keep this preserve longer than a few weeks, it is preferable to cook it with about 250 g (8 oz) sugar. This will help it to keep better. Otherwise, store it in a cool place. Add the red wine only just before serving, using just enough for the quantity being served.

≈ You can also vary the amount of walnuts, and mix some of them into the paste.

≈ An excellent variation is made by adding 2 sweet apples, peeled and grated, about 30 g (1 oz) ground almonds, 1 teaspoon ground cinnamon and ½ teaspoon ground mixed spice to the soaked fruits before cooking them.

≈ Another is to add about 250 g (8 oz) chopped dried and pitted cherries and prunes, which should be soaked together with the dates and sultanas. If you do so, reduce the quantity of sultanas by about half.

≈ *Harosset* can be made into a thicker and drier paste by using less water. Allow it to cool and roll it into marble- or walnut-sized balls. Serve sprinkled with ground almonds or walnuts.

Coconut Jam

This fragrant, brilliantly white coconut jam is another of my mother's traditional Passover recipes. Make it at least a day before serving.

500 g (1 lb) desiccated coconut
2 tablespoons orange blossom or
   rose water
500 g (1 lb) sugar

1 tablespoon lemon juice
60 g (2 oz) pistachio nuts or
   blanched almonds, chopped

Put the coconut in a bowl and sprinkle with orange blossom or rose water and a little fresh cold water, fluffing it with your fingers as you do so, until it is just moist. Leave the coconut overnight to absorb the moisture. It will swell and become soft.

Make a thick syrup by simmering the sugar with the lemon juice and 150 ml (¼ pint) water for a few minutes. Add the softened coconut to the hot syrup and bring to the boil again slowly, stirring constantly with a wooden spoon. Remove from the heat as soon as it boils. Overcooking will make the coconut harden and become slightly yellow. It should be a pure, translucent white. Allow to cool. Mix in the nuts, pour into a glass bowl and serve.

If it is not to be used within a day or two, store in a tightly sealed glass jar. Serve as a dessert or to accompany coffee.

Pumpkin Jam

1 large pumpkin
Sugar
1 tablespoon lemon juice

¼ teaspoon mastic
60 g (2 oz) blanched almonds,
   slivered

Peel the pumpkin and discard the seeds. Grate the flesh in thick shreds. Weigh the grated flesh.

Make a syrup with the same weight of sugar as grated pumpkin, half this volume of water, and the lemon juice. Bring to the boil stirring, and simmer gently until the syrup is thick enough to coat a spoon thickly. Stir in the grated pumpkin, and continue to simmer until it is soft and transparent.

Pound the mastic to a powder with a little sugar and mix well with the jam. Cook for a few minutes longer, then stir in the slivered almonds.

Pour into clean, warmed glass jars and close up as usual.

Quince Jam

1 kg (2 lb) quinces   500 g (1 lb) sugar

Peel, quarter and core the quinces, and then slice them. Simmer in a little water until just tender; then remove them carefully with a flat perforated spoon and set aside.

Measure the water left in the pan and make it up to 300 ml (½ pint) with more water. Add the sugar and heat gently, stirring, until the sugar is dissolved. Simmer the syrup gently until it is thick enough to coat the back of a spoon. Return the quince slices to the pan and continue to simmer until they are very soft. Mash them with a wooden spoon and cook for a little while longer, stirring, until the jam thickens.

A more jelly-like jam can be made by tying the peel and cores up in a thin muslin bag, and simmering them in the syrup with the quince slices. In this case, the water should be made up to 600 ml (1 pint) instead of 300 ml (½ pint). Remove the muslin bag before mashing the fruit.

Pour into clean, warmed glass jars and close up as usual.

Quince Paste

1 kg (2 lb) quinces   A few blanched almonds, to
500 g (1 lb) sugar   decorate
Juice of 1 lemon

Wash the quinces and quarter them but do not peel or core them. Boil them with very little water, or steam them for 20 to 30 minutes, until very soft. Rub through a fine sieve.

Heat the sugar and lemon juice with about 150 ml (¼ pint) water, stirring constantly, until the sugar has dissolved. Bring to the boil and simmer for a few minutes to thicken the syrup. Add the quince purée and cook over very low heat, stirring constantly with a wooden spoon, until the paste thickens and comes away from the bottom of the pan.

Turn the paste into a wide, shallow mould or tray and spread it out evenly. Leave it to dry for several days. The drying period can be shortened by placing the tray in a cooling oven several times or in an airing-cupboard.

Store the jelly-like sheets of paste wrapped in grease-proof paper or foil.

Servé with coffee, cut into small squares or triangles, with a blanched almond stuck in the centre of each one.

≈ An interesting variation is to spread a layer of chopped or halved blanched almonds between two layers of paste before it is cooled and dried.

Rose-petal Jam

An exquisitely delicate jam which I have not been able to prepare successfully with the roses from my own garden. The petals remained tough under the tooth, whereas they should offer only a slight resistance.

I have, however, recently been told that certain varieties of rose exist such as the 'wild eglantine' which would be suitable for jam-making. I am therefore giving the recipe for those who are fortunate enough to have a rose which will make a good jam.

500 g (1 lb) fresh rose petals, preferably red	500 g (1 lb) sugar
Juice of 2 or more lemons	2–3 tablespoons rose water (optional)

Pick fresh, mature, red petals. Make sure they have not been sprayed with insecticide. Cut off their white ends. Wash and drain them. Leave them whole if you like, or mince them finely with some of the lemon juice.

Simmer the petals in 600 ml (1 pint) water until tender. It may take only a few minutes or much longer, according to the variety of rose used. Add the sugar and lemon juice, and cook until the syrup thickens – usually about 10 minutes. Add a little rose water if the petals do not have a strong perfume of their own.

Sweet Aubergine Preserve

This has a pleasant bitter-sweet flavour.

1 kg (2 lb) small, thin, long
   aubergines
1 kg (2 lb) sugar

1–2 teaspoons cloves
½ teaspoon ginger (optional)
Juice of ½ lemon

Wash the aubergines. Trim the stem end, leaving a little piece. Cut one or two thin strips of peel so that the vegetables keep their shape while their flesh is exposed better to absorb the syrup. Some people leave them in water (changed daily) for three days to remove excessive bitterness, but it is sufficient to poach them in lightly salted water for 10 to 15 minutes until they soften (you will need to hold them down with a smaller lid) and then to let them drain very well before cooking them in syrup.

In a large saucepan make a syrup by boiling the sugar in about 900 ml (1½ pints) water with the spices and lemon juice. Gently press the juice out of the aubergines and throw them in. Simmer for about an hour until the aubergines are very tender and gorged with syrup. Let them cool before you put them in a jar, and cover them with syrup which should be thick enough to coat a spoon. If it is not, reduce it by boiling fast. If it is too thick or caramelized, add a little water.

≈ If you cannot find small aubergines, you may use large ones cut into cubes. In this case, sprinkle with salt and leave for about an hour, press the juices out gently, rinse and poach in unsalted water before adding to the syrup.

Sherbets and Drinks

Sharbat

The Egyptians have various kinds of sherbets or sweet drinks. The most common kind is merely sugar and water, but very sweet; lemonade is another; a third kind, the most esteemed, is prepared from a hard conserve of violets, made by pounding violet-flowers and then boiling them with sugar. This violet-sherbet is of a green colour. A fourth kind is prepared from mulberries; a fifth from sorrel. There is also a kind of sherbet sold in the streets which is made with raisins, as its name implies; another kind, which is a strong infusion of liquorice-root, and called by the name of that root; a third kind, which is prepared from the fruit of the locust tree, and called in like manner by the name of the fruit. *

I have long been haunted by the cries and songs of the street vendors in Cairo in my childhood. Most often, it was drinks that they were selling, to quench the thirst of passers-by or, as they sometimes chanted, to give them strength and health. As the vendor went by,

* Lane, *Manners and Customs of the Modern Egyptians.*

people would rush down from their flats to drink several glasses as though the thirst for wine of which Omar Khayyam sang could be quenched by the heavenly sherbets. The vendors carried a selection of sherbets in gigantic glass flasks, two at a time, held together by wide straps and balanced on their shoulders. The flasks glowed with brilliantly seductive colours: soft, pale, sugary pink for rose water, pale green for violet juice, warm, rich, dark tamarind and the purple-black of mulberry juice. As they went through the street, the vendors chanted their traditional, irresistible calls of *'Arasous!'* and *'Tamarhindi!'*, accompanied by the tinkling of little bells and the clanking of the metal cups which they carried with them.

Water-vendors, too, had a large clientèle. They carried their water in large earthenware jars, whose porous surface helped to keep the water cool by its constant evaporation. The water-vendor has a powerful position in Middle Eastern folklore. A story is told of the vendor who, greedy of power, established himself by a desert road, displaying cool and curvy earthenware jars. As a thirsty traveller approached and asked for a drink, the vendor would take a very long time to reply, then he would point to a jar. When the traveller approached the jar, the vendor would snap: 'Not that one! The one next to it!' Then, as the unfortunate man took this one up to his lips, he would be sworn at again: 'Not that one, you fool! That one, I said!' This would go on until the poor traveller was on his knees, begging to be allowed to buy a drink. As a protection from this sort of experience, an Arab proverb advises: 'The water of the well is better than the favour of the water-vendor.' However, beggars are never refused water, which is considered the most blessed of alms.

Sherbets are also served at home at all times of the day, and when guests have already had Turkish coffee and it is time to have something else. A fragrant almond drink and a rose syrup were favourites in my home. They were bought ready-made.

In *Manners and Customs of the Modern Egyptians*, E. W. Lane goes on to describe how the sherbet is served.

The sherbet is served in coloured glass cups, generally called *'kullehs'*, containing about three-quarters of a pint; some of which (the more common kind) are ornamented with gilt flowers, etc. The sherbet-cups are placed on a round tray, and covered with a round piece of embroidered silk, or cloth of gold. On the right arm of the person who presents the sherbet is hung a large oblong napkin with a wide embroidered border of gold and coloured silks at each end. This is ostensibly offered for the purpose of wiping the lips after drinking the sherbet, but it is really not so much for use as for display. The lips are seldom or scarcely touched with it.

Although this description was written a hundred years ago, the same customs still go on, as I remember from my own childhood.

Sherberts, or syrups, as they are sometimes called, are very sweet and are meant to be diluted with ice-cold water. A tablespoonful is usually enough for one glass. Use a wooden spoon when stirring. A metal one may give a metal tang to the drink.

To measure a volume of sugar equivalent to that of a liquid is not hard. Pour the liquid into a measuring jug. Measure how far up the jug it comes, then pour it into a saucepan. Wipe the jug clean, and pour sugar into it until it reaches the same level as the fluid did.

Orange Syrup

This is rather sweet, as syrups are apt to be, particularly if compared to orange juice or orange squash, but to my taste, delightful. Use the smallish, slightly acid oranges with thin skins.

Wash the oranges and squeeze them in the usual manner, removing the pips. Strain the juice if you like – I prefer not to. 10 oranges will yield about 600 ml (1 pint) juice. Add sugar, between 1 and 1½ times the volume of juice, according to taste, and stir briskly until the sugar is completely dissolved. Use an electric blender to achieve this if you have one.

Pour the sweetened juice into a saucepan, add the juice of ½ lemon, and bring slowly to the boil. Remove from the heat as soon as it reaches boiling point. Cool and pour into thoroughly washed and dried bottles.

≈ If you wish to store the syrup for a long time, here is a traditional method for preserving it. Grate the rind of 1 or 2 oranges, then squeeze it through a piece of fine muslin. Float a teaspoon of this oily 'zest' at the top of each bottle. It will act as a perfect protection. Before starting the bottle, remove the oily crust with the point of a knife.

Serve diluted with ice-cold water.

Milk of Almonds

The proportions for this excellent syrup vary according to taste. Here is one recipe.

250 g (8 oz) ground almonds
900 ml (1½ pints) water
1 kg (2 lb) sugar, or more

1 tablespoon cornflour (optional)
2 tablespoons orange blossom
    water

Put the ground almonds in a thin muslin cloth or bag. Tie it at the top, leaving a lot of free space inside for the ground almonds to move freely.

Soak the ground almonds in the water in a large bowl for about 1 hour, rubbing, squeezing and shaking the muslin with both your hands at intervals. Allow the water to penetrate the almonds and soak them, then squeeze it out again, taking with it the milk of almonds, beautifully white and fragrant.

When you feel that the almonds have given out as much 'milk' as possible, squeeze them dry. Pour the almond milk into a saucepan, add sugar and bring to the boil slowly, stirring until the sugar has dissolved. *Use 1 kg (2 lb) sugar at least if the syrup is being made to last.* Simmer gently until the syrup thickens enough to coat the back of a spoon.

Some people like to add a tablespoon of cornflour diluted in a little water, stirring it in gradually, then allow the syrup to simmer and thicken even further. But I do not feel that this is necessary.

Two minutes before removing the pan from the heat, perfume the syrup with orange blossom water. Allow to cool, pour into clean, dry bottles and close tightly.

Serve diluted with ice-cold water.

≈ A few apricot kernels (shells removed), ground and mixed with the almonds will give the drink a special taste.

Rose Water Syrup

500 g (1 lb) sugar
300 ml (½ pint) water
1 tablespoon lemon juice

2 teaspoons red food colouring
60 ml (2 fl oz) rose water

Make a thick sugar syrup by simmering the sugar, water and lemon juice together slowly, stirring, until it coats the back of a spoon. Add the colouring and stir well. Then stir in the rose water and simmer for 1 or 2 minutes longer. Allow to cool and pour into a clean, dry bottle. Close tightly.

To serve, dilute with ice-cold water.

Mulberry Syrup

Pick very ripe, black mulberries. Extract their juice by putting them in a thin muslin bag and squeezing them tightly. Alternatively, squash them with a wooden spoon through a hair sieve. Measure the volume of juice in a measuring jug and pour it into an enamelled pan. Add double the volume of sugar and a tablespoon of lemon juice per 300 ml (½ pint) juice, and bring to the boil slowly, stirring constantly. Simmer gently, stirring occasionally, until the syrup thickens and coats the back of a spoon. Skim off any froth as it rises to the surface. Let the syrup cool and pour it into thoroughly washed and dried bottles. To serve, dilute about 1 tablespoon of syrup in a glass of iced water.

Apricot Drink

Soak dried apricots or *amardine* in a little water for several hours. Put through a blender and dilute with more water. Add sugar to taste if required.

Tamarind

In Egypt, this dark, thick, rich, sweet-and-sour syrup was usually bought ready-made. It was diluted with ice-cold water to make a superb and refreshing drink, and also used in small quantities as a flavouring for stews and other dishes like stuffed leeks (page 382). The syrup is also very common and extremely popular in Italy, where it is sold by chemists. I have not yet been able to find it in London in its syrup form, but dried, cinnamon-coloured tamarind pods are sold in many Indian shops under the name of *imli* or sometimes *tamarindo*, usually cracked open and with their seeds removed. They require preliminary cleaning and careful washing (as they are often gritty) before lengthy soaking. The syrup made from these is not as dark as that made from the pods in the Middle East.

500 g (1 lb) tamarind pods
500 g–1 kg (1–2 lb) sugar, or more

Clean and wash the pods thoroughly. Soak overnight in 1 litre (1¾ pints) cold water. They will become very soft. Rub the pods through a fine sieve, squashing them with a wooden spoon. Hard seeds and fibres will be left behind. Sieve the pulp back into the soaking water. Now strain the diluted pulp through a muslin cloth into a saucepan, squeezing the pulp as much as possible with your hands. Add 500 g (1 lb) sugar if you like a sour tamarind, increase the amount if you prefer a sweeter one. (Add the larger quantity if the syrup is to last.) Bring to the boil slowly, stirring constantly until the sugar has dissolved, and simmer gently until the syrup thickens. Cool and pour into clean, dry bottles. Close tightly.

Sekanjabin

A Persian vinegar and sugar syrup. The proportions for this refreshing drink, in which one can detect a similarity to the English mint sauce for lamb, vary from one family to another.

600 ml (1 pint) water
1 kg (2 lb) sugar

300 ml (½ pint) white wine vinegar
6 sprigs fresh mint

Bring the water to the boil with sugar, stirring constantly until the sugar has dissolved. Add the vinegar and simmer for 20 minutes longer. Remove from the heat and submerge the sprigs of mint in the syrup. The flavour of the mint will penetrate the syrup as it cools. Serve diluted in ice-cold water.

≈ Sometimes a little peeled, grated cucumber is added to the drink.

☐ *Riddle: What is sweeter than honey?*
Answer: Free vinegar.

Yoghourt Drink

An excellent and deliciously refreshing drink, called *abdug* by Persians, *ayran* by the Lebanese, and *laban* by others. It is consumed extensively all over the Middle East and particularly in Turkey and Persia, prepared in homes and cafés, and sold by street vendors.

600 ml (1 pint) yoghourt
475–600 ml (¾–1 pint) cold water
Salt

1–3 tablespoons dried crushed mint, or to taste (optional)

Beat the yoghourt well in a large bowl. Add water and continue to beat vigorously until thoroughly blended together. Use an electric blender if you have one. Season to taste with salt and dried crushed mint if you like.

Serve chilled, preferably with a lump of ice.

Sahlab

An excellent winter drink made with milk and a powdered resin called *sahlab* (*saleb* in Greek).[*]

600 ml (1 pint) milk
1 tablespoon sahlab

2 teaspoons finely chopped pistachios
Ground cinnamon

Heat the milk. Add the powdered *sahlab*, beating vigorously, and cook over very low heat, stirring all the time, until it thickens (about 5 to 10 minutes). Serve in cups, sprinkled with finely chopped pistachios and cinnamon.

≈ As *sahlab* is so expensive, cornflour makes a reasonable substitute. Mix 1½ tablespoons with a little cold milk and stir it into the rest as it cooks.
≈ It is now common to add grated coconut.

[*] This is sometimes available in a hard dry form, in which case it must be pulverized, preferably in an electric grinder.

Zhourat
Infusions

Infusions are extremely popular throughout the Middle East and are recommended as a winter drink, particularly for those suffering from colds. Boiling water is thrown over dried crushed leaves of mint (*mentha viridis*), verbena, sage, sweet basil, sweet marjoram, amber, jasmin, black elder and rose petals. They are drunk very hot, sometimes lightly sweetened.

Kahwa
Turkish Coffee

Coffee first became popular in the Middle East in the Yemen and Saudi Arabia. It was probably transplanted there from Abyssinia, where it grows wild. According to legend, it was particularly favoured by the Yemeni Sufis, who believed that its effects facilitated the performance of their religious ceremonies, hastening mystical raptures. Accordingly, it came to receive a ceremonial character.

Today, the serving and drinking of coffee is still surrounded by tradition and ceremony. Walking past cafés, one cannot help but remark on the almost mystical ecstasy with which coffee-drinking still affects people.

Coffee-drinking is a very important activity in the Middle East. Men spend hours during the long summer nights, and whenever they can during the day, sitting in cafés, sipping coffees one after the other, sometimes accompanied by a *lokum* or pastry, while they sharpen their wits entertaining each other, telling jokes or tales of Goha, setting riddles, and playing charades and *tric-trac* (backgammon).

Business and bargaining are never done without coffee. At home, it is served as soon as visitors arrive, always freshly brewed, usually with freshly roasted and pulverized coffee beans. It is always prepared in small quantities as each visitor arrives, in small, long-handled copper or brass pots called *kanaka* or *ibrik*, holding from one to five cups.

Coffee cups are very small, usually cylindrical. In some countries they have no handles; in others, china cups fit into small metal holders which match the serving tray made of copper, brass or silver. The tray is usually beautifully ornamented. Traditional patterns and Arabic writing (often blessings and words in praise of God) are chiselled into the metal. Sometimes the carvings are inlaid with a thin silver thread.

People have their favourite blends of coffee beans. Mocha beans from the Yemen are popular, so are Brazilian and Kenya beans.

Rules of etiquette are observed in the serving of coffee. A person of high rank is served first, then a person of advanced age. Until a few years ago, men were always served before women, but today in the more Europeanized towns women take precedence.

Since sugar is boiled at the same time as the coffee, guests are always asked their preference – whether they would like sweet (*helou* or *sukkar ziada*), medium (*mazbout*) or unsweetened (*murra*) – and they are served accordingly. In cafés, it is customary for waiters to take thirty orders for coffee at a time, all varying in sweetness, and supposedly never to make a mistake. There is a well-known joke about the waiter who takes an order for a large gathering of inevitably differing tastes, makes them all exactly the same, medium-sweet, brings them all together on a huge tray and hands them round with a show of concentration, saying: '*Helou, mazbout, helou, murra, murra, helou* . . .'

The occasion may determine the amount of sugar added to the coffee. At happy ones, such as weddings and birthdays, the coffee should always be sweet, while at a funeral it should be bitter, without any sugar at all, regardless of the tastes of the people. At deaths it was customary for some families in Cairo to erect huge tents, which stretched right across the narrow streets. The ground was carpeted and filled with gilt chairs and the tents were decorated with sumptuously coloured appliqués. Relatives, friends and passers-by came to pay their respects. They sat on the gilt chairs, solemnly drinking black, unsweetened coffee to the wailing of the professional mourners.

An excellent account of how coffee was made in Egypt in the last century is given by E. W. Lane in *Manners and Customs of the Modern Egyptians*:

In preparing the coffee, the water is first made to boil; the coffee (freshly roasted and powdered) is then put in and stirred; after which the pot is again placed on the fire, once or twice, until the coffee begins to simmer, when it is taken off, and its contents are poured out into the cups while the surface is yet creamy. The Egyptians are excessively fond of pure and strong coffee thus prepared, and very seldom add sugar to it (though some do so when they are unwell) and never milk or cream; but a little cardamom seed is often added to it. It is a common custom, also, to fumigate the cup with the smoke of mastic; and the wealthy sometimes impregnate the coffee with the delicious fragrance of ambergris. The most general mode of doing this is to put about a carat weight of ambergris in a coffee-pot and melt it over a fire; then make the coffee in another pot, in the manner before described, and when it has settled a little, pour it into the pot which contains the ambergris. Some persons make use of the ambergris, for the same purpose in a different way – sticking a piece of it, of the weight of about two carats, in the bottom of the cup, and then pouring in the coffee: a piece of the weight above mentioned will serve for two or three weeks. This mode is often adopted by persons who always like to have the coffee which they themselves drink flavoured with this perfume, and do not give all their visitors the same luxury.

Here is my method.

PER PERSON

1 very heaped teaspoon pulverized coffee	1 heaped teaspoon sugar, or less to taste
	1 small coffee cup water

Although it is more common to boil the water and sugar alone first and then add the coffee, it is customary in my family to put the coffee, sugar and water in the *kanaka* or pot (a small saucepan could be used though it is not as successful), and to bring them to the boil together. By a 'very heaped teaspoon' of coffee I mean, in this case, so heaped that it is more than 2 teaspoons. A level teaspoon of sugar will make a 'medium' coffee.

Bring to the boil. When the froth begins to rise, remove from the heat, stir, and return to the heat until the froth rises again. Then remove, give the pot a little tap against the side of the stove, and repeat once again. Pour immediately into little cups, allowing a little froth (*wesh*) for each cup. (Froth is forced out by making your hand tremble as you serve.) Serve very hot. The grounds will settle at the bottom of the cup. Do not stir them up or drink them.

Try flavouring the coffee with a few drops of orange blossom water, cardamom seeds (called *heil*) or a little cinnamon, adding the flavouring while the coffee is still on the stove.

≈ It is common practice for people in some circles to turn their coffee cups upside down on their saucers when they have finished drinking. As the coffee grounds dribble down the sides of the cup they form a pattern or image from which at least one member of the company can usually read the fortune of the drinker. A friend has a coffee cup which she brought from Egypt and has kept in a cupboard in England for many years now, carefully wrapped in fine tissue paper and rarely disturbed. She is convinced that it bears the protective image of Rab Moshe (Moses) traced out in coffee grounds at the bottom of the cup.

Moroccan Mint Tea

A refreshing infusion of green tea and mint, the preparation of which is considered an art. It is traditionally served in a richly engraved silver pot, and poured from a great height into ornamented glasses. The mint must be of the *mentha viridis* variety. The infusion is sweetened in the teapot.

1½ tablespoons green tea	Lump sugar, to taste (about
Handful of fresh or dried whole	150–180 g/5–6 oz)
mint leaves	

Heat the teapot. Add the tea leaves and pour a little boiling water over them. Swirl round and quickly pour the water out again, taking care not to lose the leaves. Add mint and sugar to taste, and pour in about 1 litre (1½ to 2 pints) boiling water. Allow to infuse for about 5 to 8 minutes, then skim off any mint that has risen to the surface. Taste a little of the tea in a small glass, and add more sugar if necessary.

Serve in glasses.

White Coffee

Put 1 teaspoon orange blossom water in a small coffee cup and pour boiling water over it. Sweeten with sugar if you like. It is a very soothing drink of the Lebanon.

When I was a child in Egypt we used to take to bed a glass of cold water with a few drops of the flower water to make us sleep.

Chai
Tea

Tea is generally drunk strong and black and spices are often added. Make tea in the usual way and put a stick of cinnamon with 3 slices of lemon in the pot. Alternatively add 2 teaspoons aniseed and garnish each cup with finely chopped walnuts.

Chai Hamidh
Lemon Tea

A hot lemon drink is made by breaking open dried limes (*noumi basra*, see page 63) and pouring boiling hot water over them. Strain and sweeten to taste.

Miglee
Spiced Drink

An Arab drink traditionally served to visitors when a baby is born.

Boil 1 litre (1¾ pints) water in a saucepan for 5 minutes with the following spices: 2 cinnamon sticks, 3 cloves, 1 tablespoon aniseed, a 3-cm (1-inch) piece of ginger root cut up, or 1 teaspoon ground ginger.

Let everyone sweeten to taste.

☐ *Someone asked Goha what was his favourite music and he replied, 'The clanging of pots and pans and the tinkling of glasses.'*

Appendix

About Early Culinary Manuals

As early as the eighth century, writings on food were abundant and popular. So much so that the scientist Salih b. Abd al-Quddus, who was to be executed as a heretic, complained bitterly: 'We live amongst animals who roam in search of pastures without seeking to understand. If we write about fish and vegetables we are invested in their eyes with great merit, but truly scientific subjects are for them painful and boring.'

Many early cook-books are mentioned in various works but they have unfortunately been lost to us. Al Nadim, the well-known bibliographer who lived in Baghdad in the tenth century, lists eleven 'Books Composed about Cooked Food' dating from between the eighth to the tenth century and gives the names of their authors.

At the Bodleian Library in Oxford there is a hand-written manuscript of one of the earliest existing Arabic cook-books, copies of which are at the University Library of Helsinki and Topkapi Saray in Istanbul. It is an anonymous work adorned with poems and gastronomic anecdotes about famous men. It was written in the tenth century and is entitled *Kitab al-Tabikh wa-Islah al-Aghdhiya al-Makulat*. It quotes recipes from older books such as those of Ibn al-Masawaih and Ibn al-Mawsili of the early ninth century. In Istanbul there are two manuscript copies of a book called *Kitab al-Atima al-Mu'tada* which was written in the thirteenth century. Two very important books of the same period have received special attention from European scholars. I have featured some of their recipes and will deal with them here at greater length.

A series of articles by Charles Perry from California in *Petits Propos Culinaires* and elsewhere is currently throwing new light on the kind of information to be gleaned from these early sources.

The Kitab al-Tabikh

In 1934 the Iraqi scholar, Dr Daoud Chelebi, discovered two manuscripts written in Baghdad in the year 1226 by a certain Muhammad ibn al-Hassan ibn Muhammad ibn al-Karim al Katib al-Baghdadi, who died in 1239 A. D. Dr Chelebi published it in Mosul with the same title *Kitab al-Tabikh* (Cookery Book). The late Professor A. J. Arberry translated it into English and included it in his article entitled 'A Baghdad Cookery Book' published in the periodical *Islamic Culture* 13 (1939).

In the preface, after the obligatory praises to God and some remarks on the importance of good wholesome eating, the author says he wrote the book for his own use and for those interested in 'the Art of Cooking'. He divides pleasure into six classes: food, drink, clothes, sex, scent and sound. Of these, he says, the noblest and most consequential is food and he subscribes to the doctrine of the pre-excellence of the pleasure of eating above all other pleasures. For that reason he composed the book. Al-Baghdadi chose to include from among the recipes popular at the time only those which he personally liked, and discarded what he describes as 'strange and unfamiliar dishes, in the composition of which unwholesome and unsatisfying ingredients are used'. There is general advice about the necessity of keeping nails trimmed and pots clean, or rubbing copper pans bright with brick dust, potash, saffron and citron leaves, and on such things as the value of using fresh and strongly scented spices ground very fine.

One hundred and sixty recipes follow, divided into ten chapters, which include 'sour dishes', some of which are sweetened with sugar, syrup, honey or date juice; and milk dishes with 'Persian' milk which is actually curdled milk or yoghourt. The 'plain dishes' are not at all plain. The 'fried' or 'dry' dishes do not have much broth or sauce. The 'simple' and 'sweet' dishes are not puddings but meat dishes. Those grouped under 'harissa' are of meats cooked with meal. There are fresh and salted fish dishes and recipes for fish caught in the lake of Wan in Armenia. And there are recipes for sauces, relishes and savouries, vegetable pickles and salads, desserts, pastries and sweetmeats.

The recipes are remarkable in their variety and in the imaginative combinations of a wide range of ingredients including apples, prunes, quinces and currants, almonds and pistachios, with vegetables and meats. They bear Persian names and they are in the Persian tradition. Their delicate flavouring is the result of the subtle blending of herbs and spices, roots, resins and essences of flowers. Their preparation requires skill and patience, and their presentation calls for taste and artfulness. They are all perfectly explained and precise, but although they often give quantities of spices and aromatics they do not usually give measures when dealing with main ingredients. A certain knowledge and experience on the part of the cook are assumed, but they are easy to follow in a modern kitchen more than seven centuries after they were written, and they are delicious if interpreted with taste.

The Kitab al Wusla il al Habib fi Wasfi t-Tayyibati wat-Tib
(Book of the bond with the friend, or description of good dishes and perfumes)

This book exists in at least ten handwritten copies, each with minor variations and additions. One manuscript is in the British Library (shelfmark Or. 6388). Others are in Aleppo, Damascus, Cairo, Bursa, Mosul, Paris and Bankipore in India. Professor Maxime Rodinson describes and analyses the manuscripts at length in his study 'Recherches sur les documents Arabes relatifs à la cuisine' in the *Revue des études islamiques* in 1949. Unfortunately circumstances prevented him from giving a full translation of the recipes. Charles

Perry is now working in the United States on a full edition and translation.

The true origin, date and authorship of the original manuscript are uncertain; but it is very likely that it dates from before 1261 in the Ayyoubid period in Syria, and that it was written by someone close to the courts because of the many references to the Sultan, his cooks and the royal kitchens. It may have been a Prince or a grandson of Safadin and great-nephew of Saladin, or the historian Kamal ad-din ibn al-Adim or the poet and historian Ibn al-Jazzar.

It is in two parts, one of which is on table manners, while the other contains the recipes. A chapter is devoted to perfumes and incense, another to drinks and juices. There are seventy-four recipes for cooking chicken and recipes for fried and roast meats as well as omelettes and stews. Vegetables, rice, wheat, fruit and yoghourt dishes are featured; and there is a chapter on desserts and pastries.

My father's family originally came from Aleppo in Syria and I was thrilled to trace the origin of several of our own dishes.

Spanish Arabic Cook-books

Another source of old Arabic cook-books is Spain of the period when the Moors were there. Two manuscripts have been recently published, both from the thirteenth century. The first, the *Kitab Fadalat al-Khiwan fi Tayyibat al-Ta'am wal-Alwan*, translated by Fernando de la Granja, was published in Madrid in 1960 under the title *La Cocina Arabigoandaluza segun un Manuscrito Inedito*. Another translation by Huici Miranda, published in Madrid in 1966, is the *Traduccion Espanola de un Manuscrito Anomimo del Siglo XIII sobre la Cocina Hispano-Magribi*.

American Conversion Tables

1 quart	= 2 pints	=	32 fl oz
1 pint	= 2 cups	=	16 fl oz
	1 cup	=	8 fl oz
	1 tablespoon	=	⅓ fl oz
	1 teaspoon	=	⅛ fl oz

APPROX. EQUIVALENTS

British	American
1 quart	2½ pints
1 pint	1¼ pints
½ pint	10 fl oz (1¼ cups)
¼ pint (1 gill)	5 fl oz
1 tablespoon	1½ tablespoons
1 dessertspoon	1 tablespoon
1 teaspoon	⅓ fl oz

American	British
1 quart	1½ pints + 3 tbs (32 fl oz)
1 pint	¾ pint + 2 tbs (16 fl oz)
1 cup	½ pint − 3 tbs (8 fl oz)

Bibliography

Malja-at-tabbahin. Translated from Turkish into Arabic, by Muhammad Sidqi Effendi, Cairo, 1886.

A Cookery Book, by Ekrem Muhittin Yegen, Inkilàp-Kitabeir, Turkey. Third Impression, 1951.

Middle Eastern Cooking, by Patricia Smouha. André Deutsch, London, 1955.

In a Persian Kitchen, by Maideh Mazda. Charles E. Tuttle Company, Rutland, Vermont, and Tokyo, Japan, 1960.

Art of Lebanese Cooking, by George N. Rayess. Librairie du Liban, Beirut, 1966.

Treasured Armenian Recipes, by The Detroit Women's Chapter of the Armenian General Benevolent Union Inc., New York, 1963.

Food from the Arab World, by Khayat and Keatinge. Khayats, Beirut, 1965.

Contributions to the Culinary Art: A Collection of Family Recipes and Cookery Clues, by Monah Oppenheim for the Young Peoples Group of Congregation Shearith Israel. New York, 1961.

Fès vu par sa cuisine, by Madame S. Guineadeau. Morocco, 1958.

'A Baghdad Cookery-book', by Professor A. J. Arberry, in *Islamic Culture*, No. 13, 1939.

'Recherches sur les documents Arabes relatifs à la cuisine', by Maxime Rodinson, in *Revue des études islamiques*, Nos. 17–18, 1949.

'Ghidha', by Maxime Rodinson, in the *Encyclopédie de l'Islam.* Second edition, Livraison 39, 1965. This edition now out in the Encyclopedia of Islam – volume II 1057–1072.

Manners and Customs of the Modern Egyptians, by E. W. Lane. John Murray, London, Fifth edition, 1860.

Modern Lebanese Proverbs, by Anis Frayha. American University of Beirut, 1953.

Contes persans en langue populaire, by Arthur Christensen. Andr. Fred. Høst & Son, Copenhagen, 1918.

Chansons populaires recueillies dans la Haute-Egypte. De 1900 à 1914, by Gaston Maspéro. Imprimerie de l'Institut Français d'Archéologie Orientale, Cairo.

Recueil d'énigmes arabes populaires, by le R.P.A. Giacobetti des Pères Blancs. Adolphe Jourdan, Algiers, 1916.

Bibliography

The Wit and Wisdom of Morocco: A Study of Native Proverbs, by Westermarck. London, 1930.

The Wild Rue, by Bess Allen Donaldson. Luzac & Co., London, 1938.

Folk Medicine in Modern Egypt, by 'A Doctor'. Translated by John Walker, 1934.

The Exploits of the Incomparable Mulla Nasrudin, by Idries Shah. Jonathan Cape, London, 1966.

Watermelons, Walnuts and the Wisdom of Allah and Other Tales of the Hoca, by Barbara Walker. Parents' Magazine Press, 1967.

Tales of Nasr-ed-Din Khoja, translated from the Turkish text by Henry D. Barnham. C. M. G. Nisbet and Co. Ltd, 1923.

Three Centuries – Family Chronicles of Turkey and Egypt, by Emine Foat Tugay. Oxford University Press, Oxford, 1963.

La Nouvelle Cuisine marocaine, by Fettouma Benkirane. J. P. Taillandier, 1979.

A Gourmet's Delight, by Aida Karaoglan. Dar An-Nahar, Beirut, 1969.

Les Secrets des cuisines en terre marocaine, by Frette Guinaudeau-Franc. Jean-Pierre Taillandier Vilo, Paris, 1980.

Couscous and Other Good Food from Morocco, by Paula Wolfert. Harper and Row, USA, 1973.

La Cuisine arabe, by Rene Khawam. Albin Michel, Paris, 1970.

240 Recettes de cuisine marocaine, by Ahmed Laasri. Jacques Graucher, Paris, 1976.

250 Recettes classiques de cuisine tunisienne, by Edmond Zeitoun. Jacques Graucher, Paris, 1977.

Recipes From Baghdad (with contributions from more than a hundred ladies), edited by May H. Beattie. The Indian Red Cross, Baghdad, 1946.

Index

Index

Index

Index

Index

Index

Index

Index

Index

549

READ MORE IN PENGUIN

In every corner of the world, on every subject under the sun, Penguin represents quality and variety – the very best in publishing today.

For complete information about books available from Penguin – including Puffins, Penguin Classics and Arkana – and how to order them, write to us at the appropriate address below. Please note that for copyright reasons the selection of books varies from country to country.

In the United Kingdom: Please write to *Dept. EP, Penguin Books Ltd, Bath Road, Harmondsworth, West Drayton, Middlesex UB7 0DA*

In the United States: Please write to *Consumer Sales, Penguin USA, P.O. Box 999, Dept. 17109, Bergenfield, New Jersey 07621-0120*. VISA and MasterCard holders call 1-800-253-6476 to order Penguin titles

In Canada: Please write to *Penguin Books Canada Ltd, 10 Alcorn Avenue, Suite 300, Toronto, Ontario M4V 3B2*

In Australia: Please write to *Penguin Books Australia Ltd, P.O. Box 257, Ringwood, Victoria 3134*

In New Zealand: Please write to *Penguin Books (NZ) Ltd, Private Bag 102902, North Shore Mail Centre, Auckland 10*

In India: Please write to *Penguin Books India Pvt Ltd, 706 Eros Apartments, 56 Nehru Place, New Delhi 110 019*

In the Netherlands: Please write to *Penguin Books Netherlands bv, Postbus 3507, NL-1001 AH Amsterdam*

In Germany: Please write to *Penguin Books Deutschland GmbH, Metzlerstrasse 26, 60594 Frankfurt am Main*

In Spain: Please write to *Penguin Books S. A., Bravo Murillo 19, 1° B, 28015 Madrid*

In Italy: Please write to *Penguin Italia s.r.l., Via Felice Casati 20, I–20124 Milano*

In France: Please write to *Penguin France S. A., 17 rue Lejeune, F–31000 Toulouse*

In Japan: Please write to *Penguin Books Japan, Ishikiribashi Building, 2–5–4, Suido, Bunkyo-ku, Tokyo 112*

In South Africa: Please write to *Longman Penguin Southern Africa (Pty) Ltd, Private Bag X08, Bertsham 2013*

READ MORE IN PENGUIN

A SELECTION OF FOOD AND COOKERY BOOKS

The Fratelli Camisa Cookery Book   Elizabeth Camisa

From antipasti to zabaglione, from the origins of gorgonzola to the storage of salami, an indispensable guide to real Italian home cooking from Elizabeth Camisa of the famous Fratelli Camisa delicatessen in Soho's Berwick Street.

Roald Dahl's Cookbook   Felicity and Roald Dahl

Roald Dahl's Cookbook, liberally spiced with lively anecdotes, recreates the many wonderful meals that have been enjoyed by the Dahl family and their friends around the farmhouse table at Gipsy House. 'Full of fun and lovely recipes' – *Sunday Times*

The Best of Floyd   Keith Floyd

Food magician and master chef, Keith Floyd has drawn his favourite recipes from a lifetime devoted to good eating and cooking, inspired by the local ingredients and traditions of the countries he has visited while filming his hugely successful television series.

Classic Cheese Cookery   Peter Graham

From soups and entrées to main courses and desserts, *Classic Cheese Cookery* is a deliciously varied tour of cheese dishes from around the world. 'A satisfying thick bible of cheese ... Peter Graham clearly knows and loves his subject' – *Sunday Times*

The Dinner Party Book   Patricia Lousada

The Dinner Party Book hands you the magic key to entertaining without days of panic or last-minute butterflies. The magic lies in cooking each course ahead, so that you can enjoy yourself along with your guests.

Easy Cooking in Retirement   Louise Davies

The mouth-watering recipes in this book are delightfully easy to prepare and involve the least possible fuss to cook and serve.

READ MORE IN PENGUIN

A SELECTION OF FOOD AND COOKERY BOOKS

Traditional Jamaican Cookery Norma Benghiat

Reflecting Arawak, Spanish, African, Jewish, English, French, East Indian and Chinese influences, the exciting recipes in this definitive book range from the lavish eating of the old plantocracy to the imaginative and ingenious dishes of slaves and peasants.

The 30-Minute Cook Nigel Slater

'The whiff of kaffir lime leaves, cumin and ginger wafts from the pages . . . Slater is a very relaxed and relaxing kitchen companion – and I can think of no one more likely to coax timid cooks into a spirit of culinary adventure' – *Financial Times*

From Anna's Kitchen Anna Thomas

Anna Thomas, whose classic book *The Vegetarian Epicure* has long been a bestseller, has now put together over sixty mouth-watering vegetarian menus. From simple suppers to festive dishes, there is something for everyone, all year round, in Anna's kitchen.

Jane Grigson's Fish Book Jane Grigson

A new edition of Jane Grigson's imaginative and comprehensive guide to the delights of cooking and eating fish. 'A splendid book ... Most Britishers are rather shy of fish and how to cook it ... This book will change all that' – *Evening Standard*

Flavours of Greece Rosemary Barron

From the sharp olives, the salty feta and the delicate seafood of the first courses to the fragrant honey pastries and luscious figs of the desserts, Greek food offers a feast of variety that changes with the seasons. With wit and enthusiasm Rosemary Barron shows us how to recreate them in our own kitchen, for family meals or when entertaining.

READ MORE IN PENGUIN

A SELECTION OF FOOD AND COOKERY BOOKS

Real Fast Puddings Nigel Slater

'Nigel Slater has produced another winner in *Real Fast Puddings* ... Slater has great flair for flavour combinations and he talks much sense. The book is snappy and fun' – *Financial Times*. 'Delectable ... Slater is an unashamed spoon-licker' – *Daily Telegraph*

Floyd on Italy Keith Floyd

Travelling around Italy in search of authentic local dishes, Keith Floyd has brought his own inimitable style and expertise to the recipes, which are interspersed with lively accounts of the places he visited and the people he encountered.

Simple French Food Richard Olney

'There is no other book about food that is anything like it ... essential and exciting reading for cooks, of course, but it is also a book for eaters ... its pages brim over with invention' – *Observer*

Onions Without Tears Lindsey Bareham

Handled with care, alliums – onions, shallots, garlic, leeks and chives – can bring savour, aroma and harmony to any dish, from the Indian dopiaza to the French quiche and the South American salsa. 'Calm, measured, assured, sensible, clever, useful, amusing and jam-packed with spot-on recipes' – *Guardian*

The Chocolate Book Helge Rubinstein

'Fact-filled celebration of the cocoa bean with toothsome recipes from turkey in chilli and chocolate sauce to brownies and chocolate grog' – *Mail on Sunday*

The Rituals of Dinner Margaret Visser

'Margaret Visser's superlative analysis of table manners begins with the idea that eating together is a terrifying and hazardous ordeal' – *Independent*

READ MORE IN PENGUIN

FROM THE COOKERY LIBRARY

In Praise of the Potato   Lindsey Bareham

'A marvellously rich cottage pie of a book dealing in every aspect of the noble spud: its historical pedigree, its ups and downs in culinary fashion, its supposed powers of sexual invigoration, and the seemingly endless variety of recipes invented to exploit its unique texture' – *Sunday Times*

The Foods and Wines of Spain   Penelope Casas

'I have not come across a book before that captures so well the unlikely medieval mix of Eastern and Northern, earthy and fine, rare and deeply familiar ingredients that make up the Spanish kitchen' – *Harpers and Queen*. 'The definitive book on Spanish cooking . . . a jewel in the crown of culinary literature' – Craig Claiborne

An Omelette and a Glass of Wine   Elizabeth David

'She has the intelligence, subtlety, sensuality, courage and creative force of the true artist' – *Wine and Food*. 'Her pieces are so entertaining, so original, often witty, critical yet lavish with their praise, that they succeed in enthusing even the most jaded palate' – *Vogue*

Modern British Food   Sybil Kapoor

The availability of fresh produce and the willingness of British cooks to experiment with new ideas have transformed our national cuisine, enabling us to enjoy dishes with pure fresh flavours that are quick and easy to prepare. 'Unique and refreshing . . . I shall be trying out many of the recipes' – Alistair Little

Caribbean Cooking   Elisabeth Lambert Ortiz

Caribbean cooking is a delightfully eclectic blend of textures and tastes, influenced by ingredients and cooking techniques from Europe, Asia and Africa. Here are tried and tested recipes gathered from Trinidad to the Virgin Islands – carefully ensuring that the more exotic ingredients are easily available.

BY THE SAME AUTHOR

Published in hardback by Viking and forthcoming in Penguin:

The Book of Jewish Food

In this collection of over 800 glorious recipes interwoven with stories, reminiscences and history, Claudia Roden traces the fascinating development of Jewish cooking over the centuries. The recipes – many of them never before documented – are the treasures garnered by the author during almost fifteen years of travelling around the world.

Beginning with a loving recollection of her childhood in Egypt, Claudia Roden takes us on a journey through the Jewish world, from the inventive cooking of Ashkenazi Jews in Russia, Poland, Germany, England, France and America to the sensuous and colourful food of the Sephardim throughout the Orient, in Syria and Morocco, India and China, Greece and Israel.

Claudia Rosen presents the finest of her myriad dishes and leavens them throughout with tales of her travels. The result is a book unlike any other: a learned, loving and delicious tribute to the variety and vivacity of Jewish culture. An astonishing and hugely important work, it is sure to become the definitive book of Jewish cuisine, a must for every Jewish household and indispensable for anyone interested in culinary history.